Nicolas Nabokov

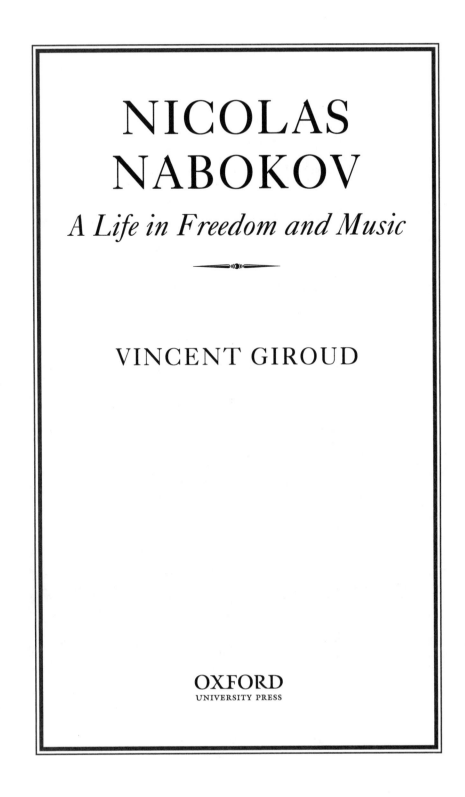

NICOLAS NABOKOV

A Life in Freedom and Music

VINCENT GIROUD

OXFORD
UNIVERSITY PRESS

OXFORD
UNIVERSITY PRESS

Oxford University Press is a department of the University of
Oxford. It furthers the University's objective of excellence in research,
scholarship, and education by publishing worldwide.

Oxford   New York
Auckland   Cape Town   Dar es Salaam   Hong Kong   Karachi
Kuala Lumpur   Madrid   Melbourne   Mexico City   Nairobi
New Delhi   Shanghai   Taipei   Toronto

With offices in
Argentina   Austria   Brazil   Chile   Czech Republic   France   Greece
Guatemala   Hungary   Italy   Japan   Poland   Portugal   Singapore
South Korea   Switzerland   Thailand   Turkey   Ukraine   Vietnam

Oxford is a registered trademark of Oxford University Press
in the UK and certain other countries.

Published in the United States of America by
Oxford University Press
198 Madison Avenue, New York, NY 10016

Library of Congress Cataloging-in-Publication Data
Giroud, Vincent.
Nicolas Nabokov : a life in freedom and music/Vincent Giroud.
pages cm
Includes bibliographical references and index.
ISBN 978–0–19–939989–5 (hardcover : alk. paper)   1. Nabokov, Nicolas, 1903–1978.
2. Composers—Biography.   I. Title.
ML410.N2G47 2015
780.92—dc23
[B]
2014021569

1 3 5 7 9 8 6 4 2
Printed in the United States of America
on acid-free paper

For Dominique
and in memoriam Elliott Carter

Contents

Acknowledgments

THIS BIOGRAPHY GREW out of my long friendship with Dominique Nabokov, Nicolas's widow, whom my longtime companion and I came to know through our late friend Eileen Finletter; and with Ivan and Claude Nabokoff, his son and daughter-in-law, whom we met through Francine du Plessix Gray. Though I would hesitate to describe it as an authorized biography, it goes without saying that it would not have been written without Dominique's constant support and cooperation and her patient and unfailing willingness to share with me her memories of her life with Nicolas. If I have at all succeeded in making him come alive in these pages, all credit should go to her. No less invaluable have been my many conversations with Ivan and Claude, whose advice, wisdom, and help I owe more gratitude than could be expressed.

Another great believer in this project from the outset was the late Elliott Carter, whose close friendship with Nabokov dated back to the mid-1930s. Sadly, he did not live to see the book completed, but he read the first half and I am immensely indebted to his generosity and assistance (as well as to the kindness of his personal assistant Virgil Blackwell). It is only fitting that the book should be dedicated to his memory.

I am profoundly grateful to other members of the Nabokov family for sharing reminiscences with me and encouraging me at various stages of my work: to Nabokov's other two sons, Peter, and his wife Linda, and to Alexandre, his wife Catherine, and their son Constantin, whose hospitality in the Provence Alps I enjoyed in March 2013; and to Nabokov's niece the late Marina Ledkovsky and his grandnephew Constantine Fasolt. I also thank Jean-Marie Grunelius and his wife for their hospitality in Kolbsheim, Nabokov's only real French home and his final resting place.

I wish to acknowledge with equal gratitude the help of all those who knew Nabokov and kindly responded to my requests: Anne Arikha, Keith Botsford, Allegra Chapuis, Jean Daniel, Frances FitzGerald, Cornelia Foss, the late Martine Franck, Francine du Plessix Gray, Marie-Ange Grunelius, John and Chantal Hunt, the late Étienne Jaudel, Florence Malraux, the late Madeleine Malraux, Alexandra Schlesinger, and Robert Silvers.

For various kinds of assistance, from a brief conversation to technical help, I am grateful to Vladimir Alexandrov, Vincent Arlettaz, Merrill Ashley, Christopher Bishop, Ambassador Avis Calleo, my colleague and friend Rudy Chaulet, Mary Sharp Cronson, Christine Evans, Michele Girardi, Tom Gold, Rita Gombrowicz, Geneviève Honegger, Bruce King, Piotr Kloczowski, Leonid Litvak, J. D. McClatchy, Anka Muhlstein, Fiamma Nicolodi, Barbara Page, Stephen R. Parks, Robert O. Paxton, Sarah Plimpton, Tatiana Ponomareva, Alexander Schenker, Stacy Schiff, Julien Segol, Evert Sprinchorn, Michael Struck-Schloen, Emma Sweeney, Ambassador William Vanden Heuvel, Érik Veaux, Tim Weiner, Richard and Adene Wilson, Andrew Wylie, and Adam Zagajewski.

Several friends read parts or the entirety of the manuscript and were kind enough to pass on suggestions for improvement. I am particularly thankful to Carol Archer and am also indebted to Eleanor Chai Beer, Leon Botstein, Barbara Horgan, Piotr Kloczowski, Jeannette Seaver, Jennifer Vorbach, Thomas C. Wallace, and James Graham Wilson.

Much of the research and part of the writing were conducted while on a one-year fellowship at the Center for European and Mediterranean Studies, New York University, for which I wish to thank, especially its director, Larry Wolff. I am also highly grateful to the Harry Ransom Humanities Research Center at the University of Texas in Austin for offering me a short-term fellowship and making their splendid facilities available to me in the summer of 2011. I acknowledge with much gratitude the staff of the various libraries where my research was conducted: the special collections of the Joseph Regenstein Library at the University of Chicago; the Beinecke Rare Book and Manuscript Library (with special thanks to Timothy G. Young) and Irving S. Gilmore Music Library, Yale University; the Elmer Holmes Bobst Library and the Tamiment Library, New York University (with thanks to Timothy Naftali, director of the Tamiment Libray, and Sarah Moazeni); the New York Public Library, especially the Berg Collection of English and American Literature and the Library for the Performing Arts, Dorothy and Lewis B. Cullman Center; the Music Division, Library of Congress (with special thanks to Kevin LaVine); the Vassar College Library; the Département de la Musique, the Bibliothèque-Musée de l'Opéra, and the Département des Arts du Spectacle of the Bibliothèque nationale de France; and the library of the École normale supérieure, Paris.

At Oxford University Press, I am grateful to Suzanne Ryan and Norm Hirschy for their support and encouragement. I am no less thankful to Andrew Westerhaus for his scrupulous and helpful copy-editing, to Lisbeth Redfield, and to Kate Nunn of Newgen North America for her assistance at all stages of the book's production.

Excerpts from Nabokov's published and unpublished writings are quoted with the kind permission of Dominique Nabokov, who has also been exceptionally generous in allowing me to reproduce her photographs. I also wish to thank the following individuals and institutions for permission to cite published or unpublished material: for Ernest Ansermet, Laurent Kasper-Ansermet, Seillans, France; for George Balanchine, the George Balanchine Trust (with thanks to Barbara Horgan); for Isaiah Berlin, the Isaiah Berlin Literary Trust, Oxford (with thanks to Henry Hardy, Alice Dill, and Nicolas Hall); for Nadia Boulanger, the Centre international Nadia et Lili Boulanger, Paris (with thanks to its president Dominique Merlet and its déléguée générale Alexandra Laederich); for Alain Daniélou, the India-Europe Foundation for New Dialogues (find.org.in/fr, with thanks to Jacques Cloarec); for Witold Gombrowicz, Rita Gombrowicz, Paris; for Constantin Jelenski, Piotr Kloszowski, Warsaw; for Michael Josselson, Jennifer Josselson Vorbach, New York; for George Kennan, the Princeton University Library special collections; for Nicole Klopfenstein, Hervé Klopfenstein, Lausanne; for Gabriel Marcel, Henri Marcel, Paris; for Igor Markevitch, Allegra Chapuis, Lausanne; for Arthur M. Schlesinger, Stephen Schlesinger on behalf of the Schlesinger family; for Christopher Sykes, Peters Fraser & Dunlop, London; for Virgil Thomson, the Virgil Thomson Foundation, New York. I am grateful to Suzanne Farrell for allowing me to quote her letter to Nabokov. Letters and material by Stephen Spender are reprinted or cited by kind permission of the Estate of Stephen Spender (with thanks to Sarah Williams, Ed Victor Ltd); and letters by Igor Stravinsky are quoted with the permission of the Fondation Igor Stravinsky, Geneva (with thanks to Marie Stravinsky).

Finally, I should mention the help and support I received throughout this project from my life partner, Robert Pounder, who was, as always, my first reader, and whose contribution could never be sufficiently acknowledged.

Introduction

WHEN, AT THE twilight of his life, Nicolas Nabokov characterized his century as an age of emigres and exiles, he was describing his own condition. Born to a famous liberal family in imperial Russia, he was an adolescent when historical circumstances forced him to trade a life of wealth and privilege for one of rootlessness and uncertainty. The remainder of his existence was an uninterrupted Wanderjahre, in Western Europe first, then in the United States, and after the war constantly back and forth between the old and the new worlds. A self-professed cosmopolitan, he was acutely aware that he had not become one by choice. The cosmopolite, he once told a television audience, is above all a homeless person. His real fatherland, he added, was music.

Exile and emigration are themselves a crucial part of twentieth-century music history. By contrast with the previous age, when issues of nationality and nationalism were paramount, some of the leading figures of modern music—Bartók, Hindemith, Schoenberg, Stravinsky, to name the greatest four—spent part of their careers away from their native soil. The present biography is thus largely the story of the struggles of a composer who found himself cut off from the support structures normally available to musicians in a national environment and which make possible performance and recognition.

Yet, for all the hardship that came with it, exile did not break Nabokov. It made him a free spirit in every possible sense—morally, philosophically, politically, aesthetically—by broadening his perspectives and stimulating his intellectual curiosity. As his more famous cousin Vladimir was able to reinvent himself as an American writer after resettling in America (in part with Nicolas's help), so Nicolas Nabokov, in the 1950s, emerged as an international cultural force, taking on political responsibilities few if any composers have ever assumed. His life thus intersects with a vast array of people in a great variety of fields, well beyond the confines of classical music, and in every part of the world.

Indeed, rather than as a musician, Nabokov today is probably remembered above all for his association with the Congress for Cultural Freedom, the Paris-based international organization he headed from 1951 until 1966. However, while the Congress has received much attention from historians in the past three decades, much of the discussion has focused on its financing, largely—though not exclusively—through American funds channeled through the CIA. This has unfortunately resulted in biased, unfair accounts of this remarkable institution. Nabokov's own image has suffered owing to this state of affairs, and in two ways: first because his own role within the Congress has been misunderstood and misrepresented; and secondly because the exclusive focus on his political activities has caused his achievements as a composer to be ignored and minimized. By telling the whole story for the first time, this biography proposes to rectify a double misperception.

It does Nabokov a grave injustice to see him primarily—or only—as a Cold War cultural warrior, which he never really was in any case, being above all passionately hostile to fascism and totalitarianism in all their forms. Nor is he a mere footnote in twentieth-century music history. By 1933, when he moved to the United States, his name was frequently mentioned, in France and elsewhere, as one of the rising stars of the younger generation of contemporary composers. He thus entered the Larousse dictionary well before his cousin Vladimir, who, under the pseudonym Sirin, was little known beyond the limited readership of the Russian emigre community in Berlin and Paris.[1] Launched, like so many others, by Diaghilev, his career is yet another proof of the far-reaching importance of the Ballets Russes in the history of artistic modernism. It will be no surprise to see that Nabokov's life is intertwined with those of several of the great names that emerged in the wake of this movement: George Balanchine, Jean Cocteau, Serge Lifar, Leonide Massine, and, above all, Stravinsky, as well as with more peripheral figures such as Harry Kessler and Henri Sauguet. However, those unfamiliar with Nabokov's musical career will be surprised by the size and range of his production, as documented in the checklist that will be found at the end of the volume. They will discover that his works were performed by the likes of Maurice Abravanel, Claudio Arrau, Leonard Bernstein, Antal Dorati, Roger Désormière, Serge Koussevitzky, Evelyn Lear, Igor Markevitch, Nathan Milstein, Dimitri Mitropoulos, Pierre Monteux, Charles Münch, Eugene Ormandy, Hermann Prey, Mstislav Rostropovich, Gérard Souzay, and Shirley Verrett, among others.

More generally, reliving Nabokov's life often feels like going through a Who Was Who in the twentieth century, so vast and diverse were his friendships and acquaintances. From Serge Prokofiev to Virgil Thomson; from Henri Cartier-Bresson, who once referred to Nabokov as his "spiritual father,"[2] to Robert Oppenheimer; from Alexis Léger—the poet Saint-John Perse—to W. H. Auden and Robert Lowell; from Jacques Maritain to Isaiah Berlin; from Yehudi Menuhin to Leontyne Price; from Willy Brandt to Indira Gandhi: the list could go on and on of the artistic, intellectual, and political figures whose path crossed Nabokov's and who will be encountered at some point in the following pages. As the reader will discover, Nabokov's expansive personality—"witty, creative, warm-hearted, and irrepressible," in the words of William Glock—seldom failed to fascinate those who came into contact with him.[3] While admitting he himself wore "the outer shell of an undemonstrative person," George Kennan felt compelled to write to Nabokov in 1972 that, after a friendship of three decades, he felt towards him "a mixture, deep and abiding, of admiration, of real affection, and of a very special sort of gratitude." Singling out what he described as Nabokov's "enormous power of instinctive understanding for the rest of humanity," he praised him for having exerted it "gallantly, graciously, generously," never ceasing to give of himself to others, "never yielding to pettiness or despair."[4]

This biography hopes to give as complete a picture as possible of the struggles, successes, and failures of an uncommon man. What it could not possibly achieve is to give more than a glimpse of the rich and fascinating personality which dazzled Kennan along with so many others. At least I hope to have gone part of the way in fulfilling the late Elliott Carter's wishes when he encouraged me in my task. "Nicolas," he said, "deserves a large book."[5]

Note on Transliteration of Russian Names and Phrases

RUSSIAN PROPER NAMES are given according to the Library of Congress authority system, either in the form sanctioned by usage (Tchaikovsky, Tchelitchew) or in transliteration, except when the system departs from standard scholarly usage (Meyerhold, not Meĭerkhol'd). For the sake of typographical clarity, double capitalization (Tsvetaeva, not TSvetaeva) and diacritics (Suvchinskii, not Suvchinskiĭ) are omitted. Also, to avoid confusion, names of family and friends nevertheless appear as cited in the sources (Onya rather than Oniia; Tolya rather than Tolia).

Nicolas Nabokov

I

The Lubcza Years

NICOLAS NABOKOV, AS he came to spell his name—combining the French version of his given name and the English version of his family name—was born Nikolai Dmitrievich Nabokov on April 4 (old style) or April 17 (new style), 1903. Lubcza, his birthplace, now in Belarus, was his mother's estate on the Niemen river, halfway between Minsk and the current Polish and Lithuanian borders. Borders, however, have moved much over the centuries in that part of Eastern Europe, where one tended—and still does—to think of oneself less in terms of citizenship than of ethnicity, religion, or mother tongue. Before the region was incorporated into the Russian empire at the end of the eighteenth century, Lubcza had thus once been part of the Grand Duchy of Lithuania and the Polish-Lithuanian Commonwealth. Fifteen miles south, Novogrudok, the district capital—Navahrudak in Belorussian—was where Adam Mickiewicz, the great national Polish poet, was born in 1798. Occupied by the German troops during the First World War, the area was given to the newly formed Polish Republic by the treaty of Riga in 1921. Invaded by the Red Army in 1939, it briefly became part of the Soviet Republic of Belorussia. Two years later, when Hitler declared war on Russia, the Nazi troops occupied it and annexed it into the Third Reich's Ostland, exterminating most of its Jewish community.

The tragic, chaotic history of the region where he was born is not without similarities with Nabokov's own destiny: an exile from the age of sixteen onwards, he had from then on a keen sense of his homelessness. While seeing himself a citizen of the world, as indeed he was, with his fluency in several languages and the range of his contacts in all continents, he retained throughout his life, like many fellow exiles of his generation, a deep-seated attachment to his roots. A "Russian cosmopolitan," as he described himself in the subtitle of his memoirs, he saw himself also as "forever a 'Beloruss.'"[1] Yet, paradoxically—as if to foretell his uprootedness in later life—none of the family roots were in Lubcza.

Made world-famous fifty-five years later by *Lolita*, the bestselling novel by Nicolas's first cousin Vladimir, the name Nabokov was widely known and respected in early twentieth-century Russia. As readers of Vladimir Nabokov's autobiography *Speak, Memory* will remember, family legend has it that the Nabokovs originated from the historical city of Pskov, to the south of St. Petersburg, where a certain "Nabok Murza (*floruit* 1380), a Russianized Tatar prince" was supposed to have settled in the fourteenth century.[2] This mythical ancestor, reputed to be a tribute collector for the Khan, would have then married into a local Russian family and converted to Christianity. Musing, many years later, over this rumored exotic ancestry when writing his memoir, Nicolas Nabokov could not help extending the range of possibilities, as if to inscribe his own uprooted cosmopolitanism into his family tree: "Maybe he was a Tartar, maybe he was a Persian, or an Arab, or an Armenian, or a Jew."[3]

Whereas the family origin remains shrouded in myth, a well-documented feature of the Nabokov family tree, and a particularly relevant one from the point of view of this biography, is the Nabokovs' descent, on their German side, from a distinguished lineage of Saxon musicians, the Grauns, initially from Wahrenbrück in southwestern Brandenburg. The most prominent member of this family, Carl Heinrich Graun (1703 [or 1704]–1759), was first attached to the court of Brunswick-Wolfenbüttel, for which he wrote his first operas. He then joined his brother Johann Gottlieb—their elder brother August Friedrich was also a musician—in the employ of Crown Prince Frederick, the future Frederick II. When his royal protector ascended the throne in 1740, Graun was put in charge of the court opera in Berlin, where many of his own works were staged. The one most familiar today, *Montezuma* (1755) had a libretto adapted from Voltaire's tragedy *Alzire* by Frederick the Great himself.[4] Vladimir Nabokov, while acknowledging his lack of personal interest in music, was nonetheless evidently proud of this artistic background, pointing out in his autobiography that Graun's features, as reproduced in the portrait hanging in the Berlin Opera House, resembled those of his composer cousin Nicolas.[5] Carl Heinrich Graun's granddaughter Antoinette married a Prussian officer, Baron Nikolaus von Korff: their great-grandson was Nicolas Nabokov's father.

On the Russian side, the first illustrious Nabokov was Aleksandr Ivanovich Nabokov (1749–1807), who rose to the rank of general under the reign of Paul I. His youngest son Nikolai (1795–1873) retired in the Pskov province after a brief military career; his wife Anna Nazimova was the sister of Mikhail Aleksandrovich Nazimov (1801–88), who in 1825 had participated in the Decembrist uprising against Nicholas I. The second of thirteen children of Nikolai and Anna, Dmitri Nikolaevich Nabokov (1826–1904) reached greater prominence than any of his forebears, since he became the Russian Minister of Justice in 1878 when Czar Alexander II dismissed Count Pahlen. During his seven-year tenure,

D. N. Nabokov fought attempts to abolish or water down the relatively liberal judicial reform of 1864, which had brought the Russian legal system closer to Western standards. His position, however, became more and more untenable after Alexander II was assassinated by nihilists in St. Petersburg in March 1881. In 1885, he was forced to hand in his resignation to Alexander III, preferring a generous financial compensation to the title of count offered him by the Czar. Contrasting with this uncompromising political stance, his alliance with the Korff family was not devoid of scandal: it was preceded by an affair with the fiancee's mother—who in fact arranged the marriage.[6] D. N. Nabokov and his wife had nine children. Dmitri Dmitrievich, the father of our composer, being the eldest of the four sons, inherited the family *majorát*, an estate in Southern Poland, near Cracow, which the Czar had given Dmitri Nikolaevich to be passed on to his eldest son.

Nicolas Nabokov's mother, née Lydia Eduardovna Falz-Fein, had acquired the Lubcza estate from two of her brothers, who in the early 1890s had purchased large pieces of land (about 100,000 acres) previously owned by the German princely family of Hohenlohe—the Lubcza castle itself having been their occasional residence. As their name suggests, the Fein-Falz were of German origin. One Fein ancestor had settled in the eighteenth century in Southern Ukraine, where he and his descendants had amassed a large fortune from the breeding of Merino sheep, purchasing vast estates in Crimea and around the Sea of Azov. "Falz"—a corruption from Pfalz—had been added to the name in the early nineteenth century when the only daughter of a wealthy Fein had married a man of much humbler status. By the early twentieth century, the name of Falz-Fein had attained an even greater prominence than that of Nabokov, internationally at least, owing to the fame of the natural park that Frederick Falz-Fein (1863–1920), Lydia's elder brother and Nicolas's uncle, had developed on his estate of Askania-Nova in Ukraine. Situated on the Taurian steppes, to the north of Crimea, Askania-Nova— the "old" Askania was a castle in the Harz Mountains—had been purchased by Falz-Fein's father from yet another German princely family, the Anhalt-Köthens— whose ancestor had been the patron of Johann Sebastian Bach from 1717 to 1723— with a view to making it a horse and sheep ranch. Frederick Falz-Fein had studied natural sciences at Dorpat University (the present-day Tartu) in Estonia. Upon inheriting the property in 1883, he made ambitious plans to create a vast natural preserve. By the end of the nineteenth century, it included a zoo (second in size to London and Amsterdam only) and, more importantly, long before the name was coined, a "biosphere" which gradually earned him the admiration of zoologists worldwide as well as official recognition in his own country: he was made a baron when Czar Nicholas II visited the estate in 1914. Though the Falz-Feins were expropriated at the time of the Revolution, Askania-Nova, miraculously, survived and is now recognized as a landmark in the history of ecology.[7]

Nabokov's parents separated when he was two. Whether the separation was caused by Dmitri Nabokov's infidelities (he was having an affair with the game-keeper's wife, whom he subsequently married) or by his wife's own infatuation with Nicolas von Peucker, the man who would become her second husband, Lydia fled Lubcza with her three children in 1905, taking advantage of her husband's absence on a hunting expedition. An acrimonious divorce trial ensued, in the course of which accusations of adultery were made against her, bolstered by the allegation that Nicolas, the youngest child, had not been fathered by Nabokov but by Peucker. The claim came back to haunt Nicolas in his adolescence when a cousin called him a bastard to his face. Deeply troubled by the accusation, he was informed by another cousin of the rumors surrounding his birth. Understandably, he shied away from bringing it up with his mother or stepfather. Yet the topic came up much later in the course of a meeting with his mother on the German side of Lake Constance, a meeting he tentatively dates from the mid-1920s.

> After a long silence, without looking at me, she said somewhat solemnly but calmly: "Sometime before I die, I must tell you about yourself and your father . . ."
> Then she paused, as if hesitating.
> "But not now," she added. "Another time. Yes, later . . . Let us now go to the station.
> "Another time" never came. She never spoke to me about it again.[8]

Confronting the possibility of one's illegitimate birth is, obviously, a traumatic experience for a child—or indeed an adult. Reviewing the facts of the case in his autobiography *Bagázh*, Nabokov concluded by stating his firm belief "that the allegation made by the lady relative at the trial was gratuitous and utterly false."[9] Manuscript and typescript drafts of the autobiography, which contain a more extended discussion of the case than the published version, while wordier, are curiously more equivocal. Looking for evidence of his legitimate birth, Nabokov finds one in what he describes as a profound difference in temperament between him and his stepfather: "He: orderly, proper, un-hedonistic, non-intellectual and in no way interested in the arts; me: disorderly, shifty, sensual, unconventional and, on the whole, enjoying the air of artistic and intellectual stables." Another proof, a more convincing one according to him, is "the unusual relations that existed between my stepfather and my mother even after their marriage. They were so pure and at the same time tender, so profoundly respectful of each other and yet completely united in all the affairs of life, so penetrated by a kind of 'law-fulness' and rectitude (somewhat conventional and conservative, of course) that it is difficult for me to imagine either of them committing an act of adultery." That his mother and her second husband did not go to bed together until her divorce

was pronounced is finally ruled by Nabokov "not only possible but definitely probable, if not certain." As proofs go, one has to admit that these are certainly far less
convincing, say, than cousin Vladimir's comment on the physical resemblance
between Nicolas and their common paternal ancestor Graun. Even more persua-
sive, not to say definitive, is the striking facial similarity between Nabokov and his
father as an adolescent, as photographed with his three brothers when he was a
student at the Imperial School of Jurisprudence. The photograph, reproduced in
Speak, Memory, shows, in particular, the peculiar Asiatic-looking eyes which characterized many male Nabokovs, especially in their youth.[10]

Many years later, when Nabokov found himself briefly reunited with his father
in postwar Berlin, he took the opportunity to question him about the rumors that
had been spread about the legitimacy of his birth. Dmitri Dmitrievich Nabokov
firmly denied having ever made such claims himself. "The allegation, he said, had
been made not by him, but by a mischievous relative, with whom he had been
accused of having had a love affair."[11] The calumny against Nabokov's mother had
been made in retaliation.

One should not read too much into Nabokov's oddly halfhearted denial of the
claim of illegitimacy. Clearly, he was above all reluctant to convey the impression
he was rejecting the strong emotional bonds that tied him to the man he called
"Uncle Koló" and who became his adoptive father after his biological father had
receded into the background. Indeed, although acknowledging his father's physical appearance and personal charm, Nabokov, in his autobiography, hardly dis-
guises the fact that he never felt much affection towards him. On the other hand,
he draws on his "confident and loving relations" with his stepfather, adding that "to
all intents and purposes, until his death in August 1918, he was our real father."[12]
If the ill-intentioned rumors he subsequently heard proved so upsetting, it was no
doubt principally because of the shadow they suddenly cast on an otherwise cloud-
less relationship with a man who, besides, happened to be his godfather, and after
whom he had been christened.

Nicolas von Peucker, Nabokov later remembered, was a man "of conservative outlook"—a conservatism reflected in his clothes and morals as well as in
the management of his and his wife's financial affairs and in his politics. His
monarchist sympathies may have been offended by the increasingly visible role
played after 1905 by Vladimir Dmitrievich Nabokov, Nicolas's uncle (and father
of Vladimir) in the liberal opposition to Nicholas II's absolutism. "Part Balt,
part Greek, and only a bit Russian,"[13] Peucker was a neighbor of the Nabokovs at
Lubcza—a neighbor in a relative sense, since his estate of Pokrovskoe was about
thirty miles away, but a neighbor all the same, considering the size of estates
owned by the upper class in this part of the Russian empire. Built in the eighteenth century, Pokrovskoe had its own musical connections: its previous owner,
Baron Karl von Meck, a Baltic engineer who had made his money in the railroad

business, was none other than the husband of Nadezhda von Meck (1831–94), Tchaikovsky's longtime protector and "beloved friend" as well as the young Debussy's employer in the early 1880s.[14] Both of these composers, to a different degree, remained important references for Nabokov in later years: in particular, he fully shared his friend Stravinsky's profound admiration for Tchaikovsky.

Nabokov's earliest years were of the peripatetic kind enjoyed by many such prosperous Russian families in the pre-Revolutionary period, with winters on the French Riviera and occasional stays in Dresden. He and his siblings—Sonia, the first-born, and Dmitri, his senior by two years—were looked after by a small army of Russian preceptors, German governesses, and French Mademoiselles in a perpetual multilingual environment. His earliest memories are of Czemin, another large family estate near Pilsen in Bohemia which belonged to another brother of his mother; there the Nabokov children and their mother spent an extended period before returning to Russia in 1908. From this period dates the episode he remembered as his first encounter with sexuality. Being the youngest in the group of children, he was asked to keep watch on certain afternoons when the other children held secret meetings in the playhouse. One day, unable to resist curiosity, he left his watch post and peeped in. The account he drafted, more graphic than the one published in *Bagázh*, evokes the boys masturbating while staring at the girls' genital organs. Inevitably, capping the fantasmatic character of the scene, the mother then appeared in the door frame. General punishment ensued, save for the little voyeur, who nevertheless met his own retribution by getting severely beaten up by two of his cousins.

Sometime in 1908, by which time the Nabokovs' divorce had been finalized and Lydia and Peucker had married—a daughter, named Lydia like her mother, was born in 1909—the family moved back to Russia, settling first at Pokrovskoe. This involved a long train journey which ended at Molczadz, on the line from Lida to Baranowichi, a major junction, located forty miles south of Nowogrudok, where the St. Petersburg to Odessa line met the one going from Moscow to Western Europe. There ensued a twenty-mile horse-drawn carriage ride to the former von Meck summer residence. The exiled Nabokov's later recollections of this return to Russia—his earliest memories of his native land—are colored with an intense nostalgia, as if the landscape, smells, and noises had remained vivid in his memory. A few months later, in the fall of 1908, Nabokov's mother fell ill and left for Vilnius with her husband to undergo surgery, while the remainder of the household departed by sleigh to Lubcza, which had just been renovated. Even more than Pokrovskoe, this return to the house where he had been born but which he had never consciously seen, filled him with a sense of "unique and overwhelming happiness."[15] Lubcza was to remain the family's main residence until the beginning of the First World War.

Since Nabokov's parents were often absent, the children were looked after by Aunt Karolya (Caroline Muller), a widowed cousin of their mother's; young Nicolas, the last-born, was her favorite, whom she nicknamed Nikooshka or Poompsie. There was no question, at that stage, of going to school. Language teaching, which came naturally through daily contact with governesses of various nationalities, chiefly consisted in learning short poems by heart—a habit Nabokov, like many Russians, kept alive throughout his life. In those days, he later recalled, Russian children from a well-to-do milieu like his were expected to speak French to their mother, Russian to their father, in German to one governess, and in English to another one.[16] The children also had a tutor, Piotr Sigismundovich Tsetsenevsky (a curious name apparently deriving from the African fly), "a blond young man with President Taft-like moustaches."

> He was of medium-height, wore a starched "Kitel," a uniform-jacket with a stiff collar, and the colors of the St. Petersburg University. He was to become our most beloved tutor. Intelligent, patient, at times exacting, but always kind and resourceful. He treated my brother and myself as his younger friends and immediately won our lasting affection.[17]

It was Tze-Tze, as Piotr Sigismundovich was called, who read to Nicolas the first book he remembered, a Russian translation of Raffaele Giovagnoli's *Spartaco*, the popular account of the revolt of Roman slaves in the early first century BC, first published in 1874 and greatly beloved in Russia long before Aram Khachaturian's 1958 ballet based on the same theme. On a visit to Italy many years later, Nabokov, looking for a copy of the original, realized to his surprise that his Italian contacts had never heard of the novel. Worse still, once he had managed to locate a copy in a "dingy public library," he realized that, his childhood recollections notwithstanding, the book was "a bore": "Irretrievably old-fashioned, grandiloquent and unabashedly sentimental: it was unreadable."[18]

The other person the adult Nabokov remembered as the most important person in his educational development was the cataloguer and bookbinder of the Lubcza library, an elder of the village's Hassidic community named Moisei Iosifovich, whose last name he never knew. A meticulous person, Moisei offered to rearrange the books by subject until Aunt Karolya made him put them back as they were, shelved according to size and binding color. To little Nicolas's requests to read something in Hebrew or comment on the star that had supposedly appeared in the Christmas sky when Jesus was born, he would respond with evasiveness. Perhaps Nabokov's ardent, lifelong philosemitism should be traced back to the affection he felt as a child towards the kindly librarian.

An avid reader from an early age, Nabokov was exposed to Russian and foreign classics, especially French, such as Dumas *père* and Maupassant. He loathed, however, the novels written in French by the Comtesse de Ségur (née Rostopchin), which were immensely popular among Russian upper classes, and proudly recalls snatching *L'auberge de l'ange gardien* from the hands of the French governess and throwing it into the pond, declaring that it was as *bête* as his *caca*.[19] A great favorite, on the other hand, was Longfellow's *Hiawatha* in Ivan Bunin's translation, which he always preferred to the original.

Instruction in the orthodox faith—Russia's official religion, though it is worth noting that Nabokov's mother had been raised a Lutheran—took the form of twice-weekly sessions with the local priest and consisted essentially in learning to recite by heart prayers in Old Church Slavonic. As for religious services, there were Saturday Vespers and High Mass on Sunday in the village church. Later in life, Nabokov remembered with distaste the bastardized music heard on those occasions, which had nothing to do with the authentic Russian chant traditions and consisted, instead, of cheap adaptations of popular tunes from Italian opera. On the special occasions—Christmas Vespers and midnight Resurrection service at Easter—when he was able to hear the real thing, it left a profound impression, and one he would remember as having exerted a major influence on his own musical development. By the same token, he blamed composers like Rachmaninov and even his beloved Tchaikovsky for writing religious music that was too obviously indebted to Western European models and ignoring "a large body of ancient Russian church chant that was still being sung in remote monasteries, mostly in northern Russia, like Valaam on the Lake Ladoga or at Solovki, which has since become a Communist jail."[20]

According to a story he later told the Franco-Dutch musicologist Fred Goldbeck, Nabokov's first musical shock, which prompted his decision to become a musician, was hearing his mother play a Rachmaninov Prelude on the upright family piano at Lubcza.[21] Another family favorite was Mendelssohn's *Venezianisches Gondellied*, which "stuck to [his] memory like fly-paper."[22] Some degree of musical instruction was, of course, expected to be part of the upbringing of a child in his milieu. Yet the daily piano lessons under the supervision of the stern Fräulein A.[23] were subsequently remembered as a dreary chore, altogether unrelated to the future composer's calling. He responded much more, he recalled, to everyday sounds like the lumberjacks' evening songs on the Niemen river, which he compares to an antiphon filling the air "with solitude and desolation,"[24] or the gay ditties of peasant women returning from the harvest on summer evenings. The domestic repertory, both at Pokrovskoe and at Lubcza, varied from salon pieces played by his mother to pseudo-Fibich or Kreisler tunes scratched by sister Onya and brother Mitya on their fiddles. Children's songs in four different tongues were part of the language instruction. While granting that the Russian folk songs he and his siblings enjoyed were not of the most "authentic" kind, Nabokov retained a softer spot for them than for the "phony" hymns heard in church. On birthdays and saints' days, Jewish musicians from the local community were invited to perform festive music and played "an extraordinary variety of music: potpourris of famous operas, military marches, Viennese waltzes, and the ooziest gypsy songs and Jewish dances, rampant with glissandos, tremolos, and tearful vibratos." "I particularly loved the violinists of these orchestras," he added, "for I enjoyed their scratchy, edgy tone, their ability to slide all over the bridge of their instrument, and their clumsy, harsh ways of intoning double stops (that Stravinsky so ingeniously copied in the *Histoire du Soldat*)."[25] In his enthusiasm, Nabokov asked his stepfather whether he could trade the piano for the violin but his request was turned down. By then, however, he had already started to learn playing the cello, for which he was secretly being coached by his mother.

Another testimony to the young Nabokov's fondness for the violin is a reminiscence he included in the second chapter of his 1951 memoir *Old Friends and New Music* but omitted from his 1975 autobiography. In the winter of 1910 his stepfather took him and his sister to Vilnius—or Vilna, as the Lithuanian capital was called in Russian—to visit their mother who was recovering from her operation. There, in the living room of the Jewish owner of a music store, the Nabokovs heard a child violinist with intense blue eyes wearing "a dark velvet suit and a Lord Fauntleroy collar," who was about to pursue his studies at the St. Petersburg Conservatory and whose miraculous playing "enraptured and overwhelmed" Nicolas:

> A big, mellow, round tone fills the room, penetrating the darkest corners of the stuffy apartment, shaking the windowpanes under its powerful impact. Its force, its warmth, the fullness of life which it represents are such that I feel as if an extraordinary, a miraculous gift were being received by my ears. It makes me tremble with sensuous pleasure and choke with delight.[26]

In *Old Friends and New Music*, Nabokov claims that he recognized, in this young violinist, Jascha Heifetz, when he heard him two or three years later at a concert in the Russian capital. The date and place would match: born in Vilnius in 1901, Heiftez, in 1910, was indeed about to enter the Petersburg Conservatory to study with Leopold Auer. Yet, revisiting the episode for possible inclusion in *Bagázh*, Nabokov was less conclusive, especially since Heifetz, when he had asked him about their youthful encounter, had no recollection of it. Had Nabokov, in his 1951 memoir, followed with too much abandon his lifelong penchant for telling a good story?

Once Nabokov's mother had recovered, it was at long last possible for the family, beginning in 1910 or 1911, to start paying regular summer visits to their maternal relatives in Ukraine, especially the Falz-Fein grandmother. Née Sophia Bogdanova Knauff, and known to the children as Omama, she comes out as one of the most colorful characters evoked in the composer's memoir. Originally from

Yekaterinoslav, the modern Dnepropetrovsk, in central Ukraine, she belonged to one of those many German families that had established themselves in that country in the late eighteenth and early nineteenth century. Her father, Nabokov recalled, had started a sewing-machine business but had run into financial difficulties. Prior to her marriage with Eduard Falz-Fein, she had been courted by his youngest brother Gustav, whom she would have favored, but the match was vetoed by his father. While seven children, one of them Nabokov's mother, were born during the ten years of her union with Eduard, Sophia Falz-Fein remained close to her brother-in-law, who had settled in Vienna, and rumors suggested that her youngest two sons were by him. Whatever may have been the case, after her husband died, she married Gustav, and as a result ended up inheriting two-thirds of the Falz-Fein fortune. She lived in a rococo mansion built for her by her husband at Preobrazhenka, a few miles from the Black Sea port of Khorly. There she lived in a grand style which Nabokov describes as "immutable and ceremonial" and in which religious ritual, including interminable Orthodox services in her private chapel (even though she had been raised a Lutheran), played an important part.[27] To reach Preobrazhenka, the family, always carrying large quantities of *bagázh*, took the train from Baranowichi to Odessa, where they boarded Omama's private steamer to get to Khorly, where the party was met by a caravan of landaus, victorias, and other horse-drawn carriages.

Despite the stuffy etiquette that reigned at Preobrazhenka, Nabokov came to enjoy those yearly visits to his formidable grandmother (who, in 1913, sternly lectured him against the perils of self-abuse).[28] Yet he liked even more his visits to Askania-Nova, where the atmosphere was infinitely more relaxed and informal, despite the presence of a constant flow of scholars and zoophiles from all over the world who came to discover the fabled wonders of the place and pay homage to its creator. An abstemious man, whose only apparent interest was his extraordinary creation, Uncle Frederick was a genial host as well as a competent and benevolent administrator. Something about him, however, made his nephew slightly uneasy, which he could not explain at the time but subsequently related to the traffic of young servant women recruited to provide their employer with their sexual favors. What put off Nabokov, once he was aware of what went on during his uncle's "naps," besides the exploitative aspect, was the contrast between his uncle's well-organized sexual routine and "the moralizing tone he took when a younger member of the family would get caught having a love affair with a member of his harem."[29] If he thus had reservations about the moral character of Askania-Nova's owner (and these strictures were, in any event, expunged from the published version of his autobiography), Nabokov had none about the place itself. By his own admission, he fell in love with it at first sight. "It excited me, amazed me, made me happy. [. . .] It even surpassed in charm and beauty my beloved Lubcza. [. . .]My mind, my senses, my emotions were on the alert, watching, observing, loving."[30]

When writing his memoirs decades later, Nabokov, in fact, remembered his entire childhood as a "charmed life," free of material constraints, and from which only happy memories emerged: day-long excursions culminating in elaborate picnics in the woods; boat trips on the Niemen on the Black Sea; the natural, zoological, and ornithological wonders of the "Noah's Ark" that was Askania-Nova; lavish birthday and name-day celebrations; copious meals; and outdoor pastimes—even though, as he readily confessed, he was never any good at sports and preferred fishing. Only several years later did he begin to realize that this privileged, sheltered existence hid one of the most inegalitarian societies in Europe, bolstered by a tyrannical political system which as of 1905 started showing fissures. Of this reality, a child could get only glimpses: a rebellious coachman being brutally beaten by his stepfather, village fires that reduced the peasants to misery, and occasional remarks overheard which indicated that the Jews living in the Pale of Settlement within which they were forced to reside (and which included the Minsk Province) were considered pariahs. But what remained in Nabokov's memory was a prelapsarian universe, in which music took possession of him—as he saw it—not through dry piano exercises, but naturally, through the "open window"[31] which let him absorb the sounds, smells, and rhythms of the surrounding world. The personality of a musician, he always claimed, is formed at an early age, almost unconsciously, by the natural environment in which he grows. Like many exiles, the adult Nabokov retained an acutely sensuous memory of his native land, and this in turn colored the way he viewed himself as predominantly a Russian composer: not so much owing to any musical or even intellectual influences as because of a profound attachment to his roots. By the same token, music-making was never for him an intellectual pursuit but a way—the only way—he could reconnect with his "golden age," the lost paradise of his early Belorussian years.[32]

2

The Petersburg Years

IN SEPTEMBER 1911, the Nabokovs moved to St. Petersburg, where Onya, since the previous summer, had already been enrolled in the Yekaterinenskii Institut, the city's leading boarding school for girls. The family occupied a large apartment on the *piano nobile* of a three-story house with a facade on the Fontanka canal and another on Karavannaia Street, a few steps away from the recently rebuilt Anichkov Bridge, with its famous horse-tamer sculptures. While his brother Dmitri entered the Imperatorskii Aleksandrovskii Litsei, Nicolas started going to school, for the first time, at the Reformatskoe Uchilishche, an exclusive private school for boys run by the German Lutheran Church and, for this reason, frequented chiefly by Germans, Balts, and scions of well-to-do Jewish families. Having hitherto been taught by preceptors and governesses, he was ill-prepared to deal with school discipline and its attendant brutality and bullying. His first year was, by his own admission, a disaster. Faced with the choice between expulsion and repeating, his mother decided to resume intensive home instruction by tutors. Nicolas was then able to return to school and, in the spring of 1914, pass the entrance examination to get admitted into the above mentioned Imperial Gymnasium where brother Mitya was already a student.

The move to Petersburg had another, happier consequence for Nicolas: it brought him into contact, for the first time, with the Nabokov side of his family. In April 1912, he was thus ceremoniously introduced to his paternal grandmother, the widow of Alexander II's Justice Minister. Babushka Nabokova, as she was known to him, spent the winter months in a spacious villa near the imperial palace of Gatchina, about thirty miles south of St. Petersburg. In the summer, she moved to the Korff family estate at Batovo, on the shore of the Gulf of Finland. Batovo, which had once belonged to the Decembrist leader Kondratii Fedorovich Ryleev, was adjacent to the Pushkin family estate of Mikhailovskoe, the inspiration for one of the poet's late poems, which Nabokov himself was to turn into a cantata in the mid-1940s. Babushka Nabokova had distinctive, angular features, a well-defined chin, and deep-set eyes. The portrait Nabokov left of her in his autobiography caused much annoyance among his relatives—his cousin Vladimir for one—when it was published in 1975.[1] It presents her as an authoritarian, eccentric woman, who kept some pubic hair in a medallion (not that of her husband, whom she described as "too small" in every respect) and once admonished her homosexual son Konstantin to stop looking at his younger brother with hungry eyes and redirect his attention, instead, towards the household's male servants.[2] Yet, notwithstanding the satirical touches he brought to his recollections of her, Nabokov seems to have been genuinely fond of his paternal grandmother, whom he found less formal and intimidating than Omama Falz-Fein:

> Despite her eccentricities (and to me because of them) and completely "anti-intellectual" character she had an extraordinary, earthy charm about her. She was warm-hearted and foolish, kind and intuitively intelligent and represented to me and to most of us a link with a past of Russia, that, alas, I had never known. She was the embodiment of a continuity in our family, our environment, our caste and our class.[3]

Another member of the Nabokov clan with whom Nicolas came into contact was his aunt Nina, Babushka Nabokova's eldest daughter. First married to a general in the Russian army, she had divorced him to marry a two-star admiral. Yet the three of them formed a trio of inseparables. From her first marriage to General Baron Rauch von Traubenberg (literally "drunken from a grapemound," a name Nabokov found highly comical),[4] Nina had a son named Iurii. Born in 1897, handsome and dashing, he quickly became Nicolas's favorite cousin; he joined the imperial horse guards and was to perish during the civil war.[5]

This integration into the Nabokov clan was a gradual process. Thus Nicolas had little or no contact during his Petersburg years with his uncle Vladimir Dmitrievich, whom his stepfather probably considered a little too politically liberal for comfort, and first cousins Vladimir and Sergei. Even with his own father, of whom he had no recollections before 1911, relations were limited to a yearly visit at the Hotel d'Angleterre, where Nabokov senior stayed when in St. Petersburg.

It was during the Petersburg years that Nabokov's musical vocation took shape. Not only did he succeed in mastering the piano, thanks to his new teacher, "a frail and charming Jewish lady" of infinite kindness and patience,[6] but he began to enjoy playing it. A fine new Becker instrument had been acquired for the ballroom of the Fontanka apartment. On this new piano he started deciphering scores picked up from the family's music shelves, such as Tchaikovsky's salon pieces and Schumann's *Albumblätter*. He was also by then studying the cello seriously with a member of the Imperial Court Orchestra named Osip Osipovich Piorkovsky. With the three-quarter-size instrument he received as an eighth-birthday present, he started participating in the family string quartet, occasionally supplemented by one or two pianists. Onya, who was then studying the violin with Joseph Auer, Heiftez's teacher, played the violin, as did Mitya—who occasionally shifted to the viola—and his teacher.

Nabokov's first compositions date from these prewar years. The only one he specifically remembers was a *Berceuse* for piano in G minor, written in honor of his mother's birthday in 1912. Tinged with a Caucasian orientalist color, it was, he recalled, "a curious mixture of B flat major and G major."[7] The painstakingly rewritten manuscript was rapturously greeted by its recipient. The piano teacher was enlisted at once to give the budding composer basic instruction in harmony and music theory. These lessons consisted chiefly in going through the slow movement of a Tchaikovsky symphony, analyzing it page by page, especially from the point of its harmonic structure, and realizing a piano reduction. They resulted in the composition of more pieces, including some for cello and piano, the two instruments Nabokov played. None of these juvenilia have survived.

Reviewing his early musical tastes, Nabokov liked to compare them to the series of diseases a child was meant to go through in order to bolster his immune system. They were, he also remarked, typical of a domestic musician raised in an upper-class Russian family of the period. A short-lived infatuation with Grieg was followed by a prolonged passion, shared with Nabokov's mother, for Chopin—or, more precisely, the Chopin that was accessible to him, given his modest technical abilities: a few easy Preludes, Nocturnes, and Mazurkas. Though he subsequently discarded Chopin, along with much of the music of the Romantic period—distaste of which was widespread among composers in the 1920s and 1930s—Nabokov came to rediscover him in the 1940s, praising him as "one of the very few composers of his time who did not give in completely to the debauches of unbridled Romanticism."[8] Bach and Viennese classicism, on the other hand, left him cold as a child and an adolescent—with the exception of the early Beethoven string quartets that were played by the family ensemble.

Russian music, with one exception, did not elicit more enthusiasm. There were many opportunities to hear it at symphony concerts, especially since 1912 and 1913 were both jubilee years: the first marked the centenary of the defeat of Napoleon's invading armies, the second the three hundredth anniversary of the Romanov dynasty. In the fall of 1913 there began, in particular, a series of bimonthly concerts by the Imperial Court Orchestra entitled "Historic Concerts in Russian Music." They consisted of a chronological survey of Russian music throughout the nineteenth century. Nabokov remembered these Wednesday evenings at the St. Petersburg Conservatory, conducted by the orchestra's music director, Reinhold von Wahrlich, as "long and fairly dreary affairs."[9] Patriotic works were given priority, and "nationalist" composers were preferred to the so-called "Westernizers." Thus, with the exception of his *1812 Overture*, ubiquitous in the jubilee year, Tchaikovsky was underperformed by comparison with the "Mighty Five"—Balakirev, Borodin, Cui, Mussorgsky, and Rimsky-Korsakov. One of them, Cesar Cui, was still alive (he died in 1918). Nabokov recalled seeing him, in conversation with Aleksandr Glazunov, at a concert he attended, and at which he heard Heifetz. The "Mighty Five" were never among his favorites, and even Tchaikovsky was yet to become one.

Nabokov was hardly more impressed when, in early February 1913, in the company of his German governess, he went to hear Richard Strauss conduct his tone poems *Also sprach Zarathustra* and *Tod und Verklärung* in St. Petersburg.[10] The second work, in particular, seemed to him "indefatigably earnest and loud," and bored him to death. Yet he recalls enjoying the few lieder for soprano that were also featured on the program, even though "Nacht" was the only word he could make out of the text.

The one musical event Nabokov, in retrospect, saw as a defining moment in his musical development was a Sunday evening concert which took place in 1912 or 1913 in a garden pavilion at Pavlovsk, the magnificent imperial estate located twenty miles south of St. Petersburg, where the Imperial Court Orchestra performed during the warm months. As befitted the summer setting, programs tended to be the standard fare: a popular overture followed by a familiar symphony or concerto, and, after the intermission, short pieces from the lighter repertory, which Nabokov usually found tedious. It was thus a shock to hear, in the second half of such a concert, "a brief, weird, and bumpy piece of music, the like of which I had never heard before. The instruments whizzed, shrieked, trilled, shot up and down their registers, sparkled, and clattered, and before I could realize what was happening, the piece came to an abrupt end with a tremendous thud on the bass drum."[11] The piece was Igor Stravinsky's orchestral scherzo *Feierverk* (Fireworks), his opus 4, which the Ukrainian conductor Aleksandr Ilich Ziloti had premiered in January 1910. It was Nabokov's first contact—and, during his Russian years, only contact—with the music of the composer he came to be associated with more than any other.

His Ballets Russes fame in Western Europe notwithstanding, Stravinsky was then hardly a household name in his native country, and his reputation in musical circles was far from unanimously positive. When a few days later Nabokov quizzed his cello teacher about *Fireworks*, he was sternly admonished to stay away from "that kind of music," which the Imperial Court Orchestra musician likened to a dangerous "abyss" one was at risk of falling into. When Nabokov subsequently asked Sergei Diaghilev's half-brother Valentin Pavlovich why Stravinsky's music was not performed in Russia, the answer was that Stravinsky was compromised because of his association with the Ballets Russes. Diaghilev was *persona non grata* at the court of St. Petersburg: this meant that the Imperial Court Orchestra couldn't play Stravinsky's music, nor could his three great ballets, no matter how famous in Western Europe, be performed in court theaters. Neither was the name of Serge Koussevitzky—who not only conducted Stravinsky's music with his orchestra but published his works in the Éditions Russes de Musique he had founded in 1909—heard in the Nabokov home.

Nabokov's introduction to the world of opera took place in early May 1913, still in conjunction with the Romanov Jubilee. For the feast of St. Nicholas, the czar's patron saint, the Mariinsky Theater presented a gala performance of Glinka's *A Life for the Tsar* in the presence of the imperial family. The cast was in keeping with the solemnity of the occasion. The legendary bass Fyodor Chaliapin sang the role of Ivan Susanin (after which the opera was renamed following the collapse of the monarchy); the soprano Antonina Nezhdanova sang the part of Antonida, in which she was particularly renowned; the veteran tenor Ivan Vasil'evich Ershov and the fabled contralto Evgeniia Zbrueva completed the cast. The orchestra was in the hands of the equally famous Czech-born conductor Eduard Napravnik—who had conducted the premieres of Mussorgsky's *Boris Godunov* and Tchaikovsky's *Pikovaia dama* as well as several of Rimsky-Korsakov's operas. The extended act 2 ballet was danced in a choreography by Marius Petipa by the stars of the company, led by the Polish ballerina Matil'da Kshesinskaia, who many years before had been the mistress of Nicholas II, and, despite her association with Diaghilev, Tamara Karsavina of Ballets Russes fame. The children's three tickets for this spectacular event had had to be secured on the black market. Trying to recollect this momentous occasion many years later, Nabokov could remember little of the music of Mikhail Glinka, of whom, in adult age, he became an ardent admirer. What he remembered was, above all, his childish excitement at being able to catch a glimpse of Russia's absolute monarch—for whom he later expressed total contempt. Yet all he could manage to see was the autocrat's white gloves clapping in polite applause at the end of each musical number.[12] Still, Nabokov was dazzled by the act 2 Mazurka as danced by the Imperial Ballet, a famous display of character dancing, which he recalled as coming close to perfection; likewise, at the end of the opera, he went along with the audience's enthusiasm for the power, color, and flexibility of the voice of Chaliapin, whose mannerisms and liberties with the music he nonetheless later came to view as major irritants.

The other opera Nabokov saw at the Mariinsky before the war, *Die Walküre*, did not leave much of a musical impression either. All that remained was the memory of the staging of the "Ride of the Valkyries": an enormous metal cloud on which stood "incredibly fat and incredibly blonde females in winged copper helmets."[13] Nabokov, save for a very brief period, never became a Wagnerite.

Helmets of a less decorative kind became an everyday sight after Germany declared war on Russia on August 1, 1914. The Nabokov family was then vacationing at Lubcza, as they did every summer. Nicolas's mother and her husband returned at once to St. Petersburg, and the children and the rest of the household, save for Piotr Sigismundovich, their tutor, who enlisted as a volunteer, left by train for Crimea. They were not to see Lubcza again until the 1920s. Most of the staff working at the estate was drafted, and very soon, following the defeat of the Russian army at Tannenberg in the last days of August, the area was under threat of an imminent German invasion: indeed, by the end of 1915, Lubcza was behind the front line, which stopped to the east of Baranowichi, the town where the Nabokovs boarded the train on their way to Odessa. It remained there until the December 1917 armistice.

The August 1914 journey to Crimea, in overcrowded railroad carriages constantly stopped in their progress by freight trains transporting troops towards the West, took several days. The first stop was Preobrazhenka, grandmother Falz-Fein's estate in Southern Ukraine. From there the children and their suite made their way to Askania-Nova, where they remained until October before returning to Petersburg, or rather Petrograd as it had been restyled. Imitating this patriotic, anti-German gesture, Aunt Karolya changed her German patronym, Müller, to Melnikova (*mel'nik* being the Russian for miller). Caught up in the nationalist fervor which swept the whole of Europe, Nicolas decorated the walls of this bedroom with images of famous compatriots, including Czars Peter the Great and Alexander II. Uncle Koló was named head of the Red Cross for Southern Russia, while Nabokov's mother and sister did volunteer work for the organization. Otherwise, life in the Russian capital continued relatively unperturbed. Though he now took the tram rather than being taken to school in a private carriage (horses were given to the army as a patriotic gesture), Nicolas continued to attend his Imperial *litsei* as a day pupil, practice the piano and cello, and study the orchestral scores of Tchaikovsky symphonies. On Sunday afternoons, he and his siblings took part in chamber music concerts held at the home of Valentin Pavlovich Diaghilev, who was a cousin of his stepfather, and whose sons Aliosha and Pavlik played the violin. Supplemented by family friends, this string orchestra performed trios, quartets, and quintets, as well as arrangements of large-scale works. Nabokov's mother continued to receive and occasionally host a grand dinner party. As in the previous years, the summer of 1915 was spent at Preobrazhenka and Askania-Nova, where Piotr Sigismundovich, whose mother lived in the Black Sea resort of Evpatoria, came to visit in his military uniform.

Yet, despite the censorship imposed on any kind of news coverage, there were signs that the political situation was fast deteriorating along with the military one. Already, in the fall of 1914, accompanying his mother to the studio of a sculptor on Gorokhovaia Street (one of the main arteries of Petersburg), Nicolas had noticed in the door frame of one of the apartments "the tall figure of a man in a white peasant blouse," bearded and with long black hair, who stared at them intently.[14] The following year, the same man, by then famous not only in Russia but throughout the world, appeared behind the hostess at a children's party and Nabokov, alone in the room while the older children were dancing, once again encountered the angry gaze of Grigori Efimovich Rasputin. By the fall of 1916, a new tutor with Communist sympathies,[15] who instead of coaching him in Latin and mathematics as he was supposed to, tried to indoctrinate him by bringing him Bolshevist pamphlets, showed him pictures of Rasputin with society ladies or the imperial family, whose devotion to the peasant healer had by then become a constant feature of Bolshevist propaganda. On December 29, 1916, on his way home from the Narodny Dom theater, where he had heard *La Traviata*, starring the famous lyric soprano Maria Kuznetsova, Nabokov noticed the newspaper headline announcing that Rasputin was missing. There was some agitation in the Fontanka apartment in the middle of the night, and the following morning, seeing that his stepfather's office was uncharacteristically closed, Nicolas peeped inside and saw, despite the obscurity, that someone, wrapped in sheets, was sleeping on the sofa. Nabokov's mother was acquainted with Vladimir Mitrofanovich Purishkevich, the monarchist deputy from Bessarabia—well known for his anti-Semitic views—who, along with Prince Yusupov, Grand Duke Dmitri Pavlovich, and an army doctor, had carried out Rasputin's assassination the previous night and dumped his body in the Neva, where it was recovered three days later. Though he was never able to elucidate the episode—one more legend about this legend-filled night—Nabokov later assumed that, fearful of the police, one of the assassins—possibly Perushkevich himself—had sought refuge at their home.[16] Such were, in any event, his personal connections with the mythical figure he later made into the subject of his first opera, *Rasputin's End*.

By 1916 Nabokov's musical taste had evolved. Perhaps in connection with wartime propaganda, which discouraged interest in German music and promoted, instead, the cultural production of Russia's military allies, he discovered some of Ravel's easier pieces (such as the *Sonatine*). The main discovery, however, was the music of Aleksandr Scriabin, which soon turned, in his own words, into a severe case of "Scriabinosis."[17] For a Russian adolescent who was emerging from a passion for Chopin, this was a perfectly natural development: Scriabin's early piano music itself derived from Chopin and Liszt. Besides, at the time of his death in Moscow in April 1915, at the age of forty-three, Scriabin was the most famous living Russian composer; Nabokov had caught a glimpse of him at the Heifetz concert he attended with his tutor in 1913 or 1914.[18] It was also natural that at this point in his intellectual and artistic development, Nabokov should have been fascinated by what later seemed the most dated aspect of Scriabin, but which then captivated the imagination of many music lovers in Russia and abroad: the mystical, theosophic symbolism in which he clothed his choice of musical structures, such as his choice of forms, keys, and harmonies. Indeed, having found his way into Scriabin via the opus 8 *Études* and first three piano sonatas, Nabokov soon fell under the spell of the more esoteric later piano sonatas and the great synesthetic pieces such as the 1914 piano "poem" *K plameni* (known as "Vers la flamme") and the tone poems *Poema ekstasa* ("Poème de l'extase") and *Prometey* (also known as "Le poème du feu"). Nabobov's passion for Scriabin—whose music he later admitted held him "in total subservience for at least three years"[19]—came, according to him, to an abrupt end in 1919: "One morning I woke up with the realization that Scriabin's eroticism was good only for highstrung adolescents, that his orgasms were a fake, and that his musical craft was singularly old-fashioned, dusty, and academic."[20]

This sweeping abjuration may seem unduly harsh towards a composer who exerted so much influence on so many twentieth-century Russian musicians and intellectuals. It was admittedly phrased at a time (1950) when Scriabin's reputation was at a low ebb. Yet two decades later, when drafting his autobiography, as Nabokov reflected on his youthful infatuation, he was hardly more forgiving, suggesting that Scriabin's appeal in milieus like the Petrograd bourgeoisie was a reflection of the apocalyptic times they were going through, "and in such times bogus mysticism is usually rampant."[21]

It was, in any event, in conjunction with Scriabin that Nabokov first caught a glimpse of another composer who subsequently became an important friend. The occasion was a benefit concert for Scriabin's widow, a few months after the composer's death, given at the Petrograd Conservatory by Sergei Rachmaninov. The composer and pianist, then in his early forties and at the height of his fame, had been Scriabin's fellow student at the Moscow Conservatory and the latter's death affected him deeply. Nabokov, who had never heard Rachmaninov play, attended the concert in the company of his tutor Piotr Sigismundovich, on leave from his military duties. Nicolas's attention was caught by a group of spectators who kept whispering during the music. Among them was "a thin young man with fleshy, protruding lips and an extraordinary large blond head precariously fitted to a thin stem."[22] The young man, Piotr Sigismundovich explained, was Sergey Prokofiev. Himself in his mid-twenties, Prokofiev, as he later told Nabokov when recalling the event, did not share his fellow Petrograd melomanes' disdain for Rachmaninov's precise and cool rendering of Scriabin's music. Yet Prokofiev managed to offend the pianist when he went to the green room to congratulate him after the performance, telling the indignant star that his playing was "not bad at all."[23] Nabokov had one more opportunity to catch a glimpse of Prokofiev during his Petersburg years, at a chess tournament which he attended, also with Piotr Sigismundovich. The star on that occasion was Aleksandr Alekhin (1892–1946), one of the greatest chess players of all time, who won all the games of the evening, save one he lost to Prokofiev.[24]

The first precise memory Nabokov retained of the events of the so-called "Great Bloodless Revolution" of February 1917, which brought down the czarist regime, was that one day classes at his *litsei* were abruptly stopped in late morning and students were sent home because trams would stop working at noon. But he remembered people "embracing and congratulating each other" and an exhilarating atmosphere of freedom.[25] Himself "elated by the downfall of the inept Romanovs,"[26] as he subsequently recalled, he participated in the jubilation by putting on a red armband with a ribbon and milling with the crowds that gathered on Nevskii Prospekt and the neighboring streets, or, climbing on the pedestal of one of the horses of the Anichkov Bridge, watched them go by. "There was in the air a state of euphoria, a grandiose, perpetual *prazdnik* [feast], and even a boy like me could not help feeling himself a part of it."[27] Classes at the now ex-Imperial *litsei*, however, were soon suspended.

> I was glad to be out of school, removed from my boorish, noisy, teasing schoolmates, most of whom, because of their parental upper-class status, hated the New Times. I, on the contrary, was filled with adolescent pride and patriotic fervor. To me these were Russia's finest days, days for which the best people of Russia had nurtured hopes for more than a century.[28]

The students were given the option to take their final examinations, but Nabokov didn't. Nor was he able to resume his schooling at home. Foreign governesses were trying to get repatriated by their respective consulates. The piano and cello teacher vanished. As for the Bolshevist tutor, he was "much too busy with 'urgent revolutionary tasks'" to waste any time on his pupil and his studies.

> He had to organize party cells in the Petrograd garrison, recruit party members from among the soldiers, give pep-talks and indoctrination lectures. He would breeze in, preferably at meal times, and, to the dismay of Kolo and Aunt C[arolina], would hold fiery agitprop "lectures," barely noticing my presence at the table (but making good use, of course, of its food).[29]

Servants started disappearing for days to attend parades, and Fritz, the despondent house doorman traded "his gold-braided cap and his smart green livery" for "a homely sheepskin jacket with a sodden-looking stocking over his head."[30] Nabokov's mother fell ill with influenza, which turned into pleurisy, and was advised to recover in a sanatorium in Yalta. Koló, reinstated in his Red Cross responsibilities, went with her, as did Onya and Mitya, while Nicolas, his stepsister and Aunt Karolya were sent to Helsinki (then still called Helsingfors, its Swedish name, in the not-yet-independent Finland), to wait for the turmoil to subside. His group was the first to leave Petrograd on April 10—March 28 old style. One week later, Nabokov celebrated his fourteenth birthday in "a neat Swedish pension in Helsingfors in a street called Kaaivoipuistaaa."[31] During the two or three weeks he remained in Finland, he read the books he had brought with him (*Tom Sawyer* was among them). He also improvised a piano sonata, his first attempt at the genre, on the pension's upright piano.

Soon, Aunt Karolya decreed it was safe to return to Petrograd. They found the Fontanka apartment with the carpets and rugs stacked up in a pile and all the furniture covered up; all paintings and bibelots had been locked away. The servants being all gone, a "taciturn person of undecipherable age and sex, with a crumpled green-apple face, who did not know how to cook," was hastily recruited by Fritz, the porter, who was himself getting ready to return to his native Sweden.[32] In the streets of the city, the jovial, celebratory crowds had been replaced by glum lines outside food stores and bakeries. The day after the return from Finland, Valya Diaghilev came to visit with his three sons, and soon the chamber music sessions resumed, thanks to the hospitality offered by Boris Sheremetev, a member of the group, in the grand ballroom of the family palace on the other side of the Fontanka (in a wing of which Anna Akhmatova subsequently lived). Apart from these sessions, there was nothing to do, except sit in the Summer Garden and read a book, or "take the steamer to Yelagin Island at dusk and sit on one of the Strelka's benches, the arrow-like end of the island that darts into the Gulf of Finland, and watch the faraway lights of the Kronstadt lighthouse."[33]

It was, however, during those six or seven weeks Nabokov spent in Petrograd before going south that he had for the first time the revelation of Debussy's piano music. The only one of his works he had heard so far was the *Prélude à l'Après-midi d'un faune*, which Ziloti (or possibly Koussevitzky) had conducted in Petrograd that winter, and it had not made any particular impression. When, in revolutionary Petrograd, Nabokov acquired the first book of the piano *Preludes*, he approached it "with mixed feelings, part awe, part excitement, part apprehension."[34] Would Debussy dethrone his admiration for the Mighty Five, or kill his infatuation with Scriabin, whose late piano sonatas exerted such a powerful influence on Nabokov's own juvenilia? "Rarely have I felt again in my life," he recalled, "the same feeling of *total* discovery as when I started painstakingly to decipher the first *cahier* of Debussy's preludes."

Not with Stravinsky, not with Schoenberg, Webern, Berg, perhaps only with Machaut and Monteverdi (but many years later).

At first I did not know where I was. Then my ten fingers (so clumsy, so inefficient!) began to tell me something about a new universe of sound, a new way of building tone structures, a new way of perceiving and expressing feelings, emotions, images, and daydreams. And everything in this new universe was like creation itself, simple, direct, yet fully invented, from the tiniest particle of a melodic outline to the grandiose beauty of chordal progressions moving freely across the keyboard in a completely unorthodox motion; obeying their own intrinsic laws and contradicting, counteracting against the rules of harmony textbooks. Besides, this music was successfully describing, or rather inscribing, and with scrupulous *precision* (or intentional *imprecision*) images, objects, states of the mind, visions of nature, or rather of a nature revisited by a painter of sounds, that is a totally novel subject-matter for music that so far had been the private domain, or preserve, of painters and poets.[35]

A few other memories remained vivid in Nabokov's mind from the last weeks he spent in the Russian capital. One was the Easter service in the chapel of the Sheremetev Palace, followed by the traditional reception in the splendidly illuminated ballroom. At a sign from old Count Sheremetev, the military band on the balcony played the Imperial anthem, with all present standing to attention and singing "God Save the Czar" as if the February Revolution had not occurred.[36]

In late April or early May, Nabokov's Bolshevist tutor offered to take him to hear Lenin.[37] The exiled revolutionary leader, whose name was little known in Russia until then, especially in Nabokov's milieu, had made a triumphant return to Russia on April 3 (old style). He was to make a public address on the other side of the Neva, from the balcony of the confiscated villa of Matil'da Kshesinskaia, the ballerina and former imperial mistress Nabokov had admired at the Mariinsky four years before. While the tutor sported a large red armband over his military uniform, Nabokov, not to excite curiosity and possible hostile reactions from the crowd, was advised not to wear his Imperial *Litsei* uniform; instead, he was dressed, he recalled, like a Russian Tea Room waiter, in a tunic and blue trousers tucked into riding boots. His tutor, to whom those figures were familiar, was able to point out to him Bukharin, Zinoviev, and other Bolshevist leaders standing on the balcony.

> Then suddenly, Lenin appeared, dressed in a winter coat and a worker's cap. He had mounted a platform which made him look taller than anyone else on the balcony. Immediately he started to speak. He spoke in a shrill, high-pitched voice, rolling his r's in the manner of upper-class salon snobs and using many "barbarisms," words of foreign extraction gleaned from the vocabulary of socialist political tracts.[38]

This contrast between Lenin's posh diction—"like a Baltic baron," as Nabokov later put it—and the brutal, radical program he was presenting, and which became known as the "April Theses"—peace, demobilization, wholesale confiscation of landed property and privately owned factories, revolutionary takeover by "soviets" (i.e., councils) of peasant and workers—seemed, Nabokov sensed, both ludicrous and ominous.[39]

The other episode that remained, more confusingly, in Nabokov's memory was a poetry reading the same tutor took him to one evening in early May. It was held in the hall of the municipal Duma on Nevskii Prospekt, and marked the first appearance in Petersburg of two prominent members of the Muscovite avant-garde, Boris Pasternak and Velimir Khlebnikov. Osip Mandel'shtam also read some of his latest work. Nabokov, however, had little interest in modern Russian poetry at the time and, despite his tutor's attempts to point out to him the literary celebrities present, he fell asleep.[40]

3

The Road to Exile

BY THE TIME of the Bolshevist putsch on November 7, 1917, the entire Nabokov family had fled south and resettled in Yalta. The fashionable resort on the southern tip of Crimea, within easy reach of both Askania-Nova and grandmother Falz-Fein's Preobrazhenka estate, appeared at the time a safe haven, far removed from both the Soviet threat and the theater of war. As a result, many well-to-do families, acutely aware that they had everything to fear from the new regime, converged there after the October coup, making it temporarily, in Nabokov's words, "a miniature St. Petersburg on the shore of the Black Sea."[1] His uncle Sergei and his family were already in town, and the sons of his uncle Vladimir were about to settle nearby.

Yet, this climate of apparent security, which could give the impression that the Communist takeover would not last, deteriorated quickly. Peace negotiations between the new regime and the Central Powers were soon underway in the Belorussian city of Brest-Litovsk. Taking advantage of this truce, the Reds, as they were already called, advanced towards Yalta and bombarded it in mid-January 1920, forcing Sergei's family, after their house was hit, to seek refuge at the Peuckers' home, while violence, some directed towards army officers, spread throughout the city.[2] It may be around that time that Nicolas heard that his tutor Piotr Sigismundovich had been shot in the face by mutinying soldiers of his regiment.[3]

The peace negotiations broke down in February 1918. The Austro-Germans, who had been holding separate talks secretly with separatist Ukrainians, resumed their military pressure on Russia and were able to demand drastic conditions that were granted to them by the peace treaty signed at Brest-Litovsk on March 3. Under its terms, Ukraine, including Crimea, became independent, on paper at least, but in fact fell to the Austro-Germans, who were already in control of much of the territory. Yalta itself was under their control by the end of April. During the bombing, the Nabokovs sought refuge in the basement of the house, where they played chamber music.

Despite these dramatic developments, Nabokov continued his studies in Yalta. He was enrolled in the city's gymnasium and furthered his musical education by taking private instruction with a local composer, Vladimir Ivanovich Rebikov (1866–1920).[4] Born in the Siberian city of Krasnoiarsk, Rebikov had studied at the Moscow Conservatory with Nikolai Semyonovich Klenovsky (1857–1915), Tchaikovsky's pupil.[5] He himself subsequently taught in Moscow and Kiev, while pursuing an international career as a pianist before settling in Yalta in 1909. Like other musicians of his generation, he had shown a keen interest in correspondences between various artistic forms, especially painting. A friend of the symbolist writer Valery Bryusov (1873–1924), best known today for his novel *The Fiery Angel*, on which Prokofiev based his 1923 opera, Rebikov had set some of Bryusov's poems to music. But Rebikov's aesthetics were also influenced by Tolstoy's views on music: he had advocated what he termed "musical psychography" in a manifesto published in 1900, and his works bore cryptic subtitles such as "melomimics," "musical-psychological tableau," "meloplastics," and "musico-psycholographic drama." His greatest success was *Yolka* ("The Christmas Tree"), a fairy-tale opera after Dostoyevsky, Hans Christian Andersen, and Gerhard Hauptmann; premiered in Moscow in 1903, it remained popular for a while, being staged as far away as Prague and Berlin.

Nabokov remembered Rebikov as an eccentric bachelor, who collected his hair with a view to making a wig for himself in his old age. Moody, unpredictable, he was also a stickler for etiquette, who got angry if his official calls were not returned by Nabokov's stepfather. Instruction consisted mostly in studying Rebikov's own compositions. He was by then an embittered man, convinced that Debussy, Scriabin, Stravinsky, and other modernist composers had "stolen" his technical innovations, such as whole-tone scales, parallel chord progressions, and superimposed fourths.[6] "*C'était moi, l'avant-garde!*" he protested in front of his pupil.[7] As for Nabokov's student efforts, they were mercilessly rejected as worthless. Rebikov would also try to dissuade him from becoming a composer, encouraging him, instead, to turn to conducting and thereby earn enough money to buy himself the favors of any women (or boys). Nabokov's testimony implies that he did not benefit much from his teacher's lessons. Yalta, besides, was cut off from the outside musical world, and even music paper became rare. For his composition exercises, Nabokov had to use wrapping paper, on which staves were drawn with the help of a rudimentary gadget borrowed from his teacher. Fortunately Rebikov had a good music library, especially rich in modern French music, in addition to Rebikov's own works. It did not, however, include a single score by Stravinsky, and the one time when Nabokov mentioned this name, he was told that Stravinsky's music was "much too barbarous." "I don't like it," Rebikov concluded firmly, "and I don't think you should like it."[8] Prokofiev, whose piano music Nabokov had just discovered, was rated no higher. Having acquired in Yalta two of his scores—one of them the four, recently published *Skazki staroi babushki* (Old Grandmother's Tales) of 1918, the other possibly the *Four Pieces* issued in the same year—Nabokov proudly brought them to the attention of his teacher. After voicing his disapproval of Prokofiev in general terms, Rebikov began to go through the music, muttering expressions of disgust. "Suddenly, in the middle of one of the prettiest and most lyrical pieces from the *Grandmother's Tales*, he picked up the music from the piano rack, got up, went to the window and without saying a word threw it out. I rushed to stop him, but the music was already floating down to the street."[9] After which Rebikov, putting an end to the lesson, showed his pupil the door while rebuking him for heaping "insult and indignity" upon his master. Rebikov did not survive the miseries and food shortages of the civil war: he died in Yalta in August 1920.[10]

In Crimea, Nabokov, finally, got to know his first cousins Vladimir (born in 1899) and Sergei (born in 1900), who had been sent south by their father a few days after the Bolshevist coup. They were staying with Countess Panin, who like their father was an active member of the Constitutional Democrat opposition: her Gaspra estate was located five miles to the west from Yalta, near Livadiia, the imperial summer palace which in 1945 was the seat of the famous Allied Conference.[11] In Petrograd, V. D. Nabokov, who together with other Constitutional Democrats had tried to resist the Bolshevik takeover, was briefly arrested, but managed to join his wife and family in mid-December. Of the two brothers—there was a third, Kirill, born in 1911—Nabokov was more immediately attracted to the gentle, bespectacled, stuttering, artistic Sergei, who lent him anthologies of contemporary Russian verse and literary journals.[12] Under Sergei's influence, Nabokov read much poetry during his eighteen months in Crimea. His favorites were Blok and the symbolist poet Maksimilian Voloshin, who lived in Crimea and was also much admired by his cousin Vladimir.[13] Thanks to Sergei, Nabokov also discovered the work of the Acmeist poets: Akhmatova, her husband Nikolai Gumilev (soon to be shot by the Bolsheviks), Pasternak, and Mandel'shtam.

Vladimir's company Nabokov initially found less congenial. Vladimir did not wear his already formidable erudition lightly and appeared to his cousin "haughty, conceited, and snobbish."[14] He was already, at the age of eighteen, a published author: his poetry had appeared in literary magazines and his first verse collection, simply entitled *Stikhi* (Poems) had been published in 1916.[15] Slightly older than the others, he did not participate in their games and had pastimes of his own, among which hunting butterflies already occupied pride of place. Unlike his brother, he showed little interest in music and shunned his cousins' domestic music-making. Yet, the only documented composition by Nicolas from this period was a setting of a poem by Vladimir on the subject of the Last Supper, "written in a lilting anapest meter with elegantly carved dactylic rhymes."[16] Neither the poem nor the music have survived.

Another memory of the stay in Yalta was the visit Nabokov paid with one of his uncles to the sister of Anton Chekhov, Maria Pavlovna, who was a family acquaintance and lived in the villa she had shared with her brother on the outskirts of the town from 1899 until the time of his death. She gave them tea and showed them the writer's room, which had been left untouched, and from which the view extended to the Yalta harbor.[17]

Nabokov and his siblings spent the summer and early fall of 1918 at Askania-Nova. Uncle Frederick, who had moved to Moscow after the February Revolution, had been arrested by the new authorities after the October takeover; he fortunately benefited from fairly lenient detention conditions and was reported to be giving lectures to his fellow prison inmates on zoology and wildlife. In his absence, Nabokov and his family stayed in the main house: the guest house, known as the "Green House," where they usually resided, had been requisitioned by the occupying German forces for the officers of a Saxon regiment. For the Nabokov household, there was, at first, no question of having any social contacts with the Germans. In the eyes of all patriotic Russians, who had been dismayed by the "Bolshevist sellout" at Brest-Litovsk, the war was not over and the Germans remained the enemy. "No truce with the occupants!" was the family motto.[18] It was thus purely by accident that the fifteen-year-old Nicolas formed an unexpected friendship with one of the Saxon officers.[19] In the park surrounding the Green House was a favorite spot of his, a secluded bench where he enjoyed reading Russian classics while fishing the carp that populated the adjacent pond. One day, he found, seated there, "a shortish man with a large round head," wearing a German officer's uniform and reading Goethe's *Wilhelm Meister*. Despite his initial reluctance, he gradually fell into conversation with the "enemy."[20] Named Martin Richard Möbius, the Dresden-born officer came from a well-known family in Chemnitz, a city embellished during the first quarter of the century by his namesake (and, presumably, relative) the architect Richard Möbius (1859–1945). This first contact developed into an intense intellectual friendship which lasted for the four months Nabokov and his family spent at Askania-Nova. Though he spoke German fluently and had attended a German school in St. Petersburg, Nabokov knew little about German literature and art. Through his new friend, he first heard names such as Rainer Maria Rilke, Stefan George, Christian Morgenstern, and the Mann brothers. Möbius read aloud to him passages from *Wilhelm Meister* and *Italienische Reise*, a book that always remained one of Nabokov's favorites. Under Möbius's guidance he learned by heart poems by Goethe, Hölderlin, and Rilke. He was shown a German translation of Marinetti's Futurist Manifesto and reproductions of German Expressionist paintings. In short, the adolescent Nabokov, whose education had so far been entrusted to governesses, private tutors, and schoolteachers, had now found a mentor. He introduced Möbius to his family, and it seems that Möbius was not insensitive to the beauty and lively personality of Nabokov's sister.

The happiness and relative serenity of the summer of 1918 was brutally interrupted in August when the news came that Nabokov's stepfather had died suddenly of a heart attack while on Red Cross business in Simferopol, the Crimean capital. The loss of a man he considered his real father must have affected Nicolas deeply. Meanwhile the military and political situation, of which he was being informed by his new German friend, was rapidly deteriorating. As the German and Austrian forces were retreating on the Western front, Ukrainians began to rise against the occupying forces. Worrying, not without reason, that the region was becoming unsafe, and further worried by the typhoid epidemic that had broken out in Southern Russia, by then on the brink of famine and civil war, Nabokov's mother decided to repatriate the household to Yalta. A caravan of horse-drawn cars and wagons left in mid-October, bringing food supplies for the winter, and, after a ten-day stop at Preobrazhenka, brought them back to the Crimean resort in the first days of November. By that time the Germans forces were in full retreat. None of this, however, is perceptible in the contemporary photograph that shows Onya and Nicolas (unidentified in the caption, but clearly recognizable behind his sister) with a large group of Bavarian officers after a St. Hubert's hunt at Preobrazhenka on November 3, 1918.[21] One of the latter, Viktor Fasolt, who can also be seen on the photograph, fell instantly in love with Onya and his feelings were reciprocated in the course of this short visit.

Nabokov himself, who was still mourning the loss of his beloved Koló, had parted with sadness with Richard Möbius on leaving Askania-Nova. A few weeks later, the commander of the Saxon regiment contacted Nicolas's mother with terrible news: having come down with typhoid, their young German friend was being evacuated to Germany when his sanitary Red Cross train, stopped at a small railroad station, had come under crossfire. Retreating Germans were by then attacked from all sides by the Reds, Ukrainian separatists, and the so-called Green Army (formed by peasants) and the Black Army (led by the anarchist leader Nestor Makhno). The Red Cross train, full of dead bodies, had been found the next day by a retreating German regiment. Nabokov and his family arranged for a requiem service for the young German at the Yalta Orthodox cathedral.

After the Germans' departure, a new Crimean regional government was constituted at Simferopol, headed by Solomon Samoilovich Krym, a rich Karaite who was a friend of the Nabokov family. Appointed Justice Minister, Uncle Vladimir moved his family to a house on the grounds of the imperial palace at Livadiia. By the end of December 1918, when the Armed Forces of South Russia were constituted under the command of General Denikin, who himself, as a monarchist, strongly distrusted the regional government to which Uncle Vladimir belonged, Ukraine was in a state of civil war. Nabokov's cousin Iurii Rausch von Traubenberg, an ardent monarchist, joined Denikin's forces as a cavalry officer. He was killed in battle on March 8 and was buried in Yalta six days later. To Nicolas, who admired and loved him, it was a hard blow. "I went through my first loss of a beloved friend," he later remembered.[22] Vladimir, who considered Yuri his closest friend, later paid tribute to him by using a musical simile: "All emotions, all thoughts, were governed in Yuri by one gift: a sense of honor equivalent, morally, to absolute pitch."[23] Meanwhile Lydia Peucker was frantically pleading with her eighty-four-year-old mother for her to join them in Yalta and leave the country with them. In late March, having fled her estate when the area was invaded by the Red Army, "Omama" Falz-Fein sought refuge in Khorly. Two Red Army guardsmen (or, according to her grandson, agents of the Cheka, the Communist secret police) raided her house there and shot her to death.[24] Her body was found the next day when the port was retaken by the Whites.

Following these dramatic developments, the decision was made to emigrate. In mid-April Nabokov and his mother took the boat to Sevastopol, along with Odessa the principal port in Crimea. The Hotel Rossiia, where they found a room, was full of people preparing to leave the country. Vladimir and his family were already there, in a different hotel, having been evacuated from Livadiia. So was Uncle Sergei, who was waiting for the remainder of his family to make its way down from Yalta. Nabokov's mother hoped at first to obtain French visas through the intervention of an officer known to them who had landed with the French expeditionary corps. The French military authorities, however, were under strict orders not to provide assistance except to their fellow citizens. The next hope was to obtain passes for the family to embark on the Greek boat which was supposed to evacuate the members of the late regional Crimean government to Constantinople and Athens. Thanks to the intervention of Krym, the former head of the ephemeral Crimean government, a car was sent to Yalta to fetch the other three children, Aunt Caroline, and one maid. Meanwhile, Krym treated Nabobov and his mother to a sumptuous dinner in a private salon of the Hotel Rossiia, with caviar and other delicacies which their host admitted he had purchased from the Bolsheviks.[25] The next day, the children arrived from Yalta, without Aunt Karolya, who had decided she did not want to leave, but with various supplies hastily assembled. No cello, and, instead of a pair, three shoes for the right foot.[26] Within hours, news came that the French commandant had succeeded in obtaining passes for the entire Nabokov group. On April 12, 1919,[27] the party of exiles boarded a tug that took them to the *Trapezund*. That boat turned out to be a "burned-out shell" that the fleeing Germans had abandoned in their flight before it could be repaired. Two cabins, devoid of running water, were secured for Nabokov's mother and his aunt Dolly, Sergei Nabokov's wife, while the men and children installed themselves in the hold. Despite these uncomfortable conditions and the prospect of leaving their home country for a long time if not forever, the Nabokov siblings and their cousins sat in a circle at the stern and sang.

At dawn the next morning, the boat was swept over by a crowd of Greek refugees, furious to realize that the *Trapezund* was already partially occupied. By the evening, the captain, "a former vice-admiral of the Baltic Fleet, unctuous and unpleasant," had decided that the presence of the Russians, their passes notwithstanding, was illegal and they ought to be disembarked, since the boat had now been chartered by the Red Cross for the Greek refugees. Uncle Sergei had to arrange the situation with a bribe in foreign currency. On April 15, 1919 (new style), as the Bolshevik forces were bombarding Sebastopol, the *Trapezund* sailed off towards Istanbul, as did the *Nadezhda* (Hope), the smaller, and equally dirty, boat carrying Vladimir Nabokov's family after they and those of the other former government members had been prevented by the French from boarding the *Trapezund*. Two days later, Nabokov celebrated his sixteenth birthday. "I remember well, sitting on the aft of the old Trapezund," he later reminisced, "my feet clad in the two right foot brown shoes that my brother brought me from Yalta, gazing at the pallid April sunset behind Constantinople's Golden Horn, with all those inchoate thoughts and feelings going through my mind and my heart. Even now, more than half a century later, they fill me with the same joy and exhilaration. [. . .]In front of me, all seemed promises, discovery, adventure, and the fullness of life."[28]

Such optimism was remarkable, considering that Nabokov and his family, whether they realized it or not, were entering a new condition. Rich until then in land and money, surrounded by servants and with all the amenities of life at their easy disposal, they were now among the millions of displaced people that were a new feature of Europe in the immediate aftermath of the First World War and the Bolshevist takeover and civil war in Russia. Awaiting them were reluctant adoptive countries, professional uncertainties, and financial precariousness. Refugees, as Nabokov would later phrase it, had become the Third Estate of the twentieth century.[29]

The period that follows, until the beginning of 1920, when Nabokov resumed his musical studies in Stuttgart, is the least documented of his existence. Whereas the Vladimir Nabokovs left Athens on May 18, boarding the Marseilles-bound *S.S. Pannonia* with a view to settling in London, the Peuckers remained in the Greek capital until July 1919, staying at a hotel in the residential seaside suburb of Phaleron. According to a later curriculum vitae, Nicolas found his first job in the Greek capital, doing secretarial and interpretation work, at a salary of $75 a month, for the US Trade Commissioner, then busy liquidating World War I stocks that had been accumulated in Greece and Turkey.[30] In July, he then boarded a Greek ship bound for the Netherlands, paying for his passage by working as a seaman, and subsequently lived in The Hague for a few months. According to a story recorded by Fred Goldbeck, he became, to his surprise, an able seaman, and won the Dutch captain's favor with his flute playing, thereby getting a better berth (or perhaps even a cabin for himself). Years later, in 1931, the same captain remembered his flute-playing seaman so vividly that he came to attend a performance of Nabokov's First Symphony when Pierre Monteux conducted it in Holland.[31]

The choice of The Hague as a destination was no doubt motivated by the fact that Nabokov had relatives there: his uncle Putia Peterson, who had married his father's sister Nataliia, was a career diplomat. He was the Russian Consul General in the Dutch capital and, amazingly, still held his position despite the change of regime—as did, for a while, his brother-in-law Konstantin Dmitrievich Nabokov at the Russian embassy in London. Peterson's sons, Nabokov's cousins, about to enter Oxford or Cambridge, were accordingly staunch Anglophiles. As for "Aunt Nata," she was, Nabokov recalled, "a wiry, thin woman in her early sixties."

> She wore masculine clothes, spoke in a deep husky bass voice, chain-smoked Players cigarettes and rode a bicycle in conformity to the custom of Dutch Aborigines. Although not as tall in stature and as eccentric as my grandmother Korff, she nevertheless looked very much like her and had inherited her mother's quick wit with an additional dose of personal sharpness and a worship of all "things of the mind." Politically, as I remember her, very much like her two younger brothers, uncle Vladimir and uncle Konstantin Nabokov. All in all, aunt Nata was quite a remarkable woman, a person of firm character and *droiture d'esprit* and, at times, could be (when she liked someone) of an exceptional charm.[32]

Nata Peterson spoke a mixture of Dutch, English, French, and Russian, and held firm views on many subjects. For example, she considered that the late czar was a total imbecile but was also of the opinion that Lenin and Trotsky ought to be hanged on the nearest lamp-post "before it is too late." In literature, anticipating the views later expressed by her nephew Vladimir, she could not abide Dostoyevsky, whom she viewed as "a middling detective-story writer," not even in the same class as Baroness Orczy. Her contempt, sparing only Pushkin and Turgenev, also embraced Tolstoy, whose *War and Peace* she considered "a novelette for twelve-year-olds."[33]

When a German diplomat posted in The Hague approached Nataliia about taking Russian lessons with her, there was an outcry among the patriotically minded males of the household. Nabokov himself was in two minds about it, having not yet shed the prejudices against Germans and Germany that the war had inculcated in him. However, perhaps remembering the friendly Saxon officers he had met in

Ukraine and the friendship he and his family had struck with Richard Möbius, he took his aunt's side and kept her company when the diplomat came for tea.

> The surprise was complete and completely baffling. The person who came into the room was young and good-looking, somewhat stocky and of medium height. He was dressed in dapper yet unostentatious clothes of an obviously English cut. His manner was mild and somewhat timid, his voice soft and pleasant and the expression on his face and in his clear blue eyes was that of gentle kindness and of a special kind of goodness mixed with a certain amount of *Verlegenheit*.[34] But what astonished me most of all—for it was the opposite of what I had expected—the person spoke exquisite French, devoid of any accent at all, and with an apparent ease and freedom of vocabulary which neither my aunt nor myself possessed. [. . .]I had expected to be confronted by a brutal, sub-human face, a dangerous *boche*, and instead I saw, sitting on my aunt's sofa, this mild, urbane-looking man, with gestures and manners that betrayed refined upbringing and what the French call *la politesse du cœur*.[35]

An immediate, lifelong friendship was struck that afternoon. When tea was over, the German diplomat walked Nabokov home and, since he himself lived nearby, invited him for a drink. His name was Alexandre Grunelius.[36] Born in 1890, he belonged, on his father's side, to a banking family, originally from Frankfurt-on-Main, which had established itself in Alsace after the province was incorporated into the newly proclaimed German Reich in 1871. His mother came from old Alsatian stock. He had studied at Oxford, where he was active in the Hanover Club, a discussion group formed before the war to promote mutual understanding between English and German students. During the war, he had served as an officer in the German army in Palestine. The world conflict, and its disastrous outcome for Germany, had triggered in him a crisis of conscience. An altruistic, idealistic, profoundly moral man, with what Nabokov described as a Tolstoyan sense of his responsibility towards other human beings, Grunelius, like other Germans of his generation, came to the conclusion that "there was in the very nature of the Wilhelminian society a hidden *hubris*, a *hubris* of tragic dimensions of which the reliance on military might (the Army and its *Generalstab*) was only an outward sign of an inward corruption and hollowness."

> And that corruption, that hollowness, they believed, had reached far beyond the ruling oligarchy of imperial Germany. It penetrated most of its bourgeois class. It cut through the fat of its *Spiessertum* [philistinism], through its bureaucracy, its academic world, and contaminated with a spirit of resigned helplessness the sparse liberal elements of the Wilhelminian

Reich. Alone the working classes of Germany's industrial capitals and a small segment of the educated and Europeanized aristocracy and intelligentsia were free from those nineteenth-century taints. Alone they could be relied upon for the building of a new, democratic Germany.[37]

Yet, Grunelius had also lost faith in the liberal ideals he had grown up with and which his Oxford education had further nurtured. What was needed, he felt, was a new faith, new ideals. And this was the source of the interest in Russia and the Russian language that had prompted him to contact Nataliia Peterson. Could the "great light in the East" (to borrow the title of Jules Romains's 1945 novel) be a path to salvation? Dostoyevsky, whose works Grunelius had just read in German translation, came up during that very first conversation.

> He was overwhelmed and taken in by what so many Western "discoverers" of Dostoyevsky find in him (and probably rightly so): his ability to describe with compelling persuasion a range of human passion, human suffering, anguish and despair, searching for them in the furthest recesses of the soul and reaching to the limits of the absurd. At the same time, and perhaps even more strongly, he admired Dostoyevky's and his protagonists' constant search for a living faith, their power of compassion, and their tragic, Manichean dilemma of perpetual internal combat between good and evil.[38]

At the same time, and to an even greater extent, Grunelius was struck by the Messianic tone of Dostoyevsky's great novels, by his belief in Russia's essential goodness and spiritual superiority to the decadent, materialistic, atheistic West.

> Thus Grunelius was taken in by what traditional, old-fashioned liberals (like for example my two uncles and my aunt Natalie) would have decried as Dostoyevsky's most obscurantist, reactionary, "Black-Hundred" beliefs. Grunelius, on the contrary, saw in these aspects of Dostoyevsky's writings a kind of special "message" to the world at large and this, of course, in the light of the events that followed the "October Revolution," of which he, like most foreigners at the time, knew very little. To him—at least in those days of the early twenties—Russia seemed a new and luminous beacon, a hope for a better world, an example of faith and courage, a thing to emulate, and above all a place where life was true and real.[39]

Those early conversations with Grunelius made a deep impression on Nabokov. Not only was the young German diplomat the only friend he made in the course of his stay in the Dutch capital; he was also, by Nabokov's own admission, the only person with whom he had had any serious kind of intellectual intercourse since leaving Russia. And for the first time, he realized the difficulties Russian emigres were going to face, for several decades, in their dealings with the liberal intelligentsia of their adoptive countries. No matter how well informed they were on the brutal, repressive, totalitarian nature of the Bolshevist police state, Western elites long remained convinced that there was, at its core, something fundamentally good which gave reasons to hope. In Grunelius's case, and thanks to Nabokov's influence, those illusions were not to last. Despite the age difference, a deep personal bond was formed between the two men. The young Russian exile, who was already experiencing feelings of isolation and loneliness, felt drawn towards the courteous, reserved junior German diplomat, himself unjustly ostracized in The Hague because of his nationality. This first contact taught Nabokov to distrust the generalizations and caricatures spread by official propaganda and to realize that, no matter what the political context was, there would always be men of culture and principles one could associate with. His view of Germany, already modified by his encounter with the young German officer at Askania-Nova, was forever transformed by this new friendship. It would never again be tainted by chauvinistic prejudice, even during the darkest days of the Nazi era. When, in early 1920, Nabokov left The Hague and moved to Stuttgart, where he was about to enter the music conservatory, Grunelius gave him letters of introduction to friends there and in Berlin. The latter, in particular, resulted in a few other long-lasting friendships.

4

In Stuttgart and Berlin

FOR A BUDDING composer of Nabokov's generation to pursue studies in composition, Germany was a natural choice. As he would later recall, one went to Germany to study music as a matter of course, just as one went to France to study painting and to Italy to study archeology and architecture: such were the prevailing assumptions among the Russian upper class.[1] Yet, in later life he also wondered whether that had been the best choice for someone of his disposition. In those days, Stravinsky, Bartók, Schoenberg, Berg, and Webern were far from having gained acceptance in Germany or Austria. The orthodoxy embraced Straussian post-romanticism, a lifelong aversion for Nabokov, or Brahmsian classicism, with which he felt no affinity either. The Royal Academy in London or the Paris Conservatoire might thus have been better choices than the Hochschule für Musik in Stuttgart, where he enrolled in January 1920. This was, at least, the conclusion he reached at the end of his life.

During his three semesters in Stuttgart, Nabokov studied counterpoint, orchestration, and music history, while taking additional courses in philosophy and medieval and Renaissance history. He also continued to study the piano with Max von Pauer (1866–1945). The son of Ernst Pauer (1826–1905), who had taught for many years at the Royal Academy of Music in London, von Pauer had just served, until 1918, as director of the Stuttgart Conservatory. He had the reputation of an excellent teacher. As for Nabokov's composition teacher, Joseph Haas (1879–1960),[2] he was an ardent disciple of Max Reger, with whom he had studied in Munich from 1904 onwards; he followed him to Leipzig three years later. Appointed at the Stuttgart Hochschule in 1916,[3] Haas had had so far a modest career as a composer. His output comprised a few piano and instrumental pieces and his reputation was above all that of a miniaturist. Only in the 1930s did he attain celebrity with his "folk oratorios" *Die heilige Elisabeth* (1931), *Christnacht* (1932), and *Das Lebensbuch Gottes* (1934), all involving audience participation, as

well as the opera *Tobias Wunderlich* (1937). Nabokov remembered his teacher as
"a gentle, round-faced man with frizzy, black cat's whiskers and an easy grin."[4]
A devout Roman Catholic, Haas was also devoted to the principles he had learned
from Reger: he taught his pupils to emulate his master's technique, forms, and
style, based on the great German tradition of polyphony and counterpoint, from
J. S. Bach to Brahms, and, of course, to emulate Reger himself. Modern composers he disapproved of—especially the Second Viennese School—were labeled
"cacophonists." Nabokov, in his memoirs, does not acknowledge much of a debt
to Haas's teaching. He particularly laments the fact that the musical examples
analyzed in class were limited to bits from Bach, Mozart, Beethoven, and Reger.
This prolonged exposure to Reger inspired in Nabokov a deep-seated dislike. In
a 1931 interview he singled him out as the one composer he truly detested and
referred to him as "the lowest point in music."[5] When it came to contemporary
music there was, as in Rebikov's days, "a lot too much" (as Stravinsky liked to say)
of Haas's own music. One suspects, however, that Nabokov received in Stuttgart,
"bourgeois, sedate, and provincial" as he may have found it, much more solid
instruction than he had in Yalta from his former mentor. Haas was, indeed, a
respected teacher, whose students included such fine musicians as the conductors
Eugen Jochum and Wolfgang Sawallisch.

Stuttgart had, at least, one positive effect on Nabokov's musical development.
According to his later recollections, there he fell in love with the music of Wagner.[6]
This brief but intense infatuation was, he recalled, "like a cyclone." "I can still picture myself seated at the piano, hammering down on the keyboard for hours on
end with a zeal worthy of Oberammergau, improvising on *Tristan* in a style somewhat reminiscent of Scriabin."[7] *Die Walküre*, as we have seen, had not made much
of an impression when Nabokov had seen it staged at the Mariinsky Theater. There
had been no further opportunities to hear more, since shortly afterward Wagner's
works were banned from opera houses while Russia was at war with Germany.
Stuttgart boasted a first-class opera house, where Strauss's *Ariadne auf Naxos* had
its world premiere in 1912. Its music director, as of 1918, was the distinguished
conductor Fritz Busch. Though Nabokov is unfortunately not specific in his recollections, it can be presumed that he attended Wagner performances in this house,
where Busch mounted, notably, *Das Rheingold* with revolutionary sets and lighting
by Adolphe Appia.[8] Nabokov may well have attended also, in early June 1921, the
Busch-conducted premiere of Paul Hindemith's one-act operas *Mörder, Hoffnung
der Frauen*, and *Das Nusch-Nuschi*, a major *succès de scandale*.

Nabokov's eighteen months in Stuttgart were a time of financial hardship.
War was going on between the newly independent Poland and Russia, with the
consequence that the Falz-Fein properties either remained under Soviet control or were in disputed territories. As a foreign student, he was ineligible for
the resident permits delivered by the Wohnungsamt (Housing Office) which

controlled all apartments in the city, and thus was not entitled to bread coupons in those days of rationing and ersatz food. To pay for his accommodation and food, Nabokov sold newspapers at the train station and worked as secretary to an emigre Armenian stamp collector and dealer named Fred Merovitch, writing his foreign correspondence. He also recalled having "helped," for a fee, less gifted but more prosperous conservatory classmates with their homework. But in this period of high inflation—even though the notorious "hyperinflation" did not begin until 1921—this proved insufficient to pay for meals at the pensione where he lived for several months. This pensione was owned by the Anthroposophical Society, the organization founded in 1913 by Rudolf Steiner, the Austrian philosopher, following his break with Annie Besant's Theosophical Society. After the war Stuttgart became one of the centers of Steiner's activities: the first Waldorf School, based on his progressive pedagogical principles, opened there in 1919. Eventually Nabokov was able to have his meals subsidized by playing the piano for several hours in the evening while the women of the pensione practiced their eurhythmics exercises ("eurhythmy" being one of the activities prescribed by the Anthroposophical system). Chopin was often requested, but even more popular was Scriabin, in view of his theosophical leanings. Nabokov thus had to play Scriabin etudes, preludes, and sonatas *ad nauseam*, while women in black tights or long dresses danced as in a trance, and a bespectacled reader, who claimed the privilege of having made the acquaintance of Scriabin, declaimed, "in a sing-song baritone and an appalling Dutch accent," theosophical poems by Morgenstern and others. Nabokov was thus able to familiarize himself with the tenets of Scriabin's musico-mystical system, which he later summarized in the following terms:

> Mankind's auditive and visual senses were to be aroused to a state of frenzied love for the male on the part of the female by Scriabin's music, based on the permutations of his "mystical chord" with which he experimented (but never quite succeeded in bringing into existence). These two factors— the "chord play" and the "color play"—were supposed to act as "super aphrodisiacs" and bring these two beings into a state of erotic ecstasy, leading via a sexual act to a state of permanent "oneness."[9]

One assumes that the evenings at the Anthroposophical pensione, along with the discovery of Wagner, went some way towards curing Nabokov's adolescent "Scriabinosis."

The happiest episode Nabokov remembered from his Stuttgart stay was an unexpected reunion with someone he never expected to see again. Early in 1920, he went, out of curiosity, to visit a Dadaist exhibition which had been savaged by the local press. As he was contemplating the Schwitters-like "objects" made of wire, cotton, and newspaper clippings, he heard behind him a familiar voice.

To his astonishment, he recognized Richard Möbius, whom he and his family had presumed dead.[10] Indeed, after the attack on his convoy, the young German officer had spent twenty-four grueling hours among dead or dying soldiers, but had managed to escape and had been rescued by a peasant woman. Evacuated to Germany with a retreating regiment, after several weeks he had found his way back to Saxony. He was now living in a house in the hilly southern part of Stuttgart and was writing a novel based on his Russian experience. He and Nabokov resumed their friendship at once and during the latter half of Nabokov's Stuttgart stay saw each other on a quasi-daily basis. Nabokov had by then left the Anthroposophical pensione and rented a small room at the home of a kindly working class family at no. 12, Seidenstrasse, in the city center. Möbius's main interests had shifted from literature to politics. His sympathies appeared to be with the Spartakus movement, the ancestor of the German Communist Party, whose main leaders, Karl Liebknecht and Rosa Luxemburg, had been murdered following the failed January 1919 Communist uprising in Berlin. Möbius introduced Nabokov to their writings and suggested he read Marx and Engels's *Communist Manifesto*, along with classic political thinkers such as Montesquieu and Rousseau.

Poland's victory over the Soviets in March 1921 had a positive consequence for Nabokov's family: their properties, long part of the Russian empire, were no longer under Soviet control; Novogrudok (its name changed to Nowogrodek) and Baranowice now belonged to Poland. His mother was soon able to sell a forest and settle in Berlin with her other two children, between stays at Lubcza and in the South of France. On September 8, 1920, in Berlin, Onya got married to Viktor Fasolt, the Thurigian officer she and Nicolas had met and befriended two years previously at Preobrazhenka. After his return and demobilization, Fasolt had kept contact with Onya, while beginning a business career in the film industry. Nabokov attended his sister's wedding, as did his cousins Vladimir and Sergei, who had just completed their first undergraduate year at Cambridge—Sergei had first gone to Oxford but after an unhappy first term joined his brother at the "other place"—, and all the Nabokovs and Falz-Feins who had resettled in Germany. Among them was Uncle Frederick, now living in a sanatorium, where he died two years later, a broken man pining away for his beloved Askania-Nova.[11]

By contrast with Stuttgart, there was nothing provincial about the German capital, which was in fact entering one of the great periods of its cultural history. It was, in the early 1920s, the main center of the Russian emigration, with a community which by 1923 numbered half a million people, who lived mostly in the city's western sections. "There were," Nabokov recalled, "Russian newspapers, Russian theaters, Russian schools and churches, Russian cabarets and libraries, Russian literary clubs and publishing houses, Russian foreign-exchange speculators, Russian bookstores, Russian art galleries, grocery stores, confiseries and antique or bargain stores that sold false and real Fabergé jewelry and a lot of genuine and fake icons."

> All around, on the walls and on the advertising pillars, one saw announcements, sometimes in Russian, not only of Russian opera performances and concerts given by Russian artists, but also of Russian political meetings, officers' clubs, welfare committees. Dowager ballerinas opened ballet schools, writers held forums and public readings of prose and poetry. Above all, there was (as there always is when Russians meet) a flow of benefit functions: concerts, dinners, and balls, to which natives and other foreigners were lured by the promise of "authentic" Russian entertainment, and which helped replenish the ever dwindling funds of Russian welfare committees and concomittantly increase the meager incomes of those who worked for them.[12]

When he moved to Berlin in the summer of 1921 to pursue his musical studies at the conservatory, Nabokov, whose childhood and adolescence had been dominated by the Falz-Fein side of his family, at last became a full-fledged member of the Nabokov clan. His mother's spacious flat, furnished in Jugenstil and Moorish styles, was at no. 16, Landhausstrasse, in the fashionable western suburb of Wilmersdorf. Nearby, on Sächsische Strasse, lived the family of his uncle Vladimir, who had left London in the fall of 1920 and founded in Berlin the important Russian emigre daily called *Rul'* (The Rudder). Babushka Nabokova had been able to escape from Soviet Russia with the retreating White Army and also lived in her son's flat. Whereas in Crimea, Nabokov had felt a degree of reticence in his uncle and aunt's attitude towards him, which he attributed to rumors about his illegitimacy, by the time he moved to Berlin all traces of uneasiness had vanished, and he was a regular guest for lunch or dinner. The Nabokov home in Berlin was a center of emigre cultural life, with "a constant flow of visitors: writers, scholars, artists, politicians, and journalists."[13] Some had newly arrived from Russia, either to remain in Berlin or Germany, or on their way to Paris, London, or New York. Others, more or less halfheartedly, were on their way back to Russia. The table talk was "gay and lively," especially when Vladimir and Sergei visited from England.[14] His cousin Vladimir he continued to find often intimidating and occasionally intolerant, not least when it came to linguistic matters. (Years later, Nicolas remained persuaded that, notwithstanding his cousin's peremptory denial, *klubnika* meant "garden strawberry" and *zemlianika* "wild strawberry.")[15] He was also disconcerted by Vladimir's irrepressible mischievousness, as when egging on the Nabokovs' oversexed dog towards his cousin's leg.[16] Sergei, on the other hand, remained a favorite as well as a literary and artistic mentor. Nicolas also grew fond of their sister Elena, his junior by three years, to such an extent that they were almost considered engaged. His own mother, however, was not in favor of the alliance and any matrimonial dreams there might have been were nipped in the bud.[17]

At his uncle and aunt's, Nabokov frequently saw members of the Moscow Art Theater. Part of the troupe, led by Konstantin Stanislavsky, its founder, had left Russia during the civil war, and before they returned to Moscow, as they did in 1923, they performed Russian plays, in Russian, for the Berlin emigre community. The company's female star was Olga Knipper-Chekhova, Chekhov's widow, who had taken part in the premieres of *The Seagull, Uncle Vanya, The Three Sisters,* and *The Cherry Orchard.* She befriended Nicolas, who would walk her back to her pensione after performances. They disagreed on Strindberg, one of whose plays Nabokov had seen performed at Max Reinhardt's Deutsches Theater, but whom she found "much too hysterical," especially when played by German actors. Many years later, though, when Nabokov saw her again in Paris on the occasion of a triumphant tour of the Moscow Art Theater, she admitted that she had come around on the Swedish playwright—provided, she added, he wasn't performed in the German manner.[18] As for Stanislavsky, Nabokov found his acting masterful, yet in a style that struck him as already old-fashioned, and even "stale."[19] On one occasion Stanislavsky came to tea at the Nabokovs with Alexander Moissi, the Austrian-Albanian actor and one of the leading members of Reinhardt's troupe, with Nicolas acting as interpreter. When the conversation came to Moissi's interpretation of Fedor in Tolstoy's *The Living Corpse,* his signature role, Stanislavsky could not refrain from expressing reservations about Moissi's extrovert performance, leaving the Austrian mortified and disappointed. Decades later, seeing a poorly directed play about Chekhov in Moscow, Nabokov could not help commenting in his diary that Russians were "*born* actors."[20]

The Berlin Hochschule für Musik, where Nabokov enrolled as a student in the fall of 1921, was directed since the previous year by the eminent Austrian composer Franz Schreker (1878–1934), whose operas *Die ferne Klang* (1912) and *Der Schatzgräber* (1920) then rivaled Strauss's own in popularity. Schreker's name does not appear in Nabokov's autobiography, but it is unlikely that he found the luscious post-romantic language of these works congenial. Nabokov's counterpoint and composition teacher, Paul Juon (1872–1940), was a Russian-German musician.[21] Born in Moscow to a family of German and Swiss descent, he had studied the violin and composition at the Moscow Imperial Conservatory, the latter with Arensky and Taneev, before moving to Berlin, where he settled permanently in 1897. Juon was the author of a treatise on harmony, published in 1901 and reissued into the 1940s. He had taught at the Berlin Hochschule from 1906, becoming full professor in 1911. Unlike Joseph Haas, who was best known for his piano music and later established his reputation with his oratorios and operas, Juon had written little for the piano and never wrote for the stage. His output comprised a fair amount of orchestral music, including two symphonies and two violin concertos (a third would follow in 1931), which earned him the nickname "the Russian Brahms." Like Brahms, he also devoted himself to chamber music: violin sonatas, piano trios, quartets, and quintets. He shared with his student an interest in Tchaikovsky: indeed Juon had translated into German Tchaikovsky's *Guide to the Practical Study of Harmony* as well as Modest Tchaikovsky's biography of his brother. This background would suggest he might have been a more sympathetic teacher than Haas had been. Yet, on the scant evidence of his later recollections, Nabokov does not appear to have greatly enjoyed studying with Juon. Like Haas a highly respected teacher, he trained his pupils in the most time-honored fashion: harmony, fugue, counterpoint, orchestration. Palestrina, a figure that had been recently popularized in the musical world by Hans Pfitzner's 1917 opera, was held as a supreme model; Nabokov remembers being asked to write a fragment of a mass in exact imitation of his style, or of the "isorhythmic" motets of the Flemish Renaissance polyphonist Heinrich Isaac—and hating the "stilted and lifeless" results.[22] Even in the area of early music, he regretted not being exposed to a greater variety of early masters like Guillaume de Machaut, Josquin des Prez, or other Burgundian, English, Flemish, or Italian masters. Yet, much later in life, he admitted that as a teacher of modal counterpoint Juon was known as being better than anyone in Berlin and that he learned a great deal from him. Summarizing his musical apprenticeship in Germany, he told an interviewer: "I owe Professor Haas my thorough knowledge of traditional harmony, and Paul Juon my knowledge of counterpoint and fugue."[23]

A potentially more exciting presence in Berlin was that of Ferruccio Busoni. After spending the war years in exile in Switzerland, the famous Austro-Italian composer had been invited in 1920 to teach a masterclass in composition at the Akademie der Künste; he also entertained young musicians at his home on Viktoria-Luise-Platz. Of his teaching, however, Nabokov only recalled "endless ramblings about aesthetics, styles of performance, ways to transcribe organ and cembalo music to the pianoforte."[24] He seems to have derived more benefits from the lectures on the history of music given by Georg Schünemann (1884–1945), Schreker's deputy and successor when the latter resigned under Nazi pressure, until his own dismissal by the Nazis.[25] In Berlin, Nabokov also heard lectures by Erich von Hornbostel (1877–1935), the Austrian-born pioneer of ethnomusicology, who later briefly taught at the New School of Social Research in New York.[26] Nabokov also mentioned the name of the Russian-born pianist Leonid Kreutzer (1884–1953), a noted interpreter of Chopin, who taught at the Hochschule from 1921 until 1933, but he is not more specific about his studies with him.[27]

In Berlin, however, Nabokov had numerous opportunities to meet fellow composers and other musicians. There was Kurt Weill, his senior by three years, who,
having previously studied at the Hochschule with Humperdinck, returned in 1921
especially to study with Busoni. If he frequented Busoni's salon, Nabokov, at the
time, could have rubbed shoulders with Hindemith (born in 1895), whom he got
to know well in the late 1920s; and also with Ernst Krenek (born in 1900) as well
as the future conductors Jascha Horenstein (1899–1973), like Krenek a student
of Schreker, and the Greek-born Dimitri Mitropoulous (1896–1960), who, in the
1930s and 1940s, was to conduct Nabokov's music.

Nabokov's uncle Vladimir was a music lover and this created one more bond
between them. He and his nephew started attending public dress rehearsals of
the Berlin Philharmonic Orchestra on Sunday mornings, bringing pocket scores
to follow the music. "It was at those Sunday morning concerts (and the discussions with Uncle Vladimir that followed) that I received the first truly useful
and lasting part of my musical education," Nabokov subsequently claimed, perhaps a little unfairly toward Haas and Juon.[28] Uncle and nephew did not agree
on every musical topic: Vladimir, who put Beethoven above all others, thus did
not share his nephew's love for Tchaikovsky. Yet, even he was won over when
they both heard Tchaikovsky's Fifth Symphony performed by the Philharmonic
under its permanent conductor, Arthur Nikisch, whose reading Nabokov remembered as admirably precise and devoid of sentimentality.[29] Wary (like his own
son Vladimir) of anything smacking of romanticism, Uncle Vladimir, for his
part, preferred to stress the "lyrical" beauty of what they heard; Nicolas was to
remember this aesthetic distinction between lyricism and romanticism as one
he always found especially useful.[30] This concert must have been one of the
great Austro-Hungarian conductor's last, since he died in January 1922. Nabokov
and his uncle also heard Nikisch's successor Wilhelm Furtwängler, with whom
Nabokov was to enter into personal contact in the years immediately following
the Second World War.

Another music lover was Nabokov's cousin Sergei, with whom he attended
concerts and opera performances—including one of Götterdämmerung at which,
so he told Isaiah Berlin, Siegfried's undernourished horses, in those days of
hyperinflation, ate Hagen's beard.[31] While Sergei was an ardent Wagnerite, Nicolas
had already lost his enthusiasm for the Bayreuth master. They both, however,
loved Verdi, and heard his operas performed in German, as was the custom, at one
or the other of the three opera houses active in Berlin in the 1920s: the Deutsche
Staatsoper on Unter der Linden, then headed by the composer Max von Schillings;
the Kroll Oper, which was to become an outstanding avant-garde theater when
Otto Klemperer was appointed its music director in 1926; and the Deutsches
Opernhaus in Charlottenburg, renamed Städtische Oper in 1925, under the leadership of Bruno Walter. It was in the company of his cousin Sergei, early into his

Berlin stay, that Nabokov heard, for the first time, Stravinsky's *Rite of Spring*, conducted by Klemperer. Yet the work, at the time not well known in Germany, was
not, as he recalled, "the shock that I expected it to be."

> I was stunned by its power and its originality, but it seemed outside, or
> beyond any personal experience of mine. It did not fit into any of the
> musical landscapes I had been wandering in and was accustomed to, nor
> had I acquired at that age any kind of yardstick by which I could measure
> Stravinsky's art.[32]

With his family in close proximity, Nabokov's material circumstances were better than in Stuttgart. He made a little money by giving private lessons in music
and languages (French, German, and Russian). For a short while, he worked as
accompanist to a high Russian tenor who produced himself in a series of "soporific" recitals entitled "History of Russian vocal music in twelve concerts," featuring songs from Glinka to Grechaninov.[33] More interestingly, he was quickly
hired by his uncle, at the instigation of his cousin Sergei and his aunt Elena, as
a contributor to *Rul'*. His initial review of a recital given by a young Russian pianist having been accepted, he became the daily's junior music critic. By his own
account, he soon tried to abuse this position by requesting tickets for concerts
the senior critic had reserved for himself, but when this was found out and his
job was in jeopardy, his uncle and aunt prevented him from being fired and got
him promoted instead. As a result, Nabokov was able to take his uncle to more
concerts of symphonic and chamber music, which he remembered as some of
the best he ever heard.[34]

This happy situation tragically came to an end on March 28, 1922. That evening, Pavel Miliukov, who as Foreign Minister had been a colleague of Nabokov's
uncle in the Russian provisional government in 1917, just back from an American
tour, addressed a large audience at the Philharmonie Hall on the subject of
"America and the Restoration of Russia." In the middle of Miliukov's lecture,
around 10 p.m., a right-wing extremist by the name of Peter Shabelsky-Bork fired
several shots at him, that missed. V. D. Nabokov got hold of the would-be assassin
and pinned him to the floor, but was himself shot at once by Shabelsky's accomplice, a certain Sergei Taboritsky, and died on the spot. Reached by telephone, V. D.
Nabokov's wife and son Vladimir, who was on holiday from Cambridge, rushed to
the Philharmonie but they were not allowed by the police into the room where the
body lay and Miliukov kept an all-night vigil.[35] To Nicolas, who received the news
at about midnight, was left the gruesome task of identifying his uncle's corpse at
the morgue the next morning. On April 1, he attended the funeral at the Russian
cemetery at Tegel where, as he noted in his autobiography, Glinka, who had died
in Berlin in 1857, had initially been buried before his ashes were repatriated.[36]

The dramatic disappearance of an uncle he had come to love and revere was nearly as devastating to Nicolas as to his cousins' family. As he puts it in *Bagázh*, his "vital center," his "Russian home in Berlin," was no more. Vladimir and Sergei returned to England to complete their university studies. The following year, his aunt Elena moved to Prague with her daughters and younger son, and he never saw them again. As for Babushka Nabokova, she moved to Dresden after her son's death. There she was courted by a senator ten years her junior, and after his accidental death was invited by Queen Marie of Romania to live in her palace on the Black Sea coast. She soon longed for Berlin and might have returned there had she not died within a few months, in her late eighties, as the result of a fall.

Fortunately Nabokov's social and intellectual life in Berlin was not limited to Russian emigre circles. Soon after his arrival, he sent the letter of recommendation Alexandre Grunelius had given him in The Hague to its recipient, who belonged to the highest circles of German society. Count Albrecht von Bernstorff[37] was the scion of an enlightened family of Prussian diplomats: his uncle, Johann-Heinrich von Bernstorff (1862–1939) was German ambassador to the United States from 1908 until the declaration of war. Born in 1890, Albrecht had read political economy as a Rhodes scholar at Trinity College, Oxford, in 1909–11. Like Grunelius, his junior by two years, he was a member of the Hanover Club. He then enrolled as a law student at the Christian-Albrechts-Universität in Kiel. Around that time, he fell passionately, if platonically, in love with his cousin Elly Reventlow, who was from an aristocratic background in Schleswig-Holstein. Following the family tradition, he entered the diplomatic service and was initially posted in Vienna in 1914. Bernstorff thus became acquainted with such figures as Hugo von Hoffmannsthal, Rainer Maria Rilke, and Arthur Schnitzler. When Nabokov met him, he was working as a volunteer at the Berlin bank of Delbrück, Schickler & Co, at a particularly troubled time for German finances.

One of Bernstorff's closest friends, killed in action during the war, was Friedrich, the elder son of Theobald von Bethmann-Hollweg, who served as German chancellor from 1909 until 1917. Through Bernstorff, Nabokov became acquainted with Friedrich's younger brother Felix, who came on his bicycle to introduce himself at Lydia Peucker's flat in Wilmersdorf. A person of culture and taste, yet exceptionally modest, handsome, and charming, combining warmth and a sense of humor, he immediately won Nabokov's friendship—a friendship that lasted until Bethmann-Hollweg's death in 1972.

Tall, slender, shy and timid, extremely well mannered, speaking excellent French and fair English, he was the image of a Gothic aristocrat, with an elongated, handsome face, as if hewn out of a well-seasoned oak. He had large blue eyes with a ready, humorous twinkle in them, though always concealing a deep-seated hue of *malinconia*.[38]

Nabokov was soon invited to visit Hohenfinow, the Bethmann-Hollweg family estate in Brandenburg, to the north of Berlin. Felix had inherited it on the death of his father in January 1921 and shared it with his maternal aunt.

It was a seventeenth-century castle in that simple, baroque style that had been developed by Danes, Swedes, and North Germans. The house was square, large with a grand oaken staircase going up three floors in a hall-way under a skylight. The most lived-in room of the house was a grand multilingual library with a commodious open fireplace. Next to it was Felix's office, also largely paneled with books.

Beyond the house was a formal terrace surrounded by rosebeds and on one of its sides an open loggia, where breakfast and afternoon tea was served in the summer. Beyond the terrace, for several hundred acres stretched a park boarded by allees of ancient linden containing a fish-pond, a trout-farm, and a running little stream whose name no one seemed to remember. All of this stood in the midst of thousands of acres of well tended farmland and forest.[39]

The Bethmann-Hollwegs were by tradition a family of bankers, scholars, civil servants, and politicians. Felix, born in 1898, had chosen a different path: when Nabokov met him, he was studying agronomy at the University of Berlin. He devoted himself to the development and embellishment of the estate and made Hohenfinow into a model farm. The "charmed castle" of Hohenfinow, where Bethmann-Hollweg maintained an atmosphere of elegant informality, became for Nabokov one of the few places where he could feel at home. As Nabokov subsequently wrote, "it was rare at that time for Russian refugees to have friends among Germans, especially of the societal strata to which Felix belonged. Russians lived largely outside the German circles and even Russian writers, com-posers, painters and poets saw few Germans."[40] Without Nabokov's chance meet-ing with Grunelius in The Hague in 1919, one doubts this almost miraculous admission into the highest, most enlightened spheres of German society would have occurred.

Though dating from a few years later, an unpublished set of songs Nabokov composed at Hohenfinow is a telling testimony to the atmosphere of leisure and culture Bethmann-Hollweg liked to surround themselves with. It is a series of six short pieces Nabokov composed in the early fall of 1927 as a gift to Felix on his twenty-ninth birthday. The songs are settings of Aesop's fables in French ver-sions by the seventeenth-century court poet Isaac de Benserade, who wrote them in 1675 to accompany hydraulic sculpture groups in the gardens of Versailles; the choice may thus have been a tribute to Bethmann-Hollweg's agronomic pursuits. Nabokov's songs were presented to Felix along with watercolors by Heinz

Boese, a young artist who was also a regular guest at Hohenfinow, where one of his frescoes adorned the master bedroom. Trained as a painter at the Akademie der Künste in Berlin, Boese was especially gifted as a cartoonist and caricaturist, whose satirical wit was often directed at the Prussian military culture. His style, Nabokov thought, was in "the same baroque manner that has characterized so much German draftsmanship, for example the nineteenth-century cartoons of Wilhelm Busch, the macabre drawings of George Grosz of the 1920s and, lately, the brilliant etchings and drawings of Horst Janssen."[41] One of Nabokov's songs is dedicated to Boese; another to a Miss von Pfuel, a cousin of Bethmann-Hollweg on his mother's side (one Pfuel had been a Prussian prime minister); and two more to Count Julius von Zech-Burkersroda (1873–1946), a diplomat and former right arm of Felix's father, and his wife.[42]

When the German version of Nabokov's autobiography came out in 1975, Nabokov was taken to task for having "fabricated" the account of his relations with Count Harry Kessler.[43] That Nabokov came to know the art collector and Ballets Russes patron is not in doubt: there are substantial references to him in Kessler's published diaries, and a few letters from Kessler to Nabokov have survived. Even Kessler's American biographer, while characterizing Nabokov as an "unreliable source" and calling his account "vivid and wholly implausible," admits that the gist of his reminiscences is corroborated by other testimonies.[44] There is no doubt, on the other hand, that Nabokov embellished details and reinvented, or more precisely transposed, the chronology and history of their friendship, with the result that it cannot be easily reconstituted.

When he started drafting his recollections of Kessler, Nabokov couldn't remember precisely when and where he first met him.[45] Was it, he wondered, at a luncheon hosted by Bernstorff at the Automobil-Club on Leipziger Platz, as he subsequently chose to report it in *Bagázh*?[46] Or was it at Bernstorff's home? A third, equally likely possibility would be that they met through Helene von Nostitz, who "ran the most attractive and most international artistic and literary salon of Berlin," where Nabokov was introduced, through either Bernstorff or Bethmann-Hollweg, soon after his arrival in the city.[47] Born Helene von Beneckendorff und Hindenburg in 1878, she was the niece of Paul von Hindenburg, the general and future German president, and in 1904 had married Alfred von Nostitz-Wallitz, one of Kessler's closest friends from his student days at the University of Leipzig. Helene herself was an intimate of Kessler, who once referred to her as "the only woman [. . .] he could ever imagine marrying."[48] Wherever it may have taken place, this initial meeting between Nabokov and Kessler apparently did not go well. Was Nabokov, as he claims in *Bagázh*, self-conscious about finding himself in the presence of the famous cosmopolitan aesthete, whose friends included Diaghilev, Strauss, and Max Reinhardt? Born in 1868, Kessler was then fifty-three.

He looked more German-Junkerish than I had expected, but, at the same time, smaller and frailer than in the photographs I had seen in the papers. His hair was brown-blond and was as carefully glazed as the shine in his light blue eyes. His hands were small, with dainty fingers and well-manicured nails. His clothes were dark, tweedy, and dapper. He spoke in a soft monotone, as upper-class Germans often do, and as he spoke his face did not move at all, only his eyes blinked at rhythmic intervals, very fast, like camera shutters.[49]

As reconstituted by Nabokov, the conversation resembled a botched job interview. Kessler wanted to know whether he was acquainted with Diaghilev, whom Nabokov had yet to meet; whether he liked Maillol, an artist Kessler was particularly close to but whom Nabokov had never heard of; whether he preferred Rilke to Valéry, neither of whom Nabokov had read; and similar questions about Meyerhold, Trotsky, Nijinsky, and Pavlova. At least Nabokov had seen the last named dance her signature *Dying Swan* at a benefit performance in Berlin, but he had not liked it. Having run out of questions, Kessler lost interest. That was the way, Bernstorff explained to Nabokov, he usually behaved towards strangers.

The next meeting with Kessler, according to *Bagázh*, occurred a few months later under lively circumstances, the details of which Nabokov probably embroidered to some extent.[50] Although he does not appear to have had any strong ties with members of the emigre literary community, one exception was Aleksei Remizov. Born in Moscow in 1877, Remizov was already reputed before the war as a modernist, satirical novelist, and short-story writer. He was thus, his notorious eccentricity notwithstanding, one of the prominent Russian figures living in Berlin. Nabokov met him, early in his Berlin stay, in the offices of *Rul'*, and was in turn introduced to his wife Serafina, shortly after their own arrival from Russia. They befriended him and he made it a weekly habit to visit them in their flat on his way back from his classes at the Hochschule. "I liked to come and talk to Aleksei Mihailovich and Serafina Pavlovna," he later reminisced, "and not only because he was one of Russia's best known writers, but because I had discovered in both of them, but especially in him (and quite intuitively, of course), an authentic morsel of a Russia I had not known before."[51] Physically, Remizov, whom Andrey Bely famously compared to a "tiny devil," was unprepossessing: "a gnome-like, hunchbacky creature out of a world of Russian or even pre-Russian saga."

His features were distinctly Mongolian. He had upward slit eyes hiding behind thick lenses (he was cross-eyed and shortsighted). His eyebrows were bushy, black, triangular, and his button nose was turned upward—a "rain nose," as one used to say in Russia. His ears were oversized, fawn-like,

his lips thick and meaty, over a receding chin. An elf-like smile hovered in
the corners of his mouth—childishly playful and a bit mischievous.

All of these facial "gimmicks" were collected in the center of something
that resembled a pale melon, and though the head was small it seemed too
large for the neck and the frail, diminutive body that carried it. He was like
a fairy tale, sylvan creature, part fawn, part sorcerer, who belonged to the
world of mosses, fern, and juniper, rather than to the Berliner Wohnung
in which he lived. [. . .]He drank great quantities of tea and shuffled noise-
lessly, catwise in felt babooshes through the rooms of his tiny flat.[52]

On Nabokov's nineteenth birthday in 1922, Remizov, whose taste for calligra-
phy bordered on the obsession, presented him with a document on parchment
appointing him to a high rank in the imaginary simian world presided over by His
Majesty Asyka (i.e., Remizov himself), ruler of the monkeys. Such jokes, which
permeate Remizov's writings, were not to everyone's taste, least of all to Nabokov's
cousin Vladimir, who mortally offended Remizov with his devastating review of
his collection *Zvezda nadvieznaia* when it came out in Paris in 1928.[53] Ivan Bunin,
the dean of emigre Russian letters (and 1933 Nobel Prize in literature) could not
abide him either; even Nina Berberova, who liked Remizov as a writer, found his
quirks insufferable when she got to know him in Berlin.[54] To Nicolas, such quirks
were the harmless manifestations of a mind living in fantasy, its natural element,
much as he liked to surround himself with amulets and seemingly took every
form of superstition with the greatest seriousness. Though his own admiration for
Remizov as a writer was not unqualified, on a personal level Nabokov had a soft
spot for him and his wife and was grateful for the hospitality they always extended
to him in Berlin. He never lost touch with Remizov—he thus took Prokofiev to
visit him in Paris in March 1928.[55] Much later,, he found a way to come to his help
at the end of his life with a subsidy from the Congress for Cultural Freedom.

In Berlin, Remizov frequented a literary society known diversely as the
Russian Club or *Dom Iskusstva* (House of the Arts), which had its quarters on
Nollendorfplatz in the Schöneberg district. It included a restaurant, the Café
Landgraf, where readings were held every week. Organized by the veteran symbolist poet Nikolai Maksimovich Minsky (1855–1937), these soirees were one of the
few points of contact between emigre writers and those visiting from the Soviet
Union or about to return there. Nabokov, who had met Minsky when visiting the
sculptor Archipenko at his flat, was not a regular attendant at these soirees: despite
the occasional recital, the Dom Iskusstva programs were mostly literary and artistic. Yet he once accompanied the composer Aleksandr Glazunov, visiting from
the Soviet Union, to hear Bunin read some of his latest short stories.[56] Sometime
during the first months of 1922, Minsky implored Nabokov and Remizov to attend
the next Friday meeting and help him entertain Isadora Duncan, who was about

to stop in Berlin for a couple of days on her way back from Russia and en route to Paris in the company of Sergei Esenin, her boyfriend and fiancé. Nabokov's original account of this episode is even more picturesque than the published version, in which Remizov and his wife were edited out.

When Nabokov came to pick up the Remizovs in the evening of the following Friday, neither of them was ready. When they finally arrived at the Café Langraf, an apprehensive Minsky informed them that Esenin and Isadora were in their cups and had already had a fight. Nabokov had no trouble spotting the smartly dressed young poet, who looked "astonishingly young and pretty—the freckled face of a Russian peasant."[57] Isadora, conversely, had the appearance of "a Roman matron after revels." Having deliberately snubbed Remizov, whose name and reputation were surely familiar to him, Esenin similarly ignored Minsky's invitation to read some of his poems and was soon heard making a scene at the bar. Appalled by his bad manners, Remizov and his wife fled and Nabokov was about to imitate them, when Esenin, running after him, begged him to accompany him and his "mare" to a gay club nearby; indeed the area around Nollendorfplatz was during the Weimar years—and still is—the center of Berlin gay life.

Having found a club of the kind Esenin had in mind on Bülowstrasse, Nabokov sat down with him and Isadora at a table close to the dance floor. While the poet ordered bottles of champagne and vodka, the composer, to his dismay, realized that Kessler was seated at a nearby table, in the company of two other people: one was a blond young man—Max Goertz, Kessler's sometime lover and factotum— and a very young dark-haired woman wearing a male suit jacket and a top hat.[58] As Esenin got drunker and noisier, Nabokov was alarmed to see Kessler, who had recognized Isadora, making his way towards their table and asking to be introduced. Contrary to Nabokov's apprehensions, "the evening ended in general fraternization."[59] Having overcome his initial mistrust, Esenin proceeded to mix vodka and champagne for everyone around. While Kessler and Isadora exchanged reminiscences about prewar Paris, Kessler's young woman companion took an interest in Nabokov and put her arm around his neck. According to an early manuscript draft of the episode, when all finally departed in their respective taxis, Kessler was waving Nabokov's handkerchief, "upon which Esenin had written, with Isadora's lipstick, in a large bloody letters, a grandiose Russian obscenity."[60]

Despite, or perhaps because of, the liveliness and precision of Nabokov's account, the authenticity of this unexpected encounter with Kessler in a gay cabaret is open to doubt. It is hard to believe that Kessler, a celebrity collector and compulsive name-dropper, would not have mentioned in his diary meeting Duncan and Esenin, even without specifying the locale. As for internal evidence, certain puzzling, conflicting variants in the manuscripts drafts for *Bagázh* seem to suggest that the episode might have resulted from a collage of several episodes that occurred at different times and in different places.[61] One of the unverifiable questions Nabokov's account raises is the identity of Kessler's young woman companion that evening. A character straight out of Christopher Isherwood's *Good-Bye to Berlin*, she is simply referred by the diminutive Doderl in *Bagázh*, but earlier, extensive drafts, where her family name is also hidden, give her name as Judith or Ruth. She was, Nabokov recalls, the daughter of prosperous German Jewish merchants.[62] In the uninhibited climate of the Weimar Republic, she was sexually free with both men and women and was fond of talking openly about sex. Although she flirted with Nabokov on that first night and on other occasions, they did not become lovers but rather friends and confidants. Nabokov, in any event, credits her for "forcing" him on Kessler by taking him or getting him invited to Kessler's receptions. As for Kessler, according to Nabokov, he began to show some interest in his protege's friend and even offered to show his music to Richard Strauss. Nabokov declined to pursue the offer, having no music ready to be shown and, besides, caring little for the opinion of a composer he never particularly liked.[63]

In *Bagázh*, "Doderl" is also credited for getting Nabokov invited—as a stand-in for her boyfriend, who was ill—to visit Kessler at his house in Weimar in May 1922, when Rilke was staying for a week. This equally lively episode, enhanced by Nabokov's preference for "dramatic" storytelling and reconstituted dialogues, cannot have taken place as reported. For one thing, the date of the visit conflicts with the evidence found in Kessler's diaries, which came to light in 1983 and have now been published in their entirety: in the spring of 1922 Kessler was in Genoa from April 10 until May 17, and then in Rome until June 2. The only times he was at his villa were March 29–31 and July 15–20. Furthermore, even if one assumes that Nabokov's visit to Weimar took place in a different month or in a different year,[64] no stay of Rilke at Kessler's villa is recorded in the early 1920s (or at any other time).[65] As the distinguished literary scholar Hans Mayer pointed out when the German edition of *Bagázh* was published, Rilke left Germany in 1919 and spent the rest of his life in Switzerland, Paris, and Venice. He knew Kessler, but evidently had no contact with him after 1918.[66]

Nabokov's account, on the other hand, strongly suggests that he *did* visit Kessler in Weimar, but in all likelihood this visit took place several years later, by which time he was on reasonably friendly terms with Kessler: in fact an April 1929 letter from Kessler in the handful preserved at Yale specifically refers to such an invitation, and there could have been earlier ones.[67] A clue can actually be found in *Bagázh* at the passage where Nabokov recalls being shown books published by Kessler's private press, the Cranach Presse (named after the street on which the Weimar villa was located): the reference to *Hamlet* being printed at the time, while it once again rules out 1922, suggests late 1927 or the following spring, since the book came out in 1928.[68] Be that as it may, Nabokov has left a vivid description of Kessler's house: designed before the First World War by the celebrated Belgian architect Henry van de Velde (1863–1957), the villa was, both inside and outside, a masterpiece of Art Nouveau style. It was surrounded by a garden in which, as Nabokov remembered it, all the flowers were white, with statues by Rodin, Maillol, and other sculptors patronized by the host.

This leaves the issue of the meeting with Rilke as reported in *Bagázh*. If it is not entirely apocryphal (and references scattered in Nabokov family letters tend to confirm its authenticity), one has to assume it took place at a different venue. The likeliest possibility is that the encounter occurred in Paris in 1925 or 1926, towards the very end of Rilke's life, through one of the literary hostesses Nabokov came to know in the French capital, such as Marguerite Caetani or Misia Sert. This later date would fit with the sickly appearance of the poet as Nabokov recalled him, "huddled up in shawls and a Scotch plaid."

> Only the face, a very pale, emaciated one with drooping mustaches and light-gray, watery eyes, was visible inside the woolen package. The package looked as if someone were trying to comfort a very sickly lap dog, and if the creature would start whimpering if deprived of its woolen warmth.[69]

As Nabokov recalls the conversation, Rilke—who, as Hans Mayer pointed out, does sound a little silly in this account—found it hard to believe that a young Russian like him would not want to return to his home country after the "great Revolutionary years." Nor did the German poet seem to comprehend why people should have anything to fear from the Bolshevist takeover. He considered Lenin "a great man of our time" and seemed puzzled when Nabokov explained that he had come to power illegally. He quizzed Nabokov about Mayakovsky, whose name he had trouble remembering, and about Blok, whom he had been asked to translate into German though he was not sure he could do it, not knowing more than two words of Russian. This puzzling detail raises more doubts about the authenticity of the encounter as reported—at the very least about Nabokov's accurate memory of it, since Rilke knew enough Russian to have written a handful of poems in that language.[70]

Curiously, the most "authentic" detail about Nabokov's encounter with Rilke—and a further indication that it can have occurred only at a later date—was left out of the English-language edition of *Bagázh*. In the German edition, Nabokov claims to have endeared himself to the poet by reciting to him his translation of a sonnet by Louise Labé.[71] Rilke had indeed published his *Vierundzwanzig Sonette der Louise Labé, Lyoneserin* with the Insel Verlag in 1918; Nabokov's own interest in Renaissance Lyonnaise poetry, however, is unlikely to predate his studies at the Sorbonne in the mid-1920s.

As for the positive image of Lenin and the optimistic, hopeful picture of Soviet Russia conveyed in Rilke's conversation, a cursory study of Nabokov's drafts suggests that they were put in Rilke's mouth as an afterthought and actually came from other remembered conversations, possibly with Kessler, who was not nick-named the "Red Count" for nothing.[72] Even Grunelius, as we saw at the end of the previous chapter, had a similar attitude when Nabokov met him in Holland. By making Rilke the spokesman for such views, it is as if Nabokov had wanted to cast the poet as the first among many distinguished Western intellectuals he was to meet throughout his life, who harbored a romantic, but ill-informed view of the Bolshevist revolution and were blind to its brutal, totalitarian aspects.

5

Paris Debuts

IN THE SUMMER or early fall of 1923, his studies at the Berlin Hochschule für Musik behind him, Nabokov moved to Paris; not, as one might have assumed, to enroll at the Conservatoire as a student in composition, but to resume his general education in the humanities. This in itself was not surprising: the October Revolution, which had occurred when he was fourteen, had forced him to interrupt his schooling at the Imperial *Litsei* and prevented him from entering university. But why Paris? Berlin, to be sure, had been the capital of Russian emigration in the early 1920s. However, in 1923 Germany was in the grips of an unprecedented financial crisis and Russians began to leave, many of them for Paris. From half a million, the Berlin Russian community shrank to less than 50,000 by the early 1930s. In Nabokov's case, there were personal factors in addition to economic ones. His mother now divided her life between the French Riviera and Lubcza, which, though close to the Soviet border, was, for the time being, safely under Polish control. His uncle Vladimir, who had almost become a second father to him at the beginning of his Berlin years, was now dead, and his aunt Elena settled permanently in Prague that autumn. Of her two sons, Vladimir decided to remain in Berlin, but his brother Sergei, after graduating from Cambridge, opted for Paris. Having been brought up speaking three languages in addition to Russian, Nicolas was no less fluent in French than in German. Nor was Paris, in the mid-1920s, less exciting a cultural metropolis than the German capital during the Weimar Republic.

Nabokov's first impulse, however, appears to have been to study divinity at the University of Louvain in Belgium, where in the fall of 1923 he successfully applied for a Cardinal Mercier fellowship. These plans were thwarted when he went to the Paris Préfecture de Police to apply for a Nansen passport, then the only internationally recognized travel document for stateless refugees, named after the Norwegian polar explorer Fridtjof Nansen, who introduced it in 1921 in his capacity as High Commissioner for Refugees to the League of Nations. When Nabokov arrived in Paris, all he had was German identification papers stamped by the

French Consulate in Berlin. The Préfecture bureaucrats responded to his request for a Nansen passport by demanding, on pain of expulsion, that he produce a residence certificate, signed by his landlord and countersigned by the concierge and the local police precinct. A *permis de séjour* and temporary ID would then have to be issued, at the Préfecture's discretion, and only after the three-month ID had been renewed for a year could the Nansen passport be petitioned for. Although the young Nabokov, at the time, no doubt viewed this bureaucratic hurdle as a major annoyance, his life would probably have taken a different turn if he had moved to Belgium instead of settling in Paris.[1]

Thus forced to change his initial plans, Nabokov registered as a student in a Paris Russian gymnasium, where he prepared himself for the French Baccalauréat, a prerequisite for enrolling as a full-fledged university student, and which he took in October 1924. To ready himself for that frightening perspective, he spent the preceding summer closeted, along with a fellow Russian emigre sufferer, "in the dilapidated commons of a lugubrious French château" occupied by Grand Duke Nikolai Nikolaevich, cousin of Nicholas II and ex-commander of the imperial army, and his household.[2] After passing the test, Nabokov registered as a humanities student at the Sorbonne, where he read literature and history with a view to a *licence ès lettres* (the equivalent of the B.A.) and graduated in 1926. Other than the fact that he wrote his senior essay on poetry in Lyons in the sixteenth century (hence his interest in Louise Labé), those two years of study have left few traces in what survives of his papers. One senior professor he remembered studying with was Victor Basch (1863–1944), the Hungarian-born philosopher and human rights activist, who, twenty years later, was assassinated with his wife by the anti-Semitic Vichy-sponsored *Milice*.

The mystery surrounding Nabokov's early years in Paris, for which little documentation survives, is compounded by the revelation found in his FBI file that sometime in 1923 or 1924, he suffered from a serious "emotional illness"—perhaps a kind of nervous breakdown—which interrupted his studies for two months, during which he stayed with his mother at Villefranche, near Nice.[3] The FBI's source—a physician who treated Nabokov in the 1930s and got the information from him—is reliable. Unfortunately, no other evidence has turned up that might shed light on this episode. Was the breakdown precipitated by the collapse of Nabokov's plan to study in Belgium? Was it connected to some kind of religious crisis? Was Nabokov in doubt about his musical vocation? These are all plausible explanations that cannot be verified.

During his Paris student years, Nabokov had several addresses. The earliest, or one of the earliest, was in the Latin Quarter, near the Sorbonne, at no. 2, place du Panthéon, across from the church of Saint-Étienne-du-Mont. There he rented a room from a French Communist couple, who were delighted to harbor a Russian, little suspecting he actually was a *White* Russian. The woman was a granddaughter of Karl Marx—possibly the daughter of his daughter Caroline, who had married the French socialist Charles Longuet. Nabokov found her and her husband so charming that he never revealed to them that he was a victim, rather than an admirer, of Lenin and Trotsky, whose portraits graced the wall of his bedroom next to that of his landlady's illustrious ancestor. The room, however, had no heating. After acquiring a small stove that consumed vast quantities of wood, Nabokov decided he was better off working in cafes.[4]

At some point in 1924, Nabokov left the Place du Panthéon to share an apartment with a Russian friend from Berlin, the painter Pavel Tchelitchew, his American lover Allen Tanner, and Tchelitchew's sister Alexandra, known as Shura. Born near Moscow in 1898, Tchelitchew had spent two years in Kiev after the Bolshevist Revolution. In 1919, he emigrated, first to Istanbul, then Bulgaria, and finally Berlin, where he worked as a set designer for the Russian Romantic Theater. There, in June 1923, he met Tanner, a pianist, born like him in 1898, and the two men began a liaison that lasted ten years. Just before moving to Paris, Tchelitchew designed an acclaimed production of Rimsky-Korsakov's *The Golden Cockerel* at the Staatsoper in June 1923.[5] Nabokov may have become reacquainted with him in Paris through his cousin Sergei, with whom the painter and his menage briefly shared a small flat on Rue Copernic, on the Right Bank, when they first settled in the French capital at the end of August 1923.[6] The new premises into which they moved when Nabokov joined them the following year were located at no. 150, boulevard du Montparnasse.[7] The apartment was on the ground floor, overlooking a dark courtyard. One room was occupied by Shura Tchelitchew. It was equipped with a sewing-machine at which she busied herself during the daytime. The room of Pavlik and "Allousha" (as Tanner was nicknamed by the three Russians) doubled as Tchelitchew's studio. In the smallest room, where Nabokov slept, there was an out-of-tune upright piano shared by the two musicians. During the day, Tanner gave piano lessons and coached women singers. Tchelitchew himself made ends meet by designing batik silk fabrics for a Parisian couture house.[8] When he was not in class, Nabokov, having no room of his own, worked in the neighboring cafes, which were as quiet in the daytime as they were busy at night. There were the Dôme, the closest to his place, favored by painters, the Rotonde, where writers tended to gather, and the Select, which particularly attracted gay men. At lunchtime, Nabokov was often joined by his cousin Sergei, who made a living by giving private tuition in Russian and in English, and brought papers to grade, or English newspapers and magazines to read.

As we know from Hemingway and others, the 1920s were the heyday of Montparnasse, which had become what Montmartre had been in the late nineteenth century and what Saint-Germain-des-Prés would be after the Liberation. Cafes were frequented by a cosmopolitan bohemia and new contacts were easy to make. At the Dôme, Nabokov recalls meeting, or at least spotting, Alberto Giacometti, Federico García Lorca, the young Bertold Brecht, the Polish poet

Julian Tuwim, and Tristan Tzara, the Romanian-born Dadaist, whom he remained on friendly terms with until Tzara became a Communist fellow-traveler and Stalin enthusiast in the early 1930s. Through Tchelitchew he also became acquainted with the group of artists who in 1926 were presented by their dealer, the Galerie Druet, as "The Neo-Romantics": the Moscow-born brothers Leonid and Eugene Berman, the Dutch Kristians Tonny, and the Parisian Christian Bérard. Nabokov even recalled having drinks with James Joyce at the terrace of the Café Francis, on the Place de l'Alma, and being asked by the Irish writer whether he was familiar with the poetry of Alexis Léger, which Joyce recommended to him as "quite delectable" and "in some ways quite un-French."9 To Nabokov, the works of Léger, a.k.a. Saint-John Perse, always remained an acquired taste, but he subsequently came to know personally the author of *Anabase* and *Vents*.

American expatriates, though numerous in Montparnasse, were less easy to meet. As Nabokov remembered, they "led their own gay, carefree, luxuriant life, having their own bookstores, magazines, newspapers and churches, but using for their fun plush and lush French places, inaccessible to the impoverished refugees like myself."10 Apart from Tanner, he recalled meeting Gershwin, though he did not remember or specify under what circumstances, noting simply that the American composer impressed him "enormously with his charm, by the tender lyricism of his songs, and the percussive way he played the piano."11 Although he dated this meeting from the early part of his Paris years, it did not likely take place until Gershwin's visit to Paris in the spring of 1928. The two composers were to renew their acquaintance after Nabokov moved to America. The other American he remembers meeting is the poet Bravig Imbs (1904–44), who, like Tchelitchew, became, for a while, close to Gertrude Stein. Stein herself, however, does not figure in Nabokov's Parisian memories.

A momentous meeting took place in Paris in the summer of 1924, according to Nabokov's dating, when he and his mother, who was visiting from Poland or the South of France, were having lunch at a Russian restaurant, and she suddenly recognized "a big man with a monocle and a flower in his buttonhole" eating at another table in the company of a young man, and in whom Nabokov had no trouble recognizing Diaghilev.12 Being related to him through her late husband, Lydia Peucker introduced herself and Nicolas to the famous impresario, suggesting that he might be interested in listening to her son's music. But Diaghilev was politely evasive and nothing came out of this initial encounter, save for the powerful impression made on Nabokov by Diaghilev's physique, especially his head, which looked "even more majestic, more lordly, than it appeared in the pictures I had seen." He was also struck by the way he spoke "in a high-pitched, nasal and capricious tone" and the way "he dropped unaccented syllables of long Russian words as if he had swallowed them up."13

Nabokov's breakthrough finally occurred in 1926, coinciding with the completion of his Sorbonne education. The earliest evidence we have of his growing reputation is an entry dated March 23 in Harry Kessler's diaries, describing him as a "lively and musically talented young man," whom he heard perform some of his music at the salon of Helene von Nostitz in Berlin: two movements from a piano sonata and songs on texts by Pushkin and Omar Khayyam.[14] In the same entry, Nabokov is described as a friend of Cocteau, Prokofiev, and Stravinsky. "He told me," Kessler recalls from the conversation, "that when he left Berlin for Paris, he thought he was ready; and there he realized that everything he wanted to do had already been done. That gave him a blow which it took him two or three years to get over. Typical," the Francophile Kessler concludes, "of the current musical standing of Berlin compared to Paris."[15]

One element in this otherwise invaluable testimony—Nabokov's first appearance in Kessler's diaries—raises doubt: Nabokov, at that time, hardly qualified as a friend of Stravinsky, since, by his own account, he was introduced to him more than a year later. Could there have been some wishful thinking on Kessler's or his interlocutor's part? Cocteau and Prokofiev, recent acquaintances both, were yet to become close friends: the first mention of Nabokov in the latter's journals is in late December 1927 and shows that they were not, at that stage, on intimate terms.[16] On the other hand, the negative comments Nabokov made to Kessler on his musical education in Germany are confirmed by similar statements in the interview the composer gave to José Bruyr in 1931: in it he rails against the "reactionary" state of music in Germany and implies that, without Tchelitchew's encouragement—and also, it seems, that of Grand Duke Nicolas—he might have given up a career as a composer. This would seem to confirm that the nervous breakdown he went through shortly after settling in France was caused, at least in part, by despondency over his artistic future.[17]

Kessler's testimony also informs us about Nabokov's musical output just as his career was about to take off. His first published work, the Piano Sonata in A Major, the first of two he completed, follows the classic Allegro-Lento-Presto pattern. From the indication at the end of the score as issued later that year by the Parisian firm of Rouart-Lerolle, it was written in 1925–26 in Paris and at Grunelius's house in Alsace. Prokofiev, always hard to please, frowned at the "deliberately vulgar-sounding (Cocteauesque) tune for the Andante" when Nabokov gave him the score in March 1928. But he found the first subject of the opening movement attractive, the major-minor development of the Andante sophisticated, and the Finale "technically very assured [. . .] albeit with a derivative theme unpleasantly reminiscent of Bach."[18] Nabokov himself was sufficiently pleased with his effort to bring the score to the attention of Stravinsky through Vladimir Dukelsky's good offices when his Russian friend, after the success of his ballet *Zéphyre and Flore*,

mounted by Diaghilev in 1925, was invited to dinner by Stravinsky in Nice the following year. Stravinsky, not before having made Dukelsky "intensely uncomfortable" by an anti-Diaghilev tirade, looked attentively at the score by his unknown
compatriot and pronounced it "not stupid."[19]

The sonata's first public performance was given in Paris on November 12, 1926,
by Claudio Arrau.[20] How and when Nabokov became acquainted with the Chilean
pianist is not known, but they presumably met via one of Nabokov's Berlin connections during one of his regular visits to the city, where Arrau was appointed
in 1924, at the age of twenty-one, as piano instructor at the Stern Conservatory.
Arrau's earliest surviving letter to Nabokov, dated March 25, 1926, suggests
that they were already on friendly terms.[21] Held at the Salle des agriculteurs de
France on Rue d'Athènes, near the Gare Saint-Lazare, Arrau's Paris recital also
included Carl Maria von Weber's Piano Sonata no. 2 in A-flat major, opus 39, and
Stravinsky's *Sérénade*. Nabokov dedicated to Arrau another piano composition,
also published by Rouart-Lerolle in the fall of 1926, a four-movement suite entitled
Short Stories, dated, like the sonata, 1925–26.[22]

At Helene von Nostitz's, as noted by Kessler, Nabokov also played (and possibly
sang) a few of his songs. The ones on poems from the Rubaiyat, translated into
French from Edward Fitzgerald's English version, were about to receive their first
public performance in Paris; there is no evidence, however, that they were ever
published, nor has a manuscript been located. Nabokov had then set two poems
by Pushkin, *Strekotun'ia beloboka* ("The Magpie") and *Pora, moi drug, pora* ("It's
time, my friend, it's time"). These were published only in 1929, along with two
other Russian songs.

Nabokov's acquaintance with Cocteau was due to the friendly ties he established at the time with Georges Auric, along with Poulenc the youngest of the
so-called *Les Six*. According to the aforementioned 1931 interview, Auric got in
touch with Nabokov after a German composer friend had told him that a piece by
Nabokov had been hissed by the audience at a concert in Berlin. Unfortunately,
neither the identity of the piece, nor the name of the German composer in question, nor the exact circumstances of this concert can be established. Auric had also
learned about Nabokov's yet unpublished *Chants à la Vierge Marie* and expressed
interest in looking at the score. Though only twenty-seven in 1926, Auric's was
already well known and commonly viewed as one of the rising stars of the new
generation, a position reinforced by the two commissions he had received from
the Ballets Russes, the ballets *Les Fâcheux* (1923) and *Les Matelots* (1924).

Next to Auric, the other composer who introduced Nabokov to the French
musical world was Henri Sauguet. They met in 1926, by complete chance, at a
Mi-Carême costume ball both attended in Montparnasse. Nabokov mentioned
that he was in the company of an elderly Russian writer whose name he left
unidentified. Born in Bordeaux in 1901, Sauguet, a passionate admirer of Erik

Satie, belonged to a small group of musicians named the École d'Arcueil (after the city where Satie lived), and which included Roger Désormière, who had just been hired by Diaghilev as Ballets Russes conductor, as well as Henri Cliquet-Pleyel and Maxime Jacob. Though he was still, at the time, completing his musical instruction with the modernist composer and theoretician Charles Koechlin, Sauguet's career had already taken off when his one-act opera buffa, *Le plumet du colonel*, had been staged in December 1924 at the Comédie des Champs-Élysées, as a double bill with Stravinsky's *Soldier's Tale*. In his posthumous memoirs, he has left a lively account of his encounter with Nabokov, whom he first mistook for the mystical Russian emigre composer—and inventor—Nicolas Obouhow:

> As we were strolling around the ball, I was approached by a young man, himself in the company of distinguished, aristocratic-looking people, wearing neither costumes nor masks; after asking me if I truly was Henri Sauguet, he introduced himself. I thought I heard Nicolas Oboukov [*sic*], a quarter-tone pioneer, some works by whom had been performed shortly before at the Salle Gaveau. I was astonished to come across this severe, even mystical, artist in such surroundings. A few days later, on the telephone (I had given him my number), I heard a deep, melodious voice: the Oboukov in question actually was Nabokoff, who came from Berlin, where he had worked with illustrious teachers, among them Busoni, and who had been attracted by Paris, as all young artists were then.[23]

Nabokov, according to Sauguet, was at the time "irresistible."

> I had to take off my glasses precipitously when he kissed me, in Russian fashion, for fear that they might get broken by his animal-like impetuousness; he was the embodiment of the Russian of one's imagination, as described by Gorky or Dostoyevsky: exuberant, lyrical, impassioned and lively.[24]

Sauguet soon introduced Nabokov to his friends of the École d'Arcueil, Désormière—who became a friend and musical mentor—and Jacob, who, a few years later, converted to Catholicism and became a Benedictine monk under the name Dom Clément Jacob.[25] Through Sauguet, Nabokov also got to know Darius Milhaud, to whom Sauguet was particularly close, and Poulenc. Another new friend was Vittorio Rieti, the Egypt-born Italian composer, who had come to prominence in 1924 when his Concerto for Wind and Orchestra was performed at the International Society of Contemporary Music Festival in Prague. Nabokov also came to know Marcelle Meyer, the *Six*'s favorite pianist: "Sonate," the last piece in the *Short Stories*, is dedicated to her.

By the spring of 1926, Nabokov had moved to different premises, two blocks away from the Place du Panthéon, at no. 3, rue de l'Estrapade, an eighteenth-century house where Diderot had once lived. It would nowadays qualify as a highly desirable address, but at the time it was nothing but "a wretched pension," as described by Kessler, who paid Nabokov a visit on June 6 that year.

> A dirty, evil smelling staircase leads to a tiny room containing nothing but a piano, a rumpled couch which evidently serves him as a bed, a chair, and a few photographs on the walls. The impression of ghastly poverty is one that his appearance in public, his well-groomed exterior and his air of *grand seigneur*, never so much as hints at. Nor did he show the slightest embarrassment, receiving me as though I were a guest in his mansion [. . .]. Nabokov really does give the impression of being an inspired young giant.[26]

As Kessler's neat vignette suggests, Nabokov by then cut an impressive figure: nearly six-foot tall and big, with distinctive, slightly Oriental features, brown eyes, and a striking mane of dark hair, he had an aristocratic, yet unaffected, demeanor and an attractive, well-placed voice which was ever ready to boom in fits of gaiety. "An engaging young man with an open Russian face and the disarming clumsiness of adolescence," recalled his compatriot and coeval Dukelsky (the future Vernon Duke), who met him, through Tchelitchew, soon after his own arrival in Paris in 1924.[27] In Nabokov there was none of the self-pity which, for understandable reasons, to be sure, became characteristic, in various degrees, in Russian expatriates of the period. This mark of his personality, which struck Kessler in 1926, remained true for his entire life. Though acutely aware of his condition as an exile, Nabokov also considered that exile had made him free.

Kessler was evidently unaware of a darker side to Nabokov's life at the time: he was subject to epileptic seizures which terrified him and plunged him into fits of despair, while setting off certain forms of erratic behavior. This aspect has been vividly evoked by Jaroslaw Iwaszkiewicz, the Polish poet and novelist, then in his early thirties. Himself trained as a musician—he wrote the libretto to his cousin Karol Szymanowski's opera *King Roger*—Iwaszkiewicz met Nabokov at one of the Tuesday evening gatherings in the offices of the *Revue musicale*, the monthly founded in 1920 by Henry Prunières, the leading French musicologist of the period. Like Sauguet and Kessler, Iwaszkiewicz was captivated by Nabokov's charm and vast culture; many years later, in his autobiography, he remembered him as being "as animated and brilliant as only a Russian can be." The two men became close, to the point that Nabokov, when in Poland to see his mother, visited Iwaszkiewicz at Stawisko, his newly built house outside Warsaw, where Nabokov did not fail to dazzle his host's family and friends. The Polish writer subsequently recalled an Australian staying at Stawisko who declared she could listen to Nabokov's conversation with Mrs. Iwaszkiewicz "until the end of the world."[28] But Iwaszkiewicz, once he became aware of Nabokov's epileptic condition, also witnessed in him "some latent cruel reality, some secret melange of holiness, despair, drunkenness, and wantonness emanating total enchantment."

> Seizures could assault him on the street, on the steps of the metro, or in a restaurant. He tried to stifle his fear of them by scandalizing behavior, heavy drinking, or typically Russian brawls which, in the strictly organized Western world, were frightening.[29]

According to Iwaszkiewicz's reminiscences, the approach of these seizures often coincided in Nabokov with uncanny "moments of clairvoyance." In a cafe, he would point to someone he had never seen before, tell his friend that this person was Tolstoy's son and was about to stop at their table to introduce himself, which invariably happened. But Nabokov's condition also made him prone to quasi-suicidal despair, as it drove Sauguet's young friend Christian Hardouin, also an epileptic, to killing himself in August 1928.[30] And even though the seizures had stopped by the time Nabokov was in his mid-twenties, the hyper-emotional sensitivity and proneness to grand gestures that struck friends and colleagues in later life may have originated from this episode.[31]

Thanks to Auric and Sauguet, the circle of Nabokov's social acquaintances miraculously expanded. He began, especially, to be introduced to art and music patrons, without whom no career could be launched in Paris at the time.[32] Through his Polish connections, he came into contact with Misia Sert (1872–1950), the Petersburg-born hostess, née Godebska, who knew everybody who was anybody in the French artistic avant-garde, from Ravel to Stravinsky and from Vuillard to Picasso. First married to Thadée Natanson, editor of the influential *Revue blanche*, she had then been the wife of the newspaper magnate Alfred Edwards. Her third husband was the Catalan painter Jose Maria Sert. When Nabokov met her, she was living in a duplex apartment at the Hotel Meurice, on the Rue de Rivoli. "What was so enchanting about Misia and her family was that once she adopted you," Nabokov later recalled, "you became, in a manner of speaking, not just a member of the family but a full-fledged member of her vast circle of friends."[33] By June 1926, as an entry in Kessler's diaries shows, Nabokov was evidently a regular guest at Misia's soirees.[34] The following year, he gave an audition of his oratorio *Ode*, before Diaghilev, in her salon.[35]

Another Paris hostess Nabokov became acquainted with was Kessler's sister, Wilma (Wilhelma), Marquise de Brion, and subsequently Duchesse de Frioul, whose French husband was a descendant of Duroc, one of Napoleon's generals. At her home on Avenue Kléber, near the Étoile, Kessler heard Nabokov give a "stunningly personal" performance of Bach on the piano at a late-night musicale on May 31, 1926.[36] Another of Nabokov's early patrons, and the dedicatee of his piano sonata, was Emily de La Grange, the American-born wife of Baron Amaury de La Grange, a Senator and former minister, with a strong interest in aviation; their son, Henry-Louis, born in 1924, was to become a musicologist and world authority on Gustav Mahler.

A very different, but even more important encounter occurred in 1926 when Nabokov was introduced to the Catholic philosopher Jacques Maritain and his wife Raïssa. Was the introduction made by Auric, as Nabokov recalled in 1931, or by the same Polish friends through whom he had met Misia, as he subsequently claimed?[37] The earlier is plausible, since Auric was close to the Maritains, whom he had met in 1916, when he was seventeen, through the pianist Ricardo Viñes. But the introduction could also have been made by another of Nabokov's closest friends at the time, Aleksander Rzewuski. Born in St. Petersburg in 1892, Rzewuski belonged to a noble Polish-Ukrainian family of officers: his grandfather had been aide-de-camp to four czars, from Alexander I to Alexander III; his paternal aunt had married a Radziwill, and he was also distantly related to the Italian princes Caetani. After the Bolshevist takeover, he spent two years in Kiev, where he became a close friend of Tchelitchew, who appears to have exerted on him a veritable fascination.[38] Settling in Paris in 1919, he started a career as caricaturist and society painter. Soon after his arrival, at a dinner at Boni de Castellane's, Rzewuski was introduced to Misia, to whom he remained close until her death.[39] He evidently resumed his friendship with Tchelitchew and it was presumably through the latter that he and Nabokov met. Rzewuski's own introduction to the Maritains was through another compatriot, the Polish painter Józef Czapski, who had moved from Warsaw to Paris in 1924. Czapski's and Nabokov's paths crossed again, more than two decades later, at the time of the establishment of the Congress for Cultural Freedom.

In 1926, Maritain was forty-four. Born in Paris to a Protestant family, he had converted to Catholicism in 1905 together with his Jewish-born wife, née Raïssa Umantseva in Rostov-on-Don in 1883. A professor at the Institut catholique in Paris, Maritain spearheaded the rediscovery and revival of the theological writings of Thomas Aquinas. He also became a spiritual beacon for a whole generation of artists, writers, and intellectuals, especially after the trauma of the First World War. His and Raïssa's home at no. 10, rue du Parc in Meudon, on the southwestern outskirts of Paris, which they shared with Raïssa's sister Vera and their Russian mother, was little short of a pilgrimage site, equipped, besides, with a chapel on the second floor. Maritain, according to Rzewuski's own recollections, "was of middle height, with a small salt-and-pepper goatee and a scarf around his neck. He really was the type of the intellectual as I imagined it. But what struck me was the extreme beauty of his eyes. Narrowly slit, half-closed eyes, but radiating immense goodness."[40] Maurice Sachs, like Cocteau one of their temporary "converts," has left a memorable portrait of the Maritain household in his autobiography *Le sabbat*:

> They had, first of all, those two qualities rarely found together: firmness of mind and tenderness of heart, from which all the rest follow: clear reasoning, rectitude, loyalty, justice, generosity, absolute devotion, along with those of imagination, gaiety, charming impulses, a taste for poetry, and no bigotry.[41]

On the other hand, as Sachs also noted, their irrepressibly impulsive, generous nature "misled them into imprudent admirations, where they suddenly betrayed that naivety all specialists reveal once they leave their specialty."[42] Jacques and Raïssa held an open house on Sunday afternoons, and Nabokov became one of their regular visitors. He is listed as such by Maurice Sachs, who tried to persuade him to collaborate with him on an unspecified project.[43] Others of the Maritains' Sunday "regulars" listed by Sachs were Henri Massis, the *Action française* critic; Henri Ghéon, an old friend of Gide who had "repented" and looked "like an old carriage driver straight out of *The Three Musketeers*";[44] the literary critic Stanislas Fumet and his wife; Charles Du Bos, another prominent critic; church dignitaries of various ranks and descriptions, such as the Abbé Henrion, who had been put in charge of Cocteau's "conversion", and the Abbé Pressoir, to whom had been entrusted the even more hopeless Sachs; Mgr. Vladimir Ghika, a charismatic Moldavian prince and Greek Orthodox convert, who after World War II returned to Romania, where he died in 1954 as a result of persecutions suffered under the Communist regime. Naturally, Maritain's circle included future priests, such as the Egyptian-born Jean de Menasce, a convert from Judaism, whose brother Jacques was to be one of the dedicatees of Nabokov's *Studies in Solitude*; or Jean Daniélou, the future Jesuit and cardinal, then in the process of preparing the Latin text of Stravinsky's *Œdipus Rex*. Daniélou's younger brother Alain, then a dancer and (briefly) the lover of Maurice Sachs, was, three decades later, to become one of Nabokov's closest friends. At Meudon, Nabokov also came into contact with the Sinologist, musicologist, and occasional librettist Louis Laloy, who, three years before, had introduced Cocteau to opium. Laloy's son Jean, Debussy's godson, became a Slavicist and diplomat and he and Nabokov remained friends.[45] There was also Marie-Alain Couturier, then a young Dominican novice and theology student, who was destined to play an important role in involving modernist artists— Chagall and Matisse, among others—in religious art; and Max Jacob, the Breton poet, like Raïssa a convert from Judaism, who divided his time between Paris and the Benedictine abbey of Saint-Benoît-sur-Loire, and with whom Nabokov was to collaborate on several occasions.

Though not trained musically, both Maritain and his wife were ardent music lovers. More importantly, the Neo-Thomist philosopher's reflections on aesthetics, though seldom discussing music, were influential on contemporary musicians— Nabokov one among many.[46] Maritain's stance against artistic experimentation for its own sake and his call for a return to order in the artistic sphere, expounded in 1922 in his essay *Antimoderne*, have been paralleled to the neoclassicism of composers such as Stravinsky and Poulenc.[47] For Maritain and his wife, with her own Russian background, the presence of a young Russian musician in their circle was especially welcome. They began to join him at concerts or the ballet, such as Satie's *Mercure* at the Ballets Russes, a performance Maritain remembered as "miraculous."[48] The fact that their friendship was well established by 1926 is evidenced by the fact that the second and third pieces of Nabokov's *Short Stories* are dedicated to them in the printed score: "Ritournelle" to Jacques, "Valse" to Raïssa.

Although, for reasons one can understand, he does not touch on this topic in his autobiography, Nabokov himself clearly experienced at the time a deep personal and religious crisis. According to Igor Markevitch, Maritain even rescued Nabokov from the temptation of committing suicide.[49] While brought up in the Orthodox faith, he had not so far shown any deep personal involvement in religious matters; or at least this is the impression subsequently conveyed by his own written recollections. The first sign of a spiritual awakening was his abortive attempt to become a divinity student at Louvain. Did he flirt for a while with the idea of converting to Roman Catholicism, like many others who fell under the Maritains' spell? Certainly Maritain hoped he would, as an allusion in a letter reveals.[50] Kessler, when he visited Nabokov at his pension in June 1926, was struck by the tone of "excessively Catholic radicalism" in some of his remarks, and reported that Nabokov considered Maritain "the most interesting personality France has to offer."[51] Two days later, when Nabokov joined Kessler and Helene von Nostitz on a car trip to Chartres, by way of Meudon, where they stopped to visit Rodin's tomb, Kessler had the same impression of religious intensity; he noted that Nabokov crossed himself when leaving the cathedral and commented ironically on his "new-fangled Catholicism."[52] Kessler's impression is contradicted to some extent by that of Rzewuski, who in his memoirs remembered a Nabokov "enthusiastic about the Orthodox religion."[53] Similarly, Iwaszkiewicz was struck by Nabokov's "fervent Russian Orthodox religiosity."[54] Indeed, while the postwar years in France gave rise to a Roman Catholic revival, by the same token, the trauma of revolution and exile triggered a comparable Orthodox revival in the Russian community in France. One of its manifestations was the opening in the northern parts of Paris, in 1925, of the Institut Saint Serge, created by Sergei Bulgakov with a view to promoting theological and liturgical studies.[55] Nabokov appears to have been deeply impressed by the sudden decision made in 1926 by one of his former classmates at the Imperial *Litsei*, Dmitri Alekseevich Shakhovskoi, to abandon a promising literary career for the clergy. Born in 1902, Shakhovskoi, whose princely family had sought refuge in Ukraine after the Bolshevist takeover, had enlisted with the Whites at a very young age. During the civil war, he had barely escaped being slaughtered when his train, in the Ukraine, was captured by Makhno's forces. After his graduation from the University of Louvain, where he studied theology, he had begun to publish poetry and at the age of twenty-four was appointed editor of the short-lived Paris-based literary review *Blagonamerenny*, "the emigration's most luxurious,"[56] whose contributors included Bunin, Remizov, Marina Tsvetaeva—and Nabokov himself, who, in the spring of 1926, contributed a short essay on "Word and Sound" to the second (and last) issue. By then, Shakhovskoi had left Paris to become an Orthodox monk at Mt. Athos in Greece, taking the name John. By his own admission, made only a few years later in the interview he gave to José Bruyr, Nabokov was tempted to follow his example.[57]

Though Rzewuski's name appears nowhere in Nabokov's autobiographical writings, he and Nabokov were on particularly close terms during the summer of 1926. Rzewuski had rented a restored medieval priory at Chênehutte-les-Tuffeaux, in Touraine, to which he invited a few close friends, Czapski among them. Rzewuski too was in the middle of a religious crisis, precipitated by a sexual "lapse" that prompted him to retire from the world.[58] In November 1926, after having hosted a final reception, ostensibly to say goodbye before sailing to New York to attend a Broadway production he was to design, he secretly took the train to Provence and entered the monastery of Saint-Maximin, where he became a Dominican monk under the name of Brother Marie-Ceslas.[59] Only four people, whom he considered his closest friends, had been informed of this decision: the Maritains, Czapski, and Nabokov. It was, in fact, at Nabokov's Latin Quarter apartment, that morning, that Rzewuski bid farewell to the four of them.[60]

Nabokov's religious crisis, such as it was, and his friendship with the Maritains, found a musical outlet in the five *Chants à la Vierge Marie* for soprano and piano he composed in late 1925 or early 1926, reworking the bilingual Russian and French texts in the following year in collaboration with Raïssa Maritain.[61] He himself prepared the Russian words, Raïssa being credited for the French version. After an introductory prayer, marked Largo, the Wedding at Cana is the subject of the second song, the tempo of which is left to the performer; a mournful "Pietà" and meditative "Dormition" are followed by a song of triumph to conclude the cycle. The score, published by Rouart Lerolle, came out in 1928 with a printed dedication to Father Jean Schlumberger, a relative of Alexandre Grunelius's wife, and "brother M.C.R.," initials under which one can recognize the name of Marie-Ceslas Rzewuski. Along with the piano sonata, this cycle was the first major composition he completed.

No matter how sincere and deep Nabokov's spiritual awakening, it clearly had a strong aesthetic dimension. At Chartres, in front of the northern portal,

Kessler reports that his young Russian friend exclaimed impulsively: "*Bientôt nous aurons de nouveau un art comme celui-là*" ("We shall soon have art of this kind again").[62] His attraction towards sacred music was obviously stimulated by his frequenting the Maritains and their circle. The peak of musical achievement, he also told Kessler at the time, "is when music '*entre [dans] le temple*,' attains the level of religion."[63] His undeniable enthusiasm for the Orthodox faith at the time was due, to some extent, to his discovery of old Slavonic chant, which was being revived at the Institut Saint-Serge, where he befriended Mikhail Osorgin, the choir leader.[64] Late in that 1926 summer he spent in Touraine with Rzewuski, Nabokov was also introduced to the Benedictine monastery of Solesmes, cradle of the Gregorian Chant revival at the end of the nineteenth century. Maritain, in the letter of recommendation he wrote for both of them to the abbot, Dom Gabriel Tissot on September 2, described Nabokov as "an ardent and profound soul." And he added: "I believe (based on his reputation, since I have yet to hear anything by him) that he is a highly talented musician and one of great promise."[65] Nabokov paid several visits to Solesmes, where he discussed the Gregorian tradition with the Prior and Dom Jean Claire, the choir leader.[66] Yet, with the *Chants à la Vierge*, as he himself explained, he did not intend to write in the style of religious music: "My intention," he wrote, "was to write religious music which would be in no way church-related in the strict sense of the phrase. It is not a work for church use, but a freely conceived religious conception outside cult precincts, in other words remaining faithful to the Orthodox tradition and dogma; prayers said outside the temple walls."[67] In other words, his own music was not ready to "*entrer dans le temple*," notwithstanding what he declared to Kessler.

Discussing his musical enthusiasms with Kessler, Nabokov, in the spring of 1926, singled out Bach and Mozart, especially the former.[68] This cult of Bach, in particular, accompanied his strong interest in religious art. It went along with a rejection of all forms of exoticism and folk influences, not excepting jazz. By the same token, and though he had himself written songs set to Persian poetry, he claimed to despise Orientalist influences in Russian music, especially Rimsky-Korsakov. The one member of the "Mighty Five" who then found favor in his eyes was Borodin. Of Mussorgsky, he claimed to like only fifty percent, rating him below Glinka and Tchaikovsky; this was a view he retained throughout his life.[69] Curiously, if one assumes Kessler reported their exchanges accurately, he had, at that time, little good to say about contemporary French music, even Ravel and Satie. This contradicts Nabokov's later testimony, according to which he fell in love with Satie's music when he discovered it in 1923. Admittedly it would be hard to detect Satie's influence in the piano sonata, where that of Scriabin is still present. *Short Stories*, on the other hand, is arguably more in the manner of the author of *Gymnopédies*. Nabokov's exposure to Satie obviously increased through his contacts with Sauguet, Milhaud, and Désormière, all Satie enthusiasts. "It is

Satie's art and his ideas," he wrote in 1951, "that taught me how to exercise a restraint and an economy of means in my own music, to prefer brevity and conciseness of musical discourse to the ramblings and rumblings of impressionism; how to limit myself to the absolutely indispensable, the minimum needed for an adequate formulation of a musical sentence and reject the camouflage of floridity and grandiloquence."

> Above all, Satie's art taught me that one should not be ashamed of being simple, intimate, "puerile," and even naïve to the point of appearing childish (provided one remains sincere), and to regard all these qualities as virtues rather than vices.[70]

The reservations expressed by Nabokov on musical impressionism—the dubious labeling under which Debussy and Ravel were typically paired at the time in France—were more understandable in the light of his new musical enthusiasms. For his enormous admiration for Debussy, he was never really influenced by him as a composer. As for Ravel, he does not appear to have thought of him as highly as did Prokofiev, who, on the other hand, despised both Debussy and Satie.[71]

Nabokov had an opportunity to express himself in writing on the situation of music in France in an article he contributed, in German, to the January 1927 issue of the influential musical journal *Melos*, published by the Mainz- and Leipzig-based firm Schott.[72] Headed "Thoughts about New Music: Observations from Paris," Nabokov's piece first describes the confusion produced by the recent developments in music. Singling out *Le sacre du printemps* as both a turning-point and a liberation, he also mentioned "the less talented but more ideologically conscious" Satie as well as *Les Six*, though he warns Auric and Poulenc against the risk of falling into frivolity—a risk he contrasts with the German propensity for excessive seriousness (the detested name of Reger is brought up twice). Congruently with his membership in Maritain's circle, he salutes the movement favoring a return to cadential harmony. The ballet, he claims, is "the most appropriate form to express new musical thoughts": by contrast with the more open-ended forms favored by post-Romantic musicians, dance requires precision and clarity of melody, rhythm, and dynamics. The article ends on an optimistic note: the new music in France rests on "healthy values" and the success of someone like Honegger seems to herald a "resurgence of large forms" like opera and the cantata.

Though he was then working on a cantata himself, Nabokov, in an unpublished draft for his autobiography, attaches much symbolic significance to the song he composed at that time after Pasternak's "*Slozha vesla*" ("With Oars at Rest"). The poem had been brought to his attention, he recalls, by his cousin Sergei when it first appeared in 1918 in *Vesennii Salon Poetov*. He rediscovered it in 1924, on a train journey from Warsaw to Paris, in an emigre printing of Pasternak's 1922 collection *Sestra moia zhizn* (My Sister Life), and jotted down the first musical idea on a billion-mark bill he found in his wallet. Two or three years later, in Paris, on the upright piano he rented at his Latin Quarter pension, he wrote out the entire song "on a sheet of prettily adorned music paper (blue, lacy frames printed upon a glazed surface)"; the music paper was a gift from Sauguet but had originally been in the possession of Debussy, who had given it to Satie.[73] According to Nabokov, everyone to whom he played the song liked it, even his cousin Vladimir, despite the latter's lack of interest in music. Prokofiev even suggested he should select several more poems from Pasternak's collection and write a song cycle. But none inspired him in the same way and the manuscript was lost.

The first documented public performance of Nabokov's music took place on June 4, 1926, at a chamber music concert of the Société de musique indépendante, the organization founded in 1909 by Fauré, Koechlin, Ravel, Florent Schmitt, and others, with a view to promoting contemporary works in a more diversified fashion than at the Société nationale de musique. The concert was held at the Salle des agriculteurs. Other composers represented on the program, which consisted entirely of world or Paris premieres, were Robert Casadesus (1899–1972), who subsequently abandoned composition to pursue a career as a pianist; Arthur Hoérée (1897–1986), the Belgian composer and critic, a disciple of Albert Roussel; the Greek composer Georgios Poniridis (1887?–1982); and the lesser-known Marc Mény de Marangue and Albert-Joseph Febvre-Longeray. Nabokov's works were his *Trois poèmes d'Omar Khayam* and an otherwise undocumented *Vocalise* for soprano and two flutes, clarinet, and piano.[74] Kessler, who attended the performance with his sister Wilma and Helene von Nostitz, noted in his diary that the pieces struck him by their "intensity" and "size," which suggests that the performance did them justice.[75] Nabokov had quite a different recollection. The singer, whose name is disguised in his autobiography, was Marguerite Babaïan, a noted classical folk singer and voice teacher of Armenian origin, who in 1906 had premiered Ravel's *Cinq mélodies populaires grecques*. Nabokov claims she had come to his attention through her uncle, "an elderly gentleman, a hunchback, and a relentless music lover,"[76] to whom he had been introduced by one of his women patrons; it is equally plausible that he came into contact with her through Louis Laloy, who was her brother-in-law. In any event, Nabokov recalled that the concert went disastrously: after angering his singer, who had a wooden leg, by nearly tripping her up in the narrow passage that led to the platform, he offended his impoverished fellow pension inmates by presenting to her the lilac bush they had purchased for him after pooling their modest savings.

If one follows Nabokov's account in *Bagázh*, the audience at the concert included, in the front row, Prokofiev as well as Diaghilev, whom Prokofiev had dragged along to hear their compatriot's music. Diaghilev had some kind words for Nabokov's music after the ordeal was over and invited him to visit him at the

Grand Hôtel, where he stayed, and play for him more of his music. The audition, as reported by Nabokov in his memoirs, gathered, beside Diaghilev, his close friend and future biographer Walter Nouvel; Prokofiev; the twenty-two-year-old Boris Kochno, Diaghilev's secretary and right arm; and the even younger Serge Lifar (born in 1905), a pupil of Bronislava Nijinska, who had just been promoted to first dancer in the Ballets Russes. Nabokov played his piano sonata and excerpts from the yet-unfinished cantata he was working on. Diaghilev, on the pretext of an urgent rehearsal, took his leave without expressing an opinion, but Nouvel reassured the composer: such was his usual reaction.

Whether things took place exactly as reported in *Bagázh* is difficult to prove or disprove. Would Diaghilev have attended a concert to hear music by an unknown composer in the middle of the Ballets Russes Parisian season at the Théâtre Sarah-Bernhardt? That was technically not impossible, since there was no performance on June 4. If Prokofiev—who was in Paris at the time—did attend the concert, he made no record of it in his diaries.[77] If the audition happened at the Grand Hôtel as reported, it must have taken place within the next few days, as the Ballets Russes London season began on June 14. All we know, based on Nabokov's much earlier and therefore more reliable testimony, is that it was in Monte-Carlo, and not until the following spring, when the Ballets Russes were rehearsing Sauguet's ballet *La chatte*, that he met with Diaghilev and "sold" him the idea of a *spectacle féerique* based on his still-unfinished cantata.[78] Nabokov's correspondence with Kochno confirms that he was in Nice, visiting his mother, on and around April 20, 1927, and made plans to meet with Kochno during that week.[79]

Nabokov's cantata, which thus became his first ballet, under the title *Ode*, was never intended as such. It is a setting of a celebrated poem of Mikhail Vasil'evich Lomonosov (1711–65), the famous scientist, linguist, and founder of the Moscow University. Entitled *Evening Meditation on God's Majesty on the Occasion of the Aurora Borealis*, it is both a didactic poem and an allegorical celebration of the 1741 coronation of Empress Elizabeth, daughter of Peter the Great and herself czarina until 1762. The idea of setting this ode to music came to Nabokov as early as 1923 when, as he recalled, he opened a volume of Lomonosov's verse for the first time since school. He was, he said, struck by "the beauty and primitive faith" of the poem, which he described as "one of those rare flowers of the eighteenth century where man still is seen as an indivisible unit—intellectual, spiritual, moral—and science, poetry, and faith form one single world."[80] The composition evidently occupied him for more than a year in 1926. When Kessler visited Nabokov on Rue de l'Estrapade on June 6, he heard fragments of it. More than a year later, Nabokov reported to Kochno, from Alsace, that he was making slow progress in the work, but was hoping to present it in a finished state by the end of the month, even though the next letter, ten days later, makes clear that nothing had been concluded with Diaghilev at that stage. The short-score draft, though dated "Paris-Kolbsheim,

May to September 3, 1927," was completed on September 1 at Hohenfinow, where Nabokov also began the orchestration.[81]

Set for soprano solo, baritone solo, and mixed chorus, *Ode* was Nabokov's first large-scale work as well as his first orchestral composition. Even though it was not written with the Ballets Russes in mind, there were two reasons, one aesthetic and one personal, why it could appeal to Diaghilev. Aesthetically, Diaghilev instinctively saw it as a period piece, in the spirit of the eighteenth-century court divertissement which particularly appealed to him in the neoclassical 1920s. On a personal level, because of the references to the coronation of Peter the Great's daughter, it discreetly bolstered the rumor that he was himself descended, on his mother's side, from one of Elizaveta Petrovna's illegitimate children.[82] In the fall of 1927, Nabokov signed a contract with Diaghilev, prepared by Nouvel, under whose terms the oratorio would form the basis of a "ballet-spectacle," and in October 1927, the Monte-Carlo correspondent of the music weekly *Le Ménestrel* announced that the next season of the Ballets Russes would include "an *action scénique* in three parts entitled *Ode*, music by M. Nabokoff."[83]

Nabokov always felt that Diaghilev's decision to take on *Ode*, which in effect launched his musical career, was sealed once he had found a new ally in Igor Stravinsky, to whom he was finally introduced in October 1927. The occasion was a luncheon at Prunier, the exclusive fish and seafood restaurant near the Place de la Madeleine.[84] In addition to Stravinsky and Diaghilev, Kochno, Nouvel, and Lifar were in attendance. Diaghilev had made it a ritual obligation for every junior composer enrolled with the Ballets Russes to be presented to the great master. While not having met Nabokov personally, Stravinsky certainly knew about him and his work: in a letter from the previous month, Cocteau had told him about Nabokov's cantata, which he found "very touching."[85] That October morning Stravinsky arrived half an hour late, complaining about the dreadful Paris fall weather. Nabokov immediately noticed his signature light-gray spats and the gold chains he wore on his waistcoat. He was struck by his unusually small size, which made the head look disproportionately big, and his "bird-like, beaky" face. The young, apprehensive composer found the lunch "long and dreary." The conversation, he vaguely recalled, was about *Apollon musagète*, which Stravinsky was then writing. His only comment about *Ode* was to wonder why Nabokov had chosen such a "stilted," academic poem.

The audition that afternoon, on the company's rehearsal upright piano, went far better than Nabokov feared. He played the introductory chorus and one of the ariettas, singing the vocal lines "in a mixture of bass and falsetto." (Maritain, for one, remembered Nabokov as the only composer of his acquaintance who could sight-read vocal music with a real singing voice.)[86] Soon Stravinsky and Balanchine, who had just come in, joined in the singing. Stravinsky responded to the "unmistakably and naïvely Russian" character of the music. According to

Nabokov's delightful, if obviously slightly embellished, account of the scene in *Bagázh*, Stravinsky was spontaneously reminded of the salon songs by Italianate Russian composers of the generation of Glinka, such as Aleksandr L'vovich Gurilev (1803–58), or the generation immediately preceding, like Aleksandr Aliab'ev (1787–1851). Why was it that Nabokov was so familiar with this unfamiliar repertory? The young composer was not sure what to answer. That is, at least, the way he reported it in *Bagázh*. His earlier account, in *Old Friends and New Music*, suggests, rather, that he had quite consciously sought inspiration in this repertory, unknown then and now in Western Europe, but with which he had grown up as a child and adolescent.[87] In any event, it appears that the audition ended with Stravinsky declaring to Diaghilev, "Of course you should perform this music"—or words to that effect. Stravinsky also urged the composer and the impresario to make sure that the orchestration be realized in the Italian, not the German style, suggesting that Rieti might offer valuable advice.[88] Offering Nabokov a taxi ride, he quizzed him on his family origins and musical training, and advised him to beware of Prokofiev's influence, since it could be harmful to the tender, nostalgic, and lyrical vein he had sensed and liked in his music.

How much of Stravinsky's music did Nabokov know at the time of this first meeting? Apart from his half-remembered, youthful exposure to *Fireworks*, he had heard Klemperer conduct *The Rite of Spring* in Berlin. In Paris, he could have attended the premiere of the Octet, which Stravinsky himself conducted at the Opéra in October 1923, and the Concerto for Piano and Winds, which Koussevitzky conducted at the same place in May 1924, not to mention *Oedipus Rex*, first heard under the composer on May 30, 1927. None of these events is mentioned in Nabokov's published or manuscript reminiscences. *Apollon musagète* was premiered in 1928 as part of the same Ballets Russes season as *Ode*. Nabokov, however, was preoccupied by his own ballet and subsequently admitted that, while admiring George Balanchine's choreography, he misunderstood the "lyrical beauty" of Stravinsky's music, which he found "too artificially restrained" and stylistically derivative.[89] Only several years later did he fully appreciate the music of *Apollon*. The performance of the string orchestra conducted by Désormière he found less than adequate, and he definitely did not like the neo-primitive sets and costumes by André Bauchant, who had been more or less forced on Stravinsky by Diaghilev, whereas Stravinsky would have favored Giorgio De Chirico.[90]

Rather than *The Rite of Spring*, the Octet, *Oedipus*, or *Apollo*, the one Stravinsky work Nabokov subsequently singled out as responsible for the shock of discovery was the "Russian choreographic scenes" *Svadebka*, generally known by its French title *Les noces*.[91] Nabokov was in Berlin when the work was premiered, under Ernest Ansermet, in May 1923 at the Théâtre de la Gaîté. It was revived the following year. Nabokov may have seen it then, but the reminiscences he published late in life are muddled: the 1924 performance was not at the Théâtre Sarah-Bernhardt but at the Théâtre des Champs-Élysées, nor was it conducted by Désormière, who joined the Ballets Russes only the following year.[92] These details suggest a confusion with the 1928 revival, still in Bronislava Nijinska's choreography and with sets and costumes by Nataliia Goncharova, and which Nabokov certainly saw, since *Noces* was given on the same program as Nabokov's own *Ode*. But Nabokov also claimed he acquired a copy of the piano-vocal score, published in 1922, at the time he lived with Tchelitchew and Tanner, and that he heard *Noces* again in the fall of the same year, in Frankfurt, conducted by Hermann Scherchen. He was certainly familiar with the music by 1926, since he makes a brief reference to *Noces* in his 1927 article in *Melos*. He eventually came to consider Stravinsky's "astute, near-miraculous reconstruction of ancient Russian marriage ritual" "the last and ultimate masterpiece of Russian music."[93]

Nabokov's own oratorio is in thirteen parts. After a brief fanfare-like introduction, the opening chorus (*Litse svoe skryvaet den'*, "Day hides its face"), with interventions of the soprano and bass soloists, is in the *ben marcato* mode that characterizes much of the work. Then follows a delicate, *romance*-like duet for soprano and bass (*Peschinka*, "Like a grain of sand"), accompanied by solo woodwinds, and ending in a passage in unison. The chorus returns for an Adagio maestoso, in the same, strongly marked, homophonic manner (*Usta premudrykh nam glasiat*, "The mouths of wise men tell us"). The next number (*No gde zh, natura, tvoi zakon?*, "But, nature, where are your laws?") is also choral, with a middle section for the solo soprano. A slow interlude comes next, its square melodic pattern rather reminiscent of a chorale. It is followed by a chorus (*O vy, kotorykh bystryi zrak*, "O you, whose penetrating gaze"), in a style reminiscent of Glinka, with a slower, quieter middle section for the bass; like much of Lomonosov's poem, it forms a rhetorical question. The same text is repeated in the next section, leading to more questions: the charming, salon-like character of the opening Andantino dialogue for the two soloists, with its guitar-like accompaniment, contrasts with the bombastic words of the sung lines. The eighth section, for the bass solo, is a long recitative, preceded by an extended introduction (*Tam sporit zhirna mgla s vodoi*, "There the dense mist contends with water"); it corresponds with a moment of darkness and uncertainty, and ends with a crescendo, sustained by the piano and percussion. A jubilant chorus of celebration (*Chto zyblet iasnyi nochyio luch?*, "Why do bright rays shimmer in the night?") greets the apparition of the Aurora Borealis: it has a marked Russian character, and it is the only chorus featuring polyphonic elements. There follows an intermezzo, in which a pastoral introduction, with solo oboe, leads to a long crescendo, with a choral-like character. The jubilant chorus is repeated and developed, ending in a tremendous blaze of sound, where the percussion is heard in full force. It segues without interruption into a brief, slightly dissonant chorale. The final chorus, marked Largo (*Somnenii polon vash otvet*, "Your answer is full of doubt"), introduced by a suspenseful passage for percussion and brass, does not end in triumphant mode, but with two question-like short motifs for the brass, as if the many questions asked in the poem could not be answered.

As Nabokov himself pointed out, *Ode* is at once strongly Russian in character, a homage to the age of Glinka and his predecessors, and couched in a form—the oratorio—not typically cultivated in Russian music—at least (as Nabokov mischievously conceded in the late 1940s) before the need to glorify Stalin was impressed upon Soviet composers and a flood of cantatas ensued. More lyrical than melodic in character, *Ode* is also striking by the directness and forcefulness of its rhythms—another aspect that must have appealed to Stravinsky. Less obvious to the listener, but equally crucial to the composer, was the element he claimed to have learned from Satie: a kind of falsely naïve simplicity which can be found, for instance, in the oratorios and other religious works by Honegger and Poulenc. In comments he made only a few years later, Nabokov explained that his intention, especially when setting the part of the poem devoted to the Aurora Borealis, was "to replace entirely the dynamic principle"—in other words thematic development in the sonata tradition—"by that of volumes and masses of sound."[94]

Turning the oratorio into a ballet involved several steps, the first of which was to devise a plot. The *Ode* scenario is credited to Kochno, who had done similar service for Auric's *Les fâcheux* and *Les matelots* and Sauguet's *La chatte* (1927), having previously penned, at a very young age, the libretto of Stravinsky's *Mavra* (1922). However, the correspondence between Kochno and Nabokov shows that the broad outline of the scenario was suggested by the composer himself in early September 1927.[95] It put into presence a female figure, representing Nature, and a student in eighteenth-century costume. The student begs Nature to explain to him the secrets of the universe. Stepping down from her pedestal, Nature shows him various phenomena: constellations, flowers and fruits, a river, etc., ending with a spectacular fete, the crowning point of which is the Aurora Borealis. In his enthusiasm, the student rashly attempts to penetrate into the vision, but the charm is broken and everything vanishes. The lesson is over; Nature steps back on her pedestal, and the ballet ends with her apotheosis.

Shortly after the contract was signed, Nabokov, as he reported to Nouvel, from Alsace, on December 5, sold his score, as it then stood, to the Parisian publisher Sénard.[96] It did not include three additional dance numbers Diaghilev requested to expand the second act Divertissement, and which were composed by mid-February 1928. By then, Nabokov had also completed the instrumentation, for which, as he told Kochno, he sought the opinion and advice of Milhaud, Rieti, and Désormière.[97]

The next step was the choice of choreographer. Kochno, according to Nabokov, would have favored Balanchine, as did the composer, who immediately bonded with the young ballet master, his junior by less than one year. But Diaghilev presumably wanted Balanchine to focus his attention on *Apollon musagète* and designated Leonide Massine, at thirty-one the company's senior choreographer, whose impressive resume already included *Parade, Le tricorne*, and *La boutique fantasque*. "Fortunately," Nabokov recalled, "Massine liked my music at once and seemed to understand its somewhat sentimental, lyrical spirit."[98] As for the cast, there was no doubt that the role of the student was to be given to Lifar, the company's rising male star.

The real difficulties started when Diaghilev made the decision to hire Tchelitchew as designer. He had seen and admired the Russian painter's sets for the ballet *The Wedding Feast of the Boyar* in Berlin in 1922 and had resolved to enlist his collaboration for the Ballets Russes.[99] Being an intimate of Nabokov, Tchelitchew already knew the music of *Ode* and liked it. He had, however, no sympathy whatsoever for the eighteenth-century court divertissement aesthetic dear to Diaghilev or the implied glorification of imperial Russia and (least of all) Diaghilev's purported family ties to Elizabeth. The revised scenario, prepared with the help of his technical assistant Pierre Charbonnier, a filmmaker as well as a painter, had nothing to do with Diaghilev's initial conception, which would have been based on contemporary representations of court balls and coronations. It was, instead, a daring reinterpretation of Kochno's outline. In place of the eighteenth-century court pageantry— the only remaining eighteenth-century elements were Lifar's costume and a few touches in the final Divertissement—it called for geometrical forms, cinematographic projections, and dazzling neon lighting effects.[100] In short, as Nabokov later summarized, "from the outset there were three different and in a way irreconcilable points of view involved in the *Ode* project":

> First there was Diaghilev's notion about a grand Elizabethan period piece, a tribute to the epoch of the great Russian poet Lomonosov; second there was Tchelitchew's view of Ode as a modern surrealist experiment; and third there was my music, which did not fit into either of the first categories.[101]

Diaghilev's reactions to Tchelitchew's bold, modernist vision were predictable. According to the painter's later recollections, as transmitted by Parker Tyler, the impresario was "petrified with horror and surprise"; he left the matter in the hands of Kochno, while warning him that they would end up with a "monster."[102]

Before their June Paris premiere, new ballets were typically prepared at Monte-Carlo during the spring, while the troupe performed its repertory in the beautiful opera house designed in 1879 by Charles Garnier, the architect of the Paris Opera. Nabokov thus spent a month in Monaco in April–May 1928. Work on the choreography with Massine, superficially at least, went well. Nabokov, of course, had no technical experience in such matters. It therefore took him a while to realize that "with the exception of two or three lovely lyrical dances, Massine's choreography, although probably very good in itself, had very little to do with my music and with the whole eminently romantic mood of *Ode*."[103] Nabokov sensed Diaghilev's dissatisfaction with the way things were going. Tchelitchew, in keeping with his "difficult and morbidly superstitious character," had yet to produce any sketches for his sets and costumes and was momentarily on nonspeaking terms with Nabokov.[104] Nevertheless, Nabokov enjoyed his stay in the Monegasque resort. He was sympathetically treated by Alexandrina Trussevich, Diaghilev's secretary, and by Sergei Grigoriev, the Ballets Russes stage manager. He was on friendly terms with the painter André Derain, who, beginning with *La boutique fantasque*, had become a favorite Ballets Russes designer, and above all he formed with Balanchine a friendship and complicity that endured for the rest of his life. With his new friends, he explored the region's picturesque villages and restaurants. There were visits from Prokofiev, Matisse, Sauguet, and Rieti. There were ballet performances in the evening, which familiarized him, in particular, with what survived of the Ballets Russes of the prewar period. There was, above all, Diaghilev, who, after a cool reception, took him under his wing and regaled him with anecdotes and reminiscences, tales he himself later transmitted in one of the liveliest chapters of his 1951 memoir *Old Friends and New Music*. However, when the subject of *Ode* came up, Diaghilev remained silent. One orchestral read-through, conducted by Marc-César Scotto, the troupe's resident conductor, went disastrously. Nabokov returned to Paris "filled with apprehension and dark forebodings."[105] The next few weeks were spent revising and reorchestrating parts of the score in collaboration with Désormière, the conductor in charge of the premiere, who more or less locked him up to protect him from the publicity surrounding the new work.

Towards the end of May, Diaghilev and his troupe returned from Monte-Carlo. Ten days remained before the opening of the season on June 6, *Ode* being part of the first program. Rehearsals resumed, still without any involvement on Diaghilev's part. The Ballets Russes' new venue, since 1926, was the rather decrepit Théâtre Sarah-Bernhardt, on the Place du Châtelet, built in 1862 to house the Théâtre-Lyrique, "a barn of a place," in Richard Buckle's words, and acoustically better suited to opera than ballet.[106] Only four days before the premiere did Diaghilev finally take charge, summoning everybody concerned and supervising every visual and musical detail of the production. As Parker Tyler, citing Tchelitchew, astutely pointed out, Diaghilev was both anxious to avoid producing a "monster" and eager to make sure the Ballets Russes, when it came to the avant-garde, "should lead the way."[107] "From that moment on and for the next three days," Nabokov recalled, "until the last curtain had fallen on a highly successful performance of *Ode*, I lived in a state of frenzy. Like everyone else connected with the production, I worked day and night, in an agony of sleeplessness and exhilaration the like of which I never experienced before or since."[108] Cecil Beaton, who attended the dress rehearsal, at which the chorus got "tangled beneath the meshes of an enormous net," thought that "it seemed impossible that, out of such chaos, order could be regained in time for the premiere."[109]

Ode was given as a triple bill with revivals of two famous Ballets Russes productions: Prokofiev's *Pas d'acier* and Stravinsky's *Noces*—the latter, as critics pointed
out, a ballet-oratorio like Nabokov's work. Being the new work on the program,
Ode received considerable attention. Despite the intensity of the last-minute
efforts demanded by Diaghilev, the musical performance clearly left much to be
desired. Nabokov himself described what he heard as "under-rehearsed, ill-sung,
ill-orchestrated," sounding "awful" in the unflattering Théâtre Sarah-Bernhardt
acoustics, and he was relieved that Stravinsky, absorbed by his own new ballet, did
not attend.[110] As the *Ménestrel* critic drily pointed out in his detailed review, what
was heard on the first night sounded like a rehearsal rather than a premiere; the
second of the two Paris performances, the following night, went much better.[111]
The same critic was, otherwise, sympathetic towards the new piece, correctly noting its romantic character and mentioning Glinka, whose works had been introduced to Parisians by none other than Diaghilev twenty years before. Comparing
Nabokov's relation to his early nineteenth-century inspiration to Auric's and
Poulenc's debt to romantic French music, he added:

> The work is striking at first by its melodic quality and choral simplicity; and
> the spare character of the musical devices used, far from being a sign of
> sterility, becomes an expression of strength—the strength of a young musi-
> cian who already knows how crucial are, in music, directness of utterance
> and the perpetual presence of song. The very austerity of this art—in the
> choice and arrangement of the material, in a kind of sonic rarefaction—is
> an appropriate conduit for the subject, which is a kind of hymn to nature,
> but a nature in which "the greatness of God" shines through. Icebergs,
> fights between mist and water, Aurora Borealis: all these natural wonders,
> far from getting us to forget about everything else as we witness them, pro-
> claim the existence of God—and by the same token, those operatic arias,
> that melodic sensuousness, far from being cause for distraction, brings us
> back towards the most substantive and concentrated elements music can
> contain. And since I was among those who imprudently used the term
> "masterpiece," let me justify it by noting how rare are the works which,
> while focusing on their supposedly superficial artistic aspects, direct us
> towards serious feelings and bring about a certain religious solemnity.[112]

Another sympathetic reviewer, Maurice Brillant, writing in *Le Correspondant*, was
sensitive to the "Italian charm" of the work, which he correctly placed in the tradition of Glinka and Tchaikovsky, contrasting it with the orientalist tendencies of the
Mighty Five; he also compared *Ode* to the Stravinsky of the pre-neoclassical period.[113]

The cast of *Ode* was headed by Lifar as the student, while Nature was danced by
Irina Belianina (also known as Ira Belline), Stravinsky's niece—and the mistress

of Louis Jouvet. The other soloists were Aleksandra Danilova, Felia Dubrovska, Alice Nikitina, and Massine himself. While the dancing was generally praised, Massine's choreography, despite the adjustments demanded by Diaghilev, did not please everyone. As for Tchelitchew's sets, projections, puppets, masks, and spare costumes, and Charbonnier's inventive lighting, they divided opinion. "The setting," Beaton remembered,

> consisted of ropes and of two lines, which mounted from either wing to meet high above the centre of the back of the stage, on which were hung small dolls, dressed exactly as the female dancers were dressed. Against a blue void the still, small dolls gave the scene vast size and depth, while the black, white and grey dancers formed with triangles of rope, strange mechanical designs.[114]

Some critics, inevitably, were put off by this abstract concept, which they described, in their confusion, as "constructivist" or even "surrealist." Others were captivated, like Stravinsky (not an easy judge in such matters), who, when he finally saw *Ode*, recognized Tchelitchew's talent as a stage designer.[115] So was Émile Vuillermoz, the music critic of *Le Temps*:

> It is impossible to describe all there is of curious and ingenious new-ness in the different tableaux which compose this strange fantasy. [. . .] Mr. Tchelitchew has created an extremely evocative atmosphere from the further dimensions of outer space and of terrestrial realms beyond reality. [. . .]It is really disconcerting to witness the timidity and the slowness our scenic designers have shown in utilizing up to now an element [the cin-ema] so efficacious in evoking fantasy, and which in its suppleness permits of realizations that can be varied in style virtually to the infinite.[116]

Nabokov himself admitted that it took him a while to appreciate the beauty and inventiveness of Tchelitchew's blue gauze sets—Brillant called them a "sym-phony in blue"—but he was eventually won over, even if he deplored that the Paris police, by banning the use of neon lighting, had deprived the production of its most novel effects.[117] *Ode*, to be sure, was no ballet in a conventional sense but, to quote Donald Windham, "a spectacle capable of encompassing an Aristotelian unity of choral speech, melody, pantomime and dance."[118] Even Balanchine, who cared little for Massine's choreography, later went so far as to declare that *Ode* was "far ahead of its time."[119] All in all, this is just what Diaghilev wanted to hear.

6

Successes and Frustrations

THE YEAR OF Nabokov's major musical debut also marked his marriage, on February 2, 1928, to Nataliia Alekseeva Shakhoskaia, the sister of his school friend Dmitri Shakhovskoi. Usually referred to by the French form of her name, Natalie—or by the Russian diminutive Natasha—she was born, like her fiance, in 1903. The daughter of Prince Aleksei Shakhovskoi, a state counselor and court chamberlain, she also had German roots on the side of her mother—née Anna von Kninen—as well as Italian blood, being also descended from Carlo Rossi, one of the great architects of eighteenth-century St. Petersburg.[1] Natalie was educated at the Levitzky School in Tsarskoe Selo. Like the Nabokovs, she left Russia with her family in 1919. The Shakhovskois spent four years in Constantinople, where Natalie and her younger sister Zinaida, born in 1906, completed their schooling at the Arnaut-Keuw American college. In 1923 Natalie moved to Nice, where she lived with a cousin of her mother. Nabokov's mother usually spent the winter in Nice, and it was probably through her that the two young people, who knew each other from their early adolescence in Petersburg, got reacquainted at that time. In 1926, Natalie's sister married Sviatoslav Malewsky-Malevich; she eventually became a writer, writing and publishing in both French and Russian under the name Zinaida Schakovskoy and the pseudonym Jacques Croisé. As for Natalie and Zinaida's brother Dmitri, whose return to religion has been mentioned in the previous chapter, he was named Archimandrite in 1937. He emigrated to the United States after the war and was appointed, successively, bishop of Brooklyn and San Francisco, becoming archbishop in 1961. With his marriage, Nabokov, himself issued from a prominent family—claiming to be descended from Genghis Khan, no less—thus allied himself with an equally distinguished lineage. After a civil wedding at the eighteenth arrondissement town hall, the religious ceremony took place at the Paris Russian cathedral on Rue Daru. Sauguet was the bride's best man, holding the candle over Natalie's head, as prescribed by the Orthodox ritual.[2]

Even before *Ode* was premiered, Nabokov's forthcoming Ballets Russes debut had generated a good deal of publicity. Diaghilev made sure that "his" musicians received maximum social exposure. Nabokov had already been introduced, as we have seen, into the circle of Misia Sert, whose personal influence with the Russian impresario may well have done more to capture Diaghilev's favor than the latter's presence with Prokofiev in the Salle des Agriculteurs for Nabokov's first concert and even than Stravinsky's subsequent imprimatur. Nabokov's close friend Rzewuski was related to Roffredo Caetani, Prince of Bassiano, whose American wife Margaret, née Chapin, was herself an important art patron; she befriended Valéry and Saint-John Perse and helped subsidize the handsome literary journal *Commerce*. She and her husband entertained on Sundays at the Villa Romana, in Versailles (not too far, therefore, from the Maritains), and at their summer home in Deauville. Another prominent musical hostess Nabokov met was Princesse Edmond de Polignac; née Winnaretta Singer, she was the daughter of the American sewing-machine industrialist. Also on the scene were her cousin by marriage Marie-Blanche de Polignac, daughter of the designer Jeanne Lanvin, and, no less importantly, Coco Chanel, friend and rival of Misia, who designed the costumes for the first production of *Apollon musagète*. Through Diaghilev, or possibly Cocteau (though the latter, by 1928, had fallen out of favor with the Ballets Russes founder), Nabokov was introduced to Count Étienne de Beaumont and his wife.[3] He also attended soirees held at the Place des États-Unis mansion of Vicomte and Vicomtesse Charles and Marie-Laure de Noailles, patrons of the Surrealists. The Noailles invited Nabokov to stay, with other composers and artists, at their villa in Hyères, on the Mediterranean, designed by the modernist architect Robert Mallet-Stevens.

Nabokov was the first to admit that he found the "societal traffic" surrounding Diaghilev and his world "terribly seductive," all the more so, he later confessed, without being any more specific, for the sexual opportunities it afforded.[4] For obvious reasons, marriage brought at least a temporary halt to his heady, frivolous lifestyle. In October 1928, to protect themselves against the pressure and distractions of Paris society, the newlyweds temporarily settled in Brussels, where Natalie's mother lived. So did her sister, after spending two years in the Belgian Congo where her husband had been posted. A baby daughter was born to the Nabokovs in the summer 1929, but the child was of a sickly constitution and, tragically, died in November of the same year, perhaps as a result of medical negligence.[5]

When not in Paris or Brussels, Nabokov and his wife often stayed with Alexandre Grunelius and his wife Antoinette in Alsace. Grunelius had abandoned his plans to serve in the German diplomatic service in 1920 when his dying father begged him to return home to care for his aging mother. Becoming a French citizen, as all Alsatians were offered to after 1918, he began a business career, and raised a family. From then on, and until his departure for America, Nabokov paid at least one annual visit to Kolbsheim, the small village, located about ten miles to the southwest of Strasbourg, where the Grunelius family had a château, from 1929 their permanent residence. Dating from the early eighteenth century, it had been enlarged and redecorated in the nineteenth, especially by Jean-Georges Humann (1780–1842), a French Finance Minister under Louis-Philippe, and his son Théodore, who became mayor of Strasbourg. It was from this family that the Gruneliuses acquired it after Alsace became part of the German Empire in 1871.[6] Destroyed during the First World War, the extensive gardens were restored and redesigned by Alexandre, partly in the French style, partly à l'anglaise, on a series of terraces overlooking the plain of Alsace. Grunelius redecorated the château's main wing in a simpler style than the one favored by his nineteenth-century predecessors.

To an even greater extent than Bethmann-Hollweg's house at Hohenfinow, Kolbsheim became Nabokov's real home in Europe. After Nabokov's marriage, Grunelius put at his and his wife's disposal a house on the outskirts of the village. It was appropriately christened "Villa Ode" and, over the next five years, Nabokov invited writer and musician friends to stay with him there: Sauguet spent several weeks there in the summer of 1928. Prokofiev and his wife did so in subsequent years, as did Hindemith, Cocteau, and Désormière, among many others. It was in Alsace that the Nabokov's son Ivan was born in January 1932. In October that year, Vladimir Nabokov and his wife Véra were Nicolas's guests at Kolbsheim, along with Natalie's mother. This stay resulted in an invitation, arranged by Zinaida, for Vladimir Nabokov to lecture in Brussels.[7] At Kolbsheim, through the Grunelius family, Nabokov became acquainted with some famous Alsatians, such as Albert Schweitzer, the future Nobel Peace Prize winner; Schweitzer's cousin the violinist Charles Münch, the future conductor of the Boston Symphony Orchestra, then concertmaster of the Leipzig Gewandhaus; and Münch's elder brother Fritz, a choral conductor in Strasbourg, who regularly put Nabokov's works on his programs. But Kolbsheim, for Nabokov, was not so much a place to socialize as a haven of peace, where he could concentrate and compose. The Piano Sonata, as noted in the printed score, was largely written there.

Antoinette Grunelius, née Schlumberger, belonged to a prominent and prosperous Alsatian family, of Protestant German stock, with ties to the banking, industrial, and wine sectors. Her uncle Jean Schlumberger (1877–1968), a well-known and prolific writer and critic, was among the founders of the Nouvelle Revue française; two other uncles were prominent scientists. She and her husband were introduced by Nabokov to Jacques and Raïssa Maritain at a concert in Paris in 1927, and were at once invited to Meudon the following Sunday. The ties between Maritain and Grunelius became closer in September 1931, when Maritain visited Kolbsheim, where Nabokov was residing. Under the Maritains' influence, Grunelius and his wife eventually converted to Catholicism: Antoinette was baptized in the Meudon chapel in March 1932, and her husband the follow-ing year. Though Nabokov probably never intended to take such a step himself, his own closeness to Maritain and his wife as well as his intimate friendship with Grunelius made him a privileged witness to this spiritual quest, which had begun when Grunelius had confided in him his doubts and hopes in 1919 in The Hague. As for Nabokov himself, a draft letter to Maritain, dated Kolbsheim, September 21, 1929, shows that his religious fervor had not diminished since 1926.[8] Meeting him on a Sunday afternoon in Meudon, the philosopher Emmanuel Mounier recalled Nabokov speaking on "the phenomenon of inspiration in music," and stressing "the distinction to be made between natural inspiration and spiritual inspiration, which today is missing more and more."[9]

Paris, evidently, remained for Nabokov a constant pole of attraction, even though, for a while, he no longer maintained a permanent address in the city. For his short, regular visits, he had to depend on the hospitality of friends, such as Jacques Février, son of the successful opera composer Henry Février and himself a distinguished pianist: in a letter probably dating from September 1929, Février apologizes for not being able to put Nabokov up as he had offered to, his mother having already rented the room, and hopes Nabokov might be able to stay with the Maritains. By the summer of 1930, Nabokov had reestablished a part-time residence in Paris at no. 9, rue Jacques Mawas, a cul-de-sac in the then affordable fifteenth arrondissement on the Left Bank. There he hosted his cousin Vladimir, on a visit from Berlin, for three weeks in the fall of 1932.

One of the liveliest and most memorable chapters of *Old Friends and New Music*, first published in 1949 in the *Atlantic Monthly*, is Nabokov's account of the evening when he sat in Diaghilev's box at the Paris Opera when Nijinsky was taken out of a sanatorium on the outskirts of Paris for one evening to attend a performance at which Lifar appeared. Diaghilev's purpose, by bringing the two dancers together, was to get Nijinsky, by his sole presence, to "anoint" Lifar as his successor. Nabokov's lively account begins with Diaghilev sending him to fetch Nijinsky, along with Vasili Zuikov and Sergei Grigoriev, and ending, back at the sanatorium, with Nabokov overhearing Nijinsky say, in Russian, "in a gentle, halt-ing, and somewhat tearful voice: 'Tell him that Lifar jumps well.' "[10] Some details in Nabokov's account, however, are difficult to reconcile with other testimonies. For one thing, the performance at the Opéra did not take place in October 1928 but on December 27 of that year; nor did Lifar appear in *The Firebird*, but as the Moor in *Petrushka*.[11] Lifar, admittedly not the most reliable witness (he himself gets the date wrong),[12] does not mention Nabokov's name in his own account, according to which it was he who, before the performance, went to fetch Nijinsky at the clinic; nor was the clinic in Villejuif, as Nabokov has it, but in Passy. Certainly, it is dif-ficult to believe that Kessler, who was with Diaghilev at the end of the performance and saw Nijinsky board the car that was to take him back to the clinic, would not have noted Nabokov's presence if he had been part of the expedition.[13] That being said, it is still possible that Nabokov was at the Opéra that night and saw, with his own eyes, "the Specter of Nijinsky."[14]

In the summer of 1928, the press mentioned that Nabokov was preparing a new cantata-ballet for Ida Rubinstein on an ancient Greek text.[15] No title is given, but in May 1928 Nabokov had told Kochno he was at work on a ballet called *Aphrodite*; in another letter to the same correspondent, he refers to it as his "Greek ballet epic," adding that it "is going well and is really quite new musically but is not [like] *Ode* and yet very Russian."[16] The news cannot have pleased Diaghilev, who considered Rubinstein an annoying rival, especially since "Idka," as Prokofiev noted, "has greatly more money than he has."[17] The Russian dancer had evidently approached composers whose works had been rejected by the Ballets Russes and offered to stage them with her newly formed company, for which she recruited Nijinska as ballet master. In any event, whether or not Diaghilev made his displeasure known—Sauguet suggests he may have threatened Nabokov to drop *Ode* over the matter—the project went nowhere.[18] No scenario has been traced. Based on the title, it can be noted that the Greek mythological theme belongs with the same vein as *Apollon musagète* and the *Perséphone* Rubinstein commissioned from Stravinsky and André Gide five years later; on an even closer subject was Honegger's *Les Noces de Psyché et de l'Amour*, which opened the first season of the Ballets Ida Rubinstein at the Opéra on November 22.[19] Whether the Russian dancer lost interest or changed her mind about *Aphrodite*, there are indications that the ballet had been properly commissioned, with a down payment of 1,000 francs, and that Nabokov completed and delivered the piano score.[20] In an undated letter, evidently in response to an inquiry from the composer, Étienne de Beaumont told Nabokov that Rubinstein had failed to communicate with him, even though the date of the scheduled performances was approaching. Later in the fall, Désormière was still urging Nabokov to try to get Rubinstein to pay him the balance due, or, at the very least, to confirm the commission so that Nabokov could register it with the Society of Authors and get an advance on royalties.[21] In late April 1929, Nabokov told Kochno Rubinstein did not answer his letters and still owed him 4,000 francs.[22] That is not the last-known reference to *Aphrodite*: as late as 1948, in a Boston Symphony Program, Nabokov still listed it among his works.[23] The score, however, cannot be traced. Prokofiev, who had seen it, did not think it was a good piece and would have improved Nabokov's reputation.[24]

Ode had definitely put Nabokov's name among the avant-garde composers one talked about. Only a few days before the premiere, Milhaud, in an interview he gave to the daily *Comœdia*, listed him, along with Honegger, Poulenc, Auric, Prokofiev, Stravinsky, Hindemith, Webern, and Rieti, among the names of contemporary musicians that had to be reckoned with.[25] Shortly after its two performances at the Théâtre Sarah-Bernhardt, *Ode* was premiered in London on July 9 as part of the Ballets Russes' four-week season at His Majesty's Theatre, where it was seen six times in total. Some appeared to have been surprised and charmed in equal measure by the lack of correlation between the visual, choreographic, and musical aspects: "Never before," A. V. Coton recalled ten years later, "were the senses so delightfully assaulted with unrelated and unrelatable forms of movement, music, lighting and colour." Above all, he was left with the memory of "the unearthly beauty created by a revolutionary use of light never before seen in any form of Theatre."[26] The balletomane bookdealer Cyril Beaumont, present at the premiere, has left an invaluable and detailed account of the occasion.[27] While calling *Ode* "the strangest of all the Diaghilev productions" and "certainly the most extraordinary of a host of unusual works," he was captivated by Tchelitchew's conception. The highly positive comments he makes on Massine's choreography suggest that the artistic realization in London far surpassed what had been seen (and heard, probably) in Paris.[28] "It is not easy," Beaumont concludes, "to convey the strange character, the celestial beauty, and the intellectual appeal of *Ode*." It "could never become a popular ballet," he concedes, "yet this stark conception attempted the boldest flight of all—to attain the infinite, and, more wonderful still, seemed at times to reach it."

The vocal score of *Ode* was issued that year by the Parisian music firm of Maurice Sénart. Almost at the same time, Rouart Lerolle published that of the *Chants à la Vierge Marie*. These songs received their first performance in December 1928 at the Salle Chopin, as part of a Pro Musica concert also featuring works by Hindemith and Frank Barlow. In April 1929 they were included in a concert of the Société internationale de musique contemporaine in Geneva. Reporting for *Le Ménestrel* on the success of the performance, André Schaeffner recalled that the work had attracted him from the start "by the way it heralded the forthcoming style of *Ode*" and the writing "at once dissonant and chromatic"; he also detected the influence of Stravinsky's Piano Sonata of 1924 and Serenade in A of 1925—the latter work a favorite of Nabokov, who once singled it out as "the joy of a skilled music lover."[29] The *Chants à la Vierge*, however, predate his meeting Stravinsky and there is no indication that he was familiar with these two works at the time. Writing in *The Musical Times*, Edwin Evans was less favorably impressed: he deplored the lack of "musical amenities" and found the vocal part "very trying" and the piano accompaniment "clumsy and heavy-footed."[30] Present in the audience at Geneva was Roger Sessions, then living in Rome, whose Symphony in E minor was performed during the same festival. He was sufficiently impressed with Nabokov's work to approach him, via a mutual friend, the Belgian composer Jean Binet, to explore the possibility of having his music performed in New York.[31]

Shortly before the Geneva performance, a concert devoted entirely to Nabokov's music took place in Berlin on March 7, 1929. It was held at the art gallery of Alfred Flechtheim, the prominent avant-garde dealer and collector, subsequently vilified by the Nazis as one of the main purveyors of "degenerate art." Presumably the connection with Flechtheim was arranged by one of Nabokov's German friends, such as Kessler or Wilhelm Uhde, or possibly at Helene von Nostitz's salon. The program included the Berlin premieres of the *Chants à la Vierge Marie*, sung by the Viennese coloratura soprano Hedwig Francillo-Kaufmann (1878–1948), then at the end of her career.[32] Nabokov uncharitably reported to Kochno that she looked like a barrel and sounded like a consumptive.[33] Also, four Russian songs by Nabokov were sung in German translation by the young tenor Boris Greverus, then attached to the Mannheim National Theater, where he had recently made his debut as Hermann in Tchaikovsky's *Queen of Spades*.[34] In addition to the two Pushkin poems of 1925, this group of songs included settings of poems by two contemporaries of Pushkin: *Na chto vy, dni* . . . ("Sad days"), on a text by E. A. Baratynskii (1800–1844), and *Khloe* ("To Chloe"), on a text by Ivan Ivanovich Dmitriev (1760–1837). These four Russian songs were issued by Rouart Lerolle, under the title *Quatre romances*, and with the indication that they were intended for a soprano or mezzo-soprano, not a tenor. Sauguet is credited with the French words, while the German version is attributed to a certain "von Wistinghausen."[35] Arrau, who served as accompanist in the two sets of songs, closed the Flechtheim Gallery concert with the piano sonata, which he had evidently performed in Berlin before, and opened it with a "Suite from a ballet, transcribed for the piano by the composer." Described as a world premiere (*Erstaufführung*), the work can be tentatively identified as the *Trois danses* issued in Berlin the following year by the Russischer Musik Verlag, with a posthumous dedication to Diaghilev. These were, in a piano reduction, the numbers added to *Ode* in 1928 and not included in the published score. One month after this Berlin concert, in April 1929, Marcelle Meyer gave the first London performance of the Piano Sonata at a BBC chamber music concert, at which she also played Stravinsky's *Serenade*. Neither work found favor with the conservative *Musical Times* reviewer, who referred to the Sonata as "probably the most irritating piece of music heard in London for some years," singling out the "obvious *salon* atmosphere of the slow movement."[36]

In mid-February 1929, *Ode* was heard in concert when it was played by the newly formed Orchestre symphonique de Paris conducted by Ernest Ansermet; the program began with Mussorgsky's prelude to *Khovanshchina* and also included Stravinsky's *Le baiser de la fée* and *Noces*. As Nabokov told Prokofiev on the day of the concert, most of the rehearsal time had been taken up by *Le baiser* (towards which Nabokov was therefore badly disposed); nor was his work helped by an inadequate soloist, the undernourished chorus, and the dreary acoustics of the Salle Pleyel. "What a pity!" wrote Sauguet in *L'Europe nouvelle*. "The work by Nicolas Nabokoff is very moving, highly poetic, at times carried away by stirrings of tender or tragic passion that come from the deepest recesses of the heart." Pointing out the score's variety, he singled out the orchestral interludes as being "among the finest passages." "It is a limpid, melodic score," he added, "technically not difficult, yet, to express its genuine qualities, beating time is not sufficient [. . .]; you have to feel and participate in the intense life that animates and drives it throughout."[37]

It must have been a bitter disappointment for Nabokov to hear, sometime in May 1929, that Diaghilev decided not to revive *Ode* as part of what was to be his last Ballets Russes season.[38] The decision may have been prompted by the departure of Massine, jealous of Balanchine's rising influence, and who left the company in late 1928.[39] According to Désormière, however, the motivation was purely financial: Diaghilev was reluctant to face the additional expense of the chorus. "I am very upset about it," the conductor wrote to Nabokov. "I was, in all sincerity, certain to be able, this year, to get *Ode* to take the sensational revenge it deserved. If I had money, I would organize a concert at once. But I have none . . ."[40] Désormière had all the more reason to be disappointed since he had been preparing for this revival by helping Nabokov to revise the orchestration. His senior by five years, he had—like Sauguet—studied composition with Koechlin and was also an accomplished flutist. He was clearly Nabokov's principal musical mentor at the time, if a frequently severe one. An undated letter shows him, in the words of his wife Colette, "completely possessed by *Ode*" and working on it, section by section, "eight or ten hours a day." "Some spots," he complained to the composer, "are tricky to fix, because the music is too sloppily written out. I beseech you, do be more careful about the way you arrange your lines. Do not be satisfied with a good harmonic sonority (or at least a sonority you are pleased with as you go along), be more severe towards what you write. You will orchestrate your music more easily once it is more strictly written."[41] In the end, Désormière, absorbed by his other Ballets Russes commitments, had to give up the task and suggested that Nabokov should get assistance from the Belgian band conductor Arthur Prévost.[42] The premiere of the revised version of *Ode* took place in Strasbourg, under Fritz Münch, on December 9, 1931.[43]

Whatever he may have felt after Diaghilev dropped *Ode* from the Ballets Russes repertory, Nabokov seems to have remained on friendly terms with him until the end. He encountered him for the last time in late July 1929 at the Baden-Baden Festival, where Diaghilev had come for the premiere of Hindemith and Brecht's *Lehrstück*; he was accompanied by the Princesse de Polignac and by the seventeen-year-old Igor Markevitch, his "*nouveau petit ami*,"[44] whom he was on his way to introducing to Richard Strauss. He asked Nabokov about his current musical projects and, on hearing that he was working on a symphony, expressed interest in hearing it. A few weeks later, when Nabokov returned from Berlin on his way to Kolbsheim, he saw the announcement in a newspaper that "the dancer Diaghilev" had died in Venice on August 19.[45] Aside from his personal sense of loss, which was patently genuine, Nabokov must have realized that this disappearance meant the end of the Ballets Russes and any hopes composers of his generation might have had for future collaborations. This was Prokofiev's immediate diagnosis: "From a professional point of view his death, so it appeared to me, would not impact on me as it undoubtedly would on other, younger composers: Rieti, Nabokov, Dukelsky. For them, of course, many of their hopes now lay in ruins."[46] Nabokov's correspondence with Kessler hints that they had been toying with such a new project for Diaghilev in the spring of 1929, although no specifics are given.[47]

Nabokov's first symphony was his major undertaking after *Ode*. Based on the opus number, its composition was immediately preceded by that of a symphonic overture after Pushkin, entitled *Le fiancé*. It was published as Nabokov's opus 9 by Koussevitzky's Russian Musical Editions, which Nabokov joined at the time, to Prokofiev's satisfaction. The composers represented in the catalogue, the latter joked in 1930, were either Koussevitzky's legitimate children, sanctioned by Prokofiev and Stravinsky—a group in which Prokofiev ranged Nabokov—or his illegitimate ones.[48] Whether or not it is the same work as the "overture in the Satie manner" Dukelsky heard Nabokov play on Alan Tanner's piano in the mid-1920s, *Le fiancé* was a piece Prokofiev particularly liked: when Nabokov played it for him in February 1929, he warmly recommended it to Diaghilev the next day.[49] When it was finally premiered in Brussels, in May 1931, under François Ruhlmann, it was well received, as it was in Strasbourg in March 1933, under Fritz Münch.[50]

The Symphony, Nabokov's opus 10, was undertaken in late 1928 or early 1929, and the orchestration was completed in mid-September 1929.[51] As early as April he had been contacted, via Sauguet, by Marcel Cuvelier of the Brussels Philharmonic Society with a view to a Belgian premiere. "You know it is a tradition for Russian composers," Cuvelier explained in tongue-in-cheek fashion, while inquiring subsequently about the work's progress, "to introduce their works in either Brussels or Liège."[52] In early October 1929, Nabokov played his new work on the piano to Stravinsky, who immediately recommended it to Ansermet, adding about Nabokov: "He really has a gift that I find pleasant."[53] The symphony's premiere took place, as planned, in the Belgian capital on November 30, 1929, at the Palais des Beaux-Arts, conducted by Désormière. The program began with fragments of Rameau's *Acante et Céphise*, in a Désormière realization, followed by Mendelssohn's Violin Concerto; the second half of the concert featured another premiere, Igor Markevitch's *Sinfonietta*, followed by Satie's *Mercure*, and ending with Nabokov's symphony. By all reports, the performance was a success. A few months later, Pierre Monteux performed the work in Brussels and The Hague in early 1930 and conducted the French premiere with the Orchestre symphonique de Paris in February. The American premiere took place in Boston on October 31, under Koussevitzky: "Symphony immense success. Congratulations!" the Russian conductor cabled his young compatriot on the same evening.[54] Discussing the work with Prokofiev in Paris a few months before, Koussevitzky said he liked the second and third movements best; Prokofiev himself favored the first and told Nabokov: "That's because it most resembles your music."[55] The symphony was heard in Warsaw in 1931 under the Polish conductor Grzegorz Fitelberg (who had conducted the Parisian premiere of Stravinsky's *Mavra* in 1922). Monteux conducted it again in 1931, this time at the Hollywood Bowl, before an audience of 15,000, and reported to the composer "a very big success"; he furthermore assured him he had recommended the work to his colleague Nikolai Sokoloff, who performed it Cleveland in November of the following year.

The symphony's opening Allegro starts with a brisk E minor theme, first exposed by the violins and piccolo on a sixteenth-note figuration, and then by the trumpet; the second subject, by contrast, is a graceful melody for the violins and flute. These two themes, variously restated and elaborated, form the substance of the entire first movement, which ends with a nostalgic recurrence of the second subject, played by the oboe and echoed by the English horn. The succeeding Largo is structured around a broadly flowing melody. The final Allegro starts with a tarentella-like subject played by the bassoon and clarinet, followed by a second theme in 2/4 rhythm. An extensive development leads to a brief, but eloquent epilogue which ends in a jubilant climax.

If *Ode* had launched Nabokov's career, his first symphony can thus be said to have, as it were, put his name on the map. It was well received by audiences and reviews were largely favorable. Following a highly successful Strasbourg premiere under Fritz Münch, in April 1931, at a concert at which Prokofiev performed his own Piano Concerto No. 3, the *Ménestrel* critic praised the "remarkably fresh invention" of Nabokov's work.[56] "His melodies, saturated with emotion, are especially attractive—and melodiousness is a comparatively rare quality in the moderns," opined the *Christian Science Monitor* after the Boston premiere.[57] The same reviewer detected influences of Stravinsky and Prokofiev. Similarly, after the French premiere, Sauguet wrote to the Italian composer Massino Leone: "It contains excellent things, but it is very influenced by Prokofiev in places."[58] "A somewhat muted work" (*de demi-teinte*), noted Claude Altomont after the second Paris hearing in May 1930, "but the sublime, ritual character of its final theme ends it in apotheosis."[59] Reviewing the earlier performance for *Comœdia*, the composer Paul Le Flem (1881–1984), while confirming that the work was very well received by the audience, praised its frank, unostentatious lyricism, its vigorous, precise, crisp rhythms, its clear, classic harmony, and the brilliance and bite of the orchestral writing—an indication that Nabokov had greatly benefited from Désormière's tutoring. The opening Allegro he described as rhythmical, joyful, decisive. The ample Largo, he noted, "does not languish," and ends in an atmosphere of serenity. In the final, rhythmical Allegro, he found a distant echo of the Scherzo of Beethoven's Ninth; like Altomont, he was impressed by the epilogue, "a singing theme sustained by broad, sonorous chords," which reinforced the lyricism conveyed by the work as a whole.[60] A more qualified, but by no means altogether negative appraisal, was given by Marcel Belvianes when the symphony was heard again in Paris in October 1931:

> It seems to be that the very warm, almost enthusiastic reception given to the work was excessive. To be sure, its composer has ideas, sincerity, a sense of rhythm. Yet I think he would have benefited from being more selective among the numerous motifs of which his head is full: not all are equally valuable or original. They follow each other in rather arbitrary fashion, which, arguably, might constitute a novel device and lead to picturesque effects. Yet the orchestration, already old hat in places, does not allow us to consider Mr. Nicolas Nabokoff revolutionary . . .[61]

The Catholic philosopher Gabriel Marcel, a friend and disciple of the Maritains, present at the same concert, conveyed his "excellent impression" in a letter to the composer:

> There is in your work admirable vitality (*sève*) and musical health, along with much emotion in certain places. I have the feeling that the light that once shone in the works of Prokofiev, but seems to have deserted him lately, shines in you nowadays. You are one of the very small number of musicians from whom we are expecting a lot. Are you preparing yourself for it?[62]

When he entitled his symphony *Symphonie lyrique*, was Nabokov aware of, if not necessarily familiar with, Alexander Zemlinsky's 1922–23 work of the same title? He introduced it with an epigraph by Pushkin, extracted from the 1833 poem "Osen" (Autumn), a quotation to which he clearly attached much importance, not just as a commentary on the atmosphere of the work, but, as he told José Bruyr, as summarizing his entire aesthetics: "Oppressed by a lyrical torment, the soul ferments, trembles, and seeks an outlet, as in a dream, for this torment to be expressed in concrete terms."[63] The manuscript of the symphony bears a dedication to "dear and kindhearted Denise"—almost certainly Denise Bourdet, wife of the Comédie-Française director and popular Parisian hostess.

The little that survives of Nabokov's papers from the period makes clear that, despite the success of his first major orchestral composition, he was going through serious financial difficulties. In the first year of their marriage, Natalie supplemented the couple's income by modeling for a Paris couture house;[64] but her pregnancy evidently put an end to it. In 1929, leaving his wife in Brussels, Nabokov took a part-time salaried position in Paris as assistant editor to a musical monthly entitled *La musique*, edited by Marc Pincherle (1888–1974), the eminent musicologist who spearheaded the rediscovery of Vivaldi. The journal was published and subsidized by the Pleyel piano firm and had its offices at the Salle Pleyel, the handsome Art Déco concert hall recently built by the firm near the Étoile, on the Rue du Faubourg Saint-Honoré. Nabokov assisted Pincherle in vetting the foreign-language material received by the magazine. (He also "assisted," he subsequently confessed, Pincherle's secretary, "a dark-haired and dark-eyed, Provençal girl in her early twenties" endowed with "a lovely face, a well-developed bosom, and ever-ready expert lips.")[65] His name had already appeared in the periodical in November 1928, when he responded to the questionnaire sent by *La musique* to a large group of composers, asking them about their models or masters and their principles, likes, and dislikes. To the first question, Nabokov answered, in a *crescendo* column: Mozart, "the heaven of music," followed by Bach, Tchaikovsky, Glinka, "and so many others"; and in a *decrescendo* column, Beethoven, Wagner, Scriabin, Reyer (*"la bassesse de la musique"*), "and so many others." To the second question, he replied in the form of a mini-manifesto: "Music, in my opinion, ought to be tonal or modal in a highly strict sense, yet quite free. Music, in my opinion, should have a well defined melody and *dux* and a clear rhythm . . . Above all, music should be . . . good (example: Stravinsky). This should give you a clear idea of my dislikes."[66]

After joining its staff, Nabokov contributed two pieces of his own to the journal: an obituary of Diaghilev, which came out in the November 1929 issue, and a short presentation of the Russian diplomat and musicographer Aleksandr Dmitrievich Ulybyshev (1794–1858), best known for his French-language biography of Mozart, published in 1843.[67] The Diaghilev obituary is an impassioned tribute to the Ballets Russes founder; because of its immediacy, it shows, even better than Nabokov's later published recollections, the impact and fascination produced by their contacts. "For a long time," Nabokov writes, "and more and more perhaps, we will be seeing the spirit of Diaghilev, creator of our time, watching over us and directing us as we go along." Diaghilev, Nabokov continues, had "the instinct of what is going to come about, to exist."

> Everything that happened at the Ballets Russes, everything that came out of his hands, had something captivating, disconcerting, luminous, refreshing, novel, perhaps like the operas of Wagner at the time when Liszt or Bülow conducted their first performances.[68]

Diaghilev, Nabokov argues, was no mere organizer, but a genuine creator. He was an eclectic, to be sure, but his eclecticism was radical, revolutionary. He also had a genius for discovery. Surprisingly, when listing Diaghilev's discoveries, Nabokov did not mention Stravinsky. The three main ones were, according to him, Nijinsky (as one would expect); then Massine, with "the well regulated factory of his move-ments and raw rhythms"; and finally Balanchine's "plastic constructivism" and "Lifar, who, in his admirable *Renard*, blurs the distinction between dance and acrobatics." (Nabokov's opinion of Lifar, as we shall see, considerably deterio-rated in later years.) Diaghilev, the piece concludes, "brought music out of Russia and opened it up to international horizons."[69]

This article caused a serious contretemps with Stravinsky, who objected to a sentence in which Nabokov discussed Diaghilev's input in the genesis of *Petrushka* and *Noces*. "Diaghilev's part in Stravinsky's work, in my opinion, is enormous. Two facts seem to prove this: Diaghilev appears to have given Stravinsky the idea for *Petrushka* and certainly he gave Stravinsky the original idea for the 'Liturgie,' which eventually evolved into *Les Noces*. Here the mark of Diaghilev's inspiration actually touches on the creation itself. He supplied the original idea and influ-enced the music in very definite ways."[70]

When Stravinsky read the article, he became, in Prokofiev's words, "apoplectic" at the suggestion that anyone, Diaghilev not excepted, could be reported as hav-ing dared "to give him ideas."[71] He reacted in a letter addressed to Nabokov, with instructions to publish it in *La musique*, where it indeed appear in the December issue. No, Stravinsky explained without any further comments, the idea behind *Petrushka* had not come from Diaghilev. And as regarded *Noces*, he had never intended, he explained,

> to write that "Liturgie" that Diaghilev, indeed, would have wanted me to compose, but of which I always rejected the notion, and which he discussed with me while *Noces* was already well into the working stage. Therefore no relation could possibly be established between that hypothetical "Liturgie" and *Noces*, which I wrote, on the contrary, while carefully guarding myself against any potential influence and gradually letting Diaghilev see the scenes only once they were finished."[72]

Would Nabokov, the letter concluded, kindly check his facts next time he was to write anything concerning Stravinsky?

Reactions to this put-down were evidently not all in Stravinsky's favor and show that, debatable though Nabokov's claims may have been, they were then widely—by Prokofiev, for one—believed to be true.[73] "Do you know," wrote to Nabokov a Belgian friend, the musicologist and critic Paul Collaer, "that Stravinsky revealed to me the story of *Petrushka*'s genesis and the part Diaghilev played? It was because [Stravinsky] regretted having told me so that he broke relations with me."[74] Nabokov, understandably, was utterly distressed. On December 5, he wrote to Stravinsky an apologetic letter, in which he blamed Diaghilev for his "inadvertent error" and, maladroitly, insisted that he did not intend to "hurt" or "anger" Stravinsky. "That would be the last straw!" Stravinsky replied.[75] Nabokov also got Maritain to intercede, which the philosopher did in a letter written shortly after the premiere of Stravinsky's *Capriccio* for piano and orchestra on December 6:

> There is something about which I must speak to you. I know that some unpleasant lines have appeared about you in an article by Nicolas Nabokov. Be assured that he is very unhappy about them. He is *un grand enfant sauvage*, but without a shade of malice. He deeply loves and admires you, and the thought that you are angry with him disturbs him greatly. Call it a great blunder on his part, but forgive him in the name of Christian charity and believe what I know to be true: that he never meant to offend you.[76]

Nabokov had already experienced Stravinsky's extreme touchiness—a common trait among composers of his stature—in matters concerning his own music. At the 1928 Paris premiere of *Apollon musagète*, which followed that of *Ode* by less than a week, Nabokov had found himself incapable to find the right words to congratulate Stravinsky when he went to his box to pay respects.[77] As he reported the next day to Prokofiev, he had only managed to find "something or other in it to be complimentary about."[78] As for Stravinsky, "putting on airs in front of a young composer" (as Prokofiev noted disapprovingly), he declared: "Yes, that was very successful. I don't know how God contrived to make me compose it."[79]

Insufficient enthusiasm was one thing, but the article on Diaghilev—whose name, when he was alive, could trigger Stravinsky's invective at any moment[80]—was an altogether more serious act of *lèse-majesté*. Not only did Stravinsky cold-shoulder Nabokov whenever they met, but he rebuffed Prokofiev when the latter, finding Stravinsky in a happy mood at a rehearsal of his *Capriccio*, tried to intercede on his friend's behalf. "Stravinsky immediately exploded, saying that Nabokov was not a bad composer but that he was an intriguer and we can confidently expect more dirty tricks from him."[81] A few weeks later, when Nabokov came to say goodbye to Prokofiev and Rachmaninov on their way to New York on the *S.S. Berengaria*, he reported to the former that Stravinsky, as a Christmas goodwill gesture, had sent word that he was forgiven.[82]

Notwithstanding the public contretemps with Stravinsky over the Diaghilev obituary, it was as a consequence of Nabokov's employment with *La musique* that the two composers were brought into close contact again in the summer of 1930. By arrangement by the Pleyel firm, Stravinsky had a studio in the Salle Pleyel, off the same corridor where Nabokov had his, and he used it whenever he was in Paris for any extended period. One morning, Stravinsky, accompanied by the composer Arthur Lourié, from whom he was then inseparable, burst into Nabokov's office and friendly relations were reestablished as if nothing had happened. It was then that Nabokov fell under the spell of the man he later called "the gracious master." "From that morning onwards," he recalled, "and through the three or four weeks of Stravinsky's stay in Paris, my life changed. The work for Marc Pincherle and the amusements with his Provençal beauty were forgotten. [. . .] All of my time was concentrated on being with Stravinsky, waiting for Stravinsky, and spending all the time I possibly could muster at his side."[83] In the morning, when Stravinsky arrived from Saint-Cloud, where he lived, he would take Nabokov to the corner cafe for a coffee *arosé* with a dollop of Calvados, after which they would sit at Stravinsky's piano and read through, four hands, a Bach cantata or Passion or a Handel oratorio. After a bout of work, Stravinsky and Nabokov had lunch with Lourié or with Vera de Bosset, Stravinsky's mistress and future wife, or the two of them would eat at the Russian restaurant on Rue Daru, next to the Russian Cathedral. Nabokov's reminiscences of Stravinsky's "table talk" in *Bagázh* is one of the liveliest portraits we have of the Russian composer. Thus, according to Nabokov, the idea of the chromatic passage in the final Alleluia of the *Symphony of Psalms*, which he was then composing, came to him one Saturday on hearing the sopranos of the Russian Cathedral choir make and repeat the same mistake, moving up a semitone, rather than the correct whole tone, in a particular passage they were rehearsing.[84]

This renewed friendship came to an abrupt, if temporary, end in the fall of 1930. Omitted from the published version of *Bagázh*, the episode is treated at some length in the manuscript.[85] The reason for Stravinsky's unhappiness with Nabokov was not, this time, his own music, but Nabokov's strong feelings of antipathy towards Lourié. Born in 1891 in the shtetl of what is now Slavgorod, in Belarus, Lourié had studied at the Petersburg Conservatory and, before the war, came into close contact with Russian Futurist circles. It was around that time that he converted to Roman Catholicism, changing his name from Naum Izrailevich to Arthur-Vincent (the first name in honor of Schopenhauer, the second of Van Gogh). After the Bolshevist takeover, Lourié served as head of the music division of Narkompros, the so-called People's Commissariat for Education, then headed by the relatively liberal Anatoly Lunacharsky. In Nabokov's words, Lourié "played his role imperiously as an all-powerful music potentate using his innate sarcastic wit to intimidate and to bully inoffensive people, such, for example, as the old and innocent Alexander Glazunov." In Paris, where he moved in 1928, the exiled Glazunov, Lourié's former composition teacher at the Petersburg Conservatory, told Nabokov about the reception Lourié (who clearly retained a misplaced taste for futurist jokes) gave him after Glazunov had requested an appointment:

He kept the old man waiting in the anteroom for an hour, and when Glazunov came in he saw Lourié sitting at his desk in the costume of a

Pierrot with his face painted half-white half-black, his lips red, and his eye-brows dark mauve, with a monocle in one eye. He did not ask Glazunov to sit down, and behaved very haughtily.[86]

In 1921, Lourié abruptly left his Narkompros position and moved to Berlin, where he became a follower of Busoni. Nabokov may or may not have come into contact with him at the time; but he definitely met him through the Maritains, with whom Lourié, by now a convert to Roman Catholicism, had become friends. Lourié's connection with Stravinsky was through Vera, whom he knew from his Petrograd days, when she was married to the painter and designer Sergei Sudeikin while Lourié himself had an affair with her sister Olga.[87] Nabokov thus saw Lourié often in the late 1920s, especially once Lourié had become, like him, a member of the Maritains' circle.[88] He claims he enjoyed "his wit and his sharp mind," but that at the same time, he had the feeling that "somewhere in the back of Lourié was a hidden skeleton."

No matter how personally antipathetic Lourié may have been to Nabokov, it is hard not to suspect that an equally strong factor was the secret sense of rivalry that began to develop between the two composers for the Maritains' favor. Indeed Maritain himself, by the early 1930s, came to see in Lourié the realization of his musical ideals (he praised him in an article in Prunières's *Revue musicale* in 1936), while Lourié, for his part, kept proclaiming his debt towards the Catholic philosopher.[89] Unlike Nabokov, Lourié was a Catholic convert, and the fact that he had converted from Judaism must have endeared him especially to Raïssa, who considered him, with her husband's approval, as "the greatest musician of our time."[90] She and Maritain remained fiercely loyal to Lourié until the end. Though Nabokov never fell out of favor with them, he may have felt that he no longer was the favorite son.

In any event, Nabokov made the mistake of not keeping his feelings secret and telling acquaintances of his that Lourié gave him "the Cheka creeps." The comment was repeated to Stravinsky and infuriated him. When Nabokov came to see him in his box after the festival concert honoring him in October 1930, Stravinsky, once again, turned his back on him. Ironically, several years later, Stravinsky broke off all relations with Lourié and never saw him again.

The break between Nabokov and Stravinsky was soon public knowledge. It put Nabokov in a difficult position vis-à-vis Ansermet, who, according to Prokofiev, "approved" of Nabokov and was originally scheduled to premiere the symphony in Paris. In a late December 1930 letter to Nabokov, Ansermet refers to "the unfortunate incident between you and Stravinsky" and explains why he felt he had to drop it from his program, while assuring Nabokov that his interest in his music was not affected.[91] But Nabokov was deeply wounded and for a while Stravinsky's name triggered in him, as Prokofiev reported with glee, "a stream of sarcastic comments."[92]

The publication of *La musique* came to an end with the March 1930 issue. To compensate Nabokov for the loss of a salary, Gustave Lyon and his sons, owners of the Pleyel firm commissioned him, on Pincherle's advice, to write a piece for the harpsichord. Even before the First World War, Pleyel had played a leading role in the revival of the instrument, which it promoted by encouraging modern composers to write for it, Poulenc's *Concert champêtre* (1928) and Manuel de Falla's Harpsichord Concerto (1926) being the best-known works that came out of their efforts. Though he accepted the commission and the advance he received for it, Nabokov, by his own admission, knew little about the harpsichord, nor did he care much for the instrument. Seventeenth- and eighteenth-century French harpsichord music left him cold, smacking, in his view, of "courtly officialdom"; as for Bach and Scarlatti keyboard music, he much preferred to hear it played on the piano.[93] Such views were, of course, widely shared at the time, when authentic performance practice for Baroque music was nonexistent. Still, having accepted the commission, Nabokov felt obliged to pay court to Wanda Landowska, who had presided over the harpsichord revival and was all but certain to premiere his piece once he had completed it. A Sunday afternoon visit was thus arranged to Saint-Leu-la-Forêt, the small town located about twelve miles to the northwest of Paris where Landowska had established herself in 1925. Nabokov was accompanied by the composer and Ravel disciple Roland-Manuel (1891–1966), who later paid his own dues to the harpsichord with his *Suite dans le goût espagnol* (1933). The visiting party also included the Russian-born music critic and translator Boris de Schloezer (1881–1969) and an unidentified French musicologist, both of them, in Nabokov's words, "harpsichord addicts."[94] At the Saint-Leu station, they were met at the station by "a masculine looking, cross-eyed and pale girl who was driving a large, black Citroën." Landowska, whom Nabokov had never seen or heard, seems to have inspired in him instant antipathy. In the vestibule of her villa ("small and rather ugly") he was "struck by her almost total unbeauty and, at the same time, by the manly force of her handshake and her sharp dark eyes. She was all smiles and charm with a backlash of perfidy that appeared in each remark she was making or about to make."[95] After being shown various memorabilia, including Landowska's 1903 visit to Tolstoy at Iasnaia Poliana, the visitors were treated to a dreary lunch of Polish tripe (not Nabokov's favorite delicacy), after which he hoped there would be an opportunity for him to fulfill the purpose of his visit by consulting the hostess on the subject of harpsichord writing. Instead, the party had to be treated to the ritual visit to the "harpsichord temple," the round-shaped studio containing the instruments collected by Landowska in the course of her career. "I felt propelled," he remembered, "into a keyboard cemetery with yellowish ivory or black ebony teeth glaring at me, ready to bite anyone who attempted to disturb their post mortem repose."[96] There followed a long recital, beginning with a Chopin Prelude performed on the very Pleyel piano Chopin played in Majorca. While thoroughly repelled by the "atmosphere of genteel sycophancy" that surrounded Landowska, Nabokov couldn't help being impressed with her playing:

> She played Chopin like a man, robustly, [. . .] and with no attempt towards mannered romanticism. And while she played, she looked unmoved, very matter-of-fact, like a true, first-rate professional that she was. Her strong and manly profile made one think a bit of Liszt's daughter, Cosima, a bit of Liszt himself and a great deal of those gift-bearing, sexless females faces one sees on Assyrian and Babylonian bas-reliefs.[97]

Next came a movement from an early Beethoven sonata, played on a contemporary Hammerklavier, after which the recital continued for two hours, in reverse chronological order, from early eighteenth-century harpsichords to late sixteenth-century spinets. The last piece, an anonymous fourteenth-century "Catch," was rendered on the earliest keyboard instrument in Landowska's collection.

> The sound of that "Catch" was so diminutive that it must have been intended for mosquito ears. Yet the buzzing that came out of the wooden box, with its ill-kept dentures, was precisely like a swarm of mosquitoes on a hot summer evening.[98]

After Nabokov finally had a chance to explain the purpose of his visit, Landowska took him to a room upstairs so that they could discuss the matter privately, but she was clearly reluctant to give any precise answers to his questions on how a contemporary composer could write for the harpsichord. When Nabokov registered his disappointment on the train back to Paris, a member of the visiting party explained that, generous though she was when it came to giving lessons to impecunious harpsichord students, Landowska considered that composers in need of advice ought to apply for formal instruction from her at her not inconsiderable fee, no matter if the work was commissioned by Pleyel, a firm that provided her with instruments and paid her a monthly allowance. Nabokov's harpsichord piece never got written.

Another unrealized project dating from this period was an opera on *Paul et Virginie*, the celebrated late eighteenth-century novel by Bernardin de Saint-Pierre, from which Cocteau had derived a libretto in collaboration with Raymond Radiguet in the summer of 1920.[99] It was then intended for Satie, who died before writing any music, though the work was periodically announced, with sets to be designed by Derain. Cocteau unsuccessfully tried to revive the project, offering the libretto first to Poulenc, then to Sauguet, and finally to Nabokov: a carbon copy of the typed libretto, with the designation "Opéra Comique," followed by the indication "Musiques de Nicolas Nabokoff" is preserved in his papers at Yale. There is no evidence, however, that any music was actually written.

Evidence is also lacking in the case of a fifteen-minute organ piece commissioned by Étienne de Beaumont in March 1932 for a late afternoon performance in May of that year at the Beaumonts' *hôtel particulier* on the Rue Masseran. The one letter documenting this commission suggests that Nabokov had approached Beaumont and offered to write some music for one of the Count's soirees.[100] For the organ piece, Nabokov was offered 3,000 francs, a reasonable sum for the period.[101]

One completed project, in 1930, was the stage music Nabokov wrote for *La petite Catherine*, a historical play in three acts and seven scenes, which opened at the Théâtre Antoine in Paris on October 2, 1930. Its author, Alfred Savoir (1883–1934), was a prolific, Polish-born playwright (his actual family name was Poznansky), whose career had been launched by the great director Aurélien Lugné-Poe. The play's subject was young Catherine the Great, one of its characters being Empress Elizabeth. Nabokov may have been recommended to Savoir by Kessler, who knew the playwright, as did Diaghilev.[102] The play was well received—one reviewer thought it the most interesting seen in Paris since Giraudoux's *Amphitryon 38*, premiered the year before—and went on tour in England, Germany, and Belgium.[103] The sets were by André Boll and the costumes by Nataliia Goncharova. Nabokov's music, which does not seem to have survived,[104] was occasionally mentioned by reviewers, but, as one of them sarcastically pointed out, chatty Parisian audiences were clearly unaware that, in a theater, music was meant to be listened to.[105] Kessler recommended Nabokov to Max Reinhardt, who considered mounting the play in Berlin.[106] The recommendation was apparently unsuccessful: as Kessler reported to Nabokov, Reinhardt strongly felt that in Berlin stage music needed to be "more popular and ingratiating" and that, besides, there ought to be a ballet at the end.[107]

A few months after the premiere of the Savoir play, in April 1931, Nabokov was interviewed by José Bruyr (1889–1980). A Belgian-born musicologist, Bruyr had published, in 1930, a book of conversations with contemporary French composers under the title *L'écran des musiciens*. In the second series, which came out in 1933, he expanded the selection to include a majority of foreign or emigre composers— a decision the critic André Cœuroy deplored in the stridently anti-Semitic preface he contributed to the book.[108] Nabokov was in distinguished company. In addition to the French-born Germaine Tailleferre, Jean Rivier, Olivier Messiaen, and Manuel Rosenthal, the musicians featured were the Catalan Frederic Mompou, the Czech Bohuslav Martinů, the Hungarian Tibor Harsányi, the Polish-born Alexandre Tansman, the Romanian-born Filip Lazar and Marcel Mihalovici, the German-Swiss Conrad Beck, and two fellow Russians, Markevitch and Prokofiev. The Nabokov chapter is a particularly interesting document insofar as, save for a handful of letters, we have no other record of Nabokov's prewar "voice" and opinions. Bruyr interviewed him at home in the fifteenth arrondissement.[109] "Nicolas Nabokoff is tall and strong," the interviewer noted. "He is broad-shouldered like a boxer. His face is open, quickly reactive. With his dark, negligently combed hair and his red shirt, he could be easily taken for a Bolshevist agitator." From the start, Nabokov stated: "I love Tchaikovsky and Robert Schumann," adding, moments later, that he also admired Liszt. Putting Tchaikovsky first may seem innocuous today, but it is worth recalling that in Paris in 1931, Tchaikovsky ("the least Russian of the Russians," in Ravel's absurd words) was held in low regard by the musical establishment, which rated him far below any of the "Mighty Five"; there was therefore a touch of defiance on Nabokov's part in putting him on the same level as Schumann and Liszt.[110] Bruyr noted that Nabokov had photographs of Diaghilev and Stravinsky above his working table, as well as photographs of Désormière, Cocteau, and even (another defiant gesture?) Kaiser Wilhelm II. Nabokov briefly evoked his contretemps with Stravinsky. Not mentioning Lourié's name, he did refer to Stravinsky's unhappiness with Nabokov's comments on the genesis of *Petrushka*. "I love Stravinsky," he continued, describing him as "a sphinx who has lost his secret. Stravinsky will no longer surprise us. Of all musicians, he may be the least instinctive by nature, but he is the most forward-looking man in music history. [. . .]Yes, I still love Stravinsky. [. . .]Only before the *Symphony of Psalms* does my admiration balk. What is the use, oh God, even when composing 'for His greater glory,' of those fugues, no matter how free-form, of that academic apparatus . . . .], of all that formalism . . ." Nabokov may have subsequently wished he could eat some of his words: as he would be the first to recognize, Stravinsky, of course, had not lost his capacity to surprise. Nabokov also came around on the subject of the *Symphony of Psalms*. The word "formalism," redolent of various "music purges" under Stalin, is also a surprise in Nabokov's mouth. But in 1931, he was keen above all to present himself as a romantic, lyrical composer, hostile to both neoclassicism ("a false, cold, stereotyped classicism posing as a return to Bach") and the cult of formal perfection (assuming this is what he meant by "formalism"). "Music is meant," he stated, taking a rather anti-Stravinskian stance, "only to express feelings, move one by way of sounds." Among contemporary musicians he liked, he cited, especially, Auric, Markevitch, and Sauguet, all of them personal friends, adding the names of Beck, Harsányi, and Martinů. As for modern musicians who influenced him the most, he told Bryur: "I locate my elective spiritual affinities, Stravinsky notwithstanding, somewhere between Hindemith and Prokofiev."

Nabokov's admiration for Prokofiev went along with a personal relationship which began to flourish in early 1928 and was at its warmest in the early 1930s. "There was never a misunderstanding between Prokofiev and me in all the time of our friendship," he recalled in the chapter he devoted to the Russian composer in *Old Friends and New Music*, "nor was there ever an iota of falsity in it."[111] Prokofiev's diaries confirm that he and his half-Russian, half-Spanish wife Lina saw the Nabokovs frequently: they went to concerts and the cinema and regularly had dinner together—in June 1930 with Meyerhold, visiting from Russia, with Petr Suvchinskii also in attendance.[112] In mid-June 1930, the two couples took a three-day road trip in northwestern France in Felix Bethmann-Hollweg's Mercedes cabriolet. "It was a trip of rare pleasure," Prokofiev noted in his diary, "the silence of Bethmann redeemed by the Nabokovs' boisterous gaiety."[113] They drove first to Rouen, then to Deauville, after which they visited Mont-Saint-Michel, explored Brittany ("charming but empty of people") and returned via the Loire chateaus, spending the last night in Chambord. The famously gastronome Prokofiev had carefully selected the Michelin-recommended restaurants where they would be eating, marking them on the map "as if he had been planning a military campaign" and complaining whenever a visit to a church or chateau threatened to delay their arrival for lunch or dinner.[114] In September of the same year, the Prokofievs, in their own Chevrolet, drove to Alsace at the Nabokovs' invitation. They spent four days at Kolbsheim, which Sergey found "marvellous," while noting that Nicolas and his wife were "a little too prone to indecent language."[115] Driving back to Paris without Natalie, who remained in Alsace, the three friends stopped at a picturesque spot in the Vosges mountains to improvise an amateur film:

> The conceptual problem we had to resolve was this: we had three characters, but only two could be in shot at the same time since the third (which we took in turn) had to shoot the sequence. This, then, was our scenario: Ptashka [Prokofiev's nickname for Lina] sits dreamily on the edge of the cliff; Nabokov, who is walking by, begins to pester her with unwelcome addresses; Ptashka tears herself away and runs to me to complain; I pick up a stick and approach Nabokov, threatening him with upraised arm; but . . . who should he be but my dear friend, so we sit down together side by side, clap each other on the knee and embrace. As we were filming, faces appeared in the windows of the nearby hostelry observing us with interest, taking us for a real film crew.[116]

Prokofiev, unlike Bethmann-Hollweg, was an abominable driver and, in his gastronomical obsession, was prone to fits of temper when fearing that the next meal could be compromised. The following day, after staying overnight at Domrémy, the Lorraine village where Joan of Arc was born, he behaved like a cad towards his wife until Nabokov threatened to get out of the car at the next village.[117]

In March 1931, Prokofiev and Nabokov found themselves in Alsace again for a concert devoted to their works by the Société des amis du Conservatoire in Strasbourg. Nathalie Radisse-Kaul, who taught piano at the conservatory, played

Nabokov's Sonata, while Prokofiev himself was heard in his Second Piano Sonata and Lina, a trained classical soprano, who had studied by Felia Litvinne and Emma Calvé, performed songs by both composers, including the four on poems by Pushkin that Nabokov had published with Koussevitzky's firm two years previously.[118] At the same concert Prokofiev also took part in a performance of the original, chamber music version of his *Overture on Jewish Themes*.[119]

Nabokov was impressed with Prokofiev's prodigious memory and vast musical culture, which extended from Tchaikovsky's early operas and *The Rite of Spring* to little-known parts of the Western repertory. As a composer, Nabokov clearly sympathized with what he saw in Prokofiev's music as "a reaction against an aestheticism burdened with philosophy, literature, and mysticism." As early as 1923, he had responded to the "tragic lyricism" of Prokofiev's five Akhmatova Songs, which he had heard at the Théâtre du Vieux-Colombier when they received their Paris premiere in the presence of the composer, whom he was yet to meet.[120] Prokofiev's achievement, he declared to Bruyr, "has been to bring music back to the world of pure sound." And, in a passage that could apply to Nabokov's own stylistic impulses:

> Hence, the cutting, direct, square, cheerful style in contrast to the "arpeggio-ridden" music of his contemporaries; hence the preference for simplified harmonic texture, a clear-cut melody, and the major character of the whole structure; hence also the sectional, sometimes almost mechanical, form of his music.[121]

Nabokov, on the other hand, was clearly unenthusiastic about Prokofiev's opera *The Fiery Angel*, or at least what he heard from it: on June 14, 1928, Koussevitzky conducted an abridged version of the second act, in concert version, at the Paris Opera. According to Suvchinskii, Nabokov and he left the final rehearsal without saying a word.[122] As for Prokofiev's opinion of Nabokov's music, we have seen that he had made positive comments on the Piano Sonata and thought highly of *Le fiancé*.[123] His opinion of *Ode* was mixed: "Some parts of the piece are nice, but a lot of it is boring," he wrote in his diary after the February 1929 concert.[124] In his own interview with Bruyr in the same volume, Prokofiev singles Nabokov out among other Russian emigre composers. Noting the success of the *Symphonie lyrique*, he adds, somewhat ambiguously: "He is now a serious worker, which was needed."[125] In February 1929, he reported he had lectured Nabokov "to the effect that he possesses a real gift for melody but needs to work harder at it: he employs too many formulaistically contrived figures." He also cautioned him against the influence of Tchaikovsky. "To love Tchaikovsky is an honourable trait, but it is important not to let it degenerate into the sugary-sweet, otherwise he will turn into a neo-Grechaninov."[126] Prokofiev also recommended Nabokov warmly to Olin

Downes, the *New York Times* critic, when visiting the United States in January
1930.[127]

With Hindemith, whom he may have met during his early Berlin days, Nabokov
was on sufficiently close terms by the summer of 1931 to invite him to his house in
Kolbsheim.[128] According to part of the manuscript of *Bagázh*, not retained in the
published version, Nabokov, visiting Berlin in 1930, heard in his company a performance of Brecht and Hanns Eisler's *lehrstück Die Massnahme* (The Decision).[129]
Talking to Bruyr, he granted that Hindemith was "not always good; but at least
he is almost alone in reacting, in that country where concerts resemble a restaurant scene: you consume Wagner and Pilsen, you digest sauerkraut and Bruckner.
Mustard along with 'extra sharp' music." Decades later, Nabokov was still fond
of this analogy between heavy German food and music he felt equally hard to
digest.[130]

Perhaps most interestingly, Nabokov also reflects, in the Bruyr interview, on
the situation on music in Soviet Russia:

> I am a strong believer in the future of New Russia: but it still has too many
> preoccupations other than music. Like the Germans in 1920, Russia has
> been cut off from the world. A group of proletarian composers is now
> waging a campaign against Prokofiev. Now, what have they produced?
> Milhaud-like percussion experiments . . . or nondescript little songs. They
> are still obsessed with Scriabin. Of Shostakovich I know only one work: *The
> Nose*, after Gogol. It is very well orchestrated, that's all. As for the future
> of European music, I would bank, rather than in any school—folk music
> being really dead—in the global music of the future, of which Prokofiev
> shows us an example. What he looks for, what I myself look for, is primary
> material, the daily bread of melody, the earthly sustenance of music."[131]

Music in Russia was, obviously, a topic of great interest to Nabokov, and one he
evidently discussed with Prokofiev, who had accepted an invitation to tour his
native country in 1927 and by 1931 was pondering resettling there, as he eventually did in 1936. Did Nabokov himself contemplate such a move? In September
1931 he did write to Prokofiev, presumably in the wake of several conversations
on the topic: "If I weren't a musician, I think that I'd make haste to the USSR,"
adding: "And this is not a throwaway line, but serious; I've thought a lot about it
recently."[132] "If I weren't a musician" was, of course, a strong qualifier—in the
same letter Nabokov deplored that Soviet music was "something cruder, simpler"
than what the country needed. Yet the admission suggests that he continued to
harbor lingering doubts about his choice of a musical career. It also reveals that
the relentless propaganda efforts led in Moscow by the so-called All-Union Society
for Cultural Ties Abroad (VOKS), founded in 1925 and led by Olga Kameneva

(Trotsky's sister), which had successfully targeted Prokofiev (whereas they failed completely in Stravinsky's case) were beginning to bear fruit.[133]

At the end of the Bruyr interview is a list of works by Nabokov. Among them is a song on the sonnet from Joachim Du Bellay's *L'Olive*, "Si notre vie est moins qu'une journée," composed in 1927 and published by Rouart Lerolle in 1929. There are also two yet unpublished works. The first is a piano concerto, which Nabokov told Bryur he had just completed. Dedicated to the memory of Liszt, according to a note on the manuscript, the work was commissioned by the Franco-Brazilian pianist Magda Tagliaferro (1893–1986), and a September 1931 letter from Monteux to Nabokov indicates that Monteux was eager to conduct the first performance with her.[134] To Nabokov, Tagliaferro proclaimed herself "enchanted" with the first movement, and her surviving correspondence with him indicates that they were on warm personal terms. It also reveals that, in addition to paying him 1,000 francs for the commission, she helped him financially, at least on one other occasion.[135] As it turned out, Nabokov's concerto, one of his most obscure works— the score was never printed—had two premieres: the first movement alone, with the Polish pianist Jakob Gimpel, at a Russian concert in Strasbourg on August 7, 1933, with Nabokov himself conducting; and the entire work in January 1935 in Rome, at a concert of the Accademia di Santa Cecilia conducted by Mario Rossi, with Marcelle Meyer as soloist. The Strasbourg critic noted—disapprovingly—the "jazzband" rhythms of the first movement.[136]

The second unpublished work mentioned at the end of the Bruyr interview, *Collectionneur d'échos*, is a "little cantata" for soprano, bass, "the audience as chorus," and nine instruments and percussion, on five poems by Max Jacob. All we know about the circumstances of this collaboration is that Nabokov was on friendly terms with Jacob, like him a member of the Maritain circle as well as a close friend of Cocteau and Sauguet, among others. When not at the monastery of Saint-Benoît-sur-Loire, the poet lived at the Hôtel Nollet in the Batignolles district of the seventeenth arrondissement. Sauguet and his lover Jacques Dupont also shared a room in this hotel, as did Alain Daniélou, who remembered meeting Nabokov at that time.[137] The piano-vocal score of the cantata was published in 1933 by the Russian Musical Editions, with a dedication to Charles and Marie-Laure de Noailles, the work's commissioners. It was first heard at a concert sponsored by the Noailles in April 1932 in Toulon, near their Provencal villa, in the municipal theater, decorated for the circumstance by Christian Bérard.[138] A photograph shows Nabokov at Hyères in the company of Auric, Luis Buñuel, Désormière, Giacometti, Markevitch, Poulenc, and Sauguet, among others—Salvador Dalí and Aldous Huxley were also present. In addition to Nabokov's work, Sauguet's cantata *La voyante* and Poulenc's *Le bal masqué* were premiered on the same occasion.[139] As Markevitch recalled, "the invited audience, text in hand, bravely sang its choral participation."[140] The Paris premiere took place on June 13, 1932, at the third concert of "La Sérénade," a contemporary chamber music group created in the fall of 1931, Nabokov being among its founding members. Presented as a "propaganda society" for the promotion of contemporary music, it gathered various composers Nabokov had grown close to in his Parisian years: Auric, Milhaud, Poulenc, Rieti, and Sauguet, in particular. The group's "angel" was the violinist Yvonne Giraud (1895–1984), who in 1921 had married a Spanish Marquis and friend of Marcel Proust, Illan de Casa-Fuerte. Throughout the 1930s, the "Sérénade" held a series of concerts, in Paris and other French cities, some of which featured Nabokov's music. The concert that included *Collectionneur d'échos* began with an Offenbach overture and comprised Poulenc's *Le bal masqué*, Sauguet's *La voyante*, and piano works by Auric and Markevitch—all Noailles commissions. Reviewing the concert for the *Revue musicale*, Raymond Petit, while confessing a preference for the *Chants à la Vierge*, noted that Nabokov's cantata reflected "many of Mr. Nabokov's qualities, a very specific charm, perhaps a little stiff, yet captivating and languid, and here combined with high spirits in large supply." Requiring the audience to participate by repeating, after the singers, the last line of each verse, seemed to him a legitimate and amusing device. "How much progress," he added, "the author has made in his musical writing since the *Ode* at Diaghilev's, though without losing any of his melodic gifts! I confess I would dearly love to hear these echoes again."[141] Prokofiev, whose friendship with Nabokov had cooled down by then, found the work "had some quite good parts, but was spoilt at the end by an inappropriate 'Slavonic' effusion."[142] The cantata was also performed in Paris in the 1930s by Jane Bathori, one of the finest French *mélodie* singers of the period.[143]

A few weeks previously, at the third Sérénade concert, which took place at the Conservatoire on May 19, 1932, Désormière gave the first performance of the *Chants à la Vierge Marie* in a version for small orchestra, with Renée Mahé of the Opéra as soloist. The program opened with Haydn's Trumpet Concerto and also included works by Markevitch, Prokofiev, Rieti, and Sauguet.

There was also a Sérénade concert on June 3, at which the soprano Suzanne Peignot (1895–1993), a singer particularly associated with the *Six*, sang two of Nabokov's Pushkin songs, accompanied by the composer. On the same program, Peignot performed songs by Poulenc and Sauguet, as well as Ravel's *Histoires naturelles*. The concert also featured Marcelle Meyer playing works by Rieti and Milhaud and giving the world premiere of a new piano suite by Nabokov entitled *Le cœur de Don Quichotte*. The piece, the composer's first musical encounter with a figure that fascinated him throughout his life, is in five movements: after an untitled Andante moderato comes a Scherzo-like Allegro molto subtitled "Flight," followed by an Andante ("Dulcinea"), an Allegro molto ("The Fight"), and a final "Andante cantabile" ("The Death of Don Quixote"). Writing in *Le Ménestrel*, Paul Bertrand praised the performance's "exquisite justness of feeling" and the originality of Nabokov's talent.[144] "Nicolas Nabokoff," wrote in the influential *Revue musicale* its editor Henry Prunières, "is one of the most gifted Russian musicians of the new generation." He liked the Pushkin songs less than Bertrand, but was full of praise for the piano suite:

> The style is firm and sustained. It sounds beautifully, and the most daz-
> zling virtuosity it exhibits never hampers the expression and organic struc-
> ture of the pieces. The fast ones, especially, are excellently written for the
> piano. Marcelle Meyer played the suite divinely.[145]

Le cœur de Don Quichotte was published in the same year by the Russian Musical Editions, with a dedication to Vladimir Horowitz, which suggests that the virtuoso writing was intended for him. Horowitz made several appearances in Paris in the late 1920s and gave a triumphant recital at the Théâtre des Champs-Élysées on May 29, 1931. Nabokov presumably became acquainted with him at the time, possibly through the Princesse de Polignac or the Noailles. No evidence has been found, however, that the Russian pianist ever performed Nabokov's work in public.[146] On the printed score is an unidentified epigraph, in Russian and French, emphasiz-ing its melancholy tone: "Birds wounded near the heart die on the same day." The suite was performed in Strasbourg the following January at a Sérénade concert at which works by Auric, Markevitch, Milhaud, Poulenc, Rieti, and Sauguet. A photo-graph taken by the local press shows Nabokov with his fellow composers as well as Jacques Février, who performed Nabokov's piece, Yvonne de Casa-Fuerte, and the mezzo-soprano Madeleine Vhita, who sang Sauguet's *La voyante* on that occasion.

The major work Nabokov worked on in 1932 was *Job*, a biblical oratorio on a text by Jacques Maritain commissioned by the Princesse de Polignac. According to the correspondence with Maritain preserved at Yale, the project was underway in September of 1932, and the philosopher drafted his libretto—the only one he ever wrote—in October.[147] Passages were later redrafted according to the composer's wishes and the music was written at the end of the year and at the beginning of 1933. Primitively entitled *Hiob*, to replicate the Hebrew pronunciation, the work is in three parts and with a prologue and epilogue.[148] In the prologue, the narrator, called "The Scribe"—a tenor part, possibly by reference to the Evangelist of Bach's Passions—introduces the story of Job ("Il y avait un homme dans le pays de Hus . . ."), with comments from the male chorus. The first part consists of a lengthy speech by Job ("Périsse le jour où je suis né . . ."). In the second part, Job is con-fronted by his three friends Eliphaz (baritone), Baldad (tenor), and Sophar (bass), and answers them in a second speech ("Qui ne sait les choses que vous dites . . ."). The third part is introduced by the Scribe ("Alors la colère d'Iahvé s'enflamma contre Job . . .") and leads to a speech by God, sung by the male chorus ("Qui est celui qui obscurcit le plan divin . . ."), to which Job responds ("Je sais que tu peux tout . . ."). In the epilogue, God speaks again ("Je te rétablirai dans ton état . . .").

Job was premiered on June 16, 1933, at the Théâtre des Champs-Élysées as part of the season of Ballets 1933, an ephemeral company founded by Balanchine in association with Kochno. The troupe's financial backer was Edward James, the American-born British aesthete and collector, who was then married to the Austrian ballerina Tilly Losch. James contributed a million francs to the venture.[149] *Job* shared the bill with Sauguet's ballet *Fastes*, choreographed by Balanchine, with sets by Derain, and *Errante*, another Balanchine choreography on dance music by Schubert orchestrated by Koechlin, with sets and costumes by Tchelitchew. Unlike *Errante* and Kurt Weill's *Les sept péchés capitaux*, which were the two sensations of the short Ballets 1933 season, *Job* was not successful. Kessler, after attending the dress rehearsal the previous day, described the work as being "serious music of major dimension." He explained the failure "partly because so serious a work is wholly unsuited to inclusion within the framework of a ballet season, boring and irritating the balletomane audience, partly because the chorus and soloists were mediocre. There were whistles and a part of the audience left demonstratively before the end. A major contribution to the failure was provided by the confusing and ridiculous-seeming magic lantern projections taken from Blake's illustrations of the Book of Job."[150] On paper, the musical side was in highly capable hands: Georges Jouatte, one of the foremost French tenors of the period (and a former dancer himself), baritone Gilbert Moryn, the Vlassov Choir (the Russian emigre ensemble that had premiered Stravinsky's *Symphony of Psalms*), and the Orchestre symphonique de Paris. On the two pianos were Février and Jean Doyen, both highly accomplished musicians, while the conductor was the young Maurice Abravanel, a disciple of Weill and the future music director of the Utah Symphony Orchestra. Though not altogether unsympathetic, and pointing out the "splendor" of the ending, the *Ménestrel* reviewer found the work, on the whole, "monotonous and boring," noting that the audience was sharply divided in its reactions.[151] As Kessler hinted, the music cannot have been helped by the behavior of some of the attendees: according to the *Mercure de France*, fashionable, noisy latecomers made it difficult to listen.[152] This is confirmed by the critic and musicologist Gustave Samazeuilh, who praised the work's "austere style, but by no means devoid of power," and detected influences of the Stravinsky of *Oedipus Rex* and the *Symphony of Psalms*.[153] After the second performance on June 19, *Job* was never heard again in Paris.

Job was not Nabokov's only contribution to the Ballets 1933. He also arranged and orchestrated a short ballet entitled *Les valses de Beethoven*, which was part of the final program on June 19. Despite its title, most of the music has nothing to do with Beethoven, who, unlike Schubert, and the *Diabelli Variations* notwithstanding, is not associated with the waltz as a musical genre.[154] It consisted of eight early nineteenth-century waltzes of doubtful attribution which Nabokov had found, published under that whimsical title, in a music bookstore in Leipzig.[155]

They were supplemented by one of Beethoven's Bagatelles and two Scottish songs harmonized by him. The ballet's mythological scenario has been summed up as follows:

> Eros, with an arrow shot from his bow, inflames the god Apollo with love for the maiden Daphne. Seeking to escape Apollo's embraces, Daphne prays to the gods and is transformed into a laurel tree. Apollo grieves his loss at the foot of the laurel and is mocked in song by his own shadow. The laurel is thereafter consecrated to poetry.[156]

Conducted by Abravanel, with sets and costumes by Emilio Terry, the ballet was performed by Tilly Losch, the Polish dancer Roman Jasinsky, and the British dancer Diana Gould. While remembering the ballet proper as "a rather sorry affair," Gould retained vivid memories of being taken by Tchelitchew ("with his beautiful, haggard, romantic face") and Nabokov ("a marvelous Russian with a mane of dark blond hair and witty blue eyes") taking her "all over Paris on various purposeless and very Russian outings to see friends who were usually absent or to chatter with American expatriates and have tea."[157] Later the wife of Yehudi Menuhin, Diana, like her husband, became a close friend of Nabokov.

7

New Exile

LATER IN LIFE, reflecting in general terms on the economic difficulties facing creative musicians, Nabokov asked a question that he could have applied to his own situation in 1933. "Can a 'gifted and striving' young composer make a living as a composer?"[1] He answered it firmly in the negative. Advances from publishers, he explained, even the retainer fee composers occasionally receive from them in exchange for exclusivity, are never sufficient to support one. An opera, a ballet take a very long time to write and, in most cases, receive only a few performances, after which they are seldom, if ever, revived. Commissions can be obtained but not relied upon and they never bring in enough money. What, then, were the alternatives? Nabokov listed ten possibilities. Conducting, a route followed by many composers throughout history, was seldom lucrative, unless one was famous to begin with. The second option, film music, *was* often lucrative, but for this very reason could become dangerously addictive and, ultimately, as some famous examples have shown—Malcolm Arnold and Georges Delerue, to name only two—might end one's career as a composer of "serious" music. Writing incidental music for the theater, Nabokov argued, was "probably the best and easiest way out of economic trouble," but it required a special talent he was not sure he possessed. Working for the radio in an advisory capacity was arduous, time-consuming, dull, and financially unrewarding. "Sitting on two chairs," that is trying to write at once popular and serious music, never worked: "Sooner or later, and usually sooner than later, the popular, more lucrative stuff gets the upper hand." Making money as an orchestrator or arranger—as Nabokov evidently did for a while during his early American years—was "pure hell." Teaching was, of course, for a composer, "the way of all flesh"; but composers who are good teachers, Nabokov felt, were exceptions rather than the norm. The best solution of all was, of course, to have personal sources of income (as did Poulenc, for instance). Music criticism Nabokov described as a "dreary, soporific and thankless task for a composer," a rarely lucrative one at that, and one which made you more enemies than friends.

Lastly, one could "borrow money from friends or find a patron"; yet, as Nabokov added ruefully, "wealthy friends are rare and patrons usually prefer performing artists to composers."

Life certainly became difficult for someone in Nabokov's situation in the early 1930s, when France began to be seriously hit by the Great Depression. He and his wife, especially with a young child to provide for, had reasons to worry about their future prospects and must have gone through the above list of questions and alternatives. In securing commissions, Nabokov, as we have seen, had been reasonably successful, even though he occasionally failed to fulfill them. Conducting, of which he did a great deal in his college years in the late 1930s and early 1940s, was never seriously considered as a career. Did he not consider himself particularly gifted at it? Or was he wary of the example of two fellow composers who had taken this path? Désormière, whom he greatly admired, had effectively ended his career as a composer by turning conductor; and the same happened to Markevitch a decade later. Writing film music was, on the other hand, a possibility he seriously explored at the time. A letter to Nabokov from the playwright Jacques Bousquet, whose wife Marie-Louise was a well-known Parisian hostess, mentions contacts Nabokov had in late December 1931 or early January 1932 with the screenwriter and film director Marc Allégret, a former lover of Gide's. Bousquet also promised Nabokov to recommend him, unsuccessfully as it turned out, to the assistant of Paul Fejos for the latter's adaptation of *Fantomas*, which was released that spring. As for stage music, Nabokov's comments suggest that his contribution to Savoir's play in 1931 had been a profitable undertaking. He clearly hoped to repeat the experience the following year when he wrote, at Denise Bourdet's suggestion, a *Marche des Tritons* for the last act of her husband's comedy's *La fleur des pois*, which opened with great success at the Théâtre de la Michodière in Paris on October 4, 1932. Unfortunately, Édouard Bourdet, during rehearsals, had to reduce the play's length and so went the little march and the expected profits.[2]

While Nabokov eventually did work for the radio in the following decade, he does not seem to have seriously considered earning his income by writing popular music. To prove his point that one's "serious" career inevitably suffers, he used the example of Dukelsky, whose "classical" output sank into oblivion after he became successful as a composer of light music under the pseudonym of Vernon Duke.[3] Yet, in his autobiography, Nabokov, with a note of regret, hints at missed opportunities in the early part of his American years, and recalls being urged by Gershwin to take this route.[4]

The remaining options were teaching, reviewing, personal income, and rich patrons. Many years of Nabokov's life were eventually spent in various colleges and universities; but no matter how conscientiously he devoted himself to teaching, he admitted he always found it a bore. He had dabbled in music criticism in early adulthood during his Berlin years; he might have returned to it if *La musique* had survived the Depression, but this source of income dried up as well. Personal wealth, or at least comfortable financial independence would have been his lot, had the Bolshevist Revolution not intervened. Even the fact that the family estate was in Poland, rather than under Soviet control, in the 1920s and 30s, was of little help. Always "an easy prey for crooks," Nabokov's mother, in 1924, was lured by a shady lawyer and his accomplices into disposing of "several thousand acres of forested lands" at half their market value.[5] After jewels were sold, the little income that remained barely sufficed to maintain the property. In December 1928, Nabokov reported to Prokofiev that the Polish manager had by then "effectively stolen it from them" and given their emigre status in Poland there was nothing to be done.[6] Many years later, meeting Nabokov's son at Mary McCarthy's Paris apartment, Iwaszkiewicz reminded him that he had in his possession in Poland an "immense archive" of letters concerning the fate of the family's possessions.[7]

Lastly, like many other musicians, Nabokov was reduced to borrowing money from friends, and he looked for patrons. During the Great Depression, however, borrowing became riskier and patrons were fewer. An effort, spearheaded by Grunelius and other Alsatian friends, to raise money on Nabokov's behalf in January 1933, through annual subscriptions of 500 francs, apparently failed to reach its target.[8] As the composersummed it up for an interviewer at the end of his life, "I left France for the United States because one needed to find, somewhere, a place to eat."[9] He could have added, as a further cause for uncertainty, his and his wife's status as stateless refugees, Nansen passport holders but otherwise dependent, wherever they went, on temporary residence permits renewable at the whim of petty bureaucrats, and in a climate of rising xenophobia—a telling example of which is Cœuroy's preface to the Bruyr volume in which Nabokov was interviewed.[10]

In his autobiography, Nabokov credits his wife for suggesting they emigrate and for exploring the possibility of procuring an invitation from Albert C. Barnes, the famous Philadelphia pharmaceutical entrepreneur and art collector, to lecture at the foundation he had created in Merion, Pennsylvania, and which had opened its doors in 1925. Inquiries were made via a Parisian art dealer of the Nabokovs' acquaintance, who brought Barnes to the May 1932 Sérénade concert at which Désormière conducted the instrumental version of the *Chants à la Vierge Marie*. Nabokov was introduced afterward to Barnes, whom he remembered as "a stocky fellow with a bulldog's face, tousled hair, and spectacles perched on a purple-plum nose."[11] The dealer who made the introduction is identified in *Bagázh* as Georges Keller, associate of Étienne Bignou at his Rue La Boétie gallery and "nurse" of the mercurial Dr. Barnes when he visited Paris.[12] A letter preserved at Yale suggests that a key role was also played by Pierre Colle, who owned a gallery on the Rue Cambacérès, near the Champs-Élysées, and numbered Barnes among his patrons.[13] A friend of Cocteau and the Noailles, as well as a business partner of

Julien Levy, Colle, whose associate at the time was none other than the young Christian Dior, exhibited Tchelitchew and other Neo-Romantic painters such as Bérard and the Berman brothers, as well as Derain and Dalí. He appears to have been among those Nabokov turned to for occasional loans. In July 1932, Colle informed him that "dear Dr. Barnes" was in Paris, keeping him busy, and had inquired about him.[14] A year and more conversations later, Nabokov, according to his account, was summoned to a luncheon in Paris with Barnes, Keller, and a trustee of Barnes's foundation Nabokov identifies by the improbable name of Dribblebees. This second meeting resulted in an invitation and a contract. Nabokov was reluctant at first. He had no teaching, let alone lecturing, experience; nor was he happy at the idea of leaving France, where his reputation as a composer was now in place, for the United States, where, despite a few successful performances of his music, he was largely unknown. Other possibilities were investigated, such as an engagement at the Salzburg Orchestral Academy in the summer of 1933, for which he tried to get the wife of Octave Homberg, an influential financier, to recommend him to Bernhard Paumgartner, director of the Mozarteum.[15] This having fallen through, there was no alternative but to accept Barnes's invitation. Its terms were enticing: Nabokov was to lecture in Merion every other Sunday morning, over a period of eight months, on topics relating to aesthetic trends in music and the visual arts in the past hundred years. Travel expenses would be covered by the Foundation and Nabokov was to receive a generous weekly honorarium of $250. Except for having to lecture every two weeks and arrive in Philadelphia the day before, there was no residence requirement.

Before their departure for America, Nabokov and Natalie went to Germany to attend the wedding of Felix Bethmann-Hollweg, to which they were driven by Claus von Bismarck (descendant of the Reich Chancellor) in his beautiful new car. The bride was Marie-Luise Reventlow, who was a cousin of both Felix and Albrecht von Bernstorff. Entrusting their one-year-old Ivan to Felix and Marie-Luise, they then returned to France and sailed from Le Havre to New York on August 9 on the *S.S. De Grasse*, "the slowest, smallest, oldest, and cheapest boat of the French Line."[16] The decoration was unpretentious, but the food superb and the stability remarkable: though normally prone to seasickness, Nabokov was spared during the entire trip. With stops at Lisbon and the Azores, and excursions thrown in in both places, the crossing took eleven days. On the French liner, among other academics and intellectuals, was the poet John Peale Bishop (1892–1944), who was returning to the United States with his family after spending a decade in France. Also on the *De Grasse* was the American avant-garde composer Edgard Varèse, moving back to New York, with his wife Louise, following a four-year stay in his native Paris. The two couples sympathized with the Nabokovs and "indoctrinated" them, in his words, "as to what to expect in America, where we should settle in New York, whom we should meet, and whom and what to avoid."[17]

The first contact with America went more smoothly than expected. The Barnes lectures turned out to be not of the challenging, scholarly kind (Dr. Barnes, in any event, had a well-known aversion toward scholars) but more of the amusing and anecdote-filled variety, and therefore requiring minimum preparation for someone so naturally endowed as Nabokov with a raconteur's talents. Barnes himself turned out to be "solicitous, hospitable, and compassionate," at least for the first six months. In New York, the Nabokovs found a "shabby little flat on West 55th Street," which they must have left at the end of the year, since he then gave his residence as the Hotel St. Hubert, at 120 West 57th Street. Far from being isolated, they were "overwhelmed by dinner and cocktail parties, by weekend invitations, and by offers of tickets for theaters or concerts or gallery openings."[18] Their contacts from previous acquaintance included Zosia Kochanska, whom Nabokov had met in Paris through Tchelitchew, a friend of hers since his days in Kiev, where she had posed for his first major portrait.[19] Zosia was married to the noted Polish-Russian violinist Pawel Kochanski, who died in January 1934, barely three months after giving the premiere of Karol Szymanowski's Second Violin Concerto in Warsaw. She lived on East 74th Street and there, in Nabokov's words, "kept a salon in the old-fashioned sense of the French term."[20] Through her, he met well-to-do society ladies, such as Dorothy Chadwick and Marion Dougherty and her sister Edith Fincke, who in turn facilitated contacts in his new adoptive country. One such contact was Claire Reis, the founder of the League of American Composers: a November 1933 letter from Aaron Copland to the pianist John Kirkpatrick indicates that she was trying to get Kirkpatrick to perform *Le cœur de Don Quichotte* in New York.[21] The work was, however, played not by Kirkpatrick but by Erno Balogh at the concert that took place at the French Institute on December 17, under the League's auspices. The *New York Times* critic, who found Nabokov's piano suite "beautifully played," noted simply that it was "more effective in its swift-moving 'La Fuite' than in its more meditative passages."[22] The remainder of the program included Prokofiev's Piano Sonatina, played by Nikita Magaloff (who also performed his own *Toccata*); Paul Bowles's *Sonatina* (played by Kirkpatrick); harpsichord pieces by Georges Migot and Jacques Ibert; Mitya Stillman's String Quartet no. 6; and songs by Theodore Chanler, Charles Ives, and Israel Citkowitz, sung by Ada MacLeish, whose husband, Archibald MacLeish, was one of Nabokov's new American acquaintances.

In February 1934, Nabokov made a new lifelong friend in the person of Raimund von Hoffmannsthal, a film industry executive who had begun his career as a collaborator of Max Reinhardt.[23] Born in 1906, he was one of the two sons of the Viennese poet and Strauss librettist Hugo von Hoffmannsthal; his elder brother Franz had committed suicide in 1929, causing his father a shock that killed him two days later. In 1932, Raimund married Alice Astor, daughter of John Jacob Astor IV, who perished on the *Titanic*. Alice herself was recently divorced from Prince Serge Obolensky and her separation and remarriage, firmly opposed by her brother Vincent, were much discussed in the press. Wealthy and hospitable, the Hoffmannsthals soon invited Nabokov to spend weekends at their mansion overlooking the Hudson River in Rhinebeck, New York.

Nabokov's first major musical project after his arrival in America was the ballet *Union Pacific*. Despite discrepancies between his own account and other sources, its history can be more or less reconstituted. Having kept in touch with John Peale Bishop after their Atlantic crossing, Nabokov was introduced to Archibald MacLeish, who was a close friend of Bishop. Born in 1892 in Glencoe, Illinois, MacLeish was a Yale and Harvard Law School graduate. He had spent five years in France in the 1920s, returning to the United States in 1928. In 1930 he was recruited by Henry Luce as editor of the newly founded *Fortune*, and in 1933 won the Pulitzer Prize for his poem *Conquistador*, inspired by his 1929 trip to Mexico on foot and mule back. When Nabokov met MacLeish, Nabokov was "overawed": "He seemed the image of the noble American from New England. He was handsome, manly, courteous, and quick-witted. 'This is the way all Americans should be, I thought.'"[24] MacLeish seems to have been no less charmed by Nabokov, whom he later described as "irresistible" and "just one vast chuckle about everything."[25] Whether the idea of a ballet was suggested by MacLeish, as Nabokov claims, or, as MacLeish recalled, by Nabokov, poet and musician soon agreed to collaborate on such a project. "I said," MacLeish subsequently wrote, "'I don't know anything about ballet. I've never even thought about it.' And he said, 'You write an account of what you want to happen on stage and I'll set it to music.' Well, it wasn't quite as simple as that."[26]

MacLeish's and Nabokov's accounts agree on one point: it was MacLeish who, having accumulated research material with a view to a piece in *Fortune* on the construction and completion in 1869 of the first transcontinental railroad, proposed this as a subject. "My scheme for the ballet," MacLeish recalled, "was based on the fact that the golden spike was driven by Mr. [John Pierpont] Morgan on the top of Promontory Mountain overlooking the Pacific—the Union Pacific had been built from the Pacific up toward Promontory Mountain by Chinese workmen and, from the east, west by Irish workmen."[27] Mormon missionaries, Mexican workers, "gay ladies," a barman, and a bar brawl in the big tent were thrown in, forming at once, in Harlow Robinson's words, "a socialist realist fable celebrating the triumph of technology and the building of a new industrial society" as well as a celebration of the American melting pot, with the meeting of the two locomotives and everybody posing for the celebrated photograph when the curtain falls.[28]

It then fell to Nabokov to find the person who could bring the project to fruition. This turned out to be Sol Hurok, the already powerful Ukrainian-born impresario, then in his mid-forties. Nabokov, who was vaguely acquainted with Hurok from his Parisian years, chanced upon him again in November 1933 on the train to Philadelphia as he was en route to deliver his bimonthly lecture in Merion. Hurok, as it happened, had just signed his first ballet company and was about to bring it to America. The company in question was the one formed in April 1932 in partnership between the producer René Blum (brother of the French Socialist Party leader and future prime minister Léon Blum) and a White Russian ex-officer named Vasilii Grigorievich Voskresenskii, who had restyled himself Colonel Wassili de Basil and been active in a Russian opera company active in Paris in the 1920s. Named Ballets Russes de Monte-Carlo, the new company set out to recruit as many as possible of Diaghilev's former collaborators, including Kochno and Grigoriev. Balanchine was initially hired as choreographer but left at the end of the first season, followed by Kochno, on learning that the Colonel had entered into negotiations with his rival Massine, who was then working in New York.[29] Massine himself, ever since touring in the United States with Diaghilev in 1916, had long wanted to do a ballet on an American theme, and had even made plans at the time with Ansermet on a subject based on the story of Pocahontas.[30] It was thus his old collaborator for *Ode* that MacLeish and Nabokov approached with the idea for an American ballet on the lines suggested by the poet. Massine, according to his own account, was not particularly enthusiastic about the scenario, which he found at first "lifeless and unimaginative," until it occurred to him that sleepers and rails could be figured by dancers themselves, providing innovative choreographic opportunities.[31]

But what about the ballet music? It obviously had to be American in character, yet Nabokov, at that time, as MacLeish puts it, "had no ideas about America."[32] At this point either MacLeish or Nabokov suggested using the collection of American popular music from the 1870s, 80s, and 90s owned by the painter Gerald Murphy. Famous now for having served as the model for Dick Diver in F. Scott Fitzgerald's *Tender Is the Night*, Murphy, a wealthy Bostonian and, like MacLeish, a Yale Skull and Bones man, had become a friend of his when they both lived in France. Nabokov himself had met Murphy then, possibly through Cocteau or as a Ballets Russes patron. The collection, according to Nabokov, was in the form of Edison cylinders, but, as MacLeish's account suggests, it likely consisted in equal measure of sheet music. It contained music-hall songs, early jazz, and popular songs of the "O Susanna" and "Pop Goes the Weasel" variety, all, in MacLeish's words, "incredibly exciting and foot-twitching."[33] Yet Hurok and Colonel de Basil were apparently reluctant to entrust the task to a "serious" rather than popular composer. Nabokov claims he suggested the names of Aaron Copland and Virgil Thomson. Massine, who arrived in New York with the company in mid-December, was no doubt instrumental in securing the final go-ahead. An even more powerful incentive were the funds raised by Murphy's circle: Gerald's wife Sara, her sister Hoytie Wiborg, Lila Luce (wife of Henry Luce, for whom MacLeish worked as a *Fortune* editor), and others pledged contributions towards the $25,000 budget suggested by Colonel de Basil.[34] Even Barnes, still well disposed towards his guest lecturer, offered to help and ended up purchasing all 500 balcony seats at the premiere. In short, as Amanda Vaill puts it, "it felt a little as if the sweat-equity philanthropy of the old Diaghilev days had returned."[35] An advance celebratory dinner was hosted in New York in March after a recital by Ada MacLeish. In addition to the Nabokovs and MacLeishs, the guest list included Stephen Vincent Benét and his wife, Copland, and Virgil Thomson, who was then on the East Coast for the premiere of *Four Saints in Three Acts*, and who reportedly "distinguished himself by speaking to no one, standing at the buffet table and devouring an entire serving bowl full of strawberries and cream, and leaving immediately afterward."[36]

Nabokov was already acquainted with the expatriate American composer, who after World War II became one of his closest friends: Sauguet had introduced them to each other towards the end of Nabokov's Paris years. On February 7, 1934, Nabokov attended the first performance of Thomson and Gertrude Stein's opera at the Wadsworth Atheneum in Hartford, Connecticut. At the party that followed at the house of Chick Austin, the museum's director, he reportedly "pounded out Russian folk songs on the piano in the parlor, sung by a boozy Archibald MacLeish."[37]

Once the green light finally came for the production of *Union Pacific*, there were, according to Nabokov, exactly twenty-three days left before the first performance, scheduled for April 6 at the Forrest Theatre in Philadelphia.[38] Albert Johnson, designer of the 1934 Ziegfeld Follies, was recruited for the sets, while the twenty-four-year-old Irene Sharaff (of *The King and I* fame) was engaged as costume designer. The musical side was in the capable hands of Efrem Kurtz, the Russian-born principal conductor of the Ballets Russes de Monte-Carlo, whose assistant was a twenty-eight-year-old Hungarian named Antal Dorati. Given the little time available, Nabokov asked Hurok for an orchestrator who could work under his supervision while he arranged the music. Edward Powell, Hurok's recommendation, turned out to be "sheer delight" as a collaborator, "incredibly musical besides being quick, gay, and never tiring."[39] On March 2, the day before the *Union Pacific* team was to depart for Pennsylvania, Mexican music had to be hurriedly found at the New York Public Library to placate Tamara Toumanova, the show's fifteen-year-old female star, who was unhappy with her main number: the replacement one was arranged, orchestrated, and copied out on the train the following day. In Philadelphia, nothing, musically or otherwise, seemed to get right until the final rehearsal on the morning of the performance. Yet, miraculously, all went well that evening. Once the curtain had fallen on Nabokov's rousing finale incorporating the tune of "Yankee Doodle," the ballet could be deemed a resounding success. Not content with earning plaudits for his choreography, Massine himself, wearing "a ginger wig, an apricot shirt, checked trousers, a barman's apron, and bright red high-buttoned boots," stole the show in the barman's dance.[40] The rest of the cast included André Eglevsky as the surveyor of the Irish workmen, David Lichine as the surveyor of the Chinese workmen, and Eugenia Delarova as the Lady-Gay. The only two American-born stars of this American ballet were Roland Guerard (the cameraman) and the young Japanese-American Sono Osato (the barman's assistant), but paradoxically, as Harlow Robinson has pointed out, even their participation served "to emphasize that immigration was a fundamental part of the American experience and identity."[41] The first-night audience responded enthusiastically, standing on their chairs "to applaud as the spike was driven," as reported by Siegfried Wagener, who added that it was "as refreshing as a glacial wind on a midsummer day to find somewhere in the world a public that is not completely obsessed with economic worries."[42] The only false note was unwittingly caused at curtain by Dr. Barnes's balcony claque, which called for Nabokov to take a bow. The angered Massine took his revenge, many years later, by not mentioning Nabokov's name even once when discussing the ballet in his autobiography.[43]

For the next two years, *Union Pacific* was one of the biggest successes of the Ballets Russes de Monte-Carlo. After Philadelphia, it was seen in Boston, after which it triumphed in Chicago on April 21, when Nabokov, unusually, conducted the performance, and in New York a few days later. In Los Angeles, the audience included Marlene Dietrich, who was so enthusiastic about the presentation that she offered to appear in the ballet as one of the wooden sleepers.[44] In mid-June *Union Pacific* was performed in Paris at the Théâtre des Champs-Élysées and then in London at Covent Garden, before continuing its triumphant American career. Save for a disparaging review in the May 1934 issue of the *Dance Observer*, the critical reception was largely favorable on the American side of the Atlantic.[45] In Paris, some critics were disconcerted by the music's uninhibited rambunctiousness: Reynaldo Hahn called it "dry"; *Le Ménestrel* described it as "brutal and puerile, especially given the dissonances that adorn it and the violent timbres it is laden with."[46] Such reactions, however, were typical of the French musical establishment of the time, readily irritated at the wide success jazz and American popular music already enjoyed in Paris. Anticipating Copland's *Billy the Kid* (choreography by Eugene Loring) by four years and *Rodeo* (choreographed by Agnes de Mille) by eight, *Union Pacific* was, indeed, the first ballet on a purely American theme, even though some, like John Martin in the *New York Times*, preferred to call it "a European ballet on an American theme."[47] "It was a primitive idea," MacLeish admitted decades later.

> My friend Lincoln Kirstein, who is the papa of ballet in the United States, the real founder of the New York City Ballet, said to me grimly that *Union Pacific* was not a ballet and shouldn't be called such on the program. And he was right. It wasn't a ballet. It was just a sort of a skit that had dances

arranged for it. [. . .][W]hat carried that ballet was not my idea and not the dancing of the ballerinas of the Ballets Russes de Monte-Carlo; it was Gerald [Murphy]'s music, which wasn't Gerald's but came out of the music halls of forty or fifty years before.[48]

Massine's were not the only ruffled feathers. No acknowledgment was made of Murphy's involvement in the project, and he was understandably peeved.[49] Even worse, the operation turned out to be a financial disaster for the authors and their backers. No proper contract had been signed by the poet and the musician with Hurok or "the crooked Colonel," as Nabokov called de Basil. Reluctantly, W. de Basil only deigned to pay the composer the $500 he had promised him orally. As for MacLeish, it seems that he had been given false reassurance that his copyright was protected by common law.[50] A lawsuit was eventually filed, but by the time it was won, the ballet had been dropped from the company's repertory.[51]

Just as *Union Pacific* was receiving its highly successful Paris premiere, another ballet by Nabokov, *La vie de Polichinelle*, was being rehearsed at the Paris Opera, where it was unveiled, also with considerable success, on June 22, in a double bill with *La damnation de Faust*. The project actually preceded *Union Pacific* and Nabokov's departure for New York. The violinist Joseph Szigeti, then in Paris, remembered Nabokov showing him sketches of his score in 1932, "dancing them out for me to visualize them."[52] The Paris Opera commission, officially made on behalf of Jacques Rouché, its director since 1914, was engineered by Lifar, now both the company's star dancer and ballet master. By July 6, 1933, according to a letter to Nabokov from Adrien Fauchier-Magnan, a minor writer and art historian who appears to have played a leading role in the negotiations, the work had not been formally accepted, but there were rumors that it might be mounted early the following season, provided Nabokov could get it orchestrated by October 15. As set designer, Fauchier-Magnan recommended the Spanish painter Pere Pruna (1904–77); as conductor he urged Nabokov to push for Joseph-Eugène Szyfer (1887–1947), a Polish-born musician then attached to the Opéra and whom Lifar considered its best ballet conductor.[53] By the end of August, Fauchier-Magnan had shown Pruna's first sketches to Lifar, describing them as "ravishing," and reporting to Nabokov that Lifar was confident that the work would be staged in January or February. In late October, Nabokov was still busy orchestrating and an audition was being scheduled for Rouché to make his final decision. It may be that the postponement until June 22 had to do with the composer's unavailability, given his American commitments, to supervise the final rehearsals until then.

A ballet in two acts and six scenes, comprising a full hour of music, *La vie de Polichinelle* was Nabokov's longest work to date. Credited to Claude Séran, pseudonym of Fauchier-Magnan's wife, the scenario was inspired by a set of recently discovered drawings by Giovanni Domenico Tiepolo.[54] As Reynaldo Hahn summarizes it, it is "a mimed and danced biography of that famous character," whom Lifar impersonated:

> First we see him as a child, making mischief for the first time, then as an adolescent, experimenting with buffoonery. We witness his youthful idyll with a girl friend he subsequently marries, and then abandons for a female acrobat. Now he is a popular actor, cheered by the crowd, triumphant, insolent, happy with the girl he loves. Poor Mrs Pulcinella, ill-advisedly, comes and makes a jealous scene, upon which he discovers an excellent way of getting her to shut up: he throws her into a well. He is arrested and shot. Pulcinella, however, is immortal: he resuscitates and, to everybody's joy, gets ready to resume his glorious, mischievous career.[55]

The public and critical reception was enthusiastic: the same Hahn was moved to declare that *La vie de Polichinelle* was "one of the prettiest ballets one has seen in Paris in a long time." Even more emphatically, the reviewer of the *Revue musicale* described it as "the most beautiful of all the ballets produced since the death of Diaghilev."[56] While Lifar's lively, stylish choreography and Pruna's Tiepolo-inspired sets and costumes were particularly admired, Nabokov's music was also generally liked. Inevitably, some criticized it for being too modern, and others for not being modern enough. Thus, Milhaud wrote that, while the score was "a faithful, clever commentary on the charming libretto," and its orchestration was "generally quite lively and varied," the melodic ideas were, at times, "a trifle conventional."[57] The notoriously hard to please Pierre Lalo, while admitting that "it would be unfair to say that the music is bad," described it as "singularly devoid of personality, accent, life," deploring that "it duly resorted to every harmonic and orchestral cliche" and "slavishly sacrificed to the cult of the wrong note."[58] Much fairer, Louis Schneider, himself hardly a fan of the musical avant-garde, began by reminding his readers that he had not cared much for *Union Pacific*. Detecting influences of Stravinsky and Milhaud, he found in the score of *La vie de Polichinelle* "very real qualities."

> First, its rhythmic pulse, clean, crisp, favorable both to dance and to variety, which conveys to the work a frenetic, joyful vitality; then the light, translucent orchestration, in which the timbres, often used in their pure form—a Stravinskian device—are thrown into relief on the background of a very pretty, aerial sonority. As for the melodic invention, it is not devoid of suppleness, nor does it hesitate to become sentimental whenever the plot requires it.[59]

Even the conservative Hahn, while deploring the music's lack of Venetian character and the "modern absurdities" with which Nabokov saddled his music—naïvely, in his view—found something to enjoy in its rhythmic liveliness and piquancy. From this ballet score, Nabokov extracted a symphonic suite, comprising seven movements, which was published separately.

While in Paris for the performances of his ballet, Nabokov took Misia Sert and Harry Kessler to see it. At the end of his stay in Paris, before taking the train to Austria to visit the Hoffmannsthals, he also went with Kessler to hear sung Vespers at the Melkite Greek Catholic church of Saint-Julien-le-Pauvre on the Left Bank. It was to be their last meeting. Kessler reflected pessimistically on the situation of Germany. "*Das Leben hat seine Sinne verloren*" (Life has lost its meaning), Nabokov remembers him saying. He died three years later, in Lyons, in October 1937.

The year 1934, on the whole, had turned out well for Nabokov's career: his success on both sides of the ocean appeared to vindicate the risky decision to transfer his residence to New York. His overture *Le fiancé* had had its American premiere at Carnegie Hall, with Sokoloff conducting the New York Orchestra, on February 13. The *New York Times* critic, while judging the work "naïve," noted that it was well received.[60] Even *Job*, despite its poor reception in Paris, received its American premiere that summer at the Worcester Festival in Massachusetts, under the festival's music director Albert Stoessel; the English version, modeled on the King James Bible, was prepared by the experienced translator Lewis Galantière, a friend of Virgil Thomson. Yet, for someone in Nabokov's financial situation, the inability to reap from the commercial benefits of *Union Pacific* must have been galling. Similarly, *La vie de Polichinelle* was an almost unqualified success, but, like other fine ballets of the period, it was never revived after its initial run. As for renewing the relatively advantageous arrangement with Barnes, at least for one year, this was ruled out when Barnes, suddenly and without apparent reason, put an end to it and broke all relations with his guest. As Nabokov pointed out, a similar fate awaited his successor in the position, Bertrand Russell, who took Barnes to court.[61] In Nabokov's case, the result was that he continued to find himself in a state of perpetual financial uncertainty.

Back in Paris for the French premiere of *Union Pacific* and the opening of *La vie de Polichinelle*, Nabokov remained in Europe for the remainder of the summer of 1934. He visited his sister and mother in Berlin, the Bethmann-Hollwegs at Hohenfinow, and the Gruneliuses at Kolbsheim. He was the Hoffmansthals' house guest at Schloss Kammer, the Austrian castle they shared with Eleanora von Mendelssohn and her husband on Attersee, in the Salzkammergut. He took the opportunity to attend performances at nearby Salzburg, while some of the festival's illustrious guests—Toscanini for one—came for lunch or dinner. Generous with both his connections and his money, Hoffmannsthal arranged a performance of Nabokov's *Job* at the Salzburg Cathedral that summer, having the orchestral and vocal parts copied at his own expense.[62]

Nabokov's life in late 1934 and through the first months of 1936 is difficult to reconstitute with precision, given the little documentation that has survived for the period.[63] When he returned to America in November, he did so, this time, with a proper immigrant visa for which he got sponsored by MacLeish.[64] His hope to earn money by giving lectures was, however, quickly disappointed: no new Dr. Barnes was forthcoming in depressed times, and he had to make do with whatever menial musical tasks were available. His personal life also changed. After five years of marriage, he and his wife, though remaining on amicable terms, began to lead more or less separate lives. Though little is known about Nabokov's liaisons at that time, he is rumored to have had an affair with Caresse Crosby, widow of the poet and publisher Harry Crosby and cofounder with him of the Black Sun Press. The principal source of the rumor is not an entirely reliable one: it is none other than Barnes, in the venomous testimony he gave to the FBI about Nabokov in 1946.[65] Barnes is quoted as characterizing Caresse Crosby as "a wealthy prostitute" associating "with noted artists and composers for personal fame and has illicit relations with them."[66] He also alleges that Nabokov "contracted a venereal disease from her." That Nabokov could have met Caresse Crosby is not surprising. She was an intimate friend of MacLeish, who had even attended the wake, at her request, after the sensational death of her husband in an apparent suicide pact with his lover Josephine Rotch Bigelow in 1929.[67] Until 1936 she divided her time between France and the United States, and she could have been introduced to Nabokov by MacLeish at the time they worked on *Union Pacific*. The affair, if it took place, could thus have occurred in late 1933 or early 1934, before Crosby became involved with the African American boxer (and future Broadway star) Canada Lee.

In early 1935 Nabokov moved—rent-free—to a "spacious studio" on East 39th Street, one floor above the study of an architect friend of Marion Dougherty and Edith Fincke. His society lady friends provided furniture and a contact at Steinway a baby-grand.[68] The studio was soon nicknamed "the Jungle" after two tropical creepers, given by Cecil Beaton, started covering the walls and ceiling. At the suggestion of Tchelitchew, who in the fall of 1934 had settled in New York with his new companion, the American poet Charles Henri Ford, a photographic exhibition was held in Nabokov's loft: it featured portraits by Beaton, Horst, Carl Van Vechten, and the Petersburg-born George Hoyningen-Huehne. A party was held, for which Hoffmannsthal not only paid for bar and buffet, but also recruited an Austrian band, to the tunes of which guests danced all night. If Nabokov's account is to be believed, two burly policemen who appeared around 3 a.m. to quiet things down were persuaded to join the party and were soon drunk and dancing like everybody else. "In the graying light of dawn the band went into 39th Street and, flanked by the two uniformed policemen, played soft Austrian lullabies to soothe the wrath of my neighbors."[69]

Another joyful occasion, mentioned in Beaton's diaries, was a cocktail-party, perhaps also hosted by the Hoffmannsthals, in honor of the producer and impresario Rudolf "Kaetchen" Kommer, best known for his association with Max Reinhardt: According to Beaton, Nabokov accompanied Marlene Dietrich on the piano that evening.[70] Nabokov also recalled traveling to Boston to attend the premiere of Gershwin's *Porgy and Bess* at the Colonial Theater on September 30, 1935. This time he was in the company of Mary Cushing, Kay Halle, Martha Rousseau and her brother Teddy (the future Metropolitan Museum curator), "and a friendly fellow called Spivacke."[71] All gathered the next morning around Gershwin at the Oyster Bar at Grand Central and had "large bowls of creamy oyster stew."

In the spring of 1935, Nabokov's "Jungle" hosted another illustrious photographer, though his name was virtually unknown at the time: Henri Cartier-Bresson. Nabokov's junior by five years, he was returning from Mexico and spent a few weeks in New York, where he took part in a group show held in late April and early May at the Julien Levy Gallery, along with Walker Evans and the Mexican photographer Manuel Álvarez Bravo. Looking for a place to stay in the city, Cartier-Bresson turned to Charles Henri Ford, who in turn recommended him to Nabokov. Nabokov himself had met Cartier-Bresson in Paris several years before through Tchelitchew; they had, naturally, many friends in common, beginning with Max Jacob, and including the art dealer Pierre Colle—not to mention Caresse Crosby, with whom Cartier-Bresson had had an affair in 1929.[72] The 39th Street studio was partitioned by a screen and the two men, pooling their modest resources, lived in "delicious harmony" for a few weeks. "He was very young and handsome," Nabokov remembered, "with a blond and pink head and a gently mocking smile playing around his lips that I have always liked in Norman French faces."

> But what was astonishing in Cartier-Bresson's face were his eyes. They were like darts—sharp and clever, limpidly blue and infinitely agile. "Henri has the fastest eyes I know," Pavel Tchelitchew used to say. Indeed, there was the quick spark of a shrewd *voyeur* in Cartier-Bresson's eyes.[73]

The two men had long conversations on moral and political subjects. In the latter sphere, liberal though they both were, they did not agree completely. Cartier-Bresson, like many progressive Frenchmen of his generation, refused to see Soviet communism in purely negative terms. However, as Nabokov recalled,

> from remarks Henri Cartier-Bresson made in my presence, I think that to him, like to me, *all* political systems and forms of government are potentially evil and inherently corruptible. There are only *relatively* better ones. Worst of all are those who use libertarian cant to take away from people their freedom, or disguise their many forms of oppression with lofty slogans.[74]

Nabokov did his best to promote his friend's work with his artist friends. Beaton approached the head of *Harper's Bazaar*, Carmel Snow—a name Cocteau rendered as *"Caramel de neige rousse"* (the "rousse" on account of the freckles on her nose)—and she "lent" some of her glamorous models for Cartier to photograph indoors or outdoors.

> The project was a fiasco. I remember the dismay on Pavlik's and Cecil's faces when Henri showed them the result of his labors. The glamor girls were snapped opening a garbage can, standing near a decaying wall, or entering a motorcar carcass. [. . .]As usual, in the relationship of art and fashion, Henri was several decades ahead of his [. . .] time. His photographs taken in 1935 belonged to future decades [. . .].[75]

Mrs. Snow herself was not amused.

In New York, Cartier-Bresson developed a passion for Harlem, and Nabokov occasionally accompanied him. There he met some of the friends the photographers made in the "radical elite," to whom, Nabokov realized, "Lenin was a hero and a saint whose role in history was not supposed to be challenged."[76] In the uncensored manuscript of *Bagázh*, Nabokov reveals another reason why Cartier-Bresson loved Harlem: he was sexually attracted to African American women. The two men, both firmly heterosexual despite having many gay friends, made arrangements to accommodate their respective busy sexual schedules: by his own admission "highly promiscuous and polygamous" during that period, Nabokov, unless he was "invited" by his women friends, tended to entertain them in the afternoon, when the photographer was at work, whereas Cartier-Bresson preferred nighttime adventures and tended to spend those nights out. On one occasion, though, Nabokov, on returning late from a soiree, found him and his black girlfriend already installed.[77] Shortly afterward Cartier-Bresson moved out to a room of his own. "Not only did we become friends forever," Nabokov concluded when reflecting on his happy 1935 companionship with the French photographer, who returned to France in early 1936, "but his intransigence, his *droiture*, his instinctive sense of justice and compassion, his single-minded devotion to his craft were a much-needed lesson to me, the shifty, wayward, and insecure."[78]

As these last words suggest, despite the success of his two ballets and his busy social life, Nabokov, in the mid-1930s, was at a loose end as far as his artistic career was concerned. If one is to trust the report an unidentified informant gave the FBI in 1943, before Nabokov started working for the Federal Government, he may even have considered returning to Russia in or around 1936 and unsuccessfully approached the Soviet Consulate in New York about obtaining a passport.[79]

If accurately reported, this attempt would be an indication of the depth of uncertainty into which Nabokov found himself three years after leaving Paris. Five years earlier, to be sure, he had hypothetically considered such a move, when his friendship with Prokofiev was still blossoming. In early 1936, before the first Moscow Trials, and when forced collectivization, the mass arrests that followed Kirov's assassination in 1934, and other unsavory aspects of Stalin's regime either went underreported or were misrepresented, even Soviet Russia might have appeared to offer brighter career prospects for a composer than New York during the Great Depression. Such was the message that Prokofiev's much publicized return to USSR, just at that time, was intended to convey. With hindsight, of course, it became obvious to him that a liberal White Russian bearing the name of Nabokov would have had virtually no chance of survival under Stalin.

The only notable performance of Nabokov's music in 1935 was that of *Les danses de Polichinelle*, the suite he had extracted from the 1934 ballet. It was heard at Carnegie Hall on April 30 under the Belgian-born Léon Barzin conducting his National Orchestral Association, the oldest training orchestra in the United States. "The suite," wrote the *New York Times* reviewer, "bespeaks his experience and skill with the orchestra; he uses the full instrumental battery and manages nevertheless to be light and humorous."[80] The same critic detected influences of Stravinsky.

Nabokov's one substantial composition evidently dating from 1935 is a set of piano variations entitled *Contrastes et développements*—a title that might have been suggested by Balanchine, so close is the phrase to his own aesthetics.[81] The pianist Leo Smit, then fourteen and a student of José Iturbi, has left a vivid account of his encounter with the piece. Iturbi occupied an apartment in the Hotel St. Hubert, where Nabokov himself resided in 1934. There, as Smit recalled, Iturbi "lived in an atmosphere of perpetual night, with Venetian blinds and drapes drawn over permanently closed windows and light provided by constantly burning electric bulbs. Barricaded behind locked doors, he paddled about in pajamas, robe, and slippers, exercising his powerful fingers and wrists hour after hour in slow motion Czerny, Cramer, and Moszkowski études."

> One day, a roaring giant of a Russian burst into that sombre enclave, thwacked down the manuscript of a newly completed opus, and to the obbligato of a wildly bellowed *vocalise*, proceeded to belt the devil out of his music, entitled *Contrastes et Développements*. I was enchanted with this uninhibited extrovert and his grandly turbulent music.[82]

On the spot, Smit asked Nabokov to teach him harmony and composition, and became his student for an entire year, during which, despite his own financial straits, the composer refused to accept any fee. Apart from documenting this act of considerable generosity, Smit's recollections give a memorable vignette of Nabokov as a private teacher.

> One day he asked me to compose something of my own. Finding it difficult to break out of my highly developed student psychology, I manufactured a stiff little Scarlatti facsimile in D major with correct modulations and binary repeats. He hated it and stamped and shouted his disapproval at considerable length. When I was sure he really meant what he said, I promised I would have something original for him for the following week's lesson. Days and nights of terrible joy accompanied my first efforts at original work, but after the seven days I had written a song. I can never forget the unbearable pleasure and pain of hearing Nabokoff sing the vocal line at the top of his lungs while I timidly crept along at the piano, all but drowned out by the drenching enthusiasm of his pleasure. A few days later he tore up the four flights of my apartment, lifted my father off the floor, and after a crunching bear hug in mid-air, took him to lunch at the Russian Tea Room to tell him the good news that I was a composer.[83]

Contrastes et développements, the premiere of which has not been traced, was published in 1936, earning a mixed review from *Music and Letters*: "It is a pity that the music exhibits no decided personality—the theme in particular is a very sentimental affair—for the piano writing is effective and exciting for the well-equipped pianist."[84]

As Nabokov's arrangement with Smit makes clear, private lessons, even supplemented by music classes for children he evidently taught at that time at the Mannes School of Music, were not likely to enable Nabokov to make a living.[85] On a subsequent application for employment with the federal government, he estimates his annual income between 1933 and 1936 as between 3,000 and 4,000 dollars—not an insignificant sum in those days, but hardly a princely figure, especially for someone from his milieu. In the spring of 1936, his society friends, alarmed by his lack of prospects, took the matter into their hands and decided to get him a permanent teaching job.[86] The determining role was played by Zosia Kochanska, who introduced Nabokov to Myron C. Taylor (1874–1959), a Cornell graduate and benefactor from upstate New York, then chairman and chief executive officer of US Steel and later Roosevelt's envoy to the Vatican. Taylor was, at that time, chairman of the board of trustees of Wells College in Aurora, New York. Knowing that Wells was looking for a new head of its music department, Taylor recommended Nabokov, whom a fellow college trustee interviewed in Boston. Though Nabokov got seasick on the boat (then the cheapest way of getting from

New York to Boston), the interview went well, and it was agreed that a second interview would be arranged in New York with William Ernest Weld, the college president. According to the draft of Nabokov's autobiography, when Dr. Weld and his trustee presented themselves at the 39th Street studio on a Saturday morning in late May 1936, Nabokov, who had forgotten about the appointment, was in bed with a girlfriend, whom he had to hide in the bathroom.[87] While Dr. Weld may have had "the shock of his life" on seeing Nabokov's "Jungle" and unmade bed, that second interview, over lunch at the Harvard Club, nevertheless resulted in an invitation to visit the college the following month.[88]

Wells College, originally Wells Seminary, was established in 1868 by Henry Wells (1805–78), founder of the Wells Fargo and American Express Companies, in Aurora, New York, where Wells lived; his residence, Glen Park, later became part of the campus. Now co-educational, it was, when Nabokov visited it, as in fact through most of its history, a school for women.[89] This first visit in early June 1936, still under the guidance of the unidentified Bostonian trustee, was nearly idyllic. Nabokov took the train from New York to Syracuse, where he spent the night. The following morning, he was driven by the trustee to Aurora, stopping on the way in Ithaca to take a look at the Cornell campus, where, as he noted, "the trees and shrubbery in their June splendor seemed to be hiding from the viewer's eye the horrors of the buildings."[90] Following a second interview with President Weld, he was offered a one-year, renewable contract as chair of the music department. Taken on a walk, before his departure, to admire the sun setting over Lake Cayuga, he remembers thinking: "Yes, ...] it is beautiful . . . Beautiful. But is this to be my lake, my pink clouds, my sun?"[91] On the noisy, bumpy sleeper train that brought him back to New York that night, he had second thoughts. Yet he ended up accepting the offer.

In late June 1936, accompanied by his four-year-old son Ivan, who was living with his mother in New York, Nabokov sailed to Germany on a Hamburg-Amerika liner to visit his mother. Having undergone an operation, she was staying in Berlin with her daughter Onya. In celebration of the forthcoming Berlin Olympics, the boat was decked with Olympic and Nazi flags, with portraits of Hitler ubiquitous, especially one the size of an altarpiece in the dining room. Yet, what startled him "even more than the boat's festive decor was that nearly all the passengers and visitors, most of them unmistakably American, displayed either on their seersucker lapel or on their flowery summer dress, the Olympic sign with a small swastika pendant attached to it."[92] At dinner, Nabokov and his son had to listen to the band playing the Horst-Wessel-Lied, during which the German-American couple they were seated with stood up. Another American passenger, a representative from an ammunition factory in Minnesota, was heard complaining that American newspapers were "all sold to the Jews." In Berlin, there were Nazi flags and uniforms everywhere. Otherwise the city, which Nabokov was not to see again until the end of the war, was unchanged, "still the greenest and grandest capital of Central Europe."[93]

For Nabokov, this visit was the last with his mother. Happy though the reunion with her was, he recalled, "the instant I arrived I sensed that it was too late."

> Something inside her had snapped. The illness had invaded her. Instead of the strong, willful person that she used to be, with a gay, eager smile, she was someone else—someone full of gentle sweetness but also of a kind of resigned indifference. Her memory was failing. She would repeat the same sentence twice in a row. She did not ask any questions, nor did she want to know how long Ivan and I were to stay in Berlin. She spoke only of the past, but often could not finish the sentence she had started.[94]

Difficulties started the following day when Nabokov sought to change the mark coupons purchased before his departure. Though he had by then obtained from the immigration services his "First Papers," a preliminary to permanent resident status, he was still, in the eyes of the German bureaucracy, a stateless person, and it was in his Nansen passport that his visa had been stamped by the German Consulate in New York. When he presented himself at the bank, the cashier demanded that he produce a visa issued by the Imperial Committee for the Supervision of Stateless Persons of Russian Origin. Now this committee, as Nabokov heard from his sister, was currently headed by Sergei Taboritsky, his uncle Vladimir's assassin.[95] Rather than dealing with the *Reichskomitee*, Nabokov decided to bring up the matter with one of his old contacts at the Ministry of Foreign Affairs. He remembered, in particular, meeting a music-loving Staatsecretär, who came from a prosperous family of art publishers, and who was all the more influential since he was occasionally called upon to play Wagner medleys on the piano to soothe the Führer's fits of depression. The Staatscretär (not identified by name in Nabokov's papers) was immediately sympathetic to Nabokov's plight and, after giving instructions to his staff, took him for a drink at a nearby cafe. There, in a manner that brings to mind the events narrated in Lillian Hellman's *Pentimento*, he urged him to leave the country by the end of the week and asked him for his train number, so that the border police could be instructed to give him free passage.

Did Nabokov, in the course of this short stay, try to reestablish contact with Helene von Nostitz? Although he is silent on the subject, it is hard to believe that he would not have heard that she and her entourage had become since the early 1930s, in Kessler's words, "infected with Nazism."[96] One friend he did contact was Heinz Boese, the painter and caricaturist he knew from his stays at Hohenfinow with Bethmann-Hollweg. Among sardonic comments on the atmosphere of propaganda and police surveillance now pervasive in Germany, Boese told Nabokov he could not adapt to the "new reality" and was determined to escape the country with his wife as soon as he could. This Boese eventually did, settling in Argentina.[97]

The other friend Nabokov got in touch with in Berlin was Richard Möbius, the Saxon officer he had befriended at Askania-Nova and reestablished contact with in Stuttgart, by which time Möbius exhibited left-wing and even Communist sympathies. He had settled in Berlin in the mid-1920s, got married, had a child, and published essays (*Die Krisis der Kunst*, 1923), various prefaces to architecture books, and two novels (*Verwünschtes Gold* in 1927, *Meine Schwester Inge* in 1936). Although Nabokov had kept in touch with him after moving to Paris—his name and address (Kurfürtenstrasse 49, Berlin W35) appear in an address book dating from the late 1920s—he had come to find his friend "didactic and lacking in imagination and fantasy."[98] Besides, Möbius had little if any interest in music, especially contemporary music. Nonetheless, Nabokov was far from expecting the surprise that awaited him that afternoon in Berlin, at the Biergarten near the Hallensee train station where he had arranged to meet with Möbius, who appeared in Nazi uniform. Refusing to shake the hand his friend extended to him, Nabokov fled the scene and never tried to reestablish contact with Möbius until his death in 1952.[99]

Nabokov did not see his cousin Vladimir in Berlin in 1936; he and his wife were on a butterfly hunting expedition. As for Bethmann-Hollweg, Nabokov heard from Marie-Luise that her husband had been involved in a car accident. He suffered broken ribs, cuts to his nose and face, and a brain concussion, and was recovering in Eberswalde, forty miles to the north of Berlin. Though he made the trip, Nabokov was not able to visit Bethmann-Hollweg at the clinic. Marie-Luise confirmed the worrying news of their mutual friends he had already received from Boese. She told him about the threats on Albrecht von Bernstorff, who, after ten years as German envoy in London, had resigned in 1933 to protest the coming to power of the Nazis and had since become a *bête noire* of Hitler's foreign affairs minister, Joachim von Ribbentrop. Though he remained in Germany, Bernstorff became an "emigre from within." This was also the position of Bethmann-Hollweg, who belonged to "those who believe that Germans should not go away and leave their country in the hands of pigs"—a decision Nabokov understood and respected.[100] But was his car accident, Nabokov wondered, just an accident?

On Saturday that week, Nabokov, taking his leave from his mother for the last time, departed with his son. The helpful Staatsecretär came to bid him farewell at the Anhalten Bahnhof, explaining that he had had his office change the train tickets from third- to second-class sleeping-car, as the third class was full of soldiers; he also gave him a telephone number at which he could be reached immediately if needed. Nabokov might be in a position some day, he said, to repay the favor; indeed, the Staatsecretär "defected" during the war, helped the Allies in their intelligence work, and finally settled in Canada. After a long journey and a train change at Baden Baden, the travelers reached the border at Kehl. A first interview was followed, after a long wait, by a second interview by the Grenzpolizeiamt, with the officer particularly insistent on the subject of their religion. Then came another long wait, at the end of which the SS officer explained that they should have obtained an exit visa from the *Reichskomitee*, the nearest branch of which was in Frankfurt. Only when a telegram arrived from the Staatsecretär in Berlin did the Hauptmann agree to release them and have them taken straight to the border. Once in France, Nabokov and his son found Grunelius waiting for them at the Strasbourg train station.

By Nabokov's own account, this short trip to Nazi Germany in late June 1936, and especially the realization that a former friend was now a Nazi, triggered in him a kind of political awakening. Until then, he had shown little interest in politics. Having grown up in a liberal milieu, at least when he became close to his uncle Vladimir, he had become wary of the majority of European liberals' reluctance to see or say anything wrong about the Soviet Union and refusal to consider it a totalitarian regime comparable in many ways to Fascist Italy and Nazi Germany. As a typical example of this attitude, Nabokov singled out André Malraux, whom he heard give what he thought was an extraordinarily doctrinaire speech on the Spanish Civil War in New York in March 1937, a speech he likened to the "Politgram lecture" he had been given by his Bolshevist tutor in Petrograd after hearing Lenin address the crowd.[101] Paradoxically, as Nabokov noted, some of the fiercest defenders of Communist Russia in the 1930s came around after the Second World War to opposite views, to the point of supporting the most extremist anti-Communist policies. Never an extremist himself, Nabokov began to "find himself," politically speaking, as an anti-fascist.

One of Nabokov's first political gestures, that summer of 1936, was to get Grunelius to drive him to Basel to visit a friend just released from a Nazi jail. He had no Swiss visa, but Grunelius had the right contacts—including a future Swiss ambassador to France. Nabokov spent most of the night talking to his friend and "getting first-hand information about what it was like to be a Nazi victim."[102]

While at Kolbsheim, in August 1936 Nabokov was joined for a couple of days by Cecil Beaton, whom he took to Colmar to see the Isenheim Altarpiece.[103] Shortly afterward, he was reunited with Beaton at Schloss Kammer, which, in Beaton's words, became, that summer, "a sort of kindergarten for extraordinary grown-ups; long, hilarious discussions; incongruous groups for lunch, for tea, for swimming, for sightseeing. We rode and went shooting in the mountains. At night on the lake, we ate gay dinners on rafts by torchlight, with music provided from adjoining barques."[104] Beaton's lively account also suggests that, behind its "timeless Hansel-and-Gretel quality," the chateau was also a center of "jealous intrigue and romantic complications," and there is evidence that Nabokov had an affair with one of the Hoffmannsthals' female guests that summer.[105] The house party included the writer and socialite David Herbert, son of the Earl of Pembroke, the artist Rex Whistler, and the two daughters of the Marquess of Anglesey, Lady

Caroline and Lady Elizabeth Paget; the last named was to become Hoffmansthal's second wife. The youngest guest was the seventeen-year-old Ivan Moffat, the future Hollywood screenwriter, grandson of Herbert Beerbohm Tree. Beaton's diaries, like the photographs he took of Nabokov in 1935–36, wonderfully capture the composer's ebullient personality:

> Nicholas Nabokoff arrived belatedly from Alsace, his vitality unsurpassed. Most people stagger off a night train incapable of speech for a while. But the journey has been like champagne to Nicolas. He bubbled now with great effervescence. In the early mornings, before the rest of the household had stirred, he would come into my room while I was having breakfast and read me the lectures on music that he planned to give during the winter at Wells College in New York . . . or perhaps I would find some morning's letter interesting enough to read to him.[106]

For Beaton, the magic of the summer came to an abrupt end when he received a telegram recalling him to London, where his father had suddenly died.

Nabokov's first "season in college hell," as he entitled—after Rimbaud—one of the unpublished chapters of his autobiography,[107] began in early September 1936 with another train ride: a sleeper from New York to Ithaca, where he changed to "a single ramshackle carriage pulled by an ancient engine that ran on those rusty lakeside tracks connecting Ithaca with Geneva."[108] At the Aurora train station, he was met by his music department colleague Carl Parrish and his wife Catherine, the college nurse, who took him to "the Prophet's Chambers," as the college guest rooms were called, where he stayed until "the huge Victorian house on the lakeside" the college had found for him was ready.[109] In October, Nabokov's wife and son joined him, but Natalie returned to New York after a month. He accordingly modified his living arrangements, moving into the house of the Rev. Allen, a Presbyterian minister, where he rented two rooms on the second floor. He prepared his own meals but ate them with Allen, his wife, and their two boys. Though the Rev. Allen, a teetotaler, frowned at his serving wine to his students, he was, Nabokov recalled, "immensely generous and compassionate."[110] The Allens had a housekeeper, a large, Seventh-Adventist African American woman named Mabel. Jean Allen, the Reverend's wife, completed Nabokov's culinary education, to the extent that he was soon able to entertain his landlords for dinner in their own home. To facilitate his weekend escapes to the city, he acquired a second-hand Ford soon after his arrival. When winter came, however, Nabokov realized that driving was impractical. He stopped doing it after a disastrous experience in December 1936, after a weekend spent with the Hofmannsthals at the Gladstone Hotel on the occasion of a Toscanini concert at Carnegie Hall: the return journey, in snowy weather, took more than twenty-four hours instead of the usual seven.

Did Nabokov attempt to reestablish contact with Prokofiev when the latter, just before he definitively resettled in the Soviet Union, gave a concert at Carnegie Hall in January 1937? Or on his subsequent visit, when he and Lina both performed at a musicale at the American-Russian Institute on March 28, 1938, as part of what turned out to be his last tour abroad?[111] If so, Nabokov has left no written recollections of their reunion.

In the spring of 1937, when Stravinsky was in New York to supervise the world premiere of his ballet *Jeu de cartes* at the Metropolitan Opera, Nabokov briefly resumed relations with the Russian master, from whom he had been estranged since the early 1930s. In 1935, he had contacted Stravinsky, on Balanchine's behalf, about the Stravinsky festival Balanchine was planning with Kirstein, but there is no evidence that Stravinsky responded.[112] The two performances of *Jeu de cartes*, in a program that also included *Le baiser de la fée* and *Apollo*—the retitled *Apollon musagète*—took place at the end of April. Nabokov was in New York on break from Wells, and attended one of them, no doubt at Balanchine's invitation. (It may be during that same week that he saw *The Eternal Road*, the English adaptation of Weill and Werfel's *Der Weg der Verheissung*, at the Manhattan Opera House; he found it "pretty poor as a didactic play but beautifully staged by Reinhardt.")[113] His unexpected reunion with Stravinsky took place "in a now-defunct Park-and-Tilford milk-bar, since then replaced by the diamond bar of Tiffany's."

> "What are you doing here and in God's name, what are you drinking?" Stravinsky's voice said from behind my back, as I was [. . .] sipping my beloved Acidophilus milk, now unobtainable in New York.
>
> "I thought you were a professor in a college," Stravinsky's voice continued, "impregnating American girls . . ."[114]

Stravinsky was in the company of the Polish emigre violinist Samuel Dushkin, for whom Stravinsky had written the *Duo concertant* in 1932.

> "I was pleased beyond words because Stravinsky's voice had no trace of resentment, it was gay and friendly. But I resisted the temptation to show my pleasure by embracing him as we usually did in the summer of 1930 in our Pleyel studios."
>
> "Stravinsky asked me all sorts of questions about America, about my life in it, and he told me that he was on tour with Sam Dushkin and soon ready to go home ("thank God!")."[115]

Nabokov was invited to a rehearsal of the *Duo concertant*, which he did not know, at Dushkin's home.

> "I [. . .] was amazed, as I always am, by the constancy of [Stravinsky's] imaginative power, and above all by the constancy of his Russian "essence," ever present under whatever formal or stylistic garb he chose to disguise it."[116]

This was the only contact Nabokov had with Stravinsky until the war.

At Wells, Nabokov had under his care about thirty young women, to whom he was generally known as "Nabby." He got on well with his two colleagues, Mary Duncan, the organist, who taught beginning theory courses, and Parrish, who taught the piano and the harpsichord. Nabokov himself taught harmony and theory, music history (together with Mary Duncan), and conducted the college choir; his nominal duties also included composition, except that there were no students interested or sufficiently equipped. He also taught a course in Russian history. The courses that gave him the most trouble were the ones described in the college catalogue as "Music Appreciation Survey I" and "Music Appreciation Survey II." The first was supposed to cover twelve centuries, from Greek music to J. S. Bach; the second went from Bach to the twentieth century. They were open to all students without any prerequisites, such as knowledge of musical notation or a background in European history. Since most students taking those courses could not read music, examples had to be drawn from gramophone records. Nabokov, who had no previous experience of the American educational system, considered the whole idea "intellectual humbug." "How could an unprepared youngster," he wondered, "whose musical environment at home had been whatever came out of the radio or a jukebox, acquire in two academic years (i.e., fourteen months) any kind of 'appreciation' of the whole Western musical tradition?"[117] Now, by tradition, these courses had to be taught by the department chair. His predecessor, a cellist from Germany, had found an easy way to fulfill this obligation: he would bring his instrument to class and play his examples on the cello, "whether it was a four-part sixteenth-century madrigal (he'd play the upper part), or the vocal line of a Mozart aria, or the themes of a Beethoven symphony."[118] Since there was no piano—or pianist—he would hum the accompaniment of a Beethoven or Brahms cello sonata, occasionally interrupting his recital to make some vague aesthetic comments. Nabokov found himself in the situation of having "to improvise a way of transforming these courses into something intellectually defensible and not [. . .] a more or less pleasant pastime for the victimized students."[119] He and Mary Duncan taught their charges elements of musical notation, had them follow the score while listening to musical examples, and tried to recruit as many as possible for the college choir. After the experience of his first year, to the dismay of faculty colleagues, he changed not only the title of those courses but their contents and character. They were renamed Introduction to music history I and II, and enrollment was made subject to one year of music theory. The two weekly one-hour lectures became two sessions of two hours each, consisting of a one-hour lecture followed by musical examples and discussion. "I regarded those history courses," Nabokov later wrote, "to be a complementary element to the intellectual history of Western civilization and have always pointed out in my lectures the relation of the art of music to the other arts, its role in history and in society. Instead of reading vulgar 'survey of music' history textbooks, I had my students read and discuss important classical texts on musical aesthetics using in class the Socratic or Aristotelian dialogical method"—a method to which he had been introduced by Maritain.[120]

As we have just seen, Nabokov took his pedagogical responsibilities at Wells very seriously. Yet, he claimed he was always uncomfortable with the teaching routine and did not feel equal to the task. Most of his knowledge, he thought, had come to him through life experience rather than from instruction. As a result, he realized (as any honest teacher is bound to realize at some point), there were gaps in his command of the subjects he had to teach, such as music theory and musical aesthetics.

> To fill those gaps I had to study a great deal of new material. I had to read systematically many dull books but above all analyze and memorize a large quantity of music scores. This took a great deal of my time away from my own work as a composer. Instead of composing music, I spent most of my time preparing myself for my lectures, correcting papers, rehearsing my choir, and acquiring indispensable knowledge for my teaching schedule. As a result, I felt doubly frustrated at Wells College. I felt isolated from the stimulus of life in a capital and unable to carry out my work as a composer.[121]

On a more positive note, as he later recognized, Nabokov vastly profited from the resources of the Wells College music library, which, to his delight, turned out to be surprisingly rich. Its resources included Monteverdi's complete works in Malipiero's edition, the Purcell Society edition of Purcell's works, the Leipzig edition of Palestrina, and, above all, a substantial run of the second and third Denkmäler series of medieval music (*Denkmäler der Deutschen Tonkunst* and *Denkmäler der Oesterreichischen Tonkunst*), "grandest of all universal guides through the *musique savante* of Europe, from the middle ages through the Renaissance."[122] These areas, as Nabokov confessed, were practically unknown to him. In Russia, Western music began with Bach and Handel; Monteverdi was just a mythic name; as for Palestrina, Nabokov remembered him chiefly as the pretext for dry counterpoint exercises in Juon's class in Berlin. Later, in France, he had expanded his modern musical culture; however, for the French avant-garde composers he associated with, music had to be, if not "made in," at least "approved by" Paris. The Wells College library thus suddenly opened up vast musical horizons. Discovering medieval modal music, especially, was for Nabokov a "profoundly personal experience," a way of connecting—or rather reconnecting—with a lost world which he realized had always appealed to him, since childhood, much more deeply than the tonal tradition in which he had been schooled in Germany. It was, as he put it, like discovering "a new continent, a new world of musical imagination and craftsmanship."

I marveled at the beauty of this new world, at the vastness of its horizons, the variety of its forms, its styles, and techniques, and at the incredible skill of its craftsmen. Perhaps because of my own Russian roots, the modal world of Medieval music seemed at once so attractive to me. At times, while transcribing a Motet or a Chanson, I would feel projected into the life of those remote centuries.[123]

The five years he spent at Wells were therefore an important step in Nabokov's own musical development.

Relations with colleagues outside the music department were, on the whole, pleasant. Among the Wells faculty members Nabokov befriended were the poet Richard Armour, the art historian J. J. Lankes, the historian George Ridgeway, and a Greek scholar named John Tyler. He particularly liked Jean Davis, head of the sociology and economics department; a Russophile, she was "one of the few people in those early years who was able to make the distinction between the Russian people and their Bolshevik rulers."[124] His relations with President Weld were excellent. An economist who had served as head of the American College in Beirut, Weld was "immensely shy and equally kind," and took to Nabokov and treated him "like one would treat a wayward son."[125] On the Wells student body, Nabokov had mixed views. Many of those young women, he granted, had "refined and even beautiful features and some [. . .] had bright, eager eyes that betrayed latent gifts of the mind"; but, given his own strict European upbringing, and the fact that he had had no previous contacts with American youth, he was put off by their carefree manners, slovenly speech, poor cultural knowledge (for a certain young woman from Toledo, Ohio, "Michelangelo" only meant an Italian dressing brand),[126] and gum-chewing habits, even at choir rehearsal ("I had to tell them repeatedly that gum chewing while singing does not enhance anybody's diction or enunciation").[127]

Nabokov's duties at Wells included forming and conducting a choir that sang in Chapel on Sundays at a service called Vespers, though it took place at 11 a.m. At Vespers President Weld gave a short sermon and a few hymns were sung. As soon as school started in September 1936, tryouts were held, following which about twenty women were selected. The quality of the voices, he thought, was good, but many of his singers sang out of tune and could not read music. They were, however, fast learners, and after about three weeks of intense ear-training and sight-reading he and Mary Duncan had at their disposal "a band of dedicated choir members who could sing honorably four-part *a cappella* pieces and read them, so to speak, by heart."[128] The number of rehearsals was increased, but attendance was a problem, since choir singing, though an indispensable feature of college life, was nevertheless considered an extracurricular activity. At "Vespers," in addition to the "oozy and oily Presbyterian hymns in their nineteenth-century harmonic garb,"

Nabokov had his choir perform at least one piece of "good polyphonic music."[129] He also organized four or five concerts a year, at which the choir sang pieces from various centuries, from the Middle Ages to the modern period, arranged for women's voices by Nabokov or his colleague.

A few of the arrangements of polyphonic music Nabokov realized for women's voices during his time at Wells have survived. Some are settings of poems by Joyce, Rilke, and Yeats, later published under the heading *Silent Songs*. Others are medieval Russian chants, which he harmonized. One is an English version of one of the religious choruses from Mussorgsky's *Boris Godunov*. There is also a setting of the Lord's Prayer, dated January 17, 1939, later rearranged by Nabokov for mixed choir—a version which was published in 1946.

Nabokov's first year at Wells College ended in triumph with two major public events. The first one was a "grand benefit dinner" served on the lawn adjacent to the College Inn. It was cooked by Nabokov and a team consisting of Mabel, the Allens' housekeeper, his colleague Mary Duncan, Jean Davis, the sociology professor, and a few students. The menu was beef Stroganoff and cucumber salad, followed by a fruit salad abundantly flavored with kirsch, the whole washed down with Chianti procured in nearby Auburn, Aurora being a dry town. The benefit was dedicated to all "victims of fascism." This antagonized the head of the German department, "a boorish Bavarian to whom the two masterpieces of German literature were Wagner's libretti and Hitler's *Mein Kampf*," and who, in the fall of the same year, hosted at Wells the photographic exhibition the German Consulate was then circulating to glorify the Berlin Olympics.[130] He complained to the college administration that the event violated American neutrality, but President Weld supported Nabokov.

The second event Nabokov organized in the spring of 1937 was a student production of Sophocles's *Oedipus Rex*, which he directed and designed, with the assistance of an able Oberlin graduate named Woody Woodruff, and for which he set to music choruses to be sung by his choir. Set on the Yeats translation (while the play itself was given in the 1920 translation by John Tressider Sheppard), they have a strong archaic flavor, being in unison and making abundant use of "open" intervals. Nabokov consulted with his classicist colleague John Tyler, who helped with scansion and explained to him some of the conventions of Greek drama. Presented as part of the Commencement, the play was a big success with the Wells community and the parents and families of the graduating class. Friends of Nabokov came to Aurora to see it, including Horst, who photographed it for *Vogue*. Several faculty members criticized the "filthy-looking" picture of Greece conveyed by the production, but Nabokov, who was familiar with Cocteau's own retelling of the Oedipus myth, had deliberately chosen to stay away from a sanitized, conventional idea of classical antiquity, choosing instead to present "a dirty-looking, pestiferous Mycenean Greece in its stark, hybris-laden decadence."[131] His Wells contract was duly renewed for two years.

8

Engagement and Americanization

ALTHOUGH, BY ACCEPTING an academic appointment, Nabokov had put his career as composer on the back burner, his preoccupations did not exclusively focus on teaching. He hoped, in particular, to resume his collaboration with Balanchine, with whom he had regularly been in touch since the choreographer's move to New York in October 1933. Not only did they get on perfectly—Madeleine Malraux, on being introduced to Balanchine by Nabokov more than three decades later, recalled them as being "almost like brothers"[1]—they became, in a manner of speaking, each other's student: soon after his arrival, Balanchine brushed up his harmony and counterpoint with Nabokov, who, in turn, during the six weeks he spent with Balanchine in Connecticut in the summer of 1935, learned from him how to cook ("rule no. 1: no cookbooks").[2] Balanchine was also close to Natalie Nabokov, and remained an intimate friend of hers even after she and her husband went their separate ways. In February 1936, Balanchine and Nabokov were both involved in the famous Paper Ball which marked the culmination of the Hartford Festival organized by Chick Austin at the Wadsworth Atheneum. Nabokov, along with George Antheil and Vernon Duke, was recruited to compose music for the occasion, notably a *danse des chiffonniers* performed by, among others, Balanchine, Lincoln Kirstein, and Eddie Warburg—the three founders of the New York City Ballet—costumed by Tchelitchew as beggars.[3]

Relations between Kirstein and Nabokov were difficult at the beginning, especially since Muriel Draper, Kirstein's friend and confidante throughout the 1930s, evidently took an instant dislike to the composer.[4] Yet, after Balanchine's appointment as ballet master at the Metropolitan Opera in the summer of 1935, it was Kirstein who enlisted Nabokov's collaboration for a long-standing ballet project based on *Uncle Tom's Cabin*. It was originally planned in 1934 with a scenario by E. E. Cummings, who published it in book form in 1935. At this initial stage, Virgil Thomson was approached to write the music, and Balanchine himself was slated to appear as Tom.[5] To Kirstein's disappointment, the project collapsed, partly over Balanchine's lack of enthusiasm for Cummings's scenario.[6] Though not yet involved, Nabokov himself was acquainted with Cummings, whom he had met through Caresse Crosby—if we are to believe the testimony of Barnes, whose account of Cummings is "a drunkard who has had high success as a poet and writer."[7]

Kirstein tried to revive the *Tom* project, this time with a scenario of his own and with sets and costumes by Ben Shahn. Based on the drafts preserved at Lincoln Center, this "ballet manifesto" was an ambitious work, scenically and musically, with choruses and passages sung, spoken, or in *Sprechgesang*: it was, in short, a ballet-cantata or ballet-oratorio along the lines of some of Nabokov's earlier productions, and involving singers and actors as well as dancers. Nabokov drafted a very large part, if not the entirety, of the music in short score. He, Kirstein, and Balanchine presented the work at a meeting of the 1936 Met Spring Season Committee. That meeting did not go well. *Tom* was supposed to be staged as a double bill with Gluck's *Orpheus and Eurydice*, choreographed by Balanchine and with sets by Tchelitchew. Nabokov made, according to Kirstein, a "courteous and excellent speech" when *Tom* came under discussion. Of the two projects, in fact, *Orpheus* was deemed the more controversial, since the singers were supposed to be in the pit while the dancers were on the stage—an idea that struck John Erskine (the head of the Juilliard School) and Edward Johnson, the Met director, as "the height of absurdity."[8] After the meeting, Tchelitchew and Nabokov suggested to Kirstein and Balanchine that they stage the double bill independently from the Met, with the help of a sponsor like Edward James or by forming a committee of "rich old ladies" to subsidize it.[9] In the end, *Orpheus* was mounted by the Met, where it was poorly received and withdrawn after two performances in late May 1936. As for *Tom*, unfortunately for Nabokov, it was shelved for good. The only completed part of the project is a four-part *a cappella* chorus for women's voices, *Little Eva's Death*, on words by Kirstein, recycled for the Wells College choir from the original for solo bass. When the chorus was published in 1946, a reviewer described it as a "pleasant combination of Moussorgsky and the Negro spiritual."[10] If the entire ballet had been completed, *Tom* would have been, along with *Union Pacific*, the most "American" of Nabokov's scores.

It was through Kirstein that Nabokov met a young American composer with whom he was to develop an exceptionally warm and long-lasting artistic, intellectual, and personal friendship "unclouded by professional rivalry."[11] Born in 1908, Elliott Carter, after receiving his BA and MA at Harvard, where Kirstein was his classmate, had gone to Paris in 1932 to study with Nadia Boulanger and at the École normale de musique. He had, at that time, become aware of Nabokov's music. He himself did not much care for *Short Stories*, which he had purchased by chance, but was more impressed with *Les valses de Beethoven* in June 1933, and even more so the following year with *Union Pacific*, which he found "brilliantly orchestrated" (not realizing at the time that the credit went partly to Edward Powell).[12] When Carter returned to America, he turned to Nabokov for help, at Kirstein's suggestion, with the orchestration of the *Tarantella* he wrote for the Harvard Glee Club. Every three or four weeks, in late 1936 and early 1937, Carter would visit Nabokov in Aurora and look over the orchestration with him. "Someday you will be able to orchestrate much better than I," Nabokov told his pupil, who, much later, cited this comment as characteristic of Nabokov's innate generosity.[13] As for the instruction he had given Leo Smit, Nabokov refused to take any payment, so Carter made it a habit to bring a case of wine or liquor. The premiere of the *Tarantella* took place in March 1937. "The orchestration," Carter recalls, "was very brilliant but there were problems: you couldn't hear the Harvard Glee Club. Nabokov had not thought about that aspect. Yet everyone liked it, it was very noisy."[14] The following year, at Wells, in conjunction with a student performance of *The Beggars' Opera*, Nabokov conducted his choir in the first performance of Elliott Carter's *Let's Be Gay*, for women's chorus and two pianos, on a text by John Gay.[15] A close friendship grew out of these first contacts. Nabokov introduced Carter to Natalie and Ivan, whom Carter remembered taking to the circus in New York. Similarly, when Carter married Helen Frost-Jones on Cape Cod, in July 1939, Nabokov was his best man. After the ceremony they all went to a Greek restaurant in Chatham.[16]

The serious artistic setback Nabokov suffered with the shelving of *Tom* was followed, in the spring of 1937, by a crisis of a more personal nature. In his production of the Sophocles *Oedipus*, Nabokov had cast in the title role a twenty-year-old Wells student who had impressed him with her "deep, velvety and powerful voice." Named Constance Holladay, "she was not only good-looking, but charmingly intelligent and possessed a splendid sense of humor."[17] Nabokov fell intensely in love with her, but she had a steady boyfriend. He may also have pondered the ethical problem posed by the fact that she was one of his students. The emotional strain, combined with the stress of the *Oedipus* rehearsals, resulted for Nabokov in a nervous breakdown at the end of June. After being hospitalized for a week in Rochester, he was sent to recover, thanks to a loan from the college arranged by President Weld, in a mental hospital in Hartford, Connecticut ("The Hartford Retreat").

It was an odd, a Hollywoodian, unreal place, the kind I had never seen before. It was cluttered with businessmen, film or theater producers and a whole array of presidents and vice presidents. They were all being cured either from an alcoholic addiction, or from an expensive nervous breakdown. Nearly all of them were bores.[18]

Nabokov himself was diagnosed as suffering from extreme exhaustion, his condition being described as "manic depressive psychosis—manic type."[19] Nor was the health crisis without physical sequels, since Nabokov was left with partial paralysis of the left side of his face, a trait that is apparent in some later photographs.

Despite the strict overseeing of his pavilion by an elderly matron, Nabokov, when he was not composing, managed a few escapades while at the Hartford Retreat with a "dark-eyed Irish beauty" who drove an exiguous Ford coupe. He kept in touch with her for a year, at the end of which she married the president of a bottling company. When he left the sanatorium, feeling "unhappy and guilty [. . .] like a minor Amfortas,"[20] Nabokov must have grieved at the thought of being cut off from his beloved Alsatian retreat. He was rescued from his depression by his New York patron Marion Dougherty, who took him under her wing and put him up in the summer house she owned on a tiny bay island off Southampton, Long Island.

Marion Dougherty, then in her early fifties, was a well-traveled and well-connected woman with a generous heart, who was particularly keen on helping newcomers to America. She herself had musical interests. Her main foible, according to Nabokov, was a tendency to bossiness, which she displayed in equal measure towards her staff and her house guests. When Nabokov stayed with her that summer of 1937, she tried repeatedly, but unsuccessfully, to coax him into pleasures he abhorred, like sunbathing, which did not agree with the nature of his skin, and swimming, which he had lamentably attempted in the Black Sea during his youth. Prone to seasickness, he had, besides, no affinities with the Hamptons beach crowd, a group that, with its clear lack of artistic or intellectual interests, reminded him of its pre-Revolutionary equivalent in Russia. Fortunately, the house was equipped with a piano. During his stay with Marion Dougherty, Nabokov composed a set of six songs on poems by Max Jacob, *L'aubépin et cinq autres mélodies*, which was published the following year with a dedication to her. Nothing more precise is known about this project, no correspondence between Nabokov and the poet having survived from that period.[21] But it suggests that Nabokov was keen to find ways of keeping his Parisian connections alive. Also that summer, Nabokov composed a string quartet in three movements entitled *Serenata estiva*. According to a note in the manuscripts of the violin and cello parts, it was written partly on Long Island and on Ram Island, the small island off the Connecticut coast, the site of a Victorian era hotel that did not survive the 1938 hurricane. As revealed by the inscription "about C[onstance]" in the same manuscript, the piece was inspired by his new love.

Marion Dougherty's sister Edith also had a summer house in the Hamptons. As large as Marion was thin, and less exuberant, she was equally generous and hospitable. She also had strong musical interests and chaired the board of the New York Schola Cantorum, the choir closely associated, at the time, with the

New York Philharmonic. Its British-born conductor, Hugh Ross, befriended Nabokov and he and the Schola gave New York performances of *Ode*, in January 1935, and, two years later, the *Oedipus* choruses. Reginald Fincke, Edith's husband, was a wealthy member of the New York Stock Exchange. At a luncheon at the Finckes' that summer of 1937, Nabokov was introduced to Judge Billings Learned Hand, whose wife Frances was Fincke's sister.[22] Born in Albany in 1872, Learned Hand (known to his intimates as "Bee") had served since 1924 as a judge on the Court of Appeals for the Second District, the most important federal court below the Supreme Court. He was "the first truly great American" Nabokov had met, and he put it, and he has left a fascinating account of the conversations they had that summer. Not included in the published version of *Bagázh*, this account was recently discovered in Nabokov's papers and published in 2012 in *The Yale Review*.

Learned Hand, Nabokov recalled, had an extraordinary appearance.

> I had never before in my life seen, or imagined, a face and a head like Judge Hand's. [. . .]It was the head of a thoroughbred Anglo-Saxon American. He had deep-seated, dark eyes overcast by inordinately bushy eyebrows. Over those brows was a noble forehead topped by unruly, peppery, but still largely dark hair. His whole face, but especially his eyes, had a permanent expression of poise and serenity, and a strangely compassionate sadness. Yet, when he smiled or laughed, as he often did, the expression of sadness and compassion gave way to an ironic twinkle in his eyes and a kind of childlike mischief. When he frowned, the contrary happened. His face grew stern and severe, but never cross or angry. When he raised his cloud-like brows, the expression on his face turned to what seemed to be total astonishment.[23]

Hand, who had a "boundless, voracious interest in people" and had "an unquenchable desire to learn something new from his interlocutor,"[24] clearly took a special interest in the White Russian composer befriended by his brother and sister-in-law. During the long walks they took together in Southampton, they talked about Russian literature, in which the erudite Hand had a particular interest, because, as he put it, writers like Chekhov, Tolstoy, and Turgenev had "an extraordinary dedication to truth."[25] About Russian history, he was not as well informed. Nabokov, as his account suggests, took special pride in telling Hand that, thanks to his grandfather's role as Alexander II's justice minister, pre-Revolutionary Russia had "the most liberal judicial structure of all continental Europe."[26] Unlike other intellectuals Nabokov had met in Western Europe and in New York, Hand harbored no illusions about the nature of the Soviet regime. He was especially curious to know why the Bolshevist putsch had succeeded so quickly and without stronger opposition; this was a question Nabokov was hardly equipped to answer adequately at the time.

Hand's curiosity was prompted by his concern, as a judge, about the dangers of tyrannical government and the ways such dangers could be prevented. Nor did he fail, unlike many anti-fascist intellectuals in the 1930s (the young Cartier-Bresson for one), to see that all forms of totalitarianism are similar. On Long Island, his indignation was aroused when a young neighbor of Edith and Reginald Fincke, at a Saturday luncheon, began to extol the beauties of Nazi Germany, which he had visited two years before, describing a Nuremberg parade as "stimulating." Hand sternly rebuked the young man in front of the assembled company.

A music lover, Hand had traditional tastes, bred by his attendance at Boston Symphony Orchestra concerts in his Harvard days and the New York Philharmonic since. He therefore was not much familiar with twentieth-century music, save for the "tons of Sibelius and Richard Strauss" one heard in America at the time. *Boris Godunov* had made a powerful impression on him at the Paris Opera in 1908, but Nabokov (never a totally unqualified admirer of the work in any case) could not help deplore that Hand had been exposed to it in a version "abominably deformed" by Rimsky's orchestral "manipulations."[27]

After the summer was over, Nabokov remained in touch with Learned Hand, visiting him at his East 65th Street townhouse (much later occupied by Richard Nixon, one of Hand's *bêtes noires*). On a deeper level, this encounter with one of the great names in twentieth-century American judicial history no doubt contributed to his political awakening, as had his short exposure to the realities of Nazi Germany.

After his stay at Marion Dougherty's in late August, Nabokov spent three weeks in Connecticut as the guest of Balanchine at his studio, a converted barn that had been put at his disposal by his patron Alice De La Mar. When Nabokov returned to Aurora that fall for his second year, after visiting his wife and son in New York, he found himself torn between nostalgia for the insouciant, frivolous life he had once enjoyed in the city and, on the other hand, feelings of hopelessness about "night falling over Europe," as Maritain put it in a letter Nabokov found waiting for him at Wells. Braving the opinion of the vast majority of French Catholics, Maritain had taken a public position against Franco in the Spanish Civil War; he also denounced the antii-Semitic persecutions in Nazi Germany.[28] "Then," Nabokov recalled, "very gradually, during the next two days and nights, something firm and resolute began to take shape in me, something I had very seldom felt before in my wayward, irresponsible and playful life."

> I felt that everyone now, however grand or small his station—and first of all I—even here, in Aurora—must do my duty, must carry my share of a burden that is manifold, far beyond the forces of any one single person. It is a moral obligation. It has become our lot. No one, no one should shirk it. I felt that the time is ripe, much riper than I or anyone thought it was.[29]

Another letter Nabokov found on his return came from Vilnius, the Lithuanian capital. It was from his sister and contained the news that their mother's health was declining rapidly and she asked for him. A few weeks later, a telegram informed him that she had died in Vilnius on November 11. It was thus in a melancholy frame of mind that Nabokov started working on his most ambitious work of the decade, his second symphony, which he started sketching at the end of 1937.

The Wells College community, that autumn, was being itself increasingly drawn into political controversy, with the faculty and student body divided into several camps. The Bavarian Nazi-sympathizer who headed the German Department had his own following of students, mostly from the Midwest and bearing Teutonic names. While a few faculty members had idealistic Communist sympathies, a much larger group, both faculty and students, consisted of undecided neutralists. In addition to Nabokov, the anti-Nazi camp included George Ridgeway, the historian, George Tyler, the classicist, and Jean Davis, the sociologist. Beginning in the spring of 1938, with a view to counteracting the "strong isolationist strain that prevailed among Wells students and a large segment of its faculty," Nabokov and Ridgeway held Friday evening sessions on current affairs, during which they distributed information on the political situation in Europe.[30] Students got involved as well, typing and distributing the material to be discussed at those sessions. One of the most active was a young woman named Jean, who came from a prosperous Jewish Southern family and was unusually knowledgeable in contemporary music and poetry. Offended by the German professor's pro-Hitler stance, she stopped greeting him when their paths crossed, and she argued passionately with other students about the need to fight Nazism. Nabokov befriended her from her freshman year as well as her best friend Pat, an English exchange-student. When she was a senior, Jean was caught spending the night with a college professor at a local inn. The professor was dismissed; Jean was expelled and eventually moved to Brazil, where she committed suicide during the war.[31]

Nabokov's own personal life took a happier turn. Having broken up with her boyfriend, Constance, now a junior, began to reciprocate his feelings, which prompted the inevitable gossip. President Weld, made aware in due course that the head of his music department was courting one of his students "much too ostentatiously," seems to have harbored infinite indulgence towards his Russian import.[32] Summoning him to his office, he advised him, from one man of the world to another, that it would be best if Nabokov could find a way of meeting his "lady friend" outside the Wells campus, preferably in the woods. This resulted in Constance getting a rash of poison ivy—according to Nabokov a common occurrence among Wells students from May onwards.[33]

The reforms Nabokov had introduced into the teaching of music at Wells began to bear fruit in his second year. The level of his choir rose appreciably, which made it possible to venture into a more ambitious repertory, such as Monteverdi and

Purcell, or medieval masters like Machaut and Josquin. On occasions, the choir was supplemented by male voices from neighboring colleges and a small instrumental ensemble. They were thus able to perform baroque or classical works in original form: for example, in December 1938, Nabokov conducted at Wells Mozart's rarely heard Mass in D Minor, K. 65. One of his new choral recruits turned out to be the possessor of a first-rate contralto voice, who as well was a "sweet, warmhearted, gay, and enterprising person, plumpish like her voice, but absolutely indefatigable as a co-worker and as a student"; named Mary Davenport (1919–2010), she became a professional singer and, after the war, a member of the Zurich Opera Company.[34] At the 1938 Commencement, as in the previous year, Nabokov staged a play, this time Milton's *Samson Agonistes*, for which he wrote incidental music; Constance was the Samson. The experience was repeated the following year with George Bernard Shaw's *Androcles and the Lion*, and in 1940 with Shakespeare's *The Tempest*. In this final production, Ariel was invisible, his voice seemingly coming out of a light, like a will o' the wisp. The production also made use of Bengal lights and Roman candles, thanks to a pyrotechnician Nabokov's assistant had discovered in Auburn or Syracuse. This caused alarm at the local fire department and President Wells had to obtain a special dispensation from the State Commissioner in Albany. Unfortunately, the permit arrived at the last minute and the effects could not be properly rehearsed: there was, as a result, a lot of smoke and stench, especially since the performance took place indoors.[35]

All in all, these theatricals, mounted on a shoestring budget—occasionally supplemented by his and the students' modest funds—were Nabokov's happiest recollection of Wells College.

> It was an admirable collective effort, the closest I had come to see the workings of a true "commune," although none of us dreamt of calling it that way. In more ways than one [. . .] this communal effort [. . .] brought me closer to the students of Wells than to their staid, and largely conventional teachers.[36]

In 1937–38, with Nabokov's affair with Constance in full bloom, there were fewer incentives for him to escape to the city as often as he did during his first year. Yet he made a point of being in touch with emigre musicians he knew from Germany or France when they arrived in New York. He also took the opportunity to invite musicians to Aurora. Copland came to lecture on a particularly foul day that winter and expressed his dismay at the surroundings ("I don't understand how you can stand it," Nabokov reports him as saying).

> Considering the weather Aaron's conference was well attended. The girls asked questions and seemed "politely interested." After the lecture there

was the usual, strictly "dry" music department reception (coke, ginger ale, coffee, tea, and cake). Timid, tedious, but fortunately brief.

I walked Aaron back to the Inn at the other end of town. The wind had subsided, but driving was still impossible. We waded through snow-drifts holding each other by the arm, slipping and stumbling like a pair of drunk-ards. "Boy!" Aaron exclaimed, giggling, "you should write a symphony and call it *La Sibérie américaine.*"

We were both frozen when we reached the Inn. As I was saying good-night to Aaron in the glum hallway, he looked at me solicitously: "You shouldn't stay here, Nicky," he said. "People are apt to forget about you when you are far from the centers. This is the way things are in America. And you cannot afford to be forgotten. Can't you get yourself at least a . . . warmer job?" And he giggled again. "Can't Koussie help? Should I talk to him?"

Early next morning, my colleague Carl Parrish drove him to his next lecture at Cornell.[37]

Yet, at the end of Nabokov's second year, no opportunity had arisen. He still owed the college money for the loan incurred to pay for his 1937 sanatorium stay, and there was no alternative except to remain at Wells for at least another year.

The words Nabokov put in Copland's mouth about the long-term risk his geo-graphical isolation posed for his career as a composer must have been a linger-ing preoccupation during his Wells years. *Contrastes et développements*, issued by Koussevitzky's Russischer Musik Verlag in 1936, and *L'aubépin*, issued in Paris by La Sirène musicale in 1938 (with the Max Jacob poems rendered into English by Charles Henri Ford and Elliott Carter), were the only two scores Nabokov pub-lished in the course of his years at Wells. Commissions, in the context of the Depression, were harder to get. Performances of his music also became rarer. In 1936, he extracted a second symphonic suite from *La vie de Polichinelle*. It was given in early January 1937 by the Cleveland Symphony Orchestra, under Arthur Rodzinski, to open a concert that also featured the Schumann Cello Concerto played by Gregor Piatigorsky (whom Nabokov knew from New York).[38] The same suite was heard in 1938 under Mitropoulos, who in the previous year had become principal conductor of the Minneapolis Symphony Orchestra. Mitropoulos also commissioned from Nabokov an orchestral arrangement of Bach's *Goldberg Variations*, in the manner of the transcriptions Leopold Stokowski realized in the 1930s for the Philadelphia Orchestra; the manuscript is dated March 18, 1938. Mitropoulos conducted the piece later that year in Minneapolis, as did Rodzinski in Cleveland the following year. In 1939 the music was used by the choreogra-pher William Dollar for a ballet entitled *Air and Variations*, which had its premiere by the Ballet Caravan at the Martin Beck Theater in New York on May 24, 1939.

It shared the bill with Elliott Carter's *Pocahontas* and Copland's *Billy the Kid*, the success of which overshadowed the other two works.[39]

In the summer of 1938, Nabokov took Constance with him to Europe. After a stay at Kolbsheim, where he worked on the score of his new symphony, they went "modestly chateau'ing in the excruciatingly boring Loire Valley" when, in early September, the news came that, in view of the deteriorating international situation, all American citizens were advised to return home at once.[40] Hurrying back to Paris, Nabokov and his not quite fiancée—he was not yet divorced—managed to obtain passages on the next French Line departure and rushed off to Le Havre. There, the same kind of difficulty Nabokov had faced in Berlin occurred again: the passport control officials, notwithstanding his US "First Papers," refused to let him embark unless his Nansen passport was stamped with an exit visa. Letting his companion sail on her own, Nabokov went back to Paris. When he presented himself at the Préfecture de Police, the bureaucrats he had succeeded in bribing with envelopes of cash on previous occasions proved impossible to find and he was drily informed that his request for an exit visa was turned down. He then contacted an elderly relative who worked at the passport division of the American embassy, but the embassy was besieged with calls for help from stranded US citizens and there was nothing she could do. At this point he got in touch with Misia Sert, who promptly invited him for dinner that evening. When Nabokov arrived at her Rue de Constantine apartment, near the Invalides, she told him she had arranged for him to see Alexis Léger, then Secretary General of the Quai d'Orsay, the next morning at ten. At dinner were old friends: Bérard, Denise Bourdet, Marie-Louise Bousquet, Cocteau and his lover Jean Desbordes, and Kochno (then Christian Bérard's lover). "*Imbécile!*" said Cocteau when Nabokov summarized his troubles. "Stay here and join us!"[41] Champagne had been provided by Marie-Blanche de Polignac. A few weeks later, at a November 28 La Sérénade soiree at the Salle Gaveau, Marie-Blanche, who may have overestimated her talent as a classical singer, premiered of three of Nabokov's Max Jacob songs (*L'aubépin et cinq autres mélodies*). She was accompanied by Poulenc, whose *Trois poèmes de Louise de Vilmorin* were also on the program. Reviewing the concert in *Le ménestrel*, Paul Bertrand found the Nabokov songs "disconcerting," while pointing out, uncharitably, that the amateur singer's vocal inadequacy and poor pronunciation made it impossible to pass judgment on the music she performed.[42]

Though not an intimate friend of Léger—alias Saint-John Perse—Nabokov had met him the 1920s. "At first glance," he later recalled, Léger "looked like the prototype of a French career diplomat."

> He was of medium height. His head was large, round, prematurely balding, and his forehead was broad and noble. He was suave, cold, courtly, well-groomed, impeccably dressed, and gave the impression of being

haughty. But this was only the surface. His eyes betrayed a deeper, much more fiery and complex nature. His eyes were those of a poet.

Though his manners were French, his face, despite its clipped, brush mustache, did not look French. The high cheek bones, the widely set, narrow slit eyes, the parchemin gloss of his skin, spoke of a remote, exotic blood. Léger was proud of this "exos" in his blood. He loved to remind one that he was a Caribbean nobleman, *"un homme des îles."*

Like most Frenchmen, he was vain, but not beyond endurance, not as obviously and as belligerently as some of the "poets in uniform" at the Académie française.[43]

"Chatty and charming," Léger received Nabokov in his office "as if he had nothing else on his mind but to spend some time with me in pleasant talk. He spoke of music and poetry in America. He asked me whether I had any news from Stravinsky and Prokofiev. He gave me a signed copy of *Anabase* in a bilingual edition."[44] The exit visa issue was brushed aside: all Nabokov had to do was to leave his Nansen passport with Léger and it would be ready to pick up the following day. But Nabokov pressed him. Could he find out whether there was anything in his file that could explain why he was given so much trouble? Léger promised to look into the matter and give Nabokov lunch two days later in the restaurant of the Place du Palais-Bourbon. The acceleration of the Sudetenland crisis forced Léger to cancel the lunch invitation, but, when he returned to Nabokov his stamped passport, he assured him that unless the secret services had withheld part of it, there was nothing incriminating in his file. Yet similar problems were to haunt Nabokov ten years later.

Nabokov and Constance were married on March 23, 1939, in Minneapolis, where her family originated. Despite his marital estrangement from his first wife, from whom he was divorced by an Illinois court on May 2, 1938, he and she always remained on companionable terms. The main reason for their breakup, he admitted to Elliott Carter, was that Natalie "was too connected with the grand Russian style"; she belonged with a past that was not his anymore.[45] In a sense, Nabokov's new marriage was part of his Americanization as much as the US citizenship he finally received, in Auburn, New York, on September 11, 1939. It was then that he officially modified the spelling of his name from Nabokoff, the traditional French rendering, to Nabokov. In Aurora, the newlyweds continued to live with the Allen family until the fall, when they moved into "a comfortable, spacious house—old-fashionedly perched on a mound of greens, surrounded by ancient elms, limes, and maple."[46] They were able to entertain visiting friends and, after the concert and lecture series, replace the college's "dry" receptions by "fully wet" parties at their home. A "friendly and gay mongrel dog" joined the household; he was named Twistick "because he twisted his hind part like a

Brazilian Capuerista."[47] A new Ford coupe was purchased, and Nabokov and his young wife, having a large house to furnish, initiated themselves in "the sport of antique furniture hunting"—an easy and affordable pastime in the Depression years, which had left many abandoned farmsteads in the upstate New York country-side.[48] Instead of going to Europe, by then on the brink of war, they spent the summer of 1939 on Cape Cod, which Nabokov had discovered that spring when visiting John Peale Bishop at his newly built house in South Chatham. Nabokov had remained in touch with the poet since their 1933 transatlantic crossing. He admired Bishop's wit, charm, and intellectual integrity; he liked his poetry too, while recognizing that it was "much too refined, too civilized, too skillfully epistemological, and, in a very personal way, too hermetic" to become truly popular. One of Bishop's champions was Edmund Wilson, his Princeton classmate. Through Bishop, Nabokov was thus introduced to Wilson and his new wife Mary McCarthy, who lived across the street from the house he and Constance had rented in Wellfleet. Prompted by Wilson, Nabokov, that summer, reread Goethe's *Elective Affinities* in German as well as Tolstoy and Flaubert. Around that time, he also discovered Henry James and rediscovered Melville, whom he had read in Russian as an adolescent.[49] Nabokov was immensely impressed with Wilson's views in political matters, and credits him for inspiring in him "a new, non-emotional, but fully rational, total rejection of any form of oppression, be it Nazi, Soviet, or Fascist."[50]

As Hitler's rise forced a greater number of artists, musicians, and intellectuals to seek refuge abroad, and especially in the United States, much of Nabokov's energy during his third year at Wells went into helping them to find teaching positions by using his academic connections. Among the people who turned to Nabokov for help was the Viennese painter, printer, and graphic designer Victor Hammer (1882–1967), whom he presumably knew either through Albrecht von Bernstorff (whose portrait Hammer painted in 1926) or the Bethmann-Hollwegs.[51] A member of the Secession Group before 1914, Hammer, though active in several European countries, had remained based in Vienna. After the Anschluss, however, he rightly feared for the safety of his wife Rosl, who was Jewish. In the summer of 1938, at Nabokov's suggestion, the painter and his wife were invited to Kolbsheim, where Hammer decorated the chapel.[52] In the following months, when the professor of fine arts at Wells, a depressive Quaker named J. J. Lankes, announced his intention to retire, Nabokov was able to persuade President Weld to appoint Hammer as his successor. At Wells, where he started teaching in early 1940, Hammer set up the Wells College Press (he had brought his own printing press) and continued to print under his own imprint. After his retirement, he moved to Lexington, Kentucky, where he built a studio.

A more prominent artistic figure Nabokov was able to assist was Hindemith. Nabokov, as we have seen, had known and admired him since the mid-1920s.

Persona non grata in Nazi Germany since he had been openly denounced in a speech by Goebbels in November 1934, Hindemith spent more and more time abroad, and in 1937 resigned from his Berlin Hochschule professorship. A first visit to the United States took place in the spring of 1937 under the auspices of Associated Music Publishers, Hindemith's American agent. Nabokov went to New York in mid-April to attend the local premiere of Hindemith's new viola concerto, *Der Schwanendreher*, with the New York Philharmonic. Hindemith returned for a series of recitals in March 1938, while in his native country the "Degenerate Music" exhibition in Düsseldorf was about to make him one of its targets. On his third visit, in early March 1939, Hindemith was invited to give a concert at Wells, accompanied by the pianist Lydia Hoffmann-Behrendt.[53] The two composers renewed their acquaintance on this occasion.[54] Within days, Nabokov pressed Hindemith's case with President Weld. On April 14, barely one week after his Wells appearance, the German composer reported to his wife that he had received that morning "an interminable and enthusiastic letter [. . .] from Nabokov in which his college suggests establishing summer courses especially for me."[55] Hindemith was then exploring several options—one of them working in Hollywood. Nevertheless, he thought the offer "worthy of serious consideration for next year." Nine days later, on April 23, Nabokov attended the concert at the New York Town Hall at which Hindemith premiered his new Sonata in F for Viola and Piano, with members of the Boston Symphony Orchestra performing his 1938 Clarinet Quintet. Afterward he and Hindemith went out for a few beers in the company of the Mannheim-born Karl Bauer, an AMP executive.[56]

Initial plans to have Hindemith teach a summer composition course had to be modified in the fall of 1939 when Koussevitzky offered Hindemith a teaching position at the Tanglewood 1940 summer school.[57] On September 7, Ernest R. Voigt, then head of AMP, contacted Nabokov, urging him to do his best to help "our friend Paul" get employment in the United States that would make it possible to get an immigrant visa. Nabokov got in touch with colleagues on other upstate New York campuses, notably Paul Weaver, head of the music department at nearby Cornell, to work out a different arrangement. In early December 1939 Hindemith received an invitation to teach six weeks at Wells and Cornell sometime between February and June 1940. In order to make the offer more attractive financially, the invitation was expanded to SUNY Buffalo, thanks to the intercession of Cameron Baird, a Buffalo industrialist and gifted amateur musician who had studied with Hindemith in Berlin.[58] At the last minute, a fourth invitation, which eventually developed into a permanent offer, was issued by Yale. Hindemith sailed to the United States for a fourth time in February 1940—this time for a stay of eight years. From Buffalo, his first stop, he took the train to Aurora and spent the last weekend of February with Nabokov at Wells. "That was something more like a pleasurable experience after the buffalo-town," he reported to his wife on February 27.

> Nabokov, despite a boil on his nose, was delighted to have me there. He is a good chap, a bit Russian and slovenly, and his entire household gives the same impression. His wife obviously has no feeling for such things, she is still rather *collegegirl*-ish and continues to study English literature in Ithaca. He meanwhile stays at home cooking.[59]

One person Hindemith was particularly happy to find at Wells was Hammer, whom he had met once in Austria. He noted that he "contributed much to the Europeanization of the atmosphere, especially since his wife yesterday fabricated an excellent chicken paprika—a great relief after two weeks of snakes' grub."[60] At Wells, Hindemith taught six Tuesday evening lectures between March 19 and April 30, sandwiched between Cornell and Buffalo. The lectures were given the general heading "A Composer at Work." The fact that they were attended by about seventy students—a remarkable figure considering that the student body did not exceed 500—gives an indication of Nabokov's success in making music an important part of the life of the institution. Astutely, or perhaps at Nabokov's instigation, Hindemith incorporated into his course the composition of a three-part *a cappella* chorus for women's voices, *A Song of Music*, set to a poem by Nabokov's colleague George Tyler. Hindemith could not attend the premiere, which took place at Wells in June, with Nabokov conducting. It was eventually published with Hindemith's own German version of Tyler's poem, and with an optional piano or string orchestra accompaniment.[61]

A third person Nabokov helped to move to the United States was his own cousin. Vladimir Nabokov had left Berlin in the spring of 1937, settling first in the south of France, and then Paris, where he and Véra found themselves when the war was declared. Nicolas was one of the people he appealed to for help and advice in the next few months, once he had made the decision to emigrate to the United States. Finally he and his family were able to sail to America on May 19, 1940, nine days after Hitler's armies invaded Belgium. Back in Wellfleet that summer, Nabokov recommended his cousin to Edmund Wilson, thereby triggering one of the century's best-known literary exchanges (and *brouille*).[62] Nabokov was also able to arrange an invitation for Vladimir to lecture at Wells in early February 1941. "To put it modestly, I had some success," Vladimir reported to Wilson, adding: "Nicholas was charming."[63]

In New York, Nabokov saw other recently arrived refugee friends. Among the first were Jacques and Raïssa Maritain. They had already left France immediately after the Munich Agreement, when the philosopher was invited to lecture at the University of Chicago by Robert Hutchins, its president, and went on lecturing for several months on various campuses in the Midwest and on the East Coast. On January 4, 1940, they left France a second time and remained in the United States for the duration of the war; to prevent the house in Meudon from being confiscated by the Nazi occupants, Grunelius and his wife purchased it.[64] After a few lectures in Toronto, the Maritains settled in New York at 30 Fifth Avenue. They were followed by Darius and Madeleine Milhaud, who landed in New York, having sailed via Lisbon, on July 15, 1940, and left a month later to take up their wartime teaching appointment at Mills College in California. In August of the same year, Rieti joined the group of musical emigres.

After four years at Wells, despite his new domestic arrangements and a then respectable annual salary of $5,000, Nabokov "grew more and more restless in Aurora," where he could never reconcile himself with the teaching routine.[65] In December 1939, he unsuccessfully applied for a Guggenheim fellowship. In his letter of recommendation, Lewis Galantière mentioned that Nabokov was at work on a "Nativity" about which nothing else is known, and on a setting of T. S. Eliot's *Ash Wednesday*; that project he never completed. While continuing work on his second symphony, two and a half movements of which had been completed by 1939, he resumed his collaboration with Archibald MacLeish, who in July 1939 was appointed Librarian of Congress. Nabokov was much impressed with MacLeish's *America Was Promises*, a poem inspired in a large part by its author's admiration for Roosevelt's leadership, and which first appeared in November 1939 in *The New Republic*.[66] Nabokov clearly responded to this "call to action" directed against isolationist trends in the United States. Describing it, over-enthusiastically, as "the greatest work since Walt Whitman," he approached CBS radio about turning it into a cantata.[67] "The poem," he explained to Orrin Dunlap Jr. of the *New York Times*, "is of an epic and political nature; its purpose is didactic, and thus every single word must be understood."

> Furthermore, the poem in its emotional content ranges from verses of a tender and lyrical nature to verses expressing passionate anger and contempt. Thus it became obvious that the formal structure would have to be planned around some [. . .] unifying focus point that would hold all these contrasting feelings together.[68]

Reluctant to cut any of the text, but having to remain within the prescribed twenty-five- to thirty-minute length, Nabokov had to alternate between spoken and sung passages: the more didactic lines are thus given to a speaker, while the more lyrical passages are shared by the soprano and baritone soloists and the chorus. Yet, to avoid abrupt transitions between the two, the spoken lines are noted rhythmically or delivered as a sort of incantation. Nabokov took the opportunity of this interview (his first since the one with José Bruyr in 1931) to proclaim his attachment to lyricism, to the need for "simple, straightforward, clear melodies," the scarcity of which, as he declared to Dunlap, "is one of the greatest defects of contemporary music." Since they tended to sacrifice melody to rhythm and harmony, contemporary composers, he argued, were at a loss before a text and usually resorted to "the commonplace patterns of so-called popular music." In his setting of *America Was Promises*, he had made sure that "there should be three or four songs whose melodies are clear-cut and simple, and yet the composer should not make any concessions to commonplace tricks of harmony or melodic patterns."

> I do not think it is necessary to make any concessions at all to the radio listeners. It is frequently said that the radio public is conservative and reactionary. I doubt very much that this is true, considering the great success of certain hours devoted to nothing but good music. In conclusion, the music for *America Was Promises* attempts to emphasize the meaning of the poem, augment its dramatic tenseness and embellish its epic and lyrical passages.[69]

First heard on WABC radio on April 22, 1940, the cantata had to wait until 1950 for its first concert performance.

Nabokov's forceful statements to Dunlap on the subject of text setting make one wonder why, having devoted so much of his compositional activity to vocal and choral music and expanded his interest to music for the theater, he had not yet turned his attention toward opera. As early as 1930, he had been approached by Belaieff, the Leipzig-based music publisher, about a commission to write a setting of Chekhov's short story *Romance with a Double Bass* but had passed it on to his friend Sauguet, evidently because he did not feel comfortable with the buffo style the work required.[70] Despite a vague reference to an unspecified project with Remizov, there is, in fact, no indication that Nabokov envisaged any serious operatic project until the summer of 1940 he spent in Wellfleet.[71] He seems to have toyed first with the idea of adapting John Peale Bishop's novel *Act of Darkness*, which had made an enormous impression on him, but Edmund Wilson talked him out of it.[72] Nabokov then tried to persuade Wilson himself, already then a remarkable connoisseur of Russian literature, to collaborate with him in writing a libretto based on Pushkin's unfinished novel *The Blackamoor of Peter the Great*. Nabokov already had in mind Lawrence Tibbett, then the most prominent American baritone, for the role of Peter the Great, and was confident that he could get the opera produced. Wilson, who considered Nabokov "an extremely intelligent fellow," was intrigued by the proposal, but hesitant.[73] While finding the story "a natural for an opera," he did not think of himself as a librettist. At Nabokov's prompting, he tried to get Thornton Wilder interested in the project. "I don't know," Wilson wrote to the latter, "whether there is much for a writer in doing librettos (though it may be theatrically interesting) or what your opinion is of Nabokov's music," adding: "I haven't heard any of it except a sort of cantata made from Archie MacLeish's awful poem 'America Was Promises,' which he played me the other night. It seemed to me quite good and the kind of thing which might promise an opera."[74] The work, Wilson optimistically concluded, could potentially find a place alongside *Boris Godunov, The Golden Cockerel,* and *Pique Dame* in the Russian operatic tradition. Wilder's response was evidently lukewarm, since Wilson tried to prod him once more:

> Masterpieces are written by people of remarkable ability. You are one, and I thought that Nabokov might be another (though my ideas about music are rather unreliable). After all, somebody has got to go on writing great Russian operas.[75]

Nabokov too persisted, since in March of the following year, Wilson reported to Vladimir: "[Nicolas] has pretty well persuaded me that I ought to do something about trying to provide him with a scenario for his opera on [*The Blackamoor of Peter the Great*]—though I think it really ought to be done by a Russian."[76] That is, sadly, the last reference that can be located to this tantalizing project. One wonders if Nabokov ever knew that his old nemesis Lourié, after his arrival in the United States in the early 1940s, unsuccessfully approached his cousin Vladimir about writing a libretto for him on the same subject.[77]

After four years at Wells College, Nabokov was eager to move to a different environment. Visiting Maritain in New York in March 1940, he heard about a college in Maryland that was looking for a new head of its music department. "It was," Nabokov recalled from this conversation, "a boys' college that had been taken over by a group of 'educators' with experimental, or at least unusual ideas about education." He had "read about it in the papers and remembered vaguely that these educators were talking about a true 'Liberal Arts' curriculum, based on the reading of the 'great books.' "[78] Maritain had recently lectured there and liked the dean. As he explained to Nabokov, the college was run by people "concerned with the future of the humanities in America." They found the present educational system "slipshod, superficial, and in effect pernicious." The remedy, in their view, was in a return to the sources, by which they meant Aristotle, Plato, and Aquinas. Maritain was familiar with this approach from his own contacts, in the fall of 1938, at the University of Chicago, with two of his main promoters, Robert Hutchins and Mortimer Adler. He suggested that the new place would be far less dull and depressing than Wells and offered to recommend Nabokov to the dean, especially since he knew they were looking for "someone with fresh ideas about how to teach music in a humanities college."[79] On the strength of Maritain's recommendation, Nabokov was invited to an interview with Scott Buchanan, the dean of St. John's College in Annapolis, Maryland.

Nabokov drove from Aurora to Washington during the reading period in the spring of 1940. In Georgetown, he enjoyed the hospitality of Francis Biddle, the recently appointed US Solicitor General, and his wife. Biddle had been a friend of Nabokov's uncle Konstantin, who before the Revolution had been posted at the Russian embassy in Washington. As for Biddle's wife, the poet Katherine Garrison Chapin, she was the sister of Marguerite Caetani, whom Nabokov knew from his years in Paris. Nabokov and the Biddles had become personal friends since crossing the Atlantic on the *S.S. Champlain* in the summer of 1936. From their place he drove to Maryland for his interview. "Quiet and tidy" Annapolis charmed him "with its colonial houses, its narrow streets laid out in the French manner, like a miniature Washington"; so did the St. John's campus, which struck him as "the image of a picture-book eighteenth-century Americana, with its ancient lime trees and shrubbery in nascent bloom."[80] He was no less charmed by Scott Buchanan, who had, he remembered, one of those inimitable faces "whose first snapshot remains forever clear in memory."

> He looked like a rugged worker, a miner. Yet the big eyes—I have forgotten their color—that looked at me from under bushy brows of an overly large cannonball head were those of a judge, a thinker, perhaps a prophet. I remember feeling uneasy at the penetrating gaze of those eyes.[81]

Born in 1895 in Washington State, Buchanan had majored in Greek and mathematics at Amherst College and subsequently read philosophy as a Rhodes Scholar at Balliol College, Oxford.[82] At Amherst, he had been strongly influenced by the college president, Alexander Meikeljohn, who partly inspired the conception of liberal arts education Buchanan began to develop in the late 1920s, when he taught at Cooper Union's People's Institute in New York, in association with his fellow philosophers Mortimer Adler and Richard McKeon. He first tried to put these ideas into practice at the University of Virginia, where he taught until 1936, when Hutchins invited him to be part, along with Adler and McKeon, of his newly formed Committee on Liberal Arts. The following year, he took up a position as dean at St. John's, which, though one of the country's oldest colleges, was going through difficult times and had been stripped of its accreditation. Along with Buchanan, St. John's recruited a new president, the ancient historian Stringfellow Barr (1897–1982), and both men reorganized the curriculum based on the so-called "Great Books" new program.

Nabokov's assignment, Buchanan explained, after introducing himself as an "irrational and uncontrollable" music lover, would be twofold. First, like all members of the St. John's faculty, irrespective of their fields, he would be expected to teach liberal arts in the broadest sense—literature, mathematics, ancient Greek, Latin, French or German, philosophy, history, and the natural sciences. He would also, more specifically, devise a "proper and rational" way the fine arts, and music in particular, could be incorporated into the curriculum. Buchanan's concern was that in traditional colleges the fine arts "had a tendency to run away with the liberal arts, at their expense," whereas the aim of the New Program was to establish the primacy of the liberal arts over all subjects—especially the fine arts.[83]

According to his later recollections, Nabokov did not understand, at the time, what Buchanan's proposal actually entailed. Teaching subjects he admitted he knew little or nothing about he took as an exciting challenge. As for the general philosophy behind the New Program, he was familiar only with its broad outline, even though he had noted that Maritain pronounced the name of Adler, like him a neo-Thomist, "with considerable misgivings."[84] Foremost on his mind was the wish to leave Aurora. The prospect of living near Washington, "an exciting, intensely cosmopolitan, and intellectually stimulating world center" in those years of the "Rooseveltian Renaissance," was particularly enticing, even though the salary St. John's was offering was less than he was making at Wells.[85] There was another obstacle: Wells would not release Nabokov before the end of his contract, which expired in June 1941, while St. John's needed someone who could start in the fall of 1940. Obligingly, Buchanan suggested Nabokov might think of someone who could "cover" for him in the first year and with whom he could collaborate in the meantime on the longer-term plans for the integration of music in the curriculum. Nabokov immediately approached Elliott Carter, who agreed and started teaching at St. John's that fall.

On his way to Annapolis for his interview with Buchanan in the spring of 1940, Nabokov stopped in Washington and made a new acquaintance which, as it turned out, was determining in his future postwar career. The occasion—"an accident of fate," as he remembered it—was a luncheon at the Garden Restaurant of the Mayflower Hotel, to which he was invited by his New York friend Edith Fincke to meet "a relative of theirs, a young American diplomat, who had been stationed in Moscow for quite a while," and was on leave from his new position in Tokyo.[86] The young man in a seersucker summer suit who arrived shortly after him struck him as a "thoroughbred American," in "the way I imagined those splendid late eighteenth-century and early nineteenth-century Americans whom of all us admired in the liberal Russia of my youth."

> Was it due to the fact that, though he looked young and [was] self-possessed and mature? Or that he was athletically rustic, and at the same time suave and elegant? Or perhaps it was the unconcealed glint in his eyes, keen and obviously ready to burst into peals of laughter, with dozens of little pleats forming themselves in the corners of his eyes? Or was it the noble face with all its parts

in perfect proportion to each other, well cut, or rather stonehewn, the way
I imagined early Roman Republican consuls?[87]

Nabokov's junior by a little more than a year, Charles Eustis Bohlen was born
in 1904 in Clayton, New York. His father was, in Bohlen's own words, "a gentleman of leisure who had inherited a little money";[88] his middle name was that of
his maternal grandfather James Biddle Eustis, the first US envoy to France with
ambassador rank (as opposed to minister) under President Cleveland in 1893–97.
After graduating from Harvard, Bohlen had entered the diplomatic service in
1929. In 1934, he was posted in Moscow as third secretary of the first American
embassy to the Soviet Union, working with Ambassador William Bullitt. One of
his colleagues was George Kennan; another was Charles Wheeler Thayer, a West
Point graduate, originally from Villanova, Pennsylvania. Bohlen, who was already
acquainted with Thayer's sister Avis, married her in 1935. After working briefly
in Washington for Undersecretary of State William Phillips, he had returned to
Moscow in 1937 and again in 1938–40.
    From this very first encounter, Nabokov was struck by what he described as
Bohlen's "no-nonsense intelligence, sharp, fast-working, pragmatic, and witty."

He had a deep, velvety, or rather furry baritone, and spoke a clear, distinct English, pronouncing each word, even slang words, carefully. It was
an upper-class sounding English, but free from any affectation, either
Bostonian, Oxonian, or any other. He told several good jokes at table that
made all of us laugh and were truly funny. He obviously liked quick quips.[89]

Bohlen spoke a fluent, rather than pedantically correct Russian, "deliciously punc-
tured by wrong tenses and genders, false prefixes, post-fixes, and in-fixes, of which
Russian abounds."

Yet his accent, choice of words, tone of voice made it so very attractive and
civilized. It did not betray any of that low-brow pollution, full of ill-digested
foreign terms, that has vulgarized and bedeviled my lovely mother-tongue
in the course of those neglect-filled decades of Sovietization.[90]

During lunch, Bohlen quizzed Nabokov about contemporary Russian literature,
expressing interest in writers like Isaak Babel, Mikhail Bulgakov, Iurii Olesha, and
Boris Pilniak. Afterward, when Nabokov gave him a ride to the State Department,
he touched on more political issues.

Yes, he said, he did go to Moscow with Bill Bullitt and the first post-
Revolutionary American embassy. But, contrary to rumor and legend,

not all of those embassy members were starry-eyed about Stalin's Russia. He was one of those who were not. Nor was George Kennan, whom Bill Bullitt picked up while Thayer was on a private trip to Leningrad.[91]

He and his colleagues, Bohlen explained, soon realized that direct contacts with Russians were rendered almost impossible in a police state, with KGB informants planted everywhere. As for the purges that had taken place in the wake of the Moscow Trials of 1936–38, and about which not much was yet known in the West, Bohlen revealed that they were much more extensive than anyone suspected; "the systematic terror continued and engulfed hundreds of thousands, if not millions of people of all walks of life, from top party elite to peasants and workers."[92] Bohlen also told Nabokov that, little though people in America suspected it in the spring of 1940, the conflict that was brewing in Europe was inevitably going to spread to the rest of the world.

One could not overstate the importance of this meeting for the evolution of Nabokov's political views. Indeed, for the first time, he had the opportunity to hear about Russia from a well-informed, first-hand witness. If Nabokov still harbored any illusions about the real nature and full extent of Stalin's dictatorship — Edmund Wilson, for one, thought he detected a note of involuntary admiration when the name came up—they were definitively swept away.[93]

Nabokov's final year at Wells was no doubt alleviated by the prospect of his forthcoming departure. It was marked by the birth of his second son, Peter, in the fall of 1940, and by two important musical premieres, both in New York, that followed each other by less than two weeks: those of the second piano sonata in late December 1940 and of the Second Symphony in early January 1941.

Completed in Wellfleet in August 1940, Nabokov's Second Piano Sonata, more classical in form and inspiration than the first, is in four movements. It is dedicated to Nabokov's former pupil Leo Smit, who premiered it on December 6, as part of a program that included works by Brahms, Debussy, Albéniz, and Michelangelo Rossi in a Bartók transcription. "The Nabokoff work," wrote the New York *Sun* critic, "is a soundly constructed creation, somewhat suggestive in its melodic contours and harmonic idiom of Poulenc, though more likely a product of similar influences—Debussy by way of Prokofieff and Stravinsky. It has, in any case, a good feeling for piano sonorities, especially in the opening 'Pastorale' and the 'Rondo' which follows a weakish 'Cantilena.' Its rhythmic variety was aptly emphasized by Mr. Smit, who also contributed an active dynamic sense and crisp fingerwork to its effectiveness."[94] To a modern listener, the influences of Debussy and Poulenc are the most apparent, as if Nabokov had sought to pay homage to the country of his musical débuts. When the work was eventually published by Boosey and Hawkes in 1954, the British reviewer of *Music and Letters* praised Nabokov as "a skillful composer, economical with his notes and possessing a true, though sophisticated fund of lyrical melody."

> The movements are of unconventional order—a Pastorale with a violent middle section, a Cantilena, a Rondo which paradoxically omits its last statement and runs instead into a solemn Lento which echoes the repeat chords of the Cantilena. The style is eclectic, ranging from spare counterpoint to rich harmony and from easy diatonics to harsh chromatics. The sonata sounds well, is not very difficult and is certainly worth playing.[95]

The Second Symphony, Nabokov's most ambitious work of the decade, was premiered by the New York Philharmonic (still officially called the New York Philharmonic Symphony Orchestra), conducted by Mitropoulos, in early March 1941. The program opened with Mario Castelnuovo-Tedesco's *Merchant of Venice* overture and ended with the Beethoven Violin Concerto with Jascha Heifetz as soloist. Begun, as we have seen, under the shock of the death of Nabokov's mother, and completed when Europe was already at war, the Second Symphony is grave and somber, a mood emphasized by the subtitle "Biblical Symphony." Like Nabokov's previous works with a religious inspiration, *Chants à la Vierge* and *Job*, it may also be indebted to Maritain's influence. Bordering on programmatic music, the first three movements purport to evoke a particular moment in the Old Testament. The opening Andante moderato, which begins *pianissimo* with a chorale-like theme, rises to a frantic climax, and ends on a quadruple *pianissimo*, is entitled "Ecclesiasticus (Wisdom)." The middle movement, also an Andante, is called "Solomon (Love)," and includes a fugue. Launched by a *staccato* clarinet ostinato which occurs in various forms throughout, evoking a flight, the Allegro that follows, culminating in a furious crescendo, is called "Absalom (Fear)." The brief concluding "Hosannah (Praise)," also marked Andante, begins with a dialogue between bassoons and low strings and leads to a short fortissimo tutti passage, but ends pianissimo, as the symphony began. "Mr. Nabokoff's symphony," wrote Olin Downes in *The New York Times*, "is effectively scored and written with vigor and intrepidity in the use of various of the most effective devices of modern composition. The writing is polyharmonic and polytonal too, but there is no insistence on one particular style or method of expression." Downes noted the thematic contrasts in the first movement and found in the score "considerable oriental color" and even "in places an impressive Hebraic quality." "The man who wrote this," he continued, "knows his Bloch as well as his Stravinsky and Milhaud."[96] The work, according to the same critic, was warmly received and Nabokov was called several times to acknowledge the applause. "Mr. Nabokov's Sinfonia Biblica," wrote Virgil Thomson in the *New York Herald Tribune*, "is a serious work of more than common competence. Its intentions are a trifle more eloquent, however, than its effect. It has dignity and a sound academic tone, and its orchestration is definitely more than skin deep. Short passages were even expressive, such as the opening of the 'Fear' movement; and the end of the 'Hosannah' was stylish. The work is worthy enough. Orchestrally, it is interesting without being especially difficult either to understand or to play. I should not be surprised if it became for a season or two a useful repertory piece for the provincial orchestras."[97] When the work was finally published in orchestral score in 1965, Nabokov removed the indications of mood associated with each movement, leaving only the Biblical references.

Just as Nabokov and his family were getting ready to leave Aurora and move to Annapolis came the news of the invasion of Russia by Hitler's armies on June 22, 1941. This affected him deeply, both as a Russian, no matter his views on the Soviet regime, and as someone with close relatives in Germany. Soon his adopted country would be at war as well, and he would be directly involved, completing his Americanization and coming closer to political engagement.

9

In Wartime Washington

ST. JOHN'S COLLEGE turned out to be a welcome change at first. Not only was it, by contrast with the geographical isolation of Aurora, close to Washington and Baltimore, but it also proved to be a more congenial intellectual environment. Nabokov liked Winkie Barr, the president, whose staunch anti-isolationist views matched his own,[1] and got on well with his faculty colleagues, many of whom were of a higher intellectual caliber than most Wells professors. He particularly enjoyed his contacts with the Russian-born Jacob Klein and Semyon Kaplan.[2] The student body also struck him, on the whole, as smarter and definitely more motivated. "Bright and even brilliant" was his assessment of his new academic community, which he affectionately came to call Platobad (or "Platon-les-bains").[3] Most importantly perhaps, Nabokov, during his first year, had the company of Elliott Carter, who had become and would remain one of his closest friends, and who stayed at St. John's for a second year. They both served as "liberal arts tutors" ("he brilliantly, I *médiocrement*," as Nabokov put it),[4] and worked together on establishing the college's music program.

The purpose of the "great books" program—essentially a reaction against the elective system of higher education developed at the turn of the century by Charles William Eliot at Harvard—had been popularized by one of its promoters, Mortimer Adler, in his 1940 bestseller, *How to Read a Book*. Nabokov was impressed neither by the book ("boring and poorly written slapstick") nor by its author, whom he heard lecture at St. John's. His talk, "peppered [with] obscure, scholastic terms" reminded him of "the sermons of the late Metropolitan Eulogius of the Russian Church in Paris, who loved to use words of foreign origin in noodle-length sentences, the meaning of which escaped him, but which successfully cradled his flock into spirals of cloudy rhetoric."[5] While welcoming the opportunity to read (or reread) many great classics of Western literature and thought, and much relieved to be spared language teaching, he soon had misgivings about the program itself. The Chicago committee's selection struck him as arbitrary. Why 100 books rather than 93 or 103? Why all of Homer (a three-week marathon) and Thucydides and so little Greek tragedy? Why spend so much time on Aristotle's "ridiculously out-dated" *Poetics* instead of explaining in twenty minutes what it contained? Why read *Genesis* "as if it were just another book"?[6] Why *War and Peace* and not (in his opinion) the vastly superior *Anna Karenina*? Why waste one's time deciphering an esoteric treatise by Robert Grosseteste, Bishop of Lincoln, rather than "the much more entertaining but equally obscure Horoscope of Wallenstein by Kepler?"[7] His own attempt to suggest adding Learned Hand's essay "On the Sources of Tolerance" as an appendix to the US Constitution and Federalist Papers was rebuffed by Buchanan on the grounds that Hand had "screwy" views on the liberal arts and the essay in question was "flimsy" and objectionable.[8]

While admitting that he was "only a half-baked, largely uneducated 'liberal art-ist,'" Nabokov also took issue with the program from an intellectual and peda-gogical point of view.[9] Rather than spend four years reading, "at breakneck speed," every word of those "great books," wouldn't undergraduates find more profit-able, he wondered, "to know more about contemporary thought, contemporary literature, music, and the arts?"

> To read more poetry and for poetry's sake; to study more history; learn about the world they are living in, and about the civilization of other lands; study the causes of poverty, inequality, and wars; learn about sex habits? But also learn such simple things as distinguishing one tree from another, one plant from another, edible from inedible mushrooms, the habits of birds, fish, and moths? And what about cooking habits and customs, or about ballet and modern dancing?[10]

By overreacting against the elective system, the program's creators, he thought, were dogmatic zealots, who had produced "a grand and profligate medieval extrav-aganza," or, even worse, "a straight-jacket for the mind."

The integration of music into the curriculum had been carefully prepared by Carter, liaising with Nabokov, before the latter's arrival. Students first learned about the physical aspects of music through laboratory exercises. To make ref-erences to music by the classical Greek authors "vivid and understandable," sonometers were built to illustrate in concrete terms the difference between the Pythagorean and Ptolemean systems of tuning and how equal temperament came into existence.[11] "Few people," Nabokov commented, "realize what an influence the changes in tuning systems had upon the evolution of musical techniques, musical structures, and musical thinking in general."[12] Excerpts from theoretical works, such as Descartes, Kepler, and Helmholtz, were also read and discussed. A program of works, broadly covering the entire history of Western music in the course of the four-year curriculum, was selected: it began with a Gregorian mass, followed by a polyphonic mass (Palestrina or Machaut), Monteverdi's *Orfeo*, one work by Bach (the *Goldberg Variations* or the B minor Mass), one Mozart opera (*Don Giovanni*), Beethoven's String Quartet no. 14 in C-sharp minor, and, finally, works by Debussy and Stravinsky (*The Rite of Spring*).[13] Students listened to recordings of these works, with the score in hand, and heard a lecture about them, following which they were discussed in a seminar, as "great books" were. These seminars took place "on two successive evenings for about two hours, often more because the talk became so lively."[14] As Carter phrased it when he described the course in *Modern Music*, the publication of the League of American Composers, in late 1944, "one of the recurrent topics was, naturally, the meaning of music."

> Did it, like language, refer to something else than itself and if so, what? Or was a work of music an ordered pattern of sounds that awakened feelings and thoughts in us as a by-product of our enjoyment of its beauties? Is listening to music simply a pleasant pastime or is it more? What does music bring to the meaning of the words in Gregorian chant? What relation has notation to what the composer imagines and to what the performer does? And so on through all those profound questions that naturally arise in students' minds but are so lightly, so carelessly, brushed by in most music courses. Here arguments developed, sides were taken, controversy was important. Music became a matter of interest, whether it was approached by the scientific, the literary, or the artistic and it gave one type of student an understanding of the other.[15]

The main obstacle, as became apparent from the start, was the lack of knowledge of music among undergraduates. Of the 280 or so student population of St. John's, only five percent had received any musical education. Carter and Nabokov were both convinced that for the course to make any sense, it was indispensable that the students should be taught the rudiments of music theory—in Carter's words, "simple notation [. . .] as well as the formation of modes and scales, key relationships and chord structure."[16] This was done in the form of formal lectures, given alternatively by Nabokov and Carter, with mandatory attendance for both faculty and students.

This theoretical part of the music course soon led to a rift with Scott Buchanan. In April 1942, towards the end of Nabokov's first year, after sitting in at one of Nabokov's lectures on musical notation, he summoned him to his office and voiced his discontent.[17] The lecture he had heard that morning had nothing to do with the system of education that was being implemented at St. John's; it was "pure music department stuff of an elective college." Was Nabokov trying to transform St. John's into a music school? What had been agreed on was that the music course would consist in a program of great works of music to be discussed in class in the same manner as "great books"; a lecture on musical notation had nothing to do with it. Why should the students be told how to read a score or even follow it in a basic sort of way? Shouldn't they, rather, be left to discover by themselves what was in these scores? St. John's was concerned with the liberal arts, not with the training of future music professionals, and certainly not with forcing young people to become music lovers or *amateurs*. The college's pedagogy, derived from the Socratic method, was to guide, or rather "goad" the students, like the slave boy in *Meno*, to figure things out by themselves, by their own "dialectic." This "inane conversation," as Nabokov characterized it, went on for a while. He tried to point out that it was not only absurd, but, in a sense, cruel to expect young people to discuss a musical work in any meaningful way if they did not know the first thing about how music is written. It was like expecting them to analyze a haiku in the original Japanese without any knowledge of the language or even the nature of ideograms. The dean was unimpressed by the argument. His objections, he explained, had nothing to do with the substance of Nabokov's lecture. That was not the point, nor was he competent, in any case, to pronounce on such matters. The point was that liberal education as conceived at St. John's was based on direct contact with the works to be discussed in class. The students read *Plato*, not the introduction to Jowett's translation of Plato. By the same token, they should not be listening to introductory lectures on musical notation before listening to music. Why not, rather, distribute the scores to the students and let them discuss them in class? A musical score, like a book, was a product of the mind, and like all such products could be rationally rediscovered by the mind. If this could not be achieved—whether the students actually listened to the music or not—then perhaps there was no point in incorporating music into the St. John's curriculum.

Nabokov resolved, on the spot, to take up Buchanan's suggestion with a view to pushing him "to the limit of the ridiculous and the absurd."[18] The score of Beethoven's String Quartet in C-sharp minor was distributed to the students without any preliminary lecture and discussed in a seminar, which Buchanan, half-heartedly, agreed to attend. Naturally, the students were bewildered. When, after a general discussion of signs and symbols and a reminder of the way the slave boy in *Meno* was led to the discovery of the Pythagorean equation, Nabokov asked the group what sense they made of the score they had been given, one of them, to general applause, declared it looked "like fly shit." At that point Buchanan, realizing Nabokov had made a fool of him, got up and left, to the embarrassment of the students, who idolized him.

"Buchanan never forgave me for what he called my foolish, gratuitous joke," Nabokov wrote in the published version of *Bagázh*, adding that he then sensed that his days at St. John's were numbered.[19] The manuscript gives a subtler, more detailed account of their relationship. "Before that 'seminar,'" he wrote, "I had in me a lingering fascination for the St. John's curriculum and its awesome Great Books shooting range."

> I also had a secret, but in fact quite apparent inferiority complex toward Scott Buchanan. I felt speechless, shy, and timid, and terribly uneducated in his presence. I even behaved toward him in a—to me quite unusual—subservient manner. He staggered me, not only by his intellectual superiority, but also by his enigmatic form of thinking and his manner of expressing himself. I never quite understood what he said, meant, or frowned or laughed about. He was a mystery to me. [. . .]
>
> Yet at the same time I felt tied to Buchanan by a kind of umbilical cord [. . .].[20]

All this changed after the famous Beethoven seminar. Nabokov was suddenly on his own ground again and "began to enjoy simpler, more frank, and fully ironic relations both with St. John's and its dean." At the same time, he suspected "that he, with the perverse masochist trait concealed in his character, enjoyed our new relationship, just as I did."[21] After ignoring him during the remainder of the academic year, Buchanan started speaking to him again in the fall semester. Nabokov was invited to his house, and he and his wife, in turn, invited the dean to a Russian dinner in the "palatial rooms" they occupied in the eighteenth-century Brice House, one of the three oldest on campus. Like several other American acquaintances of Nabokov—Francis Biddle, John Peale Bishop, Edmund Wilson—Buchanan was fascinated by Russia and Russian things, and that became the usual subject of their conversations. As for the issue of the liberal arts in general or the St. John's curriculum and pedagogy, it never came up again.

As at Wells, Nabokov, during his first year in Annapolis, put on a play. His first choice was *Oedipus at Colonus*, to him the most moving of Sophocles's extant works.[22] The idea was endorsed tepidly by Buchanan ("Don't you think it's better to read a play than to perform it?") once he was reassured that it would entail no schedule disruptions. It might have been shelved altogether if a sophomore student named Jack Landau had not introduced himself to Nabokov in the early weeks of 1942. Landau, Nabokov recalled, was "small, shy and smiling."

> He looked very young and boyish and had one of those pronouncedly Sephardic faces I have always liked. He was pale-skinned, dark-haired, inbredly sensitive, with much too widely spread ears, a much too fleshy and dropping nose, but with dark, sparkling, deep-set eyes. And the look of those eyes was both gay and melancholy, quick, furtive, curiously ingenious, and very, very pure.[23]

Landau had heard that Nabokov was toying with the idea of doing *Oedipus at Colonus*, but he argued against this choice. Why didn't Nabokov, instead, mount *The Tempest* again, as he had at Wells, but outdoors this time? Being about magic versus the liberal arts, with Prospero a Leonardo-like figure, *The Tempest*, Landau explained, would be much more palatable than Sophocles to the college authorities. With Constance lending support to the idea, plans went ahead, with Landau acting as assistant director. "In the course of these preparations," Nabokov recalled, "I became more and more convinced that Jack Landau's insight into Prospero [as] being ironically related to the lonely figure of Leonardo da Vinci, seemed to make sense."

> Particularly the Leonardo of the last years of his life at the court of Francis I, in banishment, at Amboise. Somewhere in his diaries Leonardo calls Amboise "my lonely island." And in Shakespearian England Leonardo was revered like the greatest personage of the Renaissance and as a kind of magician. It was interesting to toy with the idea and build up our Annapolitan Prospero as someone resembling Leonardo.[24]

Landau was "a born theater man, a professional, inventive, clever, quick, and thorough, reliable and ingenious," and the production turned out to be as much his, if not more, as Nabokov's.[25] Landau borrowed and developed Nabokov's device of making Ariel a voice coming out of a light.

> It was, as it should be, a fully convincing magical dialogue, between Prospero and a spirit. Landau installed half a dozen loudspeakers concealed in the ancient lime trees. They could alternately be switched off and on. Ariel, a boy with a very young and impersonal voice, spoke into a mike hidden behind shrubbery. All of it was done with professional skill and precision. Bengal lights of varying colors went on in those trees and the voice of Ariel seemed to be born out of those lights. The island was a round disc, an irregularly shaped platform on a dark blue shiny plastic material spread upon the ground. During Prospero's last speech, Roman candles and other silent fireworks broke out all over the place, [reflected] on the sea-like blue of the ground and shining in the warm and clear May sky.
>   Landau made up the boy who played the part of Prospero to look like the image of old Leonardo from his famous self-portrait. I taught him to speak slowly and very distinctly like a tired old man. It gave definitely a new, humane dimension to Shakespeare's personage and at least half the audience got the point.[26]

Well received by students and residents of Annapolis alike, the play was not as popular with the faculty, despite being treated, in the spirit of the place, as an allegory of the confrontation between magic and beauty (the fine arts) and truth and wisdom (the liberal arts). Despite promises made to the dean, and much to his annoyance, the college schedule had been brutally disrupted. Nabokov felt that it was on that evening "that he decided that we would have to part ways. I would never become a Liberal Artist and sooner or later would have to leave the Great Books circus."[27] As for Jack Landau, he later had a successful career as a stage and television director until, tragically, in 1966, at the age of forty-two, he was murdered in his Boston apartment.

Apart from teaching and theatricals, Nabokov also undertook to form and conduct a student choir at St. John's, all-male this time. He also put together an orchestra made up of students, both from St. John's and the Naval Academy, and amateur local musicians, supplemented by a handful of professional players attached to the Baltimore Symphony Orchestra.

As these multiple activities make clear, Nabokov kept himself very busy in Annapolis and this, in itself, was a source of frustration. There was no time left to compose, or indeed for any private life. This unhappy situation was compounded by financial and marital difficulties. The pay cut Nabokov had to take when he transferred from Aurora to Annapolis ($5,000 for the year, i.e., what he made in his first year at Wells) resulted in a serious pinch, especially with alimony payments he owed his first wife. And with his second wife he came to realize, once the first years of passion were over, that he had little in common in terms of temperament and interests; only their baby son still kept them together for a while. Still, even worse for Nabokov was to be so close to Washington, where he had old or new friends he was eager to see, and no time to do so.

In the early 1940s, evidently at the suggestion of friends in Washington, Nabokov had hoped to find a new patron in Elizabeth Sprague Coolidge, the wealthy and generous promoter of contemporary chamber music. In his earliest, undated letter to her, dating possibly from June 1939, he recalled being introduced to her in Paris through Stravinsky and Lina Prokofiev.[28] In 1940, he offered to dedicate to her his still unperformed *Serenata estiva* of 1937. Having accepted the offer, E.S. Coolidge subsidized the first performance of the piece at St. John's College, on 6 February 1942, by the Budapest String Quartet.[29] She, however, declined to commission a new chamber work by Nabokov, even though she remained on friendly terms with him and had the Coolidge String Quartet give a concert in Annapolis in March 1943.

The only music Nabokov seems to have completed in 1941, just before he became engulfed in his new teaching position, is the piano score of a new ballet, *The Last Flower*, based on the parable by the *New Yorker* cartoonist James Thurber. Published in November 1939 by Harper & Brothers, Thurber's illustrated fable was as much a denunciation of totalitarian militarism as an antiwar gesture, and it was in this respect that Nabokov clearly responded to it. He approached Thurber the following year, evidently via Edmund Wilson, and visited the humorist and his wife Helen at their home in Sharon, Connecticut, to seek permission to set the work to music. Presented in the manuscript as "a parable in words, pictures, and dances," Nabokov's score closely follows Thurber's story of a world annihilated as a result of World War XII, in which a young girl discovers the last surviving flower and, in the wake of this discovery, love. Slowly nature, and then civilization, are reborn, until, inevitably, soldiers and so-called "liberators" reappear and the world is at war again, with only one man, one woman, and one flower remaining at the end. Each section of the ballet corresponds to a sentence or group of words from Thurber's fable—the words are written out above the stave—and the musical mood is modeled on its sequences: after a brief overture, a *Lento assai* section evokes the world desolated by war. The discovery of the flower and the love between the young woman and the young man are appropriately treated in tender, expressive fashion. As the world and civilization begin to grow, a crescendo begins, lasting until the world is annihilated again. The cyclical nature of the story is paralleled in the music by the return of the tempo of the overture and the following Lento assai. Nabokov dedicated his score both to his friend and patron Dorothy Chadwick and to his newborn son, as well as to the memory of Tchaikovsky and *his* patron Mrs. von Meck, who was, it will be recalled, the one direct tie between Nabokov and the great Russian composer, being the previous owner of his stepfather's estate of Pokrovskoe.

The Last Flower remained in limbo for three years until the spring of 1944, when the Chilean-born impresario and ballet master George de Cuevas formed his company, which was first called Ballet Institute and shortly afterward was renamed Ballet International (three years later, it became the Nouveau Ballet Russe de Monte-Carlo, and in 1950 the Grand Ballet du marquis de Cuevas). Balanchine, who was part of the original team of choreographers Cuevas assembled, may have brought Nabokov's ballet to his attention. Nabokov worked on the instrumentation of the work in the first part of the year and delivered the orchestrated score that summer.[30] Announced on June 20, 1944 (with sets and costumes by Stewart Chaney) as part of the company's inaugural New York season at the International Theatre on Columbus Circle in October, the ballet was nevertheless dropped from the plans.[31] It was belatedly premiered in Berlin in 1958.

Another wartime composition was a sonata for bassoon and piano, written in 1942 for the bassoonist Leonard Sparrow. It is in two movements: an Adagio (initially entitled, according to the manuscript, "A Litany for Bassoon and Piano"), followed by an Allegro. No documentation has been found about its premiere. The work was rediscovered and published in 2008 by the Kansas bassoonist David Oyen.

Nabokov's second year at St. John's was less intellectually challenging than the first. Elliott Carter and his wife were gone, and he missed this close intellectual and personal friendship. Also, the war began to affect the life of the college, with students and teachers being drafted or taking on wartime jobs. On the other hand, Buchanan, perhaps realizing that Nabokov would sooner or later find a way out of Annapolis, became more accommodating: he insisted he should no longer feel obliged to attend all lectures and urged him to set time aside to compose. Aware of Nabokov's financial troubles, he also suggested that he take up a part-time teaching position at the Peabody Conservatory in Baltimore and offered to recommend him to the director. Shortly afterward, during the winter of 1942, at a concert in Washington, Nabokov was introduced to Alice Garrett, a well-connected hostess, whose late husband was from Baltimore. Through her, Nabokov met Reginald Stewart, "a long, tall, lean, balding and good-looking, but unsmiling Canadian," who was both Peabody director and chief conductor of the Baltimore Symphony Orchestra.[32] The two men hit it off and, with St. John's permission, Nabokov was invited to teach two courses (music theory and history of music) at Peabody beginning in October 1943. Given the misgivings he harbored about the liberal arts philosophy that prevailed in Annapolis, it must have been a considerable relief to teach a motivated, attentive group of future professionals, some of whom he found "surprisingly bright and even gifted."[33] He was rewarded in other ways as well, since Stewart programmed some of Nabokov's music (such as his *Polichinelle* symphonic suite) with his orchestra. In the fall of 1944, after three years at St. John's, Nabokov became a full-time member of the Peabody Conservatory, and left Annapolis—and his wife: he and she were by then leading more or less separate lives.[34] Before then, when he taught in Baltimore, he stayed at a hotel in the Mount Vernon area, near the conservatory, or, if Alice Garrett was in town, at Evergreen, her forty-eight-room neo-Palladian villa, located in a residential suburb. Her late husband, John H. Garrett, whose fortune partly derived from B. and O. Railroad stocks, had been appointed ambassador to Italy by President Hoover, serving from 1929 until 1933. His widow held FDR in deep suspicion and, conversely, retained fond memories of Mussolini ("not at all a dictator, mind you"). She had also spent several years in Paris, where her husband had been chargé d'affaires during the First World War, and had become acquainted with all kinds of celebrities, from Debussy to Proust and Ballets Russes stars. She had herself taken dance lessons and taken the habit of exhibiting herself in Loïe-Fuller-like solo performances, "twisting and swirling like a dervish," on the private theater she had built at Evergreen, where Nabokov saw what may have been the last of such fantasies in 1945.[35] Save for early Stravinsky (the *Sacre* definitely not included), her musical tastes—Franck, Sibelius, Ravel—were at odds with Nabokov's. Yet he seems to have enjoyed Alice Garrett's company, especially when he was the only guest. When she entertained on a larger scale, she was, he deplored, "indiscriminate in the quantity and the kind of glamorous people she entertained"; as a result, her dinner parties made him think of a performance of *Tristan* with three Heldentenors or one of *Eugene Onegin* "with half a dozen Lenskys."[36]

There was another development during Nabokov's second year at St. John's. One of his colleagues at St. John's, a Mr. Martin, a trained lawyer who, he noted, had "philo-Bolshevist" tendencies, had taken a job in the Anti-Trust Division at the Justice Department. Aware that Nabokov was looking for extra sources of income, he suggested he get part-time employment in the Economic Warfare unit, which was part of that same division. This was not Nabokov's first attempt to offer his services to the US government. As the communicable part of his CIA files reveals, he contacted the State Department in the summer of 1942 and was interviewed by an official named Calvin B. Hoover. Sending him his resume, Nabokov conveyed his hope that Hoover would soon be able to "advise me and help me to become useful to the USA in this war."[37] Among his qualifications, he listed his command of languages (including basic Dutch and Polish); his knowledge of social and political conditions in France, Germany, and Poland; his wide-ranging circle of acquaintances in France and Germany, especially in intellectual and artistic milieus; and, finally, his personal reputation as a composer. "I believe," he added, "that I might render genuine service as translator, propaganda analyst, adviser on foreign publicity, or officer in liaison or intelligence work." Among his references, beside Archibald MacLeish and Stringfellow Barr, he listed Thomas Finletter, then special assistant to Secretary of State Cordell Hull (he was to serve as Secretary of the Air Force under Truman and ambassador to NATO under Kennedy); his former Wells colleague George Ridgeway, now senior research assistant in the State Department; and a Lieutenant-Commander Ford Brown from the US Navy.

Beginning in January 1943, Nabokov was employed as a translator, at a daily salary of fifteen dollars, at the War Division of the Justice Department. Every Tuesday, he took the bus from Annapolis to Washington. The job consisted in sitting at a desk in the Department's basement and going through a selection of German- and Russian-language newspapers published in Nazi-occupied parts of Russia. The selection had been compiled and microfilmed by the US embassy in Sweden and flown over from Stockholm. Nabokov's task was to prepare a summary of what he found, illustrated with appropriate quotations. Though he had serious doubt about the value of his reports to the larger war effort, he took his duties seriously, and welcomed the opportunity to spend more time in Washington, especially since his social circle expanded in 1943.

In late spring or early summer, Kay Halle, an old friend from his New York days, then living in the federal capital with her sister Betsy (she was, in fact, employed by the OSS), invited Nabokov to lunch to meet "an extraordinary man," a Russian-born don at Oxford, who had recently taken up a position at the British Embassy and had been recommended to her by Randolph Churchill. The stranger who rang the doorbell at one o'clock sharp, carrying "a small Victorian bunch of flowers" and with "a gently embarrassed, shy smile on his pale face," startled him at first by the rapid flow of his almost incomprehensible Oxonian English. Yet, once the two of them started conversing in the street on their way to the restaurant, the same man turned out to speak "an absolutely unblemished, moderately fast, bassoonish-sounding, and perfectly articulated Russian."[38] Thus began Nabokov's acquaintance with Isaiah Berlin, which soon developed into an exceptionally close intellectual and personal friendship.

Born in Riga, Latvia, in 1908, to the family of a prosperous Jewish businessman, Berlin had emigrated to London with his family in 1920. After brilliant studies at Corpus Christi College, Oxford, he was appointed tutor in philosophy at New College and shortly afterward, at the age of twenty-five, was elected a fellow of All Souls. As of January 1941, he started working as a lobbyist attached to the New York office of the British Information Services, with the specific purpose of "getting America into the war."[39] After Pearl Harbor, he moved to the British embassy in Washington, where his main task consisted in preparing weekly surveys of US opinion as reflected in the press and through his own contacts with American journalists. From the start, Nabokov was dazzled by Berlin's intellectual agility and culture. Berlin seems to have found Nabokov's personality equally attractive. "The only interesting person I have met lately," he wrote to his parents, "is a gifted composer called Nicolas Nabokov, nephew of the late Cadet,[40] who teaches music in a nearby school. He is a person of great vitality and charm, neither White nor Red but a member of the old intelligentsia whom Rach [Berlin's close friend Solomon Rachmilevich] would enjoy meeting very much. I talk to him about music, Russia, books, persons, in fact all the subjects that I like talking about best."[41]

Recalling their friendship in the obituary he contributed in 1978 to the London *Times*, Berlin described Nabokov as "large-hearted, affectionate, honourable, gifted with sharp moral and political insight, and a well-developed sense of the ridiculous, an irresistible source of torrential wit and fancy, immensely sociable, [. . .] one of the last and most attractive representatives of the pre-Revolutionary Russian liberal intelligentsia."[42] Highly knowledgeable in musical matters, Berlin thought Nabokov understood music "far more than anybody, and in conversation at least talks about it with great magnificence and articulateness."[43] Berlin also gradually came to admire Nabokov's own music. While, in 1946, he claimed not to be impressed with what he had heard so far, by 1949 he had completely changed his opinion.

Around that time (he tentatively dates the event fall 1943), Nabokov was reacquainted with Charles Bohlen, who, after a period of internment in Japan, was back in Washington in late August 1942 and became assistant chief of the Russian section of the Division of European Affairs in the State Department. Their second meeting took place at a large dinner party, whose host Nabokov could not remember: Alice Garrett, or Francis Biddle, or Robert Bliss, the former ambassador to Sweden and Argentina and collector of pre-Columbian art, whose wife Mildred Nabokov called "Blissukha"?[44] It was then that Nabokov first met Bohlen's wife Avis, who captivated him by her elegance, beauty, and charm. On realizing that Nabokov was in town every Tuesday for his work at the Justice Department and was, like him, acquainted with Isaiah Berlin, Bohlen invited him for dinner with the philosopher at the house he had purchased in Georgetown after his return from the Far East. Nabokov quickly became a regular guest at "that charmed house on Dumbarton Avenue," which, for the first time in his American years, felt to him like home, "a center of friendship and of intellectual affinity," comparable to what Kolbsheim represented for him in France and Hohenfinow had in Germany.[45] The two-story house at 2811 Dumbarton Avenue was small ("could be in England"), but comfortable and unpretentious.[46] The food was no-nonsense American but plentiful and delicious and drinks and wine were similarly abundant. Nabokov began to think of life as "from Tuesday to Tuesday," although on occasions the Bohlens visited him in Annapolis (as did Berlin). When Bohlen was away on diplomatic work—as a fluent Russian speaker, he attended, as Roosevelt's interpreter, the Teheran and Yalta Conferences, among many others—Avis invited him, treating him like a member of the family. He thus came to know and befriend her mother, Gertrude Thayer, known as "Muzzy," and her brother Charles, who subsequently became Nabokov's boss at the Voice of America.[47]

Through Bohlen, Nabokov was introduced, along with Isaiah Berlin, to Washington's "Russian circle," a group of junior diplomats who had been posted in the Soviet Union and, after the war, were to play a major role in shaping US policies during the Cold War. The group included G. Frederick Reinhardt, future ambassador to Viet Nam, Egypt, and Italy; Elbridge Durbow, also a future ambassador to Viet Nam; and Llewellyn E. ("Tommy") Thompson, who, like Bohlen, was to become US ambassador to the USSR. It also comprised a few Englishmen, such as John (later Sir John) Galway Foster, a lawyer and, like Berlin, a fellow of All Souls, and John Russell, an officer at the British embassy known to Bohlen from his days in Moscow. The most prominent member of this circle, however, along with Bohlen himself, was George Kennan, who had been Bohlen's colleague in Moscow and was subsequently posted in Berlin, Lisbon, and London, before returning to Washington in 1943. He was one of Bohlen's closest friends—"no friendship," Kennan later stated, "has meant more to me."[48] On the other hand, as observers have noted, he "utterly lacked Bohlen's easy grace as a diplomat."[49] As Nabokov remembered it, when he first met Kennan at the Bohlens', during one of his short leaves from Portugal or London, he found him "morally grand and intellectually superior" and was intimidated by him.[50] Kennan asked him what he thought of the account of Russia under Nicholas I by Astolphe de Custine, an author who fascinated Kennan and to whom he devoted a book three decades later.[51] But Nabokov, at the time, did not have anything to contribute to the subject. Only several years later did Kennan and Nabokov strike a real friendship.

In 1943–44, a majority of Americans were, in Nabokov's words, "in a state of Sovietophilic euphoria."[52] After the invasion of Russia by the Nazi forces in June 1941, Hitler's former ally had become a US ally. Public opinion was quickly swayed by wartime propaganda and absurd films like the pseudo-documentary *Mission to Moscow* (1943), based on the memoir by Joseph E. Davies, Bullitt's successor as American ambassador in Moscow, and in which, notoriously, the victims of the Moscow trials are portrayed as spies for the Germans and the Japanese. The Dumbarton Avenue "Russian circle," obviously, harbored no such illusions. Their well-informed hostility toward Stalinism and their concerns about the political situation in Russia, in fact, put them at odds, and occasionally in difficulty, with the White House, and in particular with Roosevelt's adviser Harry Hopkins.[53] As a result, there was a slight atmosphere of paranoia within the group, an obsession with "who leaked what to whom and will it or will it not reach Lippman, or a lesser columnist."[54] Nabokov himself had never been duped, of course, by Soviet propaganda. But thanks to these weekly contacts in 1943 and 1944 with America's top Kremlinologists (as they came to be known), his political consciousness reached a new level of maturity.

> My political perspectives, which until then had been "simplistic," gradually acquired a degree of sophistication. I began to perceive the basic nature of the twentieth century's political scene: that the evil spirit of the century was double-headed. Hitler and Stalin were two parts of the same phenomenon. Stalinism was the opposite side of the same coin as Herr Hitler.[55]

Nabokov subsequently dated his decision to "take sides" and his new beginnings as a "political man" from his exposure to the Russian circle of Dumbarton Avenue.[56]

During his Washington years, Nabokov renewed his acquaintance with another diplomat, by then retired: Alexis Léger, who had been so helpful to him on his departure from France in September 1938. Fired from his position at the Quai d'Orsay in May 1940, Léger, turning down the offer of the ambassadorship to Washington, had sought refuge in the United States as an exile in July of the same year. Stripped of his French citizenship by the Vichy regime, he was hired by MacLeish as adviser to the Library of Congress for French literature. Beside MacLeish, he and Nabokov had other American friends in common, such as the Biddles and the Blisses, who briefly hosted the French poet at Dumbarton Oaks. Deeply suspicious of General de Gaulle, whom he viewed as a potential dictator (and who never forgave him for not rallying his cause), Léger was, along with Maritain, the most prestigious French figure then living in the United States. Nabokov saw him at regular intervals in Washington, either at soirees hosted by some of their friends or at the Greek restaurant in Georgetown near Léger's residence where Nabokov had his first lunch with Isaiah Berlin.

Léger's conversation, Nabokov recalled, was in fact more akin to a "captivating monologue" in the course of which all topics came up without any particular order. Like his poetry, which Nabokov began to read seriously at the time, Léger's talk was not always easy to follow; he spoke, in Misia Sert's words, "like a Chinese bonze." Nabokov remembered hearing him deplore that French poetry was too intellectual, inward-looking, lacking in wide-open spaces and refreshing winds. To Mallarmé and Debussy, whom he did not like (*La Mer*, he said, was pre-painted and already framed), he vastly preferred Pound and Eliot.[57] When the conversation turned to the war and diplomatic matters, he explained his distrust of de Gaulle ("a dangerous megalomaniac"). The priority, he argued, was for the Allies to win the war, not for a army-less general to be brought to power in a false triumph. Russia, "in a very, very abstract and poetic way," was to Léger the object of an attraction verging on adoration, even though he knew little about the country.[58] Like other Western intellectuals Nabokov had come across before, Léger considered Stalin a great man. To Nabokov's objections (what about the purges, the camps, the Katyn massacre, the show trials? . . .), Léger responded that all great men of history were killers and had to be exempted from the judgment of common morality. In music, Léger's admiration went above all to Stravinsky, whom he rated highest among other contemporary artists (and certainly much higher than Picasso) because he had not severed "his relationship to the earth and its multiple mysteries."[59]

A poet of comparable distinction entered Nabokov's life at that time in the person of W. H. Auden. Nabokov, who by the early 1940s did know know much about contemporary English poetry, had discovered Auden's work thanks to Edmund Wilson during one of his summers in Wellfleet. Auden had arrived in New York in late January 1939, accompanied by Christopher Isherwood. Shortly afterward he fell in love with the eighteen-year-old Chester Kallman, his future companion and collaborator, and decided to stay in America. In 1942–44, he taught at Swarthmore and Bryn Mawr. It was during this period that he wrote his verse commentary on Shakespeare's *The Tempest*, *The Sea and the Mirror*, which was published in late summer 1944. Nabokov's chronology in *Bagázh* is faulty: he could not have known by heart "large bits" of the poem at the time of his first meeting with Auden, which he dates "late autumn or winter of 1943."[60] However, it may well be that on the three or four occasions they saw each other then, Auden discussed his ongoing project with Nabokov. They were introduced to each other, according to Nabokov, by Isaiah Berlin, "in an exiguous living-room of a tiny house in Washington's Georgetown that Isaiah Berlin shared with another English college don who, like [me], was engaged in war work (face, name, attributes forgotten)."[61] Nabokov was struck by Auden's "nasal, noisy voice, his clumsy laughter, his assertive way of telling not quite exportable (English parsonage) jokes."[62] Brought up thinking all

Englishmen were reincarnations of Byron or Beau Brummel, Nabokov was astonished by Auden's lack of concern for his outward appearance, in terms both of
clothes and personal hygiene. Nabokov, however, was not one to be put off by
such considerations and a real friendship began. Once Auden visited Nabokov
in Annapolis; another time it was Nabokov who visited Auden on a weekend at
Swarthmore, where he occupied a "commodious, even grand looking flat."[63] On
this occasion Auden got him "completely drunk on gallons of Gallo's California
burgundy," while Auden argued with an unidentified Frenchman over the verisi-
militude of Gide's sexual prowess as self-reported in his autobiography *Si le grain
ne meurt.*[64]

One more important development in Nabokov's life had taken place in 1942.
Through Edmund Wilson, he had been introduced, in 1940 or 1941, to Edward
Weeks, editor of the *Atlantic Monthly*. Wilson, who regarded Nabokov highly,
urged him to try his hand at music criticism, an activity Nabokov had dabbled with
in his Berlin days, in Russian, and again in Paris, in French and in German, but
had never attempted in English. His first publication was a series of two articles in
The New Republic in March and April 1941 on "Music in the USSR."

"What [. . .] happens to music," Nabokov asks in the first article, "or to the
other arts in a country whose political leadership becomes every day a harsher and
tighter dictatorship?"

> Does such a state of affairs influence the artistic activity of the country and
> the productivity of its artists? How much and what kind of freedom does
> it leave to the creative artist? Does it tend to establish a new style in art, a
> sort of *style officiel*, or does it permit natural growth or free development to
> every individual?[65]

These were questions that were to remain central to Nabokov's preoccupations
for nearly four decades, and, as he pointed out in 1941, they did not apply to the
USSR, which was the focus of this initial article, but to all dictatorships anywhere.
As regarded the Soviet Union, the material situation of classical composers, he
granted (and he had very good reasons to know) was, on the whole, better there
than in the United States. That was, however, the only positive element. The
Soviet musical production in recent years was "very reactionary, provincial, and
flat in taste." There was indeed a Soviet *style officiel*, characterized by "extreme
simplicity bordering on poverty of imagination; old-fashioned and conservative
romantic fervor coupled with strained, pompous, and flamboyant optimism;
and a very insincere and stilted return to folklore[. . .]." In short, the art of the
"country of the future" looked and sounded more like the mythical Victorian
past. These tendencies, which could be detected, Nabokov claimed, in the work
of such diverse composers as Prokofiev, Shostakovich, Glière, and Miaskovskii,

were exacerbated during the 1935–38 period, coinciding with Stalin's great purge, when everything deviating from the strictest orthodoxy was prosecuted as "formalism." Nabokov summarized the most famous instance, the condemnation by Stalin of Shostakovich's opera *Lady Macbeth of Mtsensk District*, a work he himself did not care for, while recognizing its significance. As for Shostakovich's Fifth Symphony, its success should be understood above all, Nabokov claimed, as "an outburst of the public's pleasure in welcoming back one of its most gifted composers."[66] In his second article, he further argued, perceptively, that the work was "somber to the point of desolation for at least forty of its fifty minutes. Its gay and triumphant moments are few, strained, and at times frighteningly cheap."[67] What, then, were the choices offered to Soviet composers? All they were supposed to do was to stay away from everything experimental and write "simple, commonplace" music accessible to the masses; as a result, Soviet music had become anything but progressive. While recognizing as a positive feature of the Soviet musical life the efforts accomplished to collect and preserve folk music from all ethnic groups, Nabokov disparaged the excessive reliance on folklore as a source of inspiration. A consequence of this "pernicious fallacy"—Nabokov's views never changed on this subject—was the banality of melodic invention in Soviet music, which was also notable for the absence of polyphony and by the lack of the kind of harmonic audacity Prokofiev had exhibited in his early work. Orchestration was the only domain where Nabokov granted that Soviet composers, like their pre-Revolutionary predecessors, were remarkable; even that of Shostakovich's Leningrad Symphony, which he did not much like on the whole, he described as "genuinely brilliant" when he heard it the following year.[68]

The second *New Republic* article discussed individual composers, three from the older generation, three from the younger one. Among the earlier were Glière, never one of Nabokov's favorites, but redeemed in his eyes, at least, by "the sincerity of his enthusiasm for folk music"; Prokofiev's close friend Miaskovskii, then almost unknown in the Western World, but in Nabokov's view no less an able symphonist than the overrated Sibelius, and whose recent work showed the usual tendencies towards simplicity and folkloric inspiration; and Nabokov's old friend Prokofiev, "one of the greatest musicians of our time," but whose compositions after his return to Russia were characterized by more simplicity, and therefore less originality. In his recent compositions, Nabokov argued,

> the material is second-hand, sometimes of dubious taste, and of dubious freshness. The jokes are harmless, but childish, and I suggest they be tried on an intelligent film cutter in Hollywood before presentation to the public. The harmonies and some of the melodies show repetition of the old devices which we have seen in earlier music of Prokofiev. The themes are often trivial and commonplace; the rhythm is rectangular or triangular.[69]

Yet Nabokov singled out the first of the three 1937 Pushkin songs as being "Prokofiev at his best." Among Soviet composers of the younger generation, he mentioned, of course, Shostakovich, "definitely the most important and the most gifted"; Khachaturian, a composer Nabokov would befriend twenty-five years later, and in whose works, despite his reservations, he found "much charm and a sincere beauty"; and Kabalevsky, "the chief representative of the young academicians," whose lyrical gifts were spoiled by "blatant simplicity and academic conservatism."[70] Despite his strictures, Nabokov concluded his article by suggesting that the music of Soviet composers deserved to be better known and more widely performed in the United States.

Nabokov's *New Republic* articles came out at a time when the USSR was still officially an ally of the Third Reich and, therefore, if not officially an enemy, at least a suspect country. When Nabokov's next article, "Music under Dictatorship," appeared in the January 1942 issue of the *New Atlantic*, the situation had been reversed: Soviet Russia had been invaded by Hitler's forces in June 1941 and, after Germany declared war on the United States in December, Russia and America were fighting on the same side. As Nabokov ironically points out in his first sentence, January 1942, now that the country was being glorified as an American ally, did not "seem the proper time to discuss similarities in the dictatorships of Soviet Russia and Nazi Germany."[71] Yet, he insisted, it was important to remember that the two countries were both dictatorships and that this political similarity had implications in the artistic sphere. To be sure, Germany and Soviet Russia seemed to be two diametrically opposed cases: Germany, on the one hand, with its long and glorious musical tradition, its numerous and flourishing orchestras, opera houses, and choral societies; Russia, on the other hand, with its union-based state system guaranteeing that composers within that system enjoyed a social status and economic stability which, as Nabokov reminded his readers with a touch of bitterness, "few composers of so-called 'serious music' have in the United States."[72] He also stressed, as he had in *The New Republic*, the amount and the quality of musicological research recently undertaken in Russia, notably in the field of what was not yet called ethnomusicology. Behind this facade, however, and especially since the beginning of Stalin's purges, Russian composers lived in a climate of intense censorship, routinely denounced for "formalism" and "bourgeois tendencies." Artistic freedom was further impaired by a government insisting on a uniform musical style, accessible to the uneducated masses—and their uneducated leaders. As a result, most official commissions sounded "like a potpourri of military marches and a Franck symphony."[73] Soviet composers also resorted excessively to folklore of dubious authenticity, forgetting "that the musical culture of the twentieth century needs universality rather than provincialism."[74] Nabokov then discussed the two Soviet composers with an international reputation. Prokofiev, despite his fame and established position, was pressured into

Lubcza, the house where Nabokov was born and spent a large part of his early childhood (Dominique Nabokov archives).

Nabokov's mother in court dress, ca. 1910 (Dominique Nabokov archives).

Preobrazhenka, the estate of Nabokov's maternal grandmother, unidentified contemporary drawing (Dominique Nabokov archives).

The Nabokov siblings' string quartet: from left to right, Onya, Mitya, Mitya's violin teacher, and Nicolas (Dominique Nabokov archives).

Onya's wedding to Viktor Fasolt, Berlin, September 1920. Vladimir Nabokov is second from left at the top; Nicolas is below, ninth from left (courtesy of Nikolaus and Sophie Fasolt).

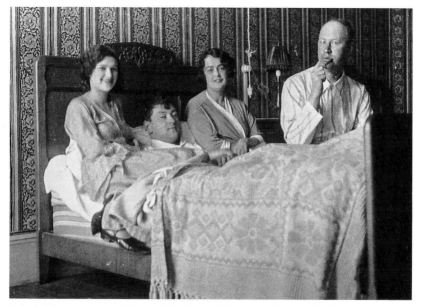

From left to right: Natalie Nabokov, Nabokov, Lina Prokofiev, and Sergey Prokofiev, during their June 1930 gastronomic tour (photograph Felix von Bethmann-Hollweg).

At a concert of La Sérénade, Strasbourg, 1932: from left to right, Vittorio Rieti, Henri Sauguet, Darius Milhaud, Yvonne de Casa-Fuerte, Nabokov, Madeleine Vhita, and Jacques Février (Dominique Nabokov archives).

Nabokov in 1934, photographed by Cecil Beaton (Dominique Nabokov archives, copyright Condé Nast).

Constance, Nabokov's second wife, at about the time of their wedding (courtesy
Peter and Linda Nabokov).

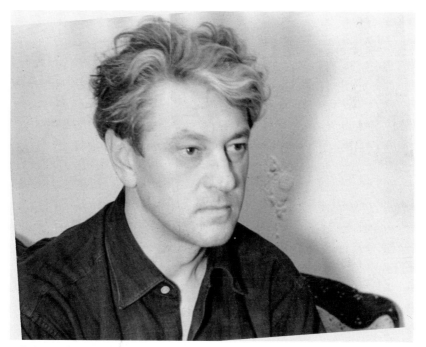
Nabokov in the early 1940s (Ivan and Claude Nabokoff archives).

Nabokov and his father, Berlin, 1945 (Ivan and Claude Nabokoff archives).

Nabokov in 1946 with Charles Thayer (right) and the head of programming at Voice of America (Dominique Nabokov archives).

Nabokov and Balanchine with Stravinsky and his wife, Hollywood, December 1947 (Dominique Nabokov archives).

Nabokov signing copies of *Old Friends and New Music*, New York, 1951. Behind him are Virgil Thomson (left), Patricia Blake, and the painter Eugene Berman (Dominique Nabokov archives).

Nabokov and Marie-Claire at their wedding,
1953 (courtesy Alexandre Nabokoff).

Nabokov and Igor Markevitch at Verderonne, 1950s (photograph by Topazia Markevitch, courtesy of Allegra Chapuis).

Nabokov with W. H. Auden, Ischia, 1950s, possibly with the poet Jules Supervielle
(Dominique Nabokov archives).

conforming to the "official style," producing works (Nabokov singled out *Romeo and Juliet*) "full of trivial and obvious themes, conventional harmonies, and a general artificial simplicity."[75] As for Shostakovich, he had emerged from disgrace with works like the Fifth Symphony ("less convincing" than his First, in Nabokov's view) that were "always reminiscent of nineteenth-century music."[76] Nabokov contrasted such "banal and even trite" products with Shostakovich's 1940 Piano Quintet, which he described as "an attractive piece, every bar of which rings absolutely true."[77] Yet, no matter how dispiriting the state of Soviet music, the situation in Nazi Germany, behind the surface glitter, was far grimmer. Citing Hitler and Rosenberg, and pointing out the "nonsense" and "confusion" of their "blood and earth" rhetoric, Nabokov explained how the reorganization of artistic life since 1933 had put music under complete control of Goebbels's Ministry of Propaganda. Quoting from Karl Gänzer's *Richard Wagner und das Judentum*, he pointed out that Wagner had become an instrument of the Nazis' anti-Semitic policies. "No doubt," he commented, "the Nazis have good reasons to admire Wagner."

> There seldom has been a more confused thinker, a more insipid and obvious poet ("torturer of the German language," as Rilke used to call him), more blatant, ungrateful, and brutal Anti-Semite than Wagner. It is quite enlightening to read his *Judentum in der Musik*, as well as his recently published *Diaries for King Louis II of Bavaria*. In both of these books Wagner foreshadows Rosenberg or even Goebbels himself.[78]

The state of contemporary music in Germany, now that prominent avant-garde composers like Hindemith had been driven into exile, was bleak. The musical establishment was dominated by "either faithful Nazis or opportunists and conformists"; Nabokov cited the names of Hermann Grabner, Paul Graener, and Julius Weismann, who could fit one or the other category.[79] Richard Strauss, having gotten over his contretemps with Goebbels over his collaboration with Stefan Zweig, seemed to "prosper as never before" in Nazi Germany, where he was "firmly entrenched as the Number One living German composer."[80] The music of Pfitzner, who was then little known in America ("and let us hope will remain so"), and famous above all for his "endlessly long and endlessly dull" *Palestrina*, was "definitely old-fashioned, 'routine-romantic,' imperfect in form and academic in spirit."[81] Save for the obvious names, music from the outside world was either *verboten*—especially if by Jewish composers—or *unerwünscht* (undesirable). Nabokov insisted on the obsessive, all-encompassing nature of Nazi antisemitism and its consequences in the musical world. He concluded his survey by stressing, once again, that in both Soviet Russia and Nazi Germany musical life was "nothing but a facade behind which lies a great despair."[82]

Nabokov returned to the cases of Prokofiev and Shostakovich in greater detail in his next two articles. Whereas his first article for the *Atlantic Monthly* made no mention of his old friendship with Prokofiev, the second, in the July 1942 issue, consists largely of personal reminiscences. Given the autobiographical tone of the piece (which was later reworked in the 1951 memoir *Old Friends and New Music*), comments on Prokofiev's new works are less acerbic than in the earlier piece. Deploring that a number of recent scores, such as the 1940 opera *Semyon Kotko*, were not accessible in the West, Nabokov also praises the sixth Piano Sonata of 1939–40. Still, he points out that Prokofiev's music has gone through "a process of simplification" and suggests that this process may have been "forced upon the composer by that particular ideological constellation now prevailing in the U.S.S.R."[83] In most of the recent works that have reached the West, there are "disconcerting signs" which "all point to the same direction." The melodic invention "begins to lose its individuality in a frame of not very well digested and often old-fashioned folk material." Even the Second Violin Concerto, for its appealing lusciousness, contains sections that are "in essence trivial and terribly old-fashioned." The article ends on a sober, respectful reflection on the plight of a musician currently living through the "Thermopylae and Verdun" of his country's history.[84]

If Nabokov's criticism of Prokofiev's music is distinctly muted in this July 1942 article, there is nothing muted in "The Case of Dimitry Shostakovich," which appeared in the March 1943 issue of *Harper's Magazine*. There too Nabokov begins with personal reminiscences, recalling how he came to discover the music of the young Soviet composer when Prokofiev had brought it to his attention in the late 1920s. At the time, he admits, Shostakovich's piano works "did not impress me as being particularly new or imaginative, nor did they seem to me to reflect a well-formed personality of the first rank."

> They sounded so orthodox, so well-behaved, and so reminiscent of older Russian piano music that it was odd to realize that they had emanated from the most revolutionary land in the world. They lacked completely the audacious experimental spirit which was sweeping through the music of central and Western Europe in the nineteen-twenties. I could not understand why this music should be rated so highly and why so much was to be expected from its young author. It did not seem better or worse than most of the older music of Russian composers that Prokofiev had brought back from the Soviet Union.[85]

This first impression was modified to some extent when Nabokov looked at the score of Shostakovich's First Symphony, which impressed him with its melodic qualities and overall developmental technique. Yet, even there, "there was something old about the music, something essentially conservative and unexperimental." It lacked personality and invention.

> There was no actual plagiarism, of course, but the whole atmosphere of the piece was synthetic and impersonal. It was like a good suit of ready-made clothes, which reminds you longingly of a good London tailor, or like one of those tidy modern cubicles in a Dutch or German workers' settlement— all perfectly built, according to the best-known techniques, very proper and neat yet infinitely impersonal and, in the long run, extremely dull.[86]

Now that Shostakovich, in 1942, has been catapulted to the pinnacle of international fame, Nabokov continues, it is legitimate to wonder whether his success is genuinely deserved or is, rather, "the result of a propitious political constellation." The article then summarizes Shostakovich's career from the beginning. He first pictures the young Shostakovich (Nabokov's junior by three years) first deciphering Haydn and Mozart on the piano with his mother, then being "swept away by an ardent passion for the esoteric music of Scriabin," yet liking Tchaikovsky "with a love often inexplicable to foreigners but natural to every Russian"; and after discovering "the great 'polyphonic miracle' of Bach" (but also "Beethoven the revolutionary"), rejecting "the Teutonic Wagnerian brew."[87] This could almost be a description of Nabokov's own musical evolution. By the mid-1920s, as Nabokov points out, Shostakovich was also unusually aware of modern trends in Western contemporary music. Yet by then he had "become an 'intellectual worker' of the Proletarian Republic, one hundred percent Stalinist-Communist, whose chief apostolate is to serve his government (and through it its people) according to his government's wishes and advices."[88] Such selflessness, Nabokov admits, is admirable; citing some of Shostakovich's wartime patriotic statements, he compares it to "the noble morality of the artisan-musician of the Middle Ages." But "as a permanent principle," this subservience of the artist to political ends is dangerous.

Nabokov's article then returns to the issue of the condemnation by Stalin of Shostakovich's *Lady Macbeth of Mtsensk District.* As in his *New Republic* survey, Nabokov, while granting that the opera is not altogether devoid of merit, dismisses it as "old-fashioned, provincial, and unimaginative," reminiscent of "many naturalistic Russian operas written in the eighties and now happily forgotten."[89] If this negative opinion may sound excessive, it was no different from Stravinsky, who had dismissed the opera as "a work of lamentable provincialism."[90] The main issue, for Nabokov, was not one of musical worth; it was that Shostakovich, confronted, on a personal level, with the real threat of his physical elimination, was then forced into the same process of simplification Nabokov detected in Prokofiev's Soviet period. In Shostakovich's case it meant that "*all* of his original musical thinking was definitely swallowed up by the 'service to the cause.' "[91]

"It is as difficult to describe the music of Shostakovich," Nabokov suggests in the last part of his survey,

> as to describe the form and color of an oyster, not because this music is by any means complicated or "inscrutable in its profundity" (as Soviet criticism puts it) but simply because it is shapeless in style and form and impersonal in color. Yet the oyster has a very individual taste of its own which Shostakovich unfortunately lacks. For one of his chief weaknesses is absolute eclectic impersonality. Even during his first period, when he still felt himself relatively free to choose or invent his own technique, his music was impersonal.[92]

Even the two positive qualities one must recognize in Shostakovich's music are ambiguous. The first, his craftsmanship and "his great versatility and efficiency in Conservatory training," conceals "a paucity of original musical ideas." The second, "the inherent optimism of his music"—a trait Nabokov argues, contrary to popular opinion, is not specific to Soviet Russia, since it can be found in foremost Russian composers of the past—takes, in his case, "a redundant, blatant, and unconvincing form."[93] For the rest, Nabokov's assessment is resolutely negative: "naive and dated formulae," "verbose and brassy style which soon becomes dreary and monotonous," "wooden 2/4 or 4/4 rhythms," "grandiloquent sentimentality and formlessness."[94] Only in the chamber music can one detect the presence of "an individual, a free artist."[95] In his conclusion, Nabokov deplores that Shostakovich's "bubble reputation" in the United States, the work of commercially minded "maestros and managers," has been achieved at the expense of more original and deserving artists, among whom he lists three Americans—Piston, Copland, and William Schuman—along with Stravinsky, Hindemith, Milhaud, and Rieti.

It should be borne in mind that Nabokov was reacting against what he viewed above all as a propaganda-driven phenomenon. As he reminded his readers, Shostakovich was then hailed as "the new Beethoven" or "the new Berlioz" (the Mahler comparison was yet to be made). The Leningrad Symphony, despite its "cumbersome length," had by then been performed more often than any contemporary work. Toscanini and Stokowski competed for its Western premiere (Nabokov reviewed the Toscanini broadcast in *The New Republic*);[96] and Shostakovich's thirty-sixth birthday, in September 1942, was celebrated in San Francisco with a festival and a congratulatory telegram signed by Charlie Chaplin, Paul Robeson, and the two star conductors just mentioned.[97] While there was, in the face of such overwhelming success, an undeniable element of provocation in Nabokov's attitude, his main point was a serious one, which corresponded to the views held by his Dumbarton Avenue friends: it was to denounce the exploitation of art for purposes of political propaganda. Much as Bohlen and Kennan were annoyed by the willingness of the Roosevelt Administration to forget the evils of Stalinism for the sake of the nation's military goals, Nabokov objected to Shostakovich's music being promoted in the United States for ideological, rather than aesthetic, considerations. By reaction, his assessment is couched in strictly musical terms. Being Russian, he was, to be sure, better informed than most people on the realities of Soviet Russia; nor does he underestimate the dangers Shostakovich (and his family) risked. But his purpose was to discuss Shostakovich as composer—a gifted composer embracing a revolutionary regime and becoming the victim of his own revolutionary zeal when the same regime turns against him. One point Nabokov comes close to making but does not quite formulate, when praising works like Shostakovich's Piano Quintet (or Prokofiev's Sixth Piano Sonata), is that the only space for relative creative freedom left to Soviet composers under Stalin was the sphere of chamber and instrumental music.

Nabokov's unpopular view of a popular composer earned him, as he recalled, "angry letters of rebuttal."[98] One reader of the article, however, was particularly pleased with it (taking particular pleasure in the "oyster" simile).[99] On September 8, 1943, from his new Southern California residence, Stravinsky congratulated Nabokov on his "brilliant articles on Prokofiev [. . .] and Shostakovich," adding that he was gratified "that these American reviews take an interest in a mentality such as yours."[100] Nabokov had resumed contact with Stravinsky a few days before this letter to indicate that he was now planning to write an article on him, outlining the main points he intended to make:

> Technique in the classical tradition is not an external adornment, but the very essence of music; if one tries to isolate technique from the musical fabric, music becomes an academic matter . . . Your music is crucial in this regard, since it brings technique and artistic meaning together again, after the estrangement brought about by the hubris of the nineteenth century.[101]

This initial exchange was followed by more letters, in which Nabokov asked for details about Stravinsky's recent works he planned to discuss in his piece.

Rejected by *Harper's* for being too technical, Nabokov's article "Stravinsky Now" appeared (possibly as a result of Edmund Wilson's recommendation) in the summer issue of *Partisan Review*, and with a dedication to Maritain. It begins with the anecdote ("true or apocryphal") of Stravinsky in a car asking the driver to turn on the windshield wipers—on a clear day—in order to record on paper their peculiar, irregular rhythm. Nabokov then turns to the central question of his piece: has Stravinsky, as skeptics claim, been on the decline since the end of his so-called "Russian period"? This question itself hinges on a more general issue, since it presupposes that "the presence of national characteristics is not only an asset but a necessary virtue of musical art." Should music, then, "reflect the 'tone color' of a national culture"?[102] If so, should Stravinsky's neoclassical works be seen as "a perverse aberration, designed to camouflage the decline of his creative powers, his loss of confidence and national deracination?"[103] Many have indeed objected to Stravinsky's evolution on musical grounds. They were puzzled by the apparent return to tradition of a composer whose early, revolutionary work had meant "a complete overturn of outmoded rules of musical writing, and a process of liberating the musician from the habit of past musical systems."[104] A further group of critics were disconcerted by a certain "aridity" in Stravinsky's new contrapuntal style, in his harmonic language, which seemed to combine conventional and modern effects, and even in his orchestration. As a result, Stravinsky, compared, for instance, to his Californian neighbor Schoenberg, had become an isolated figure and lost much of his influence. Was Stravinsky, then, "a good Russian composer with Parisian overtones who has now outlived his time"? To such views, Nabokov responds that Stravinsky's recent music is "consistent with his former genius" and "quite as 'radical' as it was at the time of the *Rites [sic] of Spring*."[105]

To bolster his argument, Nabokov first turns to Stravinsky's own exposition of his aesthetics in his Harvard lectures, written in collaboration with Suvchinskii and published under the title *Poétique musicale*, where he famously argued that music was "primarily and essentially a structural organization devoid of any conceptual meaning" and that the idea that it could teach or even express anything was an illusion, or at best a convention. Conversely, what music can achieve, Nabokov writes, is to express the present moment through measure, meter, and form, and stabilize or "petrify" it, as Goethe might have said, "in a beautiful and comprehensible form."[106] Music—and here Nabokov's analysis matches his diagnosis of the perils of ideological views of music in totalitarian systems—should not be discussed in terms of content or message, but in terms of "craft, form and style." By the same token, musical tradition acquires a special significance, beyond the mere "transmission of certain formal conventions from generation to generation."[107] It is a living continuum, the very substance of music. It should not be understood in terms of "dead scholasticism" but, on the contrary, as a series of cycles in which even "revolutions" make sense. Faithful to views he had expressed as early as 1931, Nabokov contrasts this with the negative effects of the interest in supposedly "authentic" folk elements when "national" musical schools constituted themselves, notably in Russia. Romanticism, with its emphasis on self-expression, and the leitmotif-based Wagnerian Gesamtkunstwerk, are listed as examples of other "perverse" conceptions of the meaning and function of music. Stravinsky thus represents a timely return to a rigorous understanding of tradition. In his case, it is achieved by his impeccable craftsmanship and, on the other hand, by a concern for continuous renewal. Unlike other "neoclassical" composers, who, Nabokov amusingly remarks, truly deserve to be tagged with the label of "formalism" dear to the Soviets, Stravinsky, rather than mimicking his classical sources of inspiration (Bach, for instance, in the Piano Concerto), transforms them. If Stravinsky stopped using Russian material in the 1920s, it was because he felt he had exhausted their creative potential and would only be repeating himself. Those who express disappointment with this abandonment of his Russian roots usually have the most vulgar and primitive expectations of what Russian traits ought to be. In fact, the refined polyphonic style developed by Stravinsky since 1924 transcends the dichotomy between "Russian" and "neoclassical"; it derives naturally from works like *Renard* and *Les noces*. However, Stravinsky's greatest contribution to the Western musical tradition has been as an innovator in rhythm. Melody and harmony—hitherto the two principal preoccupations of composers in the Western musical tradition—are less central concerns for him. And in this respect, Nabokov points out that far from showing a diminution of his creative powers, Stravinsky's most recent works—the Symphony in C, the *Danses concertantes*, the *Dumbarton Oaks* Concerto, *Ode*—reveal his mastery in highlighting "the monometrical unit of the measure, the single beat that determines the life of his musical organism." Their pulsation is based on "the reduction of the metrical tissue to the organic cell."[108] Nabokov equates Stravinsky's achievement in the world of rhythm to what has since been said about Debussy in the world of sound. In closing, Nabokov highlights the importance, in Stravinsky's production, of the Symphony in C, then a relatively underperformed work since its 1940 Chicago premiere (especially compared to Shostakovich's *Leningrad*!). Nabokov sees it as a perfect example of Stravinsky's achievement in terms of "perception of timelessness."

> This perception comes to one most clearly in the epilogue of the symphony. When the music begins to quiet down and the various rhythms, as it were, return to their elements, the divisions of time become longer, quieter and more serene; large, soft, subtly measured chords move slowly on the horizon of vanishing musical time. [. . .]It is as if the old Kronos, having been measured by the mind of a great Diviner and thus having received a face and a shape understandable to us humans—that shape which we call a work of music—were to dissolve itself, vanish, and in departing, give us a glimpse of that peace, that order and beauty which live above our time, our works of art.[109]

Stravinsky was very pleased with Nabokov's article, which he may have read in manuscript before its publication. In Robert Craft's words, he had "found a champion in the largely hostile American press."[110] As for Nabokov, in the space of two years, he had taken a major step by taking a public position in what would become a key issue during the Cold War—the indoctrination and persecution of artists by totalitarian regimes. To his previous careers as musician and teacher, he had added a third (which wouldn't be the last): that of a writer.

In Postwar Germany

NABOKOV CREDITED W. H. AUDEN with inspiring the next major development in his life—his decision to enlist in the US forces that had begun to occupy Germany. In fact, as he himself recalled, for more than a year he had been intending to join the Allied Armed Forces overseas "in some sort of capacity."[1] A cryptic note in a draft table of contents for his autobiography suggests that he had contacts both with the Office of War Information and OSS.[2] This is borne out by his FBI files, which show that an investigation was duly conducted in the spring of 1943 in conjunction with such an application. Save for vitriolic comments made by Barnes and his associates, its results were largely positive, especially from Nabokov's New York contacts such as Dorothy Chadwick, Maritain, and Sol Hurok. As could be expected, several Wells colleagues reported him as being "temperamental," while a confidential informant harped on the gossip caused by Nabokov's extra-marital affair with Constance, but other colleagues provided glowing testimonies. In any event, Nabokov's application was either unsuccessful or withdrawn for some reason.

What Nabokov's surviving personal files show is that on July 27, 1944, he formally applied for full employment by the Federal Government, clearly with a view to being sent to Europe. His application stated that since 1939 or 1940, he had been without news of his father, brother, sister, and stepsister ("according to rumors in a German prison camp").[3] This time, he not only listed Dorothy Chadwick and Maritain, Kay Halle, MacLeish, and Winkie Barr among his references, but also mentioned the Robert Blisses, Frederick Allen, Francis Biddle, and Bohlen among the people he knew socially. Claiming the same qualifications as in his 1942 application, he stated that he believed himself "capable of rendering genuine services as liaison officer, public relations officer, or any other duty for which I will be found fit." That OSS was among the outfits he considered joining is further evidenced by a list of possible references in this agency (one of them Avis Bohlen) prepared by Kay Halle, who, as mentioned in the previous chapter, was herself involved in OSS. Nabokov's application was, however, turned down. While he got full marks for his languages, he did poorly in economics, and his one and only attempt at parachuting was a humiliating disaster, ending with his spending five days in a hospital.[4]

After this failed attempt, another opportunity presented itself in the spring of 1945, when Auden suddenly turned up in military uniform at Isaiah Berlin's Washington flat, when Nabokov was present. Auden explained he had joined the Morale Division of the US Strategic Bombing Survey and had come to say good-bye, as he was about to be "shipped overseas."[5] On Auden's advice, Nabokov called what Isaiah Berlin apparently referred to as "that Jewish outfit at the Pentagon," consisting of a Miss Katz, who took him to be interviewed by a Mr. Kohn, following which he was cross-examined by a Mr. Kalksteen.[6] Applications were filled out, and a few weeks later Nabokov was summoned from Baltimore to Washington and flown to Europe on June 1 in a military DC4 (his first transatlantic flight). He landed in London, where he introduced himself to Isaiah Berlin's parents,[7] and from there went to Paris, where he stayed in a hotel near the Madeleine requisitioned by the US army. In the few days he had before taking the train to Hamburg, he visited friends he had not seen since 1938, such as Suvchinskii and Remizov. Of his other friends, Lifar was officially in disgrace for having taken advantage of the Occupation to advance his career, behaving, in Poulenc's words, with "an infantile imprudence because of his taste for publicity."[8] Cocteau himself was under a cloud, mostly because of his ill-advised social contacts with the occupants.[9] If he met with him, Nabokov no doubt heard about Cocteau's desperate efforts to save their friend Max Jacob, whose brother and sister had perished at Auschwitz and who himself, arrested by the Nazis in February 1944, had died in early March at the transit camp of Drancy, outside Paris.[10]

Nabokov had strong personal reasons to wish to be sent to Germany as part of the American occupation forces. His father was among the displaced people who had been driven away from Kielce, in Soviet-occupied Poland, where his property had been expropriated; he and his wife were held in a refugee camp near Weimar. Nabokov's sister Onya, whom he had not seen since 1936, had spent the war years in Berlin. She was by then separated from her husband, who had remarried and for a while was posted in Paris as part of the German occupation forces. Of their two children, the elder, Nikolaus, born in 1921, was mobilized in 1939 and, having fought on the Russian front, was seriously wounded in Finland in 1942. Marina, the younger, born in 1923, married, in 1943, Boris Ledkovsky, a musician and Russian choir director. The best man at her wedding had been their cousin Sergei Nabokov, Vladimir's brother, who also lived in Berlin. Arrested in 1941 and again in late 1943, on charges of "subversive activities," Sergei was deported to a camp near Hamburg and died there as a result of illness, exhaustion, and malnutrition. Felix Bethmann-Hollweg and his wife

had escaped the war. Shortly after landing in Hamburg, Nabokov got in touch
with him and drove to their estate of Altenhof, near the town of Eckernförde in
Schleswig-Holstein, and spent two days with them. Then he must have heard
about the fate of their friend Albrecht von Bernstorff. A member of Hanna
Solf's anti-Nazi circle, Bernstorff was arrested in January 1944 along with all
its members after they were betrayed by a Gestapo spy. Sent to the Ravensbrück
concentration camp, tortured, and subsequently tried for high treason before
Hitler's notorious "People's Court," Bernstorff was removed from jail just before
the Allied raid that destroyed the Volksgerichtshof on April 21 and shot under
circumstances that have never been fully elucidated. A different kind of loss
was that Lubcza, Nabokov's birthplace, was no more, having been destroyed
when the Soviet army took control of what had been part of Poland. To be sure,
Nabokov had long come to terms with the fact that his first home was no longer
his. "When I returned to the place where I was born," he later recalled, "it was
so sad to see that part of Russia now entirely Polonized, and to see the land crying, the forests crying. It was as if they too had lost their country. And I felt it
very deeply. I spent hours watching the sun setting over the Niemen River. And
the sun was telling me: 'Goodbye, go away, you are no longer part of this.' "[11] Yet
the news of the destruction of his childhood home—of which only the old tower
survived—must have touched him on a deep personal level.

The US Strategic Bombing Survey was established by the Secretary of War,
Henry Stimson, in late November 1944, as a body independent from the army, to
assess the effect of the air raids conducted by the Anglo-American forces in 1944
and 1945. The Morale Division, which Nabokov and Auden had joined, was headed
by Rensis Likert, an early expert on public opinion polls. Its task was to interview
civilians with a view to gathering information on how the "morale" of the popula-
tions had been affected, with questions such as, "Which bombs did you find the
most frightening?". Nabokov's unit consisted of a colonel from Nebraska ("tall,
stocky, taciturn"), a young captain from Minnesota, and a sergeant who was a refugee from the Third Reich and consequently hated Germany and all things German.
They were billeted in a spacious villa outside Lübeck, which they shared with a
group of officers from the Allied armies: Ossia Trilling, a captain in the British
Army, who spoke six languages, including Russian, and subsequently became
a respected theater critic; a Lieutenant Filonenko from France, also Russian-
speaking; and a young Soviet lieutenant named Anatolii Balakirsky, a Cossack
and survivor from the battle of Stalingrad, who spoke nothing but Russian. While
Nabokov and his colleagues were conducting surveys for the Strategic Bombing
Morale Division, the other group was the Inter-Allied Repatriation Commission
supervising the transfer of refugees from Russia and other Soviet-controlled countries from a camp outside Lübeck, in the British zone, to another camp situated
in Hardenburg, in the Soviet zone. Seeing in Nabokov a useful witness and ally,

Trilling and Filonenko urged him to take a ten-day leave, which his colonel readily granted, and join their unit.

The "transfer" took place twice a week, on Monday and Thursday. A convoy of half a dozen flatcars, full of pitiful "human cattle," as Filonenko described it—men, women, and children—arrived at what remained of the bombed-out Lübeck train station. The front of the old-fashioned locomotive was decorated with red flags and a portrait of Stalin. The hapless occupants of the flatcars were called, name by name, by a Soviet security officer and a British Member of Parliament, while the liaison officers stood by and watched. After all the names had been called, the train departed, and the Allied officers boarded two "liberated" Opels in which they were driven to the Hardenburg train station. When the train appeared, the Soviet military band played the four Allies' national anthems. The list of names was submitted to the Soviet commandant (an elderly colonel who had taught at the Leningrad Technicum) while the unloading took place. After a brief, perfunctory patriotic speech to the assembled "displaced persons," the commandant invited the Allied officers for a glass of vodka and zakuskis before the observers were driven back to Lübeck. During the three or four times he witnessed this "ceremony," Nabokov learned that the commandant's wife, "a sweet and gentle-looking elderly woman," was the daughter of his family's parish priest in St. Petersburg—she wore a cross—and that she and her husband had adopted a fourteen-year-old boy they had found in a camp, where the Nazis had knocked out all his teeth.[12]

The staff of the villa outside Lübeck consisted of young Russian or Ukrainian refugee women, supervised by a former vice-governor of Kherson named Ivan Nikolaevich Ipatov, a distant relative of Helena Blavatsky and himself a theosophist Buddhist of the Mahayan denomination.[13] Inevitably, Tolya Balakirsky, the young Soviet lieutenant, had fallen in love with Irina, one of the Russian women. As Nabokov's "leave" was coming to an end, Tolya was visited by two KGB officers who brought him his demobilization orders. Reminding him that officers on duty abroad were forbidden to marry, they informed him that he would not be allowed to bring Irina with him and she would be returned to where she came from. A distressed Tolya begged Nabokov to plead his cause with the officer in charge of the central zonal headquarters. There, Nabokov was curtly rebuffed: his visit was entirely out of place, since the case concerned an active member of the Soviet armed forces.

That same evening, Tolya and Irina were married by the theosophist ex-governor of Kherson in a Buddhist ceremony. On the makeshift altar were a bowl of rice, a candle, and images of Buddha and Blavatsky. The calligraphied marriage certificate, in four languages, was signed by Nabokov and his colonel acting as witnesses. Tolya left the next morning, his Opel full of brass instruments "liberated" from a German band, and that same afternoon two Russian officers came and picked up Irina. Nabokov never knew whether the newlyweds were actually reunited.

In the last days of June 1945, Nabokov was transferred with his unit to the European headquarters of the Strategic Bombing Morale Survey, located in Bad Homburg, a small spa town in Hesse, near Frankfurt. There, at the Kurhaus Hotel where he was billeted, he was unexpectedly reunited with Auden and spent the next eight or ten days in his company, while they were treated, along with other members of the Morale Division personnel, to debriefing sessions conducted by John Kenneth Galbraith. Having nothing to do "but enjoy being together," they spent their days "taking long walks in the pine woods that surrounded the little Middle German town" or having drinks on the terrace of the hotel, staying aloof from their USBUSS colleagues, most of whom Auden considered "crashing bores" belonging "to a world that neither you nor I can possibly like or condone."[14]

As remembered by Nabokov, his conversations with Auden, when they were not focused on the war and its consequences, turned to music, literature, and philosophy. Auden, who considered the ballet a "very, very minor art" and was yet to meet Stravinsky personally, shared Nabokov's own preference for his "post-Russian" period, and his general suspicion towards any folkloric influences in music. Auden discussed two projects dear to him: an English translation of Goethe's *Italianische Reise* (completed in collaboration with Elizabeth Mayer, it was published in 1962); and an essay on Kierkegaard, a philosopher Nabokov then knew nothing about.

Auden had by then spent six weeks in Germany, Nabokov about three. The devastation they had witnessed had made a profound impression on them both. Nabokov reports Auden as saying that the word "morale" in the name of their organization "made him squirm."

"How can one learn anything about *morals* when one's actions are *beyond* any kind of morality? *Morale* with an e at the end is psycho-sociological nonsense. What they *want* to say, but *don't* say, is how many people we killed and how many buildings we destroyed by that wicked bombing."[15]

Nabokov told Auden about visiting Nazi concentration and extermination camps in the few weeks before their meeting (Belsen, Büchenwald, Dachau, among others).[16] Auden commented on "the horror of their meticulously systematic organization," to which the Nazis had brought, in Auden's reported words, "the same pedantic organizational skills a piano tuner does when he tunes a virtuoso's concert grand."[17]

By the time Nabokov arrived in Germany, the US Strategic Bombing Survey was wrapping up its activities—"I always come at the end of lives and things,"

Nabokov noted in an early autobiographical draft.[18] The question of what to do next came up in his conversations with Auden, who himself would soon be demobilized and return to America via England. Nabokov saw him in London before his departure. On this occasion, Auden brought him as his guest to a party hosted by Stephen Spender and his wife Natasha at their house on Loudoun Road: this was the first meeting between Nabokov and his future collaborator.[19]

Apart from his desire to help his relatives in Berlin, Nabokov also had a strong political personal motivation to remain in Germany. What he had witnessed in Lübeck—"debased, dejected, exploited and hunted human beings, who lived in crowded camps in an agony of fear and despair," being turned over to the Soviets with the complicity of Western powers—was, as he subsequently saw it, a crucial stage in his political awakening.[20]

> I felt pangs of conscience and a kind of helpless misery at not being able to do something about it—something to help Americans, especially the American leadership, realize the plight of these Russian, Ukrainian, and other DP's gleaned from Soviet Russia, *now* being shipped by *us* into slavery and certain destruction.[21]

Nabokov's concerns may have originated from conversations preceding his departure with his Dumbarton Avenue friends. These conversations had solidified his belief that Nazism and Soviet totalitarianism were related forms of the same evil. Once in Germany, he resolved to remain in Berlin for a while as part of the Allied Military Government.

Through the Office of Psychological Warfare, which was also based in Bad Homburg, Nabokov applied for a position with the Information Control Division being put in place in the German capital. He was recruited on a one-year contract as a civilian attached to the War Department with the "assimilated" rank of colonel, and wearing the appropriate military uniform. The ICD was a branch of the Office of Military Government (OMGUS), headed by General Lucius D. Clay, who had served as Eisenhower's deputy in the final months of the war. Headed by General Robert A. McClure, who had previously been in charge of Psychological Warfare, the division was itself divided into several subsections, the one Nabokov joined as vice-chief being specifically concerned with theater, music, and film.

The Berlin where Nabokov arrived by jeep in mid-August 1945 was a "smoldering heap of rubble."[22] He was billeted in a comfortable villa requisitioned by the United States in Dahlem, equipped with a Blüthner grand piano, which he and his adjutant, Kurt Hirsch, shared with "two friendly colonels and a perpetually drunken 'civ' in uniform."[23] Food and supplies were, of course, abundantly available from commissaries and PX's, whereas his German neighbors "nestled in bombed out damp and unheated homes with whatever furniture they were able to save from the bombings' fires. Their diets were on the starvation level and their clothing was minimal. Many facilities were out of order and for any kind of repairs, the Allied has first-call priorities."[24] Unlike his more boorish colleagues, who shrugged it off on the grounds that the "Krauts" had brought it upon themselves, Nabokov, perhaps because he himself had German relatives then living under similar conditions, found the contrast "not only shocking, but at times insufferable." He was equally appalled by the thriving black market and "general freewheeling." Though "fraternization" was in theory forbidden, there was, of course, a fair amount. He once expelled from his billet a "beautiful German blonde" who was a regular nightly visitor of his adjutant. She turned out to be the actress—and later chanteuse—Hildegard Knef. Nabokov was best man when she eventually married Hirsch.

Once he was reunited with his sister, one of Nabokov's urgent concerns was to get her and her family out of the Soviet occupation zone. This he was able to accomplish with the help of a new acquaintance who, several years later, was to become his closest collaborator. Born in 1908 in Dorpat, Estonia (the present-day Tartu), Michael Josselson, whose father was a timber merchant, was schooled in Berlin in the 1920s and attended university there and in Freiburg.[25] His first employment was with the Berlin office of the Gimbel-May department stores, for which he arranged wholesale purchases in several European countries. In 1935, fleeing Nazi Germany, he was transferred to France and promoted to manager of Gimbel's Paris office. Two years later he emigrated to the United States with his French wife, becoming head of Gimbel's European operations in New York, until the war caused Gimbel to reassign him to a different position in Pittsburgh. Having become an American citizen in 1942, he joined the US Army the following year. Because of his fluency in French, German, and Russian, he was assigned to the Intelligence Section of the Psychological Warfare Division and worked as interpreter with the rank of lieutenant. When Nabokov met him, Josselson was attached as Cultural Affairs Officer to the American Military Government in Berlin and was able to use his connections to help Onya and her family. "Handsome, with sharp, stinging dark eyes that betrayed a quick intelligence and an instant, ever ready sense of humor," Nabokov recalled, "he was gay, full of pep, hard working, yet convivial and securely incorruptible."[26] Nabokov, by his own admission, was naturally prejudiced in favor of Balts ("to me Balts had always seemed to be people of a higher cultural standing than, for example, White Russians, or Lithuanians, or average Germans . . ."). He was further drawn to Josselson because of the strong anti-totalitarian views they shared, and which applied with equal force to Nazi Germany and Soviet Russia.[27] Because of his position as an army intelligence officer in Berlin, Josselson was "privy to a lot of confidential information and familiar with what went on in the hugely disorganized but pervasively brutal opposite camp."[28] The "opposite camp" meant not only the Soviet military government, which, as Nabokov proudly noted, had its headquarters in a suburb of Berlin named after a Prussian family he was related to (Karlshorst), but also the Soviet satellite state that was being put into place in another suburb, Pankow. There were, besides, Communist sympathizers in American uniform, some of them well-meaning fellow travelers, others more or less overtly working for the other camp. "The fight against those latter-day crooks," Nabokov recalled, "was for my lieutenant friend and for myself and for a very long time a frustrating losers game. The obtuseness of the chief American satrap in Germany, General Lucius Clay, prevented and obstructed any kind of cleanup job."[29] Given their background, Josselson and Nabokov had one other major concern in common that was clearly shared by few of their American colleagues: it was the plight of Eastern European emigres threatened with deportation to Soviet Russia with the blessing and cooperation of the Western powers. In September 1945 Nabokov signed a collective plea sent from Berlin to President Truman urging him, on behalf of all Russian-speaking Americans in uniform, not to let American authorities repatriate Soviet refugees without their personal consent.[30] The plea went nowhere, but Nabokov was impressed with the "swift, efficient, and courageous action" Josselson displayed whenever he could personally intervene and by his ability to cut through red tape, which allowed him to save lives.[31] It was thanks to him that Nabokov heard, in the winter of 1945–46, that the Soviets had begun rounding up and deporting Russians in their Berlin sector and he urgently needed to bring his sister and her family to safety.

Since 1919, Nabokov's contacts with Russians had been limited to emigres, save for the few intellectuals and artists visiting from the Soviet Union in his early Berlin and Parisian years. Now, for the first time, he had a chance to interact with Red Army officers or other Soviet officials, first in Lübeck, then in Berlin. It was, in fact, one of his chief motivations for staying in postwar Germany: "I wanted to meet Russians, speak to them, see what they are like, what they think, how they behave, what they say."[32] He clearly relished the opportunities that were suddenly given to him when, in December 1945, he was appointed coordinator of Inter-Allied negotiations, a position he kept until the following July. The writer Louis Fischer, a Soviet Union specialist and former fellow-traveler, who met Nabokov at the time, as he was working as journalist accredited by General Clay, has left a lively account of an evening when he joined Nabokov at a dinner hosted by his Russian opposite number. Fischer and Nabokov, accompanied by another Russian-born State Department official, were driven to East Berlin that evening, by way of the Tiergarten, "now a vast, treeless, burnt-out field," and Unter der Linden, "formerly Berlin's most elegant thoroughfare, today a shambles."[33] Karlshorst, however, had escaped total destruction, and the Soviet occupation forces had taken over spacious upper-middle-class villas. Nabokov and his party were met at the curb by their host, a thirty-two-year-old colonel named Gulayev and his young wife, who also wore a Red Army uniform and had the rank of lieutenant. Other guests on the Russian side included another woman junior lieutenant employed as a typist in a military office, a Soviet civilian working for the army, and another Russian couple. Vodka was poured liberally while, in the adjoining room, a copious buffet was unveiled—"an endless variety of fish and meat cold cuts, pickled cucumbers, pickled tomatoes, pickled watermelon, black olives, and several kinds of bread, from black to almost-white . . ." This turned out to be only the preliminaries to a large dinner consisting of "red beet borscht with sour cream and floating boiled potato, a meat entree plus several vegetables, and a compote of fruit succeeded by fresh fruit."[34] Food and drink also constituted, to Fischer's disappointment, the main topic of conversation, until Gulayev and Nabokov started exchanging school reminiscences once it turned out that the Soviet colonel had attended the same German-language institution as the composer. This allowed Nabokov to broach more sensitive topics.

> Skillfully, Nabokov inched over into a forbidden realm and mentioned the recent purge of Soviet writers. Gulayev said they were old and had nothing to say. Nabokov suggested that the poet Pasternak had been writing some very stimulating verse. "They must write what can be published," Gulayev proclaimed.[35]

Fischer was no more successful when he tried to steer the conversation towards the interview of Stalin by the British journalist Alexander Werth that had appeared in *Pravda*. "The party was jolly, even warm and friendly," Fischer concluded, "but, just as in Moscow, after 1936, there was no conversation, only talk, only chitchat. Before many months, even this kind of association between Russians and foreigners came to an end."[36] At one o'clock in the morning, the party of Americans returned to the American sector through "dark canyons of ruins."

Although, as Fischer's testimony shows, Nabokov did not hesitate to try to confront his Soviet counterparts on delicate issues, he was also concerned about their personal fate. "A few of them disappeared in the course of the first twelve months, God only knows where to. When one would ask their colleagues or superiors about them, they put on incredulous expressions upon their bland faces, as if those poor creatures had never existed."[37] One victim of such a "disappearance" was a lieutenant-colonel Nabokov identifies as Golubov, who, in exchange for a case of Pommery champagne and *marc* from the cellar of Marie-Blanche de Polignac—and, more prosaically, in Virgil Thomson's account, penicillin, a crucial need "in an army where venereal disease destroyed careers"—[38] had provided Nabokov's father and his wife with a permit allowing them to join him in West Berlin. It was also from Golubov that Nabokov heard about Bernstorff's fate.[39] When Nabokov subsequently inquired about Golubov, he was told he "must have been under the hallucinatory influence of liquor" when he had imagined meeting him.[40] In reminiscences published shortly after the war, Nabokov also mentions a "young, gentle, and friendly" couple to whom he took a liking; for obvious reasons of discretion, he does not name them, just referring to the woman as Tania. They entertained Nabokov at their small villa in Karlshorst, and he them at this billet in Dahlem.

> First they made one or two critical remarks about the Soviet regime, bathing them each time in a shower of awkward smiles and furtive glances, or Tania, the pale, slight wife of the officer, would take me aside and, after begging me not to repeat it, and not tell her husband, she would tell me a joke about Stalin. Finally, after several months of frequent long talks, their reticence melted away and they talked boldly and bitterly.
>
> It was the same old story, the one I had heard before from hundreds of D.P.'s: fear, and an enormous, all-consuming and totally impotent hatred of the Soviet regime.[41]

A postlude to the Lübeck episode took place in October 1945, when Nabokov heard from Ossia Trilling that the Soviet commandant at Hardenburg was being promoted and demobilized and a party was being given in his honor. Nabokov attended the event and was invited to spend the night at the commandant's lodgings. Announcing he was returning to Russia to teach at the technicum in Omsk, in southwestern Siberia, he told him he would find a souvenir under his pillow, to be opened once he was back in the American zone. It was a cigarette case and an envelope containing a message with words that said—at least as remembered by Nabokov:

> Dear N.D. [. . .], how could you lend yourself to that macabre comedy that took place here in Hardenburg, twice a week, since the end of hostilities. You were a free agent, you could say "No." As you know, we could not. But my wife and I suffered to see you participate in that monstrous crime against humanity. Didn't you know that all those hapless creatures were being shipped to an uncertain future and often, alas, straight to death. Dear N.D.—It is not too late even now to intervene, because the gruesome comedy still continues. Can't you, as a former compatriot, a Russian at heart, help stop this outrage? Don't the Allies know in what murderous an enterprise they are taking part? Please, in the name of the Lord and our short but deep-felt friendship, do something about it. Do anything you can to stop the workings of this diabolical mechanism . . .[42]

One of Nabokov's assignments in Berlin, as a Russian working on the American side, was "to coordinate Allied approaches to music control."[43] This was also the

responsibility he enjoyed the most, and the one that came closest to actual intelligence work. He was supposed to make as many contacts as he could with his
Soviet counterparts, with a view to identifying, among the many bureaucrats of
the Soviet government forces, the ones who had some measure of decision power.
McClure's plan was to reach some information control coordination between the
four powers. Through trial and error, Nabokov succeeded in meeting a Colonel
Kirsanov, who at first tried to dissuade him from pursuing his investigations, but
subsequently invited him to a reception hosted by Marshal Zhukov in Potsdam in
early November 1945. There he was introduced to a Colonel (later Major General)
Sergei Ivanovich Tiul'panov, who turned out to be one of the key players in the
system: a fluent German speaker, he was the head of the propaganda administration for the Soviet Military Administration in Germany.[44] Contacts were established with General McClure, followed by a series of informal meetings in the
early months of 1946, but Tiul'panov long remained evasive whenever the issue
of the quadripartite scheme was raised (presumably because the Russians, who
were pursuing their own agenda, were wary of the idea). Nabokov, however, got to
know Tiul'panov and was frequently his guest, at home or at his headquarters in
Weissensee. After several fruitless attempts, Tiul'panov agreed to attend a dinner
hosted by McClure, at which Nabokov and Josselson joined the Soviet guests in
singing Russian songs, and giving a rousing rendition of "We Are Working on
the Railroad."[45] This direct contact resulted, in April 1946, in the establishment
of a quadripartite Information Services Directorate.[46] When the evening was over,
Tiul'panov gave Nabokov a ride home. During the drive, the high-placed Soviet
official tried to convince him that "a man with a name like Nabokov should be in
Russia, working, toiling for the new life, for the future." Describing the "wonderful new towns in Siberia," he suggested that Nabokov "would have a good place to
live, to teach and to work."[47] But Nabokov replied that he preferred the climate of
New York. As for Tiul'panov, he fell into disgrace with Stalin in 1949 as part of the
purge of the "Leningrad Group" but, luckier than many, lived until 1987.

One of the tasks of the quadripartite commission Nabokov was part of was the
restitution of Nazi confiscations. On one such mission, he accompanied Josselson
and a Russian colonel to retrieve from a salt mine in the US zone the costumes of
the Deutsches Staatsoper to restore them to the company, provisionally installed
in the former Admiralspalast, since the Staatsoper building on Unter der Linden
had been destroyed during an air raid in February 1945.[48] On the return journey, Josselson's jeep, which preceded Nabokov's car, ran into a Soviet roadblock;
Josselson, seriously wounded, was taken to a Russian military hospital.

Along with other members of their division, Josselson and Nabokov were
also both involved in the denazification of artists and musicians accused of having, in one capacity or another, "collaborated" with Hitler's regime. Writing in
1951, still close to the events, Nabokov was careful not to mention any names

when discussing this part of his activities: "We did a good deal of successful Nazi-hunting and put on ice a few famous conductors, pianists, singers and a number of orchestral musicians (most of whom had well deserved it and some of whom should be there today)."[49] ICD members themselves were actually not making decisions in the denazification process, but they played a crucial role at the preparatory stage, notably by interviewing the musicians whose cases were brought to their attention. For anyone favoring an inclusive definition of Nazism, as was apparently the case of the intelligence section of ICD, the list of compromised names was a long one, from Richard Strauss, whose case Nabokov had discussed in his 1941 *Atlantic Monthly* article, to Herbert von Karajan, who (as Heribert Karajan, as he called himself then) had voluntarily joined the Nazi Party as early as 1933—not 1935 as he later claimed—and began his concerts in Nazi-occupied countries with the Horst Wessel Lied.[50] But it also included composers Werner Egk and Carl Orff, conductors Hermann Abendroth, Karl Böhm, Eugen Jochum, Robert Heger, Clemens Krauss, and Hans Tietjen, pianist Walter Gieseking, sopranos Elisabeth Schwarzkopf and Maria Cebotari, and many names now forgotten.[51] Nabokov's phrasing makes it clear that, though evidently not involved himself with the actual interviewing of suspect musicians, he was under no illusion about their evasions and the hypocrisy of some of their denials. He also soon realized that from one occupation zone to another, and especially with the Russians, who had other priorities, there were major differences in the treatment of even notorious Nazi sympathizers.[52] On the other hand, Nabokov strongly disagreed with the view commonly held among the Allied Powers, which was that "compromised" musicians should be banned from their profession. If their activities under the Nazi regime called for severe punishment, better punish them with a prison term, he argued, or by impounding their fees and giving them, instead, to the victims of war or racial persecution. But the stubborn refusal to let them exercise their profession seemed to him an absurdity, and one to which his own status as a musician—a musician whose current employment made it difficult for him to compose—rendered him particularly sensitive.[53]

The most publicized case Nabokov was involved with—and one that exposed the stubbornness of the American occupation authorities on this issue—was that of Wilhelm Furtwängler. The star conductor had pursued his career in Nazi Germany until almost the last minute, seeking refuge in Switzerland in early 1945. Never a member of the Nazi Party, he had been, at different times, in bad odor with some of its establishment. However, given his standing and the fact that his conducting career had flourished under Hitler, his name figured prominently on the list of people in the arts accused of serving the Third Reich. More than any other musician active in Nazi Germany, he was the target of a virulent press campaign in America. Orchestrated, among others, by Nabokov's old friend Sol Hurok, it claimed that he had actively collaborated with the regime and should therefore be considered a "big" Nazi. Yet, in the words of Furtwängler's American biographer Sam Shirakawa, admittedly a sympathetic commentator, Furtwängler's record "clearly showed that he could at best be accused of being a 'little' Nazi who had acted in a big way by giving the Nazis a respectable gloss."[54] The American authorities were therefore under pressure to make an example of him. But Furtwängler was immensely popular in Germany and Austria, where in the eyes of the public his only crime was to have continued to do the job he was paid for (and, of course, very well paid). Unlike others, Karajan for one, Furtwängler did not try to distort or hide the facts of his case; his line of defense, self-serving though it may have been, was that by remaining in Germany, he was not serving the cause of Nazi Germany, but that of "the other Germany": not the Germany of Hitler and Goebbels but that of Beethoven and Goethe.[55] A first hearing in Austria, in March 1946, concluded that Furtwängler had not acted dishonorably and should be allowed to resume his career. The Allied Powers rejected this ruling, maintaining that the conductor needed to justify himself before the appropriate committee in Berlin, and the case threatened to degenerate into "a public relations catastrophe" for ICD.[56]

Nabokov was familiar with the particulars of the affair, including some of its mitigating circumstances: it was thus from Nabokov, in 1945, that the German-born philosopher Raymond Klibansky, dismissed in 1933 for racial reasons from his lectureship in philosophy at the University of Heidelberg, learned that Furtwängler, who barely knew the young philosopher but was acquainted with members of his family, had directly contacted Goebbels to appeal on his behalf.[57] It seems that in Nabokov's own view, the one negative element that could be held against Furtwängler, as he put it in his assessment of the case, was "his position as the outstanding musician of the Third Reich"— in other words, as a symbol rather than an active agent.[58] On this and other issues, Nabokov belonged to the "moderates" within ICD rather than to the "revolutionaries." That the division was itself divided was apparent from its conflicting statements: in February 1946, Nabokov's boss, General McClure (whom Nabokov otherwise considered "a very good general") declared a ban on Furtwängler's conducting in the Western occupation zones, prompting Yehudi Menuhin to send McClure a strongly worded letter of protest and General Clay to remind ICD that denazification was not a matter for them to decide.[59] Two months later McClure admitted that a "mistake" had been made and he expected Furtwängler to be cleared shortly. However, under continued pressure from across the Atlantic, the American authorities blocked conducting offers made to Furtwängler from the British and the Russians and McClure refused to give him clearance in June 1946.[60]

That summer, the four powers finally agreed on a timetable for Furtwängler's denazification: based on his answers to a questionnaire and on his memorandum

on his activities during the Nazi years, he would appear before a German specialist subcommission, whose recommendation was to be forwarded for final clearance to the quadripartite denazification board. Nabokov explained the procedure
to Furtwängler on September 23 in response to an appeal the conductor had
written directly to him on September 7.[61] Nabokov's letter is in English and carefully worded, but the tone is sympathetic. Nabokov suggested that Furtwängler
would need someone to represent him in Berlin while he was waiting for travel
clearance from the Swiss authorities, and passed on Josselson's recommendation of Boleslav Barlog, former director of the Schlosspark Theater in Berlin,
as the right person for the task. Barlog was the first theater director to have
been denazified and he was known to be a friend of Furtwängler; he did in fact
testify movingly at the trial.[62] However, despite Nabokov's assurance that there
would be no further delay, Furtwängler had to wait another two months. In his
exasperation, according to Nabokov's later recollections, he gave a press conference in East Berlin and hinted he would go to Moscow unless cleared at once,
an incident that Nabokov later recalled as triggering McClure's "gentle fury." In
the course of that visit, Furtwängler was brought to Nabokov's billet in Dahlem
and "spent a day and two nights at Bitterstr. 16 before being packed off back to
the Villa Imperator above Montreux. I remember all about our talks with him
(especially his views on Bach, Bayreuth and Brahms)."[63] Unfortunately, Nabokov
did not record these conversations, but, much later, admittedly, he did reconstitute part of the exchange they had on the subject of the charges the conductor
was facing:

I asked: Why did you send from Cairo a patriotic-sounding cable to the N.Y.
Phil[harmonic].
HE: Why patriotic.
ME: You said: I'm not a politician, but *Ein Exponent deutscher Musik*. Why only
deutscher, you do conduct Verdi, Debussy, Stravinsky, not to speak of Vivaldi
and 18th c. Italian comp[osers].
His face showed irritation: Yes, I do conduct music of all countries, but I am
born and ombilically bound to German culture and its music.
ME: Yes but even so couldn't you send the [Hitlers] and [Goebbelses] to the dogs
and accept at once the Philh[armonic's] invitation? If you had, we would surely
not be sitting here, in this villa.[64]

Finally, on December 11, the well-publicized trial started, presided over (at the
Soviets' insistence and to Nabokov's probable dismay) by a Communist named
Alex Vogel. Though the conductor was cleared of all charges—a foregone con-
clusion—at the end of the two-day hearing, it took several months—and some
arm-twisting on Josselson's part—for him to be allowed to conduct the Berlin
Philharmonic again, which he did, triumphantly, on May 25, 1947.[65] By that time

Nabokov was back in the United States, while, in Germany, American officials remained resolutely hostile to Furtwängler.[66]

Another side of Nabokov's duties in Berlin could be described as a goodwill cultural mission: it allowed him to liaise with German musical milieus with a view to facilitating their integration within a new, Democratic Germany.[67] Some of this was achieved through lectures: thus Nabokov, in late 1945, spoke before musical audiences about music in America, introducing his audiences to names such as Barber, Copland, and Virgil Thomson. One of the first callers to Nabokov's office in September 1945 was the Austrian musicologist Josef Rufer (1893–1985), who had studied with Zemlinsky and Schoenberg and served as the latter's assistant at the Berlin Academy until 1933. The purpose of Rufer's visit, as Nabokov dimly recollected three decades later, might have been to reestablish contact with Schoenberg via the US postal services, as international mail was still not functioning in Germany. For his part, Nabokov was eager to make contacts with the German music world and offered to host a reception based on a guest list Rufer would prepare, making sure it would include no composers obviously compromised by their association with the Nazi regime.

The composer who immediately made a powerful impression on Nabokov at that reception, a few days later, was Boris Blacher. Born in China to a Baltic family, Blacher, Nabokov's senior by only a few weeks, had begun his musical education in Harbin and then studied at the Berlin Hochschule für Musik just after Nabokov had departed for Paris.[68] Partly Jewish, and considered by the Nazis as belonging to the "degenerate music" category, he was eventually forced out of his position as composition teacher at the Dresden Conservatory. When Nabokov met him, Blacher had just been appointed at the International Music Institute in Berlin-Zehlendorf. Nabokov was struck at once by Blacher's angular physique and sense of humor—two characteristics he later claimed also characterized Blacher's music—and the two composers began a friendship that lasted until Blacher's death three decades later.

> I liked his imaginative, agile mind, his amusing wit, his crisp sarcasm about his own work, about Berlin, and about the state of music in devastated Germany. He seemed so different from other Germans, with their stodgy spirit and ways, their constant laments and protests of innocence, or their embittered sense of inferiority.[69]

Despite the difficulty of their circumstances, Blacher and his young wife, the pianist Gerty Blacher-Herzog (1922–2014) seemed "light, witty, and fresh." Unlike most other people Nabokov met in Berlin, they had not lost their optimism and remained confident in the future. There is an indication that he and Blacher planned to collaborate on an opera based on a play by Ostrovsky, for which Blacher would have written the libretto (as a few years later he adapted for Gottfried von Einem Kafka's *The Trial*, in collaboration with Heinz von Cramer). This project, which may date from these Berlin years, is one more of Nabokov's operatic projects that never came to fruition.[70]

Another important contact Nabokov made when he was in Berlin was the musicologist Hans Heinz Stuckenschmidt. The two presumably met through Rufer, a close associate of Stuckenschmidt since their student days in Berlin. Born in Strasbourg in 1901, Stuckenschmidt was already well known before the war as a connoisseur and advocate of contemporary music, for which he was on bad terms with the Nazis. Enlisted in the army in 1942, he served as interpreter and was briefly imprisoned by the Allies. Upon his release in 1946, he was appointed, in early June, director of the department of new music at the Berlin Radio. On June 2, the day before he took up his appointment, he met Nabokov at a Sunday concert of the Berlin Philharmonic, then directed by the gifted Romanian conductor Sergiu Celibidache.[71] Stuckenschmidt, in his new position, quickly established himself as one of the most active and influential figures in German contemporary music. One of his immediate plans, which he discussed with Nabokov, was to launch a monthly magazine, entitled *Stimmen* (Voices). Nabokov threw his support behind this project and obtained the necessary license.[72] Co-edited with Rufer, *Stimmen* began publication in 1947. By then, Nabokov had left Germany, but he and Stuckenschmidt remained in touch; they were to have many more opportunities to collaborate in later years.

In July 1946, Nabokov was transferred from the Defense Department to the State Department to work as adviser on cultural affairs to Ambassador Robert Murphy, who, his ambassadorial rank notwithstanding, reported to General Clay. In his new capacity, which he kept until January 1947, Nabokov was able to concentrate on an important part of his former responsibilities, which was both of a concrete and charitable nature: it had to do with the reconstruction of musical life in Germany, in all aspects, beginning with the most practical.

> We had to find halls and houses for the orchestras, operas and conservatories, coal to heat them, roofing and bricks to patch up the leaks and holes, bulbs to light them, instruments for the orchestras, calories for the musicians [. . .]. The bombed-out orchestra libraries needed parts and scores, composers needed music paper and ink; opera houses needed performers and costumes; and everybody needed shelter, food, and fuel.[73]

As the correspondence of Virgil Thomson reveals, Nabokov took these duties very seriously, managing, with Thomson's own intervention, to raise the rations of musicians of the Berlin Philharmonic from 1,200 to 1,500 calories a day.[74] It was also at Nabokov's initiative that, given the shortage of music available in Germany, the Americans put forward before the four-power information committee the idea of an Inter-Allied lending music library in Berlin.[75] Housed in the Staatsbibliothek, it opened in September 1946. Unfortunately, the American contribution, which consisted of about eighty works, all on microfilms, was not on a par with the 200 supplied by the Soviets (with Shostakovich being given the lion's share) and the more than 500 that came from the British. This must have disappointed Nabokov, who in later life would be particularly mindful of such "culture gaps." Another institution Nabokov helped was Koussevitzky's Russian music publishing firm— one in which he himself had a direct interest, since Russischer Musik Verlag had issued some of his works in the 1920s and 1930s. The firm's Berlin headquarters, like much of central Berlin, had been destroyed during the bombing. Contacted by the publishing house's Parisian representative, Nabokov had to find his Berlin counterpart, provide him with material assistance, and help to reconstitute the firm's archive. The safe containing the contracts proved impossible to retrieve from the rubble, but Nabokov's efforts nonetheless earned him Koussevitzky's gratitude.[76]

Nabokov also earned the gratitude of the music publisher C. F. Peters. Founded in Leipzig in 1800, the firm had been confiscated from the Hinrichsen family and "aryanized" by the Nazis just before the war. Henri Hinrichsen's sons Walter and Max were able to resettle in the United States and reestablished the firm in New York and London (and subsequently Frankfurt). In the summer of 1946, Walter Hinrichsen, now an American citizen in US uniform, appealed to Nabokov to help him rescue the firm's precious manuscripts and copper plates. The two of them stole into Leipzig in two automobiles and managed to bring back as much of the collection as they could. A grateful Hinrichsen presented Nabokov with the short-score manuscript of Mozart's Six German Dances, K. 509, which his parents had purchased from the Berlin dealer Liepmannsohn.[77]

Also in the summer of 1946, Nabokov invited Virgil Thomson, who was then in Europe—and still under the shock of Gertrude Stein's death on July 27—to join him in Germany. Nabokov arranged his clearance in no time, and Thomson was flown to Munich in an American military plane. In Munich, Nabokov and Thomson were met by John Evarts, the newly appointed American music control officer for Bavaria. A well-connected Yale graduate, who had taught music at Black Mountain College before joining the army in 1942, Evarts, in the diary he kept at the time, described Nabokov as "an exuberant, energetic man about forty—many connections. Not shy about mentioning them."[78] Traveling through the Soviet zone, Nabokov and Thomson stopped in Berchtesgaden, where they saw Francis Biddle, who served as one of the American judges at the Nuremberg Trial. From there they went to Salzburg, where the first postwar festival was going on, as Thomson puts it, "under American protection."[79] The two musicians stayed at the Oesterreischicher Hof, the best hotel in town, which had been requisitioned as an billet for junior and middle-rank officers, while generals and the like stayed in grand palaces in and around the city. Nabokov and Thomson heard Charles Münch conduct the Vienna Philharmonic, with Münch's niece Nicole Henriot as soloist in Ravel's Concerto in G. They visited the house where Mozart was born and, in the park of Max Reinhardt's Schloss Leopoldskron, saw the bronze statues of animals seized in Paris by Goering and waiting to be repatriated. They befriended the young Austrian composer Gottfried von Einem, Blacher's student, who played for them the first act of the opera he was then working on, based on Büchner's play *Dantons Tod*. Karajan, who was still barred from appearing publicly but had rehearsed the new production of *Le nozze di Figaro*, conducted a rehearsal especially arranged at the behest of the American occupation authorities ("the best-prepared performance of Mozart's *Figaro* I have ever heard," wrote Thomson), with a cast headed by Maria Cebotari (eight months pregnant) as the Countess and Irmgard Seefried as Susanna.[80] Karajan invited Nabokov and Thomson to join him and his wife for tea "on their sumptuous mountain top."[81]

Back in Munich after three days, Nabokov and Thomson called on Carl Orff, who played for them recordings of his music. A dinner party was hosted in their honor by Heinz Norden, the German-born American publisher and human rights activist, then editor of the US occupation magazine *Heute*. Nicole Henriot, whom they had just heard in Salzburg, was there, as was Evarts, who noted with a mixture of amusement and envy how the two composers and the young pianist formed "a private triangle of musical communication," a kind of magic circle from which the others were excluded.[82]

From Munich, Nabokov and Thomson traveled back to Berlin via bomb-devastated Frankfurt and Stuttgart. In Berlin, Nabokov introduced to Thomson as many musicians he could gather, notably Blacher, who explained to the American composer-critic "why he and not Paul Hindemith should, and most likely would, take over the reconstruction of music teaching"—a prediction that proved accurate, since Blacher eventually became a longstanding director of the Berlin Hochschule.[83] Nabokov also arranged for Thomson to meet the music control officer for the Soviet military government, Major Sergei Barsky, a grandnephew of Anton Rubinstein, who took him to the music store in the Russian sector and bought him a large pile of scores by Soviet composers. Passes having been obtained in record time, thanks to Nabokov's contacts, he and Thomson spent three days traveling in the Soviet zone in an army car driven by a GI. In Dresden they stayed in the palace of Prince Heinrich of Saxony, which had been converted into a residence for foreign visitors. A Russian major accompanied them as "guide." "At first he was reserved; then he broke into faint smiles, then guffaws at Nicolas's jokes; and before we were a half-hour out of town they were slapping each other's backs to Russian stories."[84] In Dresden, Nabokov and Thomson were received royally, with white wine, red wine, champagne, and vodka—in the water glass—flowing at every meal, breakfast included. They attended performances of Kalman's *Die Czardasfürstin* and Nico Dostal's *Monika*. They were taken to see the museum's pictures stored in the Pillnitz Palace, since the museum, along with the Zwinger and the Semper opera house, was in ruins. After one last look at Berlin, which he had never visited prior to this trip, Thomson returned to the United States. This three-week visit cemented between him and Nabokov a friendship that was to last until the latter's death. It also gave Thomson material for a series of articles on music in Germany in the *New York Herald Tribune*.[85] They expressed strongly critical views on the "hard peace" attitude of the American military authorities toward the Germans ("We treat them very much as we do Negroes").[86] These views were, of course, the ones held by Nabokov himself, and the publicity Thomson's articles generated helped to speed up the denazification process.

Nabokov's administrative responsibilities in Germany left him little time to compose. Still, his contacts with the army inspired him to write a military march in the summer of 1945. Entitled *From the Beaches to Berlin* (with the alternate title "Retreat from Gettorf," which ties it to the region of Schleswig-Holstein), it is dated August 9, 1945, at the end of the manuscript, which also bears traces of Nabokov's itinerary while attached to the Strategic Bombing Survey Morale Division: Hamburg—Lübeck—Altenhof—Nauheim—London. In the spirit of the Allied victory, it combines an eighteenth-century British calvary tune, "an old American reveille from the Washingtonian period," a Soviet Russian march tune, and, by deference to the fourth quadripartite power (and, nominally at least, one of the 1945 victorious powers), a snatch from a French Revolutionary song. Although it may have been originally scored for military band, it has come to us in a version for full symphony orchestra.

Though, for obvious reasons, musicians working for the American authorities in an official capacity were not supposed to use their position to further their career, Nabokov was a sufficiently well-known composer and at least one performance of his music is recorded in Berlin: his *Serenata estiva* was included in a concert by the Berliner Philharmoniker String Quartet in January 1946, in a program that also included Mozart's String Quartet in E-flat, K. 428, and Mendelssohn's String Quartet in D major, op. 44, no. 1. The reviewer for *Das Volk*, after reminding his readers that Nabokov had studied with Haas and Busoni, wrote:

> His "Summer Reverie" is full of temperament and shows typically Russian characteristics. Some parts seem lost in reverie, whereas others are grotesque and ornate, and the light translucency of the third passage appears almost lyrically pastel-like and delicate. The string quartet (Messrs.

Bastiaan, Bethmann, Muller, and Bottermund), in an accomplished performance with and well-balanced ensemble gave an excellent interpretation,
both technically and artistically, [. . .] of this taxing work [. . .].[87]

Stravinsky's influence was detected by another German reviewer, Erwin Kroll, who
nevertheless found it "an absolutely personal work of typically Russian characteristics: original and grotesque, almost barbaric in the second part, solemnly mysterious in the third part. Although independent, the voices are melodious. There
is no 'kinetic' vacuum; everything breathes sentiment, and a strong temperament
makes itself felt everywhere."[88]

Nabokov remained in Germany until the end of 1946, save for two brief visits
to the United States in April and August and two to Paris in the winter and in
late spring. The first of these coincided with the presence in the French capital
of Marshal Zhukov, in whose box at the Opéra Nabokov found himself invited,
as he boasted to his cousin Vladimir.[89] Writing to Stravinsky ahead of his trip
to the United States on March 22, Nabokov complained he had had "enough
of discussions with representatives of the Soviets, of telephone calls from the
Soviets—though the telephone ceases to function every time Mr. Churchill
makes a speech that the Russians do not like—and enough of banquets with
Marshals Zhukov and Budennyi."[90] By the time he left Germany, Nabokov had
also evidently outstayed his welcome with the American occupation forces. Still
angry at the role played by the participation of American authorities in the forced
repatriation of Eastern European refugees, he was equally indignant when he
realized that influential positions in American-sponsored German media were
occupied by former Communists or self-professed Communist sympathizers. He had already raised the issue with Joseph Alsop, who stayed with him
when visiting Berlin.[91] His concern was shared by Ambassador Murphy's chief
of staff, Donald Heath, who, in the summer of 1946, encouraged Nabokov to
draft a memorandum on the topic for the attention of Secretary of State James
Byrnes, then attending the Peace Conference that opened in Paris at the end of
July. The memorandum eventually found its way to General Clay, who, while
not unsympathetic with the contents of the memorandum, was predictably
annoyed at being sidestepped in the transmission process. When Nabokov was
in Washington, staying with the Bohlens, to take part in preliminary discussions about launching a Russian-language service of Voice of America, he was
summoned by Clay to his office at the Pentagon and informed that his employment would not be renewed.[92]

Nabokov himself has left few personal reminiscences of his German interlude,
though he planned to cover it in great detail in the autobiography he was working
on at the time of his death. "Music under the Generals," the concluding chapter of
Old Friends and New Music, which also appeared in the *Atlantic Monthly* for January

of the same year, is a satirical account of a matinee of *Madama Butterfly* given by the Berlin Staatsoper, at its provisional Wintergarten venue, during the first of the two winters Nabokov spent in Berlin. Along with other officials from the quadripartite occupation forces, he was the guest of the Soviet Military Government for Germany. No particular fan of Puccini's masterpiece, he recalls having to explain its plot to a General X and Colonel W. as the German-language performance went on, much to the annoyance of the British, French, and Russian officers who made up the entire audience. Incensed by the poor image the opera conveys of Americans, at least as far as Lieutenant Pinkerton is concerned, the Texan general announced he would lodge an official protest with the American occupation authorities. Is this unflattering vignette of the American military establishment a reflection of Nabokov's bitter memories of his ICD experience? Did he intend to emphasize the contrast between the military brass's cultural ineptitude and the utopian loftiness of the ICD's stated claims to "reorient the German mind"?[93] Ostensibly, Nabokov, writing a few years later, now that the Cold War was at its peak, wanted to make the point that Berlin in the immediate postwar years "was the seat of the most emasculated government in the world: ineffectual, cumbersome, and absurd."[94] But his indirect exposure to Soviet rule also gave him a first-hand sense of the enslavement of culture in a totalitarian state.

> While we kept aloof, the Russians pushed the Germans around, told them what to do and how to do it, ordered them to resume opera and ballet performances on incredibly short notice, told them what to play and what not to play, made them join the Socialist Unity or the Communist Party under the threat of losing their jobs or the inducement of getting better rations, and presented to them as supreme examples of the Great Soviet culture, Russian choruses, troops of dancers, singers and virtuosi, brought to entertain the Soviet occupation troops and the officials of their military government.[95]

One such concert to which Nabokov was invited featured the great tenor Ivan Kozlovsky, who impressed Nabokov with his "small but lovely" voice of "warm lyrical quality," his breath control, and his flawless intonation, but not with his "awful provincial taste in delivery"or the "greasy outmoded sentimentality" of his interpretation.[96] The evening, which ended with choruses sung by the Red Army Chorus, reminded Nabokov of the patriotic concerts he had heard at the Ciniselli Circus in Petersburg during the First World War. "It was the same kind of music, the same kind of performance and the same kind of enthusiastic reaction in the audience. In fact, the parallel was so great that at moments it seemed that a whiff of the old nostalgic circus odor was coming to me from the stage."[97] Struck by the absence on the program of any music composed during the Soviet period, Nabokov inquired about this afterward during the reception at the officers' club. The replies he received ("we don't really *like* the music of Shostakovich and Prokofiev . . . [. . .] too complicated, too dissonant") gave him an indication of "the incredibly old-fashioned provincial and parochial taste of the new uneducated middle strata of Soviet society."[98]

Despite the humorous tone of these recollections, the year and a half Nabokov spent in postwar Germany evidently took a heavy toll on him emotionally. By the time he returned, his dark hair had turned white.

Music and the Cold War

SHORTLY AFTER NABOKOV'S return to America in January 1947, a new woman entered the composer's life. Born in 1925, Patricia Blake was, in Nabokov's words, "a thoroughbred intellectual, brilliantly intelligent and good-looking."[1] As contemporary photographs show, she was, indeed, a great beauty, though Edmund Wilson, as he reported to Vladimir Nabokov, could not help being struck by her physical resemblance to Nabokov's previous wife.[2] But unlike her two predecessors, Patricia was indeed an intellectual. A Smith College graduate, she spoke fluent French, having spent her junior year in Paris on Smith's program. Albert Camus, on meeting her in New York in April 1946, fell in love with her and the two quickly embarked on an affair that lasted until Camus returned to France in June, and developed into a lasting friendship.[3] Under Nabokov's tutelage, Patricia became fluent in Russian. Her own influence on him can be detected in the quality of the writing he published during their five-year marriage: she was, in a real sense, his editor, and he himself has acknowledged the "splendid" work she did in the autobiographical essays collected in 1951 under the title *Old Friends and New Music*.[4] It was evidently not an easy courtship, and Nabokov went through a period of depression in early 1948. Upon his return from Europe, he stayed for a few months at the Great Northern Hotel on 57th Street; he then moved to Virgil Thomson's apartment in the Chelsea Hotel, and in October to a spacious flat belonging to Patricia's aunt at 1350 Madison Avenue, across the street from the "brick crusader's castle" of the Eighth Regiment Armory, as Nabokov described it.[5] It was there that the newlyweds lived after their marriage on March 21, 1948.

On his return from Germany, Nabokov was immediately recruited by Charles Thayer, Avis Bohlen's brother, to help him to set up a Russian broadcasting service for the Voice of America on behalf of the State Department. "Good old Nika got the job which had been promised me," Vladimir Nabokov complained to Edmund Wilson on January 25, 1947.[6] For Thayer, a friend from their Dumbarton Avenue days, the choice of Nicolas over his yet relatively little-known cousin would have been perfectly natural: before Nabokov's remarriage, Thayer was even Nabokov's roommate on Madison Avenue. But there are other reasons why Nicolas was a more obvious choice than his cousin for the job. Bohlen, who was involved in the planning stages as soon as the State Department undertook the project in August 1946, contacted Nabokov in Germany and invited him to assume the position, pointing out that it was important that the Russians—for whom the broadcasts were intended—should sense that these had been planned by "one of them."[7] The task at hand was urgent: within a few weeks, a small staff had to be hired and trained, and broadcasts had to be planned. There was, in Thayer's words, "considerable amateur bumbling."[8] The fourteen-member staff, as recalled by Alan L. Heil Jr., "worked around the clock to mount the first broadcast, dropping the needle on acetate disks to isolate program excerpts."[9] Whether Vladimir—if he was ever seriously considered for the job, for which he asked Edmund Wilson to recommend him—would have been the right person under such conditions is, obviously, open to doubt.[10] Be that as it may, the inaugural broadcast in Russia—with speakers Victor Franzusoff and Helen Jacobson—took place on February 17, 1947. Then it became apparent that the broadcasts could be heard very well in Latin America—grateful Cossacks who had settled in Chile and Peru conveyed their appreciation—but not at all in Russia, because the transmitter in Munich had been accidentally reversed.[11] In addition to these technical difficulties, VOA was going through a tough financial period. Established in 1942, it had broad popular and political support as a publicly funded radio for international propaganda purposes; once the war was over, this support declined dramatically. On the contrary, both the public and Congress were of the opinion that publicly funded international radio programs should be phased out and influential Congressmen openly demanded their abolition.[12] The perception that the Cold War had to be waged on the cultural front was not generally shared, nor, one could add, would it ever be universally accepted. This situation explains in part the future controversies around the financing of the Congress for Cultural Freedom. Broadcasts to Russia were introduced at the insistence of diplomats like W. Averell Harriman, who had served as US ambassador to Moscow from 1943 until January 1946, and whose daughter Kathleen was recruited to help as an unpaid volunteer ("in violation of government regulations," as Thayer gleefully notes in his memoirs).[13]

Nabokov has left no first-hand account of his brief experience with Voice of America, although he meant to cover this episode in the second book of memoirs he was working on at the time of his death. "It remains in my memory," he wrote in his preliminary drafts, "as something hilariously funny, earnest in its aims, and as disappointing as sweet-sour pork in a third-class Chinese restaurant."[14] To his Peabody student Dominick Argento, he joked that "his most significant contribution was unmasking the radio theme song for *The FBI in Peace and War* as the work of a Communist."[15] The theme song in question was the famous march from

Prokofiev's *Love for Three Oranges*![16] One detail Nabokov mentioned in the manuscript of his autobiography is that Koussevitzky begged him to find employment with the station for Lourié, now living in New York and penniless. "I complied and a job was found for (ah! so lazy) Lourié. Now it was Stravinsky who would not come to visit me in my office at the Voice of America on West 57th Street because [he] did not want to run into Arthur Lourié."[17] In March 1947, Auden, with whom Nabokov had kept in touch since his return to New York, told Alan Ansen that Nabokov was "very depressed" and felt that there would be a war "in five or ten years."[18] He was fully convinced the Soviets were pursuing a hegemonic policy in Europe and beyond. "The only hope for peace," Auden also reports Nabokov as saying, "would be if Stalin died."[19] Thayer himself, though Nabokov's name does not figure in his memoirs, recalls that there was tension within VOA between adopting a "cool, dispassionate, almost impartial attitude" in the broadcasts, as recommended by diplomats familiar with Russia, and the temptation to fall into "bitterly sarcastic, almost vitriolic, anti-Stalinist attacks"—thereby showing Congress and the public that VOA was not "soft."[20] Nabokov would subsequently have to deal with similar internal tensions in the Congress for Cultural Freedom, with pressure coming especially from hard-liners on the American side.

The international climate had, indeed, changed dramatically around the time Nabokov returned from Germany. In the period between Churchill's "Iron Curtain" speech in Fulton, Missouri, in March 1946, and Bernard Baruch's April 1947 declaration about the United States being "in the midst of a cold war," the rift between the former allies was complete. An initiative like the VOA radio broadcasts in Russian was already part of the strategy of "containment" advocated by Nabokov's Dumbarton Avenue friend George Kennan in the "Long Telegram" he sent from Moscow in February 1946 to alert the Truman Administration to the dangers of the Soviets' expansionist designs on Eastern Europe.[21] The so-called March 1947 "Truman Doctrine" (which offered US support to countries, such as Greece, that were outside the Soviet sphere of influence but were at risk of falling under Communist control), and the European Recovery Program (the "Marshall Plan"), announced at Harvard on June 5 in that same year, were part of the same strategy. So was the establishment of the CIA by the National Security Act of July 26, 1947, to take effect six weeks later, on September 18.[22] The Agency soon recruited Michael Josselson, who was reluctant to return to civilian life in the United States after his Berlin duties ended. Having acquired an excellent reputation as a "fixer," he was approached in 1948 by an intelligence agent named Lawrence de Neufville. During one of his visits to the United States, Josselson asked Nabokov to recommend his application. Recent scholars have suggested that Nabokov "probably had a good idea of Josselson's new direction."[23] Nabokov himself subsequently claimed, in the draft of his autobiography, that he did not realize the nature of his friend's job search, nor is there is anything in their correspondence of later years that allows one to challenge this claim. "I want to join that organization, you know!" Josselson said, or words to that effect, Nabokov recalled. "I nodded, but quite frankly did not know, what he was talking about. I knew 'psychological warfare,' but had only the vaguest notion of the CIA, then still in its infancy."[24] Josselson remained in Germany as chief of the Berlin station for Covert Action: save for its "covert" aspect, the work, as Nabokov pointed out, was a continuation of the kind of psychological warfare work he and Nabokov had undertaken in Berlin.[25]

It was in this context that Nabokov himself, on the strength of his experience in Germany, and prompted, it seems, by both Thayer and Allen Dulles, decided, in the spring of 1948, to apply for a position with the Russian Policy Committee within the State Department.[26] Because of the coincidence with Josselson's own recruitment as well as the involvement (direct or indirect) of Dulles, who had played a major role in the US secret services during the war and would subsequently serve as CIA director, it has been suggested that Nabokov was actually "approached to join the CIA."[27] In theory, this cannot be ruled out, but it has been presented as a conjecture, with no evidence available to support it. Of course, one can choose not to believe Nabokov's own testimony, in his published and unpublished autobiographical writings; but the absence of any reference in his otherwise candid correspondence with Josselson inclines one to doubt it, as does the fact that, in the words of a CIA agent who knew him well, Nabokov was "not the sort of man that CIA security would have been happy about."[28] The only undisputed fact is that Nabokov failed to get his security clearance and had to withdraw his application for the Russian Policy Committee job. In an unpublished chapter of his autobiography, he has left an uproarious reconstitution of the FBI interview he underwent in an office located on the upper floor of the Central Post Office. After explaining to Nabokov that he had been "intensely investigated," wherever he went, during the past six weeks, the "synthetic-looking" Mr. Smith, as Nabokov calls his interviewer, proceeded to explain that he had to ask him a number of "indiscreet" questions. The State Department, he said, had obtained "corroborated information" of Nabokov's "homosexual tendencies." "He pronounced the last two words solemnly, like a priest saying *pax vobiscum*, but with noticeable disgust and his eyes darted straight at me."[29] Nabokov was taken aback by what seemed, in his case, an "absurd question."

> Had the [. . . .] agent accused me of polygamy, of indiscriminate, light-hearted and multiple love affairs, of free-wheeling and going out of channels while in government service, of exasperating the chief of the American satrapy [i.e., General Clay] in Germany, of keeping open KGB contacts in Berlin, of living above my means, of seeing much too many "crummy" intellectuals, of . . ., of . . . of . . .

But this particularly foolish question! Not that I *minded* it. Since childhood and my early friendship with cousin Sergei and later my collaboration with Diaghilev's ballet company, homosexuals were to me just people with *other* sexual tastes. But it seemed so completely irrelevant as far as I was concerned, with my rightly earned womanizer's reputation and just at a time when I had gone through a complex, anguish-filled third marriage!

Not realizing he was making his case worse, Nabokov explained that, though not sexually attracted to members of his own sex, he had, as an artist, "for better or for worse," frequently been in contact and had formed long-lasting friendships with homosexuals, and he and his wife, as it happened, were expecting a few at dinner that evening. Such jokes were, obviously, not at all to the taste of the interviewer, who went on to quiz Nabokov sternly about a whole list of his friends and acquaintances. "This second question," Nabokov recalled, "made me think that something else, some 'other game' was on and that the blue-serged agent was performing some special *additional* duty. I was only a minor, secondary target, a *Nebensache* [something incidental]. The real *Sache* [thing] was someone else, someone much more important and more difficult to reach."[30] More names ("queens and not queens, friends and acquaintances, colleagues and remote collaborators") came up, until a file of obvious non-American provenance was brought in, and more names came up, such as Tchelitchew, Diaghilev, and "Miss Jean Kakatoo." Nabokov concluded that police reports about his supposed homosexuality, based on his friendships (and occasional living arrangements) with well-known homosexuals, had begun to dog him in the 1930s on the other side of the Atlantic, despite Alexis Léger's assurances he had not found anything suspicious in his file in 1938.

Now it all began to fall into a pattern. Here it was—the good, old, smelly Paris police file! It was right in front of me, in the hands of this sadly uninformed American *confrère*, hauled out of the musty vaults of Mr Fouché's quadrangle [the Préfecture de police on the Île de la Cité], brought from Paris and probably even translated by courtesy of Interpol or by the services of the American Embassy with its improper transliteration of names and absurd agglunitation of falsely conjectured facts. The same one—or a copy of the one—that always prevented me from getting my papers renewed. Here it was, now at home in America, *enfin* in front of my eyes, so close, so within reach, so precious to the FBI and the SDSS, so unexpected . . .[31]

Given Nabokov's penchant for embellishment, one might be tempted to assume that his account of this interview is too good to be true. Its accuracy is, however, confirmed by Nabokov's FBI files. A memorandum from J. Edgar Hoover dated June 14, 1948, instructed his staff to conduct a thorough investigation of his case in the following two weeks. And the ensuing reports show that Nabokov was indeed interviewed by an agent handling "all investigations for his office involving homo-sexuals."[32] They confirm that, despite well documented reports on Nabokov's active heterosexual affairs, and an emphatic statement from Bohlen—along with Kennan Nabokov's main reference—that such rumors were "bunk," the FBI apparently came to the conclusion that there was a high probability that Nabokov was gay. The "specialized" agent who interviewed Nabokov was clearly convinced this was the case. He based his impression, according to his report, "on his expe-rience in having interviewed more than 500 of these people in the past," further noting that Nabokov struck him as "effeminate" and that "his manner of speech was rather odd."[33] Much was made of Nabokov's association with "ballet impres-saria" (*sic*) Diaghilev and Cocteau, "both alleged notorious homosexuals,"and of Nabokov's own jocular admission that he often attended—as the FBI phrased it—parties "at which only perverts were in attendance." Among the people inter-viewed by the FBI was a young French gay journalist named Jacques Brosse, who for a short while shared Nabokov's Madison Avenue apartment, having been rec-ommended to Patricia by Camus. Brosse, who was then covering UN affairs for the French radio, told the FBI he could not verify that Nabokov himself was gay but confirmed that he had "attended parties given for perverts and had given one in his own apartment for them."[34] An FBI informant with the Voice of America reported that Nabokov was the "laughing stock" of the International Broadcasting Unit, where he had "the reputation of being a pervert because of his actions [and] manner of speech," noting his habit of running "his hand through the hair of his acquaintances" and using "feminine terms of endearment when speaking to them."[35]

There is no question that homosexuality was then considered a security risk and rumors about one being homosexual were enough to disqualify one's appli-cation.[36] When he realized that his was at risk, Nabokov turned to Kennan, with whom he and his wife spent a weekend at the farm the diplomat owned in Adams County, Pennsylvania. Shortly afterward, on July 14, 1948, Kennan, who, like Bohlen, had recommended Nabokov's application in the most glowing terms, reported on his own investigations. His advice (which caused him, he added, "considerable sadness and a very real concern") was for Nabokov to "drop the whole matter for the time being." He should contact Thayer or Dulles and inform them that he had given up his intention to work for the government and was withdrawing his application. Pursuing it, Kennan cautioned, was likely to result in "further unpleasantness." He pointed out, diplomatically, that he had seen no files or documents—thus implying that he had been briefed orally by people who had. He added that in his opinion the denying of Nabokov's clearance by the

US Government was "ill-conceived, short-sighted, unjust, and quite inconsistent [with] any desire to utilize the services of sensitive, intelligent and valuable peo- ple."[37] Kennan's main source, according to his later conversations with Nabokov, was Robert A. Lovett, then serving as Undersecretary of State, "a man known for his forthright nobility." Alerted by Kennan, he asked to review Nabokov's file but apparently found it purged of any incriminating evidence.[38]

This bitter disappointment notwithstanding, the years 1947–49 marked a new departure for Nabokov's career. In the fall of 1947, he resumed his teach- ing responsibilities at the Peabody Conservatory, which took him to Baltimore two days a week. His teaching consisted of two music history courses ("From the Greeks to Bach" and "From Bach to the twentieth century"), supplemented by one or two courses on a broad music literature topic ("Bach and his time," "The Viennese School"), as well as composition, harmony, and counterpoint.[39] His student Dominick Argento, later in life, concluded that Nabokov was "a poor teacher" and taught him "virtually nothing about composition"—a claim Argento admittedly also makes about his six other composition teachers, including Hugo Weisgall, Luigi Dallapiccola (to whom he was recommended by Nabokov), and Henry Cowell.[40] Argento nevertheless remembered Nabokov "fondly as an extraor- dinary man"—"the only genuine cosmopolite I have ever known"—and pro- claimed himself eternally grateful to him for his encouragement to switch from a piano major to a major in composition.[41] While studying with Nabokov, Argento wrote a piano sonata which was "unashamedly modeled" on Nabokov's own— clearly, even though Argento does not specify which, the recently published sec- ond rather than the one of 1926.

> I remembered his amusement as he pointed out that the main theme of my slow movement was one note shy of being a twelve-tone row. I blushed, deeply embarrassed: Schoenberg was anathema in those days. I stam- mered, trying to explain that it had been unintentional . . . I hadn't realized . . . I wasn't . . . A sharp burst of laughter interrupted my apologies; he slapped me on the knee and said, "It's all right. It's all right. I won't tell Igor Fyodorovich."[42]

Nabokov's professorship in one of America's leading music schools gave him a much greater professional visibility than at Wells and St. John's, resulting in his being elected, in 1949, vice-chairman of the League of American Composers, a position he kept until 1952. In the summer of 1949, he was invited to teach at the Berskshire Music Center in Lenox, Massachusetts. For the first time, he received commissions from a major American orchestra (the Boston Symphony). He contributed essays to several important journals, subsequently collected in a book that appeared in 1951. And he also resumed direct, warm relations with

Stravinsky—a relationship that gradually became important to Stravinsky as well as to Nabokov himself.

"Come, come, we await you impatiently," Stravinsky had written to Nabokov, from Hollywood, in April 1946. "You can stay at our house, on the same floor and under the same canopy where Nadia Boulanger spent her nights when she came to Hollywood."[43] Nabokov, however, was then on a short leave from his duties in Germany, so his visit to Stravinsky had to wait for another year and a half. The opportunity, this time, was provided by Balanchine, who needed to see Stravinsky as part of the preparation of the ballet *Orpheus*, which was to open in New York the following April, with sets and costumes by Isamu Noguchi. Nabokov was invited to come along and bring the score of his cantata *The Return of Pushkin*, which Auden had told Stravinsky he liked very much.[44]

Nabokov's Christmas 1947 Hollywood visit forms the substance of a Stravinsky profile published in the November 1949 issue of the *Atlantic Monthly* and included, in a slightly expanded version, in Edwin Corle's new edition of Merle Armitage's 1936 *Stravinsky*. In 1951 Nabokov incorporated it into *Old Friends and New Music*. Stravinsky was displeased with the publication, probably more because he objected to anything personal to come out about him without his control over it than because of anything Nabokov's article contained. Indeed it would be difficult to think of a more humane and sympathetic portrait of the composer, and it is, justifiably, among Nabokov's most admired pieces of writing.[45]

The visit to Stravinsky was Nabokov's first trip to California. He would rather have flown, but since Balanchine and his wife, the dancer Maria Tallchief (who was to star in the new ballet), favored the train, it was agreed they would go to California by train—a sixty-seven-hour journey in a "through" car, but involving a change in Chicago from the Commodore Vanderbilt to the Grand Canyon Ltd— and Nabokov would return to New York by plane. Having left on December 19, the party arrived on December 22 and departed five days later. Nabokov has left a vivid description of life on North Wetherly Drive, where the Stravinskys occupied "a small and flat one-story house, rimmed by a narrow porch in front and a large terrace on its left-hand side," enlivened by the presence of a cat, a parrot, a canary, and a flock of lovebirds.[46] Having found in California the peace he needed to compose, Stravinsky had become a patriot of sorts. He did not "permit criticism of America in his presence." The main pleasures he retained from the Old World were a fondness for *marc* and expensive claret. In Hollywood, what Nabokov called his "White Russian inner circle" included the painter Eugene Berman, an old acquaintance of Nabokov's from his Paris years; but Stravinsky also saw much of Aldous Huxley, who joined Stravinsky and his visitors for lunch. The Christmas dinner guests were Stravinsky's daughter and her husband, André Marion, the Ballets Russes dancer Adolph Bolm and his wife, Berman, and Dr. Max Edel, Stravinsky's physician.

Beside its fascinating anecdotes about everyday life at the Stravinskys', Nabokov's essay includes comments on the composer's music, especially on *Orpheus*, a score in which Nabokov found the hallmarks of Stravinsky's genius: "a remarkable economy of means coupled with an infallible sense of proportion, time, and form."[47] He points out, in particular, how, in *Orpheus* as in other works, Stravinsky displayed his "uncanny sense of the individuality or, better, the personality of each instrument of the orchestra." In this respect, as Nabokov points out, Stravinsky breaks with the increasingly inflated orchestral sound favored by the Romantics, in their preoccupation with making music "suggest or describe [. . .] extra-musical images, expressions, ideas, or objects," and returns to the "clarity, precision and transparency" of eighteenth-century musicians—"music one could see through [. . .] with one's ears," as Diaghilev was fond of saying.[48] This allows Nabokov, as he had in his 1944 essay, to defend Stravinsky's so-called neoclassical period, so often disparaged by comparison with his "Russian" period, not so much because of the earlier works' "revolutionary" character—a characterization anathema to Stravinsky in any case—as by reference to a picture of Russia that could be reduced to a few banal cliches and stereotypes.

Order, Nabokov stresses, is the keyword to Stravinsky, both as a person and as a musician. It can be found in his meticulousness, his taste for precision and clarity, his love of dictionaries and "a clear-cut, well-defined formal structure," his contempt for unobservant conductors, "his hate of stuffy rooms, of dirt or disorder, of dusty furniture and bad odors."[49] Though full of all kinds of gadgets, Stravinsky's study is "so well organized and so functional that it gives one a sense of spaciousness and peaceful comfort."[50] Reflecting on the debt musicians of his generation owed him, Nabokov concludes that Stravinsky has shown them "new horizons in the domain of rhythm, new possibilities in the use of musical instruments, and a new concept of harmony, fuller, broader, and nobler than the sterile harmonic concepts of the late nineteenth century." Yet, he adds, "to me the most important discoveries of Stravinsky lie in his artful perception and measurement of the flow of time by means of the most complex and beautiful rhythmic patterns and designs."[51]

Stravinsky's letter of November 24, 1947, in which he confirmed to Nabokov his invitation to spend Christmas with him in Hollywood, ended with an apparently anodyne question which, however, contained the germ of a major development in Stravinsky's life: "Do you know Robert Craft? He is said to be a serious person . . . Contact him and let me know what you think of him."[52] A week later, Nabokov replied that he did not know Craft, adding that he had recently "heard something about him to the effect that he is a serious fellow."[53] In March 1948, Craft, then a choral conductor at Hunter College, entered Stravinsky's life and never left.

Having published a spirited defense of Stravinsky's neoclassicism in 1944, Nabokov had an opportunity to return to the topic in May 1948, also in *Partisan*

Review. Entitled "The Atonal Trail: A Communication," his article was a rebuttal of two essays that had appeared in recent issues of the same magazine. The first, "The State of American Music," by Kurt List, in the January number, only alluded to Stravinsky but contained derogatory comments on Barber, Blitzstein, Copland, and Virgil Thomson, only making exceptions for Ives and Sessions. The second, René Leibowitz's "Two Composers: A Letter from Hollywood," extolled Schoenberg at the expense of Stravinsky. Dismissing the List piece as "appallingly arrogant and superficial," Nabokov focused on refuting Leibowitz, a much more sophisticated critic, even though his use of Existentialist terms inapplicable to music—Leibowitz was a contributor to Sartre's magazine *Les temps modernes*—"obscures his otherwise clear but somewhat naive line of reasoning."[54] "On the whole," Nabokov declared, "it is a superficial piece, politely vicious and presumptuous and at the same time full of weak and untenable arguments."[55] To Leibowitz's principal point—that Schoenberg was not only the superior composer but also the more influential—Nabokov responded by denying that *all* composers had fallen under Schoenberg's influence. As for the claim that Schoenberg was the true innovator, because his first experimental works had preceded *The Rite of Spring* by a few years, Nabokov denounced the tendency to interpret music history solely in terms of progress. "Pioneering in music is only interesting for historians and musicologists but not to history itself and certainly not to the public."[56] He further argued that Schoenberg's discoveries, no matter how they may have appeared at the time, were "neither fantastic nor revolutionary," but, rather, the ultimate stage in the evolution of chordal harmony in Western music since the first emancipation of dissonance at the time of Monteverdi.[57] Insisting on presenting the twelve-tone system as a radical departure—Nabokov, thinking no doubt of his Stuttgart experience, likens the messianic attitude of Schoenberg's disciples to anthroposophy—has resulted in "a strange kind of fetish, a hermetic cult, mechanistic in its technique and depressingly dull to the uninitiated listener."[58] Nor was the magnitude of one's influence necessarily a good principle to assess musical worth. Rejecting as ridiculous Leibowitz's contention that Stravinsky was still mired in "hedonistic and arbitrary attitudes" and that he had been "in continuous decline since 1912," Nabokov contrasted, in his conclusion, Stravinsky's capacity for constant renewal with Schoenberg's dogmaticism.[59]

By 1948, Nabokov, who never belonged to a political party, had nevertheless become closer to the non-Communist American Left. He contributed to two of its most influential journals, *Partisan Review* and *Politics*, and he and his wife were on friendly terms with several of its prominent members, notably Mary McCarthy, now divorced from Edmund Wilson and remarried to the writer and educator Bowden Broadwater. Because of this friendship, Nabokov participated in the "Europe-America Groups," a short-lived, loose organization launched in early 1948 by Mary McCarthy with a view to raising consciousness (and money) and

promoting exchanges between nonaligned European and American liberals.[60]
Nabokov could not but agree with the groups' manifesto, which proclaimed that
Stalinism was the main threat to the freedom of culture. Other people involved
were Mary McCarthy's brother Kevin, the actor; his fellow actor Montgomery Clift;
her close friend the writer Elizabeth Hardwick; Dwight Macdonald, editor of the
magazine *Politics*; the critic Alfred Kazin; and the artist Saul Steinberg. Another
participant in the EAG venture was the young Harvard historian Arthur M.
Schlesinger Jr. Schlesinger was already acquainted with Nabokov, whom he had
met in 1947 at a dinner party given by Charles Thayer in Georgetown. The party
had started unpromisingly, with a hint of a strain between the host and his Italian
wife. Then Nabokov arrived with Bohlen and "the sad, dark room," Schlesinger
recalled, "was suddenly bathed in light and exhilaration." Like Bohlen and Isaiah
Berlin, Schlesinger was captivated by Nabokov's personality. "He overflowed with
vitality," he recalled, "was a notable raconteur in half a dozen languages, also a
notable mimic, and had, what was rare in an artist, a penetrating and ironical
political intelligence."[61] From then on, despite their fourteen-year age difference,
Schlesinger was a member of Nabokov's "inner circle." "Nicolas," he wrote many
years later, "always had the same enlivening effect on me as at that first meeting—
light and laughter in a dark age."[62] At a dinner Nabokov and Patricia hosted in
their apartment around 1950, they and Schlesinger witnessed a heated exchange
between Kennan, "the ambivalent moralist," who declared he intended to resign
from the State Department, and Bohlen, the quintessential non-quitter.[63]

   One of the fundraising events the EAG sponsored in its brief existence was a
benefit auction held at the house of Dorothy Norman, at which Nabokov played
some of his music; it also featured a short play acted by Kevin McCarthy and
Montgomery Clift.[64] EAG also sponsored a talk Nabokov gave in the spring of 1948
on "The Soviet Attack on Culture."[65] Held at the Rand School, it was followed by
a panel discussion, chaired by Mary McCarthy, with the participation of Dwight
Macdonald, Meyer Schapiro, and Lionel Trilling. Since his first *Atlantic Monthly*
article, Nabokov had established himself as an authoritative voice on the question of the state of Soviet music. Easily dismissed by some people as excessive and
biased when he first expressed them in 1941, when Soviet Russia was briefly seen
in a positive light, those views seemed to be vindicated in the climate of the Cold
War, especially after Stalin and Zhdanov, beginning in 1946, launched an unprecedented attack on the arts, and music in particular. In the 1948 spring issue of
Macdonald's *Politics*, Nabokov gave an account of the ongoing "music purge" in
the USSR.[66] "Soviet Russia," he explained from the outset, "is an autocratic oli-
garchy in which 200 million people are governed by an 'apparatus' [. . .] of two
million elected, or, better, selected people, who, in turn, are controlled by a group
of about two hundred persons."[67] The "music purge" was part of a wide-ranging
campaign waged by Stalin against every kind of Western influence in the arts and

the sciences. As his first example, Nabokov mentions the expulsion from the Soviet Musicians Alliance and dismissal from Moscow University of the music historian A. S. Ogolovets, who had had the temerity to suggest that Lenin was no expert on the subject of acoustics. Then came the February 11, 1948, decree of the Central Committee of the Communist Party, prompted by the opera *Velikaia druzhba* ("The Great Friendship") by the Georgian composer Vano Muradeli. The decree condemned as "formalist" all Western modernist trends in music—and by extension all artistic forms. Nabokov then analyzed the article "Formalism and Its Roots," in which the young composer Tikhon Khrennikov, who had succeeded Khachaturian as head of the Soviet Composers' Union, explained the Party's decision regarding the wholesale denunciation of Western music and its influence in Russia— an influence chiefly blamed on Diaghilev. This campaign, Nabokov argued, made sense considering the conventional, provincial, lowbrow musical tastes of Stalin and the vast majority of Soviet officials—as Nabokov had experienced firsthand in Berlin. But why focus on music in particular? Citing the inspector of Saltykov-Shchedrin's famous short story ("What I don't understand is undoubtedly dangerous to the security of the state"), Nabokov suggested that it was precisely because of its technical aspect, impenetrable to the layman, that music was held in such suspicion. Behind the jargon about "formalism" and "the classical tradition" was the fear of "creative individualism," which could naturally lead to "political individualism." "It is evident," Nabokov noted in his concluding paragraph, "that a closed cell within the framework of a totalitarian police state is intolerable."[68] The article was followed by a full translation of the February 11 decree, with an editorial note (probably penned by Macdonald) pointing out ironically that the text, which spoke for itself, was more damning than the *Daily Worker* seemed to realize when it had printed it in full to refute the distortions by the bourgeois press.

Nabokov updated and expanded his "brilliant" *Politics* article—as it was praised the following year by Schlesinger[69]—in "Russian Music after the Purge," which came out in the August 1949 issue of *Partisan Review*. He focused, this time, on the situation of the main composers specifically targeted by the purge, who had been invited by Khrennikov—or on his behalf—to "redeem themselves": Khachaturian, Prokofiev, and Shostakovich. (There were three more: the veteran symphonist Nikolai Miaskovskii, whom Nabokov esteemed; Gavriil Nikolaevich Popov; and Vissarion Iakovlevich Shebalin, the director of the Moscow Conservatory.) While Khachaturian, the least vulnerable, seemed to have weathered the crisis, Nabokov reminded his readers that Shostakovich had already found himself in such a situation after Stalin's condemnation of his opera *Lady Macbeth of Mtsensk District*. Although his current attempts to "redeem himself," Nabokov noted, were likely to disappoint his American admirers—"It seems that poor Shostakovich is afraid of using *any* kind of dissonance, even the most conventional ones"—[70] he was, at least, "definitely on the road to recovery."[71] Nabokov was particularly negative about the Ninth Symphony, which he had scathingly reviewed the year before as "mostly unimaginative, light-weight, and unforgivably superficial."[72] In *Partisan Review*, he praised Prokofiev's Fifth as "probably one of his best compositions, extremely thoughtful, full of imagination and thoroughly impregnated with a sincere and delightful lyricism" (the last word always a touchstone for Nabokov).[73] Yet, he pointed out that Prokofiev was the principal victim of the purge. Despite its slavishly politically correct subject ("a stilted patriotic short story about the life of a hero of the Soviet Air Force who had lost his two legs during the war") his last opera *Povest' o nastoiashchem cheloveke* (The Story of a Real Person), which Boris Khaikin had premiered, in concert, in December 1948, had been severely criticized by the authorities.[74] Citing Khrennikov's attacks, Nabokov pointed out that "in the Soviet Union, as in all bureaucratic totalitarian states, personal hatred and jealousies are of course much more intense and venomous than in the 'decadent' Western countries where the individual is not so much of a pawn in the rigid and often ruthless machinery of the State."[75] Only the deaths of Boris Asaf'ev—Prokofiev's nemesis since the 1930s—and Zhdanov himself seemed to offer a modicum of hope.

In the final part of his article, Nabokov, translating the "absurd verbiage" of the February 1948 decree into "reasonably practical terms," summarized the Soviet composers' *do*'s and *don't*'s. To be avoided at all cost were the following:

1. Discordant counterpoint (presumably the Hindemith style and atonality).

2. Introducing into the "sacred soil of pure classic Russian tradition jazz neurosis and Stravinskyan rhythmical paroxysms.

3. Inability to write "singable" melodic lines.

4. Naturalistic approaches to subject matter. (The love scene in "Lady Macbeth.").

To be "cured," the Soviet composer had to adhere to a strict regimen consisting in:

1. Avoiding "dissonance."

2. Avoiding any harmonic syntax more advanced than that of the late Sergei Rachmaninov.

3. Learning to write "easy" tunes.

4. Avoiding dependence on "abstract" instrumental and symphonic forms.

5. Writing more songs on Soviet subjects.

6. Strictly abstaining from jazz rhythms, paroxystic syncopation, "fake" (meaning dissonant) polyphony and atonality.

7. Writing operas about Soviet life.

8. Turning his attention in general to the song of the great Soviet people and forgetting about the West.[76]

The West was, indeed, the great bugaboo of the Zhdanovian system. With few exceptions—a curious one, Nabokov noted, was Walter Piston, recently lauded in *Sovietskaia Muzika*—Western composers were relentlessly attacked as "decadent formalists," "pseudo-modernists," or "cheats and scoundrels."[77] Modernist musical aesthetics were the object of a wholesale condemnation, couched at times in absurd terms, as when Hindemith was labeled as an "antiharmonic atonalist" along with Schoenberg, Berg, and Webern. Auric and Milhaud were denounced as "servile teasers of the snobbish bourgeois tastes of a capitalist city." If Poulenc was occasionally praised, it was for having set texts by "truly democratic poets" (i.e., French Communist Party members Aragon and Éluard). Among US composers, Gian Carlo Menotti and Henry Cowell were singled out for opprobrium, even though the latter had been published in the 1920s in the Soviet State Music Press.

Nabokov returned to the case of Prokofiev in a short article he published in August 1949 in the New York magazine *The Reporter*. Contrasting the seemingly "unassailable" standing of Prokofiev both in Russia and in the West with the total absence of new works by him on the concert scene, Nabokov argued that Prokofiev exemplified "the Procustean treatment that is apparently the standard fate of any Soviet artist suspected of exposure to the virus of western influence."[78] Why, he asked, had Prokofiev, a cosmopolitan musician, whose wife was half-Spanish, return to Russia? To answer his question, he gave a vignette of the composer's personality. Prokofiev belonged to the Russian middle-class, not to the soul-searching intelligentsia. He accepted the Revolution in its totality, as "a sincere and *instinctive* Russian patriot, who gives little thought to the question of justice or injustice in the Soviet government."[79] The regime, in turn, saw in Prokofiev a useful propagandist and used him as such, letting him (until 1938) keep a residence in Paris and tour around the world. When the first "anti-formalist" music purge occurred in 1932, Prokofiev had genuinely embraced it, not seeing then "any *ideological* contradiction between the aesthetic policy of the Soviet government and his own artistic philosophy."[80] Even after his halfhearted, possibly mandated, definitive return to Russia, he did his best to conform, writing a Toast Song for Stalin's sixtieth birthday, and submitting his music to "a process of great, and at times excessive, simplification."[81] Yet Prokofiev remained "one of the few Soviet composers whose music still preserved a genuine freshness, and didn't emanate the synthetic odor (like that of *ersatz* gasoline) and the dull provincialism which are the trademarks of most contemporary party-approved Soviet music."[82] Having escaped the 1936 purge and preserved his status as the dean of Soviet music, Prokofiev, in 1948, was the victim of his own preeminence. "In the eyes of those who rule the Russian people," Nabokov concluded, Prokofiev was "a symbol of Russia's association with the modern western world, an association the Kremlin now rejects, except when it has a claque as loud as the one at the Waldorf."[83]

The "Cultural and Scientific Conference for World Peace" at the Waldorf-Astoria hotel on March 25–27, 1949, provided the occasion for Nabokov's first public appearance as an anti-Stalinist cultural activist. Sponsored by a committee called National Council of the Arts, Sciences and the Professions, headed by the Harvard astronomer Harlow Shapley, a veteran Leftist, the conference was presented by its organizers as a goodwill enterprise calling for a continuation of intellectual exchange between East and West despite the worsening of the international situation. As it turned out, the conference invitation was worded in terms clearly biased towards the Eastern bloc: as Macdonald pointed out, "it denounced at length the State Department's 'cold war' policy but had not one word criticising the Russian power-moves to which this policy is a reaction."[84] The conference program, besides, excluded any possible dissenting voice. Sidney Hook, the New York University philosopher and anti-Communist activist, described it as "a family affair amongst Communists and 'honest liberals,' the quaint expression used by the Communist Party to designate formally unaffiliated individuals who were willing to echo the party line or go along with it in uncritical complicity."[85] In other words, the conference was an attempt on the part of the Soviets, following the World Congress of Intellectuals they had convened in Wroclaw in August 1948—and there were many more to come in the next four decades—to present themselves as the defenders of world peace and the United States and its allies as its enemies. It was, as Jason Epstein later put it, a "squalid attempt by Communists and fellow-travelers at cultural manipulation."[86] An impressive array of signatures had nevertheless been gathered by the sponsoring organization in support of the event: from the musical world, they included George Antheil, Leonard Bernstein, Marc Blitzstein, Aaron Copland, Lukas Foss, Morton Gould, Alexander Kipnis, Eugene Ormandy, Arthur Schnabel, Nicholas Slonimsky, Isaac Stern, and Randall Thompson, none of whom—with the exception of Blitzstein—could be labeled a fellow-traveler.[87] But there were prominent fellow-travelers among the event's organizers, and in Washington it was quickly denounced as Communist propaganda by Representative John S. Wood, chairman of the House Committee on Un-American Activities. The conference opened in a climate of tension, heightened by the denial of visas by the State Department to a number of invited delegates from Latin America and Western Europe (from Britain the writer Louis Golding and the crystallographer J. D. Bernal), a decision that prompted a protest from the American Civil Liberties Union. Visas, however, were granted to the delegation of fourteen representatives from the Soviet Union, Poland, and Czechoslovakia, headed by Aleksandr Fadeev, head of the Soviet Writers' Union, and Shostakovich.

The Waldorf-Astoria conference put liberal intellectuals such as Nabokov in a delicate position: while the event was undoubtedly in their eyes, as he put it, "a Soviet-promoted agitprop affair," and seemed to offer an ideal platform to denounce publicly the Soviet persecution of artists and musicians Nabokov himself had been denouncing in his articles, it was equally important for him and his friends, on the other hand, not to be identified with right-wing groups such as the Catholic War Veterans and the People's Committee for the Freedom of Religion, who announced they would be picketing the meeting.[88] In the version of the events he drafted many years later for *Bagázh*, Nabokov credits Mary McCarthy for bringing the conference to his attention at a dinner with two other friends at his and Patricia's place.[89] Rather than picket the event, the group decided to register as participants and "infiltrate" it along with any friends they could gather. "I felt elated," Nabokov recalled. "After so many years of frustration, something useful was in the making. At least there would be an earnest attempt to expose Stalin and Stalinism."[90] This spontaneous initiative took a more organized form when Nabokov contacted Sidney Hook, who, after being denied permission to address the conference, was already planning an action on a large scale and became, in Nabokov's words, the protesters' "chief engineer and self-appointed commander in chief."[91] As this phrasing suggests, Hook and Nabokov, by the time the latter wrote *Bagázh*, were no longer on easy terms, and Hook, in his autobiography, takes exception to Nabokov's account of the events.[92] Born in New York in 1902 to an Austrian Jewish family, Hook had studied in Germany and visited the Soviet Union, becoming a Marxist philosopher and US Communist Party member. After breaking with the Party in 1933, he gradually distanced himself from Marxism. In 1939 he founded a Committee for Cultural Freedom which issued a manifesto, signed by many prominent supporters, calling for a fight against totalitarianism in all its forms. The committee was short-lived, but the phrase "cultural freedom" was to take hold during the Cold War. By 1949, Hook, then chair of the NYU philosophy department, had become stridently anti-Communist. Though on friendly, if occasionally difficult, terms with the non-Communist Left (he had been involved in Mary McCarthy's America-Europe Groups), he later on, like other repentant Communists, moved further and further to the Right.[93]

Hook's response to the Waldorf Peace Conference was to put together a rival committee, named American Intellectuals for Freedom, which he co-chaired with his fellow philosopher and Dewey disciple George S. Counts, a professor at Columbia. To counterbalance the prestigious signatures gathered by NCASP, AIF formed its own international sponsoring committee: Benedetto Croce, T. S. Eliot, Karl Jaspers, Malraux, and Bertrand Russell—most of these later more or less loosely linked to the Congress for Cultural Freedom—gave their signatures, as did two of Nabokov's friends, Maritain and Stravinsky (who had declined an invitation to sign a telegram welcoming Shostakovich to the United States).[94] As for Albert Schweitzer, his name appeared *both* on the AIF committee and among the sponsors of the Peace Conference. Hook also arranged for the group to rent a bridal suite at the Waldorf-Astoria for the duration of the event, which became the headquarters of the protest group. He put Nabokov in touch with David Dubinsky, the anti-Communist head of the Ladies' Garment Workers Union, "a little roly-poly, humorous-looking man" with "quick, sharp eyes." Dubinsky, in turn, brought in "a small youngish-looking man with a crew cut" named Arnold Beichmann, formerly on the staff of the left-wing paper *PM*, who took care of the financial side of the operation, while relations with the press were entrusted to "a thin, sad-looking person called Mer Pitzele," an editor of *Business Week*.

When Nabokov arrived from Baltimore on Thursday, March 24, two days before the conference opened, he found Hook and his men—"the ad-Hook committee"—already installed in the Waldorf bridal suite:

> The place looked like a vacated bordello taken over by a printer or a pub-
> lisher gone berserk. One bed of the bridal suite had been removed and
> replaced by a giant mimeographing monster. The monster spewed out
> kilotons of printed matter. An attendant carried out the stuff periodically
> to one of the suite's bathrooms. There it formed tower-like structures in
> Mondrianish colors—precluding access to the john and the tub. The sec-
> ond king-size bed of the suite, with its pale-blue silk bedspread, had been
> transformed into a base for a mound of damp ladies' fur coats surrounded
> by neatly stacked mimeography in multicolored folders. [. . .]
>
> The second bathroom of the suite had been turned into a lieu for the
> in-camera meeting. When I came to the headquarters that bathroom was
> "engaged" by Beichmann, Pitzele, and Hook, with only one of them seated
> upon the john. A "Do Not Disturb" sign dangled on the door knob, but the
> door was open.
>
> There was a perpetual flow of visitors. Freedom lovers of various sizes,
> genders, and spectral colorings, squeezed their way through the cluttered
> premises in and out of doors. Some chatted excitedly, others buried their
> faces in reading matter provided by the two secretaries or the attendant of
> the mimeographic machine and its bathroom paper heap.[95]

As Nabokov's wife told him, there had been acrimonious meetings involving Mary McCarthy and her friends (Elizabeth Hardwick, Robert Lowell, Dwight Macdonald) on the one hand, and Hook on the other: Hook objected to the idea of infiltrating the event and insisted that they act according to his instructions.[96]

In his earliest account of the Waldorf-Astoria event, published in 1951 in the British edition of *Old Friends and New Music*, Nabokov evokes the press confer-ence which preceded the opening of the conference proper. There, in the Parrot Room—an appropriately named location, he could not help pointing out—Nabokov found himself seated opposite Shostakovich. He recalled watching "his

hands twist the cardboard tip of his cigarettes, his face twitch and his whole pos-
ture express intense unease. [. . .]His sensitive face looked disturbed, hurt, and
terribly shy. To me he seemed like a trapped man, whose only wish was to be left
alone, to the peace of his own art and to the tragic destiny to which he, like most
of his countrymen, has been forced to resign himself."[97]

Not content with infiltrating the Peace Conference, the protesters organized a
counter-event of their own, which was held, parallel to the conference opening,
on Saturday, March 26, at Freedom House on West 40th Street.[98] By then, the
protest was so well publicized that the hall that had been reserved was too small.
Thanks to Dubinsky's intervention with the Police Commissioner, the block was
roped off and loudspeakers transmitted the speeches. There were, according to
The New York Times, 400 people inside and about 500 in the street. Beside Hook
and Counts, the speakers included Max Eastman, Max Yeargan (one of the founders of the Council on African Relations), and Arthur Schlesinger. Speaking, for
the first time in public, on the subject of "Music and Peace," Nabokov explained
the significance of Shostakovich's presence at the conference, not as a free artist
but as "an appointed member of a political delegation, representing a government
which has repeatedly abused and mistreated him as a creative artist," a situation
that brought home "the profound and tragic irony of being a composer in a totalitarian state." He summarized the Soviet music purge, comparing Shostakovich to
"dirty laundry, [. . .] thrown in a clothes hamper, then suddenly picked up, washed,
ironed out, and sent to America with five other colleagues in blue serge suits, to
meet Dr Harlow Shapley and a motley crew of Iron Curtain parrots, each with
an olive branch . . ."[99] This mocking simile notwithstanding, Nabokov, who had
evidently been struck by Shostakovich's appearance the day before at the press
conference, evoked the composer in sympathetic terms. "No one who saw him at
that meeting," he continued, "[. . .] could help but feel compassion for the young
and timid artist, and feel an overpowering wish to take him by the arm and lead
him out of the clatter, the parody of that noisy conference, into a quiet place, far
and safe from the realities of the political world, far and safe from Stalin and his
henchmen." Nabokov also refrained from making any derogatory remarks about
Shostakovich's music, concentrating, instead, on the political significance of his
presence in New York:

> Yes, we here in America welcome the gifted and prolific Russian composer;
> we welcome him as the representative of a great and gifted people. We do
> *not* welcome him as the representative of a despotic government of which
> he and his art are helpless victims. We regret that he is forced to lend his
> name and his artistic reputation to the tortuous policies of the Soviet gov-
> ernment. But we do not point at him an accusing finger. We know that he
> is not free to choose freedom and we understand that.[100]

Stalin's government, Nabokov reminded his audience, was "responsible for the murder, deportation, exile, or disappearance from public life of [. . .] writers, scientists, poets, and artists." He listed, among others, Babel, Pilniak, Bulgakov, Meyerhold, as well as Akhmatova and Pasternak, also mentioning the vicious attacks on Prokofiev. Citing a mealy-mouthed statement from the Peace Conference, he asked, ironically, whether Harlow Shapley and his colleagues thought that such indisputable facts were a sound basis for "free and international exchange" and "peace in the world," or simply preferred to ignore them. Peace according to Stalin, he concluded, was silence: "silence of a whole people; silence of millions of slave laborers and exiles; silence of the concentration camps; silence of death."[101]

One of the people in attendance at Freedom House that afternoon, who congratulated Nabokov on his speech, was Michael Josselson, whose presence was anything but an accident: he was "covering" the meeting at the request of his boss Frank Wisner, head of the CIA's Office of Policy Coordination. The same Wisner had arranged, via Dubinsky, for the CIA to transfer funds to help pay for the Waldorf suite and other expenses associated with the protest and counter-event.[102] None of this, of course, was suspected by Nabokov and his friends.

Nabokov's other moment came on Sunday, March 27 during the conference's fine arts panel in the Starlight Roof.[103] On his way to the podium to introduce the session, Olin Downes, the *New York Times* music critic, a Shostakovich champion and one of the conference sponsors, recognized him and took him to task for associating with "black-guards and fascists."[104] The session, in Nabokov's recollection, consisted of dull, verbose papers, followed, each time, by an awkward translation into Russian or English. The "frail and strangely myopic Shostakovich" was the final speaker. Before him, Clifford Odets, the American playwright, had denounced the suggestion that Soviet Russia threatened world peace as "one of the greatest frauds ever perpetrated against the American people."[105] According to the *New York Times* report, which is at odds with Nabokov's later recollections on a few details only, Shostakovich limited himself to a few words "in high-pitched Russian" to thank the conference sponsors, after which the 5,200-word speech credited to him was read by an interpreter (identified by the *Times* as Paul Mann). The speech, obviously, had been "prepared by Agitprop agents of the Soviet Composers Union," as Nabokov suggests, or even more likely the Ministry of Foreign Affairs, at the helm of which Andreyi Vyshinskyii had just replaced Molotov. It was a typical diatribe, denouncing the United States as a warmonger and calling for "progressive" artists to rise against this new form of fascism. It also contained references to Shostakovich's past "errors" ("I departed from big themes and contemporary images, I lost my contact with the people and I failed . . .") and to the risks Prokofiev ran of "relapsing into formalism" unless he heeded the advice of the Party's Central Committee. The speech was, in fact, pieced together from three articles signed by Marian Koval, secretary of the Union of Soviet Composers, that had appeared the previous year in *Soviet Music*, and of which Shostakovich was the principal target, and from Khrennikov's 1949 new year's day message to Russian composers.[106] Among Western composers, Stravinsky was singled out for particular opprobrium: a traitor to his native land, whose "openly nihilistic writings" revealed his "moral barrenness."[107] In other words, to anyone in the audience who might have read Nabokov's articles on music in the Soviet Union, the speech must have sounded strangely familiar. "I sat in my seat," Nabokov recalled, "petrified by this spectacle of human misery and degradation."

> It was crystal clear to me that what I had suspected from the day I heard Shostakovich was going to be among the delegates representing the Soviet Government was true: This speech of his, this whole peace-making mission was part of a punishment, part of a ritual of redemption he had to go through before he could be pardoned again. He was to tell, in person, to all the dupes at the Waldorf conference and to the whole decadent bourgeois world that loved him so much that he, Shostakovich, the famous Russian composer, is *not* a free man, but an obedient tool of his government. He told in effect that every time the Party found flaws in his art, the Party was right, and every time the Party put him on ice, he was grateful to the Party, because it helped him to recognize his flaws and mistakes.[108]

The Waldorf-Astoria 800-person audience had a different reaction: it gave the composer "a resounding ovation."[109] Only a few minutes were left for the debate. Nabokov raised his hand, introduced himself in English and Russian, and asked Shostakovich his question, also in the two languages. In a recent *Pravda* article, he said, Hindemith, Schoenberg, and Stravinsky had been denounced as "obscurantists," "decadent bourgeois formalists," and "lackeys of imperialism," whose music deserved to be banned in the Soviet Union. "Does Mr. Shostakovich," Nabokov then asked, to the bewilderment of the Soviet delegation, "personally agree with this official view as printed in *Pravda*?" Prompted by his KGB "nurse," Shostakovich replied, in Russian, that he fully agreed with the *Pravda* statements on Hindemith and Stravinsky.[110] "And Schoenberg too," he added, when pressed by Nabokov.[111] "This panel rightly believes," Nabokov then asked, "that peace cannot be achieved without intellectual interchange. How come then that Western music is barred from the USSR?" "Big and significant works from Western music," Shostakovich sheepishly replied, "find their place in the repertoire of Soviet concert halls."[112] Nabokov then left the room, to "unanimous, ferocious booing" by the audience.

This confrontation—Nabokov's first encounter with the Soviet composer— has been diversely appraised. Arthur Miller, who not only figured among the conference's sponsors but chaired the panel, was still "haunted," years later, by the vision of Shostakovich and described the event as a "masquerade." However, while mentioning Nabokov's presence that morning, Miller nowhere says in his account that he disapproved of his intervention, adding, in fact, that he and Nabokov subsequently became friends.[113] Shostakovich himself—leaving aside the question of the authenticity of his memoirs—remembered this first and only trip to the United States "with horror."[114] Not mentioning Nabokov's name, he heaps scorn, not on anti-Stalinists, but on Western Communists and fellow-travelers taken in by Soviet propaganda. In other words, Shostakovich's account in *Testimony* is not in the least in contradiction with Nabokov's, as found in the British edition of *Old Friends and New Music*. More recently, however, the episode has been described as "appalling" and Nabokov accused of "throwing punches at a man whose arms were tied behind his back."[115] This criticism, which implies that Nabokov indulged in a personal attack on Shostakovich, misses the point.[116] Nabokov was much better informed than anyone in the Waldorf audience on the realities of Russia under Stalin. Members of his own family had been victims of the Soviet regime. Only two years before, his cousin Ekaterina Sergeevna, an employee of the American embassy in Bucharest, had been kidnapped by KGB agents and sent to a Gulag camp, where she still was. As his published articles show, Nabokov was well aware that Shostakovich, no matter what he thought, had no choice of answer. The purpose of his question was not to humiliate the Soviet composer, for whom, despite their aesthetic differences, he clearly felt a great deal of sympathy. It was to force Shostakovich to say what he was supposed to say and, thereby, to make a public exposure of the vacuousness and hypocrisy of the whole occasion. From this point of view, Nabokov's intervention was highly successful, perhaps even more so than the other forms of protest: even an unsympathetic writer as Frances Stonor Saunders admits the conference was "a humiliation for its Communist backers."[117] Nor did the Soviets ever try again to sponsor a similar event in the United States.[118]

While the Waldorf-Astoria conference gave Nabokov a new position as a public intellectual, his standing as a composer also grew significantly in the postwar years thanks to two major commissions. The first he received after his return from Germany came from Koussevitzky, who, as mentioned in the previous chapter, was grateful to Nabokov for his help with the reconstitution of his Berlin-based music publishing firm. Nabokov had been introduced to Koussevitzky in the late 1920s in Paris, possibly on Prokofiev's recommendation. Yet he did not know him intimately, nor had Koussevitzky conducted any of his works in Boston other than the First Symphony for its American premiere. On the other hand, Nabokov was a longtime friend of Olga Naumova, the niece of Koussevitzky's wife, Nataliia, who had died in 1942 and in whose memory the conductor established the Koussevitzky Music Foundation. Nabokov had met

Olga in the mid-1920s when she lived with her parents in Nice, near his own mother's villa. She and Koussevitzky got married in late 1947. Nabokov visited them in May of that year in Lenox, where they lived in a house called Serenak, a coinage combining the names of Serge and Nataliia Koussevitzky. At lunch, Nabokov recalled,

> Koussevitzky bombarded me with questions about Germany, about our relations with the Russians, about my experiences with the army and the military government, and listened with avid interest to my detailed account of the new music I had seen or heard in France, in Austria, in Berlin, and in particular the music of the closed concerts of the Soviet military authorities, to which I had been occasionally invited.[119]

Whether the commission, as reported in *Old Friends and New Music*, was made during that luncheon or was more likely, as the drafts for *Bagázh* suggest, offered by letter when Nabokov was still in Berlin, Nabokov proposed to write a piece he had started drafting in Germany, though he was not sure at that point about the final shape he intended to give it. It was inspired by the feelings of nostalgia prompted by his contacts with the Russians he had met in Germany, whether the anonymous refugees parked in camps and waiting for their forced repatriation or the few sympathetic Soviet officers he had been able to bond with, like Tania and her husband. Nabokov found these feelings crystallized in an unfinished autobiographical poem by Pushkin. Dating from 1835, towards the end of Pushkin's life, the untitled poem is usually referred to by its incipit "... *Vnov' ia posetil* ..." ("... I visit once again ..."), or at times as "This little plot of earth" ("*Tot ugolok zemli*"), after a phrase that occurs in the second line, or again—this was the version favored by Vladimir Nabokov—as "Mikhailovskoe Revisited."[120] Speaking in the first person, the poet, revisiting after ten years the estate where he once spent a two-year exile, evokes the surroundings (his nanny's now empty homestead, the lake, the windmill . . .), focusing especially on trees, which became a symbol for the passing of time, bringing sad reflections about lost youth, friendships betrayed, and the sting of bitter feelings. For Nabokov, the poem had a deep personal resonance: Mikhailovkoe, the estate of Pushkin's mother in the Pskov province, where the poet had been banished in 1824–26, bordered the Korff family's estate, on Nabokov's paternal grandmother's side, and the Pushkins and Korffs were acquainted. More recently, by Nabokov's own account, the poem had acquired an indirect resonance when he found himself in Germany revisiting places where he had lived twenty years before.[121] These personal connections, compounding the haunting feelings of loss and desolation that pervade the work—what Nabokov called its *toska*, an untranslatable word expressing at once "anguish, sadness and spleen"—made the poem a particularly appealing choice for a musical setting. But Nabokov was also drawn to it for reasons having to do with its form.

> On its surface, the poem is very simple. Pushkin starts by describing Mikhailovskoe's countryside, its woods, meadows and fields, the old mill, the master's house and "the furtive steps and careful watch" of his old nurse—all of it flowing, rhymeless hexameter done with gentle care and laconic, almost "Latin" precision. But as the poem advances a musician's ear perceives that the syllabic count of the hexameter is only a cover-up. Behind it Pushkin plays intricate, rhythmic word-games. Iambic pentameters (with chastised tonic accents) mingle with thwarted anapests that through unexpected *enchaînements* of words acquire an opposite, dactylic flavor. [. . .]From the middle of the poem onward and to its unintended ending Pushkin abandons the controlled lyric countenance of the rural landscape painting and lets it grow into an embittered, exuberant elegy stuffed with romantic clichés ("lost youth," "lost hopes," "*amitiés trahies*," "dark forebodings," "broken promises"). But in Pushkin's ingenious hands this romantic cant preserves a childlike innocence.[122]

Nabokov, by his own admission, hesitated between setting the poem to music and writing a symphonic poem inspired by it. He eventually decided on the former, but still gave the work a symphonic description ("Elegy in three movements"). Following the mood of the poem, the three parts are, in succession, a meditative Andante, followed by an Allegretto (corresponding to the evocation of the trees), and a melancholy final Lento Assai. The vocal line, which seldom ventures above or below the stave (rising to high B-flat only on three occasions, one of them *piano* in the opening movement), is essentially syllabic and destined to facilitate the comprehension of the text. As the composer himself said, "I had to keep under control my own musical invention in order to 'contain' and not 'exceed' the emotional flow of Pushkin's verse."[123]

Having completed *The Return of Pushkin*, as he decided to entitle his cantata, in the summer of 1947 at Kolbsheim, where he spent three weeks on leave, Nabokov devoted the next three months to the orchestration. In October he played the score to Koussevitzky at his Brookline residence. As a veiled reference in a Stravinsky letter makes clear, relations with the star conductor were not as easy as the *Atlantic Monthly* profile might suggest.[124] Nabokov initially intended his work to be sung by a tenor, and this would arguably allow for a better understanding of the text (the published score says "high voice" without specifying the gender). This was discouraged by Koussevitzky, on the grounds that audiences did not like "long solo pieces for tenor" and there were few good tenors around in any case. "Koussie" also apparently objected to the changes of meter in the first movement. The singer he proposed was the soprano Marina Koshetz—daughter of the famous Ukrainian singer Nina Koshetz, who had premiered Prokofiev's *Love for Three Oranges* in Chicago in 1921 and whom Nabokov had heard in Paris in the 1920s.[125]

Nabokov set the text of the poem in the original Russian, and it was premiered in that language. However, the score was published in trilingual Russian, English, and German performing versions. While the last is uncredited and may be by Nakobov himself, the English text—like the German a syllable-for-syllable rendering—is by none other than his cousin Vladimir. The circumstances of the latter's involvement are, unfortunately, difficult to reconstitute with precision: they are not discussed by any of Vladimir's biographers, all the more regrettably since it represents not only the only instance of a collaboration between the two cousins (save for the youthful, lost "Last Supper" composed in Yalta) but also one of the few incursions of the writer into the world of music.[126] Surviving correspondence between Nicolas and Vladimir show that the latter, assisted by Véra, worked with his customary fastidiousness. What it does not establish is whether Vladimir had anything to do with Nicolas's decision to set the poem in a longer form than its standard 51 lines and incorporate 15 lines, with a pronounced autobiographical character, that Pushkin discarded.[127]

"I wrote it with love and devotion," Nabokov wrote to Koussevitzky on September 9, 1947, reporting that the work was completed. He added that he had showed it to Virgil Thomson, Sauguet, and Suvchinskii in Paris and they had all liked it.[128]

The Return of Pushkin was first heard on January 2, 1948. It opened the Boston Symphony Orchestra program, which also included Debussy's *La damoiselle élue*, the Letter Scene from *Eugene Onegin*, and Tchaikovsky's *Francesca da Rimini* (the last apparently a last-minute substitute for Shostakovich's Sixth Symphony). Did the work, as Nabokov remembered, "fall flat"? This is certainly the impression conveyed by the *Christian Science Monitor* reviewer, according to whom "the composition made no particular impression."[129] On the other hand, the *Boston Herald* critic, while mentioning the "cordial applause" that greeted the composer, described the cantata as "an expressive and imaginative setting" and found Koshetz's performance "very moving"; his main regret, which can hardly be construed as a criticism of the work, was that lack of familiarity with Pushkin's poem made it hard to penetrate deeply into its message.[130] The work was also heard, with the same forces, at the Brooklyn Academy of Music on January 16 and at Carnegie Hall on the 17th (with Prokofiev's "Classical" Symphony replacing the Debussy in Brooklyn). It was given in Baltimore in November, conducted by Nabokov himself, and with soprano Dorothy Dittmar; though the printed program is not specific, this may have been the first hearing (and, so far as one can tell, the only one to date) of Vladimir's English version. Reviewing the Carnegie Hall concert, Olin Downes was less happy with the vocal performance than his *Boston Herald*

colleague; the *Christian Science Monitor* review had also found fault with the singer's pinched tones, Slavonic vibrato, and pitch vagaries. Yet Downes's review is far
from negative. Noting Stravinskian influences and "musical inter-relationships
between the different movements," he pointed out that Nabokov avoided the obvious pitfalls of a folkloric or antiquarian musical language in favor of a personal,
modern, at times dissonant idiom that allowed him to translate, "simply and in an
unadorned manner," what the poet said. "Between the nostalgic melancholy of the
slow movement and the music of true tenderness and introspection which makes
the final section," Downes added, "the listener is moved; he admires more the
craftsmanship and the expressive genius which brought this forth."[131]

"The music is nostalgic and poetic, serene for the most part and psychologi-
cally, rather than geographically, atmospheric," Virgil Thomson wrote in the
New York Herald Tribune. "[Nabokov's] tone is elevated, his composition elegant.
Neo-Romanticism is its school. [. . .] It is a distinguished work and a beautiful
one."[132] When *The Return of Pushkin* was given in Paris the following year, under
Désormière, and in what Nabokov described as "ghastly French," it was received
with "polite clapping at the end." Thomson, consolingly, told the composer that
his elegy was a "private" rather than a "public" affair and suggested that its inner
purpose—"to lay the ghost of Russia"—was was too intensely personal to speak
to a foreign audience but might appeal to a Russian one. "The piece," so was
Nabokov's melancholy conclusion, "is still waiting for *that* audience."[133] It always
remained his own personal favorite among all his works.[134]

When Nabokov discussed *The Return of Pushkin* with Koussevitzky, the Russian
conductor suggested at first that Nabokov write a "concerto for voice and orchestra"—which was about the opposite of what he had in mind.[135] That was, however, the subtitle Nabokov chose for his next commission from the Koussevitzky
Foundation. Instead of Russia's national poet, Nabokov turned to his Italian counterpart, selecting excerpts from Dante's *La vita nuova*, in which the poet evokes,
in a mystical tone, his love for Beatrice. The work is arranged in three parts: "The
Eating of the Heart," a recitative and aria for tenor (". . . and as I thought of her
. . ."), corresponding to the third section of Dante's work; "The Vision of Death," a
passacaglia, with the soprano voice ("Hast thou not heard it said . . ."), corresponding to section 23; and "Beatrice's Beatitude," a "Fantasia e Rota" ("Beyond the
sphere that circlest widest . . ."), a setting of the final sonnet (section 41), with the
two voices alternating and joining at the end. As in *The Return of Pushkin*, Nabokov
set the text both in the original language and in English. For the latter he used the
1861 translation by Dante Gabriel Rossetti (and Rossetti's brother Michael for the
prose passages). To make it fit the vocal line, the translation, especially the prose
passages, was modified with W. H. Auden's assistance.[136]

Initially announced for a Berskhire Music Festival concert on August 5,
1950, the premiere of *La vita nuova* took place in Boston, under Charles Münch,

Koussevitzky's successor as BSO music director, on March 2, 1951, with soprano Mary Henderson and tenor David Garen. "Nicholas Nabokov," wrote the *Boston Herald* reviewer, "has achieved that rarity: the contemporary work that makes its own way easily and naturally." While finding in the work "fleeting" influences of Prokofiev and Mahler, he emphasized its originality and variety:

> The musical language is tonal but freely moving and plastic, the structure generally chordal and monophonic with rhythms of a regular though not limited stress. The orchestral colors are usually sombre and introspective, and are remarkably well suited—as is indeed the vocal line throughout—to the character of these excerpts mingling, as they do, the rapture and mysticism of Dante's love for Beatrice, his vision of her death and his expression of sorrow.
>
> Of the three sections the second two seemed the most successful and evocative. [. . .]The Passacaglia [. . .] I found extremely beautiful, and the closing section, with its lovely final cadence, very moving indeed.[137]

The appealing program, which began with Mozart's Symphony in E-flat, K. 543, also included Schubert's Mass in G major.

The same soprano, Mary Henderson, was featured when the work was heard at Carnegie Hall, also under Münch, and in the composer's presence, on January 14, 1953. The negative review it received in the *New York Times* from "Comrade Olin Downes" (as he was cannily dubbed by Stravinsky) was probably the price Nabokov had to pay for his exchange with Shostakovich at the Waldorf-Astoria four years before.[138] Virgil Thomson, reviewing the concert in the *New York Herald Tribune*, was struck by the work's "mystical and incantatory quality" and its "nostalgic, intense" mood. Noting that the vocal parts were "expertly set for big-style declamation" and that the "neo-Romantic" orchestral writing was "rounded (rather than angular) in thematic material and suave in harmony," he concluded:

> Its strength, like that of all Nabokov's music, is the dignity of the poetic expression and its direct character. It is not the work of an expert showing off but rather of an expert speaking simply and from the heart about perfectly real feelings. This aspect of contemporary neo-Romanticism is not generally understood yet. But it will be.[139]

La vita nuova was heard several times in Europe in the early 1950s and remains, *pace* Olin Downes, one of Nabokov's most admired works.

Nabokov's other postwar compositions include a piece in two movements for violin and piano, entitled *Introduction and Allegro*. It was premiered by Nathan Milstein, accompanied by Artur Balsam, at Carnegie Hall on 17 November 1947.[140] Reviewing the concert ("one of the most delightful evenings of violin music that your announcer has experienced in some time"), Virgil Thomson praised the work's "quality of personal poetry all too rare in these days of knock-'em-out neo-classicism."

> It is a neo-Romantic piece rather than a neo-Classic one, because it is about its subject, not its form, and because the subject is personal feelings. These seem, from the melodic confrontation, to be connected with Russia—a wistful sadness, a moment of exuberance and a return to the wistful note. It is thin writing, widely spaced by moments and always conceived as a blend of piano and violin sound. It is brilliant, too, an original and effective piece of music.[141]

In 1950, Nabokov revised one of his prewar compositions, the choruses he had written for the Wells College production of *Oedipus Rex*. He rewrote and extended the second and third, and composed two new ones. The work was undertaken at the request of an old friend, Hugh Ross, formerly head of the Schola Cantorum and now director of the Marymount College Glee Club in Tarrytown, New York, where this new version, with piano accompaniment, was premiered on May 5, in a varied program that included the world premiere of Hubert Lamb's *The Annunciation* and the first New York performance of Villa Lobos's *Memorare*.

Two other works date from the same period. The first was the *Concerto Corale* for flute, strings—which the score specifies can be reduced to five solo instruments—and piano. Based on a theme by the sixteenth-century German composer Hans Leo Hassler, it was published by Belaieff in 1953 and heard for the first time in Paris in 1957. Between April 1949 and January 1950, Nabokov also wrote a song cycle comprising twelve settings of poems by Emily Dickinson. It has apparently remained unpublished. In 1949, he and Isaiah Berlin toyed with the idea of an operatic adaptation of Turgenev's novella *First Love*. Mentioning the project to Shirley Anglesey, Berlin reported that he had heard songs Nabokov had recently composed and they were "enchantingly beautiful."[142] The Turgenev project was abandoned, according to Nabokov, because neither he nor Berlin "could find an ending to the story that would turn it into an opera libretto."[143]

Another unrealized project dating from the postwar years was a film based on Tchaikovsky's *The Nutcracker*, for which Nabokov wrote the script, based on conversations with Balanchine, and evidently with some input from Lincoln Kirstein as well. Subtitled "A film fantasy," it follows the ballet's scenario, combining it with elements borrowed from the E. T. A. Hoffmann story on which it is based. David Singer, the producer who had optioned the project, did not come through with it at the time. Two decades later, when Balanchine was approached by a film producer about making his *Nutcracker* into a feature film, he and Nabokov looked at their work again and apparently agreed it was terrible.[144]

12
———

Moving Center Stage

NABOKOV AND PATRICIA spent the summer of 1949 in Europe. Rather than staying in Paris, which now seemed "glum and alien" to him, they rented a cottage in a tiny village on the edge of the Fontainebleau Forest and used it as their base.[1] At Fontainebleau, Nabokov was invited to lecture at the American summer conservatory Nadia Boulanger had opened in 1921; it had now resumed its activities after the war. A secondhand Peugeot was purchased, in which Nabokov and his wife drove through Italy, Switzerland, and the south of France, where they attended performances at the Aix-en-Provence Festival, then in its second year. On his own, Nabokov visited the Bethmann-Hollwegs at Altenhof and the Gruneliuses at Kolbsheim. In idyllic weather, the composer happily renewed his connections with Europe, visiting "old, lovely towns, cathedrals and castellos," and eating "excellent, inexpensive food in small, well-tended restaurants."[2] In September, while Patricia remained a few more weeks in Europe, Nabokov flew back to America. After this peaceful summer, he did not relish the prospect of returning to his adoptive country. Not that he minded the teaching routine at the Peabody Conservatory, which was by far his pleasantest, most stimulating teaching experience. But he did not like the political atmosphere in America, which he felt "was becoming increasingly a hunting ground for unscrupulous demagogues."[3] Much as he detested Soviet communism, he was equally opposed to the kind of witch-hunting that had begun, with Richard Nixon its most conspicuous spokesman, and would reach a hysterical pitch the following spring under Senator Joseph McCarthy.

Sometime in late 1949 or early 1950, Nabokov and his wife were invited to a press conference held in New York at the New School for Social Research. The speaker was Melvin Lasky, the young editor of *Der Monat*, the Munich-based monthly magazine founded in 1948 with the backing of the American Military Government to develop ties between German and American intellectuals. Born in New York in 1920, Lasky had made his debut as a journalist by working with Sol Levitas, editor of the anti-Stalinist magazine *The New Leader*. During the war he served as combat historian in France and Germany. After his demobilization he remained in Berlin as German correspondent of *The New Leader* and *Partisan Review*.[4] Nabokov met Lasky through Josselson when he was posted in Berlin and after his return saw him again occasionally in New York. "He was," he recalled, "a small-size, boisterous, smiling man with a well-trimmed beard, who was rumored to be a brilliant editor and journalist."[5] Though they were to collaborate for many years, there was never any chemistry between them. Nabokov was fond of Lasky's former boss, "sweet old Sol Levitas," and admired Lasky's shrewdness and sense of humor. Yet he found the latter "intellectually intimidating and somewhat man-nerless" and was made uncomfortable by what he sensed was "an aura of the American equivalent of the apparatchik."[6] Impressed by the success of Americans for Intellectual Freedom in countering the Soviets and their supporters at the Waldorf-Astoria Peace Conference, Lasky, on his return to Europe, suggested to Josselson that a similar, but much bigger, gathering of non-Communist liberal intellectuals be organized in Germany. Berlin, since the 1948 blockade a living symbol of the East-West division, was chosen as the site. Lasky, announcing the event at the New School press conference, explained that the invitations would be sent on behalf of Ernst Reuter, the Social-Democrat mayor of Berlin—a former Communist who, after being imprisoned by the Nazis, had exiled himself to Turkey and was therefore popularly known as "the Turk." The conference was to take place in June 1950 and would be largely financed by the US Military Government through "counterpart" funds—that is, on the percentage of Marshall Plan funds made available to the United States by beneficiary countries. This arrangement, Nabokov remembered, caused some controversy in the New School audience of journalists and intellectuals: the idea that what seemed to be essentially a cultural event should be financed by discretionary US funds—that is, without congressio-nal oversight—went against the natural Democratic impulse of most Americans. This was, as Nabokov later saw it, the core of the problem that would haunt him sixteen years later.

Had the American government *then* had the courage and foresight to establish a worldwide fund out of "counterpart currencies" to subsidize legally and overtly—as did the Marshall Plan in the domain of economic reconstruction—the indispensable anti-Stalinist, anti-Communist, and, in general, anti-totalitarian cultural activities of the Cold War, the whole ugly mess of 1966 or 1967 [i.e., the revelation that the Congress for Cultural Freedom was financed to a large extent with money channeled through the CIA] would not have taken place. Many reputations would have been spared, thousands of lies would have remained untold, and the eminently decent, honest Cold War period, now absurdly condemned because of a thing euphemistically called *détente* (and what a wallop of a misnomer that is!), could have been fought out, at least in the world of the intellect and culture, openly and frankly.[7]

Little did Nabokov suspect, in 1950, that the Berlin conference itself, as Lasky was in a good position to know, was to be financed, through the good offices of Josselson, with funds channeled through the CIA's Office of Policy Coordination.

Nabokov was not among the organizers of the Berlin Congress for Cultural Freedom, as the conference was called. His name is not to be found in the 41-member international committee put together by Reuter and Lasky.[8] He was, however, well acquainted with two its American members (Schlesinger and Hook). His participation was made easier by his being in Europe for four months on a formal assignment as music correspondent of the *Atlantic Monthly* to cover European music festivals. He and Patricia flew to Paris, via Luxembourg, in mid-May on a charter flight operated by the student organization "Youth Argosy." Once again they occupied their little house on the outskirts of Fontainebleau. Nabokov then flew to Berlin from Orly airport at the end of June.[9] On the DC2 were several of the Paris-based conference participants: the Austrian novelist Manès Sperber, since 1934 a refugee in France; the Resistance hero and socialist deputy Georges Altman; and the writer and human rights activist David Rousset, author of *L'univers concentrationnaire*, a study on concentration camps—both Nazi and Soviet—which had made a great impression when published in 1946. Also on the plane were Louis Fischer and Sol Levitas, with whom Nabokov was seated.[10] Next to Rousset, he noticed a "frail, diaphanous, extraordinarily sad and beautiful-looking woman," whom Rousset treated "with great deference, but also somewhat possessively, as if she were a precious object and his private property." A Dutch citizen, named Elinor Lipper, she had been arrested in Moscow in 1937 and spent the next eleven years in Soviet prison camps; the memoir she wrote in German was published in Zurich in 1950 and translated into English the following year. She spoke fluent Russian and her appearance at the Congress, as a living witness to what was not yet called the Gulag, was expected to cause a sensation. Two other Soviet camp survivors attended the Berlin Congress: Margaret Buber-Neumann, author of a 1948 memoir of Nazi and Soviet camps, *Als Gefangene bei Stalin und Hitler* (published in English in 1950 as *Under Two Dictators*); and an old friend of Nabokov from the mid-1920s, the Polish painter Józef Czapski, whose own first-hand account of Soviet camps, *Na nieludziej ziemi*, issued in 1949, appeared in English in 1951 as *The Inhuman Land*.

Before the plane landed, Nabokov had the impression that Berlin was "unchanged—just as I had left it three years ago. The same pitiful squares of vegetable gardens planted between ruins and rubble; the same treeless parks; the same naked sadness, ruin, and desolation."[11] After landing at Tempelhof, the participants were taken to their respective hotels in Charlottenburg. Nabokov's impression of the city was quickly altered.

> From the low windows of the car, I could see rows of small stores, their show windows packed with goods, and one-story dwellings, newly built and freshly painted. True enough, between them were gaping cavities, blocks of ruin, heaps of rubble. But most of the cavities had been cleared of rubble and transformed into parking lots; the ruins had been tidied and surrounded by brick walls; the rubble had been piled in orderly heaps, encased on flower beds, or framed with borders of freshly mowed grass.[12]

The first person Nabokov bumped into at the hotel am Zoo was A. J. Ayer, the British philosopher, whom he knew through Isaiah Berlin. Exchanging impressions over drinks, he and Nabokov found themselves in agreement that, despite Mayor Reuter's invitation, the conference was an "all-American" affair, carefully pre-orchestrated in Washington, DC; that it would be run smoothly and according to the organizers' designs; and that, without being exactly "had," as he put it, the participants were being gently "manipulated" by the "occult forces" behind the event. In the lobby of the hotel am Steinplatz, the conference headquarters, Nabokov encountered Josselson, who seemed "preoccupied and nervous like someone involved in organizing a prima donna's first concert in an unexplored country."

The Congress opened on June 26 in the Art Deco Titania Palast film theater, with the Berlin Philharmonic Orchestra playing a Beethoven overture,[13] in a climate of heightened international tension: the day before, troops from Communist North Korea invaded the South. The 118 foreign delegates from twenty-one countries, mostly fell into four broad categories:[14] members of the non-Communist Left who were themselves former Communists or prominent fellow-travelers; non-Communist members of European resistance movements; European Federalists; and political refugees from Soviet-dominated countries. Interestingly, Nabokov belonged to none of the above: he was not a recent exile, had never flirted with communism, and, although close to the New York Intellectuals—such as Schlesinger, who attended the event—was not a writer or an academic, but a musician.[15] The Berlin Congress was heavily tilted towards the first category. Its star, who seemed to "dominate the scene and attract everybody's interest," as Nabokov recalled, was Arthur Koestler. The forty-five-year-old Hungarian-born novelist, made famous in 1940 by *Darkness at Noon*, was one of the six disillusioned former Marxist activists or sympathizers whose testimonies had been gathered in 1949 by Richard Crossman, the Labour MP, under the title *The God That Failed: A Confession*. In addition to Koestler, three others of the book's contributors were present in Berlin: Louis Fischer, whom Nabokov had met during his postwar days in Berlin; the novelist

Ignazio Silone, one of the founders of the Italian Communist Party; and the poet Stephen Spender, whom Nabokov already knew. Rather than Koestler, who gave a rousing speech at the opening session, adopting a "proletarian manner" and addressing the participants as "comrades," Nabokov was attracted to the personality of Silone, whom he had never met previously, but whose writings he knew and admired. "His quiet manner," he remembered, "uneloquent and shy yet bitingly sardonic, was a welcome contrast to the succession of fiery bards we were exposed to during the Berlin affair."[16] One of the fieriest of these bards was James Burnham, the former Trotskyist and future neoconservative, whose speech proposed a distinction between "good" atom bombs and "bad" ones.[17] In such a context, the views of liberal "moderates" were the minority. Ayer's paper on the philosophical justifications of tolerance on the "Science and Totalitarianism" panel was coldly received, which prompted the Oxford historian Hugh Trevor-Roper to jettison the one he intended to present and limit himself to extemporized remarks. Summarizing his negative impressions of the conference for *The Manchester Guardian*, he described the proceedings as "in no sense an intellectual congress" but "a Wroclaw in reverse."[18]

Like Trevor-Roper—and unlike Hook, who remembered the event as "the most exciting conference I have ever attended, before or since"[19]—Nabokov retained an unenthusiastic memory of the Berlin Congress and later claimed he had been only a minor participant and stayed away from many sessions. Instead, he recalled, he saw friends, went to bars "with or without *Mädchen*," to the zoo, and to the National Gallery.[20] Contemporary records show that, without playing a prominent role, he was keenly aware of the political aspects of the event. For instance, he and Schlesinger took advantage of their presence in Berlin to interview refugees from the Soviet Union, with Nabokov presumably acting as interpreter. These contacts convinced them that the Soviet propaganda portraying the US foreign policy as belligerent and expansionist was working so effectively that counter-statements at the highest level were necessary—a view they subsequently tried to convey to their friends in the State Department.[21] This feeling of urgency may explain why, at the "Arts, Artists and Freedom" panel, instead of speaking about the case of Shostakovich, as he had announced, Nabokov discussed in more general and also firmer terms the future tasks of the Congress. The text of his address, in which the word *combat* (fight) recurs, shows that, like many other participants, he was caught in the aggressive rhetoric of the meeting to a greater extent than he subsequently admitted:

I think that [. . .] out of this Congress we should build our first fighting organization. We should have a standing committee. We must see to it that it seeks to identify all fighters, all fighting organizations and all methods of fighting, with a view to action. If we do not, we will sooner or later be hanged. The hour has long struck Twelve.[22]

In the context of the Korean War, such words were well received. Nabokov was appointed to the commission in charge of drafting the Berlin Congress's manifesto. This document was largely inspired by Koestler, who read it aloud on June 29 before a crowd of 15,000 at the open air Funkturm Sporthalle, in the British sector. "It reads very well even now," Nabokov later admitted. He was no doubt pleased with the manifesto's proclamation that "intellectual freedom is one of the inalienable rights of man" and the denunciation of the limits placed on the creative freedom of artists by totalitarian regimes. He may have been relieved by the removal, at the insistence of Trevor-Roper and other British delegates, joined by Silone, of an article condemning Marxism in sweeping, intolerant terms. Nabokov was also elected to the twenty-five-member "International Committee for Cultural Freedom" formed with a view to discussing the establishment of a permanent structure; it met on the last day of the conference.

On the return journey to Paris, Nabokov sat with Elinor Lipper and talked to her in Russian. It was his first opportunity to meet a Gulag survivor. She had not enjoyed the Congress, finding it "silly, ineffective, and inchoate"; she also felt she was being exploited by Rousset and others. Nabokov saw more of her during that summer in Paris and he visited her in Geneva, where she was raising the daughter born to her in a Siberian concentration camp. In the autumn, having married a French or Swiss doctor specializing in equatorial diseases, she settled with him in Madagascar, disappearing from public life. Nabokov never saw her again.[23]

Among the friends Nabokov visited in Berlin at the time of the conference were musicians he had befriended and helped during his previous stay. Out of these contacts he wrote a report on the situation of music in Germany which appeared in the June 1951 Atlantic Monthly.[24] A large part of the article is devoted to Blacher, whom he describes as "the most influential person in Central European music." Summarizing Blacher's career, Nabokov evokes, in his customary lively style, a dinner party the Russian-German composer and his wife gave for him and the Rufers at their house in the American sector. The picture Blacher and Rufer gave of the situation of composers in Berlin was bleak; music, they claimed, was, like the city itself, at an impasse. Blacher wished he could get a teaching position in America, "the only country where a composer can work fearlessly."[25] Yet, despite this pessimistic assessment, Nabokov noted many signs of improvement since his previous visit to Berlin, especially in the standards of musical performance. He praised, in particular, the work accomplished by the Hungarian conductor Ferenc Fricsay at the helm of the Berlin Radio Symphony Orchestra, "the main outlet for new German music and the only outlet for contemporary American music."[26] Like all Congress participants, Nabokov had been advised against venturing into the Soviet sector, and was therefore not in a position to assess musical life there. His article mentions with particular scorn the statements made by Hanns Eisler, after his return from his America exile, in support of the Soviet condemnation of "useless experimentation and formalistic tendencies" and "vile lackeys of impe-rialism" like Stravinsky and Schoenberg.[27] At the Municipal Opera House, in the British sector, Nabokov heard, he reports, "one of the best *Fidelios* of my life." Conducted by Fricsay and directed by Tietjen, it featured a singing and acting ensemble that "was so homogeneous, so precise, and at the same time so pro-foundly lyrical that all the moving, humane parts of Beethoven's music stood out as they rarely do in the average performance."[28] Nabokov did not care, on the other hand, for Werner Egk's ballet *Abraxas*, choreographed by Janine Charrat, which seemed to him "dull, repetitious, provincial, and terribly Central European."[29] With the Rufers, he went to hear the Berlin Philharmonic, also conducted by Fricsay. He found it "unrecognizable" and felt it had fully regained its prewar status, espe-cially in its brass section, now one of Europe's best. After the concert, he and his hosts had dinner at Fricsay's house, where the conductor played recordings he had made of modern German music. Nabokov singled out for praise a string sym-phony by Karl Amadeus Hartmann, "a vivid, dynamic piece written in personal and convincing language."[30] According to Fricsay and Rufer, the five prominent German composers currently active were Egk ("at this moment perhaps the most successful"), Carl Orff, Wolfgang Fortner, Hartmann, and Blacher himself.

After the Berlin Congress, Nabokov returned to France to complete his assign-ment for the *Atlantic Monthly*. His article on music festivals in Western Europe came out in January 1951 in a different journal, *The Saturday Review of Literature*. It is a particularly interesting piece in view of Nabokov's impending involvement in organizing festivals. He begins by comparing the postwar festival boom to the vogue of spas in the nineteenth century. "Music," he suggests half ironically, "has taken over the therapeutic role of Vichy water, which soothes, not the liver, but the troubled mind or soul."[31] More seriously, he explains the phenomenon by the need of Europeans after the war to reconnect with their great cultural traditions, espe-cially in music. As a result, whereas "so much of Europe seems to be a vast, end-less museum relegated to the past," "music alone seems alive, active, unaged."[32] Stressing that performing standards are generally higher than before the war, he lists some of the finest musicians now active: after paying homage to the recently deceased Romanian pianist Dinu Lipati, "without the shadow of a doubt one of the most authentic musical geniuses of our time," he names the Hungarian pia-nist Géza Anda and the brilliant new generation of French pianists trained by Marguerite Long (Nicole Henriot, "the excellent, if somewhat erratic" Samson François, Monique Haas, Yvonne Loriot), and their talented elders—both friends of his—Yvonne Lefébure and Jacques Février. The remarkable technical proficiency one notices in the new generation of musicians, he observes, is also found among the rising generation of conductors, among whom, as in his *Atlantic Monthly* *piece*, he singles out for praise Fricsay in Berlin. However, behind this impressive facade, Nabokov detects "a sense of fear and insecurity, of precariousness, of the inevitability of disaster which pervades all aspects of European creative and per-forming culture."³³ Some of it was due, to be sure, to the division of Europe into "two halves, with little or no connection between them," whereas European culture had always thrived on international cross-fertilization.³⁴ Europeans feared they were losing their longtime cultural leadership, and this resulted in a "sometimes ironic, despondent, self-conscious, and even violently inimical attitude towards America." This resentment was, unfortunately, combined with considerable ignorance about the state of serious American music—and "serious" American culture in general. This was particularly true in France, Nabokov perceptively pointed out, where intel-lectuals and the man in the street alike had an "incomplete or incorrect image" of America, "formed by biased reports, by irresponsible journalism, and, last but not least, by anti-American Communist propaganda."³⁵ At the same time, Nabokov noted, citing his old friend Paul Collaer, musical creativity in Western Europe, com-pared, especially, to the pre-1914 period, seemed to be stagnating. Among compos-ers currently active in Germany, Nabokov, once again, focused on Blacher, whom he saw as deriving from Hindemith and Prokofiev (which was exactly where the young Nabokov situated himself in 1931). Among the French, his article mentions Jean Françaix's "charming and elegant music," Léo Préger (like Françaix a student of Boulanger), and, especially, Henri Dutilleux, whom he perceptively describes as "perhaps the most promising of all the young French composers" and the author of "fresh, brilliantly constructed music, vigorous in its melodic outline, and abso-lutely sincere."³⁶ Among the composers of the previous generation, Nabokov cites his old friends Auric, Milhaud, and Poulenc, reserving special praise for Sauguet, whose "enormous lyrical talent remains everlastingly young and fresh." Among the twelve-toners, next to Dallapiccola, already an established figure, he mentions a brilliant newcomer, the twenty-five-year-old Pierre Boulez, whose Second Piano Sonata had already been heard in New York. "Boulez's music," Nabokov declares, "is the latest, the most complex, and the most rigorous music yet written in the twelve-tone technique."³⁷ Nabokov also mentions Tippett and Rubbra in England, deploring that their music remains unknown, owing to "the parochialism which reigns in the domain of creative music all over the Western world."³⁸ In conclu-sion, he suggests that, contrary to what was the case in the early part of the cen-tury, European musical life is dominated by "superb young performers," whereas composers still "linger in the shadow of the earlier masters of our century."³⁹

There is much in this article that anticipates Nabokov's future stance as "cul-ture generalissimo," as Stravinsky was to dub him:⁴⁰ the role music festivals should play in the postwar periods to make people feel part of their musical cul-tural heritage; the belief in the benefits of cross-cultural fertilization; the need to combat provincialism by promoting the music of other countries; and the need to fight anti-American attitudes bred by a widespread European inferiority complex combined with ignorance of American culture.

Having resumed his teaching duties at Peabody, to which he added a part-time lectureship at Sarah Lawrence College, Nabokov returned to Europe at the end of November to participate in the meeting of the international committee to which he had been elected in Berlin. He chaired one of its sessions, on November 29, and presented a report on "The principal objectives of the Congress." The new organization, he argued, ought to operate on two levels: it should, on the one hand, openly and actively fight totalitarianism in free countries—that is, counter neutralist or pro-Communist propaganda—and, on the other hand, wage "a constant, intense, secret fight against totalitarianism in countries beyond the Iron Curtain, all the way to the Soviet Union." Nabokov urged the Congress not to define itself simply in negative, defensive terms. "We should aspire for a positive, revolutionary position, based on new ideas born in the fertile soil of the free culture of Europe. We should also be in fuller agreement than we have been so far on our willingness to reject all forms of totalitarianism, all forms of dictatorship, whether from the left or from the right, because we firmly believe that any totalitarianism is essentially, fundamentally reactionary and hostile to human freedom and dignity."[41] As this last sentence makes clear, Nabokov was keen to distance himself from the bellicose, one-sided tone of some of the statements he had heard in Berlin. Similarly, in the speech he gave at the end of the meeting, he focused on his experience as a composer and an exile. Comparing twentieth-century modernism to a musical renaissance, he contrasted its cosmopolitan, experimental spirit with the conventional, provincial "pseudo-aesthetics" of German and Russian totalitarian regimes, and called for a restoration of artistic freedom.

The structure of the permanent organization (initially called "International Movement for Cultural Freedom") adopted in Brussels was proposed by Lasky in his report on the Berlin Congress: an executive committee of seven members, with seven alternates; a secretariat, to be based in Paris; and five honorary chairmen, chosen for their intellectual and moral stature: Benedetto Croce, John Dewey, Karl Jaspers, Bertrand Russell, and Nabokov's longtime friend Maritain. After Croce and Dewey died, both in 1952, they were succeeded by the anti-Franquist Spanish writer and diplomat Salvador de Madariaga and the American theologian Reinhold Niebuhr. Furthermore, national committees were to be formed around the world to support and implement the Congress's initiatives at the local level.

The outcome of the Brussels meeting was Nabokov's appointment on the permanent secretariat of the Congress, initially with the title Director of Cultural Relations, subsequently altered to Secretary General. His qualifications for the job were formidable: his fluency in several languages, including French; his standing as a composer, and the fact that he was a cultural practitioner and not simply an academic; his knowledge of Europe, both Eastern and Western; his direct experience, dating from before before the Cold War, of contacts between East and West; his extensive intellectual and artistic contacts in America and Western Europe.

Compared to other potential candidates, such as Koestler or Lasky, both of whom had dominated the Berlin Congress, he had the advantage of not being an extremist; and while there was no doubt about his anti-communism, he did not bring to it, like many ex-Communists present in Berlin, the suspicious zeal of the convert, of which Burnham (who otherwise unequivocally supported Nabokov's appointment) was a copybook example.[42] Unlike Louis Fischer, whose name also came under consideration,[43] Nabokov had powerful high-ranking supporters on the American side, such as Bohlen and Kennan. The new organization being nongovernmental, there was no need for security clearance from the US federal government. As for Nabokov's relative lack of administrative experience, it was compensated by the fact that he knew and got on well with Josselson, who, as the Congress's executive secretary (as well as the CIA contact person), would be running the operation on a day-to-day basis. It is, indeed, likely that Nabokov was Josselson's candidate and that he "lobbied hard" for his appointment.[44] In the eyes of the State Department and the CIA, which was getting ready to subsidize the new organization, Nabokov offered all the necessary guarantees: not being "one of them," he was, at the same time, sensitive to the political implications of the position. Unlike Lasky, whose name was vetoed by Wisner, and Koestler, whose arrogance and intolerance made him unfit for cultural diplomacy, he was ideally suited for the Congress's main objectives, as he himself saw them: to provide through positive, concrete programs, a counterweight to the Soviet-sponsored anti-Western (and, especially, anti-American) cultural propaganda, both in Western Europe and in the rest of the world.[45] Even his non-American birth was an asset in heading an organization that was likely to be perceived, somewhat unfairly, as being completely US-dominated.

According to Sidney Hook, whose autobiography reveals a bitter hostility towards Nabokov, the only person "who expressed strong doubts about the choice" was Sol Levitas.[46] Hook does not, however, specify the nature of Levitas's reservations nor when or in what context they were expressed, since Levitas did not attend the Brussels meeting during which Nabokov was appointed. It could be that Hook, who grudgingly concedes that "it turned out to be a perfect job for Nabokov," secretly wanted the position himself. Leaving aside the question whether he would have been a suitable candidate, there is no doubt that in his hands the Congress would have been more political than the one headed by Nabokov.

On the executive committee were several people with whom Nabokov was to work closely during the next twelve years. Its chairman was the Swiss essayist and journalist Denis de Rougemont. Born in 1906, he was well known as the author of *L'amour et l'occident*, a study of the great Western love myths, especially Tristan, published in 1939 and translated the following year as *Love in the Western World*. Never a Communist, he had, like Nabokov in America, been associated with Voice of America broadcasts (in French in his case). In 1950 he became director of the

Geneva-based Centre européen de la culture, which was to be a regular partner of CCF programs. Temperamentally very different from Nabokov, who remembered him as "witty, clever, charming, vain," and a little lazy ("a somewhat indolent sine-curian") he nevertheless proved a useful, if an occasionally touchy, collaborator.[47]

Other members or alternate members of the executive committee included the French philosopher, sociologist, and political commentator Raymond Aron, a classmate of Jean-Paul Sartre at the École normale supérieure, and one of the leading intellectual figures of postwar France; while William Phillips called him "the Sidney Hook of France," Isaiah Berlin described him as "the most impressive political observer [. . .] I've ever met."[48] There were also the Italian anti-fascist journalist and essayist Nicola Chiaromonte, whom Nabokov knew through Mary McCarthy; the German journalist Eugen Kogon; Haakon Lie, the Norwegian Labor politician; and the German Social Democrat Carlo Schmid. Also on the executive committee were Rousset, Silone, and Spender. So was Irving Brown, the powerful representative of the AFL-CIO in Europe, where he spearheaded efforts to support non-Communist trade unions, especially in France, and Italy, using for this purpose funds channeled via the CIA. Described by Nabokov as "a gay, cheerful, and very, very bright fellow,"[49] Brown, who had attended the Berlin Congress, was on the steering committee which met at Koestler's house in the summer of 1950 to lay the ground for the new organization. Another member of this informal group, the Berlin-born Swiss journalist François Bondy, was appointed director of publications in the Congress secretariat. Briefly a Communist Party member before the war, he had worked with Lasky on the staff of *Der Monat* and was to play a major role throughout the Congress's history. Koestler, on the other hand, soon cut off his ties with an organization which, by concentrating on cultural events and intellectual debates, turned its back, in his view, on the political activism he had advocated in fiery tones in Berlin.

It was through Brown that negotiations about Nabokov's salary were conducted. The 6,000 dollars he was initially offered would have meant a serious pay cut compared to the 8,000 he made from his combined teaching at Peabody and Sarah Lawrence. This was not an insignificant shortfall, considering that Nabokov had to contribute to the education of his sons Ivan, who had just entered Harvard, and Peter. Ultimately, thanks to Burnham's intercession, the difference in salary, at least for the first year, was covered by the American Committee for Cultural Freedom, which was incorporated in January 1951, Nabokov being among its first members.[50]

The issue of the funding of the Congress for Cultural Freedom through the CIA has been so controversial since it was revealed in 1966–67 that it has, regrettably if understandably, obscured or distorted discussion of the organization's activities and achievements. Given Nabokov's central position in the Congress, his own role—which is what primarily interests us here—has been particularly scrutinized, usually from a perspective that is anything but benevolent. Variously portrayed as a dupe or a disingenuous accomplice in a game of deception,[51] he has even been called "another quiet American," by reference to Alden Pyle, the middling CIA operative of Graham Greene's novel, who provides financial and technical support to a group responsible for a terrorist attack which results in the killing and maiming of innocent civilians.[52] Surely the analogy, even presented in the interrogative mode, is absurdly inappropriate. Not only was Nabokov not a CIA agent, but his own public and private testimony—in his memoirs and correspondence—never wavered on one point: neither before joining the secretariat of the Congress nor during the time he was at its helm was he officially made privy to the true sources of its financing. As we shall see, he had suspicions at various times, but he could neither verify them nor reassure himself on the subject until the early 1960s, when, as a result, he took his distance from the organization. On the substance of the issue he made himself clear: subsidizing cultural organizations like the Congress for Cultural Freedom through federal funds secretly channeled through a spying agency was, in his opinion, an "abysmal and needless impropriety."[53] If, in private, he occasionally expressed himself in slightly different terms, suggesting that the CIA's involvement had been blown out of proportion,[54] his basic point remained the same: questionable though its funding may have been, what ultimately mattered was what the Congress had accomplished. And from this perspective there was nothing to apologize for.

Nabokov was, to be sure, solidly convinced, in the first years at least, of the validity of the Congress's mission. The Soviets spent considerable sums every year (the figure of 250 million dollars has been suggested)[55] in their attempt to win the minds of Western European intellectuals, through organizations like VOKS and other similar agencies. In this they were unquestionably successful, not just in Western Europe, and it was therefore urgent, as part of the containment strategy first advocated by Kennan, to wage a counteroffensive by rallying non-Communist liberals and giving them the means to make their voices heard through publications, international meetings, and cultural events. As Nabokov himself put it, this would ideally have called for a kind of cultural Marshall Plan to bolster the culture of the West just as the Marshall Plan made it possible to restart its economy. Was such a plan realistically possible, with full congressional oversight, in the context of the traditional American resistance to state intervention in cultural matters, especially in the highly charged political climate of the McCarthy era? Many of Nabokov's close friends and associates clearly did not think so and reconciled themselves to the idea that the legitimate ends of this cultural policy (as it was not officially called) justified covert means. "Of all the CIA's expenditures, the Congress for Cultural Freedom seemed its most worthwhile and successful," Arthur Schlesinger said when interviewed in the 1980s; Kennan expressed himself in similar terms and Bohlen would no doubt have agreed.[56] As the latter wrote to Shepard Stone of the Ford Foundation, "the flap about CIA money was quite unwarranted . . . This country has no ministry of culture, and [the] CIA was obliged to do what it could to try and fill the gap."[57] This not unreasonable view was widely shared, especially among intellectual and artistic dissidents from Eastern European countries then under Soviet domination. Isaiah Berlin was evidently of this opinion, and so was Yehudi Menuhin who, at the time of the 1966 revelations, joked in a letter to Nabokov: "As a matter of fact, I would think much more of the CIA if it did associate with 'people like us.'"[58] Nabokov himself, as we have seen, felt differently. While he fully agreed that the Cold War had to be fought on the cultural front, his position, once the CCF financing was exposed, was that introducing an element of deceit in the intellectual arena, where truth and honesty should be paramount, had resulted in compromising the very cause that was being fought for. His views on the subject were thus similar to those of Jason Epstein, who deplored in 1967 that "organizations ostensibly devoted to cultural freedom and the pursuit of truth were thus based upon lies."[59] Indeed he lamented that such an impropriety had occurred "in a country that used to have a century-old tradition of what Camus called 'moral forms of political thinking.'"[60] In unpublished autobiographical drafts, he described the CIA's system of transferring money through "passing foundations" as a "reverse copy of the enemy."[61] He would thus have condoned William Phillips's severe characterization as "an attempt by a democratic nation to adopt the methods of a totalitarian one."[62]

Unfortunately, there has been a tendency, in most of the books and articles dealing with the Congress for Cultural Freedom, to become fixated on the issue of "CIA money" at the expense of everything else. Behind this obsession, which borders on demonology (to borrow Hilton Kramer's formulation),[63] is, at least implicitly, a reasoning of questionable logic: since the CIA, since its inception, has been guilty of some "crimes," it follows that nothing the CIA did could possibly be good and that everyone and everything associated with it becomes, by the same token, irredeemably tainted. If one considers that the programs of the Congress were for the most part conferences, publications, and festivals which, in Nabokov's words, "gave pleasure and joy to many and did not cost anyone's life,"[64] this seems, at the very least, disproportionate. As Alain Daniélou has pointed out, using the example of great Italian Renaissance architects and artists being patronized by tyrants, "it is perfectly possible to do good work with bad money provided one can use it as one pleases without compromising one's principles."[65]

Regrettably, there has been a parallel tendency—carried, in some cases, to ludicrous extremes—to picture the Congress as a mere tool of the Agency and all intellectuals involved in it as either agents or puppets. This distortion can be explained, in part, by somewhat self-aggrandizing recollections and testimonies of some of the CIA executives involved, notably Thomas W. Braden in a 1967 interview to the *Saturday Evening Post* and subsequent statements he made in interviews.[66] There is no need to minimize the role of Braden, who at the time the Congress was created headed the International Organizations Divisions within Wisner's Office of Policy Coordination and was instrumental in setting up the funding scheme.[67] But while the CIA served as the secret conduit for federal subsidies to the Congress, it did not "run" the Congress.[68] Everyone associated with the Congress, besides Nabokov, has firmly and consistently denied that the CIA, as has been claimed, "called the tune." As Secretary General, he was "completely unhindered by any kind of 'ideological interference' or 'secret directives.'"[69] One can, of course, choose to discard his denials as self-serving. Yet, even Hook, an unsympathetic witness, insisted that the source of the organization's funding "had absolutely nothing to do" with its policies and decisions: "It is simply preposterous to believe that men like Ignazio Silone, Raymond Aron, Nicola Chiaromonte, Michael Polyani [sic, for Polanyi], Haakon Lie, or Carlo Schmidt [recte Schmid] [. . .] would dance to anyone else's tune."[70] The omission of Nabokov's name from Hook's list may or may not be accidental: in addition to his personal dislike of Nabokov (at least by the time he wrote his memoir), Hook, like many academics who deem music unworthy to share the honors with "intellectual" disciplines, clearly thought that the cause of cultural freedom was not one to be entrusted to artists themselves. His point, however, applies to Nabokov as well as to the names he mentions. While, on a day-to-day basis, the Congress secretariat was run, with remarkable competence and efficiency, by a man who was a CIA agent and reported to the Agency, Josselson himself was well aware that Nabokov—and this was true of all members of the executive committee—was far too independent a personality to be easily controlled, let alone censored. The Congress, as Braden himself has admitted, "was on its own."[71]

Nabokov's arrival in Paris to take up his position was delayed for several months, as both Peabody and Sarah Lawrence refused to release him from his teaching contracts.[72] This meant, in effect, that planning and programming languished for several months. Instead, Nabokov took the opportunity of the spring break to visit the Stravinskys in Hollywood, from March 21 until March 26. By then Robert Craft had become a full-fledged member of the household as "the composer's assistant, musical interpreter, factotum, travelling companion, Boswell, collaborator, friend, quasi-adoptive son, even at times his musical conscience."[73] On March 22, Christopher Isherwood was the Stravinsky's guest for dinner. The following night it was Huxley, and Nabokov entertained the company with anecdotes about Auden's unhappy visit to India, where the poet had participated, at Nabokov's urging, in the third international meeting of the Congress (its first in Asia).[74] Nabokov had brought with him to California some of his recent compositions (presumably La vita nuova, and possibly The Return of Pushkin as well) and showed them to Stravinsky. The latter was sufficiently impressed to write on Nabokov's behalf to Willi Strecker, director of Schott, the prestigious music publishing firm in Mainz. "Nabokov," Stravinsky wrote, "is a serious composer, and one of value, who certainly merits publication and performances more than many many others today."[75] Though nothing came of this recommendation, it is a sufficient indication of Stravinsky's esteem, especially since such interventions were not at all habitual with him. On the flight back to New York, Nabokov lost one of his music manuscripts; he first assumed he had left it behind in Hollywood, but it was later found by a TWA employee in a copy of *Life* magazine he had been reading on the airplane.[76]

At about the same time Nabokov's first book, *Old Friends* and *New Music* was issued by Little Brown as an *Atlantic Monthly* Press Book. Dedicated to Patricia Blake, who had edited it, it collected, in revised form, articles that had appeared in the *Atlantic Monthly*: the account of the Christmas 1947 visit to Stravinsky; reminiscences of Diaghilev that had appeared, in three installments, in 1950; the evocation of Nijinsky mentioned in chapter 6; a reworked version of the 1942 article on Prokofiev; the portrait of Koussevitzky that appeared, at the same time as the book, in February 1951; and "Music under the Generals," which deals with Nabokov's postwar Berlin experience. The opening chapters are childhood memories that, in turn, were later revised and expanded in *Bagázh*. By an unfortunate coincidence, which caused some confusion in the press as to which Nabokov was which, *Old Friends and New Music* came out almost at the same time as the first version of Vladimir Nabokov's autobiography *Conclusive Evidence*.[77] But the reviews were very positive or even enthusiastic. "One of the year's most attractive books on musical matters," wrote Cecil Smith in *The New Republic*.[78] Friends of the author, naturally, agreed. In the *New York Herald Tribune*, Virgil Thomson wrote that the work had "the uncommon grace of being about its subject rather than about its author," while Auden, in the New *York Times Book Review*, suggested it was compulsory reading for "every young person considering an artistic career." The London edition was no less favorably received by British critics. Noting that a book "fitting into no clear literary species, combining elements of autobiography, reminiscence, profile-writing, essayism, musical criticism, period evocation," could have produced "an awful rag-bag," Sebastian Haffner marveled that Nabokov, instead, had "produced a literary masterpiece of a kind all its own."[79] "It is the book of a romantic, but a robust one," Tamara Karsavina perceptively observed. She found the portrait of Diaghilev, in particular, "very alive and true."

> The complexity of Diaghilev's nature is brought within the compass of his unique personality in which greatness "greatly overshadowed the faults." Diaghilev's foibles are keenly and amusingly observed: the not amiable absurdity of the ritual of "foundlings," his moods, his ruthlessness, even his, at times, unscrupulous use of the fashionable set when it could further his schemes.[80]

"An enchanting and diverting book," wrote J. S. Harrison in *Notes*, praising the chapter on Prokofiev for showing "complete understanding of the man and his music," and extended the compliment to the portrait of Stravinsky.[81] The London journal *Music & Letters* also found the chapter on Prokofiev illuminating. On Stravinsky, however, while noting that Nabokov gave the composer "more amiable traits than some have credited him with," the reviewer added wryly that even Nabokov could not "conceal the great man's extreme self-centredness." The British edition, issued by Hamish Hamilton, included a chapter not present in the American issue: entitled "The Case of Dimitri Shostakovich," it consisted of the *Harper's Magazine* 1943 article, supplemented by Nabokov's reminiscences of the 1949 Waldorf Astoria conference. Noting that this chapter made for depressing reading, the *Music & Letters* critic commented: "Here again is a composer who, however overrated at one time, is an artist and a suffering artist."[82] The *Musical Times* especially liked the Russian chapters and praised Nabokov's qualities as a writer, even when dealing with episodes from the 1920s that "have so often been told, though rarely so well as in this book. Mr. Nabokov, amid all his personal prepossessions, keeps a detached eye upon others, and dips his sharp pen into a diversity of inkpots, some filled with honey, some with gall."[83] Though clearly jaded with Ballets Russes literature, the same critic concluded that "if the next generation of devotees find one half as perceptive as Mr. Nabokov they will be lucky."

Before leaving for Europe, Nabokov had lunch at the Century Club with Learned Hand, to whom he explained the nature and purpose of the organization he would be working with. Hand, as Nabokov recalled, was not impressed. He found the phrase "Congress for Cultural Freedom" incongruous, and advised Nabokov to pursue his career as composer instead. Organizations like that, the judge cautioned, "are at best precarious things and tend to degenerate rapidly."[84] Nabokov himself seems to have been in two minds about accepting the post, perhaps anticipating the difficulties that awaited him. He took it, at first, on a temporary basis: in July 1951 he was still hoping to get employment in New York with the Free Russian Fund, an organization established at the time, with Kennan as president, to help Soviet exiles in the United States by liaising with other similar organizations. Nabokov's own responsibilities would have been as director of a proposed Center for Exile Intellectuals.[85] "I still don't know what happened," he wrote in October to Robert Joyce at the State Department. "Everything I told you and Chip [Bohlen] stands, and I quite sincerely believe that serious reconsideration of the overall approach to the Russian emigre problem (both its political and its cultural aspects) should be done as soon as possible."[86] The following year, Reginald Stewart, the head of Peabody, would urge Nabokov to consider applying for the better paid position of dean of the music school at the University of Toronto.

Nabokov flew to Paris on April 27, 1951. There he and Patricia, who had preceded him, moved into the small furnished apartment she had found near the Luxembourg Gardens, at 51, rue d'Assas. The Congress secretariat was provisionally set up at the Hôtel Baltimore, on Avenue Kléber, where Irving Brown had his own headquarters. In the spring of 1951, it moved to 41, avenue Montaigne ("opposite the luxurious salon of a great couturier," as Fredric Warburg remembered),[87] and in 1953 to spacious permanent offices at no. 104, Boulevard Hausmann, near the church of Saint-Augustin. Nabokov's schedule, however, was anything but sedentary. After spending his first week "almost exclusively in studying the operation of the Paris office and meeting a great number of people in and out of the Congress,"[88] he went to Brussels to speak at a dinner organized by the journal *Synthèses*. On May 15–16, there was a meeting of the executive committee, after which Nabokov took the train to Bordeaux, where he attended the premiere of Sauguet's ballet *Symphonie allégorique*. He then flew to England, where he visited Isaiah Berlin in Oxford and made contacts with various personalities—T. S. Eliot among others—and organizations such as the British Council and the BBC's Third Programme.[89] From there he went to Berlin to speak on a familiar topic, "Art under the totalitarian system," and make contacts with "the German field of operation"—by which we should understand Lasky, no doubt, but also Nabokov's own friends in musical milieus.[90] On the way back, he stopped in Frankfurt and in Strasbourg, where he attended the music festival. At the end of June, in Rome to establish contacts with Italian intellectuals, he gave a talk on music in the Soviet Union. In early July he took part in a seminar on new music held in Brussels at the house of Baroness Lambert. Born in Austria, Hansi Lambert was the widow of the head of the Belgian branch of the Rothschild family, and her salon on Avenue Marnix was frequented both by artists and writers and by some of the future architects of European unity.[91] Nabokov had met her through Stephen Spender and she would prove a loyal supporter over the next decade. In July, Nabokov went to England, where he attended a performance of *Idomeneo* at Glyndebourne staged by Carl Ebert, who was about to direct the Venice premiere of Stravinsky's new opera. After a week on the East Coast of the United States in early August, Nabokov visited the Hoffmannsthals in Austria and attended performances at the Salzburg Festival. He then went to Rome again to discuss the establishment of an Italian Committee for Cultural Freedom, staying at the Villa Aurelia as the guest of Laurance Roberts, director of the American Academy, and his wife.

On September 9, 1951, Nabokov arrived in Venice to attend the much-publicized premiere of Stravinsky's opera *The Rake's Progress* at the Teatro La Fenice. He was, officially, deputizing for Virgil Thomson at the *New York Herald Tribune*. He had, of course, followed the genesis of the work from the start, given his friendship not only with the composer but with the librettists, Auden and Kallman. At the end of January 1949, he was present (along with Rieti) when Stravinsky played his score for Auden in Alexander Schneider's New York apartment.[92] Nabokov was instrumental in the choice of Venice for the world premiere: in December 1950, over a luncheon discussion at Marguerite Caetani's with Mario Labroca, then director of music for the Italian radio and head of the Venice Biennale, he secured for the composer a generous conductor's fee of $20,000.[93] While Stravinsky was delighted with this arrangement, it infuriated his publishers, Boosey and Hawkes, who had been in negotiation with Covent Garden, and Nabokov was subsequently taken to task by Leslie Boosey in London.[94] By the end of April 1951, Nabokov had seen the music of the completed opera and wrote from Paris to the composer: "It is all so masterful, so clear, so infinitely beautiful, and so pleasing to the mind."[95] In Venice, Nabokov attended the dress rehearsal, led by Stravinsky's assistant Ferdinand Leitner, on September 9. The following day he recorded a talk for the radio and two days later attended the first performance. As he wrote in a review he wrote for *Preuves*, the Congress's French magazine, Nabokov described *The Rake's Progress* as "an indisputable masterpiece, whose Mozartian dimensions and lucid beauty have no equal in the lyric theater of the first half of this turbulent century."[96] He praised the freshness of the musical language, tonal throughout yet original and typical of Stravinsky's inventiveness. What he admired above all was the vocal writing, the elegance of the modulations, the beauty of the orchestration. The paradox of the work, he argued, was that it was "both subjective and objective, personal and utterly impersonal, conventional and unpredictable." It "teased our memory" with melodies reminiscent of Mozart, Handel, Tchaikovsky, Bellini, or Gounod. Poignantly moving scenes alternate with scenes "of exquisite irony and buffoonery"; yet the music can never be called programmatic or descriptive, nor does its quality ever sag. Nabokov nevertheless had reservations about the Venice premiere: like most reviewers, he was disappointed by the vocal performance of Robert Rounseville in the title role, and by the dramatic conception of Otakar Kraus, who sang Nick Shadow. He did not care for the "uninspired" sets and costumes, nor for Ebert's "appallingly banal and grotesquely old-fashioned stage direction," which reminded him of "the worst days of the worst Reinhardt period in provincial German theaters" in the 1920s.[97] Yet, all in all, the *Rake* was in his view "the first important classical opera in the English language since the middle of the 18th century."

Having left Venice immediately after the premiere, Nabokov went to Alsace to attend a seminar held in Andlau on the situation of intellectuals in Communist countries. Among the participants were Silone, Boris Souvarine (author of the first serious biography of Stalin, published in 1935), the sociologists Jules Margolin, and Jules Monnerot (author of an influential *Sociology of Communism*),[98] and the Russian-born historian and art critic Vladimir Weidlé. The star participant, unquestionably, was Czeslaw Milosz, whose defection from

Communist Poland in February 1951 had been made public on May 15 at a press conference hosted by the Congress in Paris. Until then a member of the Polish cultural services, the future winner of the Nobel Prize for Literature had attended the 1949 Waldorf-Astoria Peace Conference as an observer (he was at the time posted in Washington); as he later told Mary McCarthy, he had greatly admired the energy and exuberance of the protesters.[99] The statement he read at his press conference in Paris and the two papers he gave at Andlau already contained in germ his famous and influential 1953 essay *The Captive Mind*, which deals with the attraction of Communism for intellectuals. Milosz, already established as the leading Polish poet of the rising generation, was a major "catch" for the Congress. His own material situation, however, was difficult. Though he was taken on with open arms by the Kultura, the Polish emigre cultural center headquartered in Maisons-Laffitte, outside Paris, he felt ill at ease in the French intellectual climate, longing to be reunited with his wife and young sons that had remained in the United States. Nor was he without enemies, not only among Communists and fellow-travelers, but also in Polish emigre circles, where rumors circulated that he was a Soviet agent. His US visa application ran into difficulties, especially since his status as a former Communist made him technically ineligible under the terms of the McCarran Act.[100] Nabokov, to whom he appealed for help, used his Washington connections, especially Bohlen and Kennan. "He has been so active on our side since last May," Nabokov wrote about Milosz to a State Department official in January 1952, "that he in fact has become one of the most important assets in our fight against totalitarianism."[101]

As Nabokov was well aware, thanks to his many contacts in France, the Congress was operating under exceptionally difficult circumstances. Paris in the early 1950s was "the world capital of the fellow-travellers."[102] As Nabokov put it, it was also "Europe's most interesting but bitchy, divided, xenophobic, obstructionist, and already ardently anti-American city."[103] A telling example of the kind of intellectual climate that reigned in France at the time the Congress was established is the treatment Nabokov received from the editor of the *Revue internationale de musique* (whose advisory board included many old friends, from Nadia Boulanger to Roland-Manuel) when the journal, in its fall 1951 issue, published the French translation of Nabokov's article "On the Battle Front of Soviet Music" that had appeared the previous February in *Musical America*. The translation was preceded by a note from the editor—Jacques Chailley, a respected musicologist and Sorbonne professor—announcing that "out of a concern for objective information" Nabokov's article had been forwarded to the Communist "Association des musiciens progressistes" with an invitation to respond. Nabokov's piece was thus, in effect, downgraded to the first part of a *"tribune libre,"* the second part of which was a rebuttal, signed by Jean Prodromidès (who in the 1960s and 1970s had an esteemable career as an avant-garde opera composer)[104] and presenting an idyllic picture of the situation of music and musicians in the USSR.

> Who thus inspired and made possible such a higher cultural level of all people, who gave composers such facilities, if not the Communist Party of the USSR and, first of all, its leader, Stalin? How then should we be surprised by the gratitude and profound respect manifested towards them by Soviet musicians?[105]

To be sure, Prodromidès granted, the Party, acting in its capacity as "interpreter and guide of the Soviet masses," occasionally had to intervene in musical matters, but only in moments of crisis, as had happened in 1917, 1936, and 1948. Those crises had only occurred because composers started losing touch with the public, making such interventions necessary; yet these were made only after a prolonged, Democratic debate.[106] Rejecting the suggestion that there is any kind of artistic censorship in the Soviet Union, Prodromidès's article goes on to glorify at length the notion of socialist realism, which the author contrasts with the "false and formalist" Stravinsky, "once a great composer." Western modernists, such as Nabokov himself, are excoriated as rootless, reactionary, cosmopolitan counter-revolutionaries: "Patriotism and heroism, as sources of inspiration, seem to irritate Mr. Nabokov greatly, just as the *Marseillaise* irritated the emigres in Koblenz."[107] Citing Zhdanov at length, Prodromidès also insists that, contrary to Nabokov's assertion, the 1948 decree encourages polyphony. In his conclusion, the French fellow-traveler waxes virtuously indignant:

> Calumniating a people and its artists, presenting things in a deliberately falsified light, all that seems to us extremely grave at a time when misunderstandings between various nations can only increase current tensions. Conversely, the better one knows the culture of a people, their working conditions, and the problems of their artists can only reinforce the possibilities of rapprochement and mutual understanding. [. . .]Let us say, in conclusion, that, in spite of Mr. Nabokov, Soviet music is in fine shape; with an entire people as its audience, it is progressing towards socialist realism, in keeping with a society marching on towards the future.[108]

It is impossible to assess, of course, whether Prodromidès was the honest, deluded mouthpiece of the propaganda he was fed (some of his arguments sound depressingly familiar) or he knew more than he let on about the realities of Soviet Russia. But then, what is one to make of the self-satisfied tone of Chailley's concluding editorial note?

The RIM [*Revue internationale de musique*] has fulfilled its mission by allowing two different opinions to be freely expressed next to one another. It is now for the reader, and for the reader alone, to draw the conclusion of this debate.[109]

While Nabokov was thus treated on the Left, his standing with the Right was no better. As late as March 1954, Jacques Fontaine, writing in the conservative *Écrits de Paris*, had some unkind words for "a certain Nicolas Nobokov [sic], a recently naturalized American, appointed—with a royal compensation—[. . .] secretary general of the Congress for Cultural Freedom in order to sell psychological warfare products." Fontaine apparently assumed that anyone with a Russian name could only be a former Communist, therefore as dangerous, as he put it, as a pyromaniac turned into a fireman.[110] As for the "royal compensation," Nabokov was making less, as we have seen, than he would have made as dean of the music school at the University of Toronto.

In October 1951, Nabokov spoke on the BBC's Third Programme on the subject of "Changing Styles in Soviet Music," a talk which was published the same month in The Listener. After reminding his audience of the subservient state of Soviet music under Stalin, he raised the question of the disappearance of the experimental quality that had briefly characterized Russian music in the early years after the Communist takeover. Nabokov suggests that the most plausible explanation is the disappearance of the intelligentsia which, before 1914, had understood and encouraged the musical and artistic avant-garde. After its liquidation by the Bolsheviks, the conventional tastes of industrial workers and the lower middle class prevailed. Even the authentic popular music of the Russian peasantry was affected, losing its modal character. The lack of polyphony in Prokofiev's and Shostakovich's recent symphonies became part of the trend toward simplification Nabokov had commented upon in earlier articles. "At the present time," Nabokov concluded, "the musical output of the Soviet Union has the hallmark of a static conservatism, in form, in technique, and in invention—a conservatism unequalled anywhere outside the Soviet sphere."[111] The preparation of this talk put Nabokov in touch with Anna Kallin, the brilliant Russian-born editor and BBC producer, who at the time of her death in 1984, at the age of 88, was described as "one of the last genuine representatives of the Russian intelligentsia as it was before the Revolution."[112] Nabokov acquired enormous respect for Kallin's skills and she became and remained a trusted adviser and editor.

Masterpieces of the Twentieth Century

INITIAL PROGRAMMATIC SUGGESTIONS for the permanent Congress, as formulated in Berlin in June 1950, were fairly modest. In his report for *Partisan Review*, Hook listed four: (1) publishing White Books on the situation of writers and artists behind the Iron Curtain; (2) providing assistance to intellectuals escaping from totalitarian countries; (3) organizing radio talks in the form of "open letters" to cultural Communist leaders in the Eastern Bloc; (4) establishing a university for exiled Eastern European academics and students.[1] Of these proposals, only the first two were to some extent realized; the second was expanded to include, in some cases, helping longtime emigre writers living under difficult circumstances, such as Remizov, for whom Nabokov was able to get a subsidy from the American Committee (and other organizations) until Remizov died in 1957.[2] The third was quickly shelved, perhaps because it seemed to duplicate efforts such as Radio Free Europe. The last proposal was the brainchild of Jerzy Giedroyc, the founder of the journal *Kultura* and leader of the exiled Polish intellectual community in Paris, who had proposed it at the Berlin Congress; it was also strongly supported by his compatriot Czapski.[3] It led to the establishment, in 1951, of Free Europe University (Collège de l'Europe libre). Located in Strasbourg, the institution was largely subsidized by American funds but it did not have any real ties with the Congress, except that Nabokov was invited to sit on its board.[4] It was thus largely left to Nabokov and his collaborators to come up with the programs that made the Congress one of the most enterprising cultural and intellectual organizations of the period.

Given the national, ideological, and political diversity of the Congress's founding members, there were, from the start, inevitable differences of opinion about the directions the organization should go. Some, like Hook and Koestler, favored keeping the "spirit of Berlin" alive by holding a similar meeting in Paris. Aron, the leading French intellectual on the Congress board, firmly spoke against the suggestion at an executive committee meeting held in Versailles in February 1951: what had been accomplished in Berlin, he argued, "had been to create an international organization and then to make it work."[5] But exactly what kind of work the Congress should accomplish had yet to be determined. There was, at least, general agreement that it should undertake a program of publications. In the report he wrote on May 22 for the American committee, Nabokov announced plans for a series of pamphlets—he listed Milosz, Koestler, Schlesinger, Hook, Dos Passos, Wilder, MacLeish, among possible contributors—for which he had begun to approach French publishers.[6] But even higher on his mind was the creation of a French-language magazine, on the model of *Der Monat*, which would ideally be a foil to Sartre's neutralist *Temps modernes*, a project that had been aired before Nabokov's arrival at the Versailles executive committee meeting. Nabokov reported that he had discussed the plan with several personalities associated with the Congress or sympathetic to its objectives, such as Georges Altman, David Rousset, Manès Sperber, but his real hope was that Aron might be persuaded to take on the editorship on a full-time basis. Aron, however, was already writing a political column in *Le Figaro* and was furthermore unwilling to relinquish his academic career, which resulted in his appointment as a Sorbonne professor in 1955. While still hoping Aron might eventually be persuaded, Nabokov suggested as an alternative the writer Roger Caillois; but Caillois, a future member of the Académie française, had a lucrative position with UNESCO and was unlikely to leave it for less than an equivalent salary. In the end, the monthly newsletter *Preuves*, which since March 1951, had been edited by François Bondy, was expanded into a full-fledged magazine beginning with its November issue.[7] More magazines, of which *Encounter* remains the most important, were to be founded in the next few years.

Another objective of the Congress was to promote the creation of satellite national organizations, which would promote its ideals at the local level. Nabokov, at this early stage, seems to have had high hopes for activist, grassroots organizations, like the French "Amis de la liberté," formed in Paris in the spring of 1952. Under the leadership of Jacques Enock, a socialist, it opened centers in Grenoble, Lyons, Marseilles, Saint-Étienne, and Strasbourg in the next few years. "I am firmly convinced that these centers of 'Les Amis de la Liberté' can perhaps become the most useful instruments of anti-Communist activity in France," he wrote in his May 22 report. In the end, while national committees were established in many countries around the world, they never really became a significant grassroots movement. The Amis de la liberté petered out after 1960.

Nabokov, however, had ambitious plans of his own to put the Congress on the map. At the May 15 executive committee meeting, he proposed holding in Paris, the following spring, a major international artistic festival to celebrate the achievements of the twentieth century and highlight the importance of freedom in artistic matters, while stressing, by the same token, the negative effects of censorship under totalitarian regimes. According to Nabokov's autobiography, the idea came to him on his eleven-hour flight to Paris on "a smooth, comfortable Pan Am stratocruiser with berths."

> I wanted to start off [the Congress's] activities with a big bang and in the field of twentieth-century arts. At that time contemporary art and music were the butts and the victims of Stalin's and Zhdanov's most odious repression, just as they had been a decade earlier in Hitler's Germany.
>
> I felt that we had to reaffirm our belief in their values and that the time had come to draw an inventory of their achievements in the first fifty years of this century.[8]

As is often the case in *Bagázh*, Nabokov's chronology is confusing (he gives the date of the trip as May 23, one month late), but there is no doubt that the project was his own initiative, while contemporary sources confirm the political and ideological rationale he intended to give it, though with an additional twist. Sometime in early 1951, evidently *before* he flew to Paris, he outlined his proposal in a memorandum to Irving Brown, who at this stage handled, ostensibly at least, the Congress's funding. The festival, Nabokov explained, would be the first opportunity ever for top-ranking American cultural organizations to cooperate with their European equivalents on the highest artistic level. The effect, he argued, would be "extremely beneficial" to the cultural life of the free world "by showing the cultural solidarity and interdependence of European and American civilization. If successful," Nabokov added, the festival would "help to destroy the pernicious European myth (successfully cultivated by the Stalinists) of American cultural inferiority."[9]

According to Nabokov's later recollections, the idea of the festival was tepidly received by members of the executive committee, with the unexpected exception of James Burnham. It served as a pretext for Koestler's resignation from the committee at the end of July: he felt, in the words of his biographer David Cesarani, that "what had been founded as a political force had turned into an 'effete' arts movement."[10] It was, however, strongly supported by Josselson, and in Washington, the project, once it reached the International Organizations Division, was enthusiastically endorsed by Braden and Wisner and quickly approved for funding. Nabokov's diagnosis, in his memo to Brown, was correct: there was, in Western Europe, a well-entrenched tendency to regard America as culturally inferior, and it was constantly exploited by Soviet propaganda and its allies in the Cold War period.[11] Federally sponsored initiatives from the State Department were, in quantitative and qualitative terms, nowhere sufficient to reverse this trend. They were too timid, too conventional, and could hardly compete with the Soviet international *Kulturkampf*. The United States was seen as losing "the battle of the Festivals"[12] at the same time as it seemed to be also losing the battle for the minds of the European liberal intelligentsia. By its scope and its novelty, Nabokov's

proposal offered an exciting opportunity to try something different. That CIA officials were of this opinion and decided that the project was worth supporting with
covert funds speaks for their openness of mind and forward-looking attitude. It is
nevertheless inaccurate—and misleading—to describe the festival (or, in fact, any
of the Congress's future programs) as a CIA initiative. All testimonies, then and
since, confirm that the idea of the festival came from Nabokov. Nabokov, however,
was unaware that his brainchild had, from its inception, a secret fairy godmother.
Ostensibly, an "angel" was found in the person of Julius ("Junkie") Fleischmann,
the Cincinnati-based heir to the yeast manufacturing fortune. A Yale graduate,
Fleischmann was a well-known patron of the arts: he sat on the board of directors of the Metropolitan Opera and was a fellow of the Royal Society of the Arts
in London. He also served as a director of the Marquis de Cuevas's Ballet Russe
de Monte-Carlo and acted as financial backer of Broadway theater productions.
He was equally famous as the owner of the *Camargo*, the luxurious diesel-power
steel yacht on which he and his family sailed around the world in 1931–32. Given
his visibility in the art and music world, Fleischmann was a perfectly plausible
conduit for funds channeled through the CIA, which had previously used him
as a "front" through the Fleischmann Foundation.[13] Nabokov, to whom his brief
previous acquaintance of Fleischmann had left the memory of "a fairly stingy
Maecenas of the ballet," was astonished by this sudden largesse, but did not, at
this stage, question the sources of the funding.[14] For the purpose of financing the
1952 festival, the Farfield Foundation, incorporated on January 30, 1952, was set up
with Fleischmann as its president. Its mission was carefully framed in terms that
matched the Congress's own:

> The Foundation extends financial aid to [. . .] groups whose enterprises
> in literary, artistic or scientific fields may serve as worthy contributions
> to the progress of culture. The Foundation offers assistance to organiza-
> tions whose programs tend to strengthen the cultural ties which bind the
> nations of the world and to reveal to all peoples who share the traditions
> of a free culture the inherent dangers which totalitarianism pose to intel-
> lectual and cultural development.[15]

With its purpose established in such sufficiently broad language, the Farfield
Foundation remained, for the next fifteen years, the principal conduit for
CIA-controlled federal subsidies to the Congress for Cultural Freedom.

It is easy, from today's perspective, blasé as we tend to be with blockbuster
art shows and festivals, to deride Nabokov's 1952 plans as "elaborate, expensive, and incoherent."[16] To be sure, the vogue of international music festivals had begun before the war—as Nabokov was in a good position to know,
having gone to Salzburg in the early 1930s and explored the postwar festival

scene in 1950 on behalf of the *Atlantic Monthly*. But these festivals were inter-national in a limited sense: through their clientele and the guests conductors, vocal or instrumental soloists, and small ensembles that produced themselves. Nabokov's project was of a totally different order. It was to bring together in one place, over a few weeks, entire orchestras and troupes from Austria (the Vienna State Opera), England (the Royal Opera, Covent Garden), Germany (the Berlin Radio Symphony Orchestra), Italy (the Accademia nazionale di Santa Cecilia from Rome), Switzerland (the Orchestre de la Suisse romande), and the United States. It was no less bold from a thematic point of view: the purpose was not to highlight a handful of recognized masterpieces from the standard repertory, but to celebrate "l'œuvre du vingtième siècle," as the catchy French title of the festival encapsulated it—new works or works from a recent past, many of which had never been seen or heard in Paris.

From the point of view of the Congress's yet ill-defined mission, Nabokov's proposal reflected his preference for concrete cultural programs over ideology, and the ambivalence he felt, as secretary general of the new organization, toward the stridently political anti-Communist agenda advocated at the Berlin Congress. However, various members of the executive committee were strongly attached to this hard line, which was also the dominant view in the American Committee for Cultural Freedom. Nabokov, in the outline he prepared for his presentation before the Congress's executive committee on May 15, 1951, was therefore careful in framing his proposal in terms that stressed above all its congruence with the Congress's fundamental mission:

> No ideological polemic about the validity and meaning of free culture can equal the products of this culture itself. Let the great works of our century speak for themselves. They alone can stimulate our faith in a free civiliza-tion and provide us with a living positive example of what the imagination of free men was able to achieve in the first half of our century.[17]

In his private correspondence, Nabokov expressed himself less diplomatically. The festival, as he wrote to Arthur Schlesinger, in response to a letter in which the latter conveyed his worry about the "neurotic" anti-Communist obsessions of the leaders of the American committee, would have "much more *retentissement* than [a] hundred speeches by Arthur Koestler, Sidney Hook and James Burnham about the neuroses of our century."[18] In August 1951, Nabokov made a trip to the United States in early August 1951 in order to "sell" the festival to the American Committee. The ACCF grudgingly went along, but they never really forgave Nabokov for highjacking, as they saw it, the Congress away from their own con-ception of an anti-Communist war machine, even though how successful this war machine would have been is open to doubt.

In Paris, however, Nabokov's plans were well received and the executive committee gave its go-ahead. Astonishingly, no one seems to have doubted that such an ambitious scheme could be brought to fruition in such a short time, and it is a measure of Nabokov's dauntless energy that he managed to pull it off (something he was not to try again on comparably short notice). "My life," he wrote to Edward Weeks of the *Atlantic Monthly* in November, "has become a mixture of that of an impresario and of an administrator. I have no time to sleep, to write, to compose, I eat business-lunches and business-dinners and am in general in a state of constant neurotic euphoria."[19] Time constraints, however, forced him to reduce the scope of his initial project. As late as December 1951—with less than six months to go—he was still contemplating a festival with five components: "1—a literary program; 2—an art exhibit; 3—a musical program; 4—a film program; 5—a dramatic program."[20] As it turned out, the film and dramatic programs were jettisoned. One of the plans that fell through was to invite Laurence Olivier to present G. B. Shaw's *Caesar and Cleopatra*, never previously seen in France.[21] In late November, Fleischmann reported to the "dear boys" on the secretariat: "There is a strong feeling which I share that we are overbalanced musically and that it would be a good idea to add more drama."[22] Presumably none of the other possibilities Fleischmann suggested—an appearance by John Gielgud, Christopher Fry's *The Lady's Not for Burning*—could be successfully explored in so little time, though, until the last minute, Nabokov hoped that the festival could "provide the exposition audiences with the premiere of a play in English by an American author, and to perform in French contemporary plays by French, Spanish and Italian authors."[23] Other ambitious theatrical plans—D'Annunzio and Debussy's *Le martyre de saint Sébastien*, not staged in Paris since 1923, Brecht's and Weill's *Mahagonny*—were also considered at various stages. As for the cinema, one plan on which Nabokov was still working in January 1952 was for the festival to feature the French premiere of Charlie Chaplin's *Limelight*, with Chaplin himself in attendance. This was in itself a bold suggestion, considering that Chaplin, in America, was at the time the victim of a vicious campaign waged by Catholic War Veterans and the American Legion and was about to have his re-entry permit revoked, at J. Edgar Hoover's request, by the US Immigration and Naturalization Service; Chaplin could therefore appear as a victim, if not of totalitarianism, at the very least of political intolerance.[24] Once apprised of the plan, Fleischmann, in fact, registered his alarm—which may have been shared by some of his CIA backers— though he tried to hide it as a pure fundraising concern. "It just so happens that two of the people who are helping me out financially heard about it and, to put it mildly, they are not pleased."[25] Nabokov's response shows how he and Josselson were keen to maintain at least a semblance of independence vis-à-vis the official US hard line in such matters. "It is our concerted view here [. . .] that by accepting to appear under the sponsorship of the Congress—which is well established here as an anti-Communist organization—Mr. Chaplin does not compromise the Congress, but *compromises himself* once and for all in the eyes of [fellow-travelers] and Communist sympathizers."[26] In any event, despite the official letter of invitation Nabokov wrote to Chaplin on January 17, 1952, nothing came out of the idea,[27] and the film component of the festival was shelved.

From the start, Nabokov intended to give Stravinsky a prominent place in the festival. It would mark the composer's first appearance since 1939 in "the world's most ungrateful capital."[28] Nabokov initially hoped that the festival could incorporate the French premiere of *The Rake's Progress* at the Paris Opera, which had acquired the rights for it. Stravinsky's choice as possible director and designer was Cocteau, while Désormière was envisaged as conductor.[29] Both were, of course, old friends of Nabokov, but their participation in the festival could raise red flags, especially with the American committee jealously watching for any sign that the CCF secretariat might deviate from the Congress's strict anti-Communist line. Désormière, after the war, had joined the French Communist Party, which created a temporary rift between the two old friends ("I fear he no longer wants to conduct my music and this makes me very sad," Nabokov reported to Henry Barraud in February 1952).[30] In any event, in March 1952, Désormière suffered a massive stroke that incapacitated him for the last eleven years of his life. Cocteau was also a delicate case: perhaps to redeem himself for his wartime indiscretions, he was then flirting with French Communists and published in their literary magazine *Les lettres françaises*, edited by his old friend Aragon, a hard line Stalinist and member of the Communist Party's politburo. In January 1952, false rumors reached the Congress secretariat that Cocteau had signed the Communist-inspired Stockholm Appeal calling for a unilateral ban on nuclear weapons (and signed by the entire adult population of the Soviet Union!). Cocteau was sounded at once, on behalf of an alarmed Nabokov, via a mutual friend, Denise Tual, a well-connected film and music producer whom Nabokov had known since the early 1930s and recruited as a consultant for the organization of the festival. On January 21, 1952, Tual urged Cocteau to clear the matter with Nabokov, who needed to be reassured "since he had to report on this before the Congress's American Committee, which does not take lightly collaborations to the Festival such as yours."[31] Nabokov was right to be worried: as late as April 1952, the American Committee suggested that Cocteau's participation be rescinded on the grounds that he had signed a public protest against the execution of Communist spies in Greece.[32] By then, however, *The Rake's Progress* project had been abandoned. Maurice Lehmann, the head of the Opéra, whom Stravinsky suspected of being wary of appearing "tied in any way with all this American business,"[33] opted instead for a lavish production of Rameau's *Les Indes galantes*, which, as Nabokov reported ruefully to Stravinsky, "has waited 250 years to be staged there, and, as I observed to no avail, could surely wait a few more months."[34] The Paris premiere of *The Rake's Progress* was delayed until June 1953, under André Cluytens—not at the Opéra but in the more modest premises of the Opéra-Comique, whose acoustics Nabokov detested (not without reason). The Opéra's participation in the festival was limited to hosting the first concert of the Boston Symphony Orchestra under Charles Münch—a gala attended by the President of the Republic and Mrs. Vincent Auriol—and one performance by the New York City Ballet. The Opéra also lent its orchestra for a concert conducted by Bruno Walter, which included a performance of Mahler's *Das Lied von der Erde*, with Kathleen Ferrier; in addition, twentieth-century works on the Opéra and Opéra-Comique program at the time of the festival—Debussy's *Pelléas et Mélisande*, Strauss's *Salomé*, Emmanuel Bondeville's *Madame Bovary*—were listed in the festival's brochure.

Next to the opera, the ballet figured prominently, from the outset, in Nabokov's plans. One idea was to "re-create the *Sacre*, with new choreography by George Balanchine."[35] As Nabokov reported to the composer, Balanchine, "stunned, but pleased all the same," by the offer, announced his intention to do a "non-Russian version" with sets and costumes by Picasso. Now, Picasso was an even more delicate political case than his friend Cocteau. Not known for any political positions before 1944, save for his opposition to Franco during the Spanish Civil War, he had then, with much fanfare, joined the French Communist Party. In 1949, his drawing of a pigeon had been adopted as a symbol of the Communist-sponsored peace propaganda. Nonetheless Nabokov, in his May 22, 1951, report to the American committee, listed Picasso, whom he had met in the past, among the cultural personalities he meant to contact in Paris: "I have heard curious rumors about him which make me believe that a long conversation with him might be useful."[36] However, Picasso's well-publicized *Massacre in Korea* painting, obviously intended as anti-American propaganda, put Nabokov in an impossible position. On June 27, he reported to Stravinsky that Picasso was "out of the question for us" and made other suggestions: "Who, in your opinion, could honor the score of the *Sacre* and the choreography of Balanchine? Would it be worthwhile to ask Tchelitchew? Or old Matisse?"[37] Clearly disappointed with Picasso's elimination, Stravinsky was nevertheless happy with the idea of asking Tchelitchew, who could "always be counted on to do something unexpected and admirable."[38] However, by mid-November, Stravinsky himself changed his mind and decided on conducting one performance of *Oedipus Rex*, to be presented in a semi-staged version with costumes by Cocteau, who would also act as narrator. This alone promised an exciting event, because Cocteau, the work's librettist, who had conceived the part of the Speaker for himself, had not been invited to do it at the 1927 premiere, owing to a temporary tiff with the composer; it had been entrusted to the little-known Pierre Brasseur, then at the dawn of his brilliant career. The 1952 revival would thus bring together for the first time, as performers, the work's creators.

The special place given to Stravinsky corresponded to the political intent of the festival: here was a modernist Russian-born composer, in Nabokov's view (and in the view of many) the greatest of his century, whose music was unwelcome in his native country, where he was vilified in the official musical press. The point was emphasized in the festival program, which quoted side by side contradictory comments made on *The Rite of Spring* in the Soviet musical press in 1926 and 1948 by Asaf'ev, writing under the pseudonym Igor Glebov.[39] By the same token, the inclusion of Schoenberg, Berg, and Webern could also serve as a reminder that they too were denounced in the Soviet Union as bourgeois formalists, after being attacked by the Nazis—as an extract about Schoenberg from the *Dictionary of Jews in Music* reminded the audience in the festival brochure. Nabokov also hoped to make an even stronger case against censorship in totalitarian countries by presenting two large-scale works that he saw as victims of totalitarian censorship in their countries of origin: Falla's *L'Atlántida* and Shostakovich's *Lady Macbeth of the Mtsensk District*.

Falla's "scenic cantata," begun in 1926 but left unfinished at his death twenty years later, was actually a far less clear-cut case than Shostakovich's opera. In an article published in the May 1952 issue *Preuves* specially devoted to the festival, Nabokov argued that Falla's score, brought to Spain by Falla's sister after the composer's death in Argentina in 1946, was being withheld by Franco's regime for political reasons:[40] Falla, indeed, had shown no sympathy for Franco and adapted his libretto from the epic by the Catalan poet Jacint Verdaguer, hardly a cultural hero of the regime. An unsympathetic critic has called Nabokov's advocacy of Falla's work "the only instance known to me of Nabokov's complaining of censorship by a contemporary *right-wing* regime."[41] Leaving aside the questionable implication that Russia under Stalin was truly progressive and that anti-Stalinism, by the same token, was reactionary, the charge is grossly unfair, considering Nabokov's numerous statements, both public and private, about totalitarianism applying to both fascist and Communist regimes. As it turned out, Nabokov was probably informed that Falla had left the score of *L'Atlántida* in a state that discouraged any hopes of a performance in the near future and the project was dropped. He did not, however, lose interest in the work: in August 1952, after the festival was over, he was still inquiring about the fate of the music, and in 1957 he was still hoping to be able to present the work in concert.[42]

Nabokov hoped to score an even bigger coup with what would have been the French stage premiere—as well as the first postwar production—of Shostakovitch's *Lady Macbeth*, an opera about which, to be sure, he certainly had aesthetic reservations, but which, more glaringly than any other perhaps, illustrated the fate that a work of art could meet in a totalitarian country. As Nabokov explained in the festival brochure, as early as June 1951, attempts were made to locate a full score and instrumental parts with a view to this Paris performance.[43] However, after months of research, no copies could be found: neither the Library of Congress nor the New York Public Library had any, nor the library of the Paris Conservatoire, or any collection in England, Germany, and Switzerland. The work's original Soviet publishers informed the Congress that the score could not be made available to them. Finally, the Berlin Radio Symphony Orchestra discovered parts for the symphonic suite Shostakovich had extracted from the opera, and they performed it, under Fricsay, in a concert that also included Blacher's *Paganini Variations* and Hindemith's *Symphonic Metamorphoses on a Theme by Weber*. To emphasize the point about the ties between the selection of Shostakovich's work and the theme of the festival, the program cited, side by side, enthusiastic early Soviet reviews and the January 28, 1936, *Pravda* article that abruptly ended the opera's career. Compared to his earlier published comments on *Lady Macbeth*, Nabokov's program notes are, understandably, muted: stressing the work's resemblance to late nineteenth-century realist operas, especially in the way it incorporates folkloric elements, he points out that the writing is, in other respects, resolutely modern and reminiscent of Prokofiev's early manner, while the orchestration recalls Mahler and the polyphony Hindemith.

As he must have quickly realized, Nabokov, a musician organizing an international music festival as the head of an international organization, was putting himself in an impossible, "damned if you do, damned if you don't" position—and one in which he apparently has remained, given the tone and the substance of recent assessments of his efforts.[44] As he explained in February 1952 in a letter to Maritain, who begged him to include Lourié's Pushkin-based oratorio *The Feast during the Plague*, Nabokov had to put himself above his own personal tastes and affinities and be as just and impartial as possible.

> Now, the main objective of the musical program of our festival was, above all, to present before the public works and composers who in one way or another have definitively made their mark in the evolution of twentieth-century music and who were therefore either pioneers of new tendencies or artists representing important and new trends.[45]

This alone represented a formidable challenge, on top of which came the one of finding, in record time, star performers ready and willing to tackle the works in question, while having to deal with friendly and contradictory pressures from various quarters. While Maritain wanted more Lourié—already present with his setting of T. S. Eliot's *Little Gidding* in one of the chamber music concerts—and less Shostakovich and Prokofiev, the American Committee demanded that American music be more in evidence. Madariaga found the absence of Alexandre Tansman "scandalous" (it was remedied by the inclusion of his *Psaumes* in a choral concert)[46] while various French factions grumbled about the non-inclusion of the

Gaullist Ibert or the collaborationist Florent Schmitt.[47] The arguably more regrettable omissions of Paul Dukas and Vincent d'Indy were rectified *in extremis* in a concert of the Academia nazionale di Santa Cecilia, where *The Sorcerer's Apprentice* (though dating from 1897 and thus technically not a "masterpiece of the twentieth century") and the prelude from d'Indy's opera *Fervaal* were played under Igor Markevitch.[48]

The American participation presented Nabokov with a tricky diplomatic challenge. There he was, holding a big American-sponsored cultural event in a country recovering from a humiliating military defeat and occupation, rescued militarily and financially by the United States, and where the old atavistic anti-Americanism threatened to resurface in various forms, as it invariably did, though not so much in the general population as among the powerful and influential intellectual class (the Congress's target), then dominated by Communists and their sympathizers. The last days of the festival coincided with the arrival of General Matthew Ridgway as the new head of NATO, prompting demonstrations—based on allegations of biological warfare in Korea—against "Ridgway the Plague." The campaign protesting the Rosenbergs' conviction as Soviet spies was also in full swing. By any standards, America figured prominently in the musical part of the festival's program: not even counting emigre composers, like Krenek, Rieti, Schoenberg, Stravinsky, and Varèse, who had made the United States their home, the program included works by Barber, Copland, Ives, Piston, Schuman, and Virgil Thomson. A work by Roy Harris and Sessions's Second Symphony were also envisaged at the initial stage. American performers were also much in evidence, with the Boston Symphony Orchestra—on its first European appearance—and the New York City Ballet, and an all-black troupe performing *Four Saints in Three Acts* under the composer's direction. For this very reason, Nabokov, as he explained to Leopold Stokowski, whom he tried to recruit to conduct the final concert, wanted to avoid "anything which might be interpreted as American propaganda."[49] Instead of Copland's *Lincoln Portrait*, proposed by Stokowski, he thus recommended *El Salon Mexico*, and instead of Randall Thompson and Howard Hanson, insufficiently well known or avant-garde enough, he suggested—against his own taste—Sibelius's *Finlandia* and Strauss's *Rosenkavalier* suite.[50] As it turned out, Stokowski could not appear and the final concert was conducted by Monteux, who did include the proposed Copland and Strauss, as well as Sibelius's *Swan of Tuonela*.[51]

Gertrude Stein and Virgil Thomson's *Four Saints in Three Acts* was not part of Nabokov's initial plans.[52] It came out of discussions Nabokov had with Thomson in New York in early August 1951, Thomson even suggesting that the same troupe might be able to sing both his opera and *Porgy and Bess*.[53] But Nabokov, according to Thomson, turned down the Gershwin "as sociologically false (a white man's story) and culturally degrading to Negro actors (because sociologically false)."[54] Nabokov had strong personal reasons to favor Thomson's work: he had attended the premiere of *Four Saints* in 1934, and since then he and Thomson had become close personal friends. At that point, Thomson and Nabokov were hoping that Tchelitchew could be brought in to reconstitute the sets and costumes Florine Stettheimer had designed for the Hartford premiere. However, as Nabokov feared, Tchelitchew was no quick worker, and they turned to Francis Rose, who, like Tchelitchew, had been a Gertrude Stein protégé.[55] As choreographer, Nabokov suggested turning to Frederick Ashton, who had directed the premiere, rather than Balanchine, who was already prominently featured in the festival plans; the British participation needed to be boosted. Nabokov did intervene on one casting matter: for one of the female roles, he urged the composer to hire a ravishing twenty-five-year-old soprano from Laurel, Mississippi, endowed with a radiantly beautiful voice, named Leontyne Price. Perhaps she was brought to his attention through his many contacts in the musical world, but she may also have been recommended to him by Elizabeth Wisner, whose brother Frank headed the CIA's Office of Policy Coordination, the Wisners being originally from Mississippi.[56] Thomson, who auditioned Price in New York, must have had initial doubts, since on October 18 Nabokov pleaded his protege's case: "Please don't forget my little negro girl Leontyne Price. She can sing much better than she did the other day. Do you still have her address?"[57] On November 24, he urged Thomson again—"I beg you not to forget my negro girl, Price"—adding that he would be seeing Ashton shortly at the premiere of *Billy Budd* at Covent Garden.[58] And as late as February 26, 1952, Nabokov pleaded once more with Thomson, explaining that hiring Price would also save money, since she was coming to Paris in any case—he had suggested she might apply to the American Conservatory in Fontainebleau—and her patrons in Mississippi would be covering her trip.[59] Launched at the Paris festival thanks to Nabokov's intervention, Price's career took off later in the same year when she appeared as Bess opposite her husband William Warfield's Porgy in Gershwin's opera. As her letters to Nabokov show, the great African American soprano never forgot the crucial role he had played at that early stage.

In 1952, the very idea of an all-black cast starring in an American-sponsored international festival needed some special pleading with Fleischmann, who—or so Nabokov assumed—controlled the financing of the operation. An unsigned memorandum to Fleischmann, probably by Nabokov and likely dating from October or November 1951, while stressing that Stein and Thompson's work, unlike most American musicals or other dramatic spectacles featuring blacks, presents them "in an atmosphere of dignity and grace," emphasizes the positive psychological effects of presenting an all-black American troupe in Paris.

> It would contradict unanswerably Communist propaganda which claims that the American Negro is a suppressed and persecuted race. A performance by foreign Negroes, on the other hand, would lead immediately to derision from the Communist camp, e.g. to the effect that the U.S. would not let its Negroes "out."[60]

Whatever reservations Fleischman may have harbored on the subject, they were overcome.

Along with Stravinsky, Balanchine was one of the festival's principal honorees. In the festival brochure, Nabokov introduced him as "the perfect translator, the humble artisan of classical dance," who "bows respectfully before the musician's craftsmanship, listening to his work with infinite patience and tenderness; carefully, gracefully, he enters, like a dream, into the very heart of the musical work, and takes it into a different world, by transforming human bodies into musical bodies of extraordinary justness."[61] The New York City Ballet—in its Paris debut—presented four programs at the Théâtre des Champs-Élysées, with choreography by Balanchine, Jerome Robbins, and Anthony Tudor, many of them on twentieth-century music: Ravel's *Valses nobles et sentimentales* and *La valse*; Hindemith's *The Four Temperaments*; Prokofiev's *The Prodigal Son* (with sets by Georges Rouault); *The Pied Piper*, based by Robbins, who also starred in it, on Copland's Clarinet Concerto; and three Stravinskys: Robbins's *The Cage* (on the music of the Concerto in D), *The Firebird*, and *Orpheus*. The last work, presented in the original sets and costumes by Noguchi, was conducted by Stravinsky himself on May 14. As for *The Firebird*, it was designed by Chagall, who, however, was unhappy not to have been brought in to supervise the effect and deplored the results.[62]

As Nabokov had correctly assumed, the festival turned out to be an almost unqualified triumph for Stravinsky. *The Rite of Spring*, performed by the Boston Symphony Orchestra led by Monteux—the conductor of the riotous 1913 premiere in the same Théâtre des Champs-Élysées—was widely interpreted as a vindication, and Stravinsky's personal appearances generated the expected amount of excitement. As reported by Marcel Schneider, who described the effect produced by the Boston orchestra as "a stupor of admiration," "all the listeners rising to their feet, applauding and cheering Stravinsky, the entire audience transported and beside itself, Pierre Monteux and the Boston Symphony Orchestra almost overwhelmed by bravos and endless calls—these memories will never be forgotten."[63] Stravinsky was also feted on May 22 when he conducted the Société des Concerts du Conservatoire in his *Symphony in C*, *Symphony in Three Movements*, and *Capriccio for Piano and Orchestra*, with Monique Haas as soloist. Only the score of *Orpheus*, to the composer's chagrin, failed to win critical praise. Yet, despite Stravinsky's triumph, the festival also turned out to be an unexpected, exciting confrontation between him and the Second Viennese School. In his presentation of the festival, Nabokov had downplayed the aesthetic differences between Stravinsky and Schoenberg, claiming—repeating an argument he had used in his polemic with René Leibowitz in *Partisan Review*—that "the great creative personalities of twentieth-century music, Schoenberg and Stravinsky for instance, are not more violently in opposition than Palestrina and Gesualdo were in the sixteenth."[64] But

he may have underestimated, on the one hand, the Parisian passion for controversy, and, on the other, the extraordinary novelty value of the Second Viennese
School in postwar France.[65] The performances of Berg's *Wozzeck*, never previously
staged in Paris,[66] with Karl Böhm as conductor and the Vienna State Opera, with
a cast headed by Joseph Hermann and Christel Goltz, caused the expected sensation. "An outstanding cultural event," remembered the poet Pierre Jean Jouve, who
was inspired by the performances to embark at once on a book devoted to Berg's
opera.[67] "What a lesson for us! [. . .] We will not forget it anytime soon," Marcel
Schneider wrote in *Combat*.[68] Nabokov himself had seen the work's first production in Berlin, conducted by the young Erich Kleiber, and recalled this experience
as "the discovery of a new world."[69] The "crowning achievement" of the festival,
in Herbert Luethy's words, *Wozzeck* all but eclipsed the *Billy Budd* presented two
weeks later by the Covent Garden company, with Britten conducting.[70] As for
Schoenberg's *Erwartung*, with Irma Colassi as soloist, it proved an unexpected challenge to *Oedipus Rex* on the evening when the two works were presented together,
under Hans Rosbaud. Perhaps the audience's reaction (which the London *Times*
tactfully described as "mixed") was directed not so much at Stravinsky than at
Cocteau's masks and "new and startling *tableaux vivants*."[71] But then, as Cocteau
knew better than anyone, there is no real success in Paris without *scandale* and the
performance ended in triumph.[72] Stravinsky himself was pleased with the visual
aspect of the performance, telling a somewhat startled Henry Barraud: "It's very
good, what Jean has done, because it looks Tibetan."[73]

While concerts ended up representing the lion's share of the program, the art
and literature components were nonetheless not mere icing on the musical cake.
The former was put in the hands of James Johnson Sweeney, former curator of
the Museum of Modern Art and future director of the Guggenheim Museum.
Nabokov, however, was involved in every stage of the preparation. When he was
in New York in early August 1951, he made contact with Alfred Barr Jr., the MoMA
director, and with Monroe Wheeler, its director of publications. He even seems
to have toyed with the idea of borrowing paintings from the Barnes Collection,
though he soon realized that this was unfeasible, even though his old patron
turned nemesis was no longer on the scene, having been killed in a car crash
in 1951.[74] Like the musical side of the festival, the exhibition claimed to make the
point that the fine arts, in the twentieth century, had flourished especially when
benefiting from a climate of political freedom, whereas some of the works on
display had been variously described as "bourgeois" or "degenerate" in totalitarian countries.[75] Notwithstanding the CCF's reservations about Picasso's current political commitments, the Spanish painter, with eight works, figured most
prominently in the show, while at least one other painter featured (Matta) was a
Communist as well. American art, on the other hand, was, if anything underrep-
resented in Sweeney's show, which included Calder but not Stuart Davis, Arthur

Dove, Mardsen Hartley, Edward Hopper, or Georgia O'Keefe—but this reflected the general lack of appreciation of American painting in Europe at the time. The show opened at the Musée d'art moderne on May 7 and was subsequently seen at the Tate Gallery in London in July and August. In conjunction with the exhibition, a debate was held on May 26 on the subject of "The spirit of twentieth-century painting." Jean Cassou, head of the Musée d'art moderne, presided, and it featured Sweeney, Herbert Read, Lionello Venturi, and Edgar Windt, among others.

As for the festival's literary side, which Nabokov largely entrusted to René Tavernier, the French Resistance poet and journal editor, it took the form of three debates and two "conférences littéraires." Each debate had a particular theme. The first, on May 22, touched on "Isolation and Communication"; chaired by Tavernier, it gathered James T. Farrell, the French critic Claude-Edmonde Magny, the philosopher Jeanne Hersch, Eugenio Montale, Rougemont, and Allen Tate. The next day, Auden, Caillois, Milosz, and Glenway Wescott discussed "Revolt and Communion," with Aron chairing. Aron again, along with Louis MacNeice, and the art and literary critic Gaëtan Picon, spoke on "Diversity and Universality" on May 28, with Vladimir Weidlé presiding. The first "conférence littéraire," on May 15, on "The Writer within the City," featured Mark Aldanov, Madariaga, Guido Piovene, Katherine Anne Porter, Rougemont, and Spender. The one on May 30 on "The Future of Culture," presided over by Madariaga (who took the opportunity to publicly protest the admission of Franco's Spain into UNESCO), starred two major celebrities—William Faulkner and André Malraux—in addition to Jean Guéhenno and Silone. Faulkner had accepted the invitation with the greatest reluctance. After his arrival, he conveyed to Nabokov his annoyance at being put up in the same hotel as the black cast of *Four Saints in Three Acts*.[76] At his public appearance, he was slightly inebriated and had little to contribute, but his enormous prestige in France, as well as his words of praise for the host country, "mother of the freedom of man and the human spirit," earned him an ovation from the audience.[77] Malraux's participation had been personally solicited by Nabokov in November 1951. "It is always so good to see you," he wrote to him. "One leaves with the feeling of having accomplished in ten minutes what, in this poor dear Europe, often takes centuries."[78] In his speech, Malraux emphasized the cultural closeness between the United States and Europe and contrasted modernist creativity with the "bourgeois" quality of Soviet art—even though he made clear that there was no incompatibility, in his view, between great art and communism.

How was the festival received? It had been well publicized and certainly garnered considerable attention, with the arrival of Münch, Rieti, and Stravinsky at Orly airport on April 29 receiving front-page press coverage.[79] Interviewing Nabokov at the time for the French radio, a producer exclaimed: "One feels transported back to the days when Louis XIV opened Versailles or Louis XV hosted festivities for the wedding of his son!"[80] Janet Flanner, writing in *The New Yorker* as "Genet," opened her oft-quoted May 31 "Letter from Paris" by describing the event as being "of immense Franco-American importance." It had, she continued, "spilled such gallons of captious French newspaper ink, wasted such tempests of argumentative Franco-American breath, and afforded, on the whole, so much pleasure to the eye and ear that it can be called, in admiration, an extremely popular fiasco."[81] Explaining this double-edged compliment, Flanner suggested that, by its very weight and opulence, the festival had "vexed" the Parisian public, especially "members of the snobbish beau monde and elegant intelligentsia," who felt they had not been courted the way they were used to. Some music critics clearly felt the same way: "Are the organizers of these concerts operating according to American methods?" asked one of them in *Le Monde*.[82] If a few feathers were ruffled, the festival, *pace* Flanner, was anything but a fiasco. It was, in fact, a major critical and public success, with the Boston Symphony and the New York City Ballet garnering particular praise: reviewing the latter in *Le Monde*, Olivier Merlin ended his article by confessing that he had felt as if the times of Diaghilev had been restored and no further comments were necessary.[83] In fact, the abundant—and increasingly enthusiastic—coverage of the festival in *Le Monde* (a neutralist paper) is particularly revealing.[84] Nor is there any doubt that the art exhibition, in itself the component open to the largest and broadest audience, was extremely popular: according to Alfred Barr Jr., it attracted "the highest attendance of any [show] since the war."[85] There were, to be sure, snobs among the audiences that thronged to the sold-out concerts at the Théâtre des Champs-Élysées, as Flanner's distorted picture suggests. But much more importantly, there were also dedicated music lovers eager to discover music they had never had the chance to hear.[86] Nabokov had enlisted the full support of the French radio—where Henry Barraud was head of music programming—and broadcasts of many of the events made available to countless more, not just in Paris, but in the provinces and abroad. After it was pointed out to her that some of her comments (especially her concluding reference to Münch as having been a "collaborator") were uncalled for, a repentant Flanner wrote to Nabokov from Capri on August 7 that she was "more sorry than at any thing which has ever happened to me in my work over a quarter of a century."[87]

As expected, the Communist press, under the pen of Jean Kanapa, the Party's "intellectual" and a member of its politburo, excoriated the festival as being part of a campaign "to facilitate the ideological occupation of our country by the United States," "have French minds imbued with bellicist and fascist ideas," and promote "Yankee ideology and non-culture." Falsely reporting the participation of the "Nazi Heidegger" and the "mystico-fascist Toynbee," Kanapa also protested the decision to play, next to "the formalist Stravinsky," works by Shostakovich and Prokofiev deliberately selected among those "that have been criticized by the Soviet people and self-criticized by their authors."[88] Diffidence was also expressed in the non-Communist Left. Writing in Sartre's *Les temps modernes*, the theater critic Bernard Dort, despite a few words of praise for *Wozzeck* and Bartók's Second Piano Concerto, lambasted the whole enterprise as a political operation in the defense of "the Western neo-capitalist society and its military policies."[89] More surprisingly, *Combat*, the Resistance daily founded by Camus among others, opened its columns to Serge Lifar, whose collaborationist attitude during the war had earned him a three-year ban from the stage. On April 30, before the festival opened, *Combat* published an "open letter" from the ballet master to the festival's organizers, the real purpose of which was to complain that the Opéra ballet troupe had been "excluded" from the affair. "From the point of view of spirit, civilization and culture," Lifar concluded his preposterous diatribe, "France does not have to ask for anybody's opinion; she is the one who gives advice to others."[90] Lifar's indignation can be easily explained: not only had he not been invited to participate, but Balanchine, whom he saw as his great rival, was one of the festival's undisputed heroes;[91] and his anger was no doubt compounded once he learned that another rival, the Marquis de Cuevas, was also on the festival program, with two ballet premieres on music by Auric (*Coup de feu*) and Sauguet (*Cordélia*), given at the Théâtre des Champs-Élysées on the same evening as the stage premiere of Rieti's Lorca-based opera *Don Perlimplin*.[92] In a soberly phrased rebuttal published in the same daily two days later, the festival organizers gave a detailed account of the Opéra's involvement in the festival's program and declined to answer Lifar's "self-serving" polemic. The dancer counterattacked on May 5, still in *Combat*: this time Nabokov, "originally a Russian, like me," was personally taken to task for his "extraordinarily ambiguous attitude," which Lifar confusingly described as "putting Western culture on trial on the French soil." Lifar further accused Nabokov of revealing his "political duplicity and above all, as always, his perpetual desire to please everybody"—an extraordinary charge considering the amount of criticism Nabokov had to cope with.[93] Once again, a short communique in the next issue explained that Nabokov had no intention to respond. But Lifar's vitriol may have been on his mind when he wrote: "Of course, in any other country we would have had both more sympathy and more support."[94]

Combat, which covered the festival more extensively than any other publication, was, in fact, typical of the liberal French intelligentsia's reaction to the festival: while its music and dance reviewers, Marcel Schneider and Dinah Maggie, were bowled over by the quality of the concerts and performances they attended, the cultural and drama critic Guy Dumur, in a series of four articles devoted principally to the art exhibition, took offense at the festival's political implications: the Congress, he pointed out, was an American organization, "about which, in truth, we know very little," except that its review, *Preuves*, was "entirely devoted to anti-Bolshevist propaganda."[95] With absurd chauvinistic hyperbole—Paris, he claimed, continued to be "the one and only site of artistic creation worldwide"—Dumur argued that the ties of the festival with Cold War politics somehow compromised the beauty of its offerings.[96] In his third article, he deplored that, Malraux excepted, leading French writers—André Breton, Camus (who had been invited but declined), René Char, Sartre, and others—were missing from the debates, and he repeated in conclusion that art and politics were best kept separate.[97] Nabokov and Rougemont responded in a letter published in *Combat* on June 2 by pointing out that the festival had been subsidized by the Dutch, French, and Italian governments and a Swiss foundation in addition to its American sponsors, and, more generally, that Dumur was wrong to discuss the festival in purely Franco-American terms.[98]

But while contemporary reactions were, to a large extent, conditioned by their historical context, what about retrospective appraisals? "You would think, if you didn't know better," Hilton Kramer wrote in 1990, "that this extraordinary festival of the arts would be acclaimed in retrospect as one of the proudest accomplishments in the history of the Congress. But such it did not turn out to be in the eyes of those political stalwarts of the Congress for whom 'culture' counted for very little."[99] Writing more than three decades after the event, Sidney Hook argued that Nabokov had "highjacked" the project, which, in his view, ought to have been "ancillary to the ideals and values of the Freedom Manifesto"—a formulation one is tempted to describe as Zhdanovism in reverse, or at the very least typical of the contempt of the academic toward the fine arts, especially music.[100] Such criticism reflects the chasm that existed from the start between the Paris CCF secretariat and members of the American committee, who hoped the Congress would be the main war machine in their anti-Communist crusade.[101] Lasky's dismissive assessment ("it's unimportant whether foreigners think Americans can play music or not") may be a reflection of his personal antipathy toward Nabokov, and betrays the same general contempt toward music and musicians.[102] William Phillips was also typically dismissive in 1990, calling the festival "an impresario's dream" and claiming—without giving a source—that "the French" had "described it as the greatest couturieres' ball [*sic*]":[103] surely this kind of comment reveals more about its originator than about its target? The same could be said of Hook's testimony, especially since it contradicts his contemporary assessment of the festival in the congratulatory letter he wrote to Nabokov shortly after the event:

> My impression, from this side of the water, is that the festival was a success, that it was the only kind of thing that was possible in France at least, and indeed it was the only event that didn't turn out to be a psychological defeat for the cause of freedom. I am particularly pleased, too, because my confidence in your judgment and leadership has been vindicated.[104]

On a practical level, Nabokov had perfectly achieved one of his stated objectives: getting top-ranking American cultural institutions to cooperate with their

Western European counterparts on an equal footing. No one, after hearing the Boston Symphony and seeing the New York City Ballet perform, could deny that they were at least equal to similar French, English, or German orchestras or ballet troupes. Had the festival succeeded on a political level? From an American perspective, US officials involved in its financing clearly thought it had.[105] So did, among others, Samuel Lipman, who attended the festival "as a boy of 17" and, decades later, remembered the performances of music by Stravinsky, Prokofiev, and Shostakovich, as "a symoptic refutation of the Soviet dictatorship that wishes these works buried."[106] From a more general point of view, the question was far from clear-cut. In his perceptive report for *Commentary*, Herbert Luethy argued that, while the ideological justification—countering the Soviet charges that the West was culturally moribund by presenting the achievements of Western culture—was admirable in itself, it would have been better to be less emphatic about it.[107] But Nabokov, while doing his best to play down the political aspect in his presentation of the festival, was in no position to ignore either the strident American wing of the Congress, in the eyes of which the festival ought to have assumed the form of an anti-Communist manifesto.[108] "The most absolute art was mixed up with the most realistic politics," Luethy complained, pointing out the resulting confusion.[109] But confusion, it could be argued, is part of the price of freedom; there is no room for it in a totalitarian system. A more substantive reservation made by the same critic is that the festival was, as he put it, a "Russian festival," dominated as it was by the spirit of Diaghilev and the Ballets Russes. The charge is excessive, considering that many of the works performed— *Wozzeck, Erwartung, Billy Budd, Four Saints in Three Acts*, Bartók's Second Piano Concerto, to name but a few—had nothing to do with the Ballets Russes. Still, many did, and, from the perspective of 2014, it seems fair to say that Nabokov had not been wrong to recognize Diaghilev's place as one of the major cultural forces of the twentieth century. But were the musical choices, for this reason, too "safe" and averse to risk? For a festival that did not claim to be an avant-garde manifestation, the inclusion of Boulez's *Structures pour deux pianos* (a world premiere, with the composer and Messiaen performing) and two concerts of *musique concrète*, on May 7 and 25, tell a different story.

     To conclude this account, it may be pointed out that, despite accusations of elitism and favoritism, Nabokov had made sure that rehearsals had been open to Conservatoire students and youth musical movements. In September 1952, he thus received the collective thanks of students of Nadia Boulanger at Fontainebleau for making it possible for them to attend a number of musical performances during the festival. In transmitting the message from the group— which included Henry-Louis de La Grange, the pianist Noël Lee, and the composer Thea Musgrave—Boulanger added her own appreciation. "You did not fight and take on this frightening responsibility in vain," she wrote. Her students, she added,

> have understood all that they owe you—all that you brought them, offered them, taught them; what superior intelligence, what courage, what disinterestedness was needed to conceive, undertake, and realize this insane, yet so profoundly important project. Of course, anybody could argue, quibble, regret, criticize even. It nevertheless remains true that, thanks to you, fifty years have been condensed in their essence—masterpieces that bear testimony to those years, even as anxiety threatens to let doubts and negativity prevail—and that you succeeded where most others would have given up. Nobody is more aware than I that what I am saying is poorly expressed; do smile, criticize, but do also realize that no one appreciates, thanks, and loves you more than I.[110]

14

Culture Generalissimo

AFTER THE "MONSTER PROJECT" of the Paris festival, Nabokov felt "more or less annihilated," as he wrote to Igor Markevitch's wife Topazia.[1] In early July 1952, in Rome, he had a car accident and spent part of the summer recovering, first in Kolbsheim and then at the chalet Hansi Lambert owned in Gstaad, in the Bern Oberland, where he found himself in the company of Spender and Samuel Barber. By then, Nabokov and Patricia had separated. Moving out of the Rue d'Assas apartment, he rented a small flat on the Rue des Renaudes, near the Étoile. While Patricia embarked on an affair with Chiaromonte, Nabokov met Marie-Claire Brot, who became his fourth wife in early May 1953. The best man at their wedding was the musicologist Fred Goldbeck (husband of the pianist Yvonne Lefébure), who had coordinated the chamber music part of the 1952 festival. "My wife is half-French, half-Belgian," Nabokov reported a few weeks later to Arthur Schlesinger, "is very sweet and gay and does not speak any other language than French. She has a very charming house near Paris and an equally charming family."[2] Located an hour away from the city, Marie-Claire's house—chateau would have been a more appropriate description—was in the village of Verderonne, near Liancourt in the Oise département, and it was often there that Nabokov found the time and quiet to compose music during the next ten years.

Indeed Nabokov took the opportunity of his forced rest in the summer of 1952 to start composing again. He was approached by Raya Garbusova, the Russian emigre cellist, who had commissioned and premiered Barber's Cello Concerto in 1946, to write a piece for cello and orchestra. Subtitled "Les hommages," Nabokov's work is an exuberant, humorous piece, characteristic of the composer's upbeat mood in the wake of the 1952 festival. The homages referred to in the subtitle are to Nabokov's favorite three nineteenth-century Russian composers, to whom each of the three movements is dedicated, with themes from their music woven into the melodic structure. The opening Andante, "Serenata di Pietro," pays tribute to Tchaikovsky; the middle "Ballata di Alessandro," to Dargomyzhsky;

and the concluding "Corale di Michele" to Glinka. As Nabokov himself explained, the solo instrument is supposed to personify an aging Russian baritone, exiled in Paris, where—like the proverbial Russian emigre prince of the interwar period— he makes a living as a taxi driver, while tunes from the favorite operas of his repertoire return to haunt his memory. The work can be described as a bittersweet *plaisanterie musicale*, with an added musical joke in that a twelve-tone series makes a brief appearance in this otherwise firmly diatonic piece.

Garbusova having apparently lost interest in the project, Eugene Ormandy, whom Nabokov saw when visiting the United States in October 1952, offered to premiere the work with his orchestra and his principal cellist as soloist.[3] Because of his obligations in Paris, Nabokov, much to his annoyance, was not able to attend the Philadelphia premiere on November 6, 1953. The program began with Haydn's Symphony no. 100 (the "Military") and ended with William Schuman's Sixth Symphony. Beside Nabobov's concerto, Lorne Munroe, the soloist, performed Saint-Saëns's First Cello Concerto. "My cello concerto apparently a huge success in Philadelphia," a relieved Nabokov reported to Josselson on November 13.[4] "A pleasant surprise," noted, condescendingly, the *Philadelphia Inquirer* reviewer, adding with approval that Nabokov "unabashedly places popularity of appeal above any pseudo-profundity."[5]

"I wish that *Ode* were on the bill; not just for auld lang syne; upon its merits, wonderfully memorable," Glenway Wescott had written to Nabokov before the 1952 Paris festival.[6] But throughout his tenure at the Congress Nabokov was careful to keep his musical career separate from his duties as head of the organization. He made one discreet exception to this rule in November 1952, when the piano duo of Arthur Gold and Robert Fitzdale premiered his Waltz for two pianos in a Congress-sponsored concert at the Salle Gaveau. Leontyne Price, then singing Bess in London, also took part in the concert and offered to perform one of his songs, but Nabokov begged her not to do so, except as an encore.[7] Yet there is no question that the greater visibility he owed to his new functions brought his music to the attention of musicians and conductors. In early October 1952 *La vita nuova* was performed in London by the Hallé Orchestra, conducted by George Weldon, and broadcast on the BBC's Third Programme ("a marvelous performance," Nabokov reported to Hansi Lambert).[8] Nabokov himself—stepping in for the originally scheduled Jean Martinon—conducted the first Paris performance, with the Orchestre national, with soprano Berthe Monmart and tenor Jean Giraudeau, in December. He attended the New York premiere in January 1953, bringing with him Marie-Claire, whom he introduced to Stravinsky on the occasion.[9] Maurice Abravanel, who had premiered *Job* in Paris in 1933, now music director of the Utah Symphony Orchestra, approached the composer about reviving it in Salt Lake City—in the revised version for mixed choir Nabokov had prepared for the 1934 Worcester performances.[10]

In September 1952, Nabokov attended a UNESCO meeting in Venice. He was always wary of the mealy-mouthed rhetoric of the intergovernmental organization and the meeting itself was, in his view, "a waste of time," but he had the satisfaction of hearing considerable praise about his festival from the Italian musicians present, as he reported to Josselson with justifiable pride:

> Malipiero, Honegger, Pizzetti, Ghedini and Petrassi all spoke of the Festival as the most important event of the century, best organized and most useful, and Roland-Manuel (presiding) complimented the Congress and me in the name of the International Music Council (UNESCO) for the Festival. In fact, they were all listening to me as to someone who represent[s] the "white hope" of composers and musicians in general. [. . .]Only *here* did I realize what an *immense* success the Festival has been. Malipiero said publicly that the Congress is doing a better work for music and culture than UNESCO [. . .].[11]

The relationship between the Congress—a nongovernmental, Western organization—and the Paris-based UN agency devoted to education, science, and culture was, to be sure, rather diffident at first. But Nabokov forged good ties with the UNESCO-affiliated International Music Council. Jack Bornoff, its longtime British executive secretary, was himself a former intelligence officer who had served as "music controller" in Hamburg after the war. The collaboration between CCF and UNESCO was even easier after 1954 when, on Nabokov's recommendation, UNESCO hired John Evarts. An old acquaintance from Nabokov's postwar stay in Germany, where he had headed the Theater and Music operations in Munich, Evarts had lost his State Department job once his homosexuality was reported to his supervisors.[12] Moving to Paris, he subsisted on odd teaching jobs and playing the piano in a nightclub, until Nabokov—all the more sympathetic since he had himself faced similar accusations when seeking a State Department position in the late 1940s—used his influence to get the highly competent Evarts the position he kept for the remainder of his professional life.

One reservation about the 1952 festival, expressed by Minocheher Masani, the Indian delegate, as early as the December 1951 executive committee meeting, was that it was exclusively Western in its outlook, whereas the Congress had a worldwide scope. Nabokov had actually entertained the possibility of opening the festival to other cultures—especially that of Japan—but this proved impossible to organize in so little time.[13] After the festival, it was resolved that similar events would be held in other parts of the world—a project that was to absorb much of Nabokov's energy over the next twelve years.

Another criticism expressed about the 1952 festival was that "this brilliant show revealed no new inspiration, not one unknown talent, nothing not already consecrated."[14] That was, of course, not the intention. Yet the festival, after all, had managed to make space for Boulez and *musique concrète*. But such criticism pushed Nabokov to focus on contemporary creation for the next CCF ventures in the field of music and the fine arts. "With that festival," he told Jay S. Harrison of the *New York Herald Tribune*, referring to "Masterpieces of the Twentieth Century," "we shut the door of the past."[15] By the summer of 1952 plans were already being made for a drama competition, an international painting competition, and a music competition. "We *must* [. . .] push through our scheme with the prizes as soon as possible," Nabokov wrote to Josselson from Italy after attending the UNESCO meeting.[16] Determined to involve Stravinsky, he sounded him out in November—without success at first—about chairing the music prize advisory board.[17] Nabokov's idea, from the outset, was to combine this competition with concerts focusing largely, this time, on music by living or recently deceased composers, accompanied by a forum of composers, scholars, and critics. Rome, rather than Paris, would be the venue this time. The choice was dictated by both political and practical reasons: chief among the latter was the presence of the sympathetic and efficient Mario Labroca, now head of the RAI, which could be a major participant and financial backer of the event. Initially scheduled for September 1953, the Rome festival had to be postponed, probably to Nabokov's relief, until the spring of 1954. Plans were discussed at a meeting in Geneva in early January 1953. Attendees were Blacher, Dallapiccola, Goldbeck, Markevitch, and Sauguet. A few weeks later, Nabokov, then in New York for the local premiere of his *Vita nuova*, outlined the plans in an interview in the *New York Herald Tribune*. The manifestation would be cosponsored, with Nabokov as the chief pilot, by Rougemont's Geneva-based Centre européen de la culture, which also operated an association of European festivals. The purpose of the forum would be to "try to cover any problem with which the musician of today is faced." The concerts would be truly international and include new works or works not previously heard in Italy or in Europe. But the real novelty would be the contest: twelve young composers, preselected by an international panel, were to be invited to Rome for the performance of their work, after which a winner would be chosen by "a special jury, democratically elected by all those attending the conference." Not only would the work awarded first prize be subsequently played by three European and three American orchestras, but all the other preselected contestants would receive publication and copying of parts. The "Prix de l'Œuvre du XXe siècle," as it was initially called, was officially announced in March 1953. It consisted of a 12,000 Swiss franc prize for a violin concerto; an 8,000 Swiss franc prize for a short symphonic work; and a 5,000 Swiss franc prize for a work for solo voice and small ensemble. Members of the selection committee were Barber, Blacher, Britten, Chavez, Dallapiccola (whose *Canti di prigiona* had been, in Nabokov's opinion, "one of the great revelations" of the Paris festival),[18] Honegger, Malipiero, Frank Martin, Milhaud, and Virgil Thomson. Villa-Lobos was subsequently added to the list, and Stravinsky himself finally agreed to lend his name as chairman. The actual organization of the festival was in the hands of an executive committee, chaired by Nabokov, and consisting of Blacher, Dallapiccola, Goldbeck, Labroca (and his deputy, Count Zaffrani), Rougemont, Sauguet, and Thomson.

The most important event the Congress sponsored in 1953 was the international conference on Science and Freedom held in Hamburg in July. Nabokov sat on the organizing committee, whose chairman was the eminent emigre Hungarian physical chemist and social scientist Michael Polanyi. A professor at the University of Manchester, Polanyi was, throughout the 1950s, the scientist most actively involved in the activities of the Congress. The committee included several distinguished German scientists: the physician Arthur Jores, the zoologist and geneticist Hans Nachtsheim, and the philologist Bruno Snell. Sidney Hook and Carlo Schmid also served on the committee, as did the British biologist Cyril Darlington, professor of botany at Oxford, who had taken a firm position against Lysenkoism, and the Polish émigré physicist Alexander Weissberg-Cybulski. An international honorary committee was chaired jointly by Maritain and Bertrand Russell; it included Robert Oppenheimer, at that time under investigation by McCarthy's Senate committee and soon to have his security clearance revoked. Thus began the association with the Congress of the nuclear scientist, to whom Nabokov later became especially close. During the preparatory stages Nabokov traveled several times to Germany to discuss the participation of German scientists. After Stalin's death on March 5, serious consideration was given to inviting Soviet scientists, but this was vetoed by the mayor of Hamburg, Max Bauer, who, as Nabokov reported to Hook, feared "unfortunate political complications."[19] A tense political climate was confirmed on June 16, a month before the conference opened, when the first uprising against the Soviets in Eastern Europe took place in East Berlin. In a June 19 letter to Malraux, in which he solicited the writer's contribution to a special issue of *Preuves* on this topic, Nabokov conveyed his excitement and hopefulness about "the extraordinary events that happened in Berlin and continue in Eastern Germany."

> Indeed these events not only signify that a myth has been debunked; they are the indisputable sign that Stalinist power (at least in the satellite countries) is crumbling. When you consider that the young Russian workers in uniform, thirty-two years after Cronstadt—an event the very memory of which has been carefully expunged from their memory—are forced to shoot at their "brothers," the German workers, you truly feel you are witnessing the end of the big lies.[20]

Nabokov flew to Hamburg on July 17 ahead of the conference, which opened on July 23 and lasted through the 26th, gathering 120 scientists of various disciplines. Its purpose, as described in the conference papers, was "(1) to investigate the actual state of science in the countries behind the Iron Curtain; (2) to expose the dangers to scientific freedom of tendencies towards regimentation that may serve the interest of political tyranny; (3) to clarify and to vitalize the concept of scientific freedom in the Western world in the light of contemporary developments."[21] An outcome was the establishment, in early 1954, of a permanent committee of fourteen scientists on "Science and Freedom," chaired by Polanyi after Darlington turned it down. It published the "lively and controversial" bulletin *Science and Freedom*.[22] Once the committee was in place, Nabokov was less directly involved in the Congress's science programs.

The other important item on the Congress's agenda in 1953 was the establishment of a network of magazines, in addition to the already existing *Preuves*, while *Der Monat* was actually not officially associated with the Congress.[23] The first of these new magazines, launched in that spring, was the Spanish-language *Cuadernos*, published in Paris, edited by the anti-fascist Spanish journalist Julián Gorkin, and intended primarily for Latin American intellectuals.[24] But an even more important project was to start an English-language periodical. Originally, Nabokov and Josselson did not have an Anglo-American audience in mind, but rather India and the Far East, as well as Scandinavian countries, where neutralism was widespread.[25] As the project took shape, however, this initial model—still close to the militant anti-Communist spirit of the Berlin Congress—underwent a radical transformation. In February 1953, the London publisher Frederic Warburg, who had expressed interest in the project, took the night ferry to Paris along with Malcolm Muggeridge and Orwell's friend and *Tribune* editor Tosco Fyvel, both members of the English Society for Cultural Freedom, to discuss the matter with Bondy, Josselson, and Nabokov.[26] With his "raven black hair greying, piercing eyes, aquiline nose and a high complexion," Nabokov made a vivid impression on Warburg.[27] There was general agreement that the editorship of the new journal would be entrusted to an Anglo-American team; Spender, who had already declared himself a candidate, was also agreed on as the British editor.[28] The visitors from London, however, were worried when Nabokov, speaking for the secretariat, suggested that the magazine be based in Paris. Warburg realized that, as initially conceived by the Congress, the new magazine "was to be a carbon copy of *Preuves* but in English, again the cold-war warriors publicizing Communist theories by attacking them, giving them an audience they did not deserve and would not otherwise obtain."[29] He and Muggeridge forcefully argued that to be successful, the magazine, on the contrary, should be edited in London, carefully protected from excessive politicization, and firmly rooted in the English literary and intellectual scene. Nabokov and Josselson conceded, and suggested Irving Kristol, executive secretary of the American Committee for Cultural Freedom and former assistant editor of Elliott Cohen's *Commentary* in New York, as American editor. The result of these negotiations was *Encounter*, the first issue of which appeared in October 1953, its ten thousand copies selling out in a week. The first contributors included Albert Camus, Czapski (on Malraux), Cecil Day Lewis, Leslie Fiedler (with a controversial article on the Rosenbergs, who had been executed in June), Christopher Isherwood (who contributed reminiscences of Ernst Toller), Walter Laqueur, Rougemont, and Edith Sitwell. Not only was *Encounter* a brilliant success, it became, in Josselson's words, the Congress's "greatest asset" and surviving it for more than two decades, publishing its last issue in 1990.[30] But the American Association saw things differently. In their view, *Encounter* should have been precisely what Warburg considered a recipe for disaster: a staunch, militant anti-Communist magazine. As they saw it, Josselson and Nabokov had capitulated to the unreasonable demands of Warburg and Muggeridge. In January 1955, when the ACCF issued a memorandum, largely directed at Nabokov, in which it listed its grievances about the road the Congress had taken, *Encounter* figured prominently for "its apparent unwillingness to offend what it presumes are English sensibilities with explicit anti-Communism."[31] In other words, like the Paris festival, *Encounter* was another success of the Congress for which the New York intellectuals—who formed the core of the ACCF—never forgave Nabokov.

Nabokov himself contributed to this opening issue of *Encounter* with an article entitled "No Cantatas for Stalin?" Why, he asked, had the expected musical homages to the dead dictator failed to materialize seven months after his death? Could this absence, or delay, be related "to the sudden infrequency with which his name is mentioned in the pages of *Pravda*"?[32] Or was the positive, "uplifting" official style imposed on Soviet composers since 1948 difficult to combine with "the composition of lamentation in minor keys"? Leaving the question unanswered, Nabokov surveyed the musical scene in the Soviet Union in 1953. Save for Bartók ("a gesture of friendship to the sister republic of Hungary"), none of the great modernist composers were performed there. Except for a little Poulenc and Vaughan Williams and a handful of American composers, it was "as though the Western world had ceased to exist at some moment during the period 1905–15."[33] The repertory performed in Russia consisted mostly of Russian and Western European "great classics." Applied to Russian composers, the term "classic" had no connection to any particular musical style: taking the example of Prokofiev's posthumous canonization, Nabokov suggested that "the only indispensable qualifications for entrance" into this Pantheon were that "(1) the composer must be dead, and (2) he must on no account have composed any music that could be described as dissonant."[34] Current Soviet musical products were thus characterized by their "oppressive uniformity" ("as though they had been turned out by Ford or General Motors").[35] But why had Soviet Russia, where modern music was widely performed until 1931–32, lapsed into such conservatism? Beside the obvious reason—the general subservience of the arts in a totalitarian state—Nabokov suggested a deeper sociological explanation he had hinted at in a previous article: the disappearance in Russia—through exile or physical elimination—of the intelligentsia, which until then "set the tone of the cultural life of the nation, because it alone could understand and encourage the work of the pioneers in the arts."[36] Yet, now that Stalin had died, there were a few signs of change. The first was "the development of closer connections between the Soviet Union and its satellites"; another was that the Zhdanovian verbiage was being phased out of Soviet musical journals, just like the portraits of Stalin and Mao once ubiquitous in their pages. Perhaps, Nabokov concluded, anticipating the widespread use of the "thawing" metaphor later in the decade, "so long as the door of the refrigerator remains even slightly ajar, there will be an opportunity for some of the outer atmosphere to reach the frozen region of the interior."[37]

In August 1953, Nabokov and Marie-Claire, accompanied by Marie-Claire's daughter Caroline, vacationed in Ischia, renting a house in Forio, the village where Auden had himself been renting a house since 1948 and where he and Kallman spent their summers.[38] Auden had described the island as "one of the loveliest spots on earth" and it was likely at his suggestion that the Nabokovs joined him. "Woods," one of Auden's seven "landscape poems," written in Ischia in August of the previous year, came out with a dedication to Nabokov when it appeared as part of the group "Bucolics." Another, more recent, Ischia resident was Hans Werner Henze, who had been introduced to Nabokov by Blacher. Henze, who had dedicated to Blacher his 1950 ballet *Die Vokaltuch der Kämmersängerin Rosa Silber*, was now working on his cello concerto, inspired by Shelley's *Ode to the West Wind*, and on his opera *König Hirsch*. He himself was joined that summer by his friend the Austrian poet Ingeborg Bachmann, who was about to become one of his most important collaborators. Henze and Bachmann told Nabokov they were eager to meet Auden, and Nabokov reported this to Auden while they were seated "in a cafe in the little town's piazza." After grumbling about not wishing to meet new people, Auden consented, though he remained characteristically silent when the German composer and his female friend (both age twenty-six) were introduced to him. The next morning, Nabokov bumped into Auden at the village market. "By the way," Auden said, "I didn't like that cocky little German . . . *Not at all!* . . . But the girl seems okay . . . Nice and quiet . . ."[39] Little did Auden suspect that he and Kallman would become the librettists of Henze's *Elegy for Young Lovers* and *The Bassarids*. As for Nabokov, he liked and admired Henze, and the composer's lifelong Communist sympathies do not appear to have in any way affected their friendship, as the frank and intimate tone of their correspondence shows.[40]

After attending a seminar in Venice in September to prepare the Rome music festival and conference, Nabokov spent three weeks in Paris before going on leave from the Congress in order to take up a position as composer in residence and music director at the American Academy in Rome—a position in which he succeeded a fellow emigre, Alexei Haieff. On September 30 he left Paris by car, in the company of his father-in-law. He broke up the trip twice: first to visit Rougemont at his home in Ferney-Voltaire, near Geneva, that same evening, then in Milan on October 1. The next day, on the final leg of the journey, he stopped in Florence, where he called on Dallapiccola.

Although the purpose of Nabokov's leave was to give him time for composition, he continued to follow Congress-related matters. There was, obviously, the preparation of the festival and conference planned for the following spring, but also the international painting competition, for which he made contacts at the Galleria nazionale d'arte moderna. He was also involved in the launching of an Austrian Congress-sponsored magazine, Forum, edited by the poet and novelist Friedrich Torberg. As he candidly reported to Josselson from Rome in the last days of 1953, Nabokov had misgivings, about both Torberg's budgetary demands and the way the project was going:

> It looks to me as if it were done with typically Viennese nonchalance. As you know, I am rather skeptical about the whole affair because, fond as I am of our friend Torberg, I have no great trust in his endurance capacities and I find his mode of operating too "schampig" [sloppy].[41]

On November 26–28, Nabokov attended a meeting hosted by the Italian committee on the subject of "the working class and freedom," with Aron, Haakon Lie, and Carlo Schmid giving papers. At an executive committee meeting, Aron reported on his recent trip to India and the political difficulties encountered by the Congress in that country. This prompted Nabokov to plan a trip there himself the following year.

An important visit Nabokov received in late October was that of Shepard Stone, who, after three years in Germany, where he served as Assistant Director of Public Affairs for the American High Commissioner for Occupied Germany, John McCloy, had been appointed in 1952 Director of International Affairs at the Ford Foundation, a position he would occupy until 1967. He thus became Nabokov's principal interlocutor within what was already the world's biggest philanthropic organization. Nabokov and Rougemont had already met with him in New York at the beginning of the year. During the conversations he had with Stone in Rome, Nabokov expressed his disenchantment with the French intellectual climate, deploring that even Camus was reluctant to join a CCF-backed protest against the repression of the Berlin uprising for fear of appearing pro-American in the eyes of the Left.[42] Nabokov, at that stage, was more optimistic about the Italian situation.

Stone—who, unlike Nabokov, was aware of the CIA's role in the organization's funding—was to become a key ally of the Congress and the Ford Foundation an increasingly important financial backer.[43]

In Rome, Nabokov renewed his friendship with Elliott Carter, who, as a winner of the American Rome Prize, was spending the year as a fellow at the Academy. He also resumed his acquaintance with Wilhelm Furtwängler, with whom he had not been in contact since the painful denazification process in 1947. The German conductor spent two months in the city to conduct Wagner's *Ring*, one act at a time, for recording by the Italian Radio with a strong cast headed by Martha Mödl and Ferdinand Frantz. Thanks to Labroca, Nabokov was among the invited audience at the rehearsals and performances. He and Furtwängler had long and friendly conversations during the whole period and there was even hope that the conductor might participate in the musical forum planned for the following spring.[44]

As for his work as composer, Nabokov first had to finish orchestrating his cello concerto, soon to be premiered in Philadelphia—an urgent task made no easier by a boil in his right arm that caused considerable pain.[45] He was also beginning to explore new musical possibilities. He thus contacted Robert Whitney, the British-born founder and conductor of the Louisville Symphony Orchestra, who, beginning in 1948, had launched an ambitious policy of commissioning works by American and European composers for performance (and recording) in Louisville. Nabokov was all the more familiar with the program since Whitney had turned to him for recommendations. "I have been admiring what have you done in the last years in Louisville," Nabokov wrote to him from Paris on September 17, "and have heard from many close friends, such as Virgil Thomson, what a good time they have had in Louisville. I have only one regret, that is not to have had the opportunity of hearing your orchestra myself nor having had the pleasure to be commissioned to write a piece for it."[46] One of the indirect effects of this appeal resulted in the Louisville premiere of Nabokov's most ambitious work to date, one that would occupy him for the next five years: an opera on the subject of Rasputin. As he told the story in *Bagázh*, writing an opera—and writing one on this particular operatic subject—was suggested to him by Gian Carlo Menotti. The suggestion came when Nabokov joined Menotti and Barber for a luncheon at the house they shared in Mount Kisko, New York; another guest was the conductor Thomas Schippers. As Nabokov recalled, the topic did not greatly appeal to him at first. It was associated in his mind with "filthy films" and "American lecture tours by Prince Yusupov with their unappetizing title: 'How I Killed Rasputin.'"[47] But the idea took hold, and the next day, in a second-hand New York bookstore, he found an "excruciatingly lecherous and silly book" on Rasputin in German that set his imagination into motion.[48] Canceling appointments, he spent three days in the New York Public Library, going through books about Rasputin and the last czar and his family, and borrowing any he could to continue his reading and note-taking in the evening at the Chelsea Hotel, where he was staying in Thomson's apartment. On his flight back to Europe, Nabokov started working on a scenario.

> I sketched out several alternative outlines of what the plot of a Rasputin opera could be like. But somehow neither of the variants of the outline would fall into a pattern that would fit an opera libretto. The story was too diffuse and at the same time too cumbersome. There were too many unrelated personages in it and too much extraneous stuff. Too much politics, religion, much too close to historical and topographical variations that took one from the midst of Siberia to Tsarskoe Selo and to Yusupov's palace in Petrograd. I sensed, of course, that the center of the plot will have to be Rasputin's assassination, or rather the long night of December 29–30, with a few events preceding it. But how to shape it into an opera libretto without making it sound banal and "grandguignolesque" escaped me.[49]

The only problem with this otherwise perfectly plausible account—confirmed by a contemporary letter[50]—is the dating. According to *Bagázh*, all this took place in the spring of 1954. We know, however, that the project had "gelled" a year before, in the spring of 1953, when—not coincidentally—Stalin's death had suddenly made the future of Russia a topic of burning interest. The earliest reference to the planned opera can be found in a letter Nabokov wrote to Arthur Schlesinger on June 16, in which he announced both his new marriage and his forthcoming appointment in Rome:

> I am extremely happy about it, because it will give me time to write an opera for which I am now preparing a libretto. The subject of the opera will be close to your heart, for it is to be Rasputin. But please do not think I am writing a sex-thriller. I am rather intending to write something which will be a modern Greek tragedy.[51]

As this letter reveals, Nabokov, at this early stage, already had definite ideas about the general dramaturgy of the work and intended to fashion the libretto himself. He had even started thinking about the music, writing, for instance, in mid-July, to Gerald T. Robinson of the Music Institute at Columbia University to inquire about "hanging, tuning, and ringing of Russian church bells."[52] But he must have quickly realized that he needed a "lyricist"—someone who could translate his ideas into English verse. He evidently discussed the matter with Auden and his companion when he visited them in Ischia in August. Was Auden himself less than enthusiastic in participating in a project over which he would have only partial control? Kallman, on the other hand, agreed to get involved. "Chester Kallman [. . .] is going to write the libretto," Nabokov wrote on September 16 to his friend the publisher George Weidenfeld, asking him to find for Kallman the English translation of René Fülöp-Miller's *Der heilige Teufel*, originally published in 1927 and still widely regarded as the best book on Rasputin, "or any other biography of the gentleman with the exception of Prince Yusupov's book."[53] On the same day, he asked the same favor of Irving Kristol, now established in London. The following day, September 17, Nabokov wrote to Rougemont, urging him to lay his hands on the French translation of Fülöp-Miller in Geneva and suggesting they spend two or three hours looking at his proposed *découpage*—that is, the structuring of the plot—when Nabokov stopped at Ferney on his way to Rome. Also before his trip, Nabokov started looking into the possibility of applying for a Guggenheim Fellowship that would allow him to write the opera while in the Italian capital.[54] When the Guggenheim Foundation contacted Stravinsky for a reference, Stravinsky expressed his surprise at the choice of topic, but he nevertheless wrote to Nabokov he thought it was "an excellent subject."[55] After this period of initial excitement, the project temporarily foundered. As Nabokov reported to Stravinsky on November 17, Kallman visited him in Rome in mid-October and an outline of the libretto was agreed upon, but Nabokov was already beginning to have second thoughts about having enlisted Kallman as collaborator.

> I am expecting to receive the first scenes of his libretto, but, alas, Kallman is not very reliable as a *foutriquet*, neither as a correspondent, nor, I believe, as a worker. At any rate, I have not heard from him since he left Rome about four weeks ago . . .[56]

Sometime by the end of the year, the Rasputin project was provisionally put aside, no doubt in part because of mounting pressure relating to the preparation of the Rome festival, and possibly because Kallman decided to pull out.

Preparations of the Rome festival, indeed, occupied most of Nabokov's time in late 1953 and early 1954. Save for a brief visit to Paris in early December and a trip to Geneva in late December to meet with Rougemont. On this occasion he saw Furtwängler one last time—the German conductor died in November 1954. Remaining in Rome until February 23, Nabokov then flew to New York with Rougemont, staying on East 58th Street in the apartment of his fellow composer Charles Jones, a former colleague of Milhaud at Mills College. In the course of this two-week stay, he and Rougemont met with officers of the Rockefeller Foundation, which was one of the backers of the Rome event; Fleischmann, on the other hand, had recently suffered a heart attack—he did not attend the festival—and the future of the Farfield Foundation became uncertain for a while. Nabokov also gave a talk at Freedom House on March 2.

The purpose of the Rome festival was not simply to respond to criticisms expressed about the 1952 festivities: from a more positive perspective, it

corresponded to views Nabokov himself had published about the situation of contemporary music in the divided, increasingly compartmentalized postwar world.
As the conference document explained, in words that probably were Nabokov's
own, "one of the most outstanding facts of musical life in Europe today is that the
works of celebrated composers of the older generation are to be found in all repertories, whereas those of their juniors are in general only played in the countries
of their birth."

> Young American composers are hardly ever acquainted with the works of
> their European colleagues; similar is the case of young composers in the
> various European countries. Moreover, musicians who, before the war, had
> numerous opportunities of meeting each other and of making interna-
> tional contacts, nowadays rarely have any chance of doing so.[57]

This situation, Nabokov argued, resorting to his favorite negative qualifier, resulted
in a "provincial outlook among young composers." The problem was compounded
by the "invisible barrier" that had risen between composers and performers on the
one hand, and composers and critics on the other. The Rome events were therefore
intended to "give young composers an opportunity of having their works played
and appreciated"; "enlarge international repertories"; and "create a meeting-place
where composers, performers may have the same personal contacts which have
been enjoyed for many years by the exponents of other arts."

Officially called in Italian "The Situation of Music in the Twentieth Century"
(and, in English, "Music in Our Time"), the festival opened on April 4 with a
concert, led by Fernando Previtali, chief conductor of the Rome Radio Symphony
Orchestra, at which pieces by Gabrieli and Monteverdi were paired with works by
Malipiero, Bartók, and Roussel. And it closed on April 15 with Stravinsky conducting the same orchestra in a program comprising *Orpheus* and *The Firebird*. There
were seven symphonic and six chamber music concerts, and three recitals. The
sixty-five works performed represented thirteen world premieres, five European
ones, and eighteen Italian ones. Among these was Henze's 1952 opera *Boulevard
Solitude*, a modern retelling of the Manon Lescaut story, which was presented at
the Rome Opera House in a staging by the young Jean-Pierre Ponnelle on a double
bill with Vieri Tosatti's one-act "paradoxical opera" *Il sistema della dolcezza*, based
on Edgar Allan Poe. As with the French in Paris two years previously, Nabokov
tactfully made sure that Italian composers were well in evidence. Several omissions of 1952, such as Jacques Ibert and Carl Nielsen, were also discreetly rectified.
In addition to Previtali, the conductors involved included Rosbaud, Scherchen,
Milhaud, who conducted his Fifth Symphony, and the Swiss musician Victor
Desarzens; Markevitch was also scheduled to appear but had to cancel due to
illness; he was replaced by Ferrucio Scaglia. On April 13, Leontyne Price sang

Sauguet's *La voyante* and Barber's *Hermit Songs*, these last with the composer at the piano. Price also sang one of the works in competition—the third act of Lou Harrison's chamber opera *Rapunzel*. A sensation of the festival was unquestionably the first Italian performance of Elliott Carter's First String Quartet. Premiered in New York the previous year by the Walden Quartet, this "tumultuous and revolutionary" work—as William Glock characterized it—had been awarded the first prize at the Liège string quartet competition that autumn and Nabokov had discussed with his old friend Paul Collaer the possibility of inviting the Liège Quartet for a Rome performance.[58] As it turned out, it was played, in the composer's presence, by the reputed Paris-based Parrenin Quartet. The third symphonic concert, initially entrusted to Markevitch, was initially supposed to feature the Italian premiere of *La vita nuova*. Nabokov, however, once again uneasy about facing the reproach of a conflict of interest, convinced Markevitch to substitute Britten's *Spring Symphony* ("I personally think it is his finest work"), though it too was replaced by the symphonic suite from von Einem's opera *Dantons Tod*. Britten himself was represented by the *Michelangelo Sonnets*, sung by Peter Pears with the composer as accompanist.[59] As for the panel discussions, they were on such topics as music and contemporary society; music and the press; technique, style, and aesthetics; what makes a good program; the relationship between composers, performers, and critics; and the musical language of contemporary opera. As Allen Hughes summarized it, even though "nobody had come to Rome with a pocketful of new ideas," the debates nonetheless fulfilled their purpose by acquainting "the members of the international musical fraternity with each other."[60]

Compared to the 1952 Paris event, the originality of the Rome Festival was its focus on a music competition, with the works nominated all performed—anonymously, although it seems that who had written what was hardly a secret to anyone—on one of the programs. The composers preselected were Yves Baudrier, cofounder of the "Jeune France" group in the mid-1930s, along with Messiaen and Daniel-Lesur; the Swiss Conrad Beck, Nabokov's senior by two years, who, like him, had attained a certain prominence in the early 1930s; Bernd Bergel from West Germany, who had studied with Schoenberg in Berlin; the Englishman Peter Racine Fricker, a pupil of R. O. Morris at the Royal College of Music; the Brazilian Camargo Guarnieri, later director of the São Paulo Conservatory; the aforementioned Lou Harrison, born in Portland, Oregon, and a student of Henry Cowell and Schoenberg; the German Giselher Klebe, born in 1925, who had studied with Blacher and Rufer; Jean-Louis Martinet from France, a student of Roger-Ducasse, Koechlin, and Désormière; Mario Peragallo and Camillo Togni, Italian both and students of Casella; the Moscow-born Wladimir Vogel, now a resident of Switzerland, a participant in Busoni's masterclasses in Berlin at the same time as Nabokov, who, along with Stuckenschmidt, had been a member of the radical November Group during the Weimar years;[61] and the Missouri-born

Ben Weber. The oldest contestant, Vogel, was born in 1896; the youngest, Klebe, in 1925. Chaired by Collaer, the final jury consisted of Copland, Roland-Manuel, Rollo Myers, Goffredo Petrassi, Robert Soetens, and Heinrich Strobel (none of whom had served on the preselection committee). It awarded the first prize to Peragallo's Violin Concerto; two second prizes went to Klebe and Vogel, and two third prizes to Harrison and Martinet. The Solomonic division of the second and third prizes was widely seen as a diplomatic response to personal and political pressure: as Allen Hughes put it in *Musical America*, it turned out that "each of the countries supplying two contestants had also produced one winner."[62] Nabokov must have drawn the lessons of this disappointing process, since no more music competitions were sponsored by the Congress.

Like the Paris festival, the Roman *convegno* did not lack controversy.[63] Some of it was of a purely mundane kind. Thus, a minor scandal spoiled the premiere of *Boulevard Solitude* at the Rome Opera on April 7 when a guard refused admission to Stravinsky, Robert Craft (who conducted one of the chamber music concerts), and Ned Rorem, when they arrived in Nabokov's company, on the grounds that they were not in evening dress. "A fist-fight breaks out between Nicolas Nabokov and a guard," wrote Craft in his diary, "after which an exception is to be made for I.S., but not for me, whereupon he returns with me to the hotel."[64] Nabokov also left. At the next morning's conference session, Petrassi, on behalf of Italian musicians, apologized to Stravinsky for the incident, which made headlines on both sides of the Atlantic.[65] But there were also political difficulties. They began on April 5, at the plenary session, chaired by Rougemont, at which the competition judges were elected by the participants from a slate of fourteen proposed by the conference committee. The procedure was contested from the floor by Italian musicians and critics, both from the Right and from the Communist Left. The composers Guido Pannain and Renzo Rossellini (brother of the famous film director) voiced their refusal to take part in the vote "because the methods employed were not democratic." A similar incident occurred on April 8 in the afternoon at the session on "Music and Politics," when one of the panelists, Mario Zafred, a composer and the music critic for the Communist daily *L'Unità*, began by attacking the position paper presented by Rollo Myers, who made references to the situation of musicians in the Soviet Union. Zafred then proceeded to question the very purpose of the conference, noting the absence of Eastern European composers and the paltry representation of their works on the festival's program. Nabokov was chairing the session instead of the initially scheduled Claude Delvincourt, director of the Paris Conservatoire, who, tragically, had been killed in a car crash on his way to the conference. "Mr. Nabokov," the *New York Times* correspondent noted, "replied cogently, wittily and forcefully, and was rewarded with warm applause."[66] On the issue raised by Zafred, he pointed out that invitations had actually been sent to a number of Eastern European composers and musicians who had all turned them down: Kabalevsky, Khatchaturian, David Oistrakh, and Shostakovich from the Soviet Union; Zoltán Kodály and László Lajtha from Hungary; and Andrzej Panufnik from Poland (himself about to defect to the West). Ironically, Zafred later broke with *L'Unità* at the time of the Hungarian uprising and despite their clash at the conference, he and Nabokov resumed cordial relations.

Reactions to the event from the Italian press, while mostly favorable, were, as could be expected, far from unanimous, especially in Rome. Even before the festival began, the event had been denounced by the Communist *Il mondo operaio*, in typical Zhdanovian fashion, for its "abstraction and formalism." Five days into the festival, an open letter to Nabokov appeared in *Il giornale d'Italia*. It was signed by one of the deans of Italian music, the composer Adriano Lualdi, then director of the Florence Conservatory. After explaining that he was unable to attend the event owing to his professional obligations, he questioned some of the conference's organizational and artistic procedures, claiming that it was for the public to judge the artistic merit of musical works. "Is it absolutely certain," Lualdi asked about the works preselected, "that in this choice there are not obvious criteria of partisan, sectarian spirit and of a limited scope [. . .] to favor and shamefully advertise an art that is 'anti-social, atheistic, disaggregational, and negative in its relation to human and social values?'" Lualdi also suggested that among the composers involved in the planning of the conference included some "of the most conspicuous and authentic exponents of that 'provincialism of time, of profession, and of aesthetics,' which, in their own words, the conference organizers are purportedly fighting?"[67] Lualdi further suggested that the two Italian composers nominated for the contest belonged "to the same extreme, anti-democratic, therefore 'partisan' tendency" and were unrepresentative of the Italian musical panorama. Nabokov's reply appeared in the same newspaper on April 20.[68] The competence of the public to judge, he explained, had never been in dispute. About the type of art Lualdi argued the festival promoted, Nabokov answered that he could not answer the question because he did not understand what kind of art Lualdi had in mind. Discreetly hinting at Lualdi's former ties with fascism, he suggested that the rhetoric of his antagonist was the kind common to all totalitarianisms: "I only know that terms like that were in vogue during the recent past, under regimes which were not Democratic in any way, regimes during which persons having little theory or practice succeeded in gaining control over all cultural things." As for the attacks on the musicians involved in the planning, Nabokov listed their names and let them speak for themselves.

The activity and the works of all these music personalities are known throughout the world, wherever there is any music. We shall leave it to *the only authorized judge* [i.e., the public] to decide the tendencies of which these men are "conspicuous and authentic exponents."

Criticism also came from the musical avant-garde on the grounds that it was insufficiently represented at the festival. The charge was unfair, considering that Carter, Luigi Nono, and Guido Turchi were featured—along with Schoenberg, Varèse, and Webern—and that, besides, the purpose of the festival was to give as wide a panorama as possible of contemporary musical creativity. In fact, as Allen Hughes noted in *Musical America*, more than one-third of the music heard "had dodecaphonic characteristics."[69] The most aggressive attack, though it was not made publicly, came from Boulez, who, initially invited to take part in the panel on composers and the press (along with Thomson, Glock, and von Einem), was apparently annoyed by the presence among the competition judges of composers he disliked. He wrote Nabokov a furious letter, calling the conference and competition a "shameful travesty" and suggesting at the end that a congress on the history of condoms in the twentieth century would be a more tasteful choice for a new project. Nabokov, who, as we have seen, had brought Boulez's name to the attention of his American readers as early as 1950 and had included the world premiere of the two-piano *Structures* in the 1952 Paris festival, replied on September 14, 1954. Returning to Boulez the original of his letter in order to save him from future embarrassment (keeping, however, a copy), he upbraided him for this display of "a sectarian, pretentious, and old-fashioned spirit one might hope a man of your generation would be exempt."[70] Whether Boulez—who, referring to Nabokov, boasted at the time to John Cage of having "put the mercenary lackey in his place"—found a way of apologizing to Nabokov, their falling out turned out to be brief.[71]

It is only fair to add that few people at the time would have agreed with Boulez's assessment of the Rome festival—Glock, for one, remembered it as a "stirring event."[72] Nabokov himself felt he had reason to be happy with the fruit of his efforts. "The Rome Festival went off splendidly," he reported a few months later. Yet, he added, it was, "nevertheless, a heartbreaking affair for me because of the harrowing native *mores* and the general disorganization of the Ancient City (in Rome only the following things are organized: ruins, churches, Diplomatic Corpses [*sic*], and the Communist Party)."[73] After the festival, he remained in Rome until mid-June. One of his main preoccupations, reflected in his correspondence with Josselson, was the situation of the Italian Association for Cultural Freedom, a group dominated by the personality of Silone, who, as Nabokov reported to Josselson on May 5, operated "along 'trial and error' principles, without too much coherence between the various things he does."[74] Nabokov, bearing in mind that Maritain had been acutely uncomfortable about Croce being one of the Congress's original honorary presidents, was particularly sensitive to the political danger represented by the presence in the Italian Association of a strong anticlerical current—citing as an example the historian Gaetano Salvemini, "who eats the Pope the way Levitas used to eat Uncle Joe"[75]—which put liberal Catholic intellectuals in an awkward position.

Nabokov had all the more reason to be aware of ideological sensitivities in Italy since he was involved in the preparation of another conference to be held in that country in September of the following year on the subject of "The Future of Freedom." Silone having advised against Florence and Bologna, Nabokov, in March, made contacts in Milan. He received the enthusiastic support of the mayor, Virgilio Ferrari, a physician by training and politically a social-democrat, who in turn made useful suggestions for further contacts. Among the eminent Milanese scientists Nabokov met with were the biologist Claudio Barigozzi, the mathematician Gino Cassinis (a member of the Socialist Party as well as president of the Academia dei Lincei), and the chemist Mario Alberto Rollier. To get logistical support for the event, he turned to Luigi Morandi, vice president of Montecatini and head of the Ente manifestazioni milanesi. As Nabokov quickly realized, a delicate balance had to be found to manage political susceptibilities: the anticlerical Italian committee should not appear prominently, in order not to offend Christian democrats; nor should the tone of the event appear too confrontational, so as not to offend the extreme Left, well represented on the city council and *Ente* board.[76] An ad hoc organization committee was put together in Milan, while in Paris, another committee—Barigozzi sitting on both—selected participants and prepared the program.

Before returning to Paris, Nabokov toyed with new publication projects. In June 1954, he asked Edward Weeks: "Would you be interested in a kind of festival travelogue? Not a serious one, but a rather gay and funny one."[77] A more substantial plan was a biography of Prokofiev, for which Nabokov signed a contract with Houghton Mifflin. As he reported to the firm's music editor, however, his progress was impeded by lack of information on Prokofiev's Russian years and he seemed ready to abandon the idea. Enthusiasm was briefly rekindled when Panufnik's defection was announced in July 1954. "Panufnik has been one of the top cultural figures behind the Iron Curtain since the end of the war," Nabokov reported excitedly to his publisher on August 4, 1954. "I am seeing him next week in London. He might well be 'the missing link' in the chain of my sources of information which I was desperately looking for. If that is so, then it would render my writing of a complete biography of Prokofiev possible."[78] Alas, Panufnik, as he must have told Nabokov, had never been able, much to his regret, to meet Prokofiev, and the biography project was abandoned for good.[79] This disappointment notwithstanding, Nabokov took interest in Panufnik's difficult financial situation and did his utmost to help him: in October 1954, he informed him that the Congress had awarded him a $2,000 fellowship, and in January 1955 appealed on the Polish composer's behalf to Thomson and the Rockefeller Foundation.[80]

The summer of 1954 was plagued, for Nabokov, with health problems, presumably related to the stress of the Rome conference. Two weeks before the beginning of the festival, he had suffered a perforation of the left eardrum leaving him, as he wrote to Josselson, feeling "Beethovenized";[81] this incapacitated him for the rest of the year. The ear infection, combined with severe headaches, made it impossible for him to sleep without strong pills (of which he remained a large consumer through the rest of his life). An operation was attempted in July, but was not successful. "The ear started running again two days ago and still makes loud noises," he wrote to the violinist Alexander Schneider, adding that he feared he was in "for a serious, radical mastoid operation sometime this fall."[82] On a happier front, a son, his third, named Alexandre, was born on July 23. As the proud father reported to the same correspondent, "the child, as was [. . .] to be expected, has Mongoloid eyes, darkish hair, is fat and round and . . . has a Jewish nose!!! Where does this come from?"

A new, important musical friendship began for Nabokov that summer, when his fellow composer turned administrator Rolf Liebermann, since 1945 the music director of Radio Zurich and manager of the Beromünster Studio Orchestra, invited him to conduct and record his flute and cello concertos. The recording sessions took place on September 12–15—the Cello Concerto with Massimo Amfiteatrov, who had performed the work in Rome in April 1954, as soloist. "It went off very well," Nabokov reported to Robert Craft.[83] Liebermann, who rose to prominence that year with his Concerto for Jazz Band and Symphony Orchestra, also had his third opera, *Penelope*, premiered at the Salzburg Festival that season. Nabokov attended one of the performances, led by George Szell, with a cast that included Christel Goltz (the Marie of the 1952 Paris *Wozzeck*) in the title role, the bass Kurt Böhme as Ulysses, Anneliese Rothenberger as Telemachus, Walter Berry as Eurymachus, and the veteran Max Lorenz in a character role. Liebermann was then working on a new opera, based on Molière's *L'école des femmes*, on a libretto by Strobel (one of the competition judges at the Rome Festival), who had also written the libretto for *Penelope*. Their new opera was first staged in Louisville in 1955, in a one-act English version, and then revised for the Salzburg Festival two years later. Thanks to Liebermann, Nabokov thus came into contact with the conductor Moritz Bomhard, music director of the Louisville Opera Company, who in due course arranged a similar commission for Nabokov's *Rasputin*.

Following the recording sessions in Zurich, Nabokov and his wife and child spent two weeks in Greece, where Nabokov gave lectures and made contacts in Greek intellectual milieus. In early November, he gave more lectures in Nice, Lyons, and Saint-Étienne, and on November 17, after stops in Rome, Athens, and Cairo, he flew, for the first time, to India.

India had been the first country in Asia to show interest in the work of the Congress. As early as March 1951, an Indian Congress for Cultural Freedom had been convened, originally in Delhi, sponsored by the liberal magazine *Thought*.[84] The Indian authorities, however, alarmed by the anti-Soviet implications of the event, canceled the authorization and the meeting had to be held in Bombay instead. Nabokov, who could not attend, had persuaded Auden to speak; Rougemont and Spender were also in attendance. The Congress's main contact in the country, and a member of its executive committee, was Minocher Rustom Masani (known as Minoo), a Bombay Parsi who had studied at the London School of Economics and, after a brief flirtation with communism in the early 1930s, had become one of the leaders of the Indian liberal socialist movement, which he represented in Parliament. His prominence as a Nehru opponent, however, put both the Congress and the Indian Committee for Cultural Freedom, established as a result of the Bombay conference, in a tricky political position. The immediate purpose of Nabokov's trip was to prepare the Asiatic Conference for Cultural Freedom planned for 1955 in Rangoon, Burma. But the broader, and more important, purpose was to assess the situation of the Indian committee in the Indian political context, make new contacts, and lay the ground for programs comparable to the Paris and Rome festivals. In Bombay Nabokov was joined by the American sociologist and Japan specialist Herbert Passin, who, after occupying a junior position in General MacArthur's administration in Tokyo, became the correspondent of *Encounter* in Japan and would play an active role in the Congress's activities in Japan.

Nabokov's host in Bombay was the secretary general of the Indian Committee for Cultural Freedom, the Marathi writer Prabakhar Padhye, a "fleshless, wiry, prematurely middle-aged, or rather ageless" man, then in his mid-forties. "His face was ashen under a close-cut of peppery hair, his dark eyes were bloodshot and instead of a voice he had, alas, a chordless, toneless rasp."[85] Despite, or perhaps because of, his propensity to worry, Padhye turned out to be an invaluable ally, "straightforward, warmhearted, scrupulously honest and devoted to the cause he believed in and for which he worked." On this and subsequent visits to the Far East, Nabokov was astonished by the precision of Padhye's and Masani's organizational skills; "everything," he noted, "went according to a prearranged schedule as if planned by Cook's travel bureau."[86] On the day of his arrival, Nabokov met with the president of the Indian committee, Jayapragash Narayan, a close ally of Masani and like him one of the leaders of the Indian socialist opposition. Nabokov hoped Narayan might give the opening address at the Rangoon conference. A former fellow-traveler and the founder of the Congress Socialist Party, J. P. Narayan (as he was called), had partly retired from political life, although he enjoyed vast prestige as "India's greatest moral man," and his support for the Congress was crucial.[87] "So far as I can judge," Nabokov wrote in his report, "Narayan is the only prominent figure on the politico-cultural horizon of India who, besides Nehru, commands nationwide admiration and respect."[88]

Nabokov's first contacts confirmed what he already knew from Aron's report to the executive committee in Rome the year before:[89] the Indian committee was perceived in India as a political, rather than cultural, movement. Its secretariat was housed by the Democratic Research Service, an overtly political anti-Communist organization, opposed to Nehru and his foreign policy, which was at times neutral-ist, and at other times pro-Soviet. Masani and Padhye themselves reacted coolly to Nabokov's request to meet with the prime minister—a request that was promptly granted—because they saw it as a gesture of "appeasement." Discussions between them and Nabokov were at times difficult, with Masani offering to resign if his presence seemed a problem. Nabokov argued that the Indian committee should dissociate itself from the Democratic Research Service; move its central office to Delhi; make sure that the political positions of its members were presented as per-sonal; and, above all, develop its cultural programs along lines Nabokov himself offered to help with. Another topic for discussion was the creation of an Indian Congress-sponsored English-language cultural and literary magazine. Rather than competing with *Encounter*, which already had an audience in India, it should open its columns to Indian writers who, in Nabokov's words, were "in desperate need of channels to reach the Indian audience." It would also counterbalance the openly political, confrontational *Freedom First*, which Masani edited. Nabokov initially hoped that the new magazine would be based in Calcutta, a city whose intellectual life was dominated by Communists or fellow-travelers, and the editorship taken up by the Bengali poet Sudhindranath Datta.[90] But Datta, though sympathetic, turned down the invitation, and Nabokov suggested instead Nissim Ezekiel, the Bene Israel Jewish poet and critic from Bombay he met during his trip and who greatly impressed him. Ezekiel himself suggested the title *Quest*; its first issue appeared the following summer.

In Bombay, Nabokov gave a highly successful talk, as Passin reported to Josselson on November 25. Despite Passin's fears that comments on the "static" character of Indian music might hurt local susceptibilities, the audience was enthusiastic and Nabokov was at once in demand for "more lectures and meet-ings."[91] He met with a number of personalities, the most prominent being Huthee Singh, an Oxford-trained barrister and industrialist who was married to Nehru's younger sister Krishna. Singh, confirming Nabokov's suspicions, deplored the inactivity of the Indian committee on the cultural scene. Through the business manager of Air India, Baku Khote, and his Polish wife, Nabokov was also intro-duced to a few Indian musicians. One who impressed him was Vanraj Bathia, whom he described as "young and highly gifted Indian composer, the only Indian composer, so far as I could ascertain, who writes music in the Western tradition."[92] Bathia subsequently studied with Nadia Boulanger and became a well-known composer of film music.

After a flight in the company of "eleven turbaned Sikhs," Nabokov was met at the New Delhi airport by Stephen Spender and Eric da Costa, editor of *The Eastern Economist*, who had arranged for him to be received by Nehru. It was not their first meeting: Nabokov had been introduced to the Indian leader once, in 1949, at a party hosted in New York by a friend of Nehru.[93] Spender was also a guest at the luncheon the following day at the prime minister's residence. The others included Nehru's daughter Indira, with one of her sons;[94] Pradmaja Naidu, daughter of the poet Sarojini Naidu, the first woman to serve as Congress President as well as Uttar Pradesh governor, herself an old friend of Nehru and the former governor of West Bengal; and the historian Dinanath Gopal Tendulkar, author of an eight-volume biography of Gandhi. Nabokov was seated on Nehru's right, Spender on his left. Nabokov found Nehru "cheerful, charming and friendly."

> In fact, his charm radiated so strongly that it was difficult to resist it. His conversation at the lunch-table, though informal and general, was always interesting and had the quality of an unpretentious simplicity which is so rare in persons holding high public office. His manner is so natural and ingratiating and you feel immediately at ease in his presence. When he asks a question, as he did continuously during our lunch, he carefully and intently listens to your answer. His *amabilité* as a host is gently old-fashioned, it is somewhat donish and yet there is in it also a quality of a country gentleman entertaining his city friends.[95]

The conversation turned, in particular, to Nehru's recent trip to China and meetings with Mao and Zhou Enlai. Nabokov felt that Indira was more aware than her father of "the true nature of the Chinese Communist government."

> In talking of a newly translated Chinese novel she had been reading, she called it pure, stilted propaganda. She told me that she was appalled at the state of seclusion and isolation in which the people of China are compelled to live. "They seem to be completely cut off from the rest of the world," she said.[96]

Asked about the purpose of his visit, Nabokov explained he wanted to dispel misconceptions about the Congress, arguing that the organization did not take sides in the Cold War. " 'This is not the case,' I said, 'we do take a firm position in our ideological fight for the defense of cultural freedom, from whatever side it may be threatened, but we do not take sides in the "Cold War".' " Nehru, who may have had reasons to think otherwise, did not comment. Asked about specific projects, Nabokov mentioned one that had arisen from conversations with Malraux about his *Psychology of Art* trilogy, in which the French writer drew parallels between art objects of different kinds, times, and origins from all parts of the world. Nabokov suggested Malraux's work could inspire a traveling exhibition consisting of high-quality photographs or copies, which he called, after the title of Malraux's first volume, "an imaginary museum of reproductions."[97]

The following day, Spender and Nabokov, introduced by Da Costa, gave a joint lecture in a packed YMCA hall on the problems of cultural freedom. Indira Gandhi and Pradmaja Naidu, seated in the front row, invited them to a Sanskrit poetry reading the next day. Nabokov was understandably impressed with these first contacts with the future Indian prime minister.

> She is a very serious, attentive person, with an attractive, slightly shy manner. I felt that Mrs. Gandhi was by far the most intelligent and thoughtful woman I met in India. [. . .]Without having any concrete evidence, except a speech she made during my stay in India, in which, without mincing terms, she criticized the lack of freedom in China, I have the suspicion that Mrs. Gandhi is potentially closer to our way of thinking about international communism than her father's. [. . .]Stephen and I left the luncheon with the impression that Indira Gandhi could eventually cooperate with the Indian Committee for Cultural Freedom in some way or another.[98]

The Sanskrit reading in Nehru's garden turned into an impromptu contest, with Spender and the Indian poet reciting each other's verses. The episode inspired an amusing talk Nabokov gave the following year on the BBC's Third Programme, in which Spender was portrayed as "Dr. Fender." To Nabokov's disappointment, *The Listener* declined to publish it, as he reported to Edmund Wilson, "in order not to offend the Homintern (and in particular Dr. Fender [. . .], who enjoyed the piece very much)," while *Encounter* turned it down as well, "in order not to offend the Indians, and in particular Mr. Nehru."[99] Wilson responded that "Dr. Fender and the Guru" was "a story that ought to be told—by you—& which doesn't make the right impression when read. [. . .]In print it does sound a little anti-Indian, & also a little lacking in point—though I am sure, if I had heard you tell it, I should have been immensely amused."[100]

As in Bombay, Nabokov, while in Delhi, met with various personalities from the world of politics and culture. The highest ranking, after Nehru, was Major General Joyanto Nath Chaudhuri, Chief of staff of the Indian army, with whom he had lunch, along with Da Costa and Spender.

> He seemed very interested in the Congress, its plans, and in particular in the project of my next visit to India. He promised "all the support of the Indian army" and explained, "You do not realize what that means in India; the army can provide you with a tank, a jeep, an elephant at a moment's notice anywhere in India."[101]

Nabokov also met Nirad C. Chaudhuri, the Bengali writer (unrelated to the general), made famous in the West by *The Autobiography of an Unknown Indian* (1951), who greatly impressed Nabokov with his knowledge of such little details as the streets of Paris or Prague, even though he had never traveled outside India. In conjunction with his efforts to launch a Congress-affiliated magazine, Nabokov made contacts with the editorial team of *Thought*. He met its editor, Ram Singh, a "delightful, sweet person," who put at his disposal one of his collaborators, a student movement activist at Delhi university named Inder Parkash, who drove Nabokov around and whose intelligence and charm delighted him.

Nabokov's Delhi contacts confirmed what he had sensed in Bombay, namely that the Indian committee, notwithstanding the goodwill and efficiency of Masani and Padhye, was perceived in the capital as "a small Bombay group of anti-Congress politicians who oppose Mr. Nehru's foreign policy and who have little relation to the cultural life of India." But he also had the impression that a large section of the Indian intelligentsia was "only too ready to be seduced by the 'siren voices' of Communist propaganda" and ended his report by stating: "If India falls prey to Communism, free culture, free institutions will disappear in Asia."[102]

Nabokov's visit did result in the opening of a Congress office in New Delhi, called the "Asian bureau," with Padhye as its secretary general. But its most tangible result was the series of programs Nabokov organized in India in the course of the following decade.

15

The Rasputin *Years*

SAVE FOR A trip to Milan to prepare the "Future of Freedom" conference, Nabokov spent much of the early part of 1955 at the American Academy in Rome in his second term as composer-in-residence. This allowed him to fulfill the commission he received from the Louisville Symphony. The result was the cantata *Symboli chrestiani*, for baritone and orchestra, completed at Verderonne at the end of November. *Symboli chrestiani* can be described as a musical evocation of early Christian Rome. The idea came to Nabokov when he read about discoveries made during excavations under St. Peter's that revealed some of the secret signs pre-Constantine Christians used to recognize one another. Nabokov selected three—the anchor, the dove, and the phoenix—and built each of the cantata's three movements around one of them. The Latin and Greek sung text is a collage of early prayers, inscriptions found on sarcophagi, and quotations from two early Latin-Christian authors, namely St. Ambrose and Lactantius. The work is thus a sort of symbolic musical reconstruction of archaic Christianity—the archaic reference being manifested in the choice of the form "chrestiani" in the title, a form found on a first-century CE epitaph and believed by most scholars to be the earliest appellation used by Christians to refer to themselves.[1] By the same token, the musical style, though not "archaic" in a strict sense, has a pared down, hieratic quality. Each movement begins with an "Introit," understood here as an introductory prayer rather than in its common liturgical sense (the part of the mass sung before the Kyrie). The opening Introit, in which the voice, strikingly, enters in the very first bar, is a prayer of intercession addressed to St. Peter, who here appears not so much as a saint but as a leader or elder brother—and, on a symbolic plane, as the shepherd of his flock. After the grave, meditative "Anchora" section comes the more lyrical, expansive "Palumba in ramo" ("Dove on the bough"). The third movement, introduced by a mysterious, atmospheric "epitaph" for piano and percussion, is a setting of Lactantius's poem "De Ave Fenice" ("On the bird Phoenix"), a reinterpretation of the ancient myth in the light of Christ's resurrection. The work ends in a climate of intense serenity, with the singer repeating the words *"celestis avis"* (celestial bird).

In keeping with the work's Christian theme, Nabokov has woven into his score references to religious musical forms ("pre-Gregorian chant, Latin hymn [Ambrosian], early Lutheran choral, Hebrew chant, early Greek and Slavonic chant").[2] Similarly, the writing for the voice uses a wide expressive palette—much more so than in any of Nabokov's earlier vocal works: plain speech, spoken declamation, chant, recitative, arioso, operatic lyricism. Some passages are even notated in a manner that suggests sprechgesang, though a note for the performer specifies that these should not be sung this way but rather like the eighteenth-century *recitativo secco.*

Despite its Christian theme, *Symboli chrestiani* is not a religious piece—unlike, for instance, the *Chants à la Vierge Marie* written by Nabokov in his twenties. As he himself explained, "the work is by *no* means ecclesiastical in its mood or form."

> It deals with the spirit of a heterogeneous brotherhood of man belonging to a lowly and despised sect, in which *formal* ritual and any kind of hierarchical organization so far had not crystallized itself. It is inspired by the spirit of non-conformism and dedicated to what to me appears as the greatest spiritual upheaval of man's history—the rise of Pre-Constantinian Christendom.[3]

The work, while remaining faithful to Maritain's basic aesthetic tenets, is characteristic of Nabokov's own spiritual evolution away from any form of orthodox Christianity and the quasi-mystical exaltation of Maritain's milieu. Nevertheless he always remained attached to religious belief and even to some aspects of religious ritual. In the words of someone who was particularly close to him in the later part of his life, "Nicolas possessed a delicacy of soul that only comes with a true understanding of the sacred."[4] Nor did he ever lose touch with the friends of his exalted youth, such as Maritain and Rzewuski. When Raissa's journal was published in late 1963, three years after her death, he thus wrote to Maritain:

> [The book] overwhelmed me with its truthfulness, beauty, intimate friendship. I read it throughout in one night and was profoundly touched to find in it the two fragments of letters she wrote to me. The whole past with those beautiful years, that marvelous house, 10, rue du Parc in Meudon, where I experienced so much emotion, affection, and tenderness, came back to me. After reading the book, I would have loved to take the first train to go and embrace you. Ah, my dear Jacques, what a wonderful person she was, our (do forgive me for putting it this way) Raissa.[5]

Symboli chrestiani was premiered in Louisville on February 15, 1956, with the composer in attendance. The soloist was William Pickett, with the Louisville Symphony conducted by Robert Whitney, who subsequently recorded the work with the same singer. On the same program was Sessions's *Idyll of Theocritus* for soprano and orchestra. "My little 'Symbols,'" the visibly satisfied composer reported to the Parisian *congressisti* a few days later from Cincinnati, "had what could be called a small triumph. The audience gave me a standing ovation, shouting 'encore, encore.' The orchestra played well but the singer, alas, was a little less than first-rate."[6] To Stravinsky, the work's dedicatee, he reported "a thundering success."[7] *Symboli chrestiani* was frequently heard, and always well received, in the following years. Nabokov hoped Dietrich Fischer-Dieskau might sing the European premiere at the 1956 Venice Biennale, under Ansermet or Markevitch, but the German singer was not available. Instead, the fine Swiss baritone Heinz Rehfuss sang, and he recorded the work, under Nabokov, in Zurich in early October 1956. Markevitch conducted it in December 1957 at the Concerts Lamoureux, with Pierre Mollet as soloist—a performance Nabokov was particularly pleased with. Gérard Souzay sang it for his Philadelphia Orchestra debut in March 1959, "beautifully," according to Ormandy, who conducted.[8] Eberhard Waechter was also heard in it in Germany. As for Fischer-Dieskau, he did finally add *Symboli* to his repertory in 1959, although he gave up the idea of recording it with Fricsay for DGG.[9] In the early 1960s, the Russian-born dancer and choreographer George Skibine, a former star of the Ballets Russes de Monte-Carlo and the Marquis de Cuevas troupe—his wife Marjorie, also a dancer, was the sister of Maria Tallchief, who was briefly married to Balanchine—made *Symboli chrestiani* into a ballet, which was premiered at the Nice Opera on December 15, 1962. The following year, Nabokov corresponded with Henry Moore about the possibility of his executing drawings of the symbols for use in a production of the ballet at the Rome Opera, but the project was not realized.[10] In the late 1970s, at the suggestion of Sidney Harth, concertmaster of the Louisville Symphony at the time of the work's premiere, now teaching at the Carnegie-Mellon Music Department in Pittsburgh, Nabokov considered preparing an arrangement for two pianos and percussion, but it is not clear whether this was carried out.[11]

During Nabokov's stay at the American Academy in Rome, on May 3, 1955, the soprano Gloria Davy—who, three years later, was to be the first African American soprano to sing Aida at the Met—performed his *Silent Songs*, composed when Nabokov taught at Wells College, on poems by Joyce, Rilke, and Yeats. On the very same day, George Enesco died in Paris. Nabokov knew the Romanian composer, whom he had invited to sit in his box at one of the 1952 Boston Symphony concerts. In 1954, he had become aware of Enesco's difficult personal circumstances. Leaving his country after the 1946 Communist takeover, Enesco had resumed his career as violinist and teacher, but he suffered a stroke in 1953 and he and his wife found themselves in financial straits. In late 1954, after his return from India, Nabokov visited them in their Paris apartment and appealed to Fleischmann on Enesco's behalf.[12] Münch offered to conduct an Enesco program in Boston and invited the composer and his wife to attend, but Enesco, in poor health, had to regret. Thanks to financial help from the Farfield Foundation, the Enescos, in the first days of 1955, were able to move out of their flat into a small hotel "where they are protected against the intrusions of the Romanian embassy."[13] Nabokov then contacted various musician friends—Ormandy (who declined), Mitropoulos, Münch once again—in the hope that benefit concerts could be arranged. After Enesco's death, Monteux conducted a memorial concert with Menuhin as soloist. He asked Nabokov to put together an honorary committee, which Dallapiccola and Stravinsky agreed to be part of—though the latter, with typical disdain, could not help pointing out that the gesture was as harmless as it was useless.[14]

A project that finally came to fruition in 1955 was the international painting competition, which had been repeatedly delayed owing to the conflicting schedules of the museum directors sitting on the selection committee, Nabokov acting as its secretary. The results were finally announced in early 1955, coinciding with the Congress-sponsored "Young Painters" exhibition which opened in Rome in mid-April and was then seen at the Palais des Beaux-Arts in Brussels and finally at the Musée national d'art moderne in Paris. Among the painters who received prizes were Pierre Alechinsky from Belgium, Corneille from the Netherlands, and Richard Diebenkorn from the United States—a first-rate roster by any standards.

On September 12, 1955, Nabokov was in Milan to attend the "Future of Freedom" conference. It gathered 140 economists, philosophers, sociologists, and historians, who came from a broader horizon than the Congress's previous events, with participants from Latin American countries (Colombia, Chile, and Uruguay) as well as from Cuba, Egypt, Ghana (still named Gold Coast), Greece, India, Indonesia, Israel, Japan, Lebanon, Malaysia, Nigeria, Pakistan, the Philippines, and Thailand.[15] To be sure, some CCF habitues were there: from the United Kingdom, Richard Crossman and Polanyi—who was the driving intellectual force behind the event; Hook, Macdonald, and Schlesinger from the United States; and Aron, Caillois, Philip, Sperber, and Tavernier from France. But there were a few new faces as well: the British philosopher Stuart Hampshire, who became a close friend of Nabokov; the German-American philosopher Hannah Arendt; the Labour politicians Hugh Gaitskell, Dennis Healey, and Roy Jenkins; the French journalist and political scientist Bertrand de Jouvenel; two American "stars," Galbraith and Kennan, the latter having now left the diplomatic service following his brief tenure as US Ambassador to Moscow; and the University of Chicago political scientist Edward Shils, who was to play a prominent role in the Congress's later history.[16] The themes discussed were grouped in four broad categories: problems of the free world; the threats on free societies; the invincibility of freedom; and factors of consolidation in free societies. While Arendt—whose judgment may have been affected by the presence of her *bête noire* Hook—found the debates "deadly boring," Gaitskell told Spender that the conference was "the most interesting of its kind he had ever attended."[17]

Immediately after the conference, the Congress held its general assembly. In his report, Nabokov summarized the work accomplished since 1950. The original Congress, he argued, was born out of a historical necessity, in a tense climate created by the consolidation of the Soviet domination of Eastern Europe and the beginning of the Korean War.

> It was to fight against this climate that the intellectuals who refused to yield to this atmosphere met in Berlin and formed an association of free human beings. It was neither a monolithic gathering nor a propaganda machine, but the real presence of individual wills, freely gathered in a community. Themselves free, they only had in common the will to fight for freedom; to each of them, to each of us, it was clear that we were no Salvation Army nor a club of self-satisfied bourgeois, but fighters ready to judge freely the defects of the society we wanted to fight for.[18]

Nabokov then mentioned the changes in the international climate since 1950—or more precisely since Stalin's death and the resulting "thaw."

> We hear from all sides that things have changed, but is it true? To be sure, travel is easier, Russians are participating in more international congresses in Europe, smiles are exchanged; but aren't smiles, like yawns, reflexes almost devoid of significance? I am willing to believe that in the Soviet Union major changes are happening, but I would also want to know what has become of the Vorkuta inmates; I would want to know, with solid evidence, whether there really exists a living Russian literature, new music and thinking. We cannot accept art, thinking, literature that reflect only stagnation through formulas simply reproducing political propaganda; those who read Russian and are somewhat familiar with the Soviet press must, alas, convince themselves that, while their tone vis-à-vis the US and the West has changed, the substance of newspapers and journals shows no actual change.[19]

In his conclusion, Nabokov touched on the issue that would be the most hotly debated within the Congress in the following twelve months, that of cultural exchange between intellectuals from the East and their Western counterparts.[20] In this respect, he sounded a note of caution, which the evolution of the international situation in late 1956 was to prove justified. The next five years, he announced, would be full of temptations, deceitful appearances, and "smiles in uniform." Dialogue offers from Eastern intellectuals, he added, should not be rejected, provided the dialogue was not with agents of the Soviet government but real intellectuals such as Akhmatova, Pasternak, or Sholokhov and Zoshchenko.

> But we also need to be clear: what are we going to discuss? Will it be possible to speak freely, to criticize officialdom, criticize repressive measures, and demand the free circulation of books, newspapers, and journals? Will it be possible to attack the official aesthetic and political trends that created the stifling atmosphere in which the most gifted Russian writers, musicians, and poets have been living for more than thirty years? Will it be possible to discuss openly what is dearest to all of us: the freedom of the creative person? After the experience of three decades of Stalinism, I would like to appeal to caution before anything else. The habit of lies, the corruption of values, and the perversion of the meaning of words is so deep that they permeate all aspects of Soviet life.[21]

In early November 1955, Nabokov returned to the Far East for his longest visit to date. He first flew to Delhi, where he lectured—at the Asian Bureau on "Problems of the modern intellectuals" and at the Music Society of Delhi. He also addressed a group of 200 people under the auspices of the Office of Indian Affairs and recorded a talk for broadcast by All-India Radio over its European and American stations. Da Costa hosted a luncheon for Nabokov to meet a group of Indian journalists. He had lunch with US ambassador John Sherman Cooper, met with Sarvepalli Radakrishnan, the Vice President of the Republic, and resumed contact with Major General Chaudhuri. At the Industries Fair, he was struck by the size and lavishness of the pavilions of the Soviet Union and its satellites. Similarly, when he met with the prime minister at his office on November 11, he could not help noticing portraits of the Soviet leaders on his desk, as well as a " 'hideous' bear-driven wide wood troika at top of staircase"—a gift from President Voroshilov. With Nehru, Nabokov discussed his plans for an East-West cultural encounter in Tokyo, and brought up again his idea of an exhibition of masterpieces of world art in reproduction that would be "selected, put together, and presented by André Malraux," with parallel panel discussions on historical and cultural topics. Nabokov's impression was that Nehru was "intensely interested" in the project, which continued to occupy Nabokov's mind for several years.[22]

In Calcutta, where he arrived on November 13, Nabokov realized that the Congress was little known, if at all, which suggested to him that the Indian committee should try to set up an office. At the Calcutta School of Music he gave a a talk on "The rise of romanticism" and at the Ramkrishna Mission Institute of

Culture he spoke on the origins of Western music, a lecture subtitled "When did East and West separate?"

From Calcutta, Nabokov flew to Rangoon, where the first Asiatic Conference for Cultural Freedom had taken place in mid-February, bringing together, for the first time, forty intellectuals from ten different Asian countries. Its immediate result was the creation of an Asian CCF bureau, based in Delhi, with Padhye as its secretary general. Passin, who had attended, thought it held much promise and had encouraged Nabokov to plan this visit. The Rangoon conference had been sponsored by the Burmese Society for the Extension of Democratic Ideals, whose president was U Chan Htoon, chief justice on the Burmese Supreme Court—and one of the authors of the 1947 Burmese constitution. Before his trip, Nabokov had contacted the newly established Burmese legation in Paris and had been warned by the vice consul that the chief justice was too close to the government, "too Buddhist," and "not the best channel towards intellectuals."[23] Warning him that the country was in a state of semi-civil war, the diplomat had given Nabokov the coordinates of one liberal intellectual and warned him to be careful in the course of his visit.

Difficulties started when Nabokov and Padhye arrived at Calcutta airport, armed with an *ordre de mission* signed by Nehru, only to discover that the plane they were to board had returned to Burma owing to engine trouble. Accordingly, an old Air India aircraft, reminiscent of the kind "American generals used to fly during and after the war," was found, far too small to accommodate the forty or fifty people scheduled to fly to Rangoon. The passengers left out in the stampede showed their distemper by pelting the plane with stones, then trying to block its way on the tarmac, and had to be dispersed with gunshots. In Rangoon, where refuse collectors had been on strike for two weeks, Nabokov and Padhye found the Strand Hotel fully occupied by a Russian trade delegation. Fortunately, Nehru's letter worked miracles. The first impression of Rangoon was of a "tired and desperate city," with "disorder and despondency in every conceivable area."[24]

The following morning, the visitors were entertained by the chief justice on his motor launch in the Irawadi delta.

> The launch was by no means small. It was the size of a large Venetian *motoscaffo*. It was new and immaculately clean. The central cabin exuded a sweet, gentle scent. Two longish pots of jasmine in full bloom hung close to the ceiling with flowers cascading downward to the cabin's bar. Cooled and cooling drinks were waiting for us at the bar. They tasted of bitter almond and lemon and of spices unknown to me.
>
> The air was filled with strong and virile harbor smells. Freshly cut timber, rice granaries, tar, rubber and drying fish melted into the salty, bracing breeze that came from the sea. They brought back the feeling of life and of life's pleasures after Rangoon's stench . . .[25]

Once in the cabin, the chief justice dropped his initial impassible exterior and turned out to be a charming and cultivated man. He asked them about Auden and Stravinsky. A "suave and shrewd Mandarin," he explained to them that Buddhism was "the glue that keeps us together as people" and outlined the ongoing plans for the 2,500th anniversary of Buddha's birth in 1963. He introduced them to Professor U-Khla-Khla of Rangoon University who, the next day, guided the visitors through the new convention hall and Peace Pagoda erected outside the city with a view to these celebrations. Inside the military-looking complex was the "Cave," containing statues of Buddha and a venerable relic, described to them as one of "two, maybe three authentic teeth of Lord Buddha in the whole world." It had been given, as a long-term loan, by the Chinese. To the dismay of the local US representatives—one of whom explained to Nabokov that the shrine had been subsidized with funds channeled through the CIA—Chan Htoon, described by Professor U-Khla-Khla as "perhaps the most fiery and solid anti-Marxist and anti-Communist we have in this country," had gone to Beijing to take possession of it from the hands of Zhou Enlai. The "holy molar" itself was, of course, not what it claimed to be.

> It was lying behind its glass and gilt structure upon a piece of deep, purple brocade. It was obviously much too large for a human molar unless he were an 8-foot giant. I remembered Malraux telling me that all teeth of Buddha, whether traditionally authenticated or not, were animal molars—teeth that had been used in very early Buddhist sculptural ateliers that sprang up in North India and later in China and Korea.[26]

At lunch with the Chief Justice, the following day, Nabokov met two Baltic exiles, Karlis Tennison, the Estonian Buddhist, and his right arm Friedrich Lustig.[27] He was also introduced to two young women working as "interns" in a Buddhist monastery, one of them a cousin of Chan Htoon. They turned out to be of a more playful disposition than their current employment and shaved heads suggested: on the third day of Nabokov's visit, they invited him to a join them and a young male Burmese who drove them to disused bathhouse, where sex was combined with hashish-based "Bhan" ("like a liquid *crème caramel* with a pleasantly bitter twang to it").[28] The other young woman was related to the liberal intellectual whose name had been given to Nabokov by his Parisian contact. A London School of Economics graduate, whom Nabokov calls "Peter" in his unpublished recollections,[29] he was then Burma's leading Communist writer. Though he later repudiated Marxism, he was jailed when General Ne Win became prime minister in 1958 and was subsequently shot by one of his former associates.

Artistically, the high point of Nabokov's visit to Burma was a demonstration of *pat waing*, a group of differently tuned drums placed in a circle and played by one

virtuoso percussionist. But despite his friendly contacts with Justice Chan Htoon
and the dissident poet, Nabokov felt uncomfortable and out of place in a country
which he sensed was on the brink of civil war and reminded him of Montaigne's
phrase, "*un monde triste et lamentable.*"[30]

> To come as a tourist to a sick country is bad enough, but somehow forgiv-
> able [. . .] (don't tourists go in droves to the U.S.S.R.?). To come as a scholar
> may even be useful and justifiably reasonable. But to come to a sick world
> like Burma, as a meteoric *Kulturträger* [culture carrier], minstrelling about
> the advantages of freedom over slavery, is an imposture, a *Schweinerei*, [dis-
> grace] with Germanic overtones. But, above all, it is grotesque. It is a waste
> of those same "good intentions" with which we can just as well pave our
> own hell. No, no! Never again! . . .[31]

After a stopover in Bangkok ("a curiously mellow dictatorship") on November
21–22, Nabokov arrived in Tokyo on November 23. Save for a weekend excursion to
Kyoto, via Osaka, he remained in the Japanese capital until December 6. Following
a program meticulously prepared by Passin, Nabokov met with hundreds of political leaders, writers, artists, musicians, and students. With a strong anti-American
current among academics and intellectuals, postwar Japan was difficult ground for
the Congress. A Japanese Committee for Cultural Freedom was founded in March
1951 but was already moribund two years later. At the time of Nabokov's visit it was
being slowly reorganized on new bases by Passin.[32] Nabokov was thus introduced
to many of the personalities Passin counted on to resuscitate the Congress's presence in the country: Supreme Court justice Hideo Tanaka; Shinyo Koizumi, former
president of Keio University, who was supervising the Crown Prince's education;
the philosopher Yoshishige Abe, former Minister of Education; the legal philosopher Tomoo Otaka; and the political scientist Takeyasu Kimura. Justice Tanaka,
who had converted to Catholicism under Maritain's influence, hosted a dinner at
which Nabokov met the distinguished art historian Yukeo Yashiro, former head
of the Arts University. Through Passin, Nabokov was introduced to former officials of the defunct Japanese committee. He also took the opportunity to hear
Japanese music and meet traditional and contemporary Japanese musicians and
writers. He thus became acquainted with the composer Sadao Bekku and the poet
Tetsuro Furukaki. His contacts with Japanese musical milieus encouraged him
to pursue plans for a music festival and conference, initially scheduled for 1958,
that would bring together Eastern and Western musicians. He also hoped that the
Malraux-inspired exhibition of world masterpieces in reproduction could be presented in Japan. In the end, given Malraux's unavailability after his appointment
as France's Minister of Culture, this plan never materialized.

From Tokyo, Nabokov returned to India, via Hong-Kong, on December 9. Between the two halves of his visit, the new Soviet leaders, Khrushchev and Bulganin, had been in India on an official visit that received enormous publicity. This did not bode well for the improvement of the Congress's political standing in the country. Hardly had Nabokov landed in Calcutta than he left for Madras, where he visited the "Adyar"—the theosophy center and library founded by Helena Blavatsky—and presented a paper on "The meaning of cultural freedom" at a conference at the Music Academy. Most importantly, this visit to Madras allowed him to resume his acquaintance with Alain Daniélou, whom he had briefly met in the late 1920s. Nabokov was particularly keen to see him, given Daniélou's unique position as a Westerner who, after spending more than two decades in India, had by then become a world authority on its culture. His 1949–54 study, *Northern Indian Music*, had, in Nabokov's words, opened a "new world" for him. The lecture he heard Daniélou deliver in Madras was on "traditional music as a measure and expression of a people and its culture, and on the dangers of new development based not on the culture itself but on foreign conceptions." Fascinated by Daniélou's perspective on these issues, Nabokov asked several questions and, when the session was over, spent a long time with Daniélou "discussing problems of cultural assimilation and the ways in which India's precious heritage might be preserved." Daniélou was equally fascinated by Nabokov, whom he later remembered as "an exceptionally intelligent man, brilliant, amusing, full of fantasy, and blessed by the gods with all the possible gifts but that of moderation." Their meeting in Madras marked, as Daniélou recalled, "the beginning of a wonderful friendship and a very fruitful association."[33] Nabokov asked Daniélou on the spot to assist him with the preparation of the Tokyo Encounter.

On December 14, after brief stops in Bangalore and Mysore (where he met the rajah), Nabokov was back in Bombay. There he repeated his talk on the origins of Western music and spoke at the annual general meeting of the Indian committee. While he sensed, on the whole, that views of the Congress in Delhi had improved since the previous year, especially in Delhi, he left the country feeling that the Indian committee still remained "a small group of people whose influence has not penetrated very deeply into the cultural life of India."[34] On the other hand, he felt on a personal level, as he reported to Stravinsky, that he had spent two months "in a land of wonders."[35]

In early 1956, Nabokov spent several weeks in the United States, partly to attend the premiere of *Symboli chrestiani*. On his way to Kentucky, he stopped in Annapolis to visit his son Peter, by now "a charming, bright, wonderfully American good-looking boy" and gave a talk at St. John's.[36] While in New York in late February (staying at Virgil Thomson's), he presented his plans for the East-West music encounter and exhibition of world art in reproduction to John D. Rockefeller 2nd, who expressed particular interest in the latter.[37] While in the

United States, Nabokov received a letter from Josselson asking him to ask Little Brown in Boston about a young American novelist named John Hunt whom he had just interviewed about a job in the Congress secretariat and who had made a very good impression on him.[38] Born in a small Oklahoma town in 1925, educated at Lawrenceville and Harvard, Hunt had then worked as a schoolteacher while writing a semi-autobiographical novel, *Generation of Men*, which Little Brown had published in 1956. Looking for a change of career, he was sent by the Harvard placement service to Washington and an interview for a position with the CIA with a view to being sent to Paris to assist Josselson, who was beginning to have health problems. Nabokov was, obviously, not made privy to this detail by either Hunt or Josselson, but he liked the young writer's personality and developed an excellent working rapport with him during the years Hunt spent at the Congress secretariat.[39]

Nabokov returned to Europe on February 29, missing by less than a week the New York premiere of the revised version of his *Six Greek Choruses from Oedipus Rex*, sung at the Museum of Modern Art by the St. Cecilia's Club conducted by Hugh Ross. The program also included a work by Lou Harrison and ended with Elliott Carter's *The Harmony of Morning*. By coincidence, a few months later, Nabokov's old colleague and collaborator from Wells College, George Tyler, now teaching at Moravian College in Bethlehem, Pensylvania, asked him for permission to use the same choruses in a planned student production.[40]

Until the first days of July, Nabokov divided his time between Paris and Rome, save for a trip to Vienna, where he attended the premiere of Frank Martin's opera *Der Sturm* on June 17 and a concert of the Leningrad Philharmonic—"one of the best orchestras I have ever heard," as he reported to Elliott Carter.[41] He turned his attention again to the Rasputin opera project, interrupted in 1954. In the account he gave of the opera's genesis in *Bagázh*, Nabokov, while making no mention of Chester Kallman's initial involvement, claims that Rolf Liebermann urged him to find a German librettist, arguing that with its thirty-two opera houses, Germany was a better market for contemporary opera than the United States or the English-speaking world generally. A libretto, entitled *Der Mord* (The Murder), was indeed prepared by Heinz von Cramer, Blacher's co-librettist for von Einem's *Der Prozess* and librettist of Henze's *König Hirsch*. Cramer's typescript is undated and it is difficult to tell, from the surviving sources, whether Nabokov set any of it to music.[42] The fact that it follows the same outline as the completed opera confirms Nabokov's statement that at an early stage, "the general outline and mood of the opera plot were fairly clear in my mind."[43] It was presumably the possibility of having the opera staged in Louisville that prompted Nabokov, sometime in 1956, to resume his search for an English co-librettist and to approach Stephen Spender. Spender's first reaction was apparently negative: the topic, he declared, was boring and vulgar. But his wife Natasha convinced him to give it some thought. She urged him to put off his decision until he had read Fülöp-Miller's biography, which Nabokov left with him. According to Spender's diaries, the two men finalized their plans in Verderonne on July 8–10, 1956, and they spent two mornings on the scenario.[44] As Spender recalled, "what really happened is that [Nabokov] dictated to me the entire action of the opera, with all the scenes, all the positioning of characters on the stage, the outlines of every piece of dialogue, from the first moment to the last."

> He had a concreteness of grasping an idea from start to finish, which would be genius if it went with a corresponding grasp in every note of the music. I just hope that we may create one of those strange mad works in which a Russian genius who has apparently been leading a dispersed kind of life suddenly pulls himself together and writes a near masterpiece.[45]

Spender's contribution to the project should not, however, be minimized. It is thanks to him that the libretto of *Rasputin* is not only taut and arresting, but also blissfully free from any mock-Russian exoticism familiar to readers of Constance Garnett's translations of Dostoyevsky—of the kind mocked by Spender as: "Sergei Alexeievich, will you have a cup of tea boiling from my new samovar."[46]

In early September 1957, in Salzburg, Nabokov showed the detailed scenario to Bomhard, who pronounced himself happy with it and confirmed the terms of the Louisville commission. From there Nabokov went to Italy for the premiere of Stravinsky's *Canticum sacrum* at the Venice Biennale on September 13. It took place in the Basilica of St. Mark's, with the composer conducting, and in the presence of Archbishop Roncalli, the future Pope John XXIII. Afterward Nabokov joined Spender in London for another two-day working session.

As Nabokov phrased it, writing the *Rasputin* libretto was "an exercise in remembering," in the course of which, with Spender's help, he tried to reconnect with his memories of pre-Revolutionary St. Petersburg. Nabokov thus admitted that the partly imaginary character of Countess Marina in the opera was based on Countess Pahlen, a member of Empress Alexandra's household and friend of his mother's, who did volunteer nursing work with her during the war.[47]

> We refrained intentionally (at least on my part) from studying other libretti, not because we wanted to produce something "original," but because we felt the need of being true to our own "vision" of the Rasputin story. Both Stephen and I knew enough about opera to be able to decide when prose lines should replace rhymed poetry and when one should have arias, trios, quartets or other ensembles, how to construct a scene and what kind of *recitativo* to use.[48]

One thing was clear in the minds of the composer and his librettist: they did not intend to write a historical (or pseudo-historical) opera in the manner of nineteenth-century French *grand opéra* and, more recently, works such as Milhaud's *Maximilien* and *Bolivar*—or, more to the point, in the manner of *Boris Godunov* and *Khovanshchina*—but rather a "poetic reinterpretation" of a historical event.[49] This distance vis-à-vis history is made manifest by the generic designation of the characters: save for Rasputin himself, no last names are used in the libretto: Yusupov is called "The Prince"; Dmitri Pavlovich "The Grand-Duke"; Purishkevich "The Deputy"; Lazavert "The Doctor." The nonhistorical intent is also conveyed through the structure of the libretto: although the plot is ostensibly based on what took place at the Yusupov Palace during the night of December 29, 1916—it begins as the conspirators are making their last preparations and ends with the gunshot that kills Rasputin—a series of dreamlike sequences constantly bring us back to earlier events: Rasputin healing the Czarevich; the Prince, Grand-Duke, Deputy, and Doctor discussing the plot on the eve of the murder; Rasputin entertaining ladies of the court and being warned by Anna Vyrubova about threats on his life; a scene with a drunken Rasputin in a gypsy cabaret; Rasputin's premonitory hallucinations.

> We tried to look upon the event of Rasputin's murder poetically and build the drama around its protagonist's powerful manichean character who, in a strange and tragic way, has become a symbol of the *"Zusammenbruch"* [collapse] of a society. It is as if someone was bringing back this story out of the dark confines of a halting and faltering memory, seeing it through the vision of a repetitive dream, at times brutally real, at times dimly crepuscular . . .[50]

The point of the opera, therefore, was not to provide a plausible version of what may or may not have happened (in any case a highly disputed matter, as Nabokov was well aware), let alone to take sides on the Rasputin case; it was, rather, to impress on the audience a sense of the inherent absurdity of history.

> The gratuitous absurdity of murder, the absurdity of people's actions "in" and "out" of history, and the clumsy absurdity of so-called "good" intentions. But it was also about the inevitability of history, about the end of a historic period (those "agonic" last years of Imperial Russia) and the hapless tragedy of war.[51]

The eponymous character thus acquired—as Nabokov had determined from the beginning of the project[52]—the dimensions of a Greek tragic figure: he was not simply "a lecherous healer and an impostor," but a victim of destiny; a deeply flawed human being, not so much acting as acted upon, and an ultimately pitiful victim of "secret forces that circled around him and vied for power and influence upon the last occupant of the Imperial throne."[53]

Much of the music of the first version of the opera was drafted in the summer and fall of 1956, mostly in Gstaad, where Hansi Lambert put at Nabokov's disposal a room equipped with a piano. However, by mid-fall 1956, "real" history caught up with Nabokov's creative progress as well as his cultural plans. The Hungarian uprising began on October 23, coinciding with the Suez Crisis. A pilot meeting Nabokov had been planning in New York on November 18–21 to prepare the East-West Music Encounter was hastily called off.

Despite his cautionary words at the Milan general assembly, Nabokov had been among those arguing that the Congress should promote dialogue between East and West, especially once Khrushchev's secret denunciation of Stalin at the Twentieth Congress of the Soviet Communist Party on February 25, 1956, became known. One of his ideas was the forum of journal editors that took place in Zurich in September.[54] Though he did not attend, he must have noted with interest the participation, on the Eastern side, of his old friend Iwaskiewicz, who had rallied the Polish Communist regime and represented the magazine *Twórczosc*. The secretariat of the Congress was represented in Zurich by Constantin Jelenski, the Polish-born essayist and critic who oversaw the Eastern European side of its activities. Himself half-Italian—he was the illegitimate son of Count Carlo Sforza, one of the leaders of the anti-Fascist opposition and Minister of Foreign Affairs after the war—Jelenski had come to Nabokov's attention soon after his appointment as head of CCF.[55] Multilingual, with numerous ties with intellectual and artistic groups—from Croce to the French liberal avant-garde—Jelenski joined the CCF secretariat in 1952. He soon became a close friend and confident of Milosz and was to play a key role in the involvement of Polish and other emigre Eastern European intellectuals in the Congress's programs.

Despite Jelenski's positive assessment, the Zurich meeting infuriated Aron. Protesting the absence of *Preuves* and the presence of fellow-traveler French intellectuals "of the third order" (Roland Barthes and Georges Bataille, no less), he threatened to quit if the outrage were to be repeated.[56] The Hungarian Revolution put an end to such squabbles by exposing the limits of the thaw and prompting the Congress to focus its attention on providing assistance to refugees and victims of the repression.

For Nabokov himself, the direct outcome of the events in Hungary was a task that occupied him through most of 1957 and much of the following two years: the constitution, under CCF auspices, of an orchestra made up of professional musicians who had fled from Budapest after Soviet troops invaded Hungary on November 4, and found refuge in Vienna.[57] Most of them were in their twenties and early thirties. On their own initiative, they decided to regroup into an orchestra, initially housed in the small spa of Baden, near Vienna, and they appealed to the Congress for help. Profoundly shaken by the uprising and its tragic consequences, Nabokov was touched by their plight as well as by the exiled musicians' courage and determination. Putting nearly all other projects aside, he invested himself in this new mission. Seed money was quickly provided by the Ford and Rockefeller Foundations and the International Rescue Committee. But difficulties, personal as well as financial, soon arose, testing the diplomatic skills of Nabokov, who had to fly to Austria regularly to smooth things out. Some of these difficulties were caused by the personality of the orchestra's leader, the thirty-year-old Zoltán Rozsnyai, a student of János Ferencsik and, at the time of the uprising, an assistant conductor with the Budapest Philharmonic. At issue was the need, felt within the orchestra as well as without, to find a more prominent conductor who could serve as music director and help launch the orchestra's career. Menuhin, who, like Nabokov, immediately took the orchestra's cause at heart, recommended Sir Eugene Goossens, formerly music director of the Sydney Symphony Orchestra and the New South Wales State Conservatorium of Music, a position he had been forced to leave the previous year owing to a sexual indiscretion. Goossens, however, was given a cold reception in Baden. Rozsnyai himself raised objections to Menuhin's next recommendation, László Somogyi, also a 1956 refugee, on the grounds that Somogyi had held official functions under the Communist regime.[58] The orchestra's inaugural concert—which Nabokov attended—took place in Vienna on May 28, 1957, with Rozsnyai conducting and Menuhin as soloist in Bartók's Second Violin Concerto. Despite the warm public and critical response to this and subsequent concerts, Nabokov was concerned about Rozsnyai's failure to take steps toward improving the orchestra's standards. In July 1957, the Viennese conductor Ernst Märzendorfer, principal conductor of the Salzburg Mozarteum, reported to Nabokov that he was struck by the "tremendous heterogeneity" of the orchestra and that the double bass and second violin sections, in particular, needed to be strengthened. Noting with concern that some of the orchestra's better musicians had already departed for positions with bands of higher ranking, Märzendorfer suggested forming a nucleus chamber orchestra of thirty-five members.[59] In mid-August, Nabokov wrote a stern letter to Rozsnyai, insisting that he "weed out immediately the instrumentalists not having the necessary artistic proficiency" and threatening to withdraw the Congress's support by the end of the month.[60] Rozsnyai came to Paris on August 27 to plead his case with Nabokov and Josselson and was granted another three-month trial period. The situation improved when Antal Dorati, the Hungarian-born conductor of the Minneapolis Symphony Orchestra, was contacted at Rozsnyai's suggestion and agreed to serve as the young orchestra's music director as of mid-October. Donating his conductor's fee, he recorded with the orchestra two LPs released by Phillips. However, relations quickly deteriorated between him and Rozsnyai, who remained as permanent conductor. Nabokov had to intervene on another front when his old friend Gottfried von Einem, who served as musical adviser to the orchestra, took offense at a firm memorandum written by Dorati to the musicians. Sending the Hungarian conductor a furious letter, von Einem suggested that Dorati had behaved like a Nazi. "I really don't think you should have said those things to Dorati," Nabokov wrote to von Einem, speaking "as an old and faithful friend."[61] Reminding him that he himself had known Dorati for twenty-five years—their acquaintance went back to the days of *Union Pacific*—Nabokov explained that the conductor's memorandum was intended for a group of younger, slightly unruly musicians who occasionally needed to be addressed in sergeant-like tones. A chastised von Einem agreed to remain with the orchestra in an "advisory and supervisory capacity" and the Hungarian musicians, aware of Nabokov's tireless efforts on their behalf, expressed their gratitude by sending him, as a Christmas present, a scroll with their signatures.

Throughout 1958 and 1959, Nabokov continued to get involved in Philharmonia Hungarica matters, raising money, coordinating gifts of instruments (Menuhin donated a harp), negotiating diplomatic hurdles, and exploring future options. One of these was to find a city that would adopt the orchestra since, as Nabokov made clear to Dorati in March 1958, "the responsibility for the continued existence and future of the Philharmonia Hungarica must be taken on by an organization other than the Congress for Cultural Freedom."[62] Bonn, Passau in Southern Bavaria, and Milwaukee successively expressed interest and declined. Then Nabokov saw by chance a magazine article reporting on an experiment in city planning being conducted in the city of Marl, in the North Rhine Westphalia region. "Among other things the article said that in that planned city will be built a modern concert hall and that the mayor of the city was looking for orchestral musicians to found an orchestra there."[63] Via Carlo Schmid, vice-president of the Bundestag, Nabokov contacted the Mayor of Marl, like Schmid a Social Democrat, and appropriately named Heiland (savior); they met in Bonn on December 1.[64] Following negotiations involving Shepard Stone at the Ford Foundation, an agreement with Marl, which included a German federal subsidy, was reached in the last days of 1959.

A month ahead of the orchestra's belated first American tour in the fall of 1959, for which Nabokov had to find ways to cover a $25,000 shortfall,[65] he also had to deal with a new crisis when members of the orchestra voted by secret ballot not to retain Rozsnyai as permanent conductor. Contacted by the management, Nabokov flew to Vienna to meet with the musicians and beg them "to postpone whatever decision they wanted to take until the end of the American tour."[66] On the same occasion, he urged Rozsnyai to start looking for a different position and offered to help by contacting various opera houses. Despite these difficulties, the Philharmonia Hungarica made a successful Carnegie Hall debut, under Dorati, on October 4, 1959.[67] On their return, the musicians confirmed their earlier vote, but

Rozsnyai refused to quit, turning down an offer to conduct ten concerts a year and a position at the Düsseldorf Opera. Finally, in 1962 he was recruited by Bernstein as assistant conductor with the New York Philharmonic and went on to become music director of the San Diego Symphony Orchestra. As for the Philharmonia Hungarica, following its move to Marl in 1960, it achieved its greatest glory in the 1970s by recording the complete Haydn symphonies with Dorati. After the latter's death in 1991, Menuhin became its chief conductor. It subsequently encountered financial difficulties after losing its state subsidies and eventually disbanded in 2001.

While the Philharmonia Hungarica occupied much of Nabokov's attention in 1957, the year began with a happy family event, which he attended in Paris: the wedding of his son Ivan and Claude Joxe, daughter of the former French ambassador to Moscow (and future minister of de Gaulle). Sadly, 1957 was also the year when he lost the first of his closest friends. Tchelitchew, who had settled in Rome in 1950, suffered a heart attack on Christmas Eve, followed by a double pneumonia. While recovering at the Salvator Mundi Hospital, he wrote a long letter in French to Nabokov, urging him to slow down ("We artists are all too fragile beings, owing to our sensitivity").[68] His death on July 31 was a great blow to his old friend.

Musically, Nabokov was kept busy by the completion of his opera, for which he took some time off from the Congress in the spring, but also conducted the Paris premiere of his Flute Concerto (*Concerto corale*) on November 20, with Maxence Larrieu as soloist, on a program that included Walter Piston's *Divertimento for 9 Instruments* and Milhaud's *Aspen Serenade*, with the composer conducting.

As the Louisville premiere of *Rasputin* approached, Nabokov received warnings that probably caused him to wish he had heeded Liebermann's advice to look for a proper opera house in Germany. As the Louisville Opera Company had no theater of its own, performances took place in a high school auditorium, which had a small stage and lacked an orchestra pit. The instrumentation should therefore be reduced and brass instruments used sparingly. Choral forces had to be limited to twelve male voices. The vocal writing for parts other than the principal roles had to accommodate the fact that they would be voice students at Louisville University or amateur singers. Given the modest staging capacities of the auditorium, scene and costume changes and lighting effects would be Spartan. Last but not least, the work's duration should not exceed one hour so that the recording could fit on a single LP—it was, in the event, released on three sides. Nabokov was tempted (understandably) to call the whole thing off but was restrained by Hervé Dugardin, a former collaborator for the organization of the 1952 festival and subsequently hired by Ricordi, which was to publish the score. In February 1958, Spender and Nabokov had yet another working session at Hansi Lambert's chalet. The chronically absent-minded poet—whom Nabokov, in a letter to Stravinsky, nicknamed "*Tante Bourda*" (literally "Auntie Bummer")—returned to London with four or five of Nabokov's shirts in his luggage.⁶⁹ Finally, on March 4, 1958, the composer wrote to Liebermann that he had completed the score "this morning at 2:31 precisely. Now my dear Rasputin is well and truly murdered and all that's left is the orchestration, which I don't mind at all."⁷⁰

In Louisville, where Nabokov arrived in early April 1958 to attend the orchestral rehearsals, things began unpromisingly. The problems were not all on the Kentuckian side: as of March 17, Bomhard had not yet received the orchestral score, for which Nabokov, pressed for time, had to request the assistance of a collaborator he identifies only as "a Swiss boy."⁷¹ The hastily copied parts and conductor's score were full of mistakes and the first rehearsal went disastrously. When Spender arrived on the afternoon of the premiere on April 16, Nabokov begged him "to expect nothing from the performance," warning him that "Rasputin looked like a head waiter, the room in Yousoupov's palace like a German Bierkeller, etc."

> After lunch we went along to the opera house. This resembles a town hall and has almost none of the equipment of an opera house. Three young men in slacks, who looked like workers in an automobile factory, were rehearsing. Another youth was stage-managing. The energetic German conductor was carrying on the rehearsal. The scenery was drab, consisting of one built-in set and some crêpe curtains, and some furniture which looked as if it had come from a secondhand store.⁷²

To make matters worse, Nabokov was told that works by Copland and other American composers were being performed that same evening at a concert elsewhere in Louisville. As a result, "the hall was one-third empty, the public bewildered and tepid."⁷³ To Josselson, Nabokov described the first performance as "*really* bad,"⁷⁴ but the second, thanks to the energetic Bomhard, went reasonably well. Spender's account, written on the spot, was slightly more positive:

> The performance of Rasputin was better than we anticipated, despite the innumerable blunders of one done on a shoestring, and after only four rehearsals. The first half of the opera is powerful and carries the story forward without any break.⁷⁵

According to Nabokov, "few people seemed to like the opera, and the press (what there was of it) did not like it at all."⁷⁶ Philosophically, he surmised that "it was invaluable to be here and be able to work with the singers correcting stylistic errors and also to see what is good and what is not good in the opera."⁷⁷ A more encouraging assessment was given by the conductor. Granting that the Louisville production of *The Holy Devil* (as the work was called in Louisville, echoing the subtitle of Füllöp-Miller's biography) had been "a turbulent and not entirely happy time because we felt that we had far too little preparation for the type of presentation this work deserves," he assured his correspondent that "this fine work was received enthusiastically by audiences and critics."[78] While acknowledging the many shortcomings of this initial presentation, Nabokov, in his autobiography, made a point of paying tribute to "the zeal, the talent, the inventiveness and the total dedication of Moritz Bomhard and a small group of his collaborators" for carrying the project through.[79]

Hardly had the dust settled in Louisville that Nabokov and Spender started revising the opera. "The trouble," Spender wrote in his diary, "is that the second act is far too episodic, in fact the action is simply a series of explosive scenes. If only Nicky can be made to see this something might still come of the opera, in fact I think it might be really effective. I wrote him a letter suggesting a new scenario for Act Two, from St Louis Airport, while waiting between flights."[80] In this letter, Spender, who left Louisville immediately after the first performance, argued that the second act, as it stood, suffered from being simply "a restatement of the Prince's case against Rasputin. It is Rasputin made to look at himself through the eyes of the Prince."[81] The redrafting of act 2, though agreed on by the two collaborators, proved a more difficult task than they had envisaged, especially since, with their busy respective schedules, they could only work "in snatches," as Nabokov complained, and met only intermittently.[82] There were, understandably, moments of tension, as evidenced in a testy letter from Spender in response to Nabokov's dissatisfaction with his work.[83] As Spender pointed out, Nabokov—similar in this to many opera composers, from Mozart to Verdi or Massenet—had a very clear idea of what he wanted, but was not always able to communicate his wishes to his librettist. "To put it all in a nutshell," Spender wrote in another letter, "I am disordered, of course, you are quite right here."

> But you have not helped me to be ordered about the libretto. As professor
> A.J. Ayer would point out, there is a wrong middle to the syllogism
>> Stephen is a disorderly person
>> Therefore everything he does is disordered
>> Therefore he has been disordered in doing Nicholas his libretto. [. . .]
> And a) forgive me for all my reproaches b) eliminate, wipe out, forget all
> reproaches made by me, which are cancelled by mine to you, and let's start
> with that very English pleasure c) a clean slate.[84]

For Nabokov, there was the additional problem of writing new music and reorchestrating the work. He did so by escaping from Paris at regular intervals: to the Normandy chateau of Hansi Lambert's cousin Alix de Rothschild at Reux, or to visit her distant cousin Philippe de Rothschild and his American wife Pauline, either at their Mouton estate near Bordeaux, where Nabokov spent Christmas

1959, or their castle in the Danish countryside, where he was introduced to Karen Blixen.

Next was the question of finding a theater interested in mounting the revised *Rasputin*. In March 1958, Markevitch, from Havana, reported to Nabokov that he had seen the head of the Opera Society in Washington, DC, and they might be willing to stage the full version; yet, despite repeated attempts, this possibility fell through.[85] Meanwhile Nabokov was in contact with Karajan, now music director of the Vienna Opera. On April 25, 1958, he reported to Michael Mann, youngest son of Thomas Mann and recommended by Liebermann as possible translator for the German version, that Vienna had "definitely accepted the opera."[86] But Karajan remained elusive and, when Nabokov saw him in Salzburg in mid-August, would not commit himself until the 1960–61 season.[87] Nabokov sent the Louisville recording to Guido Valcaranghi, head of La Scala in Milan, apparently without result. Yet, having made a few more contacts at the Salzburg Festival, he was optimistic, at the end of August, about four opera companies being willing to mount *Rasputin*.[88] In January 1959, the soprano Eileen Farrell, in Louisville, asked Bomhard, on behalf of Kurt Herbert Adler, general director of the San Francisco Opera, whether the work was "grand opera enough" for San Francisco. "I told her definitely 'YES,'" Bomhard reported to Nabokov. "The whole conception of the work is such that it would lend itself extremely well for a production on a large stage. Tonight I shall see her again (she happens to be here with the Bach Aria Group) and shall continue to whet her appetite so that she can transfer this condition to Adler."[89]

In the end, the premiere of the revised *Rasputin*, retitled *Rasputin's End*, was hosted—retitled *Der Tod des Grigori Rasputins* in Fred Goldbeck's German version—by the Cologne Opera. Its state-of-the-art theater had been completed in 1957 and its new Intendant was Oscar Fritz Schuh, who had directed the 1952 *Wozzeck* in Paris and Liebermann's *Penelope* at Salzburg.

For the title role, a part written for a classic Russian *basso cantante* (a Boris Godunov or a Gremin in *Eugene Onegin*), Nabokov toyed with the idea of casting his cousin Dmitri Nabokov, Vladimir's twenty-five-year-old son, who was planning a career as a singer. He sounded out Vladimir, taking the opportunity to congratulate him on his recent fame:

> I never told you how much I liked both *Pnin* and *Lolita* and how happy
> I am about the success of the latter. The only thing that troubles me is that
> due to my vagrant, erotic past, people often think that Humbert Humbert
> is a portrait of me! I suppose that the way to profit by it is to say it openly
> and go on a lecture tour through American high schools and girls' colleges
> under the title "How I did It" . . .[90]

In the same letter, Nabokov hinted that, after *Rasputin* was completed, he and Vladimir might collaborate on an opera. "Have you any ideas? Last time I saw you, you seemed to have something in mind—or am I mistaken?" Sadly, despite this prompting, the two Nabokovs never resumed the collaboration that had begun with *The Return of Pushkin*. As for Dmitri, he was still two years away from his professional stage debut (as Colline in *La Bohème* in Reggio Emilia, opposite Luciano Pavarotti's Rodolfo) and he may have felt unprepared for a demanding leading role in a new work. Instead, the scheduled conductor of *Rasputin*, the Polish-American Joseph Rosenstock, who had just stepped down as music director of the New York City Opera, recommended the Danish bass-baritone Frans Andersson, who had sung Alberich at Bayreuth in 1958 and had been reengaged the following summer in *Tristan*. "He is undoubtedly a powerful personality (although slightly on the 'hammy' side), and with a good stage director like Schuh whom he will respect something good might come out. (By the way, Anders[s]on is a good Boris.)"[91] The choice of Andersson greatly alarmed Spender, who had not liked his Bayreuth Kurwenal, but it turned out to be justified.[92]

For the short but telling contralto part of the Gypsy singer, Nabokov first had in mind Gloria Lane, who had been in the original casts of Menotti's *The Consul* and *The Saint of Bleecker Street* and was a reputed Carmen, which she was about to sing at Covent Garden. But she was not available, and Nabokov thus picked a strikingly beautiful, but unknown twenty-eight-year-old African American mezzo-soprano who had made her stage debut at the New York City Opera the previous year in *Lost in the Stars*, the musical by Maxwell Anderson and Kurt Weill. On leave from Juilliard, and in the process of divorcing her first husband, James Carter, she had just been the victim of a humiliating racist snub: hired by Stokowski to sing the Wood Dove in Schoenberg's *Gurre-Lieder* in Houston, she had been vetoed by the Houston Symphony board. As Shirley Verrett—then still Shirley Carter—later told the story, "literally within a few weeks, Siegfried [Hearst, her first agent, formerly with Columbia Artist Management] received a call from Joseph Rosenstock. He not only liked what he had heard and seen of me but had been engaged to conduct the newly revised opera of Nicolas Nabokov's *Der Tod des Grigori Rasputins* in Cologne. Rosenstock had suggested to the composer that I play the role of the gypsy in his opera, and Nabokov had agreed."[93] After Leontyne Price, Nabokov was thus instrumental in launching the career of one of the great voices of the second half of the twentieth century.

There were other singers of note in the Cologne cast of *Rasputin*. The role of Marina was given to the French soprano Denise Duval, Poulenc's favorite interpreter, who had just premiered his *La voix humaine* in February. In a small part (one of the three princesses) was a twenty-three-year-old debutante at the dawn of a brilliant career, the Swiss soprano Edith Mathis. The Czarina was the contralto Hanna Ludwig, and Anna, the Czarina's confidante, the mezzo-soprano Elisabeth Schartel.

Despite these favorable circumstances, Nabokov was full of apprehension when the rehearsals started in early November, to the point of looking back with nostalgia to the Louisville premiere. "The parts are full of mistakes," he reported to Bomhard.

> The German translation is lousy. Denise Duval cannot sing well in German. I am nervous, Rosenstock too. Please keep your fingers crossed. [. . .] We always say ghastly things about the US music life, and particularly as regards opera, but certainly the boys and girls who sang the opera under your direction were doing a superb job, and I doubt that the *Kölner Gruppe* will do as good a job as they did.[94]

Difficulties also arose with Rosenstock, whom Nabokov credited in *Bagázh* for taking "excellent care of the music" but, on the spot, described as "a tired, disagreeable old man who hates Germany and is cordially hated by everybody."[95]

For all these apprehensions, the premiere of the revised *Rasputin* was a genuine success, followed by a lavish party hosted by Hansi Lambert and Alix de Rothschild. "Hundreds of people came from all over Europe," Nabokov wrote to his old friend Kay Halle, "and it became quite unexpectedly a kind of Nabokov festival. Cologne was transformed for two days into some sort of international centre."[96] Writing to Bomhard he was, however, less than completely enthusiastic: "I had to fight my way through Rosenstock's incompetence to a half-way decent performance."[97] "Everything went very well in Cologne," he wrote to Markevitch, "save for the orchestra, which Mr. Rosenstock conducted abominably."[98] He was, however, happy with the singing ("a superb Rasputin") and even more with the staging, "one of the most beautiful spectacles I have ever seen on the stage in a long, long time."[99] The opera and production were warmly received by the sophisticated Cologne audience and the press was largely positive, except, the composer commented ruefully, "for the American press which has been conspicuously absent—why, nobody knows."[100]

Nabokov's opera received twenty-five performances in Cologne over two seasons. In 1961, it was performed in concert version in Paris and broadcast, with Manuel Rosenthal conducting French radio forces. Andrée Esposito replaced Duval as Marina; the title-role was sung by Xavier Depraz and Anna by the distinguished mezzo Solange Michel. In February 1963, *Rasputin* was produced at the Teatro Massino Bellini in Catania, under Scherchen, then living in Italy with his Chinese wife and children—Elliott Carter remembers him, between rehearsals, making sure that they were mastering their German verbs.[101] Despite Nabokov's slight apprehensions owing to the conductor's "bellicose temperament," Scherchen led what the composer thought was an "unforgettable performance," which was subsequently broadcast on the RAI.[102] Delighted with the conducting, Nabokov was also pleased with the cast, headed by the Bulgarian bass Raffaele Arié, with the tenor Giacinto Prandelli as the Grand Duke. He was less happy with the sets and the "veristic nonsense" of the stage direction, which, among other things, insisted that Rasputin be shot onstage and not offstage as specified in the libretto.[103]

Encouraged by the success of the Sicilian production, Nabokov hoped that more would follow. "I believe the opera is now going to be given in other theaters," he wrote to Cocteau.[104] In late 1963 the possibility came up of a BBC performance under Dorati; later Nabokov was in touch with troupes in Washington and New York.[105] But Rasputin was never revived in the composer's lifetime, though as late as 1977 a hopeful Nabokov reported to Robert Silvers of the New York Review of Books that the Vienna Opera planned to do it in 1980. Ironically, the original English version has yet to be staged in its entirety. Reflecting on the failure of his opera to attract more productions, Nabokov subsequently explained it by the fact that the work, like its author, was a "rootless cosmopolitan," cut off from the national traditions—or institutions—that could promote it.[106] To some— Elliott Carter, for one, who saw the Cologne production and much preferred it to Shostakovich's Lady Macbeth of Mtsensk District, which he saw in Düsseldorf a few days later—it is Nabokov's masterpiece.[107] In the spring of 1963, Stravinsky heard a tape of the Cologne performance, alone with Nabokov in his apartment, and, according to Craft, "rather liked it"—no mean compliment on the part of one particularly hard to please.[108] Perhaps Rasputin's time will come in a Russian production—and in Russian.

Rasputin was not the only Nabokov premiere in 1958. In early September, as part of the Berlin Festival, his ballet The Last Flower, seventeen years after its composition, was mounted by the Berliner Ballet company at the Stadtische Oper with choreography by Tatjana Gvosky. The occasion was marked by a diplomatic incident: not having been informed of the rehearsal dates, Nabokov arrived in Berlin too late to attend them. He was further irritated at not being able to take a curtain call on the evening of the premiere, at which he was seated in the mayor's box.[109] Willy Brandt, who had been elected mayor in October 1957, was known to Nabokov through his predecessor Ernst Reuter, but their close relations were still in the future.[110]

Other works by Nabokov were programmed in the mid- and late 1950s: Ormandy performed his orchestration of the Goldberg Variations in Philadelphia in the fall of 1957 and Dorati the Sinfonia Biblica in Minneapolis in late February 1959. The Second Symphony was also given by the Berlin Radio Orchestra in June 1960, as a double bill with Blacher's Requiem.

Along with Lolita, which came out in the United States in the summer of 1958, the literary sensation of the late 1950s was Pasternak's Doctor Zhivago ("your competitor Zhivago," Nabokov wrote to his cousin), which earned its author the 1958 Nobel Prize for Literature.[111] A great admirer of Pasternak's poetry since his adolescence, Nabokov had all the more reason to be excited by this publication since a manuscript of the novel had been smuggled out of Russia by his close friend Isaiah Berlin. The Congress was, naturally, at the forefront of the international protests against the persecution Pasternak suffered from the Soviet authorities as a result of the novel's "unauthorized" publication in the West.[112] When the Nobel award was announced, unleashing an anti-Pasternak campaign in the Russian press, Nabokov suggested to Arthur Schlesinger that he approach Eleanor Roosevelt about sending a cable to Khrushchev in support of the dissident writer.[113] Nabokov also paid his own personal homage to the Russian writer by setting four of the twenty-four poems printed at the end of the book for low male voice and orchestra, for which Liebermann, since 1957 music director of the Nordwestdeutsche Rundfunk, arranged a commission. The poems chosen by Nabokov are the tragic opening "Hamlet," with its comparison between the Prince of Denmark and the agony of Christ at Gethsemane ("To live life to the end is not a childish task"); "Parting," another dark, melancholy song; the short, tender, humorous "Hopbines"; and the folk-like, dance-like "Wedding." Nabokov's setting is unapologetically Russian in style, with melodic and repetitive rhythmic patterns recalling songs by Mussorgsky and Tchaikovsky and, like them, incorporating popular influences. This is particularly in evidence in the final song, which is based on the theme made famous by Stravinsky's *Scherzo à la russe*—a discreet homage to the composer of *Noces?*—and climaxes on a impressive vocal and orchestral crescendo, with a long-held (optional) high G.

While using the original Russian text, Nabokov had French and German texts prepared (credited respectively to Michel Ancey and Rolf-Dietrich Keil), making necessary adjustments to the published versions to fit the vocal line.[114] He initially had a bass voice in mind. In early 1959 he was in contact with Boris Christoff, then at the height of his celebrity, but the Bulgarian bass declined on the grounds that the fee offered by Hamburg was below his usual expectations. No bass singer of comparable caliber being available, Nabokov reset the vocal line for baritone, hoping, once again, for Fischer-Dieskau. Instead, the great German baritone Hermann Prey premiered the work in Hamburg in December 1960, with Hans Schmidt-Isserstedt conducting. Prey also sang the first French performance in Paris, with Markevitch conducting the Lamoureux Orchestra. When, in the early 1960s, Nabokov met the Bosnian bass Miro Changalovich, whom he found "charming and adorable," he prepared a bass version for him.[115] This version was sung on several occasions over the next two decades, notably by Boris Carmeli in Rome and in Madrid (again under Markevitch) in the 1970s.[116]

Pasternak's death in May 1960 prompted Nabokov to pay homage to him once more in a new work commissioned by Ormandy for the Philadelphia Orchestra. *Studies in Solitude*, subtitled "Four Moods for Orchestra," consists of separate elegiac movements, each dedicated to a friend—or, in Pasternak's case, an admired writer—who had recently died. They are not identified by name in the score, where they appear only with their initials. "H. L.," whose memory the opening Lento Assai is devoted to, is Hansi Lambert, whose hospitality Nabokov had enjoyed in Belgium and Switzerland, for the last time in December 1959, shortly before her death. "P. T.," to whom the following Allegro pays tribute, is Tchelitchew. The third movement, a Cantilena with a distinctive oboe melody based on a popular song, marked Andante comodo, is an elegy for Pasternak. The final Andante moderato is dedicated to the Franco-American composer Jacques de Menasce, who also died in 1960. To emphasize the private, intimate nature of the work's inspiration, the first two and last movements contain a concealed quotation from a work by Nabokov with a particular association with the person honored, while the oboe tune in the third movement was one Pasternak himself liked to whistle.[117] The work was premiered in Philadelphia in early 1961 and recorded by Ormandy. It was programmed by several orchestras during the following decade in Europe, America, and Japan, including performances in Zagreb in 1963. In February 1970 Carlo Maria Giulini conducted the work with the Chicago Symphony Orchestra.[118] The Tchelitchew Allegro and Pasternak Andante were also extracted to form a shorter work entitled *Two Portraits*.

16

Disenchantment and New Departure

THE YEAR 1958 has been described as a turning point in the history of the Congress for Cultural Freedom.[1] Its mission had in many ways been accomplished: it had a solid program of magazines and publications; it had organized meetings of intellectuals, scientists, artists, musicians; it had sponsored prestigious festivals and exhibitions. Notwithstanding the criticisms it received from the American Association, which, in any case, disbanded in January 1957, it had fulfilled much of its original political purpose—countering the Communist influence, especially among Western intellectual milieus. To be sure, historical events—the crushing of the Hungarian Revolution, the repression in East Germany, and the political tightening in Poland after the short-lived liberalization in 1957—played a role: in France and Italy in particular, the scales fell from the eyes of some Communists and many (though by no means all) fellow-travelers. But the Congress too played its role in providing and coordinating help to dissidents and refugees, as in the case of the Philharmonia Hungarica. Nabokov, Josselson, and their colleagues had, therefore, good reasons to be proud of their work.

In later years, however, Nabokov came to view the years 1958–59 as the beginning of his "gradual disenchantment" vis-à-vis the organization he headed.[2] He felt, as he recalled, more and more isolated in an environment where, despite the Congress's name, cultural projects like the 1952 or 1954 festivals were looked down upon as frivolous or elitist by the sociologists and political scientists who formed the bulk of the executive committee. His discomfort was increased by a sense that, while being the Congress's main "P.R." person, he was treated as an outsider and some of the main decisions were made without him. By the same token, his own activities within the Congress, especially relating to music, were more and more independent from the organization's mainstream. The point has been misunderstood by recent scholars—themselves usually obsessed with the Congress's sources of funding—who, as a result, confusingly credit to the CCF (or even to the CIA) initiatives that were Nabokov's own and had nothing to do with the Congress.[3]

A case in point is Nabokov's relationship with Stravinsky and his role in the commissioning of some of his important postwar works, such as *Threni*. In mid-June 1957, Nabokov, in a letter to Stravinsky, forwarded, on Liebermann's behalf, the commission by Radio Hamburg of a work ("20 minutes or longer") to be performed in September 1958.[4] Things were finalized in October 1957 when Nabokov met in Venice with Stravinsky, Liebermann, and Alessandro Piovesan, director of the Biennale, who offered to host the new work's premiere the following year. A few months later, Piovesan—who, in November 1957 had commiserated with Nabokov on the death of his old friend Christian Dior—died himself suddenly at the age of forty.[5] Stravinsky dedicated *Threni* to his memory.

Like the *Rake's Progress* premiere in 1951, the *Threni* commission got Nabokov involved in Stravinsky's financial affairs. Within hours after its terms had been agreed on with Liebermann and Piovesan, Stravinsky called Nabokov at his hotel early in the morning, asking him to come to his room at once. Sitting "in a crumpled pajama with a *béret basque* on his head," Stravinsky explained that he had spent a sleepless night worrying about the financial arrangements.

> "Listen, Nika, you must arrange it . . . You must tell Liebermann that I can't write that piece! I simply cannot write it for the $5,000 they offer! They must pay more, or else let's forget about it. I will write it for Paul Sacher in Basel. His choir is not as good as the North German Radio Choir, but he will pay. He will pay more than Liebermann."
>
> I replied that he should not get upset and sleepless about such "bagatelles."
>
> "This is not a bagatelle!" Stravinsky shouted at me. "This is money! I need $2,500 more."[6]

Things were immediately smoothed out between Nabokov and Liebermann, and a grateful Stravinsky invited his friends to a lavish luncheon at which a substantial portion of the additional money requested was spent on expensive champagne and mountains of caviar.

Nabokov also acted as intermediary in the commission of *The Flood* by the same Liebermann, who in 1959 became director of the Hamburg Staatsoper, making it one of Europe's most exciting and forward-looking opera houses. As set designer, Liebermann first intended to approach Chagall—an artist Nabokov himself found personally charming, but whose work he did not particularly like.[7] A meeting with the painter was arranged in Nabokov's Paris apartment. Chagall arrived promptly but Stravinsky failed to show up. It turned out that, after a bibulous lunch, he had fallen asleep. Waking Liebermann up at 2 a.m., he invited him for a glass of Dom

Pérignon at his hotel but refused, in unrepeatable terms, to have anything to do with Chagall.[8]

Stravinsky's obsessional attitude toward money was due, of course, to his lifelong resentment about being deprived of royalties on his three most popular ballets owing to the fact that Czarist Russia was not a party to the Berne Convention on copyright. "Had Stravinky been born French, or English, or American," Nabokov plausibly suggested, "he would have been long ago a millionaire"—if only from the many transcriptions made of the *Firebird* Lullaby. Instead, he spent the greater part of his life in a state of economic insecurity, on the constant lookout for commissions, trying to make ends meet by conducting, recording his music himself, giving lectures, and accepting remote concert tours or individual engagements, provided they pay decently [. . .]."[9] Stravinsky's obsession with money also had to do, in Nabokov's opinion, with the memory of financially strenuous years in Switzerland during the First World War. Nabokov liked to compare Stravinsky's material situation with that of Picasso—an appropriate comparison, given their analogous standing in twentieth-century art.[10] While Picasso, as Daniel-Henry Kahnweiler, his dealer, told Nabokov, routinely made $25,000 for a painting that had taken him anywhere between three hours and three days to paint, Stravinsky was paid $10,000 or $15,000 for works that required months to write and orchestrate. The $20,000 Nabokov had arranged with Labroca for him to conduct the premiere of *The Rake*, a work completed only after "three assiduous years," seems absurdly low in this context.[11] As a result, save for a few close friends like Eugene Berman, Stravinsky resented painters, who pocketed, he claimed, "in twenty minutes what I make in three months."[12]

Stravinsky's financial frustration was compounded by his conviction that, as a US resident, he paid too much in taxes, and this was "another source of his flamboyant anger."

"Oil does not run from my nose as it does from the noses of the Rockefellers!" he would exclaim. "My nose drips drivel! . . . Why should I pay proportionately more taxes than they from the result of my hard work, while they do nothing but collect oil? . . . Why shouldn't they pay taxes for my work?"[13]

Stravinsky's postwar correspondence with Nabokov, when it comes to commissions and performances, thus often deals with tax-related schemes, as in the case of *Movements* for piano and orchestra. On March 11, 1958, still under the shock of Piovesan's death, Nabokov, after being contacted by Fricsay, forwarded to Stravinsky the offer to write a fifteen- to twenty-minute piece for piano and orchestra "for an excellent young Swiss pianist." The commission came from a Zurich industrialist named Weber, who was offering $15,000 in exchange for exclusive rights to the first season. "I am confident that this sum would be tax free," Nabokov added.[14] Even before committing himself, Stravinsky stipulated that, if he accepted the proposal, the money would have to be deposited, in his or Vera's name, on their Société des banques suisses account in Basel ("the question about the tax, as you see, has already been answered").[15] In his reply, Nabokov explained that Weber was "an extremely modest, kind, and cultured man" and that the young pianist was not, as Stravinsky had assumed, a homosexual protege but Weber's wife Margrit.[16] A grateful Stravinsky offered Nabokov ten percent of the commission, but insisted, in order not to attract the attention of the Internal Revenue Service, that it be presented as a fee "for your procuring concerts for me in 1958."[17] Stravinsky's commission for *Threni* was also paid on the Swiss bank account.[18]

Threni was Stravinsky's first composition written according to the serial system, an evolution Nabokov followed with considerable perplexity. "Is it true," he wrote with a mixture of curiosity and incredulity to Stravinsky from Bangkok in November 1955, referring to the *Canticum Sacrum*, "that your new work is a Vesper Service [. . .] and certain parts are written in *serielnaya* technique?"[19] When he visited Stravinsky in Hollywood in 1951, the latter had asked him about Boulez's debut concert in New York and, after hearing Nabokov's (indirect) report that "the hall was only half-full, that the public did not seem to like the music, and that the press reviews were largely negative," Stravinsky, visibly delighted, had opened a bottle of champagne to toast "*l'insuccès de Boulez*." At lunch afterward, he "talked about the nuisance of all those Serialist 'green geese' in Europe, about the cul-de-sac in which they were losing themselves, and about their lack of freedom in 'playing with music matter' as he himself used to do."[20] Stravinsky heard Boulez perform his *Structures* for two pianos at Nabokov's 1952 Paris Festival and attended one of the *Musique concrète* concerts that included a Boulez piece ("endless pieces whose substance was a melange of sounds and noises").[21] His opinion of Boulez improved after the younger composer was introduced to him at Virgil Thomson's New York apartment in December 1952, and, especially, after Boulez visited him in Hollywood in 1957. In his autobiography, Nabokov evokes a luncheon with Stravinsky and Boulez in Paris, possibly at the time of the Paris premiere of *Threni* in November 1958. After the meal he and Stravinsky went to Boulez's "tiny walk-up flat" and Boulez explained to Stravinsky "how to play an 'aleatoric' piece by Stockhausen, [. . .] whose structure consisted of combining at will one central element with six or eight others for an indefinite duration. Stravinsky stood in back of Boulez with a frown on his face and watched intently what Boulez was doing, occasionally interrupting him with pertinent, eagerly interested questions."[22] According to Nabokov, Stravinsky left this session intrigued and "with the appetite to dominate and make completely his own that new system of composition."

Nabokov himself was never fully comfortable with Stravinsky's "conversion" to serialism, which he compared to reversals of alliance in seventeenth-century European diplomacy.[23] He interpreted it as a sign of Craft's influence as much as "an egocentric necessity" of the composer's perpetually self-renewing genius.[24] To Ansermet, who complained to him in 1958 that "one can no longer speak with Stravinsky except as servants speak to their master or the faithful to the Pope," Nabokov confessed, *"strictly between the two of us,"* that he now kept his distance vis-à-vis Stravinsky's circle and tolerated it

> only for the sake of Stravinsky himself toward whom, *for better or for worse*— that insipid marriage phrase—I feel a lifelong attachment. It is actually very odd: since the time we became friends—and this took many years—I have only experienced personal kindness from Stravinsky. I know, on the other hand, that he can be very difficult with his friends, though I have the impression that he has considerably mellowed with age, and has become, in general, kinder and more understanding. Alas, the entourage is disappointing from many points of view.[25]

As their correspondence and Craft's own testimony show, Nabokov and Craft remained on amicable terms, despite an occasional testy exchange when Nabokov felt that Craft intruded on arrangements he had made.[26] But it is impossible not to detect a trace of resentment on the part of Nabokov, who felt that, under Craft's influence, Stravinsky had turned away from the musical aesthetics he and Nabokov had previously shared. "He never again spoke to me about my own music," Nabokov noted, with obvious disappointment, since before 1950, as we have seen, Stravinsky had expressed interest in his works and even recommended them to publishers and musicians.[27] As Craft confirms, this lack of communication over musical matters "created a certain strain."[28] Nabokov himself refrained from discussing Stravinsky's recent compositions with his old friend, even when he had been involved in the commission. "We talked about a million things, we laughed together, we ate and drank together, I listened to most of his new music at rehearsals, but he never asked my opinion of it. It was as if we had tacitly agreed to avoid some corpse in a closet."[29]

When Robert Craft's *Conversations with Igor Stravinsky* came out in 1959, Stravinsky gave Nabokov a copy and shortly afterward asked him what he thought of the book.

> I remember I answered *du tac au tac*: "Igor Fedorovich," I said, "I did not read the book nor will I read it. I never read books about you before, except your own *Musical Poetics*, and your autobiography, but nothing else."
> Stravinsky frowned. "But why?" he asked. "What is your reason for it?"

"Well," I answered, "I know you for a long time and have my own memories of you which I cherish. I remember them as tenderly as I possibly can. This book of yours and Bob's may, I'm afraid, confuse or mar my own memories so that at the end I will not know which are my own memories and which came to me from this book of Dialogues between you and Bob."[30]

A few days later, Stravinsky told Nabokov that he had not been happy with what he had told him but there would be no hard feelings ("or at least not *very* hard").

Stravinsky conducted the premiere of *Threni* in the Scuola Grande di San Rocco on September 23, 1958. Among the soloists was the young Marilyn Horne, who had already taken part in the premiere of *Canticum sacrum* the year before, and who recalls a flirtatious Nabokov taking her on a gondola ride.[31] The *Threni* premiere was preceded by a Congress-sponsored one-week seminar at the Cini Foundation on the subject of "Tradition and change in Music." Nabokov's intention was to involve writers, philosophers, and scientists in addition to musicians and musicologists. He contacted Auden, who accepted, as well as Adorno, Huxley, and Malraux, all of whom declined. Turning to Craft for suggestions, Nabokov ruled out Camus ("he does not understand anything about music") and Mauriac ("as you know, an inaudible lecturer").[32] The meeting gathered some of the usual participants: Goldbeck, Liebermann, Malipiero, the French critic Claude Rostand, Stuckenschmidt, and Thomson (who fell sick and was unable to deliver his paper). But there were also a few new faces, such as the writer and critic Guido Piovene and the Romanian-born composer Roman Vlad, then director of the Academia Filarmonica in Rome and author of the volume *Modernità and tradizione nella musica contemporanea*. Above all, the Venice seminar provided Nabokov with an opportunity to invite Daniélou, then still in India as a member of the Institut français d'indologie in Pondicherry. While not strictly the beginning of the Congress's involvement with non-Western musical traditions, Daniélou's participation was one of the first steps towards the establishment of the Institute for Comparative Music Studies he was subsequently invited to head in Berlin, and which, much later, found its permanent home within the Cini Foundation.

Possibly spurred by a letter from Fleischmann, who regretted that the Congress, though doing "a fine job politically," was not doing enough culturally ("and by this I mean *the arts*"),[33] Nabokov gave the involvement of professionals from the arts in the activities of the Congress a more official form in 1959 by constituting arts and music committees. The former consisted of museum directors—such as Cassou, Sweeney, Robert Giron from the Palais des Beaux-Arts in Brussels, Leopold Reidemeister, head of the Berlin State Museums—and art critics and historians, like Herbert Read and Malraux's close collaborator Georges Salles.

By then, however, Nabokov delegated most issues relating to the fine arts to his collaborator Ruby d'Arschot.

On the music committee were several of Nabokov's closest allies—Blacher, Goldbeck, Labroca, Liebermann, Rostand, Thomson—as well as a few well-known and influential personalities of the music world, such as Bernstein, Lord Harewood, and Ian Hunter, Harewood's predecessor as head of the Edinburgh Festival and now in charge of the Harold Holt concert agency. Carter too was apparently considered, either at Nabokov's initiative or with his support, but for some reason was not invited or declined to join.[34]

Nabokov did not, however, limit his activities to the music sector. In 1959, he was approached by two of Tolstoy's descendants, his great-grandson, Serge Tolstoy—a Paris resident—and granddaughter Tatiana Soukhotine-Tolstoi Albertini, about organizing an international conference to commemorate the fiftieth anniversary of the death of the Russian novelist. The preparation was handled by Nabokov with a small organizing committee: in addition to Serge Tolstoy (who rapidly got on his nerves), it included Isaiah Berlin, the French poet and future Académie française member Pierre Emmanuel, who had just joined the Congress's secretariat, and the literary scholar Vittore Branca, secretary general of the Cini Foundation. A large sponsoring committee was also formed, with names of Western writers as diverse as Auden, Berlin, Blixen, Caillois, Dos Passos, E. M. Forster, Huxley, Jaspers, Maritain, Mauriac, Victoria Ocampo, Leopold Sedar Senghor, J. B. Priestley, Henri Troyat, and Richard Wright. (The last named was already seriously ill—he died in November 1960—and was not able to attend.)[35] But Nabokov was no less keen to involve participants from the Eastern Bloc, and especially Russia. For fear of antagonizing the Soviet authorities, he vetoed the participation of people like his former brother-in-law John Shakhovskoy ("who speaks much too much on the *Amerikansky Golos* [Voice of America]," Nabokov wrote to Berlin), Koestler (whose name was "unpronounceable" in the presence of Russians), and even François Bondy, the editor of *Preuves*, because of the magazine's official anti-Communist line. Above all, Nabokov hoped to secure the participation of Pasternak, who in July 1959 was allowed to visit Paris, as Nabokov reported to Berlin.

> The *ci-devant* Pasternak appeared here a couple of weeks ago, called Serge Tolstoy and Mme de Proyart [French Slavicist and Pasternak specialist, who took part in the Venice event], was received by both *à bras ouverts*, ate and drank a lot, was cheerful and said that "they" know already that something has been planned in Venice, that all of them are dying to go and are expecting before they die most anxiously invitations.[36]

Pasternak's death on May 30, 1960, dashed Nabokov's hopes. Unsuccessful attempts were then made to approach Bulgakov. Nabokov was luckier with Nikolai

Gusev, the last surviving secretary of Tolstoy, who accepted, though his health prevented him from traveling to Venice. Among other names considered from Communist countries were the famous Hungarian Marxist critic György Lukacs and the Polish novelist Jerzy Andrzejewski ("Alpha" in Milosz's *The Captive Mind*), but both declined.

Odd though Venice may have been as a venue, as Isaiah Berlin gleefully pointed out—"a town that Tolstoy cordially loathed, regarded as a home of vice and luxury and never visited"—[37] the commemoration, if described by Berlin as "peculiar," was a success, not least from a political point of view: for the first time, a Russian delegation was involved in a Congress-sponsored event, despite the presence of Russian emigre writers, like Marc Slonim—not to mention that of Nabokov himself.[38] The sessions were held in the refectory of the monastery on the island of St. George. The Western participation was stellar, with John Bayley, Lord David Cecil, Dos Passos, Kennan, Madariaga, Moravia, Iris Murdoch, and Herbert Read in attendance. Nor was the East neglected, with two of India's most distinguished novelists, Raja Rao and R. K. Narayan. Perhaps the most incongruous presence—though one that actually made sense from a Tolstoyan perspective—was that of Abbé Pierre, the charismatic Catholic priest who had risen to enormous celebrity in France because of his activism on behalf of refugees and the homeless. As reported by Berlin, the Abbé Pierre gave "a rather moving address," albeit one at odds with the Congress's central tenet: "[He] talked about love and explained that according to Tolstoy freedom was not an end in itself, but that its value depended upon the purposes with which it was used—this [. . .] was vigorously taken up by the Soviet delegation, which found itself as usual in a clerical alliance against the last surviving defenders of individual liberty."[39] In his own summation of the event, Kennan recalled that when he heard Tolstoy's great-grandson talking about the family during the final session, it occurred to him that

> the figure of the old Tolstoy himself, with his massive literary and moral authority, was one of the few images imposing enough to bridge even the overriding ideological conflict of our day: neither side could afford to disown him—both of us had to do our obeisance to him and claim him for our own—a sure sign that there were things in life more fundamental than the differences between communism and capitalism.[40]

Among the younger American participants in the Tolstoy commemoration was the critic George Steiner, then teaching at Princeton, who had just published his *Tolstoy or Dostoevsky: An Essay in Contrast*. Steiner's meeting with Nabokov led to an abortive collaboration on an opera, of which only the scenario was written.[41] As the title indicates, *Alkestis in Monte-Carlo* was a Cocteau-like modern retelling of the ancient Greek myth, with an additional twist in that one of the characters is an impresario obviously modeled on Diaghilev. The hero is a rich Russian prince who is also a pathological gambler. He sponsors a ballet, *The Fire-Fly* (the allusion to *The Firebird* hardly needs pointing out), starring his mistress, a dancer named Berislova. But the Prince's health suddenly deteriorates, prompting him to wish, like Admetes in the Greek myth, that someone else would die in his stead. The Princess, his wife, accepts, despite his pleadings. She then leaves and goes on a car ride on the corniche road overlooking the Mediterranean. The next scene is an interlude, taking place after the car has crashed. Next to the wreck of the car, the chauffeur (who turns out to be the messenger of Death) is about to take the Princess to the underworld. But once she confesses she had offered her life for the Prince, he refuses to take her: "Death will have none of you. Those who come to him gladly mock his power." Act 3 takes place a few weeks later, on the first night of *The Fire-Fly*. The Princess has recovered from the accident, in which we learn that the chauffeur alone was killed, and the Prince has broken up with Berislova. But the Princess is no longer the same. The gods, she explains, "have taken part of me for their own." The Prince wants her to forgive him, suggests they return to Russia. But it is as if there were now an invisible wall between them. "So this is my damnation," says the Prince. "To lose you when I had at last found you. To lose all when I thought I had won." The Princess leaves the stage. The impresario's impatient voice is heard outside, begging the Prince to join him at the theater. Before leaving, the Prince calls his wife's name three times, but there is no answer.

Alkestis in Monte-Carlo is one of several tantalizing operatic projects Nabokov left unrealized. Sending him the detailed outline "as a Christmas present" on December 24, 1960, Steiner, while hoping that 1961 would be *"l'année d'Alceste,"* was already worrying about not having had any news and the chances of having the work commissioned. Was Nabokov too preoccupied at the time with the fate of *Rasputin*, or simply too busy with his Congress responsibilities? Did he fear Stravinsky might take offense at the allusion to *The Firebird*? No surviving documentation supplies an answer.

Another such project, which occupied Nabokov for some time in 1962, was an opera based on Evelyn Waugh's 1957 novel *The Ordeal of Gilbert Pinfold*, whose subject is the drug- and alcohol-induced hallucinations suffered by a middle-aged Catholic novelist. Anna Kallin, to whom Nabokov first mentioned the idea, suggested Christopher Sykes as librettist. Sykes, with whom Nabokov was slightly acquainted, was a friend of Waugh—as well as his future biographer. "I saw Evelyn Waugh last week," he reported to Nabokov on March 30, "and told him that I had this proposal to act as librettist for a Pinfold opera by yourself."

> After repeating his suggestion that he could sing the title role himself (basso profundissimo), he suddenly agreed to everything I asked, and said that you and I could have complete liberty as regards text, making only

one condition, that he should be given a box in Covent Garden for the first night, complete with drawing room "with coal fire!" Without any authority, I immediately agreed to this most sensible demand![42]

On April 30, Raimund von Hoffmannsthal arranged a dinner in London for Waugh to meet Nabokov (duly reminding his friend that Waugh was extremely particular about every guest wearing white tie in the evening).[43] At the end of May Nabokov mentioned the project in an interview he gave to a Ljubljana newspaper. In June and July, the two collaborators exchanged ideas about the scenario of act 1 and met in Paris. After that, the project petered out. "Are you still interested in the Pinfold opera?" Sykes hopefully wrote to Nabokov in March of the following year.[44]

In June 1960, the Congress for Cultural Freedom had solemnly feted its tenth anniversary with a large international gathering in Berlin, the site of its birth in 1950. Opened by Willy Brandt, the commemoration included a homage to his predecessor Ernst Reuter, host of the 1950 Congress, who had died in 1953, and Nabokov was part of the delegation that laid a wreath on his tomb. While mostly Western, the participation—118 Europeans, ninety-five non-Europeans, including thirty-four Americans—reflected the organization's worldwide presence. Four working groups were formed. Nabokov chaired the one on the arts, which held four consecutive sessions devoted respectively to painting and the art trade, music, and private sponsorship of the arts. As Pierre Grémion, the French historian of the Congress, has pointed out, for the first time—and the last, one can add—the artistic programs of the organization were acknowledged as being on the same footing as its intellectual, academic, and political activities.[45] At the end of the conference, a new international committee was elected. Three new honorary chairmen— Theodor Heuss, the former West German President, J. P. Narayan from India, and Senghor from Senegal—were appointed to join the four surviving from the earlier group (Jaspers, Madariaga, Maritain, and Niebuhr). The international committee, on which Nabokov sat *ex officio*, also reflected a greater geographical diversity: next to old timers like Aron, Chiaromonte, Hook, Masani, Rougemont, Schlesinger, Schmid, Spender, and Sperber, it included members from Burma, Colombia, Japan, Nigeria, Paskistan, St. Lucia, Peru, Senegal, Sierra Leone, Turkey, and Venezuela. The final declaration denounced Apartheid in South Africa as well as the Chinese domination on Tibet, criticized Franco's Spain, voiced concern about the absence of Democratic freedoms in Castro's Cuba, and expressed support for the Civil Rights movement in the American South.[46]

By contrast with this greater international acceptance of the work of the Congress, Nabokov received mixed signals in the West, and especially the United States. In February 1961, he visited New York and Washington, mostly to meet with foundation executives to raise money for future CCF programs. In the federal capital, his friend Arthur Schlesinger was now in a position of influence, having become special adviser to President John F. Kennedy. It was, Nabokov reported to his Paris colleagues, an "exhilarating and somewhat depressing visit." While he was received at the White House, where Jacqueline Kennedy gave him a tour of the second floor, on a more substantive level he had the impression that no one was seriously interested in hearing about the Congress and its activities, but only in knowing "who is getting what, when and where."[47] Yet he enjoyed visiting Robert Oppenheimer in Princeton, and, back in New York, gave a reception on February 17. Guests included Aron, Auden, Daniel Bell, Alfred Kazin, Irving Kristol, Robert Lowell, Meyer Schapiro, Isaac Stern, and Edmund Wilson. And he duly compiled for Jacqueline Kennedy, no doubt at Schlesinger's suggestion, a list of cultural personalities that could be invited to the White House.

In Paris, the Congress's daily operations underwent a significant change after Josselson, during a trip to Washington in October 1960, suffered a major heart attack.[48] After a recovery that took several weeks, it was decided he would move to Geneva, where he would continue to oversee the Congress's work, while in Paris John Hunt, who had risen to the rank of "Operations Officer," took over his day-to-day duties.

Nabokov's major undertaking remained the East-West Music Encounter planned in Tokyo. After the initial enthusiasm, the project, delayed by the Suez crisis and the events in Hungary, went through a period of uncertainty. The pilot meeting initially planned in late 1956 took place in New York in May of the following year, with a notable Eastern participant in Ravi Shankar (whose first appearance in Paris in 1953 had already been sponsored by the Congress). In Japan, some of Nabokov's 1955 interlocutors, such as Fukuraki, head of the NHK, had moved on to different positions. Thanks to Passin and the conductor Akeo Watanabe, a new sponsor was found in the Society for International Cultural Exchange (KBK), which was chaired by Kogoro Uemura, president of the Japanese Board of Trade. The KBK's secretary general, Katsujiro Bando, became Nabokov's main Tokyo contact for the organization of the event. In April 1959—when the Encounter had initially been scheduled—and again in late February and early March 1960 Nabokov went to Japan to discuss and finalize administrative arrangements. The first of these two trips coincided with Stravinsky's first visit to the country, which had been planned to coincide with the festival as originally scheduled. Nabokov joined the Stravinskys in Kyoto on April 16 and provided their trip, according to Robert Craft, with "its liveliest, most amusing, and congenial moments," entertaining Igor and Vera with Noh theater imitations and impersonations on themes such as "The Parents of an American Fulbright Student in Florence."[49] Craft noted that Nabokov was "whiter and shaggier since we saw him last" and looked "more and more like Turgenev."[50] It was during this spring visit that Nabokov attended a rehearsal of *The Firebird* at which Stravinsky, having taken a sleeping pill instead

of an awakening one, had to give up. "His arms flap about limpingly trying to follow the score and the orchestra. . . . In the intermission he leans his head on his
neighbour's shoulders and mutters: 'Now let Nembutal do the conducting' and
promptly falls asleep."[51]

The East-West Music Encounter opened on April 17, 1961, with a formal ceremony before 500 invited guests in the small auditorium of the brand new
Tokyo Metropolitan Festival Hall, built in Ueno Park by a Japanese disciple of Le
Corbusier to mark the 500th anniversary of the founding of Tokyo. To emphasize the intercultural nature of the event, a fifteen-member Gagaku ensemble performed three short classical Japanese pieces, after which a brass ensemble played
Gabrieli's *Sonata pian' e forte*. As in Rome in 1954, the Encounter was part festival,
part conference. The originality, this time, was in the combination, never tried
previously on such a scale, of Eastern and Western performers within the same
event. Along with recitals by Isaac Stern, Hermann Prey, and Zinka Milanov, there
was an evening of classical Indian music featuring the already legendary sarod
player Ali Akbar Khan. Next to the Royal Ballet, traditional Kathakali dancers from
Kerala and the Royal Dancers of Thailand were seen for the first time ever outside
their countries of origin; the former had actually never left Kerala, not even to perform in Delhi.[52] Along with twentieth-century music performed by the New York
Philharmonic, conducted by Leonard Bernstein and his twenty-six-year-old
Japanese assistant Seiji Ozawa, the Japan Philharmonic Symphony Orchestra performed works by Virgil Thomson and Dallapiccola and by contemporary Japanese
composers. As in Rome in 1954, a string quartet by Elliott Carter—his second—
caused a sensation. Premiered by the Juilliard String Quartet in New York in
March 1960, it had been awarded a Pulitzer Prize. In Tokyo, the composer found
himself mobbed by autograph-seekers.[53]

Stuckenschmidt, who attended the Encounter and describes it in some detail
in his autobiography, recalled the combination of conference and concerts as
"an indescribable vortex"—exhausting, confusing, yet exhilarating and fruitful.[54] Nabokov and his Japanese counterparts had made sure that the conference part of the festival would be a real "encounter" by inviting a large number
of Japanese and Western musicians. The latter included Luciano Berio, Blacher,
Carter, Dallapiccola, von Einem, Harrison, Bruno Maderna, and Iannis Xenakis.
Sessions had been invited and was tempted to accept, but declined after noticing
the absence of his music on the program.[55] Another American composer who
did accept was Henry Cowell. In the late 1920s and early 1930s, Cowell had been
one of the first to teach courses in comparative musicology at the New School; by
coincidence, he had also succeeded Nabokov at Peabody in 1951.[56] Cowell's piece
Ongaku—a Louisville commission—was scheduled to be performed in the course
of the festival; but it was dropped from the program when Bernstein, prompted
by Cowell himself, decided to substitute a piece by the Japanese composer Toshiro

Mayuzumi.[57] Despite his absence, Stravinsky, the centerpiece of Nabokov's previous two festivals, was represented on the musical programs.

Like the Paris and Rome events, the Tokyo Encounter, which Nabokov came to characterize as "the strangest of all my festivals,"[58] aroused much controversy. It was relentlessly denounced, in particular, by Japanese Communist intellectuals and their allies. Even before the festival started, the music critic Ginji Yamane, well known for his ties with Moscow (and he was subsequently dismissed by the newspaper), attacked the whole undertaking as American-sponsored Cold War propaganda. "I suspect he misunderstood the meaning of the words East and West," Stuckenschmidt surmised.[59] The charge was questionable, especially considering that, Nabokov's personal role notwithstanding, the Congress's financial involvement in the festival was minimal: most of the financial support came from the Rockefeller Foundation. Nevertheless, the political climate in Japan at the time was strongly anti-American, and any kind of American financing was interpreted as politically motivated. The reception by the Japanese press was mixed. The day after the Encounter ended, an article by the Japanese musicologist Ichiro Suminokura, entitled "East-West Music Conference Ends in Failure," deplored that the planning had been marked by divisions between sponsors; that many Japanese scholars and musicians had refused to participate; and that Communist countries were conspicuously absent. The truth of the matter is that musicians and musicologists from the Eastern Bloc (East Germany, Poland, and the USSR) had been invited but received instructions from their governments to cancel their participation as soon as it transpired that composers from Yugoslavia had also been invited. But Nabokov was also confronted with difficulties of a more practical nature, such as finding accommodation at the last minute, with the help of the American embassy, for the Kathakali dancers, whom no hotel in Tokyo was disposed to host.[60]

All in all, despite the political and organizational difficulties and the hostility of a large part of the Japanese intelligentsia, the East-West Encounter was far from a failure. Daniélou, for one, considered it "extraordinarily successful," as "a beginning step towards integrating the great traditions of Asia into the international music world."[61] Admittedly, there were practical problems of communication: Glock recalled that the contributions of Asian participants in the afternoon roundtables "were quite often translated into a language of fantasy."[62] Yet, in Stuckenschmidt's words, "gaps were bridged, and East and West had listened to each other in the literal and musical sense of the verb."[63] In his report for the *Frankfurter Allgemeine Zeitung*, the same Stuckenschmidt concluded that "in spite of all its weaknesses, mishaps, and improvisations, the festival was irradiated by the light of brotherhood, and this was not an empty symbol."[64] Musicians like Cowell were grateful for the stimulating chance to exchange views with fellow composers and Japanese musicians.[65] Nabokov's own assessment was that the event "would have worked a lot better, had we stretched it over a longer period of time and not tied up the conference so closely with the so-called festival."[66]

The East-West Encounter also had long-term practical consequences. It was then, thanks to Daniélou's presence, that the idea of an Institute for Comparative Musicology was first put forward. A continuity committee was formed, chaired by Menuhin, with Nabokov acting as secretary. Beside Daniélou, its members included Stuckenschmidt, the British ethnomusicologist Peter Crossley-Holland, and the Slovenian composer Dragotin Cvetko—one of the Yugoslavs whose presence had angered the Kremlin.

No sooner was the Tokyo Encounter concluded that Nabokov embarked on two new festival projects. The first was actually already on his mind before Tokyo. As he wrote to Padhye in early January 1961, the idea was to take advantage of Menuhin's going to India the following year to hold "a small but very exquisite festival of Indian and Western music."[67] Beside Menuhin, a strong supporter of musical exchanges between India and the West, Nabokov's initial plans were to involve Britten and Pears, the Juilliard String Quartet, and possibly one more singer. The hope then was that the Institute for Comparative Music Studies could in fact be established in India.[68] Nabokov visited the country again in the spring of 1961, when he saw Nehru for the last time, at a breakfast also attended by John Kenneth Galbraith, then American ambassador in India, and his wife.[69] Delays on the Indian side, however, forced Nabokov to postpone the festival project until 1964.

The other plan Nabokov formed after Tokyo was even more ambitious—indeed his most ambitious to date. It was, as he described it then, "a festival of dance and music in conjunction with a conference on the contribution of African peoples to the arts of the twentieth century."[70] As he explained to a Slovenian journalist in May 1962, he had in mind "a festival in Rio de Janeiro dedicated to the composers Villa-Lobos and Manuel de Falla," combined with an international musicological conference in Salvador, site of the University of Bahia. The festival would feature orchestras from Europe and America as well as "ritual ceremonies from north Brazil, jazz from New Orleans, Negro choruses from West Africa and an exhibition of African art."[71] As for the conference, it would gather musicians and musicologists from all over the world, and especially from Western Africa. This was perhaps Nabokov's most original scheme, since its purpose was to bring together two regions of the world where the Congress had so far made timid inroads. To be sure, national committees had been established in several Latin American countries, but their existence was largely symbolic, and the conference held by the Congress in Mexico on "The Future of Liberty" in 1956 had turned into a diplomatic fiasco, marked by virulent attacks on the United States from most Latin American intellectuals present.[72]

Nabokov's first visit to South America, in November 1961, was preceded by his first visit to Israel. In early September he went with Isaiah Berlin, who was involved as honorary adviser to the recently launched Israel Festival and hoped to enlist his friend's collaboration. Jacob Rothschild and Nabokov's old friend Raimund von Hoffmannsthal were also part of the trip. "I wonder," Berlin wrote to Robert Craft before his departure, "what impact that will make on that versatile personality."[73] As Berlin probably suspected (he once described Nabokov as "a *Judenknecht* all his life"),[74] it was a highly successful visit. "Nabokov *loves* it [. . .]: he *loves* Jews, *hates* Arabs, won't go into Jordan, loathed Nazareth & is incredibly sympathetic there," the British philosopher wrote to his wife;[75] and to Stuart Hampshire:

> Nabokov adored it more than any human being had ever adored anything. He kept exclaiming all the time how free he was, how happy he was, how much at home he felt, how he had never felt at home since 1917 to a similar extent, and this communicated well to his hosts, who reciprocated in kind. Even Jacob [Rothschild] was stirred.[76]

"The absence of strain," Berlin told the same correspondent, was probably what delighted Nabokov most: asking, with what Hoffmannsthal described as "the assurance of an aristocrat and the boldness of an artist," to be introduced by President Ben-Zvi at a concert, he was thrilled to be invited to drop by "on any day at any hour."[77] How different from Kennedy's White House, he told Berlin. Not only was Nabokov invited to become another adviser to the festival, but this first trip was to be followed by many more. Nabokov, as he told a correspondent a few years later, felt "really at home in Israel." [. . .] and not only because there are in Israel so many nice old *Russian* Jews (who were the cream of Russia in the beginning of the century) but because I like the people of Israel, because there are no classes, no castes, no social differences, and because the people are forward looking, courageous, tenacious and clear-headed. People quarrel in Israel, but they do not lie so abjectly as our g. d. administration has been doing in the last six years.[78]

Among the Israeli personalities Nabokov met during this visit were Teddy Kollek, the future mayor of Jerusalem, and Aharon Zvi Propes, the Latvian-born founder and director of the Israel Festival. Both became close allies and friends.

After a few days in New York, Nabokov flew to Brazil in early November 1961. He found Rio "surprisingly similar to Bombay in neglect and shabbiness, but grander and *simpatico*."[79] The fragmentary diary he kept shows him in a depressed and uncertain mood which reflected his misgivings and disenchantment.

> When will I be able to turn my back on it all [. . .], hide in a pretty place, and write music?
> Festival!? . . . A) is it the right thing to do here? B) it will be a gruelling, expensive job; C) Financial help? . . . I doubt that much will come . . . For

exhibitions, yes . . . But then there are so many. D) Of course a *successful* festival would mean a lot *here*, but will it not antagonize the other L.A. countries? I believe it will. Will they play ball? I believe they won't. Shouldn't
I go to Argentina? But how? Smack into a general strike. All of this world
will *inevitably* turn communist . . . That's the feeling of most people here.
But, ah! so indolent all. Not my cup o' tea![80]

Nabokov's optimism was not restored by frustrations over scheduling difficulties.
"Everything tends to go wrong in this country," he wrote to Hunt. "You phone,
cable, write, ask for appointments and then you arrive only to find that 2/3 of the
people who were 'delighted' to see you are either out of town, or 'sick,' or simply
introuvable."[81] His main purpose was to make contact with the governor of the
newly created State of Guanabara (where Rio is located), Carlos Lacerda, a bright
young politician with presidential ambitions, who happened to be a friend of the
American poet Elizabeth Bishop, then residing in Brazil, and her companion
Lota Macedo Soares. When he was finally able to arrange an appointment with
Lacerda, Nabokov's impression was positive: the governor expressed interest in
the project and liked the theme. He suggested September 1963 or May 1964 as
possible dates, and asked Nabokov to prepare a budget to include the festival in
the 1962 requests. "He urged me very strongly," Nabokov reported to Hunt, "not
to involve any local composers, conductors or other so-called 'patrons' of music
in the committee (and after two weeks of experience with him here I fully agree
with him) so as not to get involved in what he called 'musical politics and political politics.'" The festival, Lacerda told Nabokov, ought be be "a people's festival," not one reserved for the "stinking rich."[82] Nabokov sensed that Lacerda, like
left-leaning politicians in the West, held the Brazilian Association for Cultural
Freedom in deep suspicion.

Back in the United States in late November, Nabokov stopped in Washington
to discuss his festival project with the State Department and the PanAmerican
Union. At the house of Robert F. Kennedy he heard Arthur Schlesinger lecture
on "the American Constitution and Jefferson versus Hamilton" to an audience of
high-ranking diplomats and politicians, including his old friend Charles Bohlen,
who was about to be appointed US ambassador to France.[83] He then went to
Philadelphia to discuss with Ormandy the possible participation of his orchestra
in the Rio festival. Things thus seemed to be heading towards a promising start.

Nabokov was back in the United States in January 1962 for the dinner given at
the White House on January 18 to mark Stravinsky's eightieth birthday. Nabokov
had arranged the event through Schlesinger's good offices. Although Pablo Casals
had been feted at the White House the year before, it was the first time a living classical *composer* was being so honored by a US president. According to Liebermann's
recollections, the occasion was partly a ploy engineered by him and Nabokov to

make sure that Stravinsky, who had already accepted an invitation of the Union of Soviet Composers to celebrate his eightieth birthday in Russia, would not seize the pretext to renege on the contract he had signed with the Hamburg Opera for the same period.[84] Nabokov had to plead with a reluctant Stravinsky, who was annoyed to have been preceded by Casals at the White House and feared for a while that his wife might not be included.[85] In addition to the presidential couple and Schlesinger and his wife, the guest list included White House Press Secretary Pierre Salinger; Jacqueline Kennedy's sister Lee Radziwill and her friend Helen Chavchavadze ("a beauty, whom JFK monopolizes during the pre-dinner conversation," noted Craft in his diary);[86] Leonard Bernstein and his wife; the composer and Columbia Records president Goddard Lieberson; Marshall Field IV, owner of the *Chicago Sun-Times*; and the songwriter Max Freedman, who died a few months later. Apart from Nabokov, it was "more a Kennedy-circle dinner, with political payoffs, than an I.S. dinner," as dryly noted by Robert Craft—who, of course, accompanied the guest of honor. More bluntly, Nabokov wrote to Josselson that the guest list had been "handled God knows by whom and completely absurdly."[87] On the way to the dining room, Craft recalled, Nabokov made "droll and unprintable" comments on the portraits of Taft and Harding hanging on the walls.[88] At the table, Stravinsky sat next to Jacqueline Kennedy, while Vera Stravinsky (who subsequently commented that the menu of sole mousse and leg of lamb was "a perfect dinner for concierges") was seated next to the President. At the end of the meal, JFK toasted Stravinsky, who, according to Schlesinger, "responded with immense charm." He then proceeded, until Nabokov retrieved him, to follow his wife and the other ladies into the Red Room, instead of joining the President and the male guests in the Green Room—a breach of protocol which, inevitably, was reported the following day by the *Washington Post*.[89] In the Green Room, according to Nabokov's recollections, Kennedy asked Stravinsky what he thought of Soviet composers such as "X, Y, and Z" (presumably Shostakovitch, Khatchaturian, and Kabalevsky), a question, Nabokov thought might have embarrassed Stravinsky in such an "official" setting.

> Not at all. He turned to the president, in his most courtly manner, and replied: "Mr. President, I have left Russia since 1914 and have so far been in the Soviet Union. I have not studied or heard many of the works of these composers. I have therefore no valid opinion."

And the president looked at me over Stravinsky's shoulder and smiled approvingly.[90]
     "When we joined the ladies," noted Schlesinger in his diary, "I went over to talk to Stravinsky. He said, 'Lean over—I want to say something in your ear.' When I did, he said, with a smile of great content on his face, 'I am drunk.' "[91] To Vera's

relief, the composer did not bring up with Kennedy the subject of his taxes. As for Nabokov, he noted with amusement that Jacqueline Kennedy's idea of a White House hostess seemed to be a mix of Dior, Chanel, Saint-Laurent, and Broadway.[92]

In early May 1962, Nabokov went to Yugoslavia to further the contacts he had already made in musical milieus ahead of the East-West Encounter. These included the Croatian composer Milko Kelemen, chair of Zagreb Biennale (which he had founded the previous year), the Serbian composer Dragutin Gostuski, and the Slovenian musicologist Dragotin Cvetko, all three of whom had attended the Tokyo summit. It was, as Nabokov put it, an "unforgettable visit," which the presence of his old friend George Kennan as US ambassador made even more enjoyable.[93] His trip took him successively to Belgrade, Zagreb, and Ljubljana, and in the course of it he made new, long-lasting friendships. To the journalist from *Vercernji List*, the Zagreb daily, who asked him about his impression of musical life in Yugoslavia, he replied: "Absolute freedom of artistic creation—that was the fact I was most impressed with."[94] He made a similar point when interviewed in Ljubljana for the local newspaper *Delo* on May 20.

A disagreeable surprise awaited Nabokov on his return to Paris. On June 1, he felt chest spasms and pains, and an electrocardiogram confirmed that the alarm was serious. "Apparently," as he reported to Liebermann, "my coronary arteries are playing bad jokes on my heart."[95] He was sent for observation at the American Hospital for ten days. "I feel perfectly well and am absolutely sure that all of this is a hoax by those who invented the cardiograph," he protested to Christopher Sykes.[96] On June 12 he attended a concert and reception he had persuaded Suzanne Tézenas, patron of Boulez's Domaine Musical concert series, to give at her house in honor of Carter.[97] Then he left Paris to take a prolonged rest at his wife's house in Verderonne. "I have been in a state of convalescence," he wrote to his American friends Elgie and Cummins Catherwood at the end of July. "I am on a strict diet, I cannot have fun and am forbidden to walk. The only thing I am allowed to do is to drink whiskey." Next time they saw him, he added, they would have to deal "with a slow-moving, emaciated and deeply aged Nabokov."[98] During this forced rest, he contemplated new musical projects. One was a chamber cantata tentatively entitled "The Parable of the Sparrow" on a text by the emigre Polish poet Aleksandr Wat. As Nabokov described it to Kelemen at the end of August, it would be "set for a speaker, a small singing choir, two magnetophones with loudspeakers, a group of four drums, two basses, a cello, a violin, a trombone, a xylophone and vibraphone."[99] Wat, a Dadaist before the war and disaffected Communist sympathizer, had spent the postwar years in Poland before moving to Paris in 1959. He was probably introduced to Nabokov by Jelenski (or possibly Czapski). His five-page libretto, written in Russian, was completed in early September, but, like many of Nabokov's musical projects in the early 1960s, nothing came of it.[100]

Despite having suffered a serious health alert, Nabokov set off to Brazil in late August to resume plans for the Latin American festival, which he then hoped might take place in the fall of 1963. The Congress now had a permanent representative in the American novelist Keith Botsford, a friend of John Hunt, who had recruited him in November 1961. A fluent Spanish speaker—his most recent position had been as the assistant of the president of the University of Puerto Rico—Botsford had the additional advantage of a solid musical background, having been trained as a composer.[101] One of Botsford's first initiatives was to invite Robert Lowell to lecture, at the Congress's expense, in Brazil and other Latin American countries.

Though he had pushed ahead with plans for the festival—in addition to the Philadelphia Orchestra, they included a visit by the Berlin Deutsche Oper, with *Wozzeck* under the Brazilian conductor Eleazar de Carvalho, and a ballet evening on scores by Orff, Boulez, and Villa-Lobos—[102] Nabokov was not undertaking the trip without considerable misgivings. In addition to the "exasperating conditions" he had experienced the year before, he was rightly alarmed by the rising political tensions, which eventually led to the overthrow of President João Goulart by a military coup in 1964. He also sensed that the prevailing anti-American feelings among academic and cultural milieus were not propitious for a Congress-sponsored manifestation. "The climate here," he had already reported to Hunt, "is *absolutely* like the one in Paris in 1952, in Tokyo 1960–61, etc. In other words we will have to face the same attempts at sabotage, intellectual opposition, etc. as in Tokyo. Except that here it will be probably more vociferous and violent and may make things *very* difficult to organize.[103] "I fear," he wrote to Gostuski before his departure, "to find there an economic and social situation of a kind that will prevent me from realizing a 'grand' festival."[104] He hoped, at the very least, to salvage the Bahia University conference ("with a little modern music") and "Black Encounter."

From a personal point of view, Nabokov's second trip started more happily than the one the year before. Traveling with him were his stepdaughter Caroline and his secretary Gisèle Dubuis. He was happy to be reunited with Lowell and his wife Elizabeth Hardwick, old friends from the late 1940s. Along with Botsford and his wife, they all went to visit Bishop and Lota at the house they shared in Petrópolis. Nabokov was "very much taken" with Lota, as Bishop herself reported to Lowell. "He said she was 'an 18th century Russian lady,' then said she was like *him*, and belonged, just like him, to the 19th century! But Russians like Nicolas, and Brazilians, do have a lot in common."[105] On September 1 Elizabeth Hardwick took the boat back to New York. Little suspecting the disaster that lay ahead, she wrote to Nabokov on October 18, telling him what a delight it had been to be with him in Rio and what a fascinating and transforming experience the discovery of Brazil had been for her and Lowell, adding that their reunion had been "sheer heaven."[106]

As in the previous year, Lacerda proved elusive, and Nabokov's appointment
was rescheduled twice. However, the governor came to a presentation by Lowell
before Brazilian students at Bishop's house and cordial relations were resumed.
On September 2, Nabokov and Lowell visited the governor at his villa on the
island of Brocoió in Guanabara Bay—"a mix of the Casino de Monte-Carlo and
the Norman château," Nabokov reported to Josselson.[107] Two days later, Lowell
left for Buenos Aires with Botsford. That evening, Nabokov, who was not familiar with Lowell's history of manic depression, reported with alarm to Bishop and
Lota that the poet wasn't "well at all."[108] Having himself come down with a bad
cold, Nabokov nevertheless went to Bahia as planned, to discuss conference plans
with university officials. His most interesting contact there turned out to be Mário
Cravo, "the most distinguished Brazilian sculptor and connoisseur of Negro art,
who has collected an extraordinary museum in Bahia all by himself."[109] While
in Bahia, bad news came from Argentina. Nabokov received a call for help from
Botsford in Buenos Aires, but his own health and commitments made it impossible for him to leave at once. As Bishop heard on September 10 from Botsford,
who had returned to Rio, Lowell, once in Buenos Aires, had thrown out his medi-
cation and had been drinking heavily, turning his lectures into delirious political
rants. Appalled by this course of events, Bishop insisted that Botsford return to
Buenos Aires to make sure Lowell received proper medical attention. This fiasco
left Nabokov himself depressed and made him even more uncertain than after his
previous trip about the chances of holding a Latin American festival. The night
before his departure, he was able to introduce Bishop and Lota to Raymond Aron,
who was in Brazil with his wife. "He's just like the books—clever, omniscient, a
good talker," Bishop reported to Lowell.[110]

On his return to Paris, Nabokov had to take a four-week rest owing to recur-
ring heart trouble. He took the opportunity to resume work on a book project that
ended up keeping him busy for more than fifteen years. He was first contacted in
1958 by Michael Bessie, then with Harpers & Brothers, about writing his autobiography. A contract was signed in early 1959—with the Berlin publisher Fischer
Verlag acquiring an option for a German edition—and an over-optimistic Nabokov
announced he expected to finish the book in a year and a half.[111] By 1962, the project, then tentatively entitled *The Golden Egg*, was in the hands of the London publisher Martin Secker & Warburg. A first installment, a portrait of Harry Kessler,
came out in *Preuves*, in French translation, in September 1962, with a much longer
version appearing in *Der Monat* in November, in German translation and under a
different title ("The man who loved other people: In memoriam Harry Kessler").
Differing in several respects from the account of the same events published in
Bagázh, Nabokov's autobiographical essay evokes the Russian Berlin of the early
1920s; Nabokov's meeting with Grunelius (disguised under the initials W. D.) in
The Hague; and the circumstances of his acquaintance with Kessler, including

the visit to Weimar and the supposed meeting with Rilke, ending with the last encounter with Kessler in Paris in 1935. The opening section in *Der Monat* (not present in the French version) describes a pilgrimage to Rodin's Meudon house, on the way to Chartres, in June 1926, in the company of Kessler, Max Goertz, and Helene von Nostitz, and Helene's attempt to find, in the collection of the sculptor's plaster models, the bust he had made of her in the early years of the century—only to discover that it was damaged to the point of being unrecognizable.[112] This lively episode earned Nabokov a rebuke from Helene's son, who found Nabokov's portrait of his mother overly *witzig* (comical). Nabokov, in his reply, assured Oswald von Nostitz that he had not at all intended to be sarcastic or unkind to the memory of a woman he liked "very much," but simply related "the facts the way they remained in my memory."[113] Apart from Nostitz's annoyance, the publication in *Der Monat* generated a surge of interest in Nabokov's memoirs from German publishers, while the excerpt published in *Preuves* attracted that of the French publisher Julliard. Yet Nabokov made little progress on the book in the following years, prompting Warburg to demand the return of the advance. "My native Russian is rusty," pleaded Nabokov at the end of 1964, "my English is inadequate and it takes me a great deal of concentration to write a page fit to print in English. Alas, I am not endowed with the language gift, nay, the virtuosity in many tongues as is my cousin Vladimir." Begging Warburg to be patient, he promised to deliver at some point "something which would be one volume of Casanovaesque memories. In other words, I am firmly convinced that I *have* to write this book, if only to put straight a number of things which were said about a number of people whom I met in my life."[114]

Nabokov's second visit to Latin America had dimmed his hopes that the Rio festival could take place when and as planned. In December 1962, seizing as a pretext his not having received any news from his contacts in Rio and Bahia, he decided to "postpone" the planned festival until further notice. As he reported to Gostuski in January 1963, he had become convinced that Lacerda's own interest in the project was "purely for propaganda and political reasons." Having announced he would be running in the 1965 presidential elections, Lacerda, a vocal anti-Communist, had now positioned himself as the chief opponent of President Goulart. As Nabokov correctly surmised, a festival and conference officially backed by Lacerda would have been interpreted as the Congress taking sides in Brazil's internal politics, whereas, in his own view, the festival was not intended to serve anyone's political ends but only the cause of music.[115]

Nabokov may have been further alarmed by communications he received from Fleischmann, who not only had recovered from his heart problems but intended to play an active role in the planning of the event. The Cincinnati millionaire was, as Nabokov reported to Hunt, "tired of sitting, as it were, on the fence, or, rather, 'in the audience,' when we arrange a festival."[116] Nabokov had very good reasons to be wary of Fleischmann's request to be involved: he had recently become aware that the Farfield Foundation was not what it pretended to be. He knew, of course, that rumors about the Congress's financing were rife from the very beginning, and especially at the time of the Paris festival. But then, any cultural organization with American funding was routinely—and, of course, not always incorrectly—accused, in Western Europe, of being subsidized by the CIA. (In 1953, Isaiah Berlin was appalled to hear Harry Levin refer to his "poor friend, Nabokov" as "a shady international operator.")[117] Nevertheless, Nabokov couldn't help being troubled by the persistent rumors, and went so far as to confront Fleischmann with the issue.

> I remember so well the feeling of uneasiness that overcame me every time I used to be entertained in New York during those Congress years by one of those "consenting foundations." I asked myself, looking at its chairman: "Is it really this man's money that we are using?" But when I asked the chairman the awkward question, he would get red in the face and answer angrily: "I'll sue anyone who spreads these kinds of lies."[118]

Whether he was convinced or not by Fleischmann's denials, Nabokov's skepticism was rekindled in the early 1960s when he briefly flirted with Fleischmann's daughter. By then, his fourth marriage was beginning to show signs of wear. Although Nabokov and his wife had moved in late 1957 into a spacious apartment at 6, rue Jean Goujon in the fashionable eighth arrondissement (its purchase, he reported to Stravinsky, left him "flat broke")[119] and she accompanied her husband to Japan for the East-West Encounter, the couple had begun to go their separate ways. At the *Rasputin* premiere in Catania, Daniélou recalls that Marie-Claire arrived late, "accompanied by a Greek friend of hers who, not to pass unnoticed, wore an enormous cast on his leg, which he had recently broken. Whenever the hotel porter was asked for Mrs. Nabokov's whereabouts, he would answer with great dignity, 'Madame has gone out with *her* Greek.' "[120]

Through Dorette Fleischmann (known as Dielle), Nabokov not only had a confirmation of her father's notorious stinginess, which formed an odd contrast with his public facade as a lavish philanthropist, he also learned that Fleischmann had been involved in intelligence work before the war, when he was in the Navy, and that he was now connected with the CIA.[121] Nabokov thus had few doubts, by 1961, about the origin of the funds that came to the Congress through the Farfield Foundation: " 'But of course it's government money, Nicolas dear! My father has been doing this kind of thing for years. It's easy for him, because he's rich and that's the best possible cover.' "[122]

It must have become immediately clear to Nabokov that Josselson was part of the secret financial arrangement. Though there is no written trace indicating if and when Nabokov confronted his colleague on the subject—if so, he would have done it on the telephone, or face to face in Geneva—this seems likely. The revelation, in any event, explains why Nabokov began to take his distance vis-à-vis the organization and its executive secretary. Did he, at that time, share his doubts with Spender, as is suggested by an unverifiable story reported by Mary McCarthy to her biographer Carol Brightman?[123] John Hunt, for one, now believes Nabokov was both aware that the Congress was largely funded by secretly channeled federal funds and not inclined to discuss the issue.[124] In any event, while remaining, on paper, the CCF's secretary general until 1966, Nabokov was in effect, after 1962, involved in its practical operations and programs only in an increasingly selective fashion.

An opportunity, in fact, presented itself that allowed him to take his distance in a literal sense. Sometime after the Tokyo Encounter, in the late summer or fall of 1961, he found himself part of a discussion in the Congress offices in Paris between Willy Brandt, Josselson, and Shepard Stone of the Ford Foundation, on the subject of West Berlin. As mayor of the city, Brandt was concerned about its political, intellectual, and cultural isolation. "Berlin was in trouble. From being a magnet stretched out from the West to the citizens of the German Democratic Republic and to Eastern Europe in general, it suddenly became an extravagantly expensive "prestige enclave."[125] In August 1961, when the Soviets began construction of the Wall, this concern turned into alarm: everyone—the rich, artists, banks—was beginning to leave. It was urgent to do something, not just to preserve the city's cultural life, but to do something new, something sufficiently exciting to attract people to the city. In the course of the discussions, Nabokov made suggestions which everyone present urged him to put down in writing. In his memorandum, he argued, along the lines that had directed his initiatives at the Congress, that Berlin should rebuild its prestige with ambitious cultural programs.

> West Berlin should now play an important cultural game to regain some of its lost cosmopolitan glamour. Furthermore, it was clear to me that in such a game one should try to gain the support and participation of scholars and artists from the Soviet Union and from the so-called Socialist Bloc. In other words, it was my view that Berlin should stop attracting the *political* attention of the outside world and try for its *cultural* attention.[126]

Nabokov's memorandum revolved on five principles: (1) Berlin should offer cultural programs specific to the city but having lasting intrinsic value; (2) these events should be such that they would attract to the city people not just from Western Europe but from all over the world; (3) they ought to result in making the local cultural institutions more international; (4) they should be of value to the young, in Berlin and from the outside; (5) they should also be coherent programs, taking into account existing local strengths.[127] Concrete proposals listed by Nabokov included a theater seminar and opera workshop (geared, especially, towards the commissioning of new works); a television training center; a program of artists in residence; a yearly festival of contemporary music, distinct from the Berlin Festival, and which could program such ambitious works as Milhaud's *L'Orestie*, Falla's *L'Atlantida*, Henze's *Elegy For Young Lovers*, and Schoenberg's *Moses und Aaron*.

Nabokov's memorandum was enthusiastically endorsed by all parties. Stone pledged strong financial support from the Ford Foundation. Josselson, whatever misgivings he may have harbored, viewed the scheme (as Nabokov saw it) as "a good way for me to get out of the CCF, which he knows has become alien to me."[128] As for Willy Brandt, he invited Nabokov to Berlin, beginning in the fall of 1962, as the city's international adviser on cultural matters.

Berlin, Don Quixote, *and the CIA*

THE BERLIN WHERE Nabokov resettled in early 1963 was a very different city from the one he had left in January 1947. No longer in ruins, yet far from being restored to its prewar glory, it was a living symbol of the division of Europe into two blocs. Physically cut off from West Germany, it was now divided within itself by a wall separating the former Soviet sector from the parts formerly controlled by the other allies. On September 29, 1961, Nabokov and Stravinsky saw the wall being built when the latter was in the city to conduct *Oedipus Rex* and *Perséphone*. He and Nabokov were given a tour in Willy Brandt's car, starting at the Brandenburg Gate, where, as Craft noted in his diary, "the barricades, land mines and other death traps are partly, and cruelly and cynically, concealed by flowers."[1]

From an administrative perspective, Nabokov held a rather unusual status. Remaining secretary general of the Congress for Cultural Freedom, he was, as it were, "seconded" to the municipality of Berlin, as cultural adviser to the Mayor "on behalf of the CCF."[2] As agreed by the city and the Congress, he therefore continued to receive his salary as secretary general of the organization. This salary—one-third of it covered by a Ford Foundation grant to the Congress—was raised in late 1962 to a comfortable though not extravagant $18,000.[3] The Berlin government provided Nabokov with a house, rent-free, and put a car at his disposal, while the salaries of his housekeeper and driver were covered by a grant from the city. Berlin also paid for his travel and representation expenses for all matters relating to his work in Berlin, as well as the salary of his assistant Ruby d'Arschot, who followed him there. The Congress, for its part, covered Nabokov's trips to Paris on Congress business, and part of the salary of his secretary, Benita Uckert, and her own trips to Paris.[4]

In Paris, Nabokov was, *de facto*, replaced by Pierre Emmanuel, who was promoted to deputy secretary general. In Berlin, as Ruby d'Arschot reported to Sweeney, then head of the Houston Museum, Nabokov was "a sort of

Obersturmführer der Kunst, living in a palace guarded by policemen, driving in a beautiful Mercedes—with chauffeur—and, of course, drowning the Berlin people in a new wave of ideas every half hour."[5] In addition to the mayor himself, the "Berlin people" Nabokov had to work with were the heads of the city's main cultural institutions—including Karajan, Furtwängler's successor as permanent music director of the Berlin Philharmonic. He also had to work closely with the Berlin Senator in charge of Science and Art—Adolf Arndt from 1963 until 1964, and from 1964 onwards Werner Stein, who kept the position until 1975, save for a brief period in 1964–65 when he was replaced by Harald Ingensand. The Berlin Senate, indeed, rather than the mayor, controlled the city's cultural budget, which could lead to unpleasant surprises, such as the lottery subsidy to the Berlin Festival being redirected, in 1964, to the Senator for Education.[6] Nabokov also had to liaise with the Ford Foundation, which had its own representative in Berlin. By a happy coincidence, this was now the conductor Moritz Bomhard, with whom Nabokov had forged excellent relations since the Louisville premiere of *Rasputin*.

As for the ideas Nabokov showered on Berlin, to paraphrase Ruby d'Arschot's metaphor, the first to be implemented was one of the recommendations made in the memorandum he had submitted to Willy Brandt and the Ford Foundation: a program of long-term fellowships allowing writers and creative artists from all over the world to spend as long as a year in the German city at the Ford Foundation's expense. Among the artists who accepted the invitation in the first year were composers Gilbert Amy, Berio, Carter, Sessions, and Xenakis; writers Ingeborg Bachmann, Michel Butor, and Witold Gombrowicz; critics Eric Bentley and Peter Heyworth; and painters Oscar Kokoschka and André Masson.[7] The selection was made through consultation, Nabokov's "only direct suggestion," as he pointed out to Stone, being the sculptor and photographer Mário Cravo, whose work had fascinated him in Brazil.[8] To Stone, who quibbled about the "caliber" of the invitees, Nabokov, who actually had assembled an impressive array in record time, responded with a touch of sarcasm: "*Of course*, we would all have loved to have Braque, Picasso, Chagall, Stravinsky (and perhaps even J. S. Bach and Beethoven and Shakespeare) come to Berlin. But famous old artists do not *move* easily and readily. Even people of the age-bracket of Dallapicola refused to be 'displaced' from Florence, however much they may have approved or liked the general theme of the programme."[9] Beside Dallapicola, Friedrich Dürrenmatt and Henry Moore had turned down the invitation. Sessions first declined, then accepted at Nabokov's urging. Kokoschka, approached by Reidermeister, had said no, so Nabokov had to go ("*on my own and at my own expense*") and convince him personally. "But was not one of the main ideas," Nabokov reminded Stone, "to bring to Berlin not necessarily 'famous' old men, but fresh blood, fresh talent, young people and ideas?" He brushed aside similar concerns expressed by Bomhard. "When you tell me that the Berliners never heard of somebody, this does not mean anything. We should not forget that Berliners are provincial."[10]

Gombrowicz, who was Jelenski's recommendation, was a particularly inspired choice.[11] Although just beginning to be famous in the West, he was widely acknowledged, along with Milosz, as the one of the greatest of the Polish emigre writers. Born in 1904, he had lived in Argentina since 1939, at times in financially precarious conditions, and, despite his rising fame in Western Europe (and in Poland, where his work was briefly allowed to be published and his play *Yvonne, Princess of Burgundy* staged in 1957), he had never left Latin America since. On May 17, the day after Gombrowicz's arrival in Berlin, Nabokov hosted a party for him, at which he invited Butor and Masson. The year Gombrowicz spent in Berlin was a difficult time for him. He suffered from heart and respiratory problems, the latter not alleviated by the Berlin climate, and was further isolated, as Nabokov quickly realized, because he did not speak German, was unfamiliar with the German intellectual scene, and had long been absent from Europe.[12] Though he and Nabokov never became close, Nabokov was sufficiently intrigued with the personality of the Polish writer, who had a keen, if non-specialized, interest in music, to lend him recordings of *Rasputin's End* and *Symboli chrestiani.* "I have the impression that I did penetrate your sonic worlds and their inner combinations," Gombrowicz wrote to Nabokov; "and I responded intensely to the adventures of your temperament, especially in its cynical, lyrical aspects; in short, I must say I prefer your music (from the way it sounds and in a spiritual sense) to a lot of modern works that, highly respectable though they may be, are dry as pepper and cerebral to a fault."[13] Gombrowicz then proceeded to offer his own "psychoanalysis" of Nabokov. This document is worth quoting in full, for Gombrowicz acutely sensed the ambiguity that characterizes both the composer's personality and his aesthetic perspective:

> I think you are an artistic phenomenon very difficult to assess in its exact value. The difficulty comes from your being an amalgam: you are never "within" something, but always "in between." For example, you are between the spirit and the senses; between East (Russia) and West (Paris-Rome); between music and the theater; between music and words; between culture and primitivism; between art and life, etc., and there always is something in you that is a pretext for something else. For instance, in "Symboli chrestiani" Christ, almost shockingly, becomes a pretext for the artistic effect, the sacred for the secular, and vice versa. When listening to *Rasputin,* one might think at times you are Rasputin yourself . . . One feels you are so close to your doomed hero by some kind of underground demagogy.
>
> Now, it seems to me that this antinomic structure of your personality, which condemns you to be in between realities, cultures, and styles, is

basically contrary to the trends (now fashionable) toward the "purified" and the abstract. But your situation may well be far richer in possibilities. And dramatically more interesting too.

This the way I see you and maybe, my friend, it is nonsense. But as I myself like to be told how I am perceived, I thought it might be of interest to you.

I myself am strongly opposed to "the purified" and to "being within."[14]

Nabokov did try to lure Stravinsky himself to Berlin. He first proposed it in conversation in the fall of 1962, and reiterated the proposal by mail the following year.

Could you and would you *please* come and spend a month or two (or even three if you want) here in Berlin, in comfortable surroundings, in a beautiful villa (overlooking a lake), which the city of Berlin will put at your disposal free of charge? You will have a staff of servants to look after you. Vera will have her studio and you yours to work in.[15]

But Stravinsky did not take up the offer.

Another "star" Nabokov tried to attract to Berlin was Balanchine. They discussed the project of a permanent ballet school in Berlin, for students from all over Europe, which Balanchine would supervise from New York, while one of his assistants would run it on a day-to-day basis.[16] Despite the initial enthusiasm, the idea did not go beyond the planning stage.

Through no fault of Nabokov, the artists-in-residence program was only a half-success. As Carter pointed out in his report statement, it was "an important, new, and exciting experiment in city planning with a cultural goal," but it lacked an "intelligent direction" on the German side, and the participants found themselves "living in agreeable surroundings, paid, and left alone, entirely unconnected with the activities of Berlin's cultural life."[17] Sessions detected "even a certain amount of hostility toward the project itself, from people who are busy with their own *routine* and who resent (even openly) what they call America's effort to 'bring culture to Berlin.' "[18]

Much more successful, in the long term, was the establishment of the International Institute for Comparative Music Studies, an idea that went back to Nabokov's first contacts with Daniélou in Madras in 1955. By the time Nabokov moved to Berlin, Daniélou himself had left Pondicherry and settled with his Swiss companion Raymond Burnier (an heir to the Nestle fortune) in the small town of Zagarolo, near Rome. When Nabokov approached him, another offer—a tenured professorship—had come from the École pratique des hautes études in Paris. As Daniélou puts it in his autobiography, choosing to head a yet nonexistent organization over "easy work, pension, and benefits" was "a typically idealistic and unreasonable thing for me to do."[19] But he was firmly convinced, as Nabokov was, that it was important to make "the great musicians of India and other Asian countries [. . .] known to the Western world," and responded enthusiastically to the Utopian side of Nabokov's Berlin scheme. "Couldn't one make this city into a modern Athens," he wrote from Zagarolo, "an experimental city which would demonstrate, on a social, moral, religious, economic, political level what the free world ought to be, if only to deserve its name?" Berlin would thus become "the real symbol of freedom, the model that would make it possible for nations to make their institutions better. The wall is one symbol, but other, no there are no less sordid walls in every country, made of prejudices, conventions, reactionary forces, which no one dares to bring down."[20] The Institute was formally established in June 1963 thanks to a grant from the Ford Foundation which would run for the first few years until the city of Berlin was ready to take it over. Burnier joined Daniélou in Berlin to set up the new organization in an old house in the residential suburb of Grünewald. The institute's mission, as stated, was "to study the practical means of integrating the musical achievements of Asian and African cultures into world culture and of helping the preservation of authentic traditional music."[21] On its board, chaired by a Swiss diplomat, Baron Rudolph de Reding, were musicians and musicologists who were longtime allies of Nabokov (Blacher, Collaer, Menuhin, Stuckenschmidt) or recent ones, such as Cvetko, while the presence of Bornoff guaranteed UNESCO's indispensable benevolence and cooperation.

Soon after taking up their respective Berlin appointments, Nabokov and Daniélou decided to start gathering, independently from the Geneva-based Association of European Festival Directors, an informal group of like-minded festival heads. Their idea was to create a forum where views and information could be freely exchanged, along with a platform for collaborative projects, such as co-productions and cost-sharing for such expenses as transcontinental orchestral tours. Daniélou and Nabokov agreed, though, that the group should not meet in Berlin, where the atmosphere was too politically charged, but in the more inviting and congenial setting offered by the Cini Foundation in Venice. As Daniélou recalled, "the festival directors were not very enthusiastic about the project itself, but liked the idea of meeting in a relaxed, pleasant atmosphere. Thanks to the Cini Foundation, we not only enjoyed a prestigious setting but were able to entertain the participants elegantly, meet them at the airport with launches or my own personal boat, send them to good hotels, and organize dinners in the private dining rooms of Harry's Bar."[22] The group included Peter Diamond, Harewood's successor as head of the Edinburgh Festival; Charles and Aimée Kettaneh from Lebanon, for the Baalbeck Festival; Labroca for the Venice Biennale; and A. Z. Propes for the Festival of Israel. It was joined, from time to time, by representatives from the Aix-en-Provence, Holland, Montreux, and Tunis festivals. It met at regular intervals over more than fifteen years, occasionally inviting musicians, directors, and critics, such as Karlheinz Stockhausen, Jerzy Grotowski, Maurice Fleuret, and Claude Samuel.

Nabokov's proposals for Berlin involved, from the start, the Berlin Festival. When its founder and artistic director since 1951, the composer Gerhart von Westermann, died in February 1963, Nabokov was appointed his successor—after a brief interim led by Wolfgang Stresemann, son of the former German Chancellor and executive director of the Berlin Philharmonic. Nabokov set out at once to redesign and expand the festival's scope, beginning with the 1964 edition. Each festival would be centered on a broad theme, which could accommodate art exhibitions and theatrical productions as well as musical programs. On the musical side, he also suggested devoting each festival to one prominent twentieth-century composer. His first choice was, naturally, Stravinsky. Plans were discussed at the end of April 1963 when the composer visited Germany on the occasion of the Hamburg premiere of *The Flood*, choreographed by Balanchine. It was on this occasion that Nabokov and Stravinsky were filmed by a Canadian team in Stravinsky's hotel room—in Robert Craft's words "a riveting quarter-hour of unrehearsed conversation in Russian, English, and French, worth more than all printed memoirs together."[23] The two friends—Stravinsky at his most endearing, even when discussing his digestive problems[24]—exchange pleasantries, drink scotch, look up the translation of an adjective in a Russian-English dictionary, and commiserate over the stroke recently suffered by Cocteau, who was to die later that year.

To Nabokov's Berlin Festival overtures, Stravinsky initially responded with a friendly rebuff: "Though your festivals have always been the most intelligently planned and the most capably executed, and though they have always shown the greatest devotion to me and my work, I loathe festivals. Even more, I hate most of the people they draw [. . .]."[25] Stravinsky nevertheless agreed to appear in 1964 and suggested approaching Ingmar Bergman, who had directed the Swedish premiere of *The Rake's Progress* in 1961, to mount *The Soldier's Tale*, which he would himself conduct, as a triple bill with *Noces* and *Renard* ("I do not want Scherchen for these pieces, or Boulez, whose only aim is to be faster than anyone else"). Though the Bergman project did not come through, Stravinsky did conduct *Renard* in Berlin in 1964, along with the Capriccio, with Nikita Magaloff as soloist.

For the general theme of the 1964 festival, Nabokov was able to recycle, in somewhat modified form, plans he had initially made for Brazil: described as "the contribution of Negro people to the culture of the twentieth century," it was to focus on Africa, a continent in which the Congress's involvement had been limited.[26] In 1960, however, a key contact person had emerged, via Josselson, in the person of Ulli Beier.[27] A German native, Beier had emigrated to Palestine before settling in Ibadan, Nigeria, where he founded the influential magazine *Black Orpheus*, which included among its contributors some of the leading writers of the new generation in Africa, such as Chinua Achebe, John Pepper Clark, Christopher Okigbo, and Wole Soyinka. It was to Beier that Nabokov turned for advice about the two exhibitions he had in mind: one of traditional African art, the other on African influences in European and American art. He also picked Beier's brain about African writers to invite. In Paris he got in touch with the ethnologist Georges-Henri Rivière, director of the Musée de l'Homme in Paris, whom he had known since the early 1930s. For literary recommendations, he consulted Lowell, who recommended Derek Walcott, "an attractive, live young man, [. . .] and the best Negro poet writing in English that I have read."[28]

In conjunction with the theme of the festival, Nabokov even approached Stravinsky with, as he put it, an "unexpected and rather rash request":

> Would it be possible for you to consider making an orchestral arrange-
> ment or rather a transformation and adaptation for voice and orchestra
> (in the way you did do beautifully with Bach) for two, three or four Negro
> Spirituals? I have just returned from Salzburg where I heard and saw my
> dear old friend, Leontyne Price. She would be delighted and honoured to
> sing here, either under your direction or under somebody else, these adap-
> tations of Negro Spirituals, which I would like to commission you to do.[29]

Stravinsky, at first, was intrigued:

> I do not know what I can do with a "spiritual": I had to give up the idea of
> orchestrating some Mussorgsky songs recently because the music is so far
> from me now. But I will study the "spirituals" when they come, and I am
> attracted by the idea.[30]

However, Stravinsky's final answer, first conveyed by Craft and forwarded by Nabokov to Price in tactful terms, was negative ("too far away from my work now").[31] The soprano sang, instead, a Bach cantata at a Karajan-led concert.

Apart from the festival, Nabokov was directly or indirectly involved in major musical events in the German city, such as the opening of the Philharmonie Hall in October 1963, and the world premiere of Sessions's opera *Montezuma* in April 1964, coinciding with the American composer's Ford Foundation fellowship. A "very difficult" opera, by the composer's own reckoning, *Montezuma* did not fare at all well with the audience.[32] In April 1963, Nabokov attended the Deutscher Oper production of his old friend Milhaud's *Oresteia* trilogy. The work, which was one of Nabokov's initial Berlin recommendations, dated from 1913–23 but had never been staged in its entirety. On April 24, the day of the opening performance, he hosted a luncheon party for the composer, who had come from Paris for the occasion. When Nabokov entered the dining room with the guest of honor, who was paralyzed and had to be carried by two servants, Auden, whom Nabokov had also invited, loudly rebuked his host for being "twenty minutes late." This outburst astonished everyone present, particularly Milhaud's wife Madeleine, who grumbled about Auden's lack of manners as she sat down on Nabokov's right.[33] "Intractable, difficult, cranky" Auden—as Nabokov characterized him—usually stayed with Nabokov when visiting Berlin from his new residence in the small town of Kirchstetten, outside Vienna. The poet had by then become a heavy drinker: one night Nabokov found him naked, trying to force open the liquor cabinet to get himself some gin.[34]

Nabokov tried, during those days, to resurrect his old project of a musical setting of *The Sea and the Mirror*. But Auden insisted that the text should be set in its entirety or not at all: "But why, my dear? Why should you cut it? *The Sea and the Mirror* is a reasoned whole. It would be like cutting the balls out of the poems! No, no! It won't work. Forget about it."[35] Instead, Auden encouraged Nabokov to set the "Landscape Poems" he had written before leaving Ischia (dedicating one to Nabokov). But it was Nabokov, this time, who found them "inconclusive and ill-suited to a musical setting."

> Each poem, or rather each line of each poem, is itself a jewel. But those jewels are strung upon much too long lines from a composer's point of view. The prosody and meters are highly complex and the general mood is detached and serene. Besides, all of Auden's landscape poems are very carefully—and at times allusively—descriptive. It makes them cumbersomely "literary" to a composer's ear. Every word counts. It has to be heard and understood. I felt that I would be doing Auden's Landscapes an injustice by having half of their wordscapes disappear in the throbs of a singer's gullet.[36]

Auden and Nabokov saw each other even more regularly in 1964, when Auden agreed to be one of the artists-in-residence in Berlin. Despite the generous terms of the invitation, it was not a successful year for Auden, who, Nabokov excepted, had few friends in Berlin; still, he enjoyed the company of Peter Heyworth, the *Observer* music critic and Otto Klemperer biographer, who was also a guest of the Ford Foundation.

Nabokov himself, in June 1964, moved to a new Berlin address in Grünewald, at Hoehmannstrasse 11, a short distance from the Hundekehlesee; by a touching coincidence, no. 6 on the same street had once been Harry Kessler's Berlin residence. As Nabokov reported to Josselson, the house was "exactly the kind I always wanted to have here."[37] He gave a housewarming party, which was attended by the ex-Senator Arndt, Stuckenschmidt, and Helmuth Jaesrich (Lasky's successor as editor of *Der Monat*). The British ethnomusicologist Peter Crossley-Holland, who was briefly associated with the Institute for Comparative Music Studies until incompatible temperamental differences with Daniélou forced him to withdraw,[38] came with a representative of the Dalai Lama.

The Berlin appointment, as we have seen, gave Nabokov the opportunity to keep his distance from the Congress, even while formally remaining part of it. He nevertheless organized two Congress-sponsored events in 1963–64: a small seminar outside New York in June 1963, and the music conference and festival in India, which had been in the works since 1961 and eventually took place in February 1964.

The week-long seminar was the first of what turned out to be a series of several such meetings held at Seven Springs, the Mount Kisko estate of Agnes Meyer, the cultivated widow of the owner of *The Washington Post* (and mother of Katharine Graham). It was, in the words of Mark Wolverton, "a distinguished international gathering of high-powered intellectuals dedicated to discussion and learned analysis of the problems of war, peace, and poverty."[39] Lowell, who was among the participants, sent a humorous account to Elizabeth Bishop, in which he evokes Nabokov ("kind to me, but not very interested"); Oppenheimer, who chaired the discussions ("quivering like a humming-bird with difficult elliptical quotations on every field, beautiful-looking, rather like the monk in the Giorgione or Titian piano player scene"); the architect Wallace Harrison ("conservative in his craft but full of a gentle worried humane wisdom—what he would build would be the opposite of Brasília"); Stuart Hampshire ("hesitant, humorous, gossipy, pure British"); the philosopher Jeanne Hersch, then teaching at the University of Geneva ("a Jaspers student and the epitome of that kind of intellectual, Hannah A[rendt] without the genius and humor"); and George Kennan ("with views almost like Khrushchev's on the arts—in a really noble old-fashioned uninformed way, wishing the world would go back to 1800, wishing the bombs were buried"). "Nabokov said Oppenheimer was Callas, and Kennan was Robeson and the rest of us were just honest singers. Well, I felt very young, small, ignorant and fascinated, trying to play the role of the hesitant, muddled, intuitive poet."[40] *Pace* Lowell, the gathering was found sufficiently stimulating by the host and the participants for the experience to be repeated two years later—with Lowell again participating—on the subject of privacy as it applied to scientists, artists, and creative persons in the modern world.[41]

The second Congress-sponsored manifestation Nabokov organized that year was another East-West encounter in Delhi in March 1964 that had been in the planning for several years. Recalling the political susceptibilities he had sensed during his first trip to India ten years before and the good rapport he had established with Indira Gandhi, Nabokov asked her to be the conference chair. She accepted, despite her anxiety over the health of her father: indeed Nehru, who had suffered a stroke in January, was to die at the end of May. "Tradition and

Change in Indian and Western Music," as the conference was officially entitled, gathered forty-odd musicians and musicologists, half of them from India and the rest from Western Europe, the United States, and Asia. As at the Rome and Tokyo festivals, morning panel discussions alternated with late afternoon and evening concerts. Menuhin gave a recital with his sister Hephzibah and there were concerts by the Drolc String Quartet from Berlin and the Studio for Medieval Music from Munich. On the Indian side, there were performances by Ravi Shankar and Ali Akbar Khan and a Barathanatyam recital by Tanjore Balasaraswati, the legendary classical dancer from Madras. The scholarly participation was among the most diverse hitherto gathered by Nabokov, with representatives from the USSR, Hungary, and Czechoslovakia; it was also one of the most distinguished. A strong impression was made, in particular, by the Vietnamese ethnomusicologist Trân Van Khê, now based in Paris, where he headed the Centre de musique orientale within the CNRS. The London *Times* correspondent described the event as "yet another milestone on the long road to east-west understanding in the field of music."[42] Yet Nabokov's own impression of India after this trip was mixed. As he wrote to Joseph Alsop immediately on his return, he had "the feeling of being on quicker quicksands than I have ever been before. It smells all like the good old Kerensky-time, just a wee bit before the take-over."[43]

The assassination of John F. Kennedy, whose June 1963 visit had made such an impact in Berlin, came as Nabokov was preparing the 1964 festival. The festival theme, with its implied connection with the Civil Rights movement in the United States, offered an opportunity to pay homage to the slain president, a suggestion Jacqueline Kennedy received with gratitude.[44] Nabokov approached Stravinsky about including his short *Elegy for J.F.K.*, on a text by Auden. The composer turned down the request on the grounds that he had yet to hear the work, which Craft had premiered in Los Angeles in April 1964. Nabokov was more successful in arranging an invitation, issued on Willy Brandt's behalf, to Martin Luther King Jr., who agreed to give a blessing at the beginning of the concert, featuring four different gospel and spiritual choirs, that opened the festival in the morning of September 13. On his arrival in Berlin on the previous day, King found himself in the same car as Elliott Carter, whose Double Concerto for harpsichord and piano was performed as part of the festival, under Bruno Maderna. During this short visit, the civil rights leader was even able to enter East Berlin, leaving his American Express card as security, and there spoke in two churches filled to capacity.[45]

To coincide with Stravinsky's festival appearance, the Berlin publisher Colloquium issued a short monograph by Nabokov devoted to the composer. The ninety-four-page volume came out as no. 36 of a series entitled "Heads of the Twentieth Century: Small Biographies of Great Contemporaries." Heavily tilted towards writers (Hemingway, Brecht, Hesse, Ortega y Gasset, Mann, Kafka, Zweig, Camus, Sartre, Faulkner, Mayakovsky, Joyce, Eliot), the series also featured political and historical figures (Ben Gurion, Gandhi, Mao), artists (Picasso), scientists, and one architect (Le Corbusier). After Bartók, Stravinsky was only the second composer to be covered. Nabokov's initial idea was to reprint the Stravinsky chapters of *Old Friends and New Music*, which had never appeared in German, with a foreword and a chronology of Stravinsky's career. He felt reluctant to embark on a more formal study of the composer's work. "It is very difficult for me," he wrote to Roger Klein of Harper & Row in April 1964, "as a close friend of Stravinsky to speak even in the slightest way critical about his work or about his person for fear of hurting his feelings."

> On the other hand, as everybody else, I have my own ideas which I keep to myself, and which can only be told later. I belong to those people for whom personal friendship is above all other considerations. Yet I feel that if one speaks about Stravinsky now after hundreds and hundreds of books have been published about him, only a very personal and at the same time completely candid book could have any value and be of interest. Don't you agree? Such a book cannot be written by me at the present time.[46]

Whatever caused Nabokov to change his mind, the little monograph was produced in remarkably little time and succeeded in being at the same time candid and personal. In the introduction, Nabokov explains that the work is not a scientific study but, rather, the testimony of someone who has known Stravinsky for a third of his life. The copyright page, which identifies the translator (the otherwise unrecorded Gita Jopp), also acknowledges the "expert technical advice" of Thomas Höpfner as research assistant. The book was put together with the help of the indispensable Anna Kallin in London, using passages from the autobiography Nabokov had been working on during the past five years. Additional material allowed it to fit the format of the collection, including a division into sections that are not found in the original English drafts.[47] The first section, subtitled "A Partisan Chronicle," summarizes Stravinsky's life up to the *Firebird* premiere—including Nabokov's own memory of hearing *Fireworks* at one of Wahrlich's "Russian Historical Concerts." The second, "The Paris Years," is essentially devoted to *Petrushka* and *The Rite of Spring*. "Who else in this century," Nabokov asks in conclusion, "has produced so rapidly and with such precision *and* under pressure of such rigorous deadlines so many works, *all* of them of the highest quality, *all* of them thoroughly new and unmistakably his own? I do not know of anyone, not even Schoenberg, and certainly not Richard Strauss."[48] The next section, "Money Laughs—or Swiss Intermezzo,"[49] reads like a mini-pamphlet on the subject of the financial difficulties of a composer's life: beginning in question-and-answer form, it incorporates personal reflections on the precariousness of a composer's life and touches on Stravinsky's well-known aversion to paying taxes. The story of the negotiations with Liebermann over the *Threni* commission is printed in full, as is the comparison between Picasso's and Stravinsky's respective financial situations. The fourth section, "From Clarens to Paris," evokes the war years and the period leading to the premiere of the *Symphonies for Wind Instruments*, with comments on the relationship between Stravinsky and Debussy and Stravinsky and Diaghilev. The following part, "The Large Catalogue," covers the two decades from Stravinsky's return to France and his departure for America in 1939, and discusses the issue of Stravinsky's neoclassicism—up to and including the postwar *Rake's Progress*. Nabokov also evokes his own personal contacts with Stravinsky at the time he was employed by Pleyel. The final section, "To America," is the shortest. Revealingly, it refrains from discussing Stravinsky's postwar output save for *The Rake*. After evoking the dinner at the White House and the trip to the Soviet Union, Nabokov mentions Stravinsky's peripatetic life and his collaboration with (and admiration for) Balanchine. As for Craft's role in introducing Stravinsky to—and into—the postwar musical avant-garde, it is stated in the briefest terms and without any additional comments: "And it is consequently largely to the contact with Bob Craft that we owe Stravinskyan music written in the serial technique from the 'Canticum Sacrum' onwards."[50] In the book's conclusion, Nabokov suggests that Stravinsky's Picasso-like chameleon-like personality ideally embodies the genius of his age, which is change. "Yet in the case of Stravinsky," Nabokov adds, "there is an added element which, to me, enhances his stature and the validity of his art: it [is] his deep-seated, his profound Russian sense of awe before God and all God's creatures, the sense of service that art contains."[51]

"I have written the book *entirely* as an act of friendship," Nabokov warned Stravinsky before presenting him with a copy at the time of the festival.[52] A few weeks later, he urged the composer to let him know whether there were any errors so that he could correct them in the second printing as well as in the English edition, indicating that Collins, in London, was considering it for publication. In March 1965, Stravinsky reported he found the book "excellent." There were, to be sure, "a number of things [. . .] that ought to be corrected," which he did not specify, adding he would discuss them with Nabokov in due course.[53] The original English version, Nabokov explained in return, would not be issued until Stravinsky had a chance to review it.[54] When Nabokov and Stravinsky met again in Hamburg in the summer of 1965, Stravinsky told him he thought it was "the best book written about him," as Nabokov proudly reported to George Weidenfeld.[55]

At the 1964 Berlin Festival, Stravinsky was represented with twenty-two of his works, including the European premiere of *Abraham and Isaac*, conducted by Craft, with Fischer-Dieskau as soloist, struggling bravely with the text in ancient Hebrew. After the concert, Nabokov hosted a reception in Stravinsky's honor at the Kempinski, the famous luxury hotel on the Kurfüstendamm. Among the guests were Auden, Nadia Boulanger, Carter, and Spender. That evening marked the end of a difficult episode in Nabokov's sentimental life, his affair with a young German stage designer named Dagmar Hader, whom he had met in early 1963. The breakup was precipitated—and complicated—by Dagmar deliberately provoking Nabokov's jealousy by going to bed with Robert Craft, and making sure Nabokov knew about it, on the night of the reception. An embarrassing scene took place in the lobby of the Kempinski Hotel the following morning, on the day the Stravinskys and Craft left Berlin.[56]

Besides Stravinsky's participation, one of the musical highlights of the 1964 Berlin Festival was a joint appearance of Mstislav Rostropovich and his wife at a Berlin Philharmonic concert conducted by John Pritchard, at which Galina Vishnevskaya was to premiere Blacher's *Parergon zum "Eugen Onegin"*. A friendship immediately developed between Nabokov and Rostropovich. After hearing the Russian cellist again in Paris in early 1965, Nabokov wrote to Stravinsky: "Quite frankly, I believe that he is like Richter one of the most remarkable performers of our time. His playing is precise, his technique masterful, and there is no Casalsian 'Schmalz' and gypsydom." He also sounded out Stravinsky about a possible commission for Rostropovich:

> When I saw him in Paris (we spent a whole day together) he told me that he would be extremely happy to have a piece of yours, whatever the length or whatever orchestral combination, it would be and that he would pay you for it, out of his concert savings as much as you would ask. He sincerely loves and admires your present style. We went to hear together in Paris *Abraham and Isaac* which, despite what the critics say, was very well done by [Maurice] Le Roux, and the Swiss singer [Derrik] Olsen."[57]

Rostropovich, Nabokov added, would premiere the commissioned piece in Moscow and Leningrad, then give the Western European premiere at the 1966 Berlin Festival. But Stravinsky turned down the request: he was busy composing the *Requiem Canticles*, nor was he disposed to write a new work to be premiered in a country where his old works were "played free, from illegal photocopies."[58]

Artistically, the 1964 Berlin Festival, as planned, featured two exhibitions. The first, curated by William Fagg of the British Museum, "100 Tribes—100 Masterpieces," presented African bronzes never before seen in Western Europe; it then traveled to Paris. The second, curated by Reidemeister, documented the influence of African art on modernist painting and sculpture: works by Matisse, Moore, Picasso, and others were juxtaposed with examples of African art that had inspired them.

More perhaps than for its musical and artistic components, Nabokov's first Berlin festival is remembered today by cultural historians as "the most exciting international gathering of black artists in memory."[59] In addition to jazz concerts, there were performances by a Yoruba folk opera group from Nigeria and dance troupes from Cameroon and Dahomey (the modern Benin). Freezing in their colorful traditional robes, as Elliott Carter recalled, they caused a sensation in the streets of Berlin.[60] The theater—the missing link in Paris in 1952—was brilliantly represented this time, with productions of Aimé Césaire's *La tragédie du roi Christophe*, Langston Hughes's *Black Nativity*, and Jean Genet's *The Blacks*. The last named was a Blacks Co. production Nabokov had been much impressed with the previous fall in New York—the cast included Cicely Tyson, Roscoe Lee Browne, and James Earl Jones. Césaire and Hughes—an old acquaintance of Nabokov from his Paris years[61]—attended the festival, as did Soyinka; they gave readings and took part in panel discussions (one of them with Jose Luis Borges). That a number of participants had left-wing or even Communist sympathies shows that Nabokov did not feel bound by the same political restrictions as when working for the Congress. He even considered inviting one of the world's most famous fellow-travelers, but Paul Robeson's declining health made his participation impossible.

Despite his well-established anti-Communist credentials, Nabokov was indeed, as of the early 1960s, a firm believer in opening up cultural relations with the Eastern Bloc and, especially, Soviet Russia. Encouraged by Brandt, who felt that West Berlin was held hostage to a German foreign policy decided in Bonn and in Washington, he advocated these views in an early 1964 memorandum that Brandt forwarded to Bonn. One of its proposals was a Berlin festival on East and West. At the same time, Nabokov also began to be haunted by a desire, after more than four decades of exile, to visit his native country. The enormous success and impact of Stravinsky's visit to Russia, in September and October 1962, after an absence of fifty years, intensified this desire.[62] Even before Stravinsky's departure, Nabokov asked him to contact on his behalf Tikhon Khrennikov, the seemingly irremovable president of the Union of Soviet Composers—and a frequent target of Nabokov's satire in his 1940s articles on Soviet music. "I told [Khrennikov] of your wish to go to Russia," Stravinsky reported to Nabokov in January 1963, "and asked him to help, which he promised to do, if he could, but he was not certain that this was the right time."[63] A few weeks later, while attending with Isaiah Berlin a concert by Sviatoslav Richter ("a flaming fag") at the Royal Festival, Hall Nabokov brought up the matter again: "It would be good if you would confirm with Khrennikov that I wrote to him at *your* suggestion. I am afraid that I cannot go this year, but still, if you can, write."[64]

In Paris, beginning in the early 1960s, Nabokov had opportunities to meet distinguished visitors from the East, such as the poet Andrei Voznesensky and the novelists Viktor Nekrasov and Konstantin Pautovsky: all three spent time in the French capital in late 1962 and early 1963. Nabokov, as he reported to Gostuski,

invited them to his place and played his Pasternak songs, which his guests optimistically suggested might be performed in Moscow the following year.[65] Once
in Berlin, Nabokov established connections with the Soviet embassy to East
Germany, first with Iulii Kitsinzkii, the cultural attache, who came to visit him
at the Festival Office in the spring of 1963.[66] The purpose of the visit was to grill
Nabokov on his festival plans. The "Black and White festival" was the subject of
special curiosity—understandably, since the Soviets led an active propaganda
war in the so-called Third World. The conversation got off to a bad start. To his
interlocutor's aggressive questioning about the number of "niggers" who would
be present and whether bus tours around the Wall were to be part of the program, Nabokov reacted by suggesting that he would rather discuss Pushkin or
the weather.[67] Nevertheless, he seized the opportunity to tell his visitors that he
would need the embassy's support to ensure the participation of Russian artists. This first contact led to an invitation from Piotr Andreevich Abrasimov, the
Soviet ambassador, whom Nabokov knew to be one of the highest-ranking Soviet
diplomats of the postwar period. To his surprise, Abrasimov did not in the least
conform to the image of the Soviet apparatchik.

> He was handsome, trim, sportsman-like, and taller than the average Soviet
> diplomat. His face was well cut in a plain Russian way, his hair graying
> blond, his cold blue eyes looked straight into mine. There was something
> frank and open and curiously engaging in their gaze. Intuitively I felt that
> he was, after all, sizing me up, but in a different and much more subtle way
> than I had expected. There was neither hostility nor aggressiveness in the
> way he looked at me. Only interest, and perhaps a bit of caution. I found
> him attractive and un-fearsome, yet at the same time strangely distant.[68]

Abrasimov turned out to be, like Nabokov, Belorussian by birth. He proudly guided
his visitor "through the lush, fathomless horrors of his embassy":

> The marbles were real and all over the place. Malachite and lapis-lazuli
> vases stood everywhere. There were plenty of terrifying bronzes and heavy
> draperies. To top it all, in the grand hall there was a colored-glass window
> representing an ardent realist scene with Lenin or Stalin or both.[69]

These initial contacts were not only highly useful for Nabokov's cultural plans
in Berlin, making it possible for the Leningrad Philharmonic, Kirill Kondrashin,
and Rostropovich to participate in the 1964 festival; they also resulted, as Nabokov
reported to Stravinsky in early June 1964, in an invitation for Nabokov to stop in
Moscow on his return from the trip to Japan planned later that month in connection with the 1965 Berlin Festival: "However surprising it may seem, the Russians

here, at the embassy Unter der Linden, have been very eager for me to stop in Moscow on my way back from Tokyo for four days, as a guest of the Ministry of Culture."[70] Could Stravinsky, Nabokov went on, write a note to Ekaterina Furtseva, the powerful Soviet Minister of Culture and Stravinsky's official host at the time of his own visit, to introduce Nabokov as a friend of his? The request suggests that Abrasimov himself may have been uncertain about how the invitation of Nabokov would be received in Moscow, where the Congress for Cultural Freedom obviously inspired the greatest wariness and its funding through the CIA must have been, if not positively known, at least strongly suspected.

Nabokov's Russian initiatives were followed with some alarm in Geneva by Josselson, who one can suspect was kept informed throughout by his CIA contacts in Berlin. Writing to him on June 8, 1964, Nabokov was careful to present the projected Moscow visit as the result of conversations with "Willy" and Senator Stein.

> All this concerns the cultural exchanges between Berlin and the USSR. Brandt and Stein and the German Embassy in Moscow would welcome my going there and making clear to the Russians under what conditions cultural exchanges between Berlin and Moscow can happen.[71]

As it turned out, the Moscow visit was canceled at the last minute. As an official reason, Nabokov cited the fact that he fell ill during his return flight from Japan and had to be rushed to the hospital in Karachi. To Josselson, he admitted he was also concerned about current political tensions in Russia. Josselson, while applauding the decision, took the opportunity to caution Nabokov in the strongest terms he had used so far on the subject of his *Ost-Politik*:

> Some day when I get to see you, I will tell you why I so strongly objected to your proposed visit. I did not for one minute worry about your safety nor was I concerned about any consequences from your connection with the Congress. Believe me, I was only concerned about yourself and about a very embarrassing situation you could find yourself in, not immediately, but maybe in a year or two from now. I don't want to write about this, but rest assured that what I have in mind is not something I just picked up out of the air. I wish there would be no more visits by you to Karlshorst [where the Soviet ambassador's residence was located] until we meet and can talk this matter over. Also, please bear in mind that you have many enemies in Berlin who are only waiting for an opportunity to knife you, and in our own interest, you would do well to cut the ground from under these people and their malicious gossip.[72]

"As for malicious gossip and people who want to knife me," Nabokov replied on July 3, "my only response is hard work and the hope that the Festival which I have planned for this year and the one which I am preparing for next year, will be successful."[73] Nabokov knew from other sources that his presence in Berlin had given rise to malicious gossip—some of which, including absurdly inflated rumors about his salary, had come to the ears of his friend Grunelius.[74] Mentioning plans for the 1965 festival to one of his publishers, Nabokov sounded a note of discouragement: "But then again I don't know if I shall have anything to do with the festival in 1965."[75]

Josselson's fears, perhaps fueled by worry over the political change in Russia, where Brezhnev succeeded Khrushchev in October 1964, were not assuaged. An even testier exchange occurred between him and Nabokov at the end of the year. The pretext was Josselson's concern about the Congress being made to pay travel expenses that should have been covered by Berlin. He bluntly asked Nabokov to consider himself on a (paid) leave of absence from the Congress for the next few months, advising him to focus on his Berlin duties and the completion of his ballet. He also conveyed more pointed grievances. Why had Nabokov not shared with him his memorandum to Brandt, which had been brought to Josselson's attention by his own Bonn "contacts"? Why had Nabokov, when they met in Geneva after the end of the festival, failed to inform him that he had taken the opportunity of Rostropovich's presence to invite him and Abrasimov to his house? Josselson, as he reminded Nabokov, had been in two minds about the Berlin arrangement. He feared that the Soviets were about to exploit Nabokov "for their own purposes which, as I have been telling you all along, is to establish enough precedents for making West Berlin a separate entity, divorced from West Germany. This only confirms my fears that sooner or later, in one form or another, you could become an unwitting instrument of Soviet policy in Germany."[76]

Another point at issue was one of Nabokov's initiatives—in agreement, of course, with Brandt and the Berlin Senate—concerning the Berlin Festival being, as Josselson saw it, now run like "a privately run enterprise," freed from "existing arrangements on cultural exchange of West Germany." "I don't want to know anything any more," Josselson concluded, "about what you are doing either in Berlin or in Bonn."

> Let's just suspend our official relationship until May and let's keep our fingers crossed that with your doings you will not unduly damage our friendship. When I think of your repeated expressions of gratitude for my warnings when we parted at the Montreux Palace I can only regret that the idea of your going to Berlin ever came up![77]

From a strict administrative viewpoint, so long as Nabokov continued to receive his salary as secretary general, Josselson could not be blamed for insisting that the Berlin Festival was, at least to some extent, the Congress's business. This was not, however, Nabokov's position. As we saw in the previous chapter, he was dis-enchanted about his own role within the organization, and further alienated by the revelations heard about the sources of its funding. Withholding information from Josselson was a kind of *quid pro quo* for the latter's own secret role within the Congress.

From his private conversations with Willy Brandt, Nabokov was aware of—and sympathetic to—the mayor's own views on the city's "untenable" position between East and West. As for the accusation of "privatizing" the festival by making it a so-called GmbH ("company with limited liability"), Nabokov had good reasons, which he shared with Brandt and Senator Stein, to make the festival organization less bureaucratic and cumbersome, and foreign travel was only one area among many. As he pointed out to Josselson, the reason for his presence in Berlin was to make the festival "an international event with some meaning in it and not a pro-vincial festival like many others now existing in Europe."[78] As for his contacts with the Soviet embassy, Josselson's political objections notwithstanding, they became more and more frequent.

The ballet Josselson was urging Nabokov to complete was *Don Quixote*. The Balanchine commission officially dated from December 7, 1962, initially for delivery of the score by September 1963. But the project had a long prehistory, going back to Nabokov's own piano suite from the early 1930s entitled *Le cœur de Don Quichotte*. As early as 1950, a contract had been signed with Balanchine for a full-length ballet on this subject, for which Eugene Berman was to design the sets. Nabokov had begun to work on the score, completing about fifteen minutes of music, but his appointment as CCF secretary general had derailed the project. Once in Paris, engrossed in the 1952 festival plans, he had barely completed seven more after one year, instead of the ninety minutes promised.[79] Of this initial proj-ect, there remains a typed libretto in two acts, with no indication of authorship, but its similarities with the 1965 ballet suggest that it was the work of Balanchine and Nabokov. Several of the ballet's episodes are already there—the opening visions, the inn scene, Gamacho's wedding with Don Quixote disrupting the puppet show, Montesino's cave, the fight with the mills, and the death of Don Quixote—though not in the same order as in the completed ballet.[80]

After the new contract was signed with the New York City Ballet at the end of 1962, *Don Quixote* occupied much of Nabokov's time in the next three years, though slowed down as much by both Nabokov's and Balanchine's punishing schedules, which resulted in few opportunities for the two collaborators to meet. Balanchine was, in addition, a notoriously bad correspondent—"he knows neither how to read nor how to write," Liebermann quipped—and Nabokov could only reach him via his secretary Barbara Horgan.[81] The two were able to meet only on the rare occasions when Nabokov was in New York or when Balanchine was in Europe. At first, Nabokov planned to orchestrate the ballet himself and seek his inspiration from the score of Tchaikovsky's *The Sleeping Beauty*. However, pressed for time, as he had been for *Rasputin*, he had to call on the help of a collaborator for the orchestration of the ballet: most of it was realized, under his supervision, by Fernand Quattrocchi, a Paris-based Conservatoire alumnus, who had studied conducting with Manuel Rosenthal and the cello with André Navarra.[82]

In early April 1965, within weeks of the scheduled date of the premiere, Nabokov—in Berlin—and Balanchine—in New York—were still making adjustments to their ballet. "Don't worry, we'll get everything done," Balanchine wrote to the composer on April 1, "but . . . no more girls until you finish the whole thing!"[83] On April 6, Nabokov reported that all the music was written and only six numbers remained to be orchestrated.

> I have changed somewhat the titles and the character of the classical ballet of Act II. Number 13 of Act II starts with the coda of number 11 of Act I (arrival of the Prince and the Princess. It forms a Händelian prelude to the straightforward allegro movement of a Vivaldi-Haendel or Bach concerto grosso). Instead of the Gigue (number 15) I have written a fairly quick and much more amusing piece, in which I call "Danza della Caccia" (hunting dance). This kind of dance with a broken rhythm was more current in 17th century Spain than the gigue. It lasts 1'50". The "Courante", number 17, has become a "Courante sicilienne" (2'40"). Also a favorite italianization of court music in use in Spain. Instead of the "Bourrée", number 18, I have written a piece which I call "Rigaudon flamand" (2'). It is a brilliant loud number with the whole string section and the harp accompanying first two trumpets and then two woodwinds; it is very Spanish in character and I am sure will liven up the second Act by forming a stylistic contrast and separating the somewhat similar number 14 (Sarabande) and number 19 (Ritornelle). The Fugue leads us back to the more dissonant music of the beginning of the first Act. It is a very carefully worked out 12-tone double fugue which ends abruptly with the appearance of Dulcinea, using the same phrase as the beginning of Dulcinea's Variations, number 28.

"Considering that the ballet is finished," Nabokov wrote in conclusion to his letter, "I am going back to girls."[84] Yet, two days later, Balanchine requested a little more music—a prelude before the village scene, a one-minute introduction to the waltz. "If you don't have time," he added, "we can add it later, after opening night."[85]

Compared to the 1950 libretto, the scenario Balanchine and Nabokov reworked in 1964 gave, from the start, a much more important role to Dulcinea, a role in which Balanchine cast the rising star of his company, the nineteen-year-old Suzanne Farrell. When Nabokov first met Farrell in the spring of 1965, he took, as she recalled, "a long, hard look" at her and told her—in terms similar to

Balanchine's a few days later: "'You know, George has always wanted to do this ballet, for twenty-five years he has wanted to do this ballet, but he always said, 'I never found my Dulcinea.'"[86] Indeed, the ballet, as it took shape, had become the choreographer's "public declaration of adoration" for Farrell.[87] Yet, as opposed to the Petipa ballet in which the young Balanchine had appeared at the Mariinsky Theater before the Revolution, and in which Don Quixote is more a spectator than an actor, the authors also intended to restore the Don as the principal role, even if not strictly speaking a danced one. Between the June 1964 scenario and the one Balanchine and Nabokov more or less finalized in early February 1965, the main difference was that the entire third act, including the fight with the windmills, and up to the final apparition of Dulcinea as the Madonna who attends to Don Quichotte's final moments, was conceived in the shape of a long dream sequence.

As stage designer for *Don Quixote*, Balanchine, to the distress of his old friend Eugene Berman, turned to a longtime collaborator, the Spanish painter Esteban Francés, who had worked with him on *Renard* (1947), *Jeux d'enfants* (1955), and *La sonnambula* (1960), among other ballets. Yet, while the designer's national origin introduced a touch of Spanish authenticity, Nabokov's music, unlike the score Minkus composed for Petipa, is free from facile pseudo-folkloric hispanicisms. Balanchine pronounced himself to be "very pleased and satisfied," and reported that the conductor, Rovert Irving, was "very excited about your score, and likes your music very much."[88]

Nabokov flew to the United States in late April 1965 to attend the final rehearsals of *Don Quixote*, thanks to an Institute of Contemporary Arts fellowship, staying in the apartment of his friend the painter Leonid Berman (Eugene's brother) and his wife, the harpsichordist Sylvia Marlowe. The official public premiere took place on May 28, 1965, but the real premiere was the gala benefit the night before, at which Balanchine himself assumed the title-role—his first stage appearance in seven years and his last major role—to be succeeded the next night by Richard Rapp. It was a triumph for both Balanchine and Farrell, his young "muse," whose five-minute solo in act 3 was singled out by Joan Acocella as "the most remarkable piece of dancing I ever saw."[89] "We danced entirely to each other," Farrell recalled, "and in a curious way all the emotion was a relief, a release of everything that had been building up between us without any direct expression. The ballet became a kind of public courtship, a declaration, where dance, mime, and ceremony mingled with our real lives and emotions so deeply that our onstage and offstage selves became interwoven."[90] After the performance, there was a reception on the promenade of the New York State Theater. "With champagne glasses in hand, we toasted everything," Farrell recalls, "—the ballet, Nabokov, the theater, the patrons, and each other."[91]

Despite this overwhelming debut—surely one of the legendary evenings in the history of American ballet—*Don Quixote* was from the start a controversial work;

some have even called it a "problem ballet."[92] Perhaps the main problem was that it defeated expectations. It departed in striking ways from the late Balanchine style New York audiences were accustomed to. Instead of semi-abstract refinement and virtuosity, it was a full-length story. The choreography gave a large place to mime, especially at the beginning and at the end, yet it also emphasized spectacular divertissements in the manner of the late nineteenth-century romantic ballet. Since Balanchine could do no wrong in New York by then, it was the music that generally took the blame. It was, as Farrell sums it up, "condemned as unsubtle (one reviewer referred to it as 'movie music') and generally inadequate for the profound themes of faith and redemption."[93] For the critics who took the trouble to discuss the score with any precision, the main objection was what was described as its eclecticism—"an odd mixture of styles, beginning with a 12-tone introduction and then offering pastiches of 17th century composers and a smattering of Stravinsky."[94] To this objection, one could respond that musical variety was exactly what Balanchine had required. In the words of Betty Cage, the New York City Ballet's general manager, "his friendship with Nabokov was very deep, and he liked his music. He found in it exactly what he wanted for *Don Quixote.*"[95] And in fact the music had strong admirers from the beginning. Martin Gottfried, who found fault with the choreography, wrote that Nabokov's score was "by far the finest part of the new work."

> Nabokov has written a masterpiece even with its odd avoidance of the Spanish and its still odder hints at Prokofiev. But despite these peculiarities it is wonderfully melodic and perfectly danceable, deep in development and constantly inventive. Particularly at the ballet climax, when a nightmare religious processional leads into Quixote's death, beating its way dramatically to a genuinely exciting and terribly moving conclusion.[96]

One of the score's greatest admirers is the person who, other than Nabokov and Balanchine, probably knew it best, Farrell herself, who wrote to the composer in 1969:

> Four years ago I had the honor of meeting you and working with you in a ballet which has grown more dear to my heart with each performance. "Don Quichotte" was a milestone in my life both as a dancer and a person.
> The music has always inspired me, but more so this past season. Whereas I have become quite possessive toward "Don Q.," [. . .] I cannot take any credit . . . Your music conducted my feet always."[97]

In her memoir, which remains the most illuminating and moving account of the ballet—*her* ballet—Farrell singles out the moment in act 1 where the servant girl,

Mary-Magdalen-like, dries Don Quixote's feet with her hair and then climbs up
the stairs while the Dulcinea theme is stated by the orchestra.

> More than any other single element in the ballet, it was this passionate yet
> simple music that gave me the final clue to being Dulcinea. I cannot explain
> it; it was in the music—soft, gentle, mournful, and sweet, taken from an
> old Russian folk theme. When planning the ballet with Nabokov, Mr. B had
> said to him, "Don't you remember this?" and sat down at the piano and
> played a melody—or what he remembered of it—from his youth. It was
> music that had been haunting him all his life. Nabokov orchestrated it, and
> it became my theme.[98]

When Farrell revived the ballet at the Kennedy Center in Washington, DC, in 2005,
in a version that largely restored the 1965 musical text, John Rockwell, noting that
"it looked and sounded very good indeed," thought that the music "sounded far
better than most reviewers from 40 years ago heard it. This can be acerbic music,
but it matches the drama, captures the varied moods and is sometimes downright
gorgeous."[99] In the hope that the ballet might have a parallel career as a concert
piece, Nabokov extracted two symphonic works from the music for *Don Quixote*: a
set of *Symphonic Variations*, composed in 1967, and, five years later, a symphonic
suite entitled *The Hunter's Picnic*.

No sooner was the *Don Quixote* premiere behind them that Balanchine and
Nabokov began to touch it up. "In general, the orchestration worked well, but there
were things I had to redo completely, especially in the finale," Nabokov reported
to Quattrocchi in early July.[100] *Don Quixote* was revived every season in the next
thirteen years, always in a slightly different version: numbers shifted from one act
to another (the Rigaudon Flamenco was moved to act 1, then moved back to act 2 in
1972), additions (the last, a Pas classique espagnol, in 1972), or cuts (such as a variation in act 3).[101] Changes were readily agreed upon by composer and choreographer: not only were Balanchine and Nabokov close friends, they genuinely admired
each other and were in complete artistic sympathy. But the result of this constant
tinkering, according to Betty Cage, was that "the ballet was never really finished."[102]

Nabokov, who sold the score to Belaieff in Bonn, hoped, of course, that *Don
Quixote* would interest other companies and other choreographers. Exporting the
choreography was impossible, because, as Nabokov explained to Liebermann,
Balanchine was now reluctant to choreograph anything with a company other than
his own. On the other hand, the ballet was so closely identified with Balanchine
that it seemed to discourage any choreography but his. Plans for the Deutsche
Oper to mount *Don Quixote* in 1967 came to nothing. The first European production took place in 1970 at the Hessischer Staatsoper in Wiesbaden, with a choreography by Imre Keres, and was favorably received.

Nabokov and Rolf Liebermann, Paris, 1950s (Dominique Nabokov archives).

Nabokov with Artur Rubinstein and Vladimir Golschmann, Royaumont, mid-1950s (Ivan and Claude Nabokoff archives).

Nabokov with Alain Daniélou (Left) and H. H. Stuckenschmidt, Berlin, 1960s (photograph by Jacques E. Cloarec, FIND Foundation, Dominique Nabokov archives).

Nabokov and Leontyne Price, Berlin, 1963
(photograph by Hugh Dilworth, Dominique
Nabokov archives).

Nabokov and Boris Blacher, Berlin, late 1960s (photograph by Dominique Nabokov).

Nabokov and Mstislav Rostropovitch, Berlin, 1967 (photograph by Dominique Nabokov).

Nabokov discussing with Willy Brandt the program of the 1965 Berlin Festival (photograph by Harry Croner, Dominique Nabokov archives, copyright Stiftung Stadtmuseum Berlin).

Nabokov and Balanchine at Kolbsheim in 1966 (photograph by Dominique Nabokov).

Nabokov with Stuart Hampshire and Isaiah Berlin, Headington House, Oxford, 1969 (photograph by Dominique Nabokov)

Nabokov and Dominique, 1967 (photograph by Jacques E. Cloarec, FIND Foundation, Dominique Nabokov archives).

Nabokov and Virgil Thomson in Thomson's Chelsea Hotel apartment, New York, 1970 (photograph by Dominique Nabokov).

Nabokov with Jacques Maritain and an unidentified clergyman, Kolbsheim, 1967 (photograph by John Howard Griffin, reproduced with the permission of the estate of John Howard Griffin and Elizabeth Griffin-Bonazzi, Dominique Nabokov archives).

Nabokov with Balanchine and Stephen Spender, Princeton, 1967 (photograph by Dominique Nabokov).

Nabokov with Elliott and Helen Carter and Leonid Berman (Left) at the house of Berman and Sylvia Marlowe in Connecticut, 1975 (photograph Dominique Nabokov).

Nabokov with his cousin Vladimir, Montreux, 1975 (photograph by Dominique Nabokov).

Nabokov and his three sons and two of his grandchildren, Paris, 1975 (photograph by Dominique Nabokov).

For his second Berlin festival, in 1965, Nabokov decided to do in reverse what he had attempted in Japan in 1961, while drawing the lessons of what he saw as the main negative of the Tokyo Encounter—too much in too little time. As he wrote to Passin, now a professor of sociology at the Columbia University East Asian Institute and an adviser to the Ford Foundation, he intended to have a "Japanese season" along the general lines of "Japan and its relation to twentieth-century Western culture." As initially planned, this season was to extend from April through October, and included many components: a garden and flower exhibit; a traditional Japanese house; three or four major shows (architecture, pottery, textiles, lacquer work, etc.), a contemporary Japanese painting exhibition, and a touring dance company. The festival month proper would feature Nô theater, Kabuki and Gagaku groups, performances of modern Japanese music, and leading Japanese musicians.[103] With the advice of his closest Japanese contacts, especially the art historian Yukio Yashiro, Nabokov was able to present two major exhibitions: the first was eighteenth-century Zen masterpieces from the Hosokawa and Takugawa collections; the second, presented at Amerikahaus, and entitled "The Pacific Heritage," was devoted to Pacific Coast American Painters. The festival included the first European appearance of the Tokyo Kabuki Theater, while the featured composer, succeeding Stravinsky, was Bartók.

After her success in *Don Quixote*, Farrell was promoted to principal dancer and in September 1965 made her Paris Opéra debut in Stravinsky's *Agon*, choreographed by Balanchine. It was her first trip to the French capital (and indeed to Europe) and Balanchine took her to one his favorite sights, the Lady and the Unicorn tapestries in the Musée de Cluny.

> As we walked by the six huge hangings in the vaulted room he explained to me that five of them represented the senses. The last and most poignant has the beautiful but mysterious title *À Mon Seul Désir* (To My Only Desire) and depicts the young maiden embracing a coffer of jewels, a gift from a lover perhaps. Her white unicorn is seated patiently beside her with the most touching expression of innocent adoration upon its sweet face. George told me the legend that a unicorn can only be captured by a virgin; it will come and lay its head on her lap. He loved the title *À Mon Seul Désir* and said he wanted to make a ballet for me about the story of the unicorn.[104]

For this intensely personal new project, Balanchine, once again, turned to Nabokov. In early December, a contract was signed with the New York City Ballet for a score "between 30 and 60 minutes in length" for a ballet tentatively entitled *The Unicorn,* for performance in the spring of 1967. Nabokov started working on the music, composing, as he told an unidentified correspondent, one third of it.[105] In November 1966, he sent Barbara Horgan, at Balanchine's request, the one number he had orchestrated, reminding her that he had written three and that Balanchine had liked two of them in short score but had found the third "too personal."

> So far George was not clear at all about what kind of a libretto he wanted, and it is difficult, if not impossible, to write music with no clear ideas in mind as to what is going to be done on the stage, and how long each number should be. I thought that as soon as I come to America at the beginning of January, I will get to work on the Unicorn, *after* we have talked over the libretto with George.[106]

At the end of the year, Nabokov wrote to Horgan once again that he needed to have "long talks" with Balanchine on the subject of the scenario. If such talks did take place, they clearly resulted in the project being abandoned.

In the wake of the *Don Quixote* performances came an opportunity that, even more than the Berlin appointment, might have offered Nabokov a chance to take even more distance vis-à-vis the Congress: in the spring of 1965 he was invited by the program committee of the John F. Kennedy Center for the Performing Arts to formulate proposals for the center, construction of which had begun the previous December. He did so in the form of a memorandum he sent Jacqueline Kennedy in June. In it he advocated ambitious, international programming that he suggested would take a minimum of three years to put in place. The circumstances for an appointment of Nabokov as artistic director seemed to be favorable: Arthur Schlesinger headed the Program Committee and Nabokov knew several of its members, such as Goddard Lieberson. Among his referees were Bernstein and Isaac Stern. As for the board of trustees, it was chaired by the theater producer Roger Stevens, a JFK appointee. Nabokov was invited to present his views before the committee in early 1966. After a successful interview—"be at once imaginative and businesslike," Schlesinger had advised[107]—the Program Committee recommended to the Executive Committee at the end of March that Nabokov be appointed interim director; but the recommendation was tabled by the Executive Committee. In October, Schlesinger told Nabokov his name was still on the long list of people being considered for the artistic directorship. However, by the end of the year, he reported to Nabokov that the Kennedy Center job was "slipping away," largely owing to construction delays, which pushed back any hopes for an opening "until the 1969-70 season, if then";[108] indeed, the center did not open until September 1971. Bitter about the experience, Nabokov described the Kennedy Center as "the biggest White Elephant America has produced."[109] Isaiah Berlin offered words of consolation: "You must not regret Washington—you would not have emerged from it alive."[110] "Yes, yes, you are quite right," Nabokov replied, "the Kennedy job would have ruined me and killed me, but it would have given

considerable satisfaction to my pride—a kind of revenge on the sterile years
I spent working for *Il Congresso . . .*"[111]

When Nabokov wrote these words, the Congress had only a few months to
live. The story of its disintegration is well known and what concerns us here is
how Nabokov himself was affected. In 1964, a Congressional investigation into
the tax-exempt status of private US foundations, led by Representative Wright
Patman, a Democrat from Texas, revealed that eight of these were "passing foundations" for federal funds channeled through the CIA.[112] The following year, *The
New York Times* launched its own investigation into the matter. This led to the
publication, in April and May 1966, of a series of five articles, one of which, on
April 27, specifically mentioned the Congress for Cultural Freedom and *Encounter*
as the recipients of CIA funding—a mention James Angleton of the CIA, Charles
Bohlen (since 1962 ambassador to France), and Dean Rusk, Johnson's Secretary of
State, unsuccessfully tried to get the paper to suppress.[113] Nabokov's reaction, fol-
lowing, presumably, telephone exchanges with Josselson in Geneva and Hunt in
Paris, was a letter to the *Times,* dated April 30, which stated, in his official capacity
as secretary general:

> The Congress for Cultural Freedom has never knowingly received sup-
> port, directly or indirectly, from any secret source, American or otherwise.
> Grants and contributions received over the years have been in the form of
> disinterested grands-in-aid, and there has been no effort on the part of any
> donor to influence the way in which the Congress for Cultural Freedom
> carries out its international program. We have always proceeded along
> paths of our own choosing, and all our debates and discussions—in fact
> our entire program—have been a matter of public record. We have been
> completely satisfied that private American and European philanthropy was
> independent and non-governmental.
>
> However, in the light of the implications raised by the New York Times
> report, we will ask the individuals and organizations who have generously
> supported us in the past to demonstrate to our satisfaction the private char-
> acter of their support. We intend to maintain the hitherto unquestioned
> integrity of the Congress.[114]

The whole statement hinged, of course, on the adverb "knowingly." As far as
Nabokov was concerned, it was true. Also true was the claim that the Congress
had never operated according to instructions received from its financial backers.
Yet, as Nabokov was no doubt advised by Hunt and Josselson, the letter stopped
short of denying the charges. So did the open letter that appeared in the *Times* over
the signatures of Galbraith, Kennan, Oppenheimer, and Schlesinger: it stressed
the independence of the Congress's policies, the integrity of its officials (with due

acknowledgment of Nabokov's leadership), and "the value of its contributions."[115]
This letter was endorsed by many friends of the Congress (and of Nabokov's),
including Auden, Hook, Mary McCarthy, Menuhin, and Lionel Trilling. Nabokov
himself solicited Stravinsky's support.

> I can assure you that it would mean a great deal to me and to all my col-
> leagues who have been working for many years so devotedly and disinter-
> estingly for the Congress for Cultural Freedom. [. . .]You can well imagine,
> how deeply hurt I was by all these implications and how much it means to
> me and to all of us here that our friends now stand up for the sixteen year
> old record of integrity of the Congress.[116]

It is not clear whether Stravinsky reacted to this plea. Nabokov received unprompted
letters of support. The one from Menuhin has already been quoted.[117] Virgil
Thomson mused whether the "CIA allegation" might be "a move of your enemies
to hinder the Washington appointment. Likely not, but it's inconvenient."[118] The
warmest support came from a "sad and horrified" Oppenheimer:

> Overwhelmingly the good things of the Congress have been your making;
> and you have known enough to make it one of the great and benign influ-
> ences of two difficult decades, and to bind a host of people, strangers and
> friends alike, to you in gratitude.[119]

On May 10, Nabokov and Rougemont (in his capacity as Chairman of the Congress's
Executive Council) jointly signed a letter which restated the points Nabokov had
made ten days earlier: it stressed that the Congress had been founded by a group
of intellectuals and artists from all parts of the world; that it had always had a
variety of sources of financing; that no pressure had ever come from any of its
financial sponsors; and that the accusations were damaging to the intellectuals
who had participated in the Congress's activities.

The most damaging potential consequences of the 1966 revelations did
not, of course, affect intellectuals in the United States and Western Europe,
but in the developing world, where, in the new climate of anti-Americanism
spurred by the war in Vietnam, suspicions of being linked to the CIA could
put one in real danger in one's own country. Thus Tawfiq Sayigh, the editor
of the Congress-sponsored Arabic-language journal *Hiwar* (Dialogue), published in Beirut, was banned from Egypt and questioned by the Lebanese
police—prompting Nabokov to contact friends in that country to defend the
magazine.[120] In Paris, meanwhile, the Congress was preparing to reorganize
itself after the Ford Foundation, now chaired by McGeorge Bundy, expressed
its willingness to step in to cover most of its budget, at least provisionally.[121] In

August 1966, Nabokov, along with other CCF officials, was interviewed in Paris by James Perkins, President of Cornell University and Chairman of President Johnson's Advisory Committee on the US Foreign Assistance Program. In his memorandum to the Foundation, Perkins, while stressing that the organization was "led by absolutely first-class people," nevertheless noted a "disintegration of leadership"—no doubt a euphemism for the fact that Josselson was now in Geneva and Nabokov in Berlin.[122] An administrative revamping was obviously in order. A new structure, proposed by Josselson, was put in place in October. The Executive Committee and position of Secretary General were eliminated, to be replaced by a Board of Directors, which Raymond Aron agreed to chair. "I have settled my affairs with 'them' in a perfectly gentleman-like manner," Nabokov reported to Isaiah Berlin. "M.J. has been understanding, kind, and very, very friendly."[123] Yet, although he was immediately asked to join the new board, Nabokov felt, as he reported to Oppenheimer (who was also elected to the board), that he had suddenly become at once "the forgotten man" and a target for public slander.

> The poetic irony of the whole story is that I now may look to people outside (and within the Congress community) that "I" and not "others" have been an agent of a certain distinguished Agency, and had to be sacrificed to the Ford-and-Bundy money Idol. All others appear now to have been pure and had nothing to do with the "Agency" and its former help. You know of course how false this is, but it is precisely the impression that an absence of public statement on the part of Mike and Aron, and their colleagues seems to imply to the "uninitiated."[124]

"I hate to be thought of as an 'agent' and . . . I loathe bad manners," Nabokov added, suggesting that Oppenheimer might raise the issue with Josselson. To Stuart Hampshire, who wrote sympathetically from Princeton that "the Congress's atti-tude to its own past, and its own members, is so very like that of the Communist Party," Nabokov also vented his frustration:

> The interesting part of the Congress's past path is that every time that *I* had to do something, I had to raise the money myself. Hence its present purity does not affect me personally; on the contrary, you probably know by now that I have resigned as Secretary General and will remain as some sort of adviser on the arts. What bothers me is the need to look for a new job in America.[125]

As of December 1966, the reports about the CIA's involvement in the financing of the Congress were still officially treated as "allegations." But at the end of the year, *The New York Times* ran a series of three more articles on the CIA's international propaganda network.[126] And all doubts were lifted by mid-February, when the California counterculture magazine *Ramparts* (in its issue dated March) ran a well-publicized article, ostensibly on the CIA financing of the international programs of the US National Students' Association, but which took the opportunity to expose the whole network of "passing foundations," including the ones closely linked to the Congress. In the words of the Agency's historian Michael Warner, the revelations "precipitated one of the worst operational catastrophes of CIA history."[127] No denial was possible any longer. "Among the foundations named," Hunt (who, obviously, knew the entire story) reported to Nabokov, "are at least two which have in the past made contributions to the CCF. We must assume, therefore, that the Congress was possibly the recipient of funds which may have had their origin in the CIA."[128] On March 15, Nabokov, from Princeton, had a telephone exchange with Josselson, and replied to Hunt the next day: "As you know, 'Ramparts' is on a real rampage and has been approaching everyone under the sun. So far they haven't reached me, but if they do, I'll reply as per my telephone conversation with Mike yesterday morning."[129]

The denouement came at the May 13 General Assembly meeting in Paris, chaired by Masani, and attended, among others, by Aron, Bell, Emmanuel, Fisher, Polanyi, Rougemont, Shils, Silone, and Sperber. Hunt and Josselson tendered their resignations, which were "taken note of," but not formally accepted until September.[130] A press release was issued, stating, in terms which reflected Nabokov's own views, that the Assembly "condemned in the strongest terms the way in which the C.I.A. had deceived those concerned and had caused their efforts to be called into question. The effect of such action, the Assembly stated, tends to poison the wells of intellectual discourse. The Assembly repudiated entirely the employment of such methods within the world of ideas."[131]

One more nail was driven into the Congress's coffin two weeks later by Tom Braden, the former head of the CIA's International Organization Division, who published an explosive interview, provocatively entitled "I'm Glad the CIA Is Immoral," in the London *Saturday Evening Post* for May 20, 1967. Braden, who had been, as it were, present at the Creation, told the whole story of the Congress's financing. The repercussions of this "in your face" statement were unpleasant for many people, worst of all perhaps for Rajat Neogy, editor of the outstanding Congress-sponsored African magazine *Transition*, who was arrested and jailed in Kampala.[132] Less dramatically, to be sure, Nabokov himself was another casualty of Braden's "coming out": the latter's effusive words of praise for the 1952 festival made it sound as if Nabokov, whose name Braden did not even bother to mention as sole instigator and principal conceptor of the event, had acted on CIA instructions. Paradoxically, *Encounter* weathered the storm, despite Braden's claim that one of its editors was an agent. This was no doubt a reference to Lasky, who always denied it, but the fact that the charge was anonymous inevitably raised suspicions and distressed Irving Kristol.[133] Severing its connections to the Congress, the magazine, notwithstanding the departure of Spender and Frank Kermode, continued to flourish until 1990.

As for the Congress, it tried to reinvent itself under a different name: recast as the International Association for Cultural Freedom, with Emmanuel as its director, Shepard Stone as its president, and the Oxford historian Alan Bullock as chairman of its Board of Directors. For Nabokov, it was the end of an association to which he had given so much time and energy over the past seventeen years. "The flap about C.I.A money was quite unwarranted," Kennan wrote to Stone, "and caused far more anguish than it should have been permitted to cause. I never felt the slightest pangs of conscience about it, from the standpoint of the organization. This country has no ministry of culture, and C.I.A. was obliged to do what it could to try to fill the gap. It should be praised for having done so, and not criticized."[134]

18

Love's Labour's Won

THE SEVERING OF Nabokov's ties with the Congress and its successor organization closed the main chapter of his life but was hardly a closure. It was, rather, a source of anxiety that remained with him for the rest of his life. "You do seem to be entrapped by the Congress," Spender—himself badly bruised by the scandal over *Encounter*—wrote to him in 1970, adding: "I think one might write a funny Gogol-like story about a man who, whatever he did, and whoever his employer, found he was always being paid for by the CIA."[1] Had Nabokov sacrificed his career and reputation to a cause that was now distorted and discredited in the court of public opinion? Would it not have been better for him to remain a composer, instead of serving ideals that were now deliberately misrepresented and misunderstood?[2] Had he not damaged his health in addition to putting his honor at risk? Already in the fall of 1962, Isaiah Berlin reported to his wife that Nabokov was "much older; feebler, weaker," adding: "If he goes on life this, he will soon die."[3] In November 1964, after the fatigue and nervous strain of the Berlin Festival, he was sick for three weeks with angina, which developed into pneumonia. In February 1965, after an exhausting trip to Japan to prepare that year's festival, he had to take a few weeks' rest in Paris following a new heart alert. In 1966, after he canceled a medical checkup, his doctor urged him to be careful.

> We need to have this meeting, because it is indispensable that you change, in your lifestyle, what tires you and compromises your heart condition: you require some quiet, a much more reasonable regimen, a less rich diet, less frequent traveling. I know that as a friend you keep me informed of the difficult problems of your life. I do not believe they will be better solved unless you bring some order into your life.[4]

Another intimation of mortality came when Nabokov witnessed the rapid decline and death of Oppenheimer, to whom he had become particularly close in the last two years of his life.[5] In 1966, Oppenheimer invited him to become a visiting member of the Institute for Advanced Study in Princeton. "Here I am," Nabokov wrote to Anna Kallin, "installed in a kind of motel-like structure of the Institute of [*sic*] Advanced Study, where everything is made out of glass and Vladimir Nabokov-like loud and cheerful plumbing and which is inhabited, instead of numerous Lolitas, by glum and middle-aged (or, frankly, aged) mathematicians, physicists and historians (next to me lives a seven-foot-tall, lean, Swiss historian, specialist on the Roman army). The only—but very potent—consolations, as far as human beings are concerned, are the Oppenheimers, George Kennan, Stuart [Hampshire] and his wife and the dear, sweet Sessions."[6] Nabokov resided in Princeton again in the fall of 1966, when Hampshire, who was on leave, lent him his house. By then, Oppenheimer's throat cancer had begun to worsen, and Nabokov was one of his most frequent visitors during the weeks that preceded his death on February 18, 1967. A week later, he joined the large crowd that gathered in Princeton for the memorial service, the musical part of which he arranged—the slow movement of Schubert's C major Quintet, performed by the Juilliard String Quartet, and, at Oppenheimer's own request, Stravinsky's *Requiem Canticles*.[7] Other friends present included Kennan, Schlesinger, and Spender. "Now that the vigil is over," Nabokov wrote his editor at Weidenfeld & Nicholson, "there is an immense sense of loss that one feels and somehow cannot deal with."[8]

Despite worries and losses, the last decade of Nabokov's life was one of the happiest, thanks to the new woman who entered his life in late 1964 and never left it. Dominique Cibiel, a young French photographer, brought him an element of emotional stability he had lacked, and her presence at his side was gratefully acknowledged by all his friends. During the last weeks of the Congress's existence, Nabokov, with Josselson's help and advice, had made financial provisions for the education of his son Alexandre, then nearing thirteen, an arrangement contingent on postponing his divorce from Marie-Claire until their son reached the age of sixteen.[9] It was thus not until March 23, 1970, that he and Dominique were married in New York. Their witnesses were Arthur Schlesinger, Virgil Thomson, the pianist Madeleine Malraux (by then separated from the novelist and French cultural minister and living in New York), and the writer Jean Stein, then married to the diplomat William Vanden Heuvel. Nabokov and his new wife divided their lives between the United States and Europe. In Paris, where Marie-Claire kept the apartment on Rue Jean Goujon, they first rented a flat at 17 bis, avenue Beaucour, a quiet residential cul-de-sac off the Rue du Faubourg Saint-Honoré. The house belonged to a Mrs. Lebedev, the widow of a Russian aircraft designer and, after her death, passed on to her old servant, a picturesque character straight out of Tolstoy who was devoted to Nabokov. After 1971, thanks to Dominique's uncle, the Nabokovs acquired a flat on Rue Oberkampf, near the Place de la République. In New York, Nabokov had hitherto stayed most often in Thomson's Chelsea Hotel apartment. Thanks to Richard Burgi, head of the Princeton Slavic Department—and also a friend of Thomson—Nabokov heard about a flat in a townhouse located at 450 West 20th Street. As of 1967, this became his and Dominique's permanent, final New York address.

As if to assert his newly gained political independence, Nabokov, as soon as the Congress had disbanded, accepted the invitation arranged by Abrasimov to spend three weeks in Russia as a guest of the Union of Soviet Composers from June 21 until July 1, 1967. Save for a few hours between trains when he was a child, this was his first visit to Moscow. "Like the Kremlin churches, my vocabulary, my semantics were a museum," he noted at the beginning of the fragmentary travel diary he kept.[10] The Russian capital struck him as "an uncouth, disoriented, unfinished and utterly bewildering city," reminding him at first of "a kind of Delhi." In the account of the trip that closes his memoir, he evokes the precautions and friendly surveillance he was surrounded by, as if he had been "a very delicate object [. . .] to be carefully unwrapped, and then genteelly but thoroughly processed" until ready to be "rewrapped and shipped safely back to Berlin."[11] "Thank God! I am a foreigner here. A foreigner *everywhere*," he wrote down, noting little details like the pervasive smell of cheap gasoline mixed with cheap perfume, a noisy wedding party at the hotel, and the "nice young waiter" who pressed him with questions about New York. By coincidence, his old friend Sol Hurok was staying at the same hotel. Piloted by a "nurse" named Elvira, he was driven to the obligatory sites, from the Red Square ("smaller than I thought") to the Gum department store ("a mixture of Calcutta and Madras, minus the smell of spices").

"All the time I was there," he reported to Kennan, "I felt sad, harassed, often depressed and angry, on the one hand, about the neglect to which are subjected so many good people and things and, on the other hand, about the pietistic bosh they make of other things."[12] To Michael Bessie, his publisher, he wrote that he "hated the Kremlin and its empty churches: coloured wards with gilded cupolas."[13] On the other hand, he was thrilled to visit the Tretyakov Gallery and discover its unparalleled collections of Russian portraiture, and, while in Leningrad, visit the splendidly renovated imperial palace in Tsarskoe-Selo (renamed Pushkin). The American ambassador, Llewelyn Thompson, was an old friend from the Dumbarton Avenue days. Nabokov was received cordially by Furtseva, whom he saw twice—first as an impromptu meeting which he suspected had been carefully planned. She struck him as "an extremely kind and intelligent lady."[14] In both cities he had cordial meetings with composers he had not always been kind to in his past writings, such as Khrennikov and Khachaturian; with the latter ("nice, warm Armenian") and his wife Nina, in particular, he quickly established friendly relations. On Khachaturian's next visit to New York, Nabokov took him to see *Don Quixote*. "For a ballet like this one," Khachaturian told him, "you would have been awarded the Lenin Prize. Why didn't you stay?"[15] Nabokov also had lunch with Emil Gilels ("nice, calm, and efficient . . . Good man").

Rostropovich telephoned shortly after Nabokov's arrival in Moscow and, upsetting the schedule, announced he invited him to his dacha in Zhukovka that evening (June 22) to celebrate their younger daughter Elena's birthday. Blaming his wife for the delay, the cellist appeared two hours late, visibly inebriated. In the old Opel, in addition to Vishnevskaya and a "very Armenian" old lady, were two bicycles. Rostropovich drove "fast and skillfully, like drunks do," to his wife's irritation. When the party reached the house ("unfinished and very messy indeed"), Elena and her sister Olga were overjoyed at seeing the bicycles, but one of them turned out to be missing a screw and Rostropovich proceeded to try to mend it, without success. Shostakovich then arrived with his wife. "Poor, poor sick man," Nabokov noted in his diary that evening.[16] It was their first encounter since their confrontation at the 1949 Waldorf-Astoria conference; nor did Shostakovich appear not to bear Nabokov the slightest grudge for this earlier episode. Conductor Gennadii Rozhdestvenskii was also in attendance. At the birthday party—cakes and sweets washed down by gin, Bulgarian red wine, Hungarian white wine, and tea—conversation topics included Stravinsky's Russian visit and Boulez's conducting, which Shostakovich praised, while expressing reservations on Debussy's music ("No, no, I can't, I loathe it, I loathe it . . ."). After the guests had left, and while Vishnevskaya had gone for a walk, Rostropovich announced, "with constrained fury," that they would drive back without waiting for her; "*quel ménage*," Nabokov commented. That night, being prevented by his Cerberus from going out for a nightcap, he read in bed the libretto of Schoenberg's *Moses und Aaron* ("what a ghastly [. . .] highfalutin nonsense! But the music, ah! such *real* genius. Very much like the latter-day Beethoven"). The following evening he attended a concert at the Bolshoi, with Rostropovich as soloist playing Shostakovich's Second Cello Concerto, after which the composer conducted his cantata on words by Yevtushenko, *Kazn' Stepana Razina* (The Execution of Stenka Razin). The same program was to be taken to the Montreal World Fair; "not my cup of tea" was Nabokov's terse comment about the second work.

A particularly poignant moment for Nabokov must have been his reunion with Lina Prokofiev, whom he had last seen in the early 1930s. Abandoned by her husband in 1941 for a younger woman whom he eventually married—his 1923 marriage to Lina having been declared void by the Soviet authorities because it had not been registered with a Soviet consulate—she had been arrested in 1948, charged with treasonable contacts with foreign embassies, and sent to the Gulag.[17] Released only in 1956, she had been reunited with her sons Sviatoslav (born in 1924) and Oleg (born in 1928), whom Nabokov had known as children. Soon after his arrival in Moscow, he had gone to the Novodevichy cemetery to look (in vain) for Prokofiev's tomb. Having finally reached Lina by telephone, he had lunch and a long talk with her on June 26. After his return from Petersburg, he had lunch with her again, this time with her two sons, and saw her—and Oleg—on two more occasions during his short stay. Did they discuss plans to convince the French government to have a plaque placed on the house where the Prokofievs lived on Rue Valentin Haüy? Nabokov subsequently intervened to this effect, but Lina Prokofiev, who was invited for the May 1969 ceremony, did not obtain her exit visa.[18] Oleg, whose second wife was British, was able to leave the Soviet Union in 1971, and Lina herself joined him three years later.[19]

In both cities Nabokov was able to hear music by younger composers such as Edison Denisov, who called on him soon after his arrival in Moscow ("*delicious meeting*"), Alfred Schnittke, Boris Tishchenko, and the dodecaphonist Valentin Sylvestrov. "I brought back," Nabokov wrote to Elliott Carter, "a full stock of the most advanced music I have ever heard. Xenakis and Mr Bussotti are nothing in comparison with what is being done by some boys there."[20] ("Only the young talk a little," he noted in his diary, "and they create in protest.")[21] In both Moscow and Leningrad, he had the opportunity to play some of his own music at the headquarters of the Composers' Union.

The most emotionally charged moment of Nabokov's trip was the excursion he took on June 26 to the holy city of Sergiyev Posad—rebaptized Zagorsk under Soviet rule—where, in the chapel of the Trinity Lavra monastery, the burial place of St. Serge, he felt he heard, "as if coming from very, very far, like the remote sound of a harp string, the quiet beating of the Russian heart."[22] Leningrad, on the other hand, where he spent three days (June 28–30), going by train from Moscow both ways and staying at the Astoria Hotel, turned out to be "a traumatic experience."[23] Whereas Stravinsky had been bowled over by the city's architectural splendor during his 1962 visit, the beautiful facades, Nabokov told Stravinsky, "angered" him.[24] He sensed that behind this magnificent "shell," the soul of the city of his youth "was gone, gone forever."[25] "I knew in my mind that I would not find what I had left there," he later reminisced when interviewed on French television, "but I couldn't help looking for something that was no longer present."[26] One of his first visits was a pilgrimage to the family house, now much degraded, while he noted that "the proportions were exactly as he remembered them."[27] He also glanced at his old school.

"Russia was irritating, exhausting, terribly interesting, full of problems and beautiful festivals," Nabokov summed up his experience to Michael Bessie, promising him, for his autobiography, "a last chapter about the Russian trip, a chapter full of anger and irony."[28] To Stravinsky, he complained that he was "utterly worn out" and that Russia was, next to India, "the most exhausting country" he had been to.[29] As he told Carter, on his return, he had lost five kilos. He spent a few weeks recovering, in Dominique's company, first at Kolbsheim, where he was briefly reunited with Maritain, and then with the Bethmann-Hollwegs at Altenhof.

Despite this emotionally wrenching experience, Nabokov accepted a second official invitation from Abrasimov to visit the Soviet Union the following year. This time, he planned to bring Dominique (who was not part of the 1967 trip), take her to Byelorussia to see what remained of his native place, and travel to Lithuania to pay his respects with her at his mother's grave in Vilnius. Alain, the son of Madeleine Malraux from her first marriage to André Malraux's brother Roland, was to accompany them. But after Soviet troops invaded Czechoslovakia on August 20, 1968, Nabokov decided to turn down the invitation. Abrasimov, who had made the arrangements, was obviously disappointed, but this did not affect their good relations: the two men remained in contact, in Berlin and then in Paris, where Abrasimov became Soviet ambassador in September 1971.[30]

A few months before Nabokov's 1967 Russian visit, one of the most sensational defections of the period had occurred when Svetlana Allilueva, Stalin's daughter, requested political asylum at the US embassy in New Delhi.[31] Kennan, who was among those who debriefed her in Switzerland before she arrived in America, sent Nabokov an excited report and made plans for him to meet her. Nabokov, as he explained to Kennan, was diffident at first. "I am sure she is a marvelous person and those who have read her book say it is a remarkable work. But for reasons which are too long to explain here, I have divided feelings about meeting her, largely because of the complicated relations which I have established with many young people in the Soviet Union."[32] When Nabokov and Allilueva did meet in Princeton through Kennan as planned, the two emigres nevertheless hit it off splendidly, despite their widely different backgrounds. However, as with virtually everyone she initially befriended in America, Stalin's daughter found a pretext to quarrel with Nabokov and this put an end to their relations.

Nabokov continued to remain involved in Berlin cultural matters, and especially the music festival. In 1966, the general theme was the Baroque, while the featured composer was Hindemith. The 1967 festival, which featured the European debut of the Kathakali dance theater, was initially supposed to focus on East-West contacts but the subject proved too politically controversial and was altered to "Europe" in a broad sense, with Schoenberg as the composer honored. This gave Nabokov the opportunity to enlist the collaboration of Leibowitz, one of Schoenberg's principal champions in France, with whom he had differed in print two decades before. However, the departure of Willy Brandt, who became the West German Chancellor in December 1966, deprived Nabokov of his key ally in the politically fraught climate of the city. Despite his friendly relations with Egon Bahr, Brandt's right-hand man in Berlin, Nabokov stepped down as festival director in 1967, remaining only in an advisory capacity. "After three years of working with Berliners (the best of the lot)," he complained to Isaiah Berlin in a moment of discouragement, "I am warier of Germans than I was ever before."[33] As a courteous, but exasperated February 6, 1968, letter to Stresemann shows, Nabokov was not always consulted about

matters directly pertaining to his advisory duties.[34] Nevertheless, the festival continued to flourish. The 1968 edition, the last one he was directly and completely
involved in, featured, among many other offerings, exhibitions on the Wilhelmine
Period and Piotr Mondrian; plays by Molière and Feydeau performed by the
Comédie-Française; Césaire's *Une saison au Congo* in a Jean-Marie Serreau production; the Alvin Nikolais Dance Theater; the world premiere of Dallapiccola's opera
Ulisse, under Lorin Maazel; and prestige concerts by the New York Philharmonic
conducted by Bernstein and the Berlin Philharmonic under Böhm and Karajan.

As Nabokov's Berlin responsibilities became less onerous, he took on other
advisory positions. Through his former contacts in Japan, he was hired as festival
consultant to the Royal Japan Festival, though he soon realized that the organizers were not looking for innovative programs but for big, bankable names like
Callas and Richter. Monte-Carlo requested Nabokov's services, notably for a festival in 1969 commemorating the fortieth anniversary of Diaghilev's final season
in the principality. In September 1967, at Menuhin's urging, he went to Teheran
to participate in a music conference. He had misgivings—"the whole affair," he
wrote to Thomson, "will probably turn into a Menuhiada"—and was furthermore
reluctant to speak, as requested, on "infant education in music."[35] Yet this visit
led to an offer to serve as consultant to the Teheran Biennale, beginning in 1968.
For the 1969 edition, he submitted ambitious plans along the lines of his past
festivals: a broad unifying theme ("Rhythm"); groups to be invited from Africa,
Brazil, and France (the Percussions de Strasbourg); and the participation, which
he would help negotiate via Khrennikov, of two younger Soviet composers he had
befriended during his Moscow visit, Denisov and Tishchenko.[36]

Another outcome of the 1967 conference in Teheran was the founding of
the Shiraz Festival, for which Nabokov also began to serve as an adviser. In the
words of Daniélou, who was also involved, the festival was "strictly a millionaire's
idea": when the first festival was held in the fall of 1968, the hotels, hastily built in
the middle of the desert, remained unfinished, still surrounded by barbed wire;
as for musicians and performers, they had to be flown from Teheran on military planes. During the inaugural concert, a mini-tornado blew away the scores
of the Tchaikovsky symphony the orchestra was playing. Yet, while noting that
"the unexpected sounds of Schönberg, Ligeti, and Boulez must have made Darius
turn in his grave," Daniélou also noted that concerts, like the one by the Indian
oboist Bismillah Khan at the tomb of Hafiz, the fourteenth-century Persian poet,
"were intensely poetic and never to be forgotten."[37] Though wary of the political
implications of these festivals, Nabokov developed friendships with the organizers in Teheran and Shiraz and visited Iran regularly throughout the following
decade. One of his main contributions to the Shiraz Festival was to facilitate the
participation of Peter Brook. A longtime admirer of the British director's work,
Nabokov had invited him to present his production of Peter Weiss's *Marat-Sade*

at the Berlin Festival. When in 1970 Brook was invited by the French government to establish in Paris his newly created International Centre for Theatre Research, Nabokov was instrumental in securing a gift from an American patron to help launch the project. *Orghast*, the experimental play on the myth of Prometheus, written by Brook in collaboration with Ted Hughes in an imaginary language that gave the work its title, was premiered at Persepolis in the fall of 1971, with a cast of actors from nine different countries, including Iran. It was the International Centre's first public performance.[38]

Even though Nabokov, when asked to step down as secretary general of the Congress, received a financial settlement from the Farfield Foundation, he now found himself without a salary and the attached benefits, which increased his disappointment not to get the Kennedy Center appointment. Never a rich man—or even well off—since his family had left Russia, he found himself, once again, facing the familiar predicament of professional classical composers: having to find sources of income to supplement the little they made with their music. In the spring of 1967 he considered applying for the directorship of the Disney-endowed California Institute of the Arts, for which he was recommended by Ormandy.[39] Teaching, despite his professed aversion to it, remained the most obvious and safest option. Thanks to Arthur Schlesinger, he was appointed visiting professor at the City University of New York, where he taught a seminar on "The arts in their social environment" in the winter and spring of 1968. In the fall of 1969, he was recruited as adjunct professor at Old Westbury, the liberal arts college that had opened two years before in Oyster Bay, New York, as part of the New York State university system, with campus buildings designed by Buckminster Fuller. The president of the college, Harris Wofford Jr., was a former aide to President Kennedy and associate director of the Peace Corps. There Nabokov taught a music course and lectured on Communist Russia, from the 1917 Bolshevist Revolution to the post-Stalinist era. He also led a theater workshop in collaboration with Jerome Ziegler, vice president of the college. As if to revisit his undergraduate theater experience from his Wells and St. John's days, he mounted a production, that winter, of Euripides's *The Trojan Women*. Old Westbury was not spared the wind of student revolt that was blowing on most American campuses during that year, but Nabokov was determined to make the best of the experience, and the play—which involved students from underprivileged milieus and minority groups—was a success, "the best thing that's happened at Old Westbury," Wofford wrote to him.[40] In 1970, however, Wofford left Old Westbury to become the fifth president of Bryn Mawr College. The new Old Westbury president, John D. Maguire, did not renew Nabokov's appointment. In the fall of 1970, Nabokov became visiting professor at the State University of New York in Buffalo, where he taught a graduate course in aesthetics. He also had one student in composition, who "did things entirely his own way, couldn't help him at all."[41] This was his last stint as professor of composition. In February and March 1972, he lectured at Bryn Mawr and in Beirut. From September 1, 1972, until the end of February 1973 he served as composer-writer in residence at the Music Department of New York University, and in March 1973, he revisited St. John's College, where he gave a lecture. In the fall of 1975, thanks to an arrangement with the Gottesmann Foundation, he was appointed writer-in-residence at New York University for the academic year, with a salary of $22,000. Though he claimed he never liked to teach, Nabokov was not only a dedicated pedagogue—"I am redeemed by my good German blood," he liked to say—but, in fact, an excellent one.[42]

In late 1969, Nabokov began working as consultant to the Institute for Study of Humanities founded in 1949 in Aspen, Colorado, by Walter Paepcke. A Chicago executive, Paepcke had been strongly influenced by Mortimer Adler's Great Books program: Nabokov was thus in familiar territory.[43] Paepcke's dream was to assemble at the Institute, every summer, authors and artists, along with business leaders who would all participate in "executive seminars." The institute was headed by Joseph Slater, formerly the deputy of Shephard Stone at the Ford Foundation, who, in early 1970, started making plans to open a branch of the Institute in West Berlin with the foundation's support. Nabokov was asked to suggest names of European and American personalities who might be invited to join the Institute's Arts Council.[44] In a memorandum entitled "The Arts and its Makers," he outlined various proposals for the organization. Examining the current situation, in terms both of cultural heritage preservation and avant-garde experimentation, he argued that "more time should be devoted to the exploration, discussion, and as it were, an 'analysis in depth' of the present-day fallow anarchy that prevails in the life of the arts." He suggested a program of seminars, beginning with one on the theater in 1971 and followed by similar ones on composers, musical performers, and critics in 1972; painters, sculptors, dealers, and critics in 1973; poets, writers, publishers, and literary critics in 1974; and, finally, in 1975, filmmakers and film critics. He also mentioned the possibility of an art exhibition along the lines of the one the Congress had sponsored in Paris in 1960.

First involved as a consultant, Nabokov was appointed artistic adviser to the president of the Institute as well as composer-in-residence, beginning in 1970. The most enjoyable part of Nabokov's Aspen duties was the ability to get old friends invited to spend the summer at the Institute: Cartier-Bresson thus came in 1971, with his wife Martine Franck, and presented his *Vive la France* exhibition. In 1972, it was the turn of Schlesinger, Sessions, and Xenakis, while Bohlen—already suffering from the cancer that killed him two years later—was also the Institute's guest; in 1973, Carter, Stuart Hampshire, Gilbert Amy, and the Korean composer Isang Yun (now residing in West Germany) came, with Peter Brook as a special guest at the end of August. Nabokov also invited Khatchaturian and Rostropovich but they were prevented from traveling.

Much in the same way as he had become suspicious of the Great Books Program at St. John's, Nabokov quickly grew disenchanted with Aspen. "Too many cooks are cooking the Aspen cultural dinner," he wrote to Slater in the fall of 1970.[45] In his private correspondence with Josselson, he began to call the Institute "Humanities in aspic."[46] Even during his first summer, there was a strong note of irony in his comments. "This place here," he wrote to Peter Diamand, "is full of Paepcke. He invented the mountains, the Institute and of course, Dr. Schweitzer. The mountains are beautiful and teutonic."[47] As he complained to the painter Herbert Bayer and his wife, he felt increasingly allergic to "bureaucrato-charismatic memorandese" and noted that the frenzied atmosphere—perhaps a comment on his own past experience at the head of the Congress—was not conducive to creation. "The active life of the mind does not flourish at conferences and at seminars."[48] "I stay away from seminars and go rarely to lectures," he reported to Josselson in August 1973. "Instead we drove the other day in the company of Francine [du Plessix Gray] and the dear Hampshires to Monument Valley. It is the most beautiful *fin du monde* landscape I've ever seen."[49] It was Nabokov's last summer in Aspen. The following year he wrote to the same Josselson that he was "mightily glad" not to return to Colorado.[50] And in 1975, he wrote to another friend that he was happy "to be out of the Mc B[undy] + McNam[ara] + Joe MacSlate circuit with all these Nobelites."[51]

Nabokov's principal objective, after leaving the Congress, was to resume his career as composer, which, thanks to Balanchine, had been given a boost with *Don Quixote*. He immediately embarked on various new projects, not all of which came to fruition. In March 1966, he signed a contract with the Harkness Ballet, which had been incorporated in New York in 1964, for a thirty-minute score to be choreographed by George Skibine, the company's artistic director. Setting to work at once, Nabokov completed the commission in September, dedicating it to the memory of Gerald and Sara Murphy. Entitled *The Wanderer*, it was loosely inspired by the episode of the costume party in the first part of Alain-Fournier's 1913 novel *Le Grand Meaulnes*. Most of the music was written, in the summer of 1966, at Rebekah Harkness's seaside villa in Watch Hill, Rhode Island. Skibine, however, postponed the project and, by the time the company folded in 1975, the ballet had not been produced and was yet to be orchestrated. Nabokov showed the short score to Balanchine, who told him he liked it but so long as *Don Quixote* was being revived he could not have more than one Nabokov ballet in his repertory.[52] As late as the summer of 1977, when interviewed by the French radio, Nabokov mentioned the Grand Meaulnes ballet as being an ongoing project, adding that it was intended for the Vienna Opera.[53]

Another abortive project was an orchestration of Ravel's piano suite *Gaspard de la nuit*, which Karajan, in late 1966, expressed interest in commissioning. But Durand, Ravel's publisher, nipped it in the bud, arguing that if Ravel had wanted to orchestrate the work he would have done it himself.[54] In 1969 Nabokov's friend Sylvia Marlowe, on behalf of the Harpsichord Music Society, tried to get him to overcome his old antipathy toward this instrument by commissioning a composition. But she was not successful, and in early 1972, Nabokov returned his $500 advance. Also around 1969, the New York City Ballet commissioned an orchestration of the slow movement of Schubert's C major Quintet with two cellos. Balanchine, however, never choreographed it.

The news of Anna Akhmatova's death in March 1966 awakened in Nabokov a desire to pay tribute to her, as he had to Pasternak six years before. He set to music six poems from the group, most of them dating from 1939–40, that had come out in Munich in 1963 under the title *Requiem*—actually a section of the larger collection entitled *Reed*—while her work remained banned in the Soviet Union. The choice of these particular poems, which evoke the harsh realities of everyday life in Russia under Stalin, was thus doubly a plea for cultural freedom as well as a homage to a great Russian poet. The cycle was commissioned by the American soprano Evelyn Lear, herself of Russian Jewish origin (her maiden name was Evelyn Shulman) as well as a champion of twentieth-century music. Unlike Nabokov's Pasternak songs, which were intended from the start for voice and orchestra, the Akhmatova Lieder were conceived with piano accompaniment. The published score is accompanied with English and German translations, but the songs themselves (unlike the Pasternak Lieder) are set only in Russian and a note stipulates that they are not to be sung in any other language. This English translation was realized by Nabokov himself, with duly acknowledged advice from Nina Berberova, the prominent emigre writer, whom he got to know through Richard Burgi and befriended when living in Princeton, where she taught in the Slavic Department.[55] Lear premiered the cycle in Rome in 1967 and it was published by Bote & Bock in Berlin in the same year. She was also scheduled to sing it in an orchestral version at the 1968 Berlin Festival, with Bruno Maderna conducting the Residenz Orchestra of The Hague, but she canceled and her replacement was inadequate. Unjustly, the work remains among Nabokov's least performed and least known.

A consequence of Nabokov's 1967 trip to Moscow and contacts with Rostropovich was the commission of a piece for cello and orchestra. In the course of a dinner that fall at Nabokov's Paris apartment with Rostropovich and Balanchine, the idea was floated of a ballet with music by Nabokov, choreographed by Balanchine, and with Rostropovich doubling as conductor and soloist. Balanchine was sufficiently taken by the idea to send a telegram to Furtseva on October 24 to convey his interest in the project and ask for her support, while urging Nabokov to have a score ready for a premiere optimistically scheduled for early May 1968.

Nabokov conceived the work as a set of variations on a "tender and lyrical" theme that had long haunted him, Oksana's aria in act 1 of Tchaikovsky's 1887 "comic-fantastic" opera *Cherevichki* (traditionally, if incorrectly, rendered as *The Slippers*), adapted from Gogol's story "Christmas Night." It consists of a prelude, four variations, and a finale. In the prelude, Tchaikovsky's theme is heard in its entirety, transposed from the original key of E down to B-flat and in a different harmonic climate. The variations, as Nabokov explained, are not traditional variations on a theme, but rather variations in the tradition of the ballet: they comprise a scherzo; a lyrical andante ("a kind of *canzona di ballo*"); a Burlesque or *omaggio cavalesco* to Tchaikovsky, inspired by Nabokov's memories of the equestrian dances of the Ciniselli Circus in St. Petersburg; and a slow movement labeled "Pas d'action," interspersed with solo cadences, which is not based on the Tchaikovsky theme but inspired, instead, by Verdi—another composer dear to Nabokov from his early years. The Finale, which contains a cadence for cello and timpani, evokes, in Nabokov's words, "the virtuoso playing of the timpani player of the Moscow Philharmonic Orchestra." It returns to Oksana's theme, distorted, this time, by nostalgic reminiscences of early jazz of the kind that was first heard in pre-1914 St. Petersburg. "The whole work is obviously a virtuoso exercise," explained Nabokov at the time of the premiere,

> considering that it was written for Mstislav Rostropovich. The musical language of the work is tonal in a *partisan* way and, while there is a little twelve-tone dust left, it is purely accidental. By the same token, the work does not call for polyphonic procedures nor for so-called "avant- garde" contemporary techniques. It remains within the tradition of Russian harmonic writing and is nothing but a humble testimony of admiration and love for Tchaikovsky's melodic genius.[56]

After the 1968 Czech crisis, Nabokov decided that in the present circumstances "any kind of cooperation with the Soviet Union would be *immoral*"; he even suggested to Balanchine that they look for a different soloist, like Jacqueline Du Pré or Pierre Fournier.[57] Yet, in October of the same year, he flew to Moscow for four days—at his own expense, since he had turned down the official invitation—to show the score to Rostropovich and continue to explore the possibility of his appearing in it if done as a ballet. While assuring Nabokov he remained interested in the idea, Rostropovich asked him to prepare a version more lightly orchestrated for concert performance. As Nabokov reported to Barbara Horgan from Teheran on October 18, 1968, it now depended on whether Sol Hurok, who by then represented both Rostropovich and his wife, would authorize this "ballet stunt." The following winter, Nabokov and Rostropovich met once again in Canada and went over the score.

While Rostropovich's initial idea was to premiere this new "concert version" in Russia, the first performance took place in Monte-Carlo on August 5, 1970, with Rostropovich and the Orchestre philharmonique de Monte-Carlo conducted by Igor Markevitch. The all-Russian program also featured Vishnevskaya in six Mussorgsky songs orchestrated by the conductor. Nabokov was not enthusiastic about the performance. Sending a tape to Ormandy, who was to conduct the American premiere the following year, he apologized for "the puny orchestra under the direction of, alas, a (more than) half deaf conductor" and complained about some of the soloist's tempi, "especially the Third Variation (F major), which should be slower than he plays it."[58]

Whether or not Hurok objected to the gimmick, the participation of Rostropovich as soloist and conductor in the choreographic version of the Tchaikovsky Variations never took place. At the time of the Monte-Carlo concert, the ballet was still announced for the 1970–71 New York City Ballet season. But it was postponed, presumably because Balanchine's own interest had waned. Yet, as late as 1977, *Oxana*, as the ballet was entitled, was again scheduled for the fall of that year, though nothing came of it.[59] As for Rostropovich, despite his occasional irritation with his star-like behavior, Nabokov supported him unreservedly when the cellist found himself in political difficulty in the spring of 1974 and was forced into exile.[60]

At the end of 1966, Nabokov received a commission from the New York Philharmonic as part of its 125th anniversary celebrations two years later. The result was his Third Symphony, subtitled "A Prayer," and which he dedicated to the memory of Pope John XXIII and Robert Oppenheimer. The work was inspired by an article Grunelius had clipped in a Swiss newspaper in 1966 and showed to Nabokov. It quoted a prayer attributed to John XXIII, in which the Pope, supposedly a few days before he died, apologized to God for the suffering inflicted by Christians on the Jewish people throughout history.[61] At once attracted and intrigued by this little-known text, Nabokov tried, without success, to verify its authenticity. He was nevertheless satisfied with the idea that its spirit was consistent with the ideals of openness and tolerance associated with its purported author.[62] Completed in Princeton in April 1967, the symphony, the shortest of Nabokov's three, is arranged in five movements. The opening Andante (Praeludium) is followed by an Allegro moderato subtitled "Diaspora," succeeded by an Andante or "Responsorium I." Then comes an Allegro non troppo "ma feroce" ("Persecutio"), followed by an Allegro moderato or "Responsorium II." "The music," the Philharmonic program quotes Nabokov as saying, "does not adhere to any system and combines serialism, modality, tonality, and contains, at certain points, archaic melodic forms." The work was premiered, under Leonard Bernstein, on January 4, 1968, at a concert that included Weber's *Euryanthe* overture, Hindemith's *Symphonic Metamorphoses*, and Beethoven's First Piano Concerto with Martha Argerich as soloist. "My symphony had what is called here a 'very good performance,'" Nabokov reported to his assistant in Berlin, where he hoped Bernstein might include it in one of his festival concerts, but Bernstein was reluctant to perform new works on tour.[63] "The orchestra liked it, played it beautifully, Lenny conducted it extremely well," Nabokov wrote to "Grisha" Propes in Israel, sending him "one intelligent review. The two others that I saw were stupid, but this is what reviews usually are (and the best of the story was that—the program being changed around—one of the reviewers mistook Hindemith's piece for being mine, only to discover that he did not like my 'real' symphony at all."[64] In late February and early March of the same year, the symphony was performed in Paris and the industrial suburb of Kremlin-Bicêtre by the Lamoureux Orchestra conducted by René Klopfenstein. "I hope," the conductor's wife wrote to Nabokov a few days later, "that you will have heard about the great success your symphony obtained with the public."

> I must tell you that even non-specialists were profoundly moved by it and this was particularly clear with the unsophisticated audience at Kremlin-Bicêtre on Saturday. Your son came, and so did the faithful Goldbeck, Marie-Claire, Sauguet, and a few others [. . .]. I want to tell you myself that the work deeply touches me personally, with its brevity, its palpitation, and its astonishing nobility. René put an enormous amount of emotion and power into it. The work is very dear to him, he could have conducted it by heart, having studied it, penetrated it so much, but he didn't dare because of the measure changes. The orchestra followed him very well.[65]

Having once described writing film music as a potentially lucrative but dangerously addictive pursuit for a "serious" classical composer, Nabokov yielded to the temptation once in 1971 when he collaborated with Jean-Louis Bertucelli on *Paulina 1880*. Born in 1942, the young French director, who was married to Nabokov's stepdaughter Caroline Corre, had come to prominence at the age of twenty-six with *Remparts d'argile*, which told about the cultural oppression of a young woman in a small Tunisian village. Adapted from the 1925 novel of the same title by Pierre Jean Jouve, *Paulina 1880* is also the tragic story of a young woman trapped, this time, in a conservative, highly religious society in late nineteenth-century Italy, who falls in love with a married man, and eventually kills him. Nabokov was captivated both by the subject and by the film director's personality. Bertucelli himself was clearly delighted to have the opportunity to work with such an experienced composer, especially since he intended to give music a prominent place in the film. Nabokov wrote and orchestrated his score in the fall of 1971, recycling elements from *The Wanderer*, his abandoned ballet project. When it was released in France in February 1972, the film got mixed reviews—it was better received in

Germany—but the music was often singled out for praise. Nabokov considered arranging an orchestral suite from the score but apparently never realized it.

To the end, Stravinsky remained a major, constant presence in Nabokov's life. In early October 1968 Nabokov visited the aging composer, now eighty-six, in Zürich, and then saw him regularly in Paris at the end of that month, for what turned out to be his last visit to Europe.[66] Their contacts became even more frequent at the end of 1969, when Stravinsky, deciding against returning to California, settled in New York, taking up residence at the Essex House. As Craft recalls in his memoirs, Nabokov and his wife were then "more attentive to Stravinsky, more gentle and affectionate to him, than any of their other friends."[67] At one dinner, on December 18, 1969, the other guests were Balanchine and Auden. The latter gulped down Stravinsky's carefully chosen Château Margaux as if it had been *vin ordinaire*, and displayed his uncommon absence of tact by exclaiming, in front of his Russian host and fellow guests: "Everybody knows that Russians are mad."[68]

On February 12, 1971, Nabokov called on the ailing composer to say good-bye before leaving for Europe. As Craft, who was present, recorded in his diary, Stravinsky reacted angrily when Nabokov innocently asked him how he was. "'You can see how I am, miserable,' he shouts, and so angrily that N[abokov], who loves him more than anyone, leaves with wet eyes."[69] When he himself recalled the occasion in his memoir, Nabokov pictured Stravinsky "sitting in his little wheelchair, [. . .] thin and transparent, his profile of an extraordinary ancient Oriental beauty." Too weak to join the dinner party Vera Stravinsky hosted that evening at the Pavillon, with Xenakis as guest of honor, he begged Nabokov not to leave him alone *"avec les femmes de chambre."*[70] It was their last encounter. Nabokov received the news of Stravinsky's death on April 6 as he was working on his new opera. Nine days later, on April 15, he attended the funeral of his friend in Venice. During the Russian Orthodox service held, by special papal dispensation, in the Basilica of San Zanipolo, Nabokov—"the only person who could have handled this," Craft noted with admiration—stood "like an ambassadorial wall" between Vera Stravinsky and Craft, on one side, and Stravinsky's children, with whom the composer was on nonspeaking terms in the last years of his life.[71] According to Daniélou, who was present, "the two groups never exchanged a word."[72] One year later to the day, on April 15, 1972, Nabokov was in Venice again for the dedication of Stravinsky's tomb in the Orthodox cemetery on the island of San Michele. Ironically, in view of Stravinsky's politics, the design of the simple monument had been commissioned from Giacomo Manzù, the Communist sculptor and Lenin Prize recipient. A few weeks later, in June 1972, Stravinsky was honored by the New York City Ballet with a ten-day festival; Vera Stravinsky served as honorary chair and Nabokov as co-chair.

After Stravinsky's death, Nabokov began to revise and expand the essay on Stravinsky he had published in German in 1964. He gave it the new title *The*

Gracious Master and first wrote it in the second person, as a sort of open letter to the late composer. Saul Bellow, whom Nabokov had met in Aspen in the summer of 1971, while complimentary on the book in general, expressed reservations about the second-person device, which he found "confusing and unnecessary."[73] He also advised Nabokov to eliminate some of the technical discussion of *Les noces*. On a more sensitive issue, Bellow pointed out that the image Nabokov gave of Robert Craft was "not entirely clear" and suggested to the reader that much was left unsaid. "When Craft is mentioned, you fall into psychological diplomacy, ambiguity, etc. This is very different from the free mordant observation which makes the rest of your memoir so delightful."[74] Following Bellow's advice, Nabokov reverted to a third-person narrative and removed the discussion of *Les noces* for separate publication.[75] On the subject of Craft, Nabokov admitted in his reply to Bellow that in his original version he had written less kindly about him, but had toned it all down at the suggestion of Dominique and of Alexander Liberman, his main concern being not to hurt Vera Stravinsky's feelings. Perhaps, he suggested, all mentions of Craft ought to be removed?[76] In the summer of Nabokov sent the 250-page typescript to Michael Bessie at Atheneum, suggesting it might be incorporated into his autobiography and might, in the meantime, be excerpted in *The New Yorker*. By the time Nabokov died, the memoir remained unpublished.

The idea of a ballet in memory of Stravinsky was born of discussions between Balanchine and Nabokov following the composer's death. "Balanchine," Nabokov reported to Nadia Boulanger in the summer of 1971, "has asked me to write a short musical piece on a psalm Igor was particularly fond of."[77] The project did not come to fruition for another three years, when Nabokov started working on a setting of Psalm 150 ("Praise ye the Lord, Praise God in His sanctuary" in the King James version). In the contract he signed by the New York City Ballet, it had become a ballet "tentatively entitled 'The Psalms,'" lasting between twenty and fifty minutes. Nabokov wrote much of the score in April 1976 when he was on a Rockefeller Foundation fellowship at the Villa Serbelloni in Bellagio. By then, Psalm 150 had become the subject of the final movement of a seven-part composition. It started with a prelude (or "Prologomenon" in the score), featuring the horn-like instrument from the Andes known as Erchenko. Part 2 was a series of five variations ("Joy"; "King David's Song"; "Round"; "On the Rivers of Babylon"; "Praise the Lord With Dance"). Then came a Miserere, based on Psalm 51, followed by a section entitled "King David's Dance in Front of the Ark (Samuel VI)." Part 4 was a Pastorale built on Psalm 23 ("The Lord Is My Shepherd"), Part 5 an "Akathesion" ("Hours" in Greek), and Part 6 a "Processional." The concluding epilogue, based on Psalm 150, is built on a theme by J. S. Bach. The ballet was to be produced with sets designed by Alexander Liberman, and Nabokov's contract with the New York City Ballet indicated the fall of 1976 as a premiere date; yet, by the time the composer died Balanchine had not been able to turn his attention to it and it has never been staged.

Though not considering himself a musicologist, Nabokov agreed to edit a four-volume series on twentieth-century music published by Weidenfeld and Nicholson (and in the United States by Holt, Rinehart, and Winston), with Anna Kallin as his co-editor. The first volume, devoted to America, written by Virgil Thomson, came out in 1971, with an introduction by Nabokov. The second volume, devoted to Germany and Central Europe, was entrusted to Stuckenschmidt, and also came out in 1971. Nabokov was unhappy with the first outline his old friend submitted in the summer of 1966: as he complained to his London editor, Frank Martin was left out, as was Stockhausen, while only one Henze opera was mentioned.[78] Nabokov was also critical of the work of another old friend, Fred Goldbeck, whom he had put in charge of the volume devoted to France, Italy, and Spain. While finding the chapters on the French avant-garde "very good indeed," Nabokov disagreed with some of Goldbeck's positive assessments in the earlier period—the "immensely boring" Maurice Emmanuel and the "odious" d'Indy in particular. He was least happy with the chapter on Debussy and required a complete rewrite, suggesting getting help from Maurice Fleuret or Peter Heyworth. Among other points of disagreement, Nabokov criticized Goldbeck for making too much of Mussorgsky's influence, which led him to restate his reservations on the Russian composer he felt was generally overrated in the West:

> In Debussy, all is *perfection*, all is total accomplishment, i.e. there is, at every moment, a complete surrender of musical matter to the will of its inventor. In Mussorgsky, all is tentative, occasional, brilliant insights clogged by howlers of imperfection. And, what is worse, it is swamped by medleys of *populismo russo* and foul burps of Wagner via Korsakov combined with dear old Modest's immodest poor taste. It is, at best, to use a gallant phrase of Louis Laloy, "l'approximation du génie."[79]

Already annoyed with Kallin's editorial interventions, Goldbeck was understandably hurt by Nabokov's negative reaction, and the two friends were on cool terms for a short period, prompting Yvonne Lefébure to plead her husband's case.[80] Amicable relations were soon restored, and when Goldbeck's volume finally came out in 1974, the author thanked Nabokov for his kind words in the introduction he provided to the volume.[81] Nabokov was not completely happy either with the contribution of the composer Humphrey Searle to the third volume, *Britain, Scandinavia and the Netherlands*, co-authored by the music critic Robert Layton, which came out in 1972. As for Russia and Eastern Europe, the subject of what was planned to be Volume 2 in the series, Nabokov first considered giving it to Nicolas

Slonimsky. He then had second thoughts and, despite his limited enthusiasm for Soviet music, toyed with the idea of going to Russia and Poland on a research trip and write it himself. In his 1966 outline, he sketched out sections on Scriabin ("strange mixture of Chopin and Liszt with French undertones"); Rachmaninov ("a pianist-composer rather than a composer-pianist . . . the anachronistic symbol of exile combined with comfort and wealth"); Stravinsky ("the first *complete* (and so far unsurpassed) eclectic genius in music"); and Prokofiev, whose weaknesses ("a certain uncouthness of his melodic invention; repetitiveness, absence of thorough polyphonic development; satire instead of irony") were balanced with his strengths ("a personal mark on every musical sentence, despite the use of convention; an innate sense of modern lyricism").[82] Slonimsky was eventually brought in, with the suggestion that the book would incorporate in some fashion the English version of Nabokov's 1964 book on Stravinsky and that he might also cover Shostakovich himself. But in the end the book remained unwritten and the series incomplete.

Nabokov had few contacts with IACF during its brief existence. He resigned from the General Assembly in 1969, pointing out that the new organization showed no interest in the arts, though he accepted Shephard Stone's offer to keep him listed as consultant.[83] With his former colleagues in the CCF, however, he remained on amicable terms, especially with John Hunt, who for a while served as executive vice president of the Salk Institute in La Jolla, California, where Nabokov visited him in December 1969, when Slater was looking for ways of developing ties between Salk and Aspen; Hunt subsequently worked as Slater's deputy at Aspen Institute and then as an executive vice president at the University of Pennsylvania. Relations with Josselson had always been, and remained, more complicated; and a note of diffidence, and even occasional irritation on Josselson's part, frequently creeps up in their correspondence—and whenever Josselson discussed Nabokov with other correspondents. Josselson devoted his retirement years to writing a biography of the Russian general Barclay de Tolly. Completed by his wife Diana, it was published posthumously by Oxford University Press in 1980.

Beginning in the early 1970s, Josselson, Hunt, and Nabokov were involved in discussions concerning the disposition of the Congress's vast archive, which was for a while deposited with the cultural center established at the Abbey of Royaumont outside Paris. Well aware of the lack of resources of French research facilities and wary of the obstacles raised by the cumbersome French state bureaucracy, Nabokov strongly argued against keeping the archive in France, suggesting that a major American academic library—or even the Library of Congress—would be a far more suitable choice. Columbia University, where his niece Marina Ledkovsky taught in the Slavic Department, appeared the strongest contender for a while, though in the end an arrangement was made with the University of

Chicago, owing to the presence on the faculty of scholars long associated with the Congress, such as the sociologist Edward Shils. When he reviewed the archive inventory, Josselson was annoyed when he realized that Nabokov had retrieved his own correspondence files. These, Josselson claimed, properly belonged to the Congress.[84] But Josselson's own papers contain much material that had to do with the Congress, while in Nabokov's case it would have been difficult to distinguish what was strictly personal from what was strictly Congress business; and in fact copies of Nabokov's outgoing correspondence are to be found in the chronological files of the Congress's archive. The episode, however, strained the relationship.

Parallel to the disposition of the Congress's archive was the issue of the way its role and achievements would be publicly perceived. Josselson and Nabokov were both especially concerned that the Congress should not be seen only in the light of the CIA's financial involvement, a trend that began in 1968 with Christopher Lasch's onslaught in his essay on "the cultural Cold War."[85] From this perspective, Nabokov was in a delicate position, having been the organization's chief executive officer but never having been officially apprised of the CIA's role in its financing. The most effective way to counter the attacks of the New Left, he argued, was to confront the issue frankly.

> I do not feel one should be apologetic about the funding of the Congress from the CIA. Many of us suspected some sort of funding of this kind and it was the "talk of the town" in many capitals of Europe, Asia, Latin America, and Africa. The point is not the funding, but what the Congress has done in its twelve-year existence. It was a remarkably live intellectual center free of any association with totalitarianism of any kind when free-thinking intellectuals were being maligned by their totalitarian brethren.[86]

There was much discussion in the early 1970s among Congress "survivors" of plans for an oral history of the organization: the idea was to record cassette interviews of the people most closely connected with its activities. Josselson mentioned the project in letters to Silone and Walter Laqueur in the spring and summer of 1971. "We suffered from the interpretation of the CCF based on the American Committee," Josselson wrote to Hunt. "Now we will be suffering from an equation of the CCF with its bastard offspring, the AILC [Association internationale pour la liberté de la culture]."[87] In August 1971 Nabokov brought up the issue in a memorandum to Stone, in which he insisted that both Josselson and Hunt had played a role that went far beyond their association with the CIA. He was particularly insistent in the case of the former, calling him "the brains and the leading spirit of the Congress." Further discussions followed, during which Nabokov—in keeping with views he had advocated as secretary general—urged for the inclusion of artists among the people to be interviewed.[88] Despite the initial enthusiasm, however, the project never got off the ground, presumably for lack of actual direction. In early 1974 Josselson, who may have hoped it would be monitored by the University of Chicago, mentioned it to Shils as being still in the works, but by the summer of 1975 he clearly had given up on the idea.[89] By then delays in the project had prompted Nabokov to start making plans for an oral history project of his own, which would cover both his CCF experience and his contacts in the cultural and political world. In December 1972, he brought it to the attention of Frederick Burkhardt, president of the American Council of Learned Societies, and in February 1973 he reported to Saul Bellow that he had received positive feedback from Robert Rosenthal at the University of Chicago library.[90] As he described it in a grant proposal he submitted to the Gulbenkian Foundation, it was to be "a pioneer project [. . .], insofar as it attempts, through the biography of one particular person—myself in this case—and by using the most up-to-date technology, to gather material originating from the memories of others over a period of fifty years . . ."[91] In another grant proposal dating from the mid-1970s, for which Nabokov submitted a budget of $146,000 for a two-year period, the project had expanded into an ambitious oral autobiography in three parts: political and public affairs (postwar Germany, the beginnings of Voice of America, the origins of the Congress for Cultural Freedom, West Berlin and Willy Brandt's Ostpolitik); education and the arts (the revolution of liberal education in the United States; working with Balanchine; as a composer and in his relations with other composers); and as a member of the Nabokov family.[92] By then, Nabokov had recorded interviews with Daniélou and Liebermann; he planned to continue with Balanchine, Berlin, Bernstein, Boulez, Cartier-Bresson, Kirstein, Teddy Kollek, the painter Pavel Mansurov ("last living Suprematist"),[93] Menuhin, Rostropovich, Spender, and Thomson. He considered adding Sidney Hook to the list, which suggests that the two men were still on reasonably good terms. He also included Kennan, suggesting that his essay on Custine Kennan published in 1971 could be a topic for discussion, especially since Nabokov found himself not in full agreement with Kennan's views.

This last part of Nabokov's oral history project acquired a life of its own, in the form of a proposal for a television film tentatively entitled "The Destiny of the Russian Emigration (the Nabokov Family)." Television, Nabokov pointed out, had so far shown little interest in the first wave of the post-1917 Russian emigration, despite its size (two million people) and unusual social makeup compared to other large migratory movements (upper-middle class and intelligentsia). The Nabokov family was particularly representative, he argued, listing the various destinies and accomplishments of members of four different generations, including his own sons Ivan—by then chief editor at the *Reader's Digest* book section—and Peter, who had already published two books on Native American history, a subject on which he was to become a highly respected authority.[94]

Nabokov credited the birth of his second completed opera, *Love's Labour's Lost*, to Lincoln Kirstein, a man with whom his own relations were not always the smoothest.

> My relations with Lincoln have always been ambivalent, subject to sudden changes of mood. It was a kind of "on and off" game with Lincoln as the game leader. At times he would be friendly and convivial. Then, for no apparent reason, he would suddenly become distant and uncommunicative. But Auden, to whom I spoke about those changes of Lincoln's mood, said: "Nicky! You should learn to respect other people's moods. Moods change . . . Lincoln always means well . . . He's a very good man." Since then I [have] followed Auden's advice and [not worried] about Lincoln greeting or not greeting me, frowning or laughing, being brusque or amiable.[95]

Kirstein admired *Don Quixote*, both music and choreography, and when Nabokov was in New York to supervise the rehearsals of one of the ballet's revivals, he suggested a collaboration with Auden, who was looking for a new operatic project— he had unsuccessfully approached Michael Tippett and Harrison Birtwhistle.[96] Nabokov was at first coy about the idea.

> One day Lincoln Kirstein said to me, "Why don't you write an opera with Wystan?" And I said, "Well, I don't know if Wystan would want to write an opera with me. He's been writing operas with Stravinsky and with Henze. I'm another kettle of fish. I'm a old-fashioned Russian composer, a Russian lyricist with an addiction to melody." And Lincoln said, "Don't be stupid. That is precisely why Wystan likes your music."[97]

It was also Kirstein who reported to Nabokov Auden's view (which Auden apparently started expressing around 1964) that, of all Shakespeare plays, *Love's Labour's Lost* was the one that lent itself most naturally to an operatic adaptation in the English language.[98] This was, at first sight, an improbable proposition. One of the reasons why this "Pleasant Conceited Comedie" is among the less frequently staged of his works is that the "plethora of puns and now incomprehensible allusions" discourages modern audiences.[99] Puzzled at first, Nabokov—who was familiar with the young Peter Brook's famous 1946 production—reread the play, and noticed that dramaturgically it was not without similarities with Mozart's *Cosi fan tutte*, with its parallel couples and stylized, deliberately artificial plot. Even the courtiers dressed up as Muscovites recalled Mozart's Ferrando and Guglielmo disguised as Albanians, while appealing to the composer for obvious reasons, being the only reference to Russia in Shakespeare. (As Nabokov probably did not know, *Love's Labour's Lost* had actually been adapted in 1863 by Jules Barbier and Michel Carré—Gounod's librettists—as a substitute for Da Ponte's "immoral" libretto in a French production of *Cosi fan tutte* at the Théâtre-Lyrique.)[100]

> But it also contains, in a terribly powerful way, Shakespeare's habit of "souring" comedies toward the end. I adhere here to Jan Kott's view that Shakespeare was, like Cervantes in Don Quixote, a pessimistic answer to the hopes of the Renaissance. The awful seventeenth century was coming on, with its murders and cruelty and inhumanity, and the hopes of the Renaissance were dashed.[101]

Nabokov was also struck by the similarity between Don Armado, Shakespeare's "braggart Spaniard," and the hero of Cervantes—an accidental similarity since Shakespeare cannot have been familiar, at the time he wrote the play, with the first English translation of *Don Quixote*, which came out in 1612.

Nabokov first discussed the project with Auden in New York in early February 1969.[102] Auden was even more categorical than reported by Kirstein, calling *Love's Labour's Lost* "the only Shakespeare play that will do as an opera. It is structured like an opera and so much of it is already rhymed verse."[103] Nabokov's concerns about the play's euphuistic language were brushed aside.

> "Well . . . I don't think we should worry about that," he said. "Some of those words can be changed, others can just as well remain. That isn't the problem. What needs to be done is to trim the play down to opera requirements. A number of secondary characters should be eliminated. Most of the comic scenes with their banter should be cut—they won't do for opera. Maybe some of the verses could be shortened, and all of the play must get leaner. I see it," he continued, "as an *opera buffa* in a fast tempo, a kind of perpetual allegro going through to the last scene. Then everything must go solemn and slow—that is most important" and he emphasized the word "most." "The morality-play ending of *Love's Labour's Lost* and its meaning should remain quite clear and intact."[104]

Auden made his participation contingent on the acceptance of Kallman who, as usual, spent the winter in Athens while Auden stayed in New York. It was readily granted. In the course of the next few weeks, Nabokov and Auden and Kallman worked out their ideas for an outline, and separately arrived at the same conclusion that the plot of the opera should focus on the four pairs of lovers.[105] "It will be a tender, lyrical, gay, but fairly small-scale opera," Nabokov promised Massimo Bogianckino, then head of the Festival of the Two Worlds in Spoleto.[106]

On July 15–16, 1969, Nabokov spent two days with Auden and Kallman at their house in Austria to discuss plans for the scenario in greater detail. "The Bard's play has to be radically altered," Auden concluded from their conversations.[107] A sketch of acts 1 and 2 was sent to Nabokov in early August, and the libretto was completed at the end of September. In October, librettists and composer met with the Italian director and stage designer Filippo Sanjust, whom Auden and Kallman knew from his work on Henze's *Bassarids* at Salzburg in 1966, and who would also be responsible for the sets and costumes of the new opera.

As Edward Mendelson has observed, little of Shakespeare's actual text has actually survived in Auden and Kallman's libretto: "the opening and closing arias, the lovers' letters, and miscellaneous lines and phrases" (one speech lifted, in fact, from *As You Like It*, while the boisterous hunting scene that closes Act 1 is an anonymous song first printed in 1614 in Thomas Ravenscroft's *A Briefe Discourse*).[108] As Kallman put it, he and Auden "stamped Shakespeare to bits and then put it together again."[109] Initially subtitled "Operatic Pastoral"— though in its final form the opera was labeled "musical comedy"—it reduces Shakespeare's cast of eighteen to ten. An idea for which Auden credited Kallman was to turn Moth, Armado's page in the play, into "a Cupid-Ariel figure"—also reminiscent of Puck, as Nabokov pointed out. Moth also incorporates some of the traits of the play's clown, Costard, who was therefore eliminated along with other secondary characters.[110] The romantic couples are down to three from four, while Armado is upgraded to royal secretary. For reasons of vocal variety the women come in as early as the second scene—not in the second act as in the play—and join the men for the hunt at the end of the act. The plot is, symbolically, extended over the four seasons, from Moth's introductory spring song (moved from the end of the play to the beginning of the libretto) to the allusion to winter at the close of Act 3.

Nabokov was enthusiastic about the "marvelous" libretto he had to work from—an even greater achievement, he thought, than Auden and Kallman's collaboration on *The Rake's Progress*. The few changes he requested were chiefly cuts.[111] Yet, from a formal point of view, he was faced with a problem: though based on traditional operatic forms—arias, duets, trios, quartets, quintets even—the libretto left no space for recitatives to connect those numbers, which were, rather, like a series of developed scenes.

> I thought immediately, and practically intuitively, that the only way to handle it, to be adequate to the idea of comedy, was with what the French call "persiflage." There is no English word for it. Persiflage is not quite satire, but it is a little more than just a takeoff or a joke. [. . .]My persiflage is, of course, modern. The subjects of my persiflage are Kurt Weill, Bertold Brecht, the American popular song, the 12-tone gents and their technique, a great deal of the neoclassical Stravinsky. Every now and then, the mood breaks.[112]

Humorous touches include a quotation of the Toreador Song from *Carmen*—a musical symbol of virility—when Don Armado boasts about his powers of seduction, while the *Tristan* motif, treated in jazz style, is cited when Berowne sings ecstatically about love. The Muscovite Masque offered a perfect opportunity for persiflage, with Glinka, Tchaikovsky, and Mussorgsky being pressed into service, as well as a snatch from Berg's *Lulu*, duly Russianized, and even a parody of Russian jazz from the 1930s.[113] Towards the end, another, more serious, kind of musical allusion comes in when the dramatic tone suddenly changes with the announcement of the death of the King of France. "Hitherto," as Auden has written, noting that music would "make this change even more impressive," "the characters have lived in a world of pure play, flirtation and banter, where nothing serious could happen. Now, the awareness of death as a physical fact thrusts them into the real world, where personal relations are real and always involve suffering."[114] The parody is applied, this time, to classical Indian music and to the American avant-garde:

> At the very end, I have a cello that is prepared, like the instruments of John Cage, with paper and a loudspeaker. The cello zooms about like a sarod or a sitar. The orchestra always plays the same accompaniment, as in Indian music, but the voices sing something very serious and very tragic.[115]

In the opera's final measures, when Armado delivers the couplet "The words of Mercury / Are harsh after the songs of Apollo," a short quotation is heard from the prologue of Stravinsky's *Apollo*, a moment that was called "the strongest emotional effect of the entire opera."[116] In the music, as in the libretto, the world of detached persiflage is thus eventually replaced by the very serious tone of a musical tribute to a departed master who, for Nabokov, was as much a father to him, on a symbolic plane, as the one mourned in Shakespeare's play by the Princess of France.

Nabokov started drafting the music of *Love's Labour's Lost* in Aspen in 1970 during his first two months as composer in residence, completing Act 1 by the end of the summer before taking up his visiting appointment at SUNY Buffalo. He resumed work in February and April–May 1971 at Kolbsheim, where he completed the score in early September. According to a note in his hand, the Act 2 "Interludium" was composed and transcribed in fair copy on April 6, the day Stravinsky died.[117] The orchestration was realized with the help of Harold Byrns, an American conductor and former collaborator of Bernstein, who completed the work, under Nabokov's supervision, by the summer of 1971.

Nabokov remembered the composition of his second opera—perhaps by contrast with that of the first, which was constantly interrupted by his administrative duties—as being "a continuous pleasure."[118] While he himself characterized the music as "tonal, non-experimental, and consistently melodic," as well as detached "from any school of aesthetic ideology," it is not conventional by any means, occasionally resorting to polytonality and making frequent use—but always fleetingly—of whole-tone and octatonic scales.[119]

As soon as Nabokov had received Auden and Kallman's libretto, he secured an arrangement with the Deutsche Oper in West Berlin, whose troupe included native English speakers, and a contract was signed on April 19, 1971, with its director, Egon Seefehlner. However, it was also made clear from the start that, because the opera was in English, the premiere could not take place in Berlin and would have to be hosted by a different theater. Attempts were made to persuade Spoleto, Covent Garden, or Venice to be the venue. Paris was also mentioned, while Cincinnati and Washington, DC, expressed interest for the American premiere. Plans were announced to stage the opera at the 1971 Edinburgh Festival as part of the visit from the Deutsche Oper, then dropped, ostensibly for financial and scheduling reasons, but actually because the Berlin Opera was pressured into programming works by German composers when performing in Scotland. The premiere was thus postponed for another eighteen months. At the end of November 1972 the vocal score was published by the Berlin firm of Bote & Bock. Finally, *Love's Labour's Lost* was staged in February 1973, with the Berlin troupe singing the original English, at the Théâtre de la Monnaie in Brussels. Nabokov, while privately admitting that the orchestral playing was not on the same level as American orchestras, praised the production by Winifried Bauernfeind as "able and imaginative." It was not, however, to Auden's taste. "I like the music very much, the singers were good, but the stage-direction sheer hell," Auden wrote to a friend.[120] He and Kallman were particularly pleased with the singing of David Knudsen as Moth—a role librettists and composer initially intended to be sung by a soprano ("like [Edith] Mathis")[121]—calling it "one of the most remarkable vocal performances that we have ever heard."[122] The cast also included Patricia Johnson as the Princess, Lou Ann Wyckoff as Rosaline, Carol Malone as Jacquenetta, Barry McDaniel as Berowne, and George Fortune as Armado.

The February 7 Brussels premiere was an even more glamorous event than the Cologne premiere of *Rasputin*. Many of Nabokov's friends were in attendance, beginning with Willy Brandt and his wife. As Daniélou recalled, the latter "looked very bored and obviously did not enjoy the music. She complained about this to Nicolas, naively asking him the name of the composer."[123] The Nabokov family, with the exception of Vladimir, were present in force, including two of Nabokov's former wives (Natalie and Marie-Claire), his sons Ivan and Alexandre, and his stepsister Lydia, Princess Mirsky, whose daughter was now married to a member of the Furtwängler family. Isaiah Berlin, Hampshire, Spender came from England; Dutilleux, Fleuret, Goldbeck, Liebermann, Sauguet, from Paris; from Berlin, Helmut and Antoinette Becker; from Denmark, Marie-Luise Bethmann-Hollweg; and Daniélou and Jacques Cloarec from Italy. The press was generally positive. "The whole piece," Fleuret wrote in *Le Nouvel Observateur*, "remains light, fast-moving, tongue-in-cheek, at times tender, generous always."[124] Whereas Auden and Kallman's libretto was unreservedly admired, the music disconcerted most critics. They praised the "geniality" of the score, the "sympathetic" writing for the voice, and the excellence of the contrapuntal language. But the work's humor—its persiflage—was thought by some as excessive, "rather as though Messrs Kallman and Auden had thrown away Shakespeare's puns only for Mr. Nabokov to enjoy a few of his own."[125] Such reactions caused Nabokov to regret making public comments about the way he had conceived the music. "Please cut all the references I made to my own music," he instructed his German translator ahead of the Berlin premiere. "It misleads critics into writing even worse nonsense than they usually do. Instead, put the following sentence: As for the music of *Love's Labour's Lost*, I have nothing to say; it is not for the composer, but for the public to judge."[126]

Ironically, when the work was presented in Berlin a few months later—two performances during the Berlin Festival and three more performances later in the season—it was not performed in Claus Henneberg's German version, but in English, out of deference to the singers, who were reluctant to learn their roles again in a different language.[127] The production was, again, well received, but was not revived. Within the next few years, Nabokov unsuccessfully tried to have the work staged in other countries. London, San Francisco, Israel were approached. Mindful of the objections of Auden and Kallman, who suggested that the orchestration was too loud, too "Viennese," making the text difficult to follow, the composer offered to rescore it for a chamber orchestra to make it more attractive to smaller theaters. But the opera has not been staged since. Sensing, from the time of the premiere, that it was a "problem work," Nabokov concluded that the opera, with its poetic, introspective, bittersweet quality, was too subtle "for a bourgeois audience that wants to feel young and gay."[128]

A few weeks after the premiere of *Love's Labour's Lost*, Nabokov celebrated his seventieth birthday. A joyful party was held in Berlin, with John Evarts contributing a charming doggerel toast:

His peripatetic
And very eclectic
career
has carried him far and wide and clear.
Through revolutions and wars and crises
And peace!
Frequently a husband and three times a father
(And sometimes, quite possibly, a lover)
He has enriched the whole world in
One way or another
And especially the city of Berlin.[129]

There were other, more formal marks of recognition as well. At the end of May 1970 Nabokov was inducted—on the same day as Duke Ellington—as a new member of the American Academy of Arts and Letters. The same year, he was elected a member of the Century Association in New York. In December 1972 honors came, this time, from the German government, which awarded him the Grosse Verdienstkreuz des Verdienstordens des Bundesrepublik Deutschlands. In March 1976, at the French Consulate in New York, he was decorated with the Legion of Honor. In his diary, Spender, who was present, commented on the "atmosphere of comedy as the Consul made a speech, going through [Nicolas's] whole life, drawing throughout a distinction between what he called 'creation' and 'career.' Although the festivals he had organized were listed, the CCF was skirted adroitly. The hollowness of French rhetoric on such occasions is so transparent that it acquires a kind of sincerity."[130] Perhaps Spender was being a little unfair to the adroitness of the Consul, an early supporter of de Gaulle during the war, whose wife was related to Aline Berlin.

Hardly had he completed *Love's Labour's Lost* that Nabokov began to toy with the idea of a new opera, adapted, this time, from Bulgakov's *Last Days* (*Poslednie dni*)—also known by its alternative title *Alexander Pushkin*. The play had been written by Bulgakov in 1935 with a view to the commemoration of the centenary of Pushkin's death two years later. It tells the story of the events leading to the fatal duel with d'Anthès, with the dramatic twist—already used by Bulgakov in *Molière*—that Pushkin himself, though constantly mentioned, never appears. Plans for a 1937 production were dropped after Bulgakov fell from official favor in 1936 and the play was staged only in 1943, after the author's death, at the Moscow Art Theater, where it was the last production by Nemirovich-Danchenko. In the words of Ellendea Proffer, "*Last Days* is about a Russian national hero, and one cannot imagine it being a great success anywhere but Russia; it is deliberately parochial. Nevertheless it is a masterfully composed work, one which resonates in a special way for Russians. Pushkin's tragedy is Russia's tragedy, and like all of Bulgakov's historical plays, this work has contemporary relevance."[131] Josselson, with whom Nabokov discussed the project, admitted he found the play "very thin," though he saw why Nabokov could see its potential for a musical setting.[132] Spender responded more positively: "I do look forward to hearing about the Bulgakov. It sounded beautiful from your account of it."[133] Nabokov asked Henneberg to work on a scenario and, in April 1973, sent Peter Ustinov the outline, sounding him about writing the libretto and directing and designing the first staging. Ustinov having failed to respond, Nabokov, while still hoping he might agree to direct the work, had second thoughts about him as a librettist ("too lazy to do any writing") and suggested that Henneberg himself should write the libretto in German, while Spender would take care of the English translation.[134] Was Nabokov disappointed with what he saw of Henneberg's work?[135] Did he get negative reactions from

Joseph Brodsky, with whom he discussed the project that spring when staying with Alexander and Tatiana Liberman at their summer house in Connecticut?[136] Or from Arthur Miller, with whom he proposed to discuss it as well? The Bulgakov opera, in any event, was left unrealized. With Brodsky himself, Nabokov made plans for an opera based on Dostoevsky's absurdist and macabre short story *Bobok*, for which the young emigre poet would have written the libretto.[137]

Nabokov's autobiography, which finally came out in 1975, was his first book-length publication since the 1964 essay on Stravinsky—which was initially supposed to be part of it. It had been more than fifteen years in the making. Begun in the late 1950s, it had been delayed by Nabokov's Congress activities, and further delayed by his work in Berlin and his new musical projects like *Don Quixote*. The book project also went through several publishers and several forms. After Michael Bessie, who had initially approached Nabokov, left Harper & Brothers in 1959, it followed him to the newly founded Atheneum, while Weidenfeld and Nicholson retained rights, as did Fischer Verlag in Frankfurt for a German version. In 1965, Nabokov reported to the latter that he had begun drafting a book entitled *The German Manichee* about his memories of Germany in 1921–23.[138] In July 1966, he sent 125 pages to Michael Raeburn, his London editor. Work was briefly resumed in November 1967, when Nabokov and Dominique stayed with Alix de Rothschild in Normandy. In 1969, the book was announced for the following year, still with a separate British edition. In July 1971, Nabokov wrote to Jerry Ziegler, his Old Westbury colleague, that he hoped the autobiography would be finished by the end of 1972. Then he was sidetracked again by work on his memoir on Stravinsky. He resumed work the following year. "I am immersed in the horrors of trying to finish my book," he wrote to John Hunt in March 1973, "but, oh, how difficult it is to write when one has no mother tongue!"[139] Each section was first drafted in longhand, often in two or three versions, before being given to a typist, which led to a new round of corrections. The corrected draft was then sent to London to be reread by Anna Kallin, on whose editorial judgment, no matter how severe, Nabokov relied unreservedly. Portions of the work were also reread by Elizabeth Hardwick. Nabokov hesitated between different titles. Early versions are called "The All of Me: An Autobiographical Chronicle." Subsequent ones carry the heading "And It Was So," later corrected to "A Life Reinvented: An Autobiographical Chronicle and Stories." In the end, the English, German, and French versions all appeared under different titles. The German was called *Zwei rechte Schuhe im Gepäck* ("Two right shoes in one's luggage")—a reference to the hasty departure of the exiles from Sevastopol in 1919—and subtitled "Memoirs of a Russian Cosmopolite." While carrying the same subtitle, the English version retained the more evocative title of a chapter that appeared in April 1975 in *The New Yorker*:[140] *Bagázh*, the Russian word derived from the French "bagage," and referring to the enormous quantity of things of all kinds a wealthy Russian family carried around whenever traveling in pre-Revolutionary Russia. Taking on a symbolic resonance, *bagázh* referred both to the part of himself he had left in Russia, or, with equal force, the personal and cultural "baggage" emigres bring with them wherever exile takes them.

Over the years, Nabokov's memoir had grown to vast proportions. Rather than being a linear narrative, it freely mixed early recollections and more recent episodes. The most complete typescript in English comprises nine sections of unequal length. The first is devoted to early memories of Russia, before the family moved to St. Petersburg, and, though significantly longer, is the closest to the published text. The second deals with life in Petersburg before the Revolution but includes sections on Diaghilev and on the making of *Rasputin's End*. The third part deals with Germany in the 1920s and includes sections on Kessler and Rilke as well as a long portrait of Remizov, which remained unpublished. The fourth part, "America the Beautiful," also considerably longer than the printed version, dealt with Nabokov's life in New York until his recruitment by Wells College.[141] It ends with Nabokov receiving the news of the death of his mother and reminiscing about the family's departure from Russia in 1919. Part five was to incorporate Nabokov's memories of Prokofiev, the "Music Under the Generals" chapter from *Old Friends and New Music*, with additional material on Remizov. Part six, devoted entirely to Stravinsky, corresponded to the manuscript of *The Gracious Master* Nabokov had shown to Bellow and others. Part seven, "Years of *engagement*," was the longest. It began with Nabokov's 1936 trip to Berlin and included, especially, an account of Nabokov's friendship with Richard Möbius and the realization that the latter had become a Nazi. It also covered his 1938 trip to Europe, his exit visa troubles and the assistance provided by Alexis Léger, Nabokov's postwar difficulties in getting State Department clearance, and the 1949 Waldorf-Astoria and 1950 Berlin conferences. This led Nabokov to comment on the CIA's involvement with the Congress. One then moved back chronologically to his leaving Wells for St. John's, his Washington and Baltimore wartime contacts—Bohlen, Berlin, Auden, among others. It included Nabokov being reunited with Auden in Germany and their postwar relations, up to the composition of *Love's Labour's Lost*. The final part was a brief account of the festivals Nabokov had organized—mostly Paris and Berlin, but briefer references to Italy, Japan, and India—and ended with his East Berlin Soviet connections and 1967 trip to Moscow.

The manuscript emerged from the hands of Nabokov's editors at Atheneum in much reduced form. Among the main casualties were the sections featuring Remizov and the Berlin friend Nabokov calls Doderl, the visit with Kessler to Rodin's tomb, the portraits of Léger, and most of Nabokov's American friends, notably Learned Hand and Alice Garrett. But the general tone of the book suffered, perhaps to an even greater degree, from numerous small cuts within the narrative that resulted in a disconcertingly disjointed aspect. Unsurprisingly, the early Russian memories, which suffered the least from Atheneum's scissors, were picked by several critics as their favorite part. To be sure, the entire manuscript would have been a long book. There is little doubt, however, that it would have been a better one.

The German version came out first on September 15, 1975, an event marked by a concert of Nabokov's music. Translated by Henneberg and Jaesrich, it was much less drastically cut and, in many respects, reads better than the English. Enriched by passages from *Old Friends and New Music*, which was still unpublished in German, the Piper Verlag edition also benefits from the different presentation: instead of being divided into three main parts ("Russia . . . Then"; "Between Wars; "To America"), each comprising a great number of untitled shorter sections, it is in one continuous part, but with the short sections carrying headings that are not present in the English *Bagázh*. Not only is it a clearer, more elegant option; it also emphasizes, rather than awkwardly attempting to hide, the book's deliberately episodic character. Indeed, *Bagázh* is not a memoir of the conventional sort, but rather a book of autobiographical stories. As Nabokov made clear in his introduction, the intention was not to give a factual, objective account of his life but to tell a story—or a series of stories—as vividly as possible: hence the amount of "reconstructed" dialogue that, in places, makes the narrative read more like a work of fiction than an autobiography. Nabokov spelled it out clearly in his foreword: "It is a story-teller's and a story-maker's book."[142] To a French journalist who interviewed him when the French translation came out, he declared: "At first I regretted not having kept a diary or taken notes. But as I was writing, I realized that it was better this way and one should rely on one's memory, including its *déformations*."[143] Soberly entitled *Cosmopolite*—Nabobov would have preferred *Cosmopolite russe*, but the editor vetoed it as being too long—this French version was translated by Nabokov's daughter-in-law Claude and basically followed the English text, with a few passages inserted from *Old Friends and New Music*. The book did well in France, earning Nabokov an invitation to speak, in October 1976, on the popular television program *Apostrophes*.

Before the book came out, portions had appeared in various magazines. Beside the extract featured in *The New Yorker*, the reminiscences of Auden were included in the memorial volume edited by Spender, and those of Prokofiev in *Die Merkur*. Other excerpts were published in *Die Welt, Die Furche, Vogue*, and *The American Scholar*. As Nabokov had clearly foreseen—"I know that they would be the first ones to contest *my* way of remembering," he wrote in his draft introduction—Nabokov's "hawkish relatives" were infuriated by his account of their family, and especially by the portrait of Babushka Nabokova. His cousins Serge, in Brussels, and Elena and Vladimir, in Switzerland, were particularly incensed.[144] Nabokov's former Congress associates were also less than enthusiastic, perhaps because the book did not conform with their image or recollection of the author. "Reads smoothly, but left me with a taste of *flat* champagne," Josselson complained to a correspondent;[145] yet he told Daniel Bell that he thought that the CCF side of the story had been handled "quite well"—by which he probably meant as discreetly as possible.[146] Others, like Hook, never forgave Nabokov for the way they were portrayed in his memoir.[147] But most reviews were favorable. Particularly enthusiastic was Raymond Mortimer, who described the book as "an exceptional treat" in *The Sunday Times*.[148] Reviewing the book in the *Times Literary Supplement*, Gabriele Annan praised especially "the poetry and playful felicity" of the Russian reminiscences.[149] Equally positive was Clement Crisp in *The Financial Times*: "Vivid, beguiling, this first section of the book is a considerable social document as well as a touching portrait of a favoured and happy time."[150] Stuckenschmidt contributed a long, laudatory review in *Die Merkur*. "The great charm of the book," wrote the reviewer of the *Frankfurter Allgemeines Zeitung*, "lies not only in the variety of worlds and their distinct color, but also in the fact that their incompatibility—the essence of every emigrant life—is referred to only indirectly and without sentimentality, and in that Nabokov hints at the fact that, rather than a memoir, this is the book of a storyteller, that it is a teller of tales who is 'writing.'"[151] The only discordant note was sounded by the distinguished literary scholar Hans Mayer—a former Marxist—who severely took Nabokov to task for "fabricating" an implausible encounter with Rilke in Weimar in 1922.[152]

In the United States, one of the wittiest and most perceptive was penned by Ned Rorem in the *New York Times Book Review*. Noting that Nabokov, "clear-minded and farseeing" when discussing music in general, was curiously reticent when talking about his own, he contrasted, by the same token, the discretion of the references to the composer's closest friends with the detailed accounts of people Nabokov "met but once and scarcely knew," like Isadora Duncan and Rilke. Rorem's main regret was that more of the book was not devoted to America and, especially, to "the noted American composers known to be his friends." Nabokov, Rorem concluded, "has done as much as any Russian since Koussevitzky toward putting American music on the map."[153]

Whereas some readers—Josselson for one—privately expressed their relief at Nabokov's decision to leave out any in-depth discussion of his role within the CCF, some reviewers regretted it. Writing in *The Observer*, and describing the CIA funding as "a tragedy," Edward Crankshaw concluded his review with the words: "I think Nabokov should have told us more about it—or else not mentioned it at all."[154] "I could not do more," Nabokov explained to McGeorge Bundy in 1976. "The subject-matter of the book was different and, chronologically, except for the book's epilogue, it stopped when my association with the CCF began."[155] But even before *Bagázh* had been completed, he started planning and drafting a book devoted to his years with the Congress. It was not to be a history of the Congress, but a personal account of his travels and the personalities he had met in the course of those seventeen years. He mischievously planned to entitle the book "On the Wings of the CIA," with the subtitle *Les Très Riches Heures du CIA*, a suggestion to which Isaiah Berlin responded with horror ("if you were serious about this, let me earnestly advise you not to do this").[156] Although the book was never completed, Nabokov has left a detailed outline and wrote out several sections. The opening chapters ("The Abomination of Desolation") were to begin with the summer of 1945 in Germany, an experience that so profoundly affected his political outlook, and cover such topics as the denazification of Furtwängler and Karajan; the founding of Voice of America; the failed attempt to get security clearance to work for the State Department; and the circumstances that led to the CCF appointment. Part two, which was apparently never drafted, was to be an account of the festivals and conferences Nabokov had organized during his tenure as secretary general. Part three was to be called "Buddha's Tooth and Other Odds" and be devoted to Nabokov's trip to Burma, his visits to India and contacts with the Nehru family, and his experience of Japan. The book's epilogue was to be "in praise of the C.C.F."

> Its contribution to the Zeitgeist of the mid-century and its intrepid assertion of the values of the liberal tradition. Its worldwide network of dedicated participants. The excellence of its magazines and reviews. Its defense and fight for full intellectual freedom. Its enlightened opposition to communism and all forms of totalitarianism.[157]

Perhaps bearing Berlin's admonition in mind, Nabokov also considered using *Buddha's Tooth* as the title of the entire book.

Even before Nabokov turned seventy, some of his old friends had begun to disappear: Felix Bethmann-Hollweg in 1972; Auden and Maritain in 1973; in 1974 Charles Bohlen and Raimund von Hoffmannsthal, two losses—particularly Bohlen's—that affected him deeply. Blacher died of lung cancer in January 1975; one year later, Nabokov paid homage to him in Cleveland, where Maazel conducted a memorial concert, at which Gerti Herzog, Blacher's widow, performed the piano concerto her husband had composed for her in 1961.[158] The saddest blow of all was, in 1977, the death of Alexandre Grunelius, his friend of nearly fifty years. That spring, visiting his cousin Vladimir in Montreux, Nabokov was alarmed to find him in declining health and suggested to Véra that he should be moved to the United States.[159] His death on July 2, 1977, was yet another shock, "especially since some French papers had the special grace of mixing up my photo with him."[160] Nabokov and his son Ivan attended the funeral in Clarens on July 7. On January 13, 1978, it was Josselson's turn. Mourning "the friend and unique human being," Nabokov reminded Josselson's wife that, other than Lasky, he had been the first to meet him among the people subsequently associated with the Congress.

Nabokov's own health had itself long been cause for concern. In the summer of 1972, while at Aspen, he caught pneumonia and developed a bad reaction to antibiotics he was prescribed. Later that year, he was hospitalized in New York because of heart problems. In early 1974, his heart condition deteriorated again. In early September, while staying with Marie-Luise Bethmann-Hollweg at Altenhof, he suffered a heart attack and was hospitalized for a week. In March 1976, he came down with another bout of pneumonia, and in January 1978 with a protracted flu.

Despite these health-related anxieties, Nabokov kept a busy travel sched-ule until the end of his life. Beside the usual destinations—Paris, Kolbsheim, Altenhof, Berlin, Oxford (to visit Isaiah Berlin and the Hampshires), Rome (to visit Daniélou at Zagarolo)—there were new ones, such as Santo Domingo, which he and Dominique visited in the winter of 1975, staying at La Romana, the house of Oscar and Françoise de la Renta, and again in February 1978. In the winter of 1977, seeking relief from the harsh New York winter, they spent a few weeks at the plan-tation Dielle Fleischmann owned in South Carolina, where the weather, it turned out, was even worse. Israel had become a favorite country, especially Jerusalem, which Nabokov described to Teddy Kollek as "the only city I really love."[161] Kollek consulted him when planning Mishkenot Sha'ananim ("Peaceful Dwellings"), the international cultural center that opened in the summer of 1973, and invited him to be among the first scholars and artists in residence—a visit delayed by the Yom Kippur War in October 1973. Nabokov returned in October 1975 and again in the spring of 1976, this time as composer-in-residence, with two subsequent visits in April and October 1977.[162]

Nabokov's final composition was a commission—the only one he received, even after stepping down as director—from the Berlin Festival. Evidently intended as a ballet, according to a note in the manuscript, it is a playful, ten-minute piece entitled *Circus Scenes* (*Kirkus-Szenen*)—an obvious echo of Stravinsky's *Circus-Polka*—to which Nabokov gave the subtitle "Divertimento pasticciato." An alterna-tive version of the title specifies "Paris Memories." It consists of a short overture and five tiny "snapshots" (or "miniatures"). "Life is a circus," noted Nabokov on his manuscript as an epigraph. As for the composers pastiched—along the lines of the "persiflage" attempted in *Love's Labour's Lost*, they are Prokofiev; Milhaud, Stravinsky, and Kurt Weill;[163] Auric, Poulenc, and Sauguet; and, in the final miniature, Nabokov himself. Drafted in late 1977 and early 1978, the piece was performed posthumously in Berlin in September 1978.

In the spring of 1978, Nabokov and Dominique were making plans for a visit to St. Petersburg—her first, since he had gone on his own in 1967 and canceled the trip planned in 1968—after stopping in Paris first. They would fly to Helsinki and then take the boat. Before their departure, Nabokov had to undergo benign urological surgery at Mt. Sinai Hospital, in New York. The night before he was to be released, on April 6, 1978, he died suddenly of heart failure. "It seems," as Robert Craft reported, "that when Dominique left him at about 1 A.M. he was in good spirits [. . .]. Then came the brutal telephone call. My Stravinsky world—Stravinsky died seven years ago on the same day—shrinks more with this loss than with any other in the interim. [. . .]I also think of how the Stravinskys enjoyed every visit from him as they did from no one else, and how they looked forward to them. Poor Dominique, who took such loving care of him!"[164] The funeral took place two days later at the Russian Orthodox Cathedral of Our Lady of the Sign, on East 93rd Street. Natalie, with whom Nabokov had remained on amicable terms until the end, was present.[165] So were Nabokov's three sons—Ivan, the Russian (with his own son Alexis), Peter, the American, and Alexandre, the Frenchman—as well as his sister and his cousin Dmitri, Vladimir's son. Apart from Balanchine, who was recovering from a heart alert, many of his friends were present: Robert Craft came with Vera Stravinsky, to join Suzanne Farrell, Elizabeth Hardwick, George and Annelise Kennan, Lincoln Kirstein, Alexander and Tatiana Liberman, Sylvia Marlowe, Vittorio Rieti, Arthur and Alexandra Schlesinger, Robert Silvers and Grace Dudley, and Virgil Thomson. A few weeks later, another ceremony, attended by Marie-Claire, was held at the Russian Cathedral in Paris, close to the Salle Pleyel, where Nabokov and Stravinsky had spent happy moments five decades before.

Nabokov left no instructions as to his final resting place. After consulting with Antoinette Grunelius, Dominique decided that Kolbsheim, one of Nabokov's "elective homes," and the one where the exile had found more peace than anywhere else, was a choice that would have made him happy. A Russian Orthodox priest came from Strasbourg to bless the burial, which was attended by Alexandre and Ivan and his wife. Also present, among others, were the Beckers, Henri Cartier-Bresson and his wife, and Florence Malraux. It is next to the tombs of his friends Alexandre and Antoinette Grunelius and Jacques and Raïssa Maritain that Nabokov now rests in this small, peaceful Alsatian village.

Epilogue

"HE WAS A very cultivated man; I found him to be one of the most civilized men I ever met, a perfect representative of the pre-Russian Revolution intelligentsia. He had mastered vast amounts of knowledge, had wide horizons and a wonderful imagination; he was also one of the warmest and most sympathetic of men, very generous, and with a very fine character. His charm was extraordinary."[1] Thus Isaiah Berlin summarized the personality of Nabokov, whom he considered his best friend.[2] In a letter to the London *Times*, he described him as "large hearted, affectionate, honourable, gifted with sharp moral and political insight and a well developed sense of the ridiculous, an irrepressible source of torrential wit and fancy."[3] In his obituary for the bulletin of the Century Association, Arthur Schlesinger wrote that Nabokov "was a man of arresting and astonishing vitality, overwhelming charm, the highest intelligence and character and the widest range of sympathy, knowledge and friendship."[4] Kennan, who gave memorial minutes at the Institute for Advanced Study, evoked "an intensely gregarious man, delighting, basking even, in the company of a host of friends and acquaintances, knowing everyone worth knowing, speaking all the languages, familiar with every great city of the West." Nabokov, he added, "was the epitome of the cultured cosmopolitan of our age; at home everywhere, and at home nowhere, unless it be in the companionship and affections of his friends. [. . .]He enjoyed people immensely. He lived by their warmth; he reflected it. He had an unerring eye for their failings: their pretentions, their ridiculousness. He was a superb mimic, in at least four languages. Yet the criticism implied in his mimicry was seldom, if ever, cruel. It was his way of understanding others. He took life as he found it, not caring to inquire into its philosophic implications; and he loved every bit of it. He loved the whole wonder and absurdity of our contemporary Western civilization: the music, the poetry, the drama, good food, good humor, beautiful women, and above all the amusing spectacle of the impact of colorful individuals upon one another." Such uncommon generosity, Kennan added, will inevitably expose one to the accusation of spreading oneself thin. "He went through life tossing off to every side bits and pieces of himself: of his wit, his enthusiasms, his friendships, his loves—tossing them off generously, without reflection and without remorse. Each of us who thought of ourselves as his friends (and there were a great many of us) had a small part in this lavishly-dispensed bounty. The result was that, aside from his music and his books, the whole of him was probably not left in any single place. But he was not the first man to express himself in such a manner; and who is to say, after all, that the sum total of these contributions, entering like everything else into that great stream of time and forgetfulness that sooner or later embraces and absorbs all that any of us has to offer, was any the less significant for the open-handed and joyous manner in which its component parts were flung to the winds of sociability, of friendship, and of affection?"[5]

Nabokov, who lived for his friendships and described them as the *hortus deliciarum* of his life, would have been proud to be lauded in such terms by those who knew him best.[6] But to the world at large, he hoped he would be remembered above all as a musician. His career as a composer, distinguished by any standards, is all the more remarkable in retrospect if one considers that he had two more, as an educator and a cultural diplomat (for lack of a better term). Several of his works were unqualified successes: *Ode, Union Pacific*, the First Symphony, *La Vie de Polichinelle, Symboli chrestiani, Rasputin's End*. There were some, at the time of his death, who deplored that this part of his life, the most important in his eye, got short shrift in the obituaries. "I am convinced Nicolas was a great musician," Jelenski wrote to Dominique, "who will be 'rediscovered' by all those who, in music, look for imagination, wit, nostalgia and grace."[7] Among professional musicians, Markevitch was particularly forceful in his defense: "It is a type of music about which it is possible to say that it can wait. Its quality is such that it will find its place in the wake of Stravinsky and Prokofiev. If he had remained in his country, he would be among the most performed composers there."[8] Indeed, one can only hope that Nabokov's music—as Markevitch hinted in his letter of condolence to Dominique—only needs to wait until it is rediscovered (or rather, discovered) in his native country, as Russia slowly begins to claim back its emigre artistic heritage. In the West, meanwhile, it will probably remain dormant, a fate shared with so much first-rate twentieth-century music. Already in 1972, Sessions singled Nabokov out among composers whose works were unjustly underperformed.[9] Several reasons can explain this neglect. The most obvious one is that Nabokov did not write in the musical style of the avant-garde that came into prominence—and fashion—in the 1940s, 1950s, and 1960s. "I do not believe that anyone, in 1947, wrote music so simple as that of *The Return of Pushkin*," Fred Goldbeck noted when presenting the work to French radio audiences twenty years later.[10] Nabokov's musical idiom is essentially tonal, lyrical even, and remains, as Markevitch pointed out, very much in the continuity of Prokofiev and the Stravinsky of the middle period. To this argument, one could respond that the careers of composers like Dutilleux, Messiaen, and Poulenc, or those of Górecki and Lutosławski, have not suffered from their writing music that remains basically tonal. Another reason, which logically derives from the first, is that Nabokov's music is firmly rooted in the Russian tradition, at least to the same extent as Soviet composers: this was the reaction of younger Russian composers Nabokov met when visiting his native country in 1967.[11] But Nabokov was an emigre, and the situation of an emigre composer—a profession that depends, in many cases, on the possibility of having one's works performed by large symphonic forces and opera houses—is even more problematic than that of emigre writers or visual artists. Once you leave your country, you leave behind all possibilities of institutional support of a kind that is normally available only to nationals. As Nabokov pointed out, if the careers of Stravinsky and Prokofiev did not suffer in emigration—though even they occasionally found themselves in financial straits—it was in part because they found in the Ballets Russes a substitute fatherland. The untimely disappearance of Diaghilev (who was only fifty-seven when he died) deprived younger Russian composers of the same chance. As for returning to Russia, as Prokofiev did, Nabokov—even if he briefly considered it in a moment of despair—knew only too well that, being from a well-known liberal, anti-Bolshevist family, he had no chance of survival under Stalin. Being a rootless cosmopolitan was not a choice, it was the only option he had left. And yet his music remained, as he put it, anchored in his Russian past.[12]

The reputation and dissemination of Nabokov's music also suffered, paradoxically, from his very generosity towards fellow composers. In the words of Françoise Xenakis, the novelist and wife of the Greek-born composer (who himself found in Nabokov one of his most disinterested champions), "Nicolas will be remembered, among those who do not find gratitude grating, for an extraordinary love for his fellow human beings, in an art world in which ignoring the work of others is virtually *de rigueur*. Nicolas, on the contrary, while not writing avant-garde music, came to the assistance of most contemporary composers."[13] Having helped the careers of others once he found himself in a position to do so, while refraining from using this position to promote his own, Nabokov, though not lacking in friends or allies in the musical world, condemned himself to the margins.

In itself, his musical output is anything but negligible, both in quantity and in variety: two operas, three symphonies, four concertos, five oratorios or cantatas (six if one includes *Ode*), six completed ballets, chamber music of various kinds, piano music (including two sonatas), songs, and choral music. These genres show an indebtedness to the nineteenth-century tradition—a century Nabokov loved more than most of his contemporaries did, perhaps because of his deep attachment to lyricism. To quote the perspicacious Goldbeck again, speaking on *The Return of Pushkin*, it is music marked by "Russian universals": a slightly archaic flavor, with modal overtones, and a fluidity of writing in which the basses, in particular, are treated on the same footing as the other parts of the musical discourse. His music, as Elliott Carter put it, "has a neo-romantic color that was specifically his."[14] Someone new to this music, and who would expect to hear a slavish epigone of Stravinsky, will therefore be greatly surprised by how different it actually sounds from that of the modern composer he admired more than any other.

While Nabokov's musical career unquestionably suffered from his efforts in promoting the music of others, one should not belittle, let alone forget his achievement in this regard. "A modern Liszt," declared Rieti, who compared him to a Renaissance man—and, for once, this much-abused characterization seems wholly appropriate.[15] His cultural activism extended well beyond classical music in a narrow sense: to traditional music and dance from other parts of the world, contemporary theater—indeed to all forms of intellectual and artistic endeavor. The world is now so saturated with festivals that it is hard to imagine how novel and forward-looking were realizations such as Masterpieces of the Twentieth Century, the Tokyo East-West Music Encounter, and the Berlin "Black and White" festival. To people who knew him, Nabokov left the memory of a cultural force that, more than thirty-five years after his death, continues to reverberate and inspire. "Among all the luminous personalities I met in my life," the French journalist Jean Daniel recalled, "he remains one of the greatest."[16] Elliott Carter put it in fairly similar terms, describing Nabokov as "a bright light in everybody's life," and adding, "without him, the world is a duller place."[17]

Checklist of Nicolas Nabokov's Works and Writings

MUSICAL WORKS

I. WORKS FOR THE STAGE

A. Operas

I-A1. Rasputin's End

I-A1A (FINAL VERSION). Rasputin's End: opera in three acts. Libretto by Stephen Spender and Nicolas Nabokov

Act 1. Scene 1: In the Murder Room. Scene 2: The Healing of the Czarevich. Act 2. Scene 3: In the Murder Room. Scene 4: At the Palace of Countess Marina. Act 3. Scene 5: At Rasputin's House. Scene 6: At the Gypsies. Scene 7: The Dream. Scene 8: In the Murder Room.

Date of composition: 1954–59.

First performance (as Der Tod des Grigorij Rasputin): Cologne, November 27, 1959.

Manuscript: DNA (drafts); Ricordi archives.

Published: vocal score, Paris: Ricordi, 1959 (300 p., P. 1596), with words in English and German; German version by Frederick Goldbeck.

Libretto, German: Der Tod des Grigori Rasputin, Oper in 3 Akten. Deutscher Text nach dem englischen Originaltext von Stephen Spender und Nicolas Nabokov, von Frederick Goldbeck. Paris: Éditions Ricordi [1959], 91 p.

Libretto, Italian: La morte di Rasputin; opera in 3 atti. Libretto di Stephen Spender e Nicolas Nabokov. Versione ritmica italiana di Flavio Testi. [Milan] Ricordi [1963], 48 p.

Cast: Rasputin, basso cantante; the Prince, baritone; the Deputy, bass; the Grand Duke, tenor; the Doctor, tenor; the Secretary, tenor; the Empress, mezzo soprano; the daughters, two sopranos, one contralto; the Grand Duchesses, two sopranos, one contralto; Anna, contralto; Marina, soprano; three ladies, two sopranos, one contralto; Gypsy woman, contralto; silent roles, the Csarevitch, two gypsies, a monk, one of the Grand Duchesses, Rasputin's daughter, the daughter of the third lady.

Instrumentation: 2 flutes, 2 oboes, 2 clarinets in A, 2 bassoons, 2 horns in F, 2 trumpets in C, 2 trombones, timpani, percussion, pianoforte 1 and 2, celesta, harp, strings.

I-A1b (first version). The Holy Devil. Opera in two acts. Libretto by Stephen Spender [and Nicolas Nabokov]

First performance: Louisville, April 16, 1958.
Published: vocal score, Paris: Ricordi, 1958 (222 p., P. 1594/P. 1596).
Cast, instrumentation: see above.
Recording: Members of the Kentucky Opera Association; Louisville Orchestra, cond. Moritz Bomhard; Lou Records 594 and Louisville Philharmonic Society [1959], 2 LPs (3 sides). Distributed by Columbia Records.
Note: commissioned by the Louisville Philharmonic Society.

I-A2. Love's Labour's Lost

Love's Labour's Lost: comedy set to music. Libretto by W. H. Auden and Chester Kallman after Shakespeare's play = Verlor'ne Liebesmüh', musikalische Komödie von W. H. Auden und Chester Kallman nach William Shakespeare. Deutsch von Claus H. Henneberg.
Date of composition: 1970–72.
First performance: Brussels, Théâtre de la Monnaie, February 7, 1973 [Deutsche Oper, Berlin production]
Cast: Rosaline, soprano drammatico; Katherine, soprano lirico; Jaquenetta, soprano leggiero; Princess, mezzo-soprano; Moth, soprano lirico; Dumaine, tenor; Berowne, baritone; Don Armado, baritone; the King, baritone; Boyet, bass.
Instrumentation: 3 flutes (and piccolo), 3 oboes, English horn, 3 clarinets, bass clarinet, 2 bassoons, contrabassoon, 4 horns, 3 trumpets, 3 trombones, tuba, percussion (3–10), pianoforte, celesta, mandoline, guitar, harp, strings.
Manuscript: Act 1, DNA; portions in NN, Texas.
Published: Wiesbaden: Bote & Bock, 1972 (short score; 353 p.; B & B 22408[1185]), with words in English and German.
Libretto published in W. H. Auden and Chester Kallman, Libretti and other dramatic writings by W. H. Auden, 1939–73, ed. by Edward Mendelson. London: Faber and Faber, 1993.
Note: orchestration realized in collaboration with Howard Byrns.

B. Ballets

I-B1. Ode

Oda: vechernee razmyshlenie o Bozhiem velichestvie pri sluchaie velikago siev-
ernago siianiia: dlia bolshogo smieshannago khora, dvukh solnykh golosov i
simfonicheskago orkestra = Ode: méditation du soir sur la majesté de Dieu à
l'occasion de la grande Aurore boréale. Words by Mikhail Vasilievich Lomonosov;
adaptation française de Roger Désormière.

1. Introduction: Andante con moto.—2. Duetto: Andante.—3. Chorus: Adagio
   maestoso.—4. Chorus and soprano: Allegro—Andante—Tempo I.—5.
   Interlude: Andante.—6. Chorus and bass: Andantino—Tempo I—Alla breve.—7.
   Soprano, bass, and chorus (Air): Andantino.—8. Bass recitative: Adagio—
   Allegro.—9. Chorus (Celebration): Largo—Vivo—Andante molto.—10.
   Intermezzo: Andante moderato.—11. Chorus (Reprise): Largo—Tempo di
   Andante molto—Meno mosso.—12. Chorale: Lento.—13. Finale: Largo.

Date of composition: 1925–28.

First performance: Paris, Théâtre Sarah-Bernhardt, June 6, 1928, choreogra-
phy by Leonid Massine, sets and costumes by Pawel Tchelitchew and Pierre
Charbonnier, cond. Roger Désormière; with Ira Belianina [Ira Belline] (la
Nature), Serge Lifar (l'Élève), Massine, Aleksandra Danilova, Felia Dubrovska,
Alice Nikitina.

Instrumentation: soprano solo, baritone solo, mixed chorus (SATB), 2 flutes (and
piccolo), 2 oboes, English horn, 2 clarinets in B-flat, bass clarinet, 2 bassoons,
contrabassoon, 4 horns in F, 2 trumpets in C, 2 trombones, tuba, timpani, bass
drum, snare drum, tambourine, xylophone, tam-tam, cymbals, strings.

Duration: 33' (or ca. 40' with additional dances)

Manuscript: NN, Yale (short-score and full-score manuscript).

Published: Paris: Maurice Sénart, 1928 (vocal score; 81 p.; E.M.S. 7598); words
in Russian and French. Missing from this score are three additional dances
included in the original version.

Recordings: Marina Shaguch (soprano), Alexander Kisselev (bass), Russian State
Symphonic Cappella, Residentie Orchestra, The Hague, cond. Valeri Polyansky
(Chandos 9768).

Note: commission from the Ballets Russes of Sergei Diaghilev; scenario by Boris
Kochno. The vocal score bears a printed dedication, in Russian and French, to
the composer's mother.

I-B2. Union Pacific

Union Pacific. Ballet on a scenario by Archibald MacLeish.

1. Introduction.—2. Irish Workmen: Lento. Chinese Crew: Andante—Allegro
   moderato—Andante subito—Presto. Big Tent (Overture): Andante. The
   Tramblers: Allegro.—3. Intermezzo: Andante.—4. Allegro. Shuffles: Lento. Pas

de deux: Andante. The Start of the Fight: Allegro—Andante con moto—Largo—
   Lento—Allegro subito—Andante con moto.

Date of composition: 1933–34.

First performance: Forrest Theater, Philadelphia, April 6, 1934, cond. Efrem Kurtz,
   choreography by Leonide Massine, with Massine, Tamara Toumanova.

Instrumentation: 2 flutes (and piccolo), 2 oboes, 2 clarinets in B-flat, 2 bassoons,
   saxophone alto, saxophone tenor, 4 horns, 3 trumpets in C, 2 trombones, tuba,
   percussion, pianoforte, harp, strings.

Duration: 33'48"

Manuscript: Princeton; NN, Texas (missing the end?).

Unpublished?

Recordings: Residentie Orchestra, The Hague, cond. Valeri Polyansky (Chandos
   9768); with Ode (see I-B1).

Note: Orchestrated with the assistance of Edward Powell.

I-B3. La vie de Polichinelle

La vie de Polichinelle: ballet in two acts and six tableaux on a scenario by Claude
   Séran.

Date of composition: 1932–33.

First performance: Paris Opera, June 22, 1934, choreography by Serge Lifar, cond.
   Joseph-Eugène Szyfer, with Serge Lifar (Polichinelle), Mlle Simoni (Mme
   Polichinelle), Mlle Didion (la Belle Acrobate). Sets and costumes by Pere Pruna.

Duration: Act 1, 28'; Act 2, 30'.

Instrumentation: 2 flutes (and piccolo), 2 oboes, English horn, 2 clarinets in B, bass
   clarinet b in B, 2 bassoons, 4 horns in F, 3 trumpets, 3 trombones, tuba, timpani,
   cymbals, celesta, harp, piano, strings.

Manuscript: NN, Texas (also orchestral parts).

Published: [Paris] Éditions russes de musique [1934?]

Notes: see Danses de Polichinelle (III-A3)

I-B4. The Last Flower

The Last Flower: a parable in words, pictures and dances. Ballet on a scenario by
   James Thurber.

Date of composition: 1941.

First performance: Berlin, Stadtische Oper, Berliner Ballet, September [24?], 1958,
   choreography by Tatjana Gvosky.

Duration: 30'.

Instrumentation: 2 flutes (and piccolo), 2 oboes, 2 clarinets in B-flat, 4 horns F, 2 trumpets in B-flat, 2 trombones, timpani, snare drum, bass drum, pianoforte, strings.

Manuscript: original not traced; copy of holograph full-score, NN, Texas.

Published: Paris and Munich: Ricordi [facsimile of manuscript score?]

Notes: on verso of title-page: "this music is written/for my son Peter/and in the/ memory of/P. I. Tchaikovsky and Mme von Meck/and/dedicated/to/Dorothy Chadwick in/grateful friendship/and/to her this manuscript/shall belong." See also III-A6.

I-B5. Don Quixote

Don Quixote: ballet in three acts, scenario by Nicolas Nabokov and George Balanchine.

Date of composition: 1962–65, rev. 1965–73.

First performance: New York, New York City Ballet, May 27, 1965; choreography by George Balanchine, sets and costumes Esteban Frances; cond. Robert Irving; with George Balanchine (Don Quixote) and Suzanne Farrell (Dulcinea).

Instrumentation: 2 flutes, piccolo, 2 oboes, English horn, 3 clarinets, 3 bassoons, 4 horns, 3 trumpets, 3 trombones, tuba, timpani, percussion (triangle, vibraphone, xylophone, tambourine, military drum, bass drum, glockenspiel), harp, celesta, piano, strings.

Duration (in 1965): Act 1, 38'; Act 2, 30'; Act 3, 38', total 107 mins (1 hour 47 mins).

Manuscript: NYCB, portions and copies, NN, Texas.

Published: London and New York: M. P. Belaieff, 1966 (condensed score, 255 p.; 3539 Belaieff).

Notes: orchestrated with the assistance of Fernand Quattrocchi; see below III-A8 and III-A10.

References: Balanchine 1983, no 352.

I-B6. The Wanderer

The Wanderer: ballet in one act, scenario by George Skibine, inspired by *Le Grand Meaulnes* by Alain-Fournier.

Date of composition: 1966.

Unperformed.

Instrumentation: not traced, probably never orchestrated.

Manuscript: NN, Texas (short score, photocopy, 2 copies).

Notes: commissioned by the Harkness Ballet Company, of which George Skibine was director. On the title page of the manuscript: "(This score is dedicated to the memory of lost friends,/Gerald and Sarah [sic] Murphy, to whose/love and knowledge of American lore/I owe most of it.)"

Note: music partly recycled in film music for *Paulina 1880* (see below).

I-B7. Oxana

Oxana: Balletvariationen über ein Thema von Tschaikowski.

1. Praeludium (Andante).—2. First Variation (Allegro).—3. Second Variation ("Romanza"; Andante Moderato).—4. Third Variation ("Ciniselli Variation"; Allegro moderato).—5. Fourth Variation (Adagio).—6. Finale (Allegro).

Date of composition: 1970–75.

Not performed.

Instrumentation: 3 flutes (incl. piccolo), 2 oboes, English horn, 2 clarinets in B-flat or A, bass clarinet in B-flat, 2 bassoons, 4 horns in F, three trumpets in C, three trombones, tuba, 4 timpani, bass drum, cymbals, anvil, snareless drums, tambourine, maracas, bongo, gong, woodblock, whip, castanets, triangle, glockenspiel, vibraphone, xylophone, celesta, harp, strings.

Duration: 40'

Manuscript: NN, Texas (fragments and copy of full score).

Published: Mayence: Belaieff [1975?].

Notes: dedication (on manuscript) "to George and the N.Y.C. Ballet"; commissioned by the New York City Ballet.See Variations on a Theme by Tchaikovsky (III-B4).

I-B8. The Psalms

The Psalms: a symphonic commentary in seven movements.

1. Prologomenon and 5 Variations: a) joy; b) King David's Song; c) Round; d) On the rivers of Babylon; e) Praise the Lord with dance.—2. Miserere.—3. King David's Dance in front of the Ark (Samuel VI).—4. The Lord is my shepherd (a pastoral Psalm).—5. [in Greek] AKATHESION (hours).—6. Processional.—7. Praise the Lord (Psalm 150) on a theme by J. S. Bach.

Date of composition: 1975–76.

Unperformed.

Instrumentation: erkencho, 2 flutes (and piccolo), 2 oboes, English horn in F, 2 clarinets, bass clarinet, 2 bassoons, 4 horns, 3 trumpets, 3 trombones, tuba, timpani, percussion (xylophone, vibraphone, drums, triangle, bells, cymbals, temple block, castanets) harp, pianoforte, strings. (Note at bottom of short score manuscript: "Erkencho is a horn-like instrument from the Andes, resembling the Skofar, but can be blown in tune within a limited range.")

Duration:?

Manuscript: New York City Ballet; copy, NN, Texas (full score and short score).

Notes: Commissioned by the New York City Ballet to be choreographed by Balanchine. Ballet not realized.

See also Valses de Beethoven, V-1.

C. Incidental music and film music

I-C1. La petite Catherine

La petite Catherine: incidental music to La petite Catherine, play in three acts and seven tableaux by Alfred Savoir.

Composed 1930?

First performance: Paris, Théâtre Antoine, October 2, 1930; directed by Roger Rocher; sets by André Boll; cast including Henri Rollan, René Rocher, Alice Cocéa et Marguerite Pierry.

Instrumentation: not known.

Manuscript: not traced.

Unpublished, presumably lost.

I-C2. Samson Agonistes

Samson Agonistes: incidental music to the play by John Milton.

Date of composition: 1938.

First performance: Wells College, Aurora, New York, May 14, 1938.

Manuscript: NN, Texas (incomplete).

Unpublished.

Notes: in NN, Texas is an Andante ("While their hearts were jocund and sublime . . ."), scored for speaker's voice (in Sprechgesang), 2 clarinets in B, bassoon, and pianoforte.

Note: see also II-C8.

I-C3. Paulina 1880

Paulina 1880: music for the film realized by Jean-Louis Bertucelli after the novel by Pierre Jean Jouve.

Date of composition: 1970.

Film released 1972.

Instrumentation: flute, piccolo, oboe, 2 clarinets in A, clarinet in E-flat, clarinet in B-flat, bassoon, 2 horns, timpani, percussion (tambourine, snare drum, vibraphone, triangle, bass drum), pianoforte, strings.

Manuscript: not traced; copy of full score, NN, Texas.

Published: New York: Seesaw Music Corporation, 1972 (facsimile of full-score manuscript).

See also Six Choruses for Oedipus Rex (II-C).

II. VOCAL MUSIC

A. Vocal music with orchestra

II-A1. Job

Job. Oratorio for male chorus and orchestra. Text of the Bible adapted by Jacques Maritain. English version by Lewis Galantière and Albert Stoessel.

Prologue. First Part: Préface et premier discours de Job. Second Part: Discours des trois amis. Third Part: Préface du Scribe et discours de Dieu. Epilogue.

Date of composition: 1932–33.

First performance: Paris, Théâtre des Champs-Élysées, June 15, 1933, Ballets 1933: Georges Jouatte, tenor; Gilbert Moryn, baritone; Vlassov Choir; Jacques Février et Jean Doyen, pianos; Orchestre symphonique de Paris, cond. Maurice Abravanel.

Instrumentation: 3 flutes (and piccolo), 2 oboes, English horn, 2 clarinets in B, bass clarinet, saxophone soprano in B, saxophone tenor in B, 2 bassoons, contrabassoon, 4 horns in F, 3 trumpets, 3 trombones, tuba, harp, celesta, percussion (bells, cymbals and suspended cymbal, timpani, snare drum, and bass drum), 2 pianos, strings.

Duration: 35'

Manuscript: NN, Texas (short score).

Published: Boosey & Hawkes; vocal score, in copyist's hand, reproduced with stamp of Worcester Country Musical Association.

Notes: commissioned by the Princesse de Polignac. Originally for male choir, reorchestrated and revised for mixed choir in 1934. Variant title (on instrumental parts): Hiob. In the Dominique Nabokov archives is a proof of engraved vocal score with two piano accompaniment, 49 p., incomplete, as well as a complete set of instrumental parts and revised mixed chorus parts.

II-A2. The Return of Pushkin

The Return of Pushkin: an elegie in three movements for high voice and symphony orchestra = Vozvrashchenie Pushkina: elegiia v trekh chastiakh dlia vysokogo golosa i simfonicheskogo orkestra. English text by Vladimir Nabokov after Alexander Pushkin's poem "Mikhailovskoe."

I. Andante. "Vnov ia posetil tot ugolok zemli . . ." ("I have seen again that corner of the earth . . ."). II Allegretto. "Na granitse vladenii dedovskikh . . ." ("On the border of my ancestral land . . ."). III Lento assai. "V razny gody pod vashu sen . . ." ("I remember at various times . . .").

Date of composition: 1946–47.

First performance: Boston, January 2, 1948, Marina Koshetz (soprano), Boston Symphony Orchestra, cond. Serge Koussevitzky.

Instrumentation: 2 flutes, 2 oboes, 2 clarinets, 2 bassoons, 4 horns, 3 trumpets, timpani, bells, strings.

Duration: 25'.

Manuscript: not traced.

Published: Bonn: M. P. Belaieff, 1964 (short score, 32 p.; 3525 Belaieff); words in Russian, English, and German).

Notes: commissioned by the Koussevitzky Foundation and dedicated to the memory of N. K. Koussevitzky and to the Koussevitzky Foundation.

II-A3. La vita nuova

La vita nuova: concerto for soprano, tenor and orchestra on three excerpts from Dante's "The New Life."

English version by Dante Gabriel and William Michael Rossetti, adapted with the
assistance of W. H. Auden.

I.—Recitativo e Aria. Andante.—II. Passacaglia. Lento (e molto espressivo).—III.
Fantasia e Rota. Allegretto.

Date of composition: 1947

First performance: Boston, March 2, 1951, Mary Henderson (soprano), David Garen
(tenor), Boston Symphony Orchestra, cond. Charles Münch.

Instrumentation: 2 flutes (and piccolo), 2 oboes, 2 clarinets in B-flat and A, bass
clarinet, 2 bassoons, 4 horns in F, 2 trumpets B-flat, 2 trombones, tuba, timpani,
percussion (glockenspiel, triangle, snare drum, bass drum), harp, piano, strings.

Manuscript: not traced; DNA (drafts); blue print copy, NN, Texas.

Duration: 27'

Unpublished; full score and parts available from New York: Associated Music
Publishers.

Note: Commissioned by the Koussevitzky Foundation.

II-A4. Symboli chrestiani

Symboli chrestiani, for baritone and symphonic orchestra.

Introit I: "Ancora".—Introit II: "Palumba".—Introit III: "Fenice."

Date of composition: 1955.

First performance: Louisville, February 15, 1956, William Pickett, baritone, Louisville
Symphony Orchestra, cond. Robert Whitney.

Instrumentation: 2 flutes (and piccolo), 2 bassoons, 2 horns in F, 2 trumpets in C,
harp, celesta, pianoforte, timpani, percussion (snare drum, military drum, triangle, bass drum, cymbals, tam tam, xylophone), strings.

Duration: 19'

Manuscript: NN, Texas.

Published: Paris and Munich: Ricordi (facsimile of manuscript short score, 27 p.;
R. 1471).

Recording: William Picket, baritone; Louisville Symphony Orchestra, cond. Robert
Whitney (Recordings of works commissioned by the Louisville Philharmonic
Society for the Louisville Symphony Orchestra, LOU 58-1).

Note: Commissioned by the Louisville Symphony Orchestra.

II-A5. Four Poems by Boris Pasternak

Quatre poèmes de Boris Pasternak, tirés du Docteur Jivago. French words by Michel
Ancey, German words by Rolf-Dietrich Keil. For baritone and piano.

1. Gamlet = Hamlet.—2. Razluka = Die Trennung = La séparation.—3. Khmel =
Wilder Wein = Houblon.—4. Svadba (Chastushka) = Hochzeit (Tschastuschka)
= Noces (Tchastouchka).

Date of composition: ca. 1960.

First performance: Hamburg Radio, 1960, Hermann Prey, baritone, Nordwestdeutsche Rundfunk Symphony Orchestra, Hans Schmidt-Isserstedt.

Manuscript: not traced.

Instrumentation: 2 flutes, piccolo, 2 oboes, 2 clarinets in B, bass clarinet in B, 2 bassoons, 2 horns, 2 trumpets, 2 trombones, harp, gong, timpani, percussion, pianoforte, strings.

Published: unpublished in full score. For short score, see below II-B13.

Notes: Commissioned by Nordwestdeutche Rundfunk, Hamburg; also published in version with piano, see II-B13.

B. Vocal music with piano or small ensemble

II-B1. Quatre romances

Quatre romances pour piano et chant: 1. La pie (Pushkin).—2. Pora, moi drug, pora = Il est temps = S'ist Zeit (Pushkin).—3. Na chto vy, dni . . . = Ah, tristes jours = Ihr Tage, ach! (Boratinski [E. A. Baratynskii])—4. Khloe = À Chloé = An Chloja (Dimitrieff [Ivan Ivanovich Dmitriev]).

Date of composition: 1925.

For soprano or mezzo soprano and piano.

First performance traced: Berlin, Galerie Flechtheim, March 7, 1929, Boris Greverus, tenor, Claurio Arrau, piano.

Manuscript: not traced.

Published: Paris: Rouart, Lerolle & Cie, 1929 (R. L. & Cie 11662, 11663, 11666; each song has a separate title page); French words by Henri Sauguet, German words by von Wistinghausen.

II-B2. Trois poèmes d'Omar

[Three songs for high voice and piano on poems by The Rubayait of Omar Khayyam, translated into French from the English version by Edward Fitzgerald.]

Composed: 1925 [?]

First performance: Paris, Salle des Agriculteurs de France, concert of the Société musicale indépendante, June 4, 1926. Marguerite Babaïan, soprano, Nicolas Nabokov, piano.

Manuscript: not traced.

Unpublished, presumably lost.

II-B3. Vocalise

[Vocalise for soprano voice, with accompaniment of two flutes, clarinet, and piano]

Composed: 1926 [?]

First performance: Paris, Salle des Agriculteurs de France, concert of the Société indépendante de musique, June 4, 1926. Marguerite Babaïan, soprano, Nicolas Nabokov, piano.

Manuscript: not traced.

Unpublished, presumably lost.

II-B4. Chants à la Vierge Marie

Bogorodichnye piesnopiesniia: dlia vysokago zhenskago golosa i fortep'iano = Chants à la Vierge Marie: pour voix de soprano et piano. Text by Nicolas Nabokov, French words by Raïssa Maritain.

1. Slavovoslovie vstupitelnoe = Chant d'introduction. Largo.—2. Pesn' pervaia (Chudo v Kane Galileiskoi) = Chant premier (Cana). Tempo ad libitum.—3. Pesn' vtoraia (Polozhenie vo grob Spasitelia)/Chant second (Pieta). Andante (legatissimo).—4. Pesn' tret'ia (Uspenie)/Chant troisième (Dormition). Un poco andante (legato).—5. Slavoslovie zakliuchitel'noe/Chant final (triomphe). Allegro moderato.

Date of composition: 1926.

First performance traced: Paris, Salle Chopin, "Pro Musica" concert, December 19, 1928: A. Merlin and G. Copperie, sopranos, J. Ibels, piano. Also performed Geneva, 7th festival of the Société internationale de musique contemporaine, April 1929.

Manuscript: not traced.

Published: Paris: Rouart Lerolle, 1928 (14 p.; R. L. 11617 et Cie); text in Maritain 1993, 1159–61.

Notes: alternative title "Cantiques à la Vierge." Published with the printed dedication: "Bratu M. Ch. R. Ord. Prop. I i Otsu Ioanny Sh./Au frère M. C. R. [Marie Czeslas Rzewuski] o.p.; au Père Jean Sch. [Schlumberger]"

Reference: Maritain 1995, 863 (28.1).

II-B5. Quatre poésies de A. Pushkin

Quatre poésies de A. Pouchkine. 1. Razstavan'e = Départ = Parting.—2. Naprasno ia begu = En vain je fuis . . . = In vain I fly.—3. Ne stanu ia zhalet' o rozakh = Qu'importe qu'elles soient flétries . . . = I do not regret.—4. Kogda v obiatiia moi = Lorsque dans mes bras = When in my arms.

For high voice and piano.

Date of composition: [1928?]

First performance traced: Strasbourg, Conservatoire, March [10?] 1931, Lina Prokofiev, soprano; Nathalie Radisse-Kaulm, piano.

Manuscript: not traced.

Published: Berlin: Russischer Musik Verlag, 1929 (with separate pagination; R.M.V. 480, 481, 482, 483). Words in Russian, French (by Renée Vivier), and English (by D. Millar Craig).

Note: dedications at the head of no. 3: "Petru Petrovichu Suvchiskomu" [Petr Petrovich Suvchinskii] and at the head of no. 4: "à M. François Frank."

II-B6. Fables d'Ésope

Fables d'Ésope en langue française, d'après les quatrains de Benserade: six songs for high voice and piano.

1.Le corbeau et le renard: Un poco andante (ben legato).—2. Le serpent et la lime: Allegretto.—3. Le rat de ville et le rat des champs: Lento.—4. Le cerf se regardant dans l'eau: Allegretto (bene legato).—5.Le ventre et les membres: Andantino doloroso.—6. Le chat et le coq: Largo maestoso.

Date of composition: September 17–October 5, 1927.

First performance: not traced.

Unpublished.

Manuscript: DNA

Notes: inscribed on cover of manuscript "à Mon Sieur Felix de Bethmann-Hollweg, Seigneur à Hohenfinow [. . .] en témoignage d'affectueuse reconnaissance." Additional dedications: Le serpent et la lime ("à Madame la Comtesse Jules Zech"); Le rat de ville et le rat des champs ("à Mademoiselle Claire de Pfuel de tout [drawing of a heart]"); Le cerf se regardant dans l'eau ("à Mon Sieur le Comte Jules Zech, en souvenir de notre amitié commune pour les cerfs-volants et le charmant Sieur Tumpelbock ainsi que sa vénérée famille"); Le ventre et les membres ("à Mon Sieur Heinz Boese, docteur en peinture, en souvenir des vins de champagne, des vins de Bourgogne et des maux d'estomac"). Presumably intended for private performance at Hohenfinow Castle.

II-B7. Si notre vie . . .

Si notre vie est moins qu'une journée: song for voice and piano on a sonnet by Joachim du Bellay.

Date of composition: 1927.

First performance: not traced.

Published: Paris: Rouart, Lerolle & Cie, 1929 (R. L. & Cie 11644).

Note: Dedicated on the printed score to Mme André Bourgeois, née Jourdan-Savonnières.

II-B8. Collectionneur d'échos

Collectionneur d'échos: petite cantate pour soprano, basse, le chœur du public, 9 instruments et batterie. Text by Max Jacob.

1. Entrée (Andante molto), soprano solo: "À vendre! Dans le pays de Caux . . ."—2. Aria (Andante moderato), solo bass and soprano solo: "Berger, combien cette montagne?"—3. Chanson (Allegro moderato), solo bass and soprano solo with chorus: "Or c'était comme en des coulisses . . ."—4. Invention (Andante), solo bass and soprano solo: "Le vieux lord dit . . ."—5. Cantique (Allegro moderato), soprano solo and solo bass: "Mais toujours acheter des ruines . . ."

Date of composition: 1930–31.

First performance: Toulon, théâtre municipal, April 20, 1932 (performers not traced).

Instrumentation: flute, oboe, clarinet, bassoon, trumpet, percussion, violin, viola, cello, and double bass.

Published: Berlin: Russischer Musikverlag, 1933 (piano reduction by the author, 16 p.; RMV 559).

Note: dedicated to Charles and Marie-Laure de Noailles; the instrumental parts have not been located.

II-B9. L'aubépin

L'aubépin et cinq autres mélodies. Poems by Max Jacob. English words by Elliott Carter and Charles Henri Ford, German words by Hansi Gosselin.

I. L'aubépin (The Hawthorn Tree/Der Weissdorn).—II. Vos yeux clos (Your Veiled Eyes/Geschloss'ne Augen).—III. L'adultère (The Unfaithful/Ehebruch).—IV. Lune (Moon/Der Mond).—V. La crise (The Crisis/Krise).—VI. Angoisses (Anguish/Herzenangst).

Date of composition: summer 1937.

First performance traced: Paris, Salle Gaveau, November 28, 1938, concert of La Sérénade, Marie-Blanche de Polignac, soprano, Francis Poulenc, piano.

Manuscript: DNA (incomplete).

Published; Paris: La Sirène Musicale, 1938 (16 p.).

II-B10. America Was Promises

America was Promises: cantata for baritone and alto solo, male chorus, and chamber orchestra. Text by Archibald MacLeish.

Date of composition: 1940.

First performance: New York, WABC radio, April 22, 1940; Patricia Pierce, contralto, John Percival, bass, cond. Howard Barlow; first public performance: New York, April 25, 1950.

Instrumentation: not traced.

Duration: 25'

Manuscript: LC(short score, with indications of orchestration).

Unpublished?

Note: manuscript dated "Aurora, March 21, 1940"

II-B11. Silent Songs

Silent Songs: poems by Joyce, Yeats, and Rilke.

1. "Sleep" (James Joyce).—2. Alone (Joyce).—3. Moon Night = Mondnacht (Rainer Maria Rilke).—4. Dream of death (W. B. Yeats).—5. Brown Penny (Yeats).

Date of composition: 1937–41 [?].

First performance: not traced.

Manuscript: not traced.

Unpublished in solo form?

Recording: Gloria Davy, soprano, William Johnson, piano, American Academy in Rome spring concert, May 3, 1955 [Rome: American Academy, 2003]. Recorded at the Villa Aurelia.

Notes: the Rilke poem has words in English and German; English version not credited. See below II-C7.

II-B12. [Twelve Songs on Poems by Emily Dickinson]

[Twelve Songs on Poems by Emily Dickinson] for high voice and piano.

1.Nature, the gentlest mother (quite slow) [dated December 24, 1949].—2. There came a wind like a bugle (quite fast) [dated December 20, 1949].—3. Why do they shut me out of heaven? (moderately). [dated September 27, 1949].—4. The world feels dusty . . . (very slowly) [dated March 28, 1949].—5. Heart, we will forget him (very slowly) [dated April 30, 1949].—6. Dear March, come in! (with exuberance) [n.d.].—7. Sleep is supposed to be (moderately slow—with dignity) [dated October 6, 1949].—8. When they come back (moderately, beginning slowly) [dated April 23, 1949].—9. I felt a funeral in my brain (rather fast) [dated January 26, 1950].—10. I've heard an organ talk sometimes (gently flowing) [dated October 11, 1949].—11. Going to Heaven! (fast) [dated January 13, 1950].—12. The Chariot. (with quiet grace) [dated April 10, 1949].

Date of composition: 1949.

First performance: not traced.

Unpublished?

Manuscript: not traced; Independent Music Publishers blue print copy, DNA.

II-B13. Four Poems by Boris Pasternak

Quatre poèmes de Boris Pasternak, tirés du Docteur Jivago. French words by Michel Ancey, German words by Rolf-Dietrich Keil. For baritone and piano.

1. Gamlet = Hamlet.—2. Razluka = Die Trennung = La séparation.—3. Khtel = Wilder Wein = Houblon.—4. Svabda (Chastushka) = Hochzeit (Tschastuschka) = Noces (Tchastouchka).

Date of composition: 1958–59.

First performance: for the piano version, not traced.

Duration: ca. 18'

Published: Paris: Ricordi, 1961 (32 p.; R.2006, 2009, 2012, 2015). Words in French, German, and Russian.

Note: for original orchestral version, see II-A5.

II-B14. Six Lyric Songs from Akhmatova's Requiem

Shest' stikhotvoreniĭ: iz tsikla "Rekviem" Anny Akhmatovoĭ = Six Lyric Songs: from the cycle Requiem/poems by Anna Akhmatova.

1. "Tikho liotsa tikhii Don . . ." ("Slowly flows the quiet Don"), Andante moderato.—2. "Uvodili tebia na rassvete . . ." ("They led you away at dawn"), Andante (come une Marcia funebra)—Allegro—Andante.—3. Raspiatie (The Crucifixion), Andante moderato.—4. Prigovor (The Verdict), Lento assai—Andante.—5. "Uzhe bezumie krylom . . ." ("The wings of madness has covered), Allegro moderato.—6. K smerti (The Death), Allegro moderato.

Date of composition: 1966.

First performance: Rome, 1967 [?], Evelyn Lear, [accompanist not traced]

Duration: 14'10".

Published: Berlin: Bote & Bock, 1967 (23 p.; B & B 22080 [974]); Russian words with phonetic transliteration, with English and German translations on p. 2 and 3; English translation by Nabokov "with the sollicitous help of Nina Berberova, Princeton University, USA); German translation by Irene Stolz, Berlin.

Note: Commissioned by and dedicated to Evelyn Lear. An indication in the score stipulates that the cycle is to be sung in Russian only. Also exists in a subsequent orchestral version, premiered by Barbro Ericson and the Residenz-Orchester Den Hag at the 1968 Berlin Festival, under Bruno Maderna (orchestration not traced).

II-B15. Gretchens gebet

Gretchens gebet [song for soprano voice and piano]. Words by Goethe.

Date of composition not known.

First performance: not traced.

Manuscript: NN, Texas

Unpublished?

Note: incipit: "Ach neige du Schmerzensreiche dein Antlitz gnädig meiner Not!"

C. Choral

II-C1. Cantate de cour

Cantate de cour pour petit choeur d'hommes (chantée à l'entrée de la cour). Paroles de Derjawin (1760).

Incipit (ten.): Kogda iz ponma goludogo vedet . . .

Two-part chorus (TB) with pianoforte accompaniment, marked Allegro.

Date of composition: [1932?]

First performance not traced.

Manuscript: DNA.

Unpublished?

Note: pencil note on manuscript: "G. Balanchin, 11 mai 1932."

II-C2. Five Studies for A Capella Women's Chorus

Five Studies for A Capella Women's Chorus = Cinq études pour chœur de femmes a capella: 1. Brown Penny, poem by Yeats.—2. Little Eva's Death, from Uncle Tom's Cabin [words by Lincoln Kirstein].—3. [Sleep Now] Chamber Music XXXVI, poem by James Joyce.—4. Alone (from Chamber Music), poem by James Joyce.—5. Mondnacht, poem by R. M. Rilke (English Translation by Constance Rosebough).
In four parts (SSAA).
Date of composition: [1937–38?]; Mondnacht dated November 7, 1937; Sleep Now dated February 18–19, 1938 (dedication at top: "for Conny")
First performance: not traced [Wells College, 1937–38?]
Manuscript: original not traced; copy, DNA.
Published: Brown Penny, New York: Associated Music Publishers, 1957 (8 p.; A-188); others not traced, despite the indication "Copyright 1952, AMS, Inc., NY" on manuscript.
Note: 1 and 3–5 revised as Silent Songs for solo voice, see above II-B11.

II-C3. Oedipus Rex

Six Greek Choruses from Oedipus Rex:
I: On the Plague ("Alas, alas, beyond all reckoning my myriad sorrows . . .")—II. Invocation to the Gods ("Glad message of the voice of Zeus . . .")—III. On Prophecy ("The prophet wise, reader of bird and sign . . .")—IV. On the Birth of Oedipus ("Tomorrow brings full moon")—V. On Hybris ("Oedipus seemed blessed . . .")—VI. Lament ("Heartbroken Oedipus, Would you ever have come to Thebes . . .").
Original version (4 numbers) for female choir (mixed choir in no. 4); revised version for female choir (mixed choir only in no. 4) and piano.
Date of composition: spring 1937; revised 1950.
First performance: Wells College, Aurora, New York, June 1937; first concert performance of the revised version: Tarrytown (New York) Town Hall, May 5, 1950, Marymount College Glee Club, Hugh Ross director, May 5, 1950.
Manuscript: NN, Texas; drafts, DNA.
Unpublished.
Note: "Numbers 1 through 4 were composed in 1937 for a College production of the play 'Oedipus Rex' by Sophocles, given in the translation by Yeats. Numbers 2 and 3 have been re-written and extended and Numbers 5 and 6 were recently composed for this performance" (Marymount College Glee Club, concert program, May 5, 1950).

II-C4. Kondakon

" 'Kondakon of the Christmas Vespers,' a Vesper carol sung at Christmas: origin Russian or Greek, XIIIth century, traditional melody from the Codex of the Valaam Monastery in Finland, set for Four Parts [SSAA] by Nicolas Nabokoff."

Incipit: "The Viring this day brings forth Him who was before all time . . ."

Marked "Andante con moto."

Date of composition: [1936–39?]

Manuscript: not traced; copy, DNA.

Unpublished?

II-C5. Hymn for the Feast of Purification

" 'Hymn of the Feast of Purification'; origin of the melody: Greek or Russian, XIth or
XIIIth century. From the Codex of the great Znamennyi Rospyev. Free harmonisation and treatment by N. Nabokoff."

Three soloists and four-part chorus [SSAA].

No expressive marking; $\downarrow$ = 60–66.

Note at bottom about the soli: "can be sung by either three women's or three men's
voices.

Date of composition: [1936–39?]

Manuscript: not traced; copy, DNA.

Unpublished?

II-C6. Hymn for Epiphany

"A Hymn for Epiphany; origin of melody, probably 13rd century Russian. From the
Codex of the great Znamennyi Rospyev. Free harmonisation and treatment by
N. Nabokoff."

Four-part chorus [SSAA].

No expressive marking; [quarter-note] = 78–80.

Date of composition: [1936–39?]

Manuscript: not traced; copy, DNA.

Unpublished?

II-C7. Silent Light: A Prayer

"Silent Light: A Prayer from the daily Vesper service. Traditional melody from
the script of Valaam Monastery (probably 13th–14th century). Harmonized by
N. Nabokoff."

4-part a cappella chorus for SATB.

No expressive indication; [quarter-note] = 132.

Date of composition: [1936–39?]

First performance: not traced.

Manuscript: DNA

Unpublished?

II-C8. Samson Agonistes

Five choruses from Milton's Samson Agonistes, for Soprani I and II and alti, with
    piano accompaniment.
1.– 2.—3. God of Our Fathers, What Is Man.—4.—5. Go and the Holy One of Israel
    be Thy Guide.
Date of composition: spring 1938.
First performance: Wells College, May 1938.
Unpublished. Blue print copy in Dominique Nabokov archives.

II-C9. Androcles and the Lion

Incidental music to G. B. Shaw's play *Androcles and the Lion.*
Date of composition: spring 1939.
First performance: Wells College, May 1939.
Manuscript: not traced.
Unpublished.

II-C10. The Tempest

Incidental music to Shakespeare's *The Tempest.*
Date of composition: spring 1940.
First performance: Wells College, May 1940.
Manuscript: not traced.
Unpublished.

II-C11. The Lord's Prayer

The Lord's Prayer: for unaccompanied four-part male chorus.
Date of composition: [1939?]
First performance: not traced.
Manuscript: not traced.
Published: New York: Associated Music Publishers, 1946 (A.M.P. 194527-4 [M]);
    includes piano part with mention: "For rehearsal only."
Note: printed inscription on score: "Froeliche Weinachten und herzliche Gruesse
    von Nicolas Nabokoff, 1946.25.12."
Note: original two-part version, dated January 18, 1939, "set for women's or men's
    chorus." Copy, DNA.

II-C12. [Two unaccompanied four-part choruses in memory of Stravinsky]

"Pamiati I. F. S. [Igor Feodorovich Stravinsky]/Zapovedi Blazhenstva/dlia smeshan-
    nago khora/(po primeram Valaamskogo rascheva)/dlia Zhorzha Balannchina/ot
    N. D. Nabokova/Ni Iork 28go Iulia 1972g.":
Incipit: "Vo tsarstvii tvoem pomiani nas Gospodi . . ."

Date of composition: 1972.

First performance: untraced.

Unpublished?

Described from Dztec copy on a single bifolium (3 p of music), NN, Texas, and DNA.

III. ORCHESTRAL MUSIC

A. Symphonic Music

III-A1. Le fiancé

Le fiancé, overture, op. 9, after Pushkin

Date of composition: [1928?]

First performance traced: Brussels, May 2 [?], 1932, Société philharmonique de Bruxelles, cond. François Ruhlmann.

Instrumentation: 2 flutes, 2 oboes, 2 clarinets, 2 horns, 2 trumpets, 2 horns, 1 trombone, timpani, percussion, celesta, strings.

Duration: 6'

Manuscript: not traced.

Published: Munich: Russicher Musik Verlag [date?]; Berlin: Boosey & Hawkes Musik Verlag [date?].

Note: Wrongly dated 1934 in *New Grove 2* (see Carr, Preston, and Meckna 2001).

III-A2. Symphony no. 1

Symphony no. 1, op. 10, "Symphonie lyrique"

1. Allegro.—2. Largo (ma non troppo lento).—3. Allegro.

Date of composition: 1928–29.

First performance: Brussels, November 30, 1929, Société philharmonique de Bruxelles, cond. Roger Désormière (Paris premiere, February 16, 1930).

Instrumentation: 2 flutes (and piccolo), 2 oboes, English horn, 2 clarinets in C, bass clarinet in C, 2 bassoons, contrabassoon, 4 horns in C, 3 trumpets in C, 3 trombones, tuba, timpani, snare drum, bass drum, cymbals, tambourine, strings.

Manuscript: not traced; copy and orchestral parts, NN, Texas.

Published: Munich: Russischer Musik Verlag.

Notes: on title page of full score, epigraph and dedication in Nabokov's hand: "The soul feels pressed by lyrical excitement, it tumbles and sings and seeks, as in a dream, to prove itself out in free fulfilment"/Pushkin/Symphonie/lyrique/op. 10 1929./[epigraph in Russian]/à la chère et bonne Denise [Bourdet?] avec tout mon [drawing of a heart] Nicolas"

III-A3. Les Danses de Polichinelle

Les danses de Polichinelle: suite de danses pour orchestre symphonique

1. Le grand cortège—2. Les jeux d'enfance.—3. Pas de deux lyrique.—4. Les farces de
    Polichinelle.—5. Pas de deux tendre.—6. Polka lente.—7. Les Arlequins dansent.
Date of composition: 1933–34.
First performance traced: New York, Carnegie Hall, National Orchestral Association,
    cond. Leon Barzin.
Instrumentation: 3 flutes (and piccolo), 3 oboes (and English horn), 2 clarinets, bass
    clarinet, 2 bassoons, contrabassoon, soprano saxophone (or trumpet), tenor sax-
    ophone (or horn), 4 horns, 3 trumpets, 3 trombones, tuba, timpani, percussion,
    pianoforte, harp, strings.
Duration: 25'.
Manuscript: Philadelphia, Free Library (full score and parts).
Published: Munich: Russischer Musik Verlag [1934?]; Berlin: Boosey and Hawkes,
    n.d.
Note: see above I-B3. Occasionally referred to as "First Symphonic Suite."

III-A4. First Symphonic Suite

First Symphonic Suite, from *La Vie de Polichinelle*
1.The First Steps of Polichinelle.—2. The Discovery of Love. 3.—Gay Games.—4.
    The Drama.—5. The Burial of Polichinelle.—6. The Resurrection.
Date of composition: 1934–36 [?].
Instrumentation: similar to III-A3 [?].
Duration: 30'.
First performance: Cleveland Orchestra, Artur Rodzinski, January 7, 1937.
Unpublished?
Note: Occasionally referred to as "Second Symphonic Suite."

III-A5. Symphony no. 2

Symphony no. 2: "Sinfonia biblica"
1. Ecclesiasticus (Wisdom). Andante moderato.—2. Solomon. Andantino.—3.
    Absalom. Allegro.—4. Hossanah. Andante moderato.
Date of composition: 1938–40.
First performance: New York, Carnegie Hall, January 2, 1941, New York Philharmonic
    Symphony Orchestra, Dimitri Mitropoulos.
Instrumentation: 2 flutes (and piccolo), 2 oboes, English horn, 2 clarinets in B-flat, 1
    clarinet in E-flat, bass clarinet, 2 bassoons, contrabassoon, 4 horns in F, 3 trum-
    pets in B-flat, 3 trombones, tuba, timpani, percussion (bass drum, castanets,
    snare drum, cymbals, glockenspiel, triangle, tam tam, xylophone), harp, piano-
    forte, strings.
Duration: ca. 38'.
Manuscript: not traced; copy of full score (in copyist's hand), NN, Texas.

Published: Bonn: Belaieff, 1965 (study full score, 76 p.; 3569 Belaieff) and 1967 (full
score, 76 p.; 3529).
Notes: Dedicated to Dimitri Mitropoulos.

III-A6. The Last Flower, symphonic suite

Arranged from the ballet composed in 1941 [see I-B4]
First performance: not traced
Instrumentation: similar to I-B4?
Manuscript: not traced
Unpublished?

III-A7. Studies in Solitude

Studies in Solitude: Four Moods for Orchestra.
1. To the memory of H. L. [Hansi Lambert]: Lento assai.—2. To the memory of P. T.
[Pawel Tchelitchew]: Allegro.—3. To the memory of B. P. [Boris Pasternak]:
Andante comodo.—4. To the memory of J. de M. [Jacques de Menasce]: Andante
moderato.
Date of composition: 1960.
First performance: Philadelphia, Philadelphia Orchestra, Eugene Ormandy, 1961.
Instrumentation: 2 flutes, 2 oboes (saxophone soprano optional), English horn, 2
clarinets in B, 2 bassoons, 2 horns in F, 1 trumpet in C, 2 trombones, triangle,
vibraphone, crotale, snare drum, tam-tam, gong, harp, celesta, gong pianoforte,
strings.
Duration: 15'.
Manuscript: not traced.
Published: Paris: Ricordi, 1961 (full score; 55 p.; R. 2030).
Notes: Commissioned by the Philadelphia Orchestra. Also published in a piano version by the composer (Ricordi R 2164). There exists a short version, consisting of
the second and third movements, entitled *Two Portraits*.

III-A8. Symphonic Variations

Symphonic Variations [after *Don Quixote*].
Introduction (Andante).—Variation I (Allegro molto).—Variation II (Andante).—
Variation III (Allegro).—Variation IV (Allegro).—Variation V (A Russian Tango;
Andante).—Variation VI (A Mocking Fugue; Allegro).—Variation VII (Pavane
funèbre; Andante moderato).—Variation VIII (Lento assai; Andantino).—
Variation IX (Allegro).—Finale (Processional and Return of the Theme; Andante
moderato).
Date of composition: 1967

First performance: not traced

Instrumentation: 3 flutes (incl. piccolo), 3 oboes, 3 clarinets in B-flat, 3 bassoons, 4 horns, 3 trumpets, 3 trombones, 1 tuba, timpani, percussion (triangle, vibraphone, xylophone, tambourine, military drum, bass drum, glockenspiel), pianoforte, celesta, harp, strings.

Duration: 38'

Published: Mayence: Belaieff, 1966 (full score, 229 p.; 3533).

III-A9. Symphony no. 3

Symphony no.3: "A Prayer"

1. Praeludium (Andante).—2. Diaspora (allegro moderato).—3. Responsorium I (Andante).—4. Persecutio (Allegro non troppo, ma feroce).—5. Responsorium II (Andante moderato).

Date of composition: 1966–67.

First performance: New York, Philharmonic Hall, New York Philharmonic, cond. Leonard Bernstein, January 4, 1968.

Instrumentation: 2 flutes, piccolo, 2 oboes, English horn, 2 clarinets, bass clarinet, 3 bassoons, 4 horns, 3 trumpets, 3 trombones, tuba, timpani, percussion (bass drum, 3 drums, crotales, suspended cymbal, 2 large cymbals, 1 big temple gong, campani, woodblock, whip, metal sheet, triangle, xylophone, vibraphone), pianoforte, harp, strings.

Duration: 18'.

Published: [n.p.] Belaieff, 1967 (study full score, 64 p.; 3570 Belaieff).

Notes: Commissioned by the New York Philharmonic Orchestra on the occasion of its 125th anniversary.

III-A10. The Hunter's Picnic: Symphonic Suite from the Ballet Don Quixote.

1. Prelude.—2. Mazurka.—3. Pas d'action.—4. Variation for Act I.—5. New Variation for a Girl Dancer.—6. New Variation for a Male Dancer.—7. Valse "Pestchinka 1928" pour Giorgio Balanchine.—8.

Date of composition: 1972.

First performance: not traced.

Instrumentation: 2 flutes (and piccolo), 3 oboes, 2 clarinets in B-flat, bass clarinet, 2 bassoons, 4 horns in F, 3 trumpets in C, 3 trombones, tuba, timpani, snare drum, bass drum, cymbals, tambourine, castanets, tam tam, triangle, vibraphone, celesta, xylophone, glockenspiel, large bells, small chimes, gong, ratchet, anvil, whip, woodblock, harp, pianoforte, strings.

Manuscript: not traced.

Published: New York: Seesaw Music Corp. (facsimile of full score), 1973.

III-A11. Circus Scenes

Zirkus-Szenen: Ouvertüre und fünf Miniaturen für sinfonisches Bläser, Schlagzeug, Klavier und Kontrabass.

1. Allegro moderato; Allegro.—2. [♪ = 132].—3. Allegro moderato.—4. Moderato.—5. Moderato e teneroso.—6. Finale galopato, Allegro moderato.

Date of composition: 1977–78.

First performance: Berlin, Junge Deutsche Philharmonie, cond. Michael Luig, September 8, 1978.

Instrumentation: 2 flutes (and piccolo), 2 oboes, saxophone, 2 clarinets in B-flat, 2 bassoons, 4 horns in F, 2 trumpets in C, 2 trombones, tuba, timpani, percussion (4), whip, pianoforte (with loudspeaker), strings.

Duration: 10'.

Manuscript: NN, Texas (full score, copy).

Published: Mayence: Belaieff [1978?]

Notes: Commissioned by the Berlin Festwochen.

B. Concertos

III-B1. Piano Concerto

Concerto for Piano in C

1. Allegro.—2. Andante moderato.—3. Allegro.

Date of composition: 1930–31.

First performance: Strasbourg, Conservatoire, August 7, 1933, Jakob Gimpel, Orchestre municipal de Strasbourg, Nicolas Nabokov (first movement only); first complete performance traced: Rome, January 6, 1935, Marcelle Meyer, Accademia di Santa Cecilia, Mario Rossi.

Instrumentation: 2 flutes, 2 oboes, 2 clarinets, 2 bassoons, 4 horns, 2 trumpets, 2 trombones, tuba, percussion, strings, pianoforte solo.

Duration: 23'.

Manuscript: NN, Texas (short score).

Published: Berlin: Boosey & Hawkes Musikverlag, 1932; facsimile of short-score manuscript issued by Durand & Cie, Paris, n.d.

Note: on manuscript, dedication, crossed out in some copies: "ad memoriam di Franz Liszt. 1931."

III-B2. Concerto Corale

Concerto Corale for Flute, Strings, and Pianoforte [on a theme by Hans Leo Hassler]

1. Preludium (Andante).—2. Cadenza romantica (Allegro non troppo molto).—3. Rondo finale (Allegro; Corale, Andante moderato).

Date of composition: [1950?]

First performance traced: Paris, November 20, 1957, Maxence Larrieu, flute, orchestra cond. Nicolas Nabokov.

Instrumentation: strings, solo flute, pianoforte solo.

Duration: 17'.

Manuscript: NN, Texas (copy).

Published: Frankfurt, Peters and Belaieff [1953]; facsimile of full-score manuscript in copyist's hand, Belaieff, 1966 (3541 Belaieff).

Note: According to the composer's indications, the work can be performed in chamber music version, with the strings reduced to one instrument per part.

III-B3. Les Hommages

Les Hommages: concerto per violoncello e orchestra

1. Serenata di Pietro (Andante).—2. Ballata di Alessandro (Allegro).—3. Corale di Michele (Andante moderato).

Date of composition: 1952–53.

First performance: Philadelphia, Lorne Munroe, cellist, Philadelphia Orchestra, cond. Eugene Ormandy, November 6, 1953.

Instrumentation: 2 flutes, 2 oboes, 2 clarinets in F, 2 bassoons, 4 horns in F, 2 trumpets in B-flat, 2 trombones, timpani, triangle, snare drum, bass drum, gong, cymbal, vibraphone, xylpophone, bells, celesta, pianoforte (or harp), strings, cello solo.

Duration: ca. 16'

Manuscript: DNA (drafts); NN, Texas (full score, copy)

Unpublished?

III-B4. Prelude, 4 Variations and Finale

Präludium, 4 Variationen und Finale = Prelude, Four Variations and Finale, for cello and orchestra on a theme by Peter I. Tchaikovsky.

1. Praeludium: Andante moderato.—2. Prima Variazione: Allegro molto.—3. Secunda Variazione: bene cantando.—4. Terza Variazione: Allegro moderato. 5. Variazione 40 chiamato Pas d'action romantique [Testimonio a Mahler e Verdi]: Andante moderato; Andante molto moderato (bene incantando e molto expressivo); Largo.—6. Finale.

Date of composition: 1968.

First performance: Monte-Carlo, Mstislav Rostropovitch, cello, Orchestre philharmonique de Monte-Carlo, Igor Markevitch, August 5, 1970.

Manuscript: drafts, DNA.

Published: Frankfurt: Belaieff, 1977 (short score; 55 p.; M. P. Belaieff 3562; inserted cello part with bowing and fingering by Rostropovich).

Recording: Mstislav Rostropovitch, Philadelphia Orchestra, cond. Eugene Ormandy, Intaglio INCD 7521.

IV. CHAMBER AND INSTRUMENTAL MUSIC

A. Chamber Music

IV-A1. Serenata estiva

Serenata estiva (Summer Serenade) for String Quartet
1. Canzone: Lento, andante moderato (molto expressivo).—2. Sonata: Allegro.—3. Dialogo corale: Andante sostenuto e ben legato.
Date of composition: 1937.
First performance traced: Annapolis, Maryland, St. John's College, February 6, 1942, Budapest String Quartet.
Manuscript: LC; NN, Texas (violin and cello parts only)
Published: Frankfurt: Peters, n.d.
Note: dedicated on the manuscript to Elizabeth Sprague Coolidge.

IV-A2. Sonata for bassoon and piano

Sonata for bassoon and piano, in two movements
1. Adagio.—2. Allegro.
Date of composition: 1942.
First performance: not traced
Manuscript: not traced (National Blue Print copy, NN, Texas).
Duration: 10'.
Published: Manhattan (Kansas): Prairie Dawg Press, 2008 (23 p.), ed. Bruce Gbur.
Recording: David Oyen, bassoon, Chia-Ling Hsieh, piano [Morehead, Kansas: Morehead State University]. Recorded live, October 6, 2009, Duncan Recital Hall.
Note: first movement originally entitled "A Litany for Bassoon and Piano"; dedicated on the manuscript to Mr Leonard Sparrow.

IV-A3. Introduction and Allegro

Introduzione e Allegro for violin and piano
Andante moderato—Allegro.
Date of composition: 1947.
First performance: New York, Carnegie Hall, November 17, 1947, Nathan Milstein, violin; Artur Balsam, piano.
Manuscript: NN, Texas.
Published: unpublished? (penciled note on manuscript: "FO 1078, copyright 1949 by Classical Music Publishers, Inc."; registered with SACEM, Paris, 1951)

Variant titles: "Introduzione corale" (manuscript); "Choral e allegro" (SACEM copy and title at first performance).

IV-A4. Canzone

Canzone for violin and piano
Andante molto moderato
Date of composition: 1950.
First performance: not traced.
Manuscript: not traced
Unpublished? (lithographic copy deposited with SACEM, Paris, 1951)
Note: dedicated to Nathan Milstein.

B. Music for the piano

IV-B1. Piano Sonata no. 1

Sonate pour le piano [no. 1]
1. Allegro. 2. Interludium: Adagio ma non troppo. 3. Finale: Presto.
Date of composition: 1925–26.
First performance: Paris, Salle des Agriculteurs, November 12, 1926, Claudio Arrau.
Manuscript: not traced.
Duration: 12'.
Manuscript: not traced.
Published: Paris: Rouart Lerolle, 1926 (22 p.; R. L. 11615 et Cie).
Recording: Madeleine Malraux (Interludium only), DDD K 617019 M7 8651 (recorded 1992, Salle Adyard, Paris).
Notes: printed dedication on published score to Baroness Amaury de La Grange. In A major. Dated "Kolbsheim-Paris 1925–26" at the end.

IV-B2. Short Stories

Short Stories: 4 morceaux pour le piano
1. Recitativo.—2. Ritournelle.—3. Valse.—4. Sonate.
Date of composition: 1925–26.
First performance: not traced.
Manuscript: not traced.
Published: Paris: Rouart Lerolle 1925–26 (11 p.; R. L. 11616 et Cie); note misprint ("Shot" for "Short" on cover and title page). Dated "1925–26 Kolbsteim [*recte* Kolbsheim]" at the end.
Note: printed dedication to Claudio Arrau on published score; no. 2, "Ritournelle," dedicated to Jacques Maritain; no. 3, "Valse," dedicated to Raïssa Maritain; no. 4, "Sonate," dedicated to Marcelle Meyer.

IV-B3. Valse des coqs et des arlequins

Une valse des coqs et des arlequins
Date of composition: 1927.
First performance: not traced.
Manuscript: DNA.
Unpublished.
Note: the penciled manuscript is inscribed to "M. et Mme [Maurice?] Jaubert." Tempo indication: "Comme à Vienne (plutôt vite)." At the end: "Da capo al infinita."

IV-B4. Trois danses

Trois danses pour piano
1. Allegro.—2. Lento Assai.—3. Allegro.
Date of composition: 1928.
First performance traced: Berlin, Galerie Flechtheim, March 7, 1929, Claudio Arrau.
Manuscript: not traced.
Duration: 8'
Published: Berlin, New York: Russischer Musik Verlag [1930] (RMV 471, 472, 473), with dedication "à M. Serge de Diaghilew."
Note: Presumably a piano reduction of the ballet numbers added to *Ode* at Diaghilev's request and not included in the published score.

IV-B5. Le cœur de Don Quichotte

Serdtse Don Kikhota: siuita dlia f. p. v 2 ruki = Le cœur de Don Quichotte: suite pour piano à 2 mains.
1. [Untitled] (Andante moderato).—2. Begstvo = La fuite (Allegro molto).—3. Dultsinea = Dulcinée (Andante).—4. Draka = La bagarre (Allegro molto).—5. Smert' Don Kikhota = La mort de Don Quichotte (Andante cantabile).
Date of composition: 1931.
First performance: Troisième concert de La Sérénade, Paris, Salle du Conservatoire, May 24, 1932, Marcelle Meyer, piano.
Manuscript: NN, Yale.
Published: Berlin: Russischer Musik Verlag [1932] (14 p.; R.M.V. 550). With cover illustration by Christian Bérard, and epigraph: "Les oiseaux blessés dans la région du cœur meurent le jour même = Ptitsy ranenie v oblast serdtsa pogibaiut v tot-zhe den"
Note: printed dedication to Vladimir Horowitz.

IV-B6. Contrastes et développements

Contrastes et développements: pour piano

Date of composition: 1935.
First performance: not traced.
Manuscript: not traced.
Published: Berlin: Russischer Musik Verlag [1936] (18 p.), music publisher's number RMV 629.

IV-B7. Piano Sonata no. 2

1. Pastorale: Allegretto.—2. Cantilena: Andante moderato.—3. Rondo: Allegro.—4. Lento.
Date of composition: 1940.
First performance: New York, December 6, 1940, Leo Smit.
Manuscript: not traced (copy, DNA).
Published: London and New York: Boosey & Hawkes, 1948 (19 p.); music publisher's number: B. & H. 16424.
Note: dedicated to Leo Smit; dated Wellfleet, August 22, 1940, at end of manuscript.

IV-B8. Valse pour deux pianos

Date of composition: [1952?]
Manuscript: not traced (Circle Blue Print copy, NN, Texas).
Unpublished.
First performance traced: Paris, Salle Gaveau, Arthur Gold and Robert Fitzdale, November 23, 1952.
Note: marked "Tempo di Valse (Andantino)." In G major.

V. OCCASIONAL MUSIC

V-1. Marches

1. Fanfare (Allegro moderato e risoluto).—2. Workers' March (Andante).—3. In Memoriam (Andante moderato).—4. Soldiers' March (Allegro non troppo molto).
Date of composition: 1945.
First performance: not traced.
Instrumentation: 3 piccolos (or 1 piccolo and 2 flutes), 3 oboes (or 2 oboes and English horn), 2 clarinets in B-flat, 2 bassoons, contrabassoon, 4 horns, 3 trumpets in B-flat, 3 trombones, tuba, triangle, timpani, drums, cymbals, suspended cymbal, snare drum, bass drum, glockenspiel, pianoforte, strings.
Manuscript: not traced (copy of full score, NN, Texas).
Unpublished?
Note: alternative titles on manuscript or parts: "March-Suite," Parade. Dated March 1, 1945, at end of full score. Alternative title for Soldiers' March: Parade. Also exists in a version entitled "Three Marches," without the Soldiers' March.

V-2. From the Beaches to Berlin

From the Beaches to Berlin [military march]

Date of composition: 1945.

First performance: not traced.

Instrumentation: 2 flutes, oboe, English horn, clarinet in B, 2 bassoons, 4 horns in F, 2 trumpets in C, triangle, snare drum, bass drum, strings.

Manuscript: DNA (draft short score, autograph parts, and piano reduction)

Unpublished.

Dedicated on manuscript: "to my great Hamburgers Eric Maschwitz, John MacMillan, and all the officers and men of BAN, from an assimilated nearby Frankfurter." With additional note: "In this piece one can readily detect reminiscences of: a) a modified 18th-c. British cavalry tune; b) an old American reveil of the Washingtonian period; c) a Soviet-Russian marching song; d) a phrase from a French Revolutionary tune."

Alternative title: Retreat from Gettorf: A March for Symphony Orchestra (see DNA).

V-3. Variation on Happy Birthday for two celli

Arioso for two v[iolon]celli on the theme "happy birthday to you": a birthday greeting to Eugene Ormandy

Date of composition: 1969 [dated January 24, 1970, at the end of the manuscript].

First performance: Philadelphia, January 24, 1970.

Manuscript: not traced [Philadelphia Orchestra archives?].

Published in facsimile in Variations on Happy birthday. Written especially for and presented to Eugene Ormandy on the occasion of his 70th birthday celebration. The Academy of Music, 113th anniversary concert and ball, January 24, 1970. 2,000 copies for presentation to friends of Eugene Ormandy, with frontispiece illustration by Andrew Wyeth, [Philadelphia?] 1970; the presentation inscription on p. 1 reads: "Arioso for two v[iolon]celli on the theme "happy birthday to you": a birthday greeting with much love to Gene from Nicolas N."

Note: Other contributing composers were Samuel Barber, Theodor Berger, Leonard Bernstein, Aaron Copland, Paul Creston, Norman Dello Joio, David Diamond, Gottfried von Einem, Ross Lee Finney, Carl Orff, Vincent Persichetti, Walter Piston, George Rochberg, Miklós Rózsa, William Schuman, Roger Sessions, Virgil Thomson, and Eugene Zádor.

VI. ORCHESTRATIONS AND ARRANGEMENTS

VI-1. Les Valses de Beethoven, ballet

1. Introduction (alla tedesca).—2. 1ere Valse (tempo di Valza).—3. 2eme Valse (Moderato).—4. 3e Valse (Allegro molto).—5. 4e Valse (Allegro moderato).—6. 5e Valse (Lento).—7. 6e Valse (Andante).—8. 7e Valse (Allegro).—9. 8e Valse (Allegro).—10. Bagatelle (Andante moderato).—11. Finale (Allegro).

Orchestration of eight early nineteenth-century waltzes of doubtful attribution, to which are added two Beethoven arrangements of Scottish songs.

Date of composition: 1933.

First performance: Paris, Théâtre des Champs-Élysées, June 19, 1933, Ballets 1933, choreography George Balanchine, cond. Maurice Abravanel.

Instrumentation: 2 flutes (and piccolo), oboe, 2 clarinets in B, bassoon, 2 horns in F, 2 trumpets, harp, celesta, percussion (snare drum, bass drum, triangle), strings.

Manuscript: NN, Texas (viola part only); complete set of parts, DNA.

Unpublished.

References: Balanchine 1983, no 139.

VI-2. Johann Sebastian Bach. Goldberg Variations, BWV 988. Arrangement for chamber orchestra

Orchestrer Suite aus Bachs 'Aria mit Dressig Veraenderungen' J. S. Bach für Klavier, für Orchester gesetet von . . . .] = Orchestra Suite from Bach's Aria with 30 Transformation, also called The Goldberg Variations, orchestrated by N. Nabokoff.

Date of composition: dated March 13, 1938, at the end of the manuscript.

First performance: Minneapolis, Minneapolis Symphony Orchestra, cond. Dimitri Mitropoulos, 1938.

Instrumentation: solo oboe, viola sola, 2 solo celli, harpsichord (or pianoforte), strings.

Duration: 26–27'.

Manuscript: not traced (blue print copy, NN, Texas; and DNA).

Unpublished.

Note: Made into the ballet *Air and Variations*, choreographed by William Dollar, premiered at the Martin Beck Theater, New York, May 24, 1939.

VI-3. Two Choruses from Boris Godunov

"God of Truth and Justice" and "Grant Us Thy Grace," two choruses from Musorgsky's *Boris Godunov*, arranged for four-part women's choir (SSAA)

Arranged [1936–39?]

First performance: not traced

Manuscript: not traced; copy, DNA.

Unpublished?

VI-4. Franz Schubert. Quintet in C major, D. 956. Adagio.

Orchestral arrangement of Schubert's Quintet for two cellos

Date of composition: ca. 1969

First performance: not traced.

Instrumentation: 2 flutes, 2 oboes, 2 clarinets, bassoon, 4 horns, 3 trumpets, 3 trombones, timpani, harp, strings.

Manuscript: not traced (copy, NN, Texas)

Unpublished.

Note: commissioned by the New York City Ballet, but not produced.

VII. WORKS LOST, PROJECTED OR UNCOMPLETED

Aphrodite, ballet-cantata [1928], commissioned by Ida Rubinstein. Unperformed, music lost?

Paul et Virginie, opéra-comique in three acts on a libretto by Jean Cocteau and Raymond Radiguet. Projected ca. 1931, music not composed.

Marche des Tritons for Édouard Bourdet's play *La fleur des pois*, 1932. Unperformed, music lost?

Tom, "ballet manifesto" on a scenario by Lincoln Kirstein, 1935–36. Unperformed. Typescript libretto and draft short score, incomplete, NYPL.

"Orgelmusik," incomplete draft, DNA. Possibly dating from the late 1930s.

"The moon's pale silver meshes make," words by Joyce, 3-part chorus in F major, [1936–38?]. Referred to in *Bagázh* typescript, 4:74, not traced.

Ash Wednesday, song cycle on the poem by T. S. Eliot, [1939–40?] Drafts, DNA.

Alkestis in Monte-Carlo. Opera on a libretto by George Steiner, ca. 1960–61. Typescript of libretto, NN, Texas; music not written.

Pinford, opera on a libretto by Christopher Sykes after the novel by Evelyn Waugh. Music not composed.

The Lady with the Unicorn, ballet on a scenario by Nicolas Nabokov and George Balanchine. Manuscript notes, DNA.

Poslednie Dni, opera on a libretto by Claus H. Henneberg after the play by Mikhail Bulgakov, music not composed.

WRITINGS

Some of Nabokov's early contributions to periodicals have not been traced.

1926. "Slovo i zvuk." *Blagonamerennyi: Zhurnal russkoi literaturnoi kul'tury* [Paris, ed. D. A. Shakhovskoi] 2 (April): 137–41.

1927. "Gendanken über neue Musik: Beobachtungen aus Paris." *Melos: Zeitschrift für der Musik* 6:1 (January): 32–35.

1928. "Nicolas Nabokoff répond au questionnaire de *La Musique*." *La musique* 2:2 (November 15): 624.

1929a. "La vie et l'œuvre de Serge de Diaghilew." *La musique* 3:2 (November 15): 54–68.

1929b. "S. P. Diagilev." *Volia Rossii: zhurnal politiki i kultury* 8/9.

1930a. "A.-D. D'Oulibicheff (Deux lettres inédites à Fétis)" [presentation and notes by Nicolas Nabokoff]. *La musique* 3:6 (March 15): 264–70.

1930b. "Po sledam musyki." *Chisla: Sborniki* [Paris] 1.

1930c. "Prokof'ev." *Chisla* 2/3.

1930d. "Musyka v Germanii." *Chisla* 4.

1931. "Mikhaïl Wassilievitch Lomonossoff" [and Presentation of *Ode*]. Ville de Strasbourg, Palais des Fêtes. Concert program, Concerts d'abonnement de l'Orchestre municipal, IVe concert de l'abonnement, December 9, 1931.

1931a. "Musyka v Germanii." *Chisla* 5.

1941a. "Music in the U.S.S.R." *The New Republic* (March 31): 436–38.

1941b. "Music in the U.S.S.R. II." *The New Republic* (April 7): 469–71.

1942a. "Music under Dictatorship." *Atlantic Monthly* 1987 (January): 92–99.

1942b. "Sergei Prokofiev." *Atlantic Monthly*, 187 (July): 62–70.

1943. "The Case of Dimitri Shostakovich." *Harper's Magazine* 186:1114 (March): 422–31.

1944. "Stravinsky Now." *Partisan Review* 11:3 (Summer): 324–34.

1947. Review of Shostakovich, Symphony no. 9, op. 70, and Prokofiev, Symphony no. 5, op. 100. *Notes*, Second Series, 4:3 (June): 360–62.

1948a. "The Music Purge." *Politics* 5:2 (Spring): 102–6.

1948b. "The Atonal Trail: A Communication." *Partisan Review* 15:5 (May): 580–85.

1949a. "The Specter of Nijinsky." *Atlantic Monthly* 184:2 (August): 43–45.

1949b. "The Trials of a Cosmopolitan Composer." *The Reporter* (August 16): 17–19.

1949c. "Russian Music after the Purge." *Partisan Review* 16:8 (August): 842–51.

1949d. "Igor Stravinsky: An *Atlantic* Portrait." *Atlantic Monthly* 184:5 (November): 21–27.

1949e. "Christmas with Stravinsky." In *Igor Stravinsky: A Merle Armitage Book*, edited by Edwin Corle, 123–68. New York: Duell, Sloan and Pearce, Distributors.

1950a. "Sergei Diaghilev." *Atlantic Monthly* 185:1 (January): 24–29.

1950b. "Sergei Diaghilev [Part 2]." *Atlantic Monthly* 185:2 (February): 66–73.

1950c. "Sergei Diaghilev [Part 3]." *Atlantic Monthly* 185:3 (March): 64–70.

1951. *Old Friends and New Music*, Boston: Little, Brown; London: Hamish Hamilton.

1951a. "Music under the Generals." *Atlantic Monthly* 187:1 (January): 49–54.

1951b. "Festivals and the Twelve-Tone Row." *Saturday Review of Literature* 34:2 (January 13): 56–58, 83–84.

1951c. "The Composer's Conductor: Koussevitzky." *Atlantic Monthly* 187:2 (February): 46–52.

1951d. "On the Battle Front of Soviet Music." *Musical America* (February): 12, 144, 174.

1951e. "Sur le 'front de bataille' de la musique soviétique" [translation of 1951d]. *Preuves* 1:2 (April): 9–12.

1951e. "Music in Germany: Berlin Revisited." *Atlantic Monthly* 187:6 (June): 38–43.

1951f. "Changing Styles in Soviet Music." *The Listener* 46:1180 (October 11): 598–99.

1951g. "La musique en Union soviétique" [see 1951d and 1951e]. *Revue internationale de musique* 11 (Autumn): 505–11.

1951h. "Lettre de Venise: Le libertin prend son essor." *Preuves* 1:8 (October): 22–24.

1952a. "Introduction à l'Oeuvre du XXe siècle." *La Revue musicale* 212 (April), "Numéro spécial L'Oeuvre du XXe siècle," 5–8.

1952b. "Élégie funèbre sur quatre notes." *Preuves* 15 (May), "Numéro spécial: L'Oeuvre du vingtième siècle, mai 1952," 7–12.

1952c. "This is our culture." *Counterpoint* 17 (May): 13–15.

1953a. "La vie musicale en U.R.S.S. est-elle à un tournant?" [Part 1 of "No Cantatas for Stalin, see below], *Le Figaro littéraire* (August 15): 9.

1953b. "Où en est la musique soviétique . . . Des indices de libération?" [Part 2 of "No Cantatas for Stalin"], *Le Figaro littéraire* (August 29): 9.

1953c. "No Cantatas for Stalin?" *Encounter* 1:1 (October): 49–52.

1954. [A response to Adriano Lualdi's "Open Letter to Mr. Nicolas Nabokov published in *Il giornale d'Italia*, April 9, 1954]. *Il giornale d'Italia*, April 20.

1957. "Stravinsky: Fifteen and Three-Score." *High Fidelity* 7:6 (June), 33 (Stravinsky 75th Birthday issue).

1958a. "Reflections on the Moscow Art Theatre." *The Listener* (June 19): 1009–10.

1958b. "La musique des autres (carnet de voyage)." *La revue musicale* 242 (October): 79–82.

1961. "La musique en Union soviétique." *Revue internationale de musique* 11 (Fall): 505–11.

1962a. "Harry Kessler, un aristocrate européen." Translated by Christine Lalou. *Preuves* 139 (September): 31–39.

1962b. "Der Mensch, der andere liebte: in memoriam Harry Kessler." [uncredited, expanded German translation of 1962a] *Der Monat* 170 (November): 41–56.

1964. *Igor Strawinsky*. Translated from the English by Gisa Jopp, and with expert technical advice from Thomas Höpfner. Berlin: Colloquium Verlag. (Köpfe des XX. Jahrhunderts: kleine Biographien grosser Zeitgenossen, no. 36).

1965a. "Remembering Nehru." In *Jawaharlal Nehru: A Critical Tribute*, edited by A. B. Shah, 23–26. Bombay: Manaktalas (Indian Committee for Cultural Freedom).

1965b. Preface to Miyake, Shūtarō Miyake, *Kabuki, japanisches Theater*. Edited by Wolfgang Schimming, translated by Ingeborg Dalchow. Berlin: Safari-Verlag.

1971a. "Introduction: Twentieth-Century Makers of Music." In *American Music since 1910*, by Virgil Thomson, ix–xvi. London: Weidenfeld and Nicholson [*Twentieth-Century Composers*, ed. Anna Kallin and Nicolas Nabokov, vol. I: *America*, New York, Holt].

1971b. "Igor Stravinsky, esprit de notre temps." *Musiques de tous les temps* 5 (October): 2–15.

1972a. "Introduction: Twentieth-Century Makers of Music." In *Britain, Scandinavia and The Netherlands*, by Humphrey Searle and Robert Layton, ix–xvi. London: Weidenfeld and Nicholson [*Twentieth-Century Composers*, ed. Anna Kallin and Nicolas Nabokov, vol. III].

1972b. "Nicolas Nabokov: 'Le Tiers-État du XXe siècle, ce sont les émigrés.'" *L'Orient-Le Jour* (Beyrouth), new series, no 53 (June 10–16): xiii–xv.

1972c. "Stravinsky: A Partisan Chronicle", Coloquio/Artes (Lisbon) 10 (December).

1974. "Introduction: The Latin Realm of Twentieth-Century Europe." In *France, Italy and Spain*, by Fred Goldbeck, vii–ix. London: Weindenfeld and Nicolson [*Twentieth-Century Composers*, Vol. IV]

1975. *Bagázh: Memoirs of a Russian Cosmopolitan*, New York: Atheneum.

1975a. [*Bagázh*. German] *Zwei rechte Schuhe im Gepäck: Erinnerungen eines russischen Weltbürgers*. Translated by Claus H. Henneberg and Hellmut Jaesrich. Munich and Zurich: R. Piper.

1975b. "Excerpts from memories." In *W.H. Auden: A Tribute*, edited by Stephen Spender, ed., 133–48. London: Macmillan.

1975c. "Bagázh [in Russian spelling]." *The New Yorker* (April 7): 37–39.

1975d. "Erinnerung an Prokofjew." *Die Merkur* 328 (September): 844–56.

1975e. "Ein Trinklied auf den Genossen Stalin" [excerpt from 1975a], *Die Welt*, September 27.

1975f. "Russian Revolution in a Teacup." *Vogue* 165:11 (November): 210–11, 239–42.

1975g. "Days with Diaghilev." *The American Scholar* (Autumn): 620–35.

1976. [*Bagázh*. French] *Cosmopolite*. Translated by Claude Nabokov. Paris: Robert Laffont.

1976a. "Besuch bei Strawinsky." [excerpt from 1975a] *Die Furche*, January 10.

1976b. "Les tribulations de Nicolas Nabokov" [excerpt from 1976]. *Le Figaro littéraire*, October 2–3.

1976c. "Une vie dans les délices de l'amitié: propos recueillis par Gilles Anquetil. *Les nouvelles littéraires* 2554 (October 14–21).

1977. "Under the Cranberry Tree" [review of Jacqueline Onassis, ed., *In Russian Style*]. *The New York Review of Books*, March 3.

1978. "The Peasant Marriage (*Les Noces*) by Igor Stravinsky." *Slavica Hierosolymitana* (Slavic Studies of the Hebrew University of Jerusalem) 3, 272–81.

1979. [*Bagázh*. German] *Zwei rechte Schuhe im Gepäck: Erinnerungen eines russischen Weltbürgers*. Translated by Claus H. Henneberg and Hellmut Jaesrich. Munich: Deutscher Taschenbuch Verlag. [Paperback edition of 1975a]

1998. "Bagázh (Chast vtoraia. "Mezhdu voinami.")" [First Part: Between Wars.] Translated into Russian by Ye. Bolshelapova and M. Shereshevskaya. *Zvezda* [St. Petersburg] 10, 75–124.

1999. "Bagázh. (Chast pervaia. "Rossiia . . . Togda.")" Translated into Russian by Ye. Bolshelapova and M. Shereshevskaya, with an introduction by Marina Ledkovsky. *Zvezda* [St. Petersburg] 4: 92–151.

2003. [*Bagázh*. Russian] *Bagazh: memuary russkogo kosmopolita*. Translated by E. Bol'shelapovoi and M. Shereshevskoii. St Petersburg: Izd-vo zhurnala "Zvezda."

2003. "Boris Blacher." In *Boris Blacher: Im Auftrag der Stiftung Archiv der Akademie der Künste.* Herausgegeben von Heribert Henrich und Thomas Eickhoff, 11–21. Hofheim: Wolke Verlag.

2006. [*Bagázh.* French] *Cosmopolite.* Translated by Claude Nabokov. [Includes a checklist and discography of Nabokov's musical works.] Paris: Mémoire du Livre.

2011. "Star'e druz'ia I novaia muzyka" ["Christmas with Stravinsky" and "Stravinsky and Hollywood" from 1951]. Translated by M. Iamshchikov, edited by Evgenii Beloduvrovskii. *Novii zhurnal/The New Review* (New York) 263 (June): 126–60.

2012a. "Kusevitskii" ["Koussevitzky," from 1951]. Translated by M. Iamshchikov, edited by Evgenii Beloduvrovskii. *Novii zhurnal/The New Review* (New York) 266 (March): 166–90.

2012b. "The Learned Judge (A Portrait)." Edited and with an introduction by Vincent Giroud. *The Yale Review* 100:3 (July): 49–63.

Abbreviations

ACCF, NYU	American Committee for Cultural Freedom Records, The Tamiment Library and Robert F. Wagner Labor Archives, Elmer Holmes Bobst Library, New York University
Berg	Vladimir Nabokov Archive, Berg Collection of English and American Literature, New York Public Library
BnF	Bibliothèque nationale de France, Paris
BnF-Musique	Bibliothèque nationale de France, département de la Musique, Paris
BnF-Opéra	Bibliothèque nationale de France, bibliothèque-musée de l'Opéra, Paris
DNA	Dominique Nabokov archives
IACF, Chicago	International Association for Cultural Freedom Archives, Joseph Regenstein Library, The University of Chicago
ICNA	Ivan and Claude Nabokoff archives
INA	Institut national de l'audiovisuel, Paris
LC	Music Division, Library of Congress, Washington, D. C.
MJ, Texas	Michael Josselson Papers, Harry Ransom Humanities Center, The University of Texas at Austin
New Grove 2	*The New Grove Dictionary of Music and Musicians*, edited by Stanley Sadie; executive editor John Tyrrell (New York: Grove, 2001)
NN FBI files	Federal Bureau of Investigation, Washington, DC
NN, Texas	Nicolas Nabokov Papers, Harry Ransom Humanities Center, The University of Texas at Austin
NN, Yale	Nicolas Nabokov Papers, Beinecke Rare Book and Manuscript Library, Yale University
Opera Grove	*The New Grove Dictionary of Opera* (London: The Macmillan Press, 1992)

Works Consulted

Akhmatova, Anna. 1990. *Complete Poems*. Translated by Judith Hemschemeyer, edited and with an introduction by Roberta Reeder. 2 vols. Somerville, MA: Zephyr Press.

Akimova, Irina. 2011. *Pierre Souvtchinsky: parcours d'un Russe hors frontière*. Paris: L'Harmattan.

Ansen, Alan. 1989. *The Table Talk of W.H. Auden*. Edited by Nicholas Jenkins. New York: Sea Cliff Press.

Argento, Dominick. 2004. *Catalogue Raisonné as Memoir: A Composer's Life*. Minneapolis: University of Minnesota Press.

Arnaud, Claude. 2003. *Jean Cocteau*. Paris: Gallimard.

Aron, Raymond. 1990. *Memoirs: Fifty Years of Political Reflection*. Translated by George Holoch. New York: Holmes & Meier.

Assouline, Pierre. 2005. *Henri Cartier-Bresson: A Biography*. Translated by David Wilson. London: Thames & Hudson.

Auden, W. H., and Chester Kallman. 1993. *Libretti and Other Dramatic Writings*. Edited by Edward Mendelson. Princeton: Princeton University Press.

[Balanchine, George]. 1983. *Choreography by George Balanchine: A Catalogue of Works*. New York: The Eakins Press Foundation.

Barré, Jean-Luc. 1995. *Jacques et Raïssa Maritain, les mendiants du ciel: biographie croisée*. Paris: Stock.

Beaumont, Cyril. 1975. *Bookseller at the Ballet: Memoirs 1891 to 1929; incorporating The Diaghilev Ballet in London: A Record of Bookselling, Ballet Going, Publishing, and Writing*. London: C. W. Beaumont.

Beaton, Cecil. 1946. "Designing for Ballet." *Dance Index* 5, no. 8 (August): 184–98.

———. 1961. *The Wandering Years: Diaries 1922-1939*. Boston and Toronto: Little, Brown and Company.

———. 1968. *The Best of Beaton*. With notes on the photographs by Cecil Beaton. Introduction by Truman Capote. New York: The Macmillan Company.

Becker, Hellmut. "Erinnerung an Nicolas Nabokov," in 30.Berliner Festwochen 1980 [Official 1980 Berlin Festival Program], 130–133.

Bell, Daniel. 1988. *The End of Ideology: On the Exhaustion of Political Ideas in the Fifties.* Expanded ed. Cambridge, MA: Harvard University Press.

Bellow, Saul. 2010. *Letters.* Edited by Benjamin Taylor. New York: Viking.

Berberova, Nina. 1972. *The Italics Are Mine.* Translated by Philippe Radley. New York: Harcourt, Brace & World, Inc.

Berenguer, Bruno, ed. 2003. *Henri Sauguet, amitiés artistiques.* Paris: Séguier.

Berghahn, Volker R. 2001. *America and the Intellectual Cold Wars in Europe: Shepard Stone between Philanthropy, Academy, and Diplomacy.* Princeton and Oxford: Princeton University Press.

Berlin, Isaiah. 2004. *Letters 1928-1946.* Edited by Henry Hardy. Cambridge and New York: Cambridge University Press.

———. 2009. *Enlightening: Letters 1946-1960.* Edited by Henry Hardy and Jennifer Holmes with the assistance of Serena Moore. London: Chatto & Windus.

———. 2013. *Learning: Letters 1960-1975.* Edited by Henry Hardy and Mark Pottle. London: Chatto & Windus.

Bird, Kai, and Martin J. Sherwin. 2005. *American Prometheus: The Triumph and Tragedy of J. Robert Oppenheimer.* New York: Alfred A. Knopf.

Bishop, Elizabeth. 1994. *One Art: Letters.* Selected and edited by Robert Giroux. New York: Farrar, Straus, and Giroux.

Bishop, Elizabeth, and Robert Lowell. 2008. *Words in Air: The Complete Correspondence between Elizabeth Bishop and Robert Lowell.* Edited by Thomas Travisano with Saskia Hamilton. New York: Farrar, Straus, and Giroux.

Bloom, Alexander. 1986. *Prodigal Sons: The New York Intellectuals and Their World.* London: Oxford University Press.

Bohlen, Charles E. 1973. *Witness to History: 1929-1969.* London: Weidenfeld and Nicholson; New York: W. W. Norton & Company.

Botstein, Leon. 1995. "After Fifty Years: Thoughts on Music and the End of World War II." *Musical Quarterly* 79, no. 2 (Summer): 225–30.

Boulez, Pierre, and John Cage. 1993. *Correspondence.* Edited by Jean-Jacques Nattiez with Françoise Davoine, Hans Oesch, and Robert Piencikowski. Translated and edited by Robert Samuels. Cambridge and New York: Cambridge University Press.

Boyd, Brian. 1990. *Vladimir Nabokov: The Russian Years.* London: Chatto & Windus.

———. 1992. *Vladimir Nabokov: The American Years.* London: Chatto & Windus.

Braden, Thomas W. 1967. "I Am Glad the CIA is 'Immoral'," *Saturday Evening Post,* 20 May.

Bressolette, Michel. 1991. "Une grande amitié: Jacques Maritain et Jean Cocteau." In *Jacques Maritain et ses contemporains,* edited by Bernard Hubert and Yves Floucat, 99–116. Paris: Desclée.

Brody, Martin. 1993. "Music for the Masses: Milton Babbitt's Cold War Music Theory." *Musical Quarterly* 77, no. 2 (Summer): 161–92.

Bruyr, José. 1933. *L'écran des musiciens*, 2nd Series. Paris: José Corti.

Buckle, Richard. 1979. *Diaghilev*. New York: Atheneum.

Buckle, Richard, with John Taras. 1988. *George Balanchine, Ballet Master*. New York: Random House.

Caron, Sylvain. 2009. "André Caplet et Jacques Maritain: une résonance du paradigme médiéval entre la musique et les idées." In Sylvain Caron and Michel Duchesneau,eds. *Musique, art et religion dans l'entre-deux-guerres*, Lyons: Symétrie, 43–55.

Carpenter, Humphrey. 1981. *W.H. Auden: A Biography*. London, Boston, Sydney: George Allen & Unwin.

Carr, Bruce, Katherine K. Preston, and Michael Meckna. 2001. "Nabokov, Nicolas." *The New Grove Dictionary of Music and Musicians*, edited by Stanley Sadie, London: Macmillan. Vol. 17, 586.

Carroll, Mark. 2003. *Music and Ideology in Cold War Europe*. Cambridge and New York: Cambridge University Press.

Carson, Anne Conover. 1989. *Caresse Crosby: From Black Sun to Roccasinibalda*. Santa Barbara: Capra Press.

Carter, Elliott. 1944. "Music as a Liberal Art." *Modern Music* 22, no. 1 (November–December): 12–16.

Cesarani, David. 1998. *Arthur Koestler: The Homeless Mind*. London: Heinemann.

Chazin-Bennahum, Judith. 2011. *René Blum and the Ballets Russes*. Oxford and New York: Oxford University Press.

Chimènes, Myriam. 2004. *Mécènes et musiciens: du salon au concert sous la IIIe République*. Paris: Fayard.

Cockcroft, Eva. 1992. "Abstract Expressionism, Weapon of the Cold War." In *Art in Modern Culture: an Anthology of Critical Texts*, edited by Francis Frascina and Jonathan Harris, 82–90. London: Phaidon Press.

Coleman, Peter. 1987. "Sidney Hook and Cultural Freedom." *The National Interest* (Fall), 104–11.

———. 1989. *The Liberal Conspiracy: The Congress for Cultural Freedom and the Struggle for the Mind of Post-War Europe*. New York: Free Press; London: Collier Macmillan.

Craft, Robert. 1992. *Stravinsky: Glimpses of a Life*. London: Lime Tree.

———. 1994. *Stravinsky: Chronicle of a Friendship*. Revised and expanded ed. Nashville and London: Vanderbilt University Press.

———. 2002. *An Improbable Life: Memoirs*. Nashville: Vanderbilt University Press.

———. 2007. "Restoring Stravinsky: Conversations with Robert Craft." *Areté 24* (Winter): 5–80.

Crossman, Richard, ed. 1950. *The God That Failed: Six Studies in Communism*. London: Hamish Hamilton.

Daguerre, Pierre. 1954. *Le Marquis de Cuevas*. Paris: Éditions Denoël.

Daniélou, Alain. 1987. *The Way to the Labyrinth: Memories of East and West*. Translated by Marie-Claire Cournand. New York: New Directions.

David-Fox, Michael. 2012. *Showcasing the Great Experiment: Cultural Diplomacy and Western Visitors to the Soviet Union, 1921–1941*. Oxford and New York: Oxford University Press.

Donaldson, Scott. 1992. *Archibald MacLeish: An American Life*. In collaboration with R. H. Winnick. Boston [etc.]: Houghton Mifflin Company.

Downes, Olin. 1944. "Politics versus Symphonies." *New York Times*, April 30.

Duberman, Martin. 2007. *The Worlds of Lincoln Kirstein*. New York: Alfred A. Knopf.

Dufour, Valérie. 2006. *Stravinski et ses exégètes: 1910-1940*. Brussels: Éditions de l'université de Bruxelles.

———. 2009. " 'Néo-gothique et néo-classique': Arthur Lourié et Jacques Maritain." In *Musique, art et religion dans l'entre-deux-guerres*, edited by Sylvain Caron and Michel Duchesneau, 31–41. Lyons: Symétrie.

Duke, Vernon. 1955. *Passport to Paris*. Boston: Little, Brown and Company.

Dulong-Sainteny, Claude. 1996. *Notice sur la vie et les travaux de Jean Laloy (1912-1994)*. Paris: Palais de l'Institut.

Easton, Laird McLeod. 2002. *The Red Count: The Life and Times of Harry Kessler*. Berkeley, Los Angeles, London: University of California Press.

Emerson, Caryl. 2006. "Artur Vincent Lourié's *The Blackamoor of Peter the Great*: Pushkin's Exotic Ancestor as Twentieth-Century Opera." In *Under the Sky of My Africa: Alexander Pushkin and Blackness*, edited by Catherine Theimer Nepomnyashchy, Nicole Svobodny, and Ludmilla A. Trigos. Evanston, IL: Northwestern University Press, 332–67.

Epstein, Jason. 1967. "The CIA and the Intellectuals." *New York Review of Books*, April 20.

Falz-Fein, Woldemar von. 1930. *Askania Nova: Das Tierparadies: Ein Buch des Gedenkes und der Gedanken*. n.p.: Verlag von J. Neumann-Neudamm.

Farrell, Suzanne. 2002. *Holding on to the Air: An Autobiography*. With Toni Bentley. 2nd ed. Gainesville [etc.]: University Press of Florida.

Ferrand, Jacques. 1982. *Les Nabokov: essai généalogique*. In collaboration with Serge Nabokoff. Montreuil, France: J. Ferrand.

Fischer, Louis. 1956. *This Is Our World*. New York: Harper & Brothers.

Flanner, Janet ["Genêt"]. 1952a. "Letter from Paris." *The New Yorker* (May 31): 72–77.
———. 1952b. "Festival of Free-World Arts." *Freedom & Union* (September).

Gaddis, Eugene R. 2000. *Magician of the Modern: Chick Austin and the Transformation of the Arts in America*. New York: Alfred A. Knopf.

Gaddis, John Lewis. 2011. *George F. Kennan: An American Life*. New York: The Penguin Press.

Galassi, Peter. 1987. *Henri Cartier-Bresson: The Early Work*. New York: The Museum of Modern Art; Boston: Little, Brown and Company.

Galbraith, John Kenneth. 1981. *A Life in Our Times: Memoirs*. Boston: Houghton Mifflin Company.

Gillis, Daniel. 1970. *Furtwängler and America*. New York: Manyland Books, Inc.

Gladkova, T. L., and Tatiana Ossorguine-Bakounine, eds. 1988. *L'émigration russe: revues et recueils, 1920-1980: Index général des articles*. Paris: Institut d'études slaves.

Glock, William. 1991. *Notes in Advance*. Oxford and New York: Oxford University Press.

Gombrowicz, Rita. 1988. *Gombrowicz en Europe 1963-1969*. Paris: Denoël.

Gombrowicz, Witold. 2013. *Kronos*. Cracow: Wydawnictwo Literackie.

Grémion, Pierre. 1986. "Berlin 1950: aux origines du Congrès pour la Liberté de la Culture." *Commentaire 9*, no. 34 (Summer 1986).

———. 1989. *Preuves, une revue européenne à Paris*. Paris: Julliard.

———. 1995. *Intelligence de l'anticommunisme: le Congrès pour la liberté de la culture à Paris*. Paris: Fayard.

Grunelius, Antoinette. 1982. "Jacques Maritain et Kolbsheim." *Cahiers J. Maritain 4*, no. 5 (1982): 88–100.

Hamilton, Ian. 1982. *Robert Lowell: A Biography*. New York: Random House.

[Hammer, Victor Karl]. 1965. *Victor Hammer: A Retrospective Exhibition*. Raleigh: North Carolina Museum of Art.

Hand, Learned. 2013. *Reason and Imagination: Selected Correspondence 1897-1961*. Edited by Constance Jordan. Oxford and New York: Oxford University Press.

Hersh, Burton. 1992. *The Old Boys: The American Elite and the Origins of the CIA*. New York: Charles Scribner.

Hindemith, Paul. 1995. *Selected Letters*. Edited and translated from the German by Geoffrey Skelton. New Haven and London: Yale University Press.

Hixson, Walter L. 1997. *Parting the Curtain: Propaganda, Culture and the Cold War, 1945-1961*. New York: St. Martin's Press.

Ho, Allan Benedict, and Dmitry Feofanov. 1998. *Shostakovich Reconsidered*. London: Toccata Press.

Hochgeschwender, Michael. 1998. *Freiheit in der Offensive?: der Kongress für Kulturelle Freiheit und die Deutschen*. Munich: Oldenbourg.

———. 2003. "A Battle of Ideas: The Congress for Cultural Freedom (CCF) in Britain, Italy, France, and West Germany." In Geppert, Dominik, editor, *The Postwar Challenge: Cultural, Social, and Political Change in Western Europe, 1945–58*, Oxford: Oxford University Press, 319–38.

Hook, Sidney. 1950. "The Berlin Congress for Cultural Freedom." *Partisan Review 17*, no. 7 (September-October): 715–22.

———. 1987. *Out of Step: An Unquiet Life in the Twentieth-Century*. New York: Harper.

———. 1995. *Letters: Democracy, Communism, and the Cold War*. Edited by Edward S. Shapiro. Armonk, NY: M. E. Sharpe.

Horowitz, Joseph. 1982. *Conversations with Arrau*. New York: Alfred Knopf.

Howe, Irving. 1949. "The Cultural Conference." *Partisan Review 16*, no. 5 (May), 505-11.

Hughes, Allen. 1954. "Rome Conference Selects Prize Scores." *Musical America 74*, no. 7 (May): 3, 20.

Hurok, Sol. 1946. *Impresario: A Memoir*. In collaboration with Ruth Goode. New York: Random House.

Ignatieff, Michael. 1998. *Isaiah Berlin: A Life*. New York: Henry Holt and Company, Metropolitan Books.

Isaacson, Walter, and Thomas Evans. 1986. *The Wise Men: Six Friends and the World They Made*. New York: Simon and Schuster.

Iwaszkiewicz, Jaroslaw. 1975. *Ksiazka moich wspomnien*. Warsaw: Czytelnik.

———. 1976. "Cztery ksiegi pamietnikow z czasow mojej mlodosci" [Review of *Cosmopolite*, French ed. of *Bagázh*]. *Zycie Warszawy*, no. 301, December, 18–19.

Jeffreys-Jones, Rhodri. 1989. *The CIA and American Democracy*. New Haven: Yale University Press.

Jelenski, Constantin. 2007. *Chwile oderwane*. Gdánsk: Slowo/Obraz terytoria.

Johnson, A. Ross, and R. Eugene Parta. 2010. *Cold War Broadcasting: Impact on Soviet Union and Eastern Europe: A Collection of Studies and Documents*. Budapest and New York: Central European University Press.

Joseph, Charles M. 2002. *Stravinsky & Balanchine: A Journey of Invention*. New Haven and London: Yale University Press.

Journet, Charles, et Jacques Maritain. 1997. *Correspondance. Vol. 2, 1930–1939*. Fribourg: Éditions universitaires; Paris: Éditions Saint-Paul.

Juliar, Michael. 1986. *Vladimir Nabokov: A Descriptive Bibliography*. New York and London: Garland Publishing, Inc.

Karlinsky, Simon. 1977. Review of *Bagázh: Memories of a Russian Cosmopolitan, Nicolas Nabokov*. *Russian Review 36*, no. 1 (January): 115–17.

Karsavina, Tamara. 1931. *Theatre Street: The Reminiscences of Tamara Karsavina*. Foreword by J. M. Barrie. New York: E. P. Dutton & Co., Inc.

Kennan, George. 1967. *Memoirs 1925-1950*. Boston and Toronto: Little, Brown and Company.

———. 1972. *Memoirs 1950-1963*. Boston and Toronto: Little, Brown and Company.

———. 1989. *Sketches from a Life*. New York: Pantheon Books.

Kennedy, Richard S. 1980. *Dreams in the Mirror: A Biography of E.E. Cummings*. New York: Liveright Publishing Corporation.

Kermode, Frank. 1995. *Not Entitled: A Memoir*. New York: Farrar, Straus, and Giroux.

Kessler, Harry, Graf. 1971. *The Diaries of a Cosmopolitan 1918-1937*. Translated and edited by Charles Kessler. London: Weidenfeld and Nicolson.

———. 2007. *Das Tagebuch: Siebter Band 1919-1923*. Edited by Angela Reinthal with the assistance of Janna Brechmacher and Christoph Hilse. Stuttgart: Cotta.

———. 2009. *Das Tagebuch: Achter Band 1923-1926*. Edited by Angela Reinthal, Günter Riederer, and Jörg Schuster, with the assistance of Janna Brechmacher, Christoph Hilse, and Nadin Weiss. Stuttgart: Cotta.

———. 2010. *Das Tagebuch: Neunter Band 1926-1937*. Edited by Sabine Gruber and Ulrich Ott, with the assistance of Christoph Hilse and Nadin Weiss. Stuttgart: Cotta.

Kiernan, Frances. 2000. *Seeing Mary Plain: A Life of Mary McCarthy*. New York and London: W. W. Norton & Company.

Kirstein, Lincoln. 1994. *Tchelitchew*. Santa Fe: Twelvetrees Press.

Kolding, Shri Suzanne. 1998. "Nicolas Nabokov's *Love's Labour's Lost*: A Study of Its Origins, Libretto, and Musical Style." Master of Music thesis, The University of Texas at Austin.

Kollek, Teddy. 1978. *For Jerusalem: A Life*. With Amos Kollek. New York: Random House.

Kozloff, Max. 1985. "American Painting During the Cold War." In Frascina and Harris *1985*.

Kramer, Hilton. 1999. *The Twilight of the Intellectuals: Culture and Politics in the Era of the Cold War*. Chicago: Ivan R. Dee.

Kuisel, Richard F. 1993. *Seducing the French: The Dilemma of Americanization*. Berkeley: University of California Press.

Kurth, Peter. 2001. *Isadora: A Sensational Life*. Boston, New York, London: Little, Brown and Company.

Kustow, Michael. 2005. *Peter Brook: A Biography*. London: Bloomsbury.

Lacombe, Hervé. 2013. *Francis Poulenc*. Paris: Fayard.

Lafaye, Jean-Jacques. 1980. "Entretien avec Nicolas Nabokov." *Paradoxes 41* (Fall): 113–21.

Laqueur, Walter. 1996. "Anti-Communism Abroad: A Memoir of the Congress for Cultural Freedom." *Partisan Review* (Spring).

Lasch, Christopher. 1965. *The New Radicalism in America 1889-1963: The Intellectual as a Social Type*. New York: Vintage.

———. 1968. "The Cultural Cold War: A Short History of the Congress for Cultural Freedom." In *Towards a New Past: Dissenting Essays in American History*, edited by Barton J. Bernstein. New York: Pantheon.

———. 1969. *The Agony of the American Left*. New York: Knopf.

Lesure, François. 1994. *Claude Debussy: biographie critique*. Paris: Klincksieck.

Levitz, Tamara. 2013a. "Igor the Angeleno: The Mexican Connection." In *Stravinsky and His World*, edited by Tamara Levitz, 141–76. Princeton and Oxford: Princeton University Press.

———. 2013b. "Stravinsky's Cold War: Letters About the Composer's Return to Russia, 1960-1963." In *Stravinsky and His World*, edited by Tamara Levitz, 273–317. Princeton and Oxford: Princeton University Press.

Levy, Julien. 1977. *Memoir of an Art Gallery*. New York: G. P. Putnam's Sons.

Liebermann, Rolf. 1976. *Actes et entractes.* In collaboration with Bernard Sizaire and Stephen Wendt. Paris: Stock.

Lifar, Serge, 1940. *Serge Diaghilev, His Life, His Work, His Legend: An Intimate Biography.* New York: G. P. Putnam's Sons.

Lipman, Samuel. 1989. "The Encounter Group," *The Washington Post*, September 17.

Lischke, André. 1993. *Piotr Illyitch Tchaikovski.* Paris: Fayard.

Longstaff, S. A. 1989. "The New York Intellectuals and the Cultural Cold War." *New Politics* (New Series) 2, no. 2 (Winter), 156 –70.

Lowell, Robert. 2005. *The Letters of Robert Lowell.* Edited by Saskia Hamilton. New York: Farrar, Straus, and Giroux.

Lucas, W. Scott. 2003. "Revealing the Parameters of Opinion: An Interview with Frances Stonor Saunders." In Scott-Smith, Giles, and Hans Krabbendam, editors. *The Cultural Cold War in Western Europe, 1945–1960.* London and Portland, OR: Frank Cass, 15–40.

Luethy, Herbert. 1952. "Selling Paris on Western Culture." Translated by Lionel Abel. *Commentary*, 14 July, 70–75.

McAuliffe, M. 1978. *Crisis on the Left: Cold War Politics and American Liberals, 1947–1951.* Amherst: University of Massachusetts Press.

McCarthy, Kathleen. 1987. "From Cold War to Cultural Development: The International Cultural Activities of the Ford Foundation, 1950–1980." *Daedalus* 116, no. 1 (Winter), 93–117.

Macdonald, Nesta. 1975. *Diaghilev Observed by Critics in England and the United States, 1911–1929.* New York: Dance Horizons; London: Dance Books Ltd.

MacLeish, Archibald. 1972. *Reflections.* Edited by Bernard A. Drabck and Helen E. Ellis. Amherst, MA: The University of Massachusetts Press.

———. 1983. *Letters of Achibald MacLeish, 1907 to 1982.* Edited by R. H. Winnick. Boston: Houghton Mifflin Company.

McVay, Gordon. 1980. *Isadora & Esenin.* Ann Arbor, MI: Ardis.

Malraux, Madeleine, et Céline Malraux. 2012. *Avec une légère intimité: le concert d'une vie au cœur du siècle.* Paris: Baker Street and Larousse.

Mariani, Paul. 1994. *Lost Puritan: A Life of Robert Lowell.* New York and London: W.W. Norton & Company.

Maritain, Jacques, and Raïssa Maritain. 1986–2007. *Oeuvres complètes.* Edited by Jean-Marie Allion et al. 17 vols. Fribourg: Éditions universitaires; Paris: Éditions Saint-Paul.

———. 1989. *Oeuvres complètes.* Vol. 8. Edited by Jean-Marie Allion et al. Fribourg: Éditions universitaires; Paris: Éditions Saint-Paul.

———. 1993. *Oeuvres complètes.* Vol. 14. Edited by Jean-Marie Allion et al. Fribourg: Éditions universitaires; Paris: Éditions Saint-Paul.

———. 1995. *Oeuvres complètes.* Vol. 15, 1945–1960. Edited by Jean-Marie Allion et al. Fribourg: Éditions universitaires; Paris: Éditions Saint-Paul.

Maritain, Raïssa. 1974. *Raïssa's Journal*. Presented by Jacques Maritain. Enlarged ed. Albany, NY: Magi Books.

Markevitch, Igor. 1980. *Être et avoir été*. Paris: Gallimard.

Martini, Clare Joseph. 1959. *Maritain and Music*. PhD Dissertation [1958], Northwestern University.

Mason, Francis. 1991. *I Remember Balanchine: Recollections of the Ballet Master by Those Who Knew Him*. New York: Doubleday.

Massine, Leonide. 1968. *My Life in Ballet*. Edited by Phyllis Hartnoll and Robert Rubens. London [etc.]: Macmillan; St. Martin's Press.

Mayer, Denise, and Petr Suvchinskii, eds. 1966. *Roger Désormière et son temps*. Monaco: Éditions du Rocher.

Mayer, Hans. 1975. "Eine seltsame Begegnung zwischen dem Musiker Nabokov und Rilke." *Frankfurter Allgemeine Zeitung*, December 24.

Meyer, Felix, and Anne C. Shreffler. 2008. *Elliott Carter: A Centennial Portrait in Letters and Documents*. Woodbridge, Suffolk: The Boydell Press.

Miller, Arthur. 2005. *Timebends: A Life*. London: Methuen.

Moffat, Ivan. 2004. *The Ivan Moffat File: Life among the Beautiful and Damned in London, Paris, New York, and Hollywood*. Edited and with a foreword and afterword by Gavin Lambert. New York: Pantheon Books.

Moiraghi, Mario. 2009. *Paul Hindemith: musica come vita*. Palermo: L'Epos.

Monk, Ray. 2012. *Robert Oppenheimer: A Life Inside the Center*. New York [etc.]: Doubleday.

Monod, David. 2005. *Settling Scores: German Music, Denazification, & the Americans, 1945-1953*. Chapel Hill and London: The University of North Carolina Press.

Móricz, Klára. 2013. "Symphonies and Funeral Games: Lourié's Critique of Stravinsky's Neoclassicism." In *Stravinsky and His World*, edited by Tamara Levitz, 105–26. Princeton and Oxford: Princeton University Press.

Morrison, Simon Alexander. 2009. *The People's Artist: Prokofiev's Soviet Years*. Oxford and New York: Oxford University Press.

———. 2013. *Lina and Serge: The Love and Wars of Lina Prokofiev*. Boston: Houghton Mifflin.

Mousli, Béatrice. 2005. *Max Jacob*. Paris: Flammarion.

Muggeridge, Malcolm. 1982. *Like It Was: The Diaries of Malcolm Muggeridge*. Selected and edited by John Bright-Holmes. New York: William Morrow.

Nabokov, Vladimir. 1975. *Eugene Onegin, A Novel in Verse by Aleksandr Pushkin, Translated from the Russian, with a Commentary*. Revised ed. 4 vols. Princeton: Princeton University Press.

———. 1989. *Speak, Memory: An Autobiography Revisited*. New York: Vintage Books.

———. 1989a. *Selected Letters 1940-1977*. Edited by Dmitri Nabokov and Matthew J. Burccoli. San Diego, New York, London: Harcourt, Brace, Jovanovich; Bruccoli, Clar, Layman.

———. 2008. *Verses and Versions: Three Centuries of Russian Poetry selected and trans-lated by Vladimir Nabokov.* Edited by Brian Boyd and Stanislav Shvabrin. Orlando [etc.]: Harcourt, Inc.

Nabokov, Vladimir, and Edmund Wilson. 1979. *The Nabokov-Wilson Letters: Correspondence betweeen Vladimir Nabokov and Edmund Wilson 1940-1971.* Edited, Annotated and with an Introductory Essay by Simon Karlinsky. New York [etc.]: Harper & Row.

Naimark, Norman M. 1995. *The Russians in Germany: A History of the Soviet Zone of Occupation, 1945-1949.* Cambridge, MA; London: The Bellknap Press of Harvard University Press.

Nelson, Charles A. 2001. *Radical Visions: Stringfellow Barr, Scott Buchanan, and Their Efforts on Behalf of Education and Politics in the Twentieth Century.* Westport, CT, and London: Bergin & Garvey.

Nichols, Roger. 2011. *Ravel.* New Haven and London: Yale University Press.

Noss, Luther. 1989. *Paul Hindemith in the United States.* Urbana and Chicago: University of Illinois Press.

Panufnik, Andrzej. 1987. *Composing Myself.* London: Methuen.

Pells, Richard H. 1985. *The Liberal Mind in a Conservative Age: American Intellectuals in the 1940s and 1950s.* New York: Harper and Row.

———. 1997. *Not Like Us: How Europeans Have Loved, Hated, and Transformed American Culture Since World War II.* New York: Basic Books.

Phillips, William. 1983. *A Partisan View: Five Decades of a Literary Life.* New York: Stein & Day.

———. 1990. "Comment: The Liberal Conspiracy." *Partisan Review* 57, no. 1: 7–13.

Pitzer, Andrea. 2013. *The Secret History of Vladimir Nabokov.* New York and London: Pegasus Press.

Press, Stephen D. 2006. *Prokofiev's Ballets for Diaghilev.* Farnham, Surrey, and Burlington, VT: Ashgate.

Proffer, Ellendea. 1984. *Bulgakov: Life and Work.* Ann Arbor, MI: Ardis.

Prokofiev, Sergei. 2012. *Diaries 1924-1933: Prodigal Son.* Translated and annotated by Anthony Phillips. London: Faber and Faber.

Puddington, Arch. 2000. *Broadcasting Freedom: The Cold War Triumph of Radio Free Europe and Radio Liberty.* Lexington: University Press of Kentucky.

Pugliese, Stanislao G. 2009. *Bitter Spring: A Life of Ignazio Silone.* New York: Farrar, Straus, and Giroux.

Raczymow, Henri. 1988. *Maurice Sachs ou les travaux forcés de la frivolité.* Paris: Gallimard.

Raeff, Marc. 1990. *Russia Abroad: A Cultural History of the Russian Emigration, 1919-1939.* New York and Oxford: Oxford University Press.

Rampersad, Arnold. 2002. *The Life of Langston Hughes, Volume II: 1941-1967: I Dream a World.* 2nd ed. Oxford and New York: Oxford University Press.

Ricci, Franco Carlo. 1987. *Vittorio Rieti*. Rome and Naples: Edizioni Scientifiche Italiane.

Riding, Alan. 2010. *And the Show Went On: Cultural Life in Nazi-Occupied Paris*. New York: Alfred A. Knopf.

Robinson, Harlow. 1987. *Sergei Prokofiev: A Biography*. London: Robert Hale.

———. 1994. *The Last Impresario: The Life, Times, and Legacy of Sol Hurok*. New York: Viking.

Roger, Philippe. 2002. *L'ennemi américain: généalogie de l'antiaméricanisme français*. Paris: Éditions du Seuil.

Rorem, Ned. 1978. "Nabokov's Bagázh." In *An Absolute Gift: A New Diary*. New York: Simon and Schuster, 178–82.

Ross, Alex. 2007. *The Rest Is Noise*. New York: Farrar, Straus, and Giroux.

Rzewuski, Alex-Ceslas. 1976. *À travers l'invisible cristal: confessions d'un dominicain*. Paris: Plon.

———. 2006. *La double tragédie de Misia Sert*. Paris: Éditions du Cerf.

Sachs, Joel. 2012. *Henry Cowell: A Man Made of Music*. Oxford and New York: Oxford University Press.

Sachs, Maurice. 1950. *La décade de l'illusion*. Paris: Gallimard.

———. 1964. *Witches' Sabbath* [Le Sabbat]. Translated by Richard Howard. New York: Stein and Day.

Sachs, Maurice, Jacques Maritain, and Raïssa Maritain. 2003. *Correspondance (1925–1939)*. Edited by Michel Bressolette and René Mougel. Paris: Gallimard.

Sauguet, Henri. 2001. *La musique, ma vie*. Paris: Séguier.

Saunders, Frances Stonor. 1999. *Who Paid the Piper?: The CIA and the Cultural Cold War*. London: Granta Books. [American ed.: *The Cultural Cold War: The CIA and the World of Arts and Letters*. New York: The New Press.]

Schakovskoy, Zinaïda. 1959. *The Privilege Was Mine: A Russian Princess Returns to the Soviet Union*. Translated by Peter Wiles. New York: G. P. Putnam's Sons.

———. 1964. *Lumières et Ombre (Tel est mon siècle)*. Paris: Presses de la Cité.

———. 1965. *Une manière de vivre (Tel est mon siècle)*. Paris: Presses de la Cité.

Schiff, Stacy. 1999. *Véra (Mrs. Vladimir Nabokov)*. New York, Random House.

Schlesinger, Arthur M. 1949. *The Vital Center: Our Purposes and Perils and the Tightrope of American Liberalism*. Boston: Houghton Mifflin.

———. 2000. *A Life in the Twentieth Century: Innocent Beginnings, 1917-1950*. Boston and New York: Houghton Mifflin.

———. 2007. *Journals 1952-2000*. Edited by Andrew Schlesinger and Stephen Schlesinger. New York: Penguin Press.

———. 2013. *Letters*. Edited by Andrew Schlesinger and Stephen Schlesinger. New York: Random House.

Scott-Smith, Giles. 2000. "The 'Masterpieces of the Twentieth Century' Festival and the Congress for Cultural Freedom: Origins and Consolidation 1947–52." *Intelligence and National Security* 15 (Spring), 121–43.

———. 2002. *The Politics of Apolitical Culture: The Congress for Cultural Freedom, the CIA, and Post-War American Hegemony.* London and New York: Routledge.

Sert, Misia. 1952. *Misia.* Paris: Gallimard.

Sessions, Roger. 1992. *Correspondence.* Edited by Andrea Olmstead. Boston: Northeastern University Press.

Shils, Edward. 1990. "Remembering the Congress for Cultural Freedom." *Encounter* 25, no. 2 (September), 53–65.

Shirakawa, Sam H. 1992. *The Devil's Music Master: The Controversial Life and Career of Wilhelm Furtwängler.* New York and Oxford: Oxford University Press.

Shostakovich, Dmitri Dmitrievich. 2004. *Testimony: The Memoirs of Dmitri Shostakovich, as Related to and Edited by Solomon Volkov.* Translated from the Russian by Antonina W. Bouis. New York: Limelight Editions.

Sisman, Adam. 2010. *Hugh Trevor-Roper: The Biography.* London: Weidenfeld & Nicolson.

Slonimsky, Nicolas. 1994. *Music Since 1900.* 5th ed. New York: Schirmer; Toronto: Maxwell Macmillan Canada; New York [etc.]: Maxwell Macmillan International.

Smith, Julia. 1955. *Aaron Copland: His Work and Contribution to American Music.* New York: E. P. Dutton & Company, Inc.

Spender, Stephen. 1985. *Journals 1939-1983.* London: Faber & Faber.

Stoliarova, T. N. 1999. *Parish 1928: Oda vozvrashchaetsia v teatr.* Moscow: Rossiisk gos. Gumanit. un-t (Chtenia po istorii i teorii kultury, vyp. 27).

Stravinsky, Igor. 1982. *Selected Correspondence.* Vol. *1.* Edited with commentaries by Robert Craft. New York: Alfred A. Knopf.

———. 1984. *Selected Correspondence.* Vol. *2.* Edited with commentaries by Robert Craft. New York: Alfred A. Knopf.

———. 1985. *Selected Correspondence.* Vol. *3.* Edited with commentaries by Robert Craft. New York: Alfred A. Knopf.

Stravinsky, Igor, and Robert Craft. 2002. *Memories and Commentaries.* London: Faber and Faber.

Stravinsky, Vera, and Robert Craft. 1978. *Stravinsky in Pictures an Documents.* New York: Simon and Schuster.

Struve, Nikita. 1996. *Soixante-dix ans d'émigration russe (1919-1989).* Paris: Fayard.

Stuckenschmidt, Hans Heinz. 1982. *Zum hören geboren: ein Leben mit der Musik unserer Zeit.* Munich: Deutscher Taschenbuch Verlag; Kassel, Basel, and London: Bärenreiter Verlag.

Sumner, Gregory D. 1996. *Dwight MacDonald and the* Politics *Circle: The Challenge of Cosmopolitan Democracy.* Ithaca and London: Cornell University Press.

Suther, Judith. 1990. *Raïssa Maritain: Pilgrim, Poet, Exile.* New York: Fordham University Press.

Szigeti, Joseph. 1967. *With Strings Attached: Reminiscences and Reflections.* 2nd ed., revised and enlarged. New York: Alfred A. Knopf.

Tagliaferro, Magda. 1979. *Quase tudo*. Translated [from the French] by Maria Lúcia Pinho. Rio de Janeiro: Editora Nova Fronteira.

Taper, Bernard. 1984. *Balanchine: A Biography*. New York: Times Books.

Taruskin, Richard. 1992. "Nabokov, Nicholas." In *The New Grove Dictionary of Opera*, edited by Stanley Sadie, 3:543. London: Macmillan.

———. 1996. *Stravinsky and the Russian Tradition in sing*. 2 vols. Berkeley and Los Angeles: University of California Press.

Thacker. Toby. 2003. "'Playing Beethoven like and Indian': American Music and Reorientation in Germany, 1945-1955." In Geppert 2003, 365–86.

———. 2007. *Music After Hitler, 1945-1955*. Aldershot, England: Ashgate.

Thayer, Charles W. 1959. *Diplomat*. New York: Harper & Brothers.

———. 1966. *Muzzy*. New York: Harper & Row.

Thoburn, Crawford R. 1966. "Hindemith at Wells." *Wells College Bulletin*.

Thomson, Virgil. 1947. *The Art of Judging Music*. New York: Alfred A. Knopf.

———. 1966. *Virgil Thomson by Virgil Thomson*. New York: Alfred A. Knopf.

———. 1988. *Selected Letters*. Edited by Tim Page and Vanessa Weeks Page. New York [etc.]: Summit Books.

Thorpe, Charles. 2006. *Oppenheimer: The Tragic Intellect*. Chicago and London: The University of Chicago Press.

Todd, Olivier. 1997. *Albert Camus: A Life*. Translated by Benjamin Ivry. New York: Alfred A. Knopf.

Tommasini, Anthony. 1997. *Virgil Thomson, Composer on the Aisle*. New York and London: W. W. Norton.

Trenner, Franz. 2003. *Richard Strauss: Chronik zu Leben und Werk*. Vienna: Dr. Richard Strauss GmbH & Co.

Tyler, Parker. 1967. *The Divine Comedy of Pavel Tchelitchew: A Biography*. New York: Fleet Street Publishing Corporation.

Vaill, Amanda. 1998. *Everybody Was So Young: Gerald and Sara Murphy, A Lost Generation Love Story*. Boston and New York: Houghton Mifflin.

Verrett, Shirley, with Christopher Brooks. 2003. *I Never Walk Alone: The Autobiography of an American Singer*. Hoboken, NJ: John Wiley & Sons, Inc.

Vickers, Hugo. 1985. *Cecil Beaton: The Authorized Biography*. London: Weidenfeld and Nicolson.

Vishnevskaya, Galina. 1984. *Galina*. Translated from the Russian by Guy Daniels. San Diego: Harcourt Brace Jovanovich.

Volta, Ornella. 1989. "À la recherche d'un fantôme: Paul & Virginie d'Erik Satie." *Revue internationale de musique française* 29:47–70.

Wald, Alan M. 1987. *The New York Intellectuals: The Rise and Decline of Anti-Stalinist Left from the 1930s to the 1980s*. Chapel Hill and London: The University of North Carolina Press.

Wall, Irwin M. 1991. *The United States and the Making of Postwar France 1945-54*, Cambridge: Cambridge University Press.

Warburg, Fredric. 1973. *All Authors Are Equal: The Publishing Life of Fredric Warburg 1936-1971*. London: Hutchinson & Co.

Warner, Michael. 1995. "Origins of the Congress for Cultural Freedom." *Studies in Intelligence 38*, no. 5 (Summer 1995), 89–98.

———. 1996–97. "Sophisticated Spies: CIA's Links to Liberal Anti-Communists, 1949–1967." *International Journal of Intelligence and Counter-Intelligence 9*, no. 4 (Winter), 425–33.

Wellens, Ian. 2002. *Music on the Frontline: Nikolas Nabokov's Struggle against Communism and Middlebrow Culture*. Aldershot: Ashgate.

White, Edmund. 2009. *City Boy*. New York, Berlin, London: Bloomsbury.

Whitfield, Stephen J. 1996. *The Culture of the Cold War*. Baltimore: The Johns Hopkins University Press.

Wilford, Hugh. 1995. *The New York Intellectuals: From Vanguard to Institution*. Manchester: Manchester University Press.

———. 2000. "'Unwitting Assets'? British Intellectuals and the CCF," *Twentieth-Century British History 11*, no. 1, 42–60.

———. 2003. *The CIA, the British Left, and the Cold War: Calling the Tune?* London, Portland, Oregon: Franz Cass.

———. 2014. "The American Society of African Culture: The CIA and Transnational Networks of African Diaspora Intellectuals in the Cold War," *Transnational Anti-Communism and the Cold War: Agents, Activities, and Networks*, edited by Luc van Dongen, Stéphanie Roulin, and Giles Scott-Smith, Houndmills, Basingstoke, Hampshire, and New York: Palgrave Macmillan, 23–34.

Wilson, Edmund. 1977. *Letters on Literature and Politics 1912-1972*. Edited by Elena Wilson. Introduction by Daniel Aaron. Foreword by Leon Edel. New York: Farrar, Straus, and Giroux.

———. 1983. *The Forties: From Notebooks and Diaries of the Period*. Edited with an introduction by Leon Edel. New York: Farrar, Straus, and Giroux.

———. 2001. *Edmund Wilson, the Man in Letters*. Edited and introduced by David Castronovo and Janet Groth. Athens: Ohio University Press.

Wilson, Elisabeth. 2007. *Mstislav Rostropovich: Cellist, Teacher, Legend*. London: Faber and Faber.

Windham, Donald. 1944. "The Stage and Ballet Designs of Pavel Tchelitchew." *Dance Index 3*, nos. 1–2 (January-February): 4–32.

Wise, David. 2000. "Spook Art: Was the CIA really behind the rise of Abstract Expressionism?" *Art News*, September, 161–64.

Wolverton, Mark. 2008. *A Life in Twilight: The Final Years of J. Robert Oppenheimer*. New York: St. Martin's Press.

Woolf, Vicki. 2000. *Dancing in the Vortex: The Story of Ida Rubinstein*. New York: Routledge.

Wreszin, Michael. 1994. *A Rebel in Defense of Tradition: The Life and Politics of Dwight Macdonald*. New York: Basic Books.

Zimmer, Dieter E. 2001. *Nabokovs Berlin*. Berlin: Nicolai.

AUDIOVISUAL DOCUMENTS

Apostrophes 73 (October 1, 1976). Paris, INA.

"Hommage à Serge Koussevitzky par Nicolas Nabokov," French Radio, Chaîne coloniale, June 9, 1951. Paris, INA.

L'invité du lundi: Nicolas Nabokov." France-Culture, July 18, 1977. Paris, INA.

"La musique une et divisible." Produced by Fred Goldbeck, France-Culture, January 20, 1967. Paris, INA.

"Nicolas Nabokov Discusses Stravinsky" and "Stravinsky and Nabokov in Hamburg [1963]." In *Stravinsky*, directed by Wolf Koenig and Roman Kroitor, National Film Board of Canada, 1965; DVD reissue, Video Artists International, Inc., 2004.

Nicolas Nabokov ou le jardin des délices. Produced by Mildred Clary, France-Culture, 1999. Paris, INA.

"Nicolas Nabokov présente son spectacle et indique le sens qu'il lui donne" [Spring 1952], *Plein feu sur les spectacles du monde,* French Radio, Chaîne nationale. Paris, INA.

Parti pris: Nicolas Nabokov. France-Culture, October 12, 1976. Paris, INA.

Témoignages [Nicolas Nabokov], French Radio, Chaîne nationale, June 15, 1952. Paris, INA.

Notes

INTRODUCTION

1. The connection between Vladimir and Nicolas is often comically misrepresented: see for instance "the Nabokov brothers" in Hersh 1992, 302.
2. Henri Cartier-Bresson, oral testimony, *Nicolas Nabokov ou le jardin des délices*, 21, INA.
3. Glock 1991, 109.
4. George Kennan to Nabokov, December 19, 1972, NN, Texas.
5. Elliott Carter, personal testimony, May 19, 2010.

CHAPTER 1

1. See Nabokov 1975, 10.
2. Vladimir Nabobov 1989, 52. On the origins of the Nabokov family, see also Ferrand 1982, especially 123ff.
3. Nabokov 1975, 11.
4. The Prussian king also wrote the libretto of Graun's *Merope* (also after Voltaire) in 1756 and collaborated with Count Francesco Algarotti on the one for his *Coriolano* (1749) and with a less-distinguished partner, Leopoldo de Villati, on those of *Ifigenia in Aulide* (1748) and *Angelica e Medoro* (1749).
5. V. Nabokov 1985, 55.
6. See Boyd 1990, 24.
7. A history of Askania-Nova was written by one of Nabokov's maternal uncles, then living in exile in Germany: see Falz-Fein 1930). The landmark status of Askania-Nova was sanctioned by UNESCO in 1972 when it was put on the World Heritage List. Today the natural reserve attracts more than a hundred thousand visitors a year (see http://ukraineplaces.com/south-ukraine/askania-nova-reserved-land, consulted on September 20, 2010).

8. Nabokov 1975, 14.

9. Ibid., 15.

10. See the composer's comments on this physical trait in Nabokov 1972b.

11. "The All of Me," typescript, 3, DNA.

12. Nabokov 1975, 13.

13. Ibid., 12.

14. See Lischke 1993, 113–14 and 163–64; and Lesure 1994, 43–47.

15. Nabokov 1975, 31.

16. See Nabokov 1972b.

17. *Bagázh* typescript, Part 1, 35, DNA.

18. Ibid., 46.

19. *Bagázh*, typescript draft with heading "Pokrovskoye," 36, DNA.

20. Nabokov 1975, 25.

21. Nabokov 1951, 3–5. See also Fred Goldbeck, "A Note on Nicolas Nabokov," type-script, n.d. [ca. 1956], IACF, Chicago.

22. "Igor Stravinsky: A Partisan Chronicle," typescript, 2, DNA.

23. Though she is designated by an initial in *Bagázh,* her family name is given as Abzieher in Nabokov 1951, 5, 6, and *passim.*

24. Nabokov 1975, 48; see also Nabokov 1951, 25.

25. Nabokov 1975, 49.

26. Nabokov 1951, 35–36.

27. See Nabokov 1975, 56–57.

28. Ibid., 61–66.

29. *Bagázh* typescript, Part 1, 173, DNA.

30. Nabokov 1975, 68.

31. The phrase occurs both in Nabokov 1951, 21ff, and Nabokov 1975, 47.

32. See "The Golden Age," manuscript draft for *Bagázh,* DNA.

CHAPTER 2

1. See Nabokov's letter of April 4, 1976, to his son Ivan and daughter-in-law Claude, ICNA. Vladimir's sister Elena and Nabokov's cousin Sergei Sergeevich also took offense at the portrayal of their grandmother.

2. See Nabokov 1975, 115. At the insistence of one of Nabokov's cousins, the reference to the medallion was excised from the French edition of *Bagázh.* See Claude Nabokoff's testimony in *Nabokov ou le jardin des délices* 1, INA.

3. *Bagázh* typescript, Part 1, 277, DNA.

4. Ibid., 250.

5. See his portrait in Vladimir Nabokov's *Speak, Memory;* Nabokov 1989, 196–200.

6. *Bagázh* typescript, Part 6, 5, DNA.

7. Nabokov 1951, 38.

8. Ibid., 40.

9. *Bagázh* typescript, Part 6, 19, DNA.

10. Strauss conducted two concerts in the Russian capital, on February 6 and 7. See Trenner 2003, 344.

11. Nabokov 1975, 78.

12. See the chapter entitled "His Majesty's Gloves" in Nabokov 1951.

13. Nabokov 1951, 42.

14. Nabokov 1975, 84. From 1914 onwards Rasputin lived at no. 64 on Gorokhovaia Street.

15. His name is given as Arsenyev in *Bagázh* typescript, Part 2, DNA.

16. On this episode, see Nabokov 1975, 85–87.

17. The coinage is found in *Bagázh* typescript, Part 6, 7 and 35, DNA.

18. See Nabokov 1951, 37.

19. Ibid., 40.

20. Ibid., 40–41.

21. *Bagázh* typescript, Part 6, 23, DNA.

22. Nabokov 1951, 146.

23. Ibid.

24. Ibid., 147.

25. *Bagázh* typescript, Part 1, 286, DNA.

26. *Bagázh* typescript, Part 7, 5, DNA.

27. "The German Manichee I," typescript,5, DNA.

28. Ibid.

29. Ibid., 2.

30. Ibid., 3.

31. Ibid., 8.

32. "Nesrochnaya vesna (The Unhasty Spring)," typescript draft for *Bagázh*, 2, DNA.

33. Ibid., 9.

34. Ibid., 11.

35. Ibid., 11–12.

36. Ibid., 12–16.

37. The most detailed, and probably most reliable, account of this episode is in the autobiographical essay "To Meudon," *Preuves* Papers, IACF Archives, Chicago.

38. Nabokov 1975, 142. In Nabokov's autobiography, the episode is presented within the largely fictitious context of a conversation with Rilke in 1922.

39. Many years later, finding himself in Petersburg again in late June 1967, Nabokov retained such a powerful memory of this episode that he took the trouble to walk to the same spot: see "Reise in die SU," typescript, DNA.

40. "Moods of memory," typescript draft for *Bagázh*, 9–10, DNA.

CHAPTER 3

1. Nabokov 1975, 111.
2. See Boyd 1990, 141.
3. Nabokov 1975, 84.
4. On Rebikov, see Tamara Nikolaevna Levaya's entry in *New Grove 2*.
5. And not Tchaikovsky himself, as suggested in Nabokov 1975, 90. See also the portrait of Rebikov in Nabokov 1951, 148–49.
6. See the exactly contemporary testimony of M. Montagu-Nathan, "Rebikov and His Mantle," *The Musical Times* 58, no. 894 (August 1, 1917): 356.
7. Cited in Nabokov 1975, 91.
8. *Bagázh* typescript, Part 6, 39, DNA.
9. Nabokov 1951, 150.
10. This date, given in all standard sources, does not match the account given in Nabokov 1975, 92, where Rebikov is claimed to have been found frozen on his bed during the winter of 1921. According to Rebikov's death certificate (a copy of which Nabokov had in his papers, see DNA), Rebikov died, in fact, of a brain hemorrhage.
11. See Boyd 1990, 136ff.
12. *Bagázh* typescript, Part 3, 9–10, DNA.
13. See Boyd 1990, 149.
14. Nabokov 1975, 111.
15. See Boyd 1990, 118–19.
16. Nabokov 1975, 111.
17. See Nabokov 1975, 139.
18. "The German Manichee. Part I," MS draft, DNA.
19. This episode is part of the material not included in Nabokov 1975; see *Bagázh* typescript, Part 7, 54ff, and "Moods of Memory" and "The German Manichee: I," typescript drafts, DNA. In these drafts, the name of the German officer is given either as Dieter M.
20. "Moods of Memory," typescript draft, 10, DNA.
21. See Falz-Fein 1930, plate 84.
22. *Bagázh* typescript, Part 1, 251, DNA.
23. V. Nabokov 1989, 200.
24. See Nabokov 1975, 66, and Falz-Fein 1930, 296.
25. Krym subsequently emigrated to Southern France, where he managed a large agricultural estate; there he was visited by Vladimir Nabokov. See Boyd 1990, 205, 208.
26. This detail, which seems to epitomize the emigre's condition, served, slightly modified, as the title of the German version of *Bagázh* (see Nabokov 1975a): *Zwei rechte Schuhe im Gepäck: Errinerungen eines russischer Weltbürger* (Two right shoes in the luggage: Recollections of a Russian Cosmopolite).

27. The dates in the journal-like account of the events in Nabokov 1975, 93–98, are given in the old style, Julian calendar.
28. *Bagázh* typescript, Part 7, 6, DNA.
29. See for example Nabokov 1972.
30. Curriculum vitae on Wells College stationery, and "New Friends on the Cape: John Peale Bishop," MS draft for *Bagázh*, 6, DNA.
31. Fred Goldbeck, "A Note on Nicolas Nabokov," IACF archives, Chicago.
32. "To Meudon," *Preuves* Papers, IACF Archives, Chicago.
33. "Ad [sic] memoriam A. G. and F. BH. Second Story. Havens. 1. To Altenhof," MS draft, *passim*, DNA.
34. That is, a mixture of reserve and embarrassment.
35. "To Meudon" (see above n29). For a much shorter account of this crucial meeting, see Nabokov 1975, 118.
36. The name is not given in Nabokov 1975, possibly by mutual understanding with Grunelius, who was still living when *Bagázh* came out.
37. "To Meudon" (see above, n32).
38. Ibid.
39. Ibid.

CHAPTER 4

1. The point is made in Nabokov 1972.
2. See Tamara Levitz, "Haas, Joseph," in *New Grove 2*; and Erik Levi, "Haas, Joseph," in *Opera Grove*.
3. *Opera Grove* gives the year as 1911.
4. *Bagázh* typescript, Part 6, 39, DNA.
5. "Cette bassesse de la musique." Bruyr 1935, 82. Elsewhere in the same interview, he lumps Reger and Richard Strauss together in the category of bores (*emmerdeurs*); see ibid., 88.
6. See Nabokov 1951, 42.
7. Cited from *La morte di Rasputin*, program, Teatro Bellini, Catania, 1963, ICNA.
8. See Thomas Bauman and Horst Koegler, "Stuttgart," and Ronald Crichton, "Busch, Fritz," *Opera Grove*.
9. *Bagázh* typescript, Part 6, 32, DNA. The passage occurs in Nabokov's reminiscences of his conversations with Stravinsky in Paris.
10. This episode is found in *Bagázh* typescript, Part 7, 60–65, DNA.
11. On Uncle Frederick in Berlin, see Nabokov 1975, 72.
12. Nabokov 1975, 119.
13. Ibid., 106.
14. Ibid., 108.
15. *Bagázh* typescript, Part 1, 268, DNA.
16. Ibid.

17. Nabokov 1975, 109.

18. *Bagázh* typescript, Part 2, 266–67, DNA.

19. Nabokov 1975, 109.

20. "Vocabulary, Semantics, Facades" [Moscow Diary, 1967], DNA.

21. See William D. Gridger and Erik Levi, "Juon, Paul," *New Grove 2*.

22. Nabokov 1975, 174.

23. Autobiographical statement in a presentation of *Rasputin*, Nabokov to Dr. Weitz, October, 20, n.d. [but 1959], NN, Texas.

24. *Bagázh* typescript, Part 4, 84, DNA.

25. Ibid. Nabokov later paid a discreet homage to Schünemann in his first contribution to the *Atlantic Monthly*; see Nabokov 1942a, 92.

26. Hornbostel's name appears in "Days in Burma," MS, Part 1, 12, DNA.

27. See Yohanan Boehm, "A Peripatetic Musician," *Jerusalem Post*, December 7, 1973.

28. Nabokov 1975, 102.

29. Ibid., 103–4.

30. See Nabokov 1975, 104.

31. See Isaiah Berlin to Harold Rosenthal, November 7, 1974, cited from Berlin 2013, 582.

32. *Bagázh* typescript, Part 6, 41, DNA.

33. See untitled manuscript draft headed "II," 4, DNA.

34. Nabokov 1975, 107–8.

35. See the account in Vladimir Nabokov's journal in Boyd 1990, 191–93.

36. Nabokov 1975, 117.

37. The name is unfortunately misspelled "Bernsdorff" in Nabokov 1975. On Bernstorff, see the detailed article in the German version of Wikipedia, http://de.wikipedia.org/wiki/Albrecht_Graf_vonBernstorff, consulted February 28, 2012.

38. "Ad [*sic*] memoriam A. G. and F.BH. Second Story. Havens. 1. To Altenhof" MS, DNA.

39. Ibid.

40. Ibid.

41. *Bagázh* typescript, Part 7, 48, DNA.

42. The songs, however, were more than an occasional piece for presentation to a friend: Nabokov mentioned them in a letter to Boris Kochno dated September 30, 1927.

43. See Mayer 1975.

44. See Easton 2002, 454n1 and 455n10.

45. "To Meudon. In Memoriam H.K.," *Preuves* Papers, IACF Archives, Chicago. See also 1962b.

46. See Nabokov 1975, 120–22, and Easton 2002, 365–66.

47. "Ad [*sic*] memoriam A.G. And F.BH. Second Story. Havens. 1. To Altenhof" MS, DNA.

48. Kessler 2011, 107; see also 40n and 383n.
49. Nabokov 1975, 121.
50. Curiously, the episode, though it takes place in Berlin, is reduced to a few lines in the German edition of *Bagázh*; see Nabokov 1975a, 146–47.
51. *Bagázh* typescript, Part 3, 26, DNA. Remizov was entirely excised by Nabokov's editors from the published version of his autobiography.
52. *Bagázh* typescript, Part 3, 27–28, DNA.
53. See Boyd 1990, 287, 391.
54. See Berberova 1972, 262–63.
55. See Prokofiev 2012, 695.
56. Miscellaneous drafts for *Bagázh*, unnumbered page marked "insert II, p. 13," DNA.
57. Nabokov 1975, 124.
58. On Max Goertz's relations with Kessler, see Easton 2002, 368 and 454n10. As an astute reviewer pointed out when *Bagázh* came out, Nabokov's memory betrayed him when he put German words in the mouth of Esenin, who was from a peasant family and spoke no language other than Russian; see Karlinsky 1977.
59. Untitled manuscript draft for *Bagázh*, 17, DNA.
60. Untitled manuscript draft for *Bagázh*, 18, DNA. In the revised, and hence probably less reliable version published in *Bagázh*, Nabokov recalls that Kessler took Isadora home and he and Esenin, supported by Kessler's two friends, spent the end of the evening "writing huge Russian obscenities on a show window with lipsticks" and he woke up the next day at the house of Kessler's young woman friend (Nabokov 1975, 131).
61. Biographers of Isadora have repeated Nabokov's account, with various degrees of skepticism; see McVay 1980, 71–72, and Kurth 2001, 444–45.
62. Cut from the published version of *Bagázh*, the portrait of "Doderl" is found in *Bagázh* typescript, Part 3, 26–30, DNA.
63. *Bagázh* typescript, Part 3, 31, DNA.
64. Thus, in the draft typescript of his essay on Stravinsky's *Noces* (see Nabokov 1978), he claims to have seen a copy of *Malii i Velikii Znamennii Rosspiev* at Weimar in 1921 (ICNA). One can safely assume that this took place at a much later date.
65. See Kessler 2007 and Schnack 2008.
66. See Mayer 1975.
67. Harry Kessler to Nabokov, Weimar, April 22, 1929, NN, Yale.
68. See Nabokov 1975, 135.
69. Ibid., 138. The episode was also published in *Vogue* in November 1975 (see Nabokov 1975c).
70. This is pointed out in Karlinsky 1977 and Mayer 1975.
71. Unfortunately spelled Labbé in the German edition, as Mayer duly pointed out.
72. This is the way it is reported in Nabokov 1962a and 1962b.

CHAPTER 5

1. See Bruyr 1933, 85 (where the date 1923 is given) and *Bagázh* typescript, Part 4, 4–5, DNA.

2. "Moods of Memory," typescript, [6], and "Material for France," loose MS draft for *Bagázh*, 5, DNA.

3. Testimony of Dr. Charles von Salzen, July 2, 1948, NN FBI files, file 123–162.

4. See "Alexis Saintléger Léger," manuscript draft of a talk, n.d. [but ca. 1976], DNA.

5. In 1931 he referred to Tchelitchew as "an old friend from Berlin" (see Bruyr 1933, 85).

6. See Kirstein 1994, 33.

7. There is hardly any mention of Nabokov's early Parisian years in Nabokov 1975; they are, however, evoked in some detail, if clearly embellished somewhat, in "Alexis Saintléger Léger," DNA.

8. See Tyler 1967, 297.

9. Ibid.

10. "New Friends on the Cape: John Peale Bishop," MS draft for *Bagázh*, 7, DNA.

11. Ibid., 6.

12. Nabokov 1975, 145.

13. Ibid., 147.

14. Kessler 2009, 760.

15. Ibid. All uncredited translations are mine.

16. See Prokofiev 2012, 681–82.

17. Bruyr 1933, 85. The encouragement given by Grand Duke Nicholas is mentioned in the testimony of Dr. Charles von Salzen, July 2, 1948, NN FBI files, file 123–162.

18. Prokofiev 2012, 696.

19. Duke 1955, 200.

20. See Horowitz 1982, 116 (with no date supplied).

21. NN, Texas.

22. Much to the amusement of the *Musical Times* reviewer, the score came out with the title misprinted *Shot Stories*—a detail Elliott Carter, who purchased the score at the time, also remembered; see T. A., "New Music: Pianoforte," *The Musical Times* 69, no. 1028 (October 1, 1928).

23. Sauguet 2001, 230.

24. Ibid.

25. On Désormière, see Mayer and Suvchinskii 1966. The ties between Désormière and Nabokov, however, are not mentioned in this source.

26. Kessler 1971, 301.

27. Duke 1955, 109.

28. See Iwaskiewicz 1976, with thanks to Piotr Kloszowski and Érik Veaux.

29. Iwaszkiewicz 1975, 237. Translation kindly supplied by Alexander Schenker.

30. See Lacombe 2013, 324.

31. On Nabokov's hypersensitivity, see, for instance, Michael Josselson to Sidney Hook, July 21, 1975, MJ, Texas.

32. See Chimènes 2004.

33. "Alexis Saintléger Léger," MS, DNA.

34. See Kessler 1971, 298.

35. See *Bagázh* typescript, Part 6, 42, DNA.

36. Kessler 2009, 792–93.

37. "Alexis Saintléger Léger," MS, DNA. On the ties between Maritain and Auric, see Bressolette 1991.

38. According to Tyler 1967, 238, Rzewuski "adored" Tchelitchew, whom he met through the critic and musicologist Petr Petrovich Suvchinskii (often referred to as Pierre Souvtchinski), with whom Nabokov himself was on good, if never especially close terms.

39. See Rzewuski 2006.

40. Rzewuski 1976, 288.

41. Sachs 1964, 117.

42. Ibid.

43. In an undated letter of 1926, Sachs asks Maritain for Nabokov's address; the following year, on August 27, he made the same request, mentioning "a publication project strictly intended for musicians which might be of interest to him"; see Sachs Maritain 2003, 147, 217. There is no mention of Nabokov in Raczymow 1988.

44. Sachs 1950, 189.

45. On Laloy, see Dulong-Sainteny 1996.

46. On Maritain and music, see, in particular, Martini 1959, Caron 2009, and Dufour 2009.

47. See Caron 2009, especially 45–46.

48. "De quelques musiciens," Maritain 1993, 1118.

49. See Markevitch 1980, 224–25.

50. In September 1926, he referred to Nabokov as being "still Orthodox" (Sachs Maritain 2003, 316).

51. Kessler 1971, 301.

52. Kessler 2009, 800.

53. Rzewuski 1976, 198.

54. Iwaskiewicz 1975, 237.

55. See Struve 1996, 81–90.

56. Schakovskoy 1965, 100.

57. See Bruyr 1933, 85.

58. The phrasing of this episode in his autobiography may suggest that this "lapse" was homosexual in nature—Rzewuski was evidently bisexual. See Rzewuski 1976, 300.

59. Or Czeslaw in Polish; see Iwaszkiewicz 1975, 235–36.

60. See Rzewuski 1976, 324, and R. Maritain 1974, 223–24.

61. Raïssa's French version was republished in Maritain 1986–2007, 14:1159–61.

62. Kessler 2009, 800.

63. Kessler 1971, 301.

64. See *Bagázh* typsecript, Part 4, 85, DNA.

65. Maritain Sachs 2003, 316.

66. Not to be confused with his recent namesake, who led the Solesmes choir from 1971 to 1996.

67. Presentation of the *Chants à la Vierge Marie* [for the 7th ISCM Festival, Geneva, 1929?], cited from *Le Ménestrel* 91, no. 17 (April 26, 1929): 195.

68. Kessler 1971, 301.

69. See Kessler 2009, 800.

70. Nabokov 1951, 98.

71. Ibid., 144.

72. See Nabokov 1927.

73. "Moods of Memory," typescript draft for *Bagázh*, 7, DNA.

74. See the review of the concert by "A.S." in *Le Ménestrel* 88, no. 24 (June 11, 1926).

75. Kessler 2009, 795.

76. Nabokov 1951, 74. The account is Nabokov 1975, 147–49, is slightly abbreviated.

77. See Prokofiev 2012, 332.

78. See Nabokov 1931 as well as Bruyr 1933, 86. The spring 1927 date is also found in Buckle 1979, 496.

79. See Nabokov to Boris Kochno, visiting card, n.d., and postcard sent from Nice, April 20, transcripts, private collection.

80. Nabokov 1931.

81. Nabokov to Boris Kochno, September 2, 1927, transcript, private collection. See also *Ode*, manuscript short score, NN, Yale.

82. See Nabokov 1951, 81.

83. *Le Ménestrel* 89, no. 42 (October 21, 1927): 431.

84. See Nabokov 1975, 160–63. A longer version of the account of this first encounter is in *Bagázh* typescript, Part 6, 41–47, DNA.

85. Jean Cocteau to Igor Stravinsky, September 1927, cited from Stravinsky 1982, 113.

86. "De quelques musiciens," Maritain 1993, 1118.

87. See Nabokov 1951, 96–97. This passage is commented on in Taruskin 1996, 1545n76.

88. This detail is not in the printed text but in *Bagázh* typescript, Part 6, 49, DNA.

89. Nabokov 1975, 165. Nabokov may have also been influenced by Prokofiev's strong dislike of Stravinsky's work; see Press 2006, 254.

90. See Nabokov 1975, 165, and *Bagázh* typescript, Part 6, 46, DNA.

91. See Nabokov 1978, 274–75. The full title, suggested to Stravinsky by Charles-Ferdinand Ramuz, is *Les noces villageoises*.

92. See Nabokov 1978, 274. Nabokov claims he was in the company of Wilhelm Uhde, whom he did know from Berlin, and Iwaszkiewicz, whom, on the other hand, he probably did not get to know before 1926 at the earliest.
93. Nabokov 1978, 275.
94. Nabokov 1931.
95. Nabokov to Boris Kochno, September 2, 1927, transcript, private collection.
96. Nabokov to Walter Nouvel, December 5, 1927, transcript, private collection.
97. Nabokov to Boris Kochno, February 6, 1928, transcript, private collection.
98. Nabokov 1951, 92.
99. See Windham 1944, 9.
100. Tchelitchew's scenario is reproduced in Tyler 1967, 328–36.
101. Nabokov 1951, 96.
102. See Tyler 1967, 331, 335.
103. Nabokov 1951, 111.
104. The quotation comes from Stravinsky and Craft 2002, 153.
105. Nabokov 1951, 123.
106. Buckle 1979, 469.
107. Tyler 1967, 335.
108. Nabokov 1951, 125.
109. Beaton 1946, 195.
110. "The Gracious Master" MS, NN, Yale, 56.
111. S. Haeffner [André Schaeffner?], "Théâtre Sarah-Bernhardt. — Ballets Russes de Serge de Diaghilew, *Ode* de Nicolas Nabokoff," *Le Ménestrel* 90, no. 24 (June 15, 1928): 268–69. On June 7, *Ode* was still paired with *Pas d'acier*, but *Noces* was replaced by *Prélude à l'Après-midi d'un faune* and *Soleil de nuit*, on Rimsky-Korsakov's ballet music for *May Night*.
112. Ibid.
113. Maurice Brillant, "Les hommes et les œuvres," *Le Correspondant*, August 25, 1928, 620–24.
114. Beaton 1946, 194.
115. See Stravinsky and Craft 2002, 153.
116. Cited from Tyler 1967, 336.
117. See Bruyr 1933, 86. We follow this early testimony, which is confirmed by Kochno's own account, while contradicting Nabokov's subsequent account, in which he claims that Diaghilev managed to get the ban overturned; see Nabokov 1951, 125; see also Buckle 1979, 499.
118. Windham 1944, 10.
119. Tyler 1967, 336.

CHAPTER 6

1. On the Shakhovskoi family, see, in particular, Schakovskoy 1959, 14–16, and Schakovskoy 1964, 80–85.

2. See Sauguet 2001, 260.

3. A small correspondence from Étienne de Beaumont to Nabokov, in French, is preserved in NN, Yale. The earliest is a postcard dated Warsaw, July 16, 1928, as Beaumont and his wife were about to visit Soviet Russia.

4. Nabokov 1975, 166; see also "The Gracious Master," MS, NN, Yale, 54–55.

5. This is suggested in a letter from Paul Collaer to Nabokov, December 4, 1928, in French, NN, Yale; see also Prokofiev 2012, 756.

6. See Grunelius 1982.

7. See Schiff 1999, 65, and Boyd 1990, 394.

8. NN, Yale. In a July 1932 to his friend Charles Journet, Maritain asks his correspondent to "pray for Nicholas Nabokoff the musician" (Journet and Maritain 1997, 249).

9. Barré 1995, 390.

10. Nabokov 1951, 140.

11. See Lifar 1940, 347–48.

12. The date Lifar gives is January 1939 (see Lifar 1940, 345 and photo caption across from 348). The date of December 27 is confirmed in Buckle 1979, 512.

13. See Kessler 1971, 355–56.

14. It is possible that Nabokov's rewriting of the story was a way of getting even with Lifar, who claimed, improbably, that Diaghilev had mounted *Ode* for his sake, "though it did not interest him at all" (Lifar 1940, 332). As for "Tell him that Lifar jumps well," it may have been inspired by Karsavina's own account of the episode (see Karsavina 1931, 300).

15. See Maurice Brillant, "Les hommes et les œuvres," *Le Correspondant*, August 25, 1928, 620n1.

16. Nabokov to Boris Kochno, May 19, 1928, and n.d., in Russian, transcript, private collection.

17. Prokofiev 2012, 696; see also Nabokov 1951, 94.

18. See Sauguet 2001, 260.

19. See Woolf 2000, 167. Woolf makes no mention of Nabokov and the *Aphrodite* project.

20. A letter from Désormière, dated November 6, 1928, implies that, in Nabokov's view at least, the Russian dancer had not behaved in straightforward fashion: "Do compel Dame Rubinstein to pay you, *it is your right!*" (NN, Yale).

21. Désormière to Nabokov, "Lundi" [fall 1928?], in French, NN, Yale.

22. Nabokov to Boris Kochno, April 21, 1929, in Russian, transcript, private collection.

23. Boston Symphony Orchestra, Sixty-Seventh Season, 1947–48, Second Concert [program], Brooklyn Academy of Music, January 16, 1948.

24. See Prokofiev 2012, 757.

25. Interview of Darius Milhaud with Pierre Maudru of *Comœdia*, cited from "La musique française," *Le Ménestrel* 90, no. 22 (June 1, 1928): 251.

26. A. V. Coton in *A Prejudice for Ballet* (1938), cited in Nesta Macdonald 1975, 362.

27. Beaumont 1975, 381–83.

28. This is the way it was evidently reported to Nabokov by Kochno; see Nabokov to Boris Kochno, July 21, 1928, transcript, private collection.

29. "VIIe Festival de la SIMC," *Le Ménestrel* 91, no. 17 (April 26, 1929): 195. The citation is from Nabokov 1951, 218.

30. Edwin Evans, "Geneva Festival," *The Musical Times* 70, no. 1035 (May 1, 1929): 440.

31. See Jean Binet to Nabokov, September 15 [1929?], in French, NN, Yale. The Nabokov Papers at Yale contain one undated letter from Sessions to Nabokov, in Russian, dating from the same period.

32. Francillo-Kaufmann had, among other roles, partnered Caruso as Gilda in *Rigoletto* and had sung Zerbinetta at the London premiere of Richard Strauss's *Ariadne auf Naxos*, under Thomas Beecham. See K. J. Kutsch and Leo Riemens, *Grosses Sängerlexikon* (Munich: K. G. Saur, 2003), 3:1538.

33. See Nabokov to Boris Kochno, January 27, 1929, in Russian, transcript, private collection.

34. The dates of Boris (also known as Bodo) Greverus are uncertain. His birth year is usually given as 1904; the year of his death is unrecorded. See K. J. Kutsch and Leo Riemens, *Grosses Sängerlexikon* (Munich: K. G. Saur, 2003), 3:1830. He can be heard in the title role of a German-language recording of Verdi's *Don Carlos*, conducted by Ferenc Fricsay, with the young Dietrich Fischer-Dieskau as Posa (WLCD 0136).

35. Possibly Walter von Wistinghausen (1879–1956).

36. P. C. H., *The Musical Times* 70, no. 1035 (May 1, 1929): 455. The concert included Martinů's Second String Quartet and Hindemith's Viola Sonata and Fourth String Quartet, performed by Hindemith as soloist and the Amar-Hindemith Quartet.

37. Henri Sauguet, "Les concerts: Strawinsky et Nabokoff à l'O.S.P.", *L'Europe nouvelle*, February 23, 1929.

38. As late as May 4, Nabokov asked Kochno when rehearsals were to begin: see Nabokov to Boris Kochno, May 4, 1929, transcript, private collection.

39. See Massine 1968, 174.

40. Désormière to Nabokov, May 3, 1929, in French, NN, Yale.

41. Roger Désormière to Nabokov, "mardi," n.d., in French, NN, Yale. Colette Désormière added the post-scriptum quoted. The letter is unlikely to date from the weeks preceding the premiere of *Ode* in 1928 because it addresses Nabokov in the second person singular, which Désormière and Nabokov did not use in their correspondence until after that date.

42. See Paul Collaer to Nabokov, October 24, 1928, in French, NN, Yale.

43. See the review of the concert—which began with Schubert's great Symphony in C major—by Zed in *Les dernières nouvelles de Strasbourg*, December 10, 1931.

44. The phrase is in a letter from Colette Désormière to Nabokov, July 10, 1929, in French, NN, Yale. As Dukelsky later wrote in his memoirs, Markevitch eventually—if briefly—became Diaghilev's "fourth son," a position Nabokov—and Dukelsky himself—may have secretly hoped to be promoted to, if not on such intimate terms. See Duke 1955, 208.

45. Nabokov 1951, 127–30; reprinted in Nabokov 1975, 159–60. See also Buckle 1979, 536. The phrase "le danseur Diaghilev," which was used in the initial press releases, is found in a letter from Cuvelier to Nabokov, August 21, 1929, in French, NN, Yale.

46. Prokofiev 2012, 856.

47. Harry Kessler to Nabokov, May 4 and September 1, 1929, in German, NN, Yale.

48. Prokofiev 2012, 972–73.

49. See Prokofiev 2012, 781. See also Duke 1955, 109.

50. See Paul Collaer to Nabokov, May 8, 1931, in French, NN, Yale. Letters from Ansermet and Alfred Cortot (NN, Texas) suggest that they both considered including the overture in one of their concerts.

51. According to a letter to Maritain, draft, Kolbsheim, September 21, 1929, in French, NN, Yale.

52. Marcel Cuvelier to Nabokov, August 24, 1929, in French, NN, Yale.

53. Igor Stravinsky to Ernest Ansermet, October 3, 1929, cited from Stravinsky 1982, 200.

54. Serge Koussevitzky to Nabokov, telegram, NN, Yale. An undated, early letter [1932?] from Igor Markevitch to Nabokov, also at Yale, also refers to the symphony as "the great success of this past season in America."

55. Prokofiev 2012, 956.

56. "Le mouvement musical en province," *Le Ménestrel* 93, no. 18 (May 1, 1931): 195; see also Prokofiev 2012, 973.

57. Review signed "Leonid," *Christian Science Monitor*, July 4, 1930.

58. Henri Sauguet to Massimo Leone, February 22, 1930, cited in Berenguer 2003, 202.

59. Claude Altomont, "Les grands concerts: Orchestre Symphonique de Paris," *Le Ménestrel* 92, no. 20 (May 16, 1930): 229.

60. Paul Le Flem, "Les concerts," *Comœdia*, February 18, 1930.

61. Marcel Belvianes, "Concerts Poulet," *Le Ménestrel* 94, no. 44 (October 30, 1931): 454.

62. Gabriel Marcel to Nabokov [October 26, 1931], in French, NN, Yale.

63. I translate the French rendering Nabokov improvised before Bruyr in 1931; see Bruyr 1933, 89. In Babette Deutsch's Modern Library version, the lines read: "The soul oppressed with the old lyric fever / Trembles, reverberates, and seeks to pour / Its burden freely forth, and as through dreaming . . ." I am grateful to Vladimir Alexandrov for identifying the passage. Nabokov cites it slightly differently in *Bagázh*; see Nabokov 1975, 105.

64. See Prokofiev 2012, 696.

65. *Bagázh* typescript, Part 6, 60–61, DNA.
66. Nabokov 1928.
67. See Nabokov 1930.
68. Nabokov 1929, 54.
69. Ibid., 66–68.
70. Ibid., 64. Cited from Stravinsky and Craft 1978, though their English version oddly departs from the original on one point: "the mark of Diaghilev's inspiration" is not an accurate rendering of "le côté improvisateur de Diaghilev" (Diaghilev's extemporizing side).
71. Prokofiev 2012, 891.
72. "Une lettre d'Igor Stravinsky." *La musique* 3, no. 3 (December 15, 1929): 119.
73. Craft himself admits this much in Stravinsky 1978, 364. See Prokofiev 2012, 891.
74. Paul Collaer to Nabokov, January 5, 1930, in French, NN, Yale.
75. Stravinsky 1984, 368.
76. Cited from Stravinsky and Craft 1978, 293.
77. *Bagázh* typescript, Part 6, 59, DNA.
78. Prokofiev 2012, 712.
79. Ibid.
80. See the already cited passage in Duke 1955, 199–200.
81. Prokofiev 2012, 891.
82. Ibid., 893.
83. *Bagázh* typescript, Part 6, 75, DNA; see also Nabokov 1975, 167.
84. See Nabokov 1975, 169–70. See p. 58 of the Boosey & Hawkes orchestral score of the *Symphony of Psalms*; the first hearing of the passage in question occurs four bars after rehearsal number 23.
85. See *Bagázh* typescript, Part 6, 118–20, DNA.
86. Ibid., 118–19. Nabokov had met Glazunov in Berlin. That they were reacquainted in Paris is evidenced by a group photograph, reproduced in Raeff 1990, on which Nabokov and Lifar are seated next to Glazunov.
87. ıvinsky and Craft 1978, 288.
88. friendship with the Maritains began sometime in 1926; see Dufour ⌐o.
89. r la musique d'Arthur Lourié," in Maritain 1986–2007, 6:1060–66. On Stravinsky, and Maritain, see also Móricz 2013.
90. Maritain 1974, 261.
91. Ansermet to Nabokov, December 24, 1930, in French, NN, Texas; see letter of December 31. Prokofiev's testimony is in Prokofiev 2012, 727.
92. ₂v 2012, 950.
93. See *Bagázh* typescript, Part 6, 60, DNA.
94. Not included in Nabokov 1975, presumably not to offend admirers of Landowska, the chapter "Harpsichord's High Priestess" can be found in *Bagázh* typescript, Part 6, 59–74, DNA.
95. Ibid., 62.

96. Ibid., 66.
97. Ibid., 68.
98. Ibid., 69.
99. See Volta 1989 and Lacombe 2013, 363.
100. Étienne de Beaumont to Nabokov, March 6, 1932, in French, NN, Yale.
101. The Dominique Nabokov archives include the undated draft of an piece for organ, entitled "Orgelmusik," but there is no indication that it has anything to do with the Beaumont commission.
102. Kessler lists Savoir among the people he dined with in December 1928 after Nijinsky had been taken back to his Passy sanatorium; see Kessler 1971, 356.
103. See BnF online catalogue, record no. FRBNF39459406.
104. It was not used when the play was revived in 1971 on French television.
105. Pierre Bost in *La revue hebdomadaire* 39, no. 43 (October 25, 1930): 522–26.
106. See Kessler 1971, 401.
107. Harry Kessler to Nabokov, December 5, 1930, NN, Yale.
108. See Bruyr 1933, 82–89. An École normale supérieure graduate and German philologist, André Cœuroy (1891–1976) studied harmony and counterpoint with Reger and went on to found the *Revue musicale* with Henry Prunières in 1920. During the war he worked as music critic for the openly collaborationist *Comœdia*. He had already prefaced the first series of *L'écran des musiciens*.
109. Bruyr actually writes twentieth, but this is likely to be a slip of the pen or a typo (both numerous in his interview), especially since Tchelitchew, who lived in nearby Montparnasse, is referred to as a "neighbor."
110. See Nichols 2011, 261. Equally typical of the average perception of Tchaikovsky in the French musical establishment in the 1930s is the view expressed by Reynaldo Hahn—one of the great music critics of the period—in *Le Figaro* for April 10, 1935: "Louis XIV was quite surprised, according to Dangeau, when, having asked Boileau who, in literature, was the most remarkable man of his age, he got the answer: 'Sire, it is Molière.' Louis XIV, however, was quite sensible. He therefore told Boileau: 'I wouldn't have thought so; but you are more competent than I.' Similarly, when Russians assure you that Tchaikovsky is the most Russian of Russian composers, all you have to do is to assent: they are more competent than we."
111. Nabokov 1951, 160. Curiously, unlike several other chapters of *Old Friends and New Music*, this chapter was not incorporated into *Bagázh*. Nabokov's friendship with Prokofiev is briefly touched upon in Robinson 1987, 217–18.
112. See Prokofiev 2012, 954.
113. Prokofiev 2012, 958.
114. *Bagázh* typescript, Part 7, 74, DNA.
115. Prokofiev 2012, 970; see also 958.
116. Prokofiev 2012, 970.

117. The veracity of Nabokov's account is confirmed in Prokofiev 2012, 970–71. One could also cite the testimony of Dukelsky, who was close to Prokofiev, and recalls "constant quarrels between the Prokofievs, terminating in Jupiter-like shouts from Serge and copious tears from Lina" (Duke 1955, 199).

118. On Lina Prokofiev's singing career, see Morrison 2013.

119. See Zed, "Société des Amis du Conservatoire: Festival Prokofieff-Nabokoff," *Les dernières nouvelles d'Alsace*, March 11, 1931.

120. Nabokov 1942b, 62.

121. Nabokov 1951, 167.

122. See Akimova 2011, 104; this is confirmed by Prokofiev's own testimony: see Prokofiev 2012, 712.

123. See above, [134.

124. Prokofiev 2012, 782.

125. Bruyr 1933, 27.

126. Prokofiev 2012, 786.

127. See Prokofiev 2012, 905.

128. See Grunelius 1982, 88.

129. *Bagázh* typescript, Part 7, 11–12, DNA. Nabokov dates this early 1933, but the work was performed in December 1930.

130. See the comment on Richard Strauss in *Bagázh* typescript, Part 6, 9, DNA: ". . . only out of that kind of Bavarian beer pub could have sprouted those mammoth tone-poems I had heard in my childhood. This was their natural climate."

131. Bruyr 1933, 89.

132. Nabokov to Sergey Prokofiev, September 20, 1931, cited from Morrison 2013, 146.

133. On VOKS, see, especially, David-Fox 2012, in particular 40ff.

134. Magda Tagliaferro to Nabokov, January 3, 1931, and Pierre Monteux to Nabokov, September 28, 1931, NN, Yale.

135. See Magda Tagliaferro to Nabokov, October 30 [1930], NN, Yale. Nabokov's name does not appear in Tagliaferro 1979.

136. Zed, "Au Conservatoire: la première journée de la session d'études musicales et dramatiques: Musique russe," *Les dernières nouvelles de l'Alsace*, August 8, 1933.

137. See Daniélou 1987, 73.

138. There is no mention of the work—or of Nabokov's name—in Mousli 2005; the concert was reported in the June 1932 issue of *Vogue*, p. 23.

139. See Berenguer 2003, 217.

140. Markevitch 1980, 235.

141. Raymond Petit, *La revue musicale* 13 (July–August 1932): 128–29.

142. Prokofiev 2012, 1002.

143. An undated program of her concert is in DNA.

144. Paul Bertrand, "Concert Suzanne Peignot," *Le Ménestrel* 94, no. 23 (June 3, 1932): 243.

145. Henry Prunières, "Nabokoff: oeuvres nouvelles. (Concerts S. Peignot et La Sérénade," *La revue musicale* 13 (June 1932): 52.

146. The work is not listed as being part of Horowitz's repertory in Glenn Plaskin, *Horowitz* (New York: William Morrow and Company, Inc., 1983) or any other reference work.

147. Maritain to Nabokov, October 5, 1932, in French, NN, Yale. The same letter mentions the Princesse de Polignac's intervention. There is no discussion of *Job* in Martini 1959, which deals strictly with Maritain's discussion of music in his philosophical writings. The text of the oratorio is published in Maritain 1986–2007, 16:439–46.

148. The fact that the original spelling is found in Kessler 1971, 458, 459, suggests that it was changed only at the last minute.

149. See Taper 1984, 141–45.

150. Kessler 1971, 458, 459.

151. Roger Crosti, "Théâtre des Champs-Elysées.—Les Ballets 1933.—Job, oratorio pour deux voix et chœurs de M. Nicolas Nabokoff," *Le Ménestrel* 95, no. 25 (June 23, 1933): 254.

152. René Dumesnil, *Le Mercure de France* 843 (August 1, 1933): 713.

153. Gustave Samazeuilh, *La revue hebdomadaire* (July 8, 1933), 239–40. The parallel with Stravinsky (and also with Honegger) was also suggested by Henry Malherbe in his review for *Le Temps*, June 21, 1933.

154. The Beethoven catalogue does, however, include two piano waltzes, dating from 1824–25, with the respective opus numbers WOO84 and WOO85; see *Oxford Music Online*, accessed April 15, 2012.

155. According to an interview he gave to *La Libre Belgique*, February 5, 1973.

156. Cited from Balanchine 1983, 116.

157. Diana Menuhin in Mason 1991, 111.

CHAPTER 7

1. These reflections are part of a biographical sketch of Stravinsky, [ca. 1964], NN, Yale; see also Nabokov 1964, 41–43.

2. Édouard Bourdet to Nabokov, September 6, 1932, in French, NN, Yale.

3. See Nabokov 1975, 196–97.

4. Ibid., 197.

5. *Bagázh* typescript, Part 7, 5, DNA.

6. Prokofiev 2012, 757.

7. See Iwaszkiewicz 1976.

8. See J. Wenger-Valentin to Serge Koussevitzky, February 13, 1933, LC, transmitting a mimeographed proposal signed by Baronne D. de Dietrich, Alexandre Grunelius, Professor D. Pautrier, Maître Pfersdorff, Baron M. de Turckheim, J. Wenger-Valentin, and Roger Wolf.

9. Nabokov 1980, 121.
10. Such a *laisser-passer* has survived, delivered to Nabokov and his wife for a temporary stay in Belgium from February 10 to 13, 1931, and renewed on February 12 for three more days (ICNA).
11. Nabokov 1975, 184.
12. See Levy 1977, 183–84. Keller later became director of the New York branch of the Bignou Gallery on East 57th Street.
13. See Galassi 1987, 19, and Assouline 2005, 67–68.
14. Pierre Colle to Nabokov, July 13, 1932, in French, NN, Yale. The BnF online catalogue gives Colle's dates as 1909–48.
15. See Jeanne Homberg to Nabokov, March 8 and 24, 1933, in French, NN, Yale.
16. "New Friends on the Cape: John Peale Bishop," MS draft for *Bagázh*, 3, DNA.
17. Nabokov 1975, 187.
18. Ibid., 193, 188.
19. See Kirstein 1994, 26; on Pawel and Zosia Kochanski, see also Tyler 1967, 233–34.
20. *Bagázh* typescript, Part 4, unpaginated draft, DNA.
21. Aaron Copland to John Kirkpatrick, November 22, 1955, cited in Smith 1955, 154.
22. H. H., "New Music Tested in League Concert: A Trend Toward Clarity of Design Noted in Works of Contemporary Writers; Nabokov Suite Played," *The New York Times*, December 18, 1933.
23. On Raimund von Hoffmannsthal, see Moffat 2004, 121ff.
24. Nabokov 1975, 189.
25. MacLeish 1972, 92.
26. Ibid., 93.
27. Ibid. The idea, put forward in Ballets Russes de Monte-Carlo programs, that the initiative was Colonel de Basil's may be a self-promoting ploy, but it is, in fact, entirely possible that the idea of an American ballet might have germinated in more than one mind.
28. Robinson 1994, 170.
29. Balanchine subsequently characterized Colonel de Basil as "a crooked octopus, and with bad taste" (Taper 1984, 145).
30. Ibid., 168.
31. Massine 1968, 197.
32. MacLeish 1972, 93.
33. Ibid.; see also Robinson 1994, 170.
34. See Vaill 1998, 242.
35. Ibid.
36. Ibid.
37. Tommasini 1997, 258.
38. Nabokov's chronology in *Bagázh* cannot, however, be totally relied upon, as he gives March 6 as the date of the premiere, which actually occurred one month later on April 6.

39. Nabokov 1975, 192.

40. Massine 1968, 199.

41. Robinson 1994, 170.

42. Cited in Donaldson 1992, 237.

43. See Nabokov 1975, 194–95, and Massine 1968, 197–200.

44. Massine 1968, 199.

45. On the reception of the ballet, see, in particular, Chazin-Bennahum 2011, 147–49.

46. See Reynaldo Hahn, "Chronique musicale," *Le Figaro*, June 12, 1934; Roger Crosti, *Le Ménestrel* 96, no. 23 (June 8, 1934): 212–13.

47. Cited in Robinson 1994, 171.

48. MacLeish 1972, 93–94.

49. See Vaill 1998, 242.

50. See Archibald MacLeish to Robert N. Linscott [ca. January 1934], in MacLeish 1983, 265.

51. A single performance was given in New York in January 1941 at the Fifty-first Street Theater.

52. Szigeti 1967, 131.

53. Adrien Fauchier-Magnan to Nabokov, July 6, 1933, in French, NN, Yale.

54. See Nabokov's program notes, Cleveland Orchestra program, January 7 and 9, 1937, DNA. The Giandomenico Tiepolo drawings are now in the Robert Lehman Collection, Metropolitan Museum of Art.

55. Reynaldo Hahn, "Chronique musicale," *Le Figaro*, June 26, 1934.

56. Alexandrine Troussevitch, "La Vie de Polichinelle à l'Opéra," *La Revue musicale* 148 (July 1934): 126.

57. Darius Milhaud, *Le jour*, June 24, 1934.

58. Pierre Lalo, *JNL*, June 24, 1934, cited from BnF-Arts du spectacle, Rondel 11088.

59. Louis Schneider, *Miroir du monde*, June 30, 1934.

60. W. B. C., "Sokoloff Directs Russian Program; Rachmaninoff Symphony No. 2 Played Brilliantly by New York Orchestra; New Work by Nabokoff: 'The Fiancé' Has Premiere Here as Its Composer Is Greeted in a Stage Box," *The New York Times*, February 14, 1934.

61. Nabokov 1975, 188.

62. See "College Exile I. 1. To Wells College," MS, 6, DNA.

63. This reconstitution is complicated by the fact that Nabokov's own chronology in *Bagázh* is, in places, patently off by one year.

64. See "College Exile I. 1. To Wells College," MS, 4, DNA.

65. See NN FBI files, especially memo of July 1, 1948 and file no. 77-2212. Georges Keller also mentions this affair in his testimony, but since he was Barnes's dealer, it can be assumed that the information comes from the same source.

66. The phrase "wealthy prostitute" is attributed to Barnes in NN FBI files, file 77-15210 [June 1948].

67. See Carson 1989, 39. There is no mention of Nabokov in Carson's biography, nor does his name appear in the catalogue of Caresse Crosby's papers at the University of Southern Illinois in Carbondale.

68. See "College Exile I. 1. To Wells College," MS, 16, DNA.

69. Nabokov 1975, 199.

70. Vickers 1985, 182. On Kommer, see Deborah Vietor-Engländer, " 'The Mysteries of Rudolfo': Rudolf Kommer from Czernowitz, 'That Spherical, Remorselessly Shaved, Enigmatic "Dearest Friend" ', A Puller of Strings on the Exile Scene," *German Life and Letters* 51, no. 2 (April 1998): 165–84. "The Mysteries of Rudolfo" was the title of Alexander Woollcott's profile of Kommer in *The New Yorker* for March 18, 1933. After Alice von Hoffmannsthal's divorce and her remarriage to the journalist Philip Harding in 1940, Kommer became the administrator of her fortune.

71. Nabokov 1975, 209. Spivacke may be Harold Spivacke, who became head of the music division of the Library of Congress.

72. Assouline 2005, 84; Cartier-Bresson's affair with Caresse Crosby is mentioned in ibid., 40–41; the connection with Colle is referred to in Galassi 1987, 21. See also Cartier-Bresson's testimony in *Nabokov ou le jardin des délices* 21, INA.

73. Nabokov 1975, 200.

74. *Bagázh* typescript, Part 4, 23, DNA.

75. "College Exile I. 1. To Wells College," MS, 21-2, DNA; see also Nabokov 1975a, 240.

76. Nabokov 1975, 200.

77. *Bagázh* typescript, Part 4, 20, 23; see Nabokov 1975a, 240–41.

78. Nabokov 1975, 201.

79. NN FBI files, file no. 77-6072 MMS, April 22, 1943.

80. H. T., "Ballet Suite Given Its Premiere Here: Nabokoff's Polichinelle Group Presented by Barzin and His Training Orchestra," *The New York Times*, May 1, 1935.

81. See White 2009, 180.

82. Leo Smit, "Nicolas Nabokov," typescript, DNA.

83. Ibid.

84. E. R., *Music and Letters* 18, no. 1 (January 1937): 104.

85. Nabokov employment at the Mannes School of Music is mentioned in NN FBI files, file 123-924, July 22, 1948.

86. The most detailed account of Nabokov's appointment at Wells is See "College Exile I. 1. To Wells College," MS, 13ff, DNA.

87. *Bagázh* typescript, Part 4, 24–25, DNA; see also Nabokov 1975a, 242–43.

88. Nabokov 1975, 199.

89. Wells College became co-educational in 2005, a move which caused considerable controversy among its alumnae and resulted in a lawsuit.
90. *Bagázh* typescript, Part 4, 29, DNA.
91. Ibid., 31; see also Nabokov 1975a, 247.
92. *Bagázh* typescript, Part 7, 13, DNA.
93. Ibid., 24.
94. Ibid., 70.
95. See Boyd 1990, 427–28, and Schiff 1999, 77–78.
96. Kessler 2010, 383n.
97. *Bagázh* typescript, Part 7, 51–52, DNA.
98. Ibid., 65, and see address book [1928–1933?], DNA.
99. In this unpublished part of *Bagázh*, Nabokov claims that Möbius, who had kept in touch with Onya and her family, reenlisted in the army despite his age and died defending Hitler in Berlin in 1945. Möbius's third and final novel, *Flucht ins Abenteuer* (Flight to Adventure), came out in Darmstadt in 1943.
100. *Bagázh* typescript, Part 7, 52, DNA.
101. "To Rodin's Tomb," 23, *Preuves* Papers, Chicago.
102. *Bagázh* typescript, Part 7(2), 1, DNA.
103. See Beaton 1961, 286 (dated 1935 by mistake—as is made obvious on p. 290).
104. Beaton 1961, 287; see also Vickers 1985, 191.
105. Beaton 1961, 287, 289. Early plans for *Bagázh* were supposed to include an "Austrian interlude" subtitled "A love story"; see "Tentative Outline of a Book entitled: Ages of Lives," DNA.
106. Beaton 1961, 290. Beaton's photograph of Nabokov with Iris Tree is reproduced in Beaton 1968, 90.
107. *Bagázh* typescript, Part 4, 33, DNA.
108. Ibid.
109. Ibid., 34.
110. Ibid., 64.
111. See Morrison 2009, 50–52, 72.
112. See Craft in Stravinsky 1984, 364–65.
113. *Bágazh* typescript, Part 4, 169, DNA.
114. *Bágazh* typescript, Part 6, 121, DNA.
115. Ibid., 121–22.
116. Ibid., 122.
117. *Bagázh* typescript, Part 4, 53, DNA.
118. Ibid., 54.
119. Ibid., 53.
120. Ibid., 54.
121. Ibid., 52.
122. Ibid., 83.
123. Ibid., 90–91.

124. "College Exile I. 2. Games," MS, 5, DNA.
125. *Bagázh* typescript, Part 4, 59, DNA.
126. Nabokov 1975a, 252.
127. *Bagázh* typescript, Part 4, 56, DNA; see also Nabokov 1975a, 253.
128. *Bagázh* typescript, Part 4, 87, DNA.
129. Ibid., 90.
130. Ibid., 64.
131. Ibid., 109–10.

1. Malraux 2012, 180.
2. Buckle 1988, 80; *Bagázh* typescript, Part 4, 64, DNA.
3. Buckle 1988, 99, and Gaddis 2000, 304–5. See also Thomson 1966, 257. Archibald and Ada MacLeish were among the attendees.
4. See Duberman 2007, 207, 209, 303.
5. Ibid., 241–42.
6. See Kennedy 1980, 371–72.
7. NN FBI files, file 77-2212 MJM, July 9, 1948.
8. Duberman 2007, 310.
9. Ibid.
10. Jack Beeson, "*The Lord's Prayer, for Four-Part Chorus of Men's Voices, Unaccompanied*, by Nicolas Nabokoff; *Little Eva's Death, from 'Uncle Tom's Cabin,' Four-Part Chorus of Women's Voices, Unaccompanied*, by Nicolas Nabokoff," *Notes*, 2nd ser., 4, no. 1 (December 1946): 106.
11. Meyer and Shreffer 2008, 37.
12. Elliott Carter, personal testimony, August 19, 2011.
13. Elliott Carter, interview, *Nabokov ou le jardin des délices* 20, INA.
14. Elliott Carter, personal testimony, August 19, 2011.
15. Meyer and Shreffer 2008, and Elliott Carter, personal testimony, May 5, 2012.
16. Elliott Carter, personal testimony, May 5, 2012. See also Meyer and Shreffer 2008, 37.
17. *Bagázh* typsecript, Part 4, 110, DNA.
18. Ibid., 111.
19. See the testimony of Dr. Charles von Salzen, NN FBI files, file 123-162 LH, July 2, 1948.
20. *Bagázh* typescript, Part 4, 111, DNA.
21. There is no mention of the work (or of Nabokov) in Mousli 2005.
22. See Hand 2013, 7.
23. Nabokov 2012, 50.
24. Ibid., 51.
25. Ibid., 60.
26. Ibid., 57.

27. Ibid., 61.
28. See Barré 1995, 443–50.
29. *Bagázh* typescript, Part 4, 157–58, DNA.
30. Ibid., 72.
31. Ibid., 69–70.
32. Ibid., 59; see also Nabokov 1975a, 254–55.
33. See Nabokov 1975a, 255.
34. *Bagázh* typescript, Part 4, 162, DNA.
35. *Bagázh* typescript, Part 8, 28, DNA.
36. "College Exile I. 2. Games," MS, 9, DNA.
37. *Bagázh* typescript, Part 8, 2, DNA; see also Nabokov 1975a, 271.
38. See the photograph showing Nabokov and Piatigorsky singing together a song by Nabokov reproduced in Nabokov 1975a, implausibly dated "New York, 1931" [*recte* 1934?].
39. See Meyer and Shreffler 2008, 41, 44.
40. *Bagázh* typescript, Part 7, 8, DNA.
41. Ibid., 8–12.
42. Paul Bertrand, "Concerts divers: La Sérénade (Salle Gaveau, 28 novembre)," *Le Ménestrel* 100, no. 49 (December 9, 1938): 280–81.
43. *Bagázh* typescript, Part 7, 14–15, DNA.
44. Ibid., 18.
45. Elliott Carter, personal testimony, May 19, 2010, and August 19, 2011.
46. *Bagázh* typescript, Part 8, 3, DNA.
47. Ibid.
48. Ibid.
49. Ibid.
50. "New Friends on the Cape: John Peale Bishop," MS draft for *Bagázh*, 19, DNA.
51. See Hammer 1965, 59 and 85, for the portrait of Bernstorff (no. 79) and 29 and 77, for the portrait of Countless Reventlow, sister-in-law of Marie-Luise Bethman-Hollweg.
52. See the testimonies of Antoinette Grunelius and Jacques Maritain in Hammer 1965, 70–71; see also Suther 1990, 135.
53. See Moiraghi 2009, 234, and Noss 1989, 48.
54. Most biographers (e.g., Noss 1989, Moiraghi 2009) refer to this as their "first contact," not knowing that Hindemith and Nabokov, while not close, had long been acquainted.
55. Paul Hindemith to Gertrud Hindemith, March 14, 1939, cited from Hindemith 1995, 132.
56. Noss 1989, 54.
57. See Paul Hindemith to Ernest R. Voigt, November 8, 1939, in Hindemith 2005, 139.
58. See Noss 1989, 60–61, and Thoburn 1966.

59. Paul Hindemith to Gertrud Hindemith, March 14, 1939, cited from Hindemith 1995, 155–56.

60. Paul Hindemith to Gertrud Hindemith, March 14, 1939, cited from Hindemith 1995, 156. Hammer, who was not known to Gertrud, is not mentioned by name, but he is obviously the person referred to.

61. On Hindemith at Wells, see, in particular, Noss 1989, 67–68.

62. See Boyd 1992, 19, and Nabokov-Wilson 1979, 29.

63. Vladimir Nabokov to Edmund Wilson, January 9 [*recte* February], 1941, in Nabokov-Wilson 1979, 37.

64. See Barré 1995, 469–70, 537.

65. Nabokov 1975, 202. The salary figure is given in a 1939 curriculum vitae on Wells College stationery, DNA.

66. See MacLeish 1986, 234.

67. See Donaldson 1992, 330, and Orrin Dunlap Jr., "Epic poem in melody: MacLeish's Ode is Fashioned into Cantata by Nabokoff, Who Discusses the Work," *New York Times*, April 21, 1940. At the last minute, MacLeish decided to change the tense in the title to "America Is Promises," but it was too late for the modification to be made.

68. Orrin Dunlap Jr., "Epic poem in melody" (see previous note).

69. Ibid.

70. See Sauguet 2001, 278.

71. The possible collaboration with Remizov is mentioned in a loose MS draft for *Bagázh*, marked "Insert II, p. 14," DNA.

72. "New Friends on the Cape: John Peale Bishop," MS draft for *Bagázh*, 9, DNA.

73. Edmund Wilson to Thornton Wilder, August 25, 1940, in Wilson 1977, 362.

74. Ibid.

75. Edmund Wilson to Thornton Wilder, September 6, 1940, in Wilson 1977, 362.

76. Edmund Wilson to Vladimir Nabokov, March 7, 1941, in Nabokov-Wilson 1979, 40.

77. See Emerson 2006, 335. Set to a libretto by Irina Graham, the opera was completed in 1956 and orchestrated in 1961 but never staged, though it was premiered in concert at Cologne in 1992 (ibid., 336–37).

78. *Bagázh* typescript, Part 8, 4–5, DNA.

79. Ibid., 5.

80. Ibid., 8.

81. Ibid.

82. On Buchanan, see in particular Nelson 2001.

83. See *Bagázh* typescript, Part 8, 8–10, DNA.

84. Ibid., 10.

85. Ibid., 11.

86. Ibid., 6.

87. Ibid., 16.

88. Bohlen 1973, 4.
89. *Bagázh* typescript, Part 8, 18, DNA.
90. Ibid.
91. Ibid., 19.
92. Ibid.; see also "Recital by Leo Smit, NY SB, 7 Dec 1940. High Powered Music," *New York Herald Tribune*, March 3, 1941.
93. See Wilson 1983, 76.
94. "Recital by Leo Smit," *New York Sun*, December 7, 1940.
95. I. K. in *Music and Letters* 35, no. 3 (July 1954): 264.
96. Olin Downes, "Sinfonia Biblica Is Given Premiere: Philharmonic Plays Nicolas Nabokoff Work with Dimitri Mitropopulos Conducting," *The New York Times*, January 3, 1941.
97. Virgil Thomson, "High Powered Music," *New York Herald Tribune*, March 3, 1941.

CHAPTER 9

1. See Nelson 2001, 77.
2. The two names are singled out in *Bagázh* typescript, Part 5, 57, DNA.
3. Nabokov 1975, 205; also Nabokov's testimony in *Nicolas Nabokov: L'invité du lundi*, INA.
4. *Bagázh* typescript, Part 8, 12, DNA.
5. "From Aurora to Annapolis," manuscript draft for *Bagázh*, 10A, DNA.
6. *Bagázh* typescript, Part 8, 31, DNA.
7. Nabokov 1975, 204.
8. "The four S's," MS draft for *Bagázh*, 55, DNA.
9. See "The Heart of the Matter and Matters of the Heart," MS draft for *Bagázh*, 13, DNA.
10. *Bagázh* typescript, Part 8, 31, DNA.
11. See Carter 1944, 15.
12. Nabokov 1975, 206.
13. See Nabokov 1975, 205, and Carter 1944, 15 (with slight variants).
14. Carter 1944, 16.
15. Ibid.
16. Ibid., 15.
17. See Nabokov 1975, 207. Briefly summarized the published version of *Bagázh*, the episode occupies several pages in the manuscript and typescript drafts.
18. *Bagázh* typescript, Part 8, 39, DNA.
19. Nabokov 1975, 207.
20. *Bagázh* typescript, Part 8, 46–47, DNA.
21. Ibid.
22. See "The Tempest in the Windmill," manuscript, 25, DNA.

23. *Bagázh* typescript, Part 8, 27, DNA.

24. Ibid., 32.

25. Ibid.

26. Ibid., 33.

27. Ibid., 34.

28. See Nabokov to Elizabeth Sprague Coolidge, n.d., LC.

29. See Nabokov to Elizabeth Sprague Coolidge, January 30, 1942, LC.

30. See the correspondence and August 3, 1944, contract with the Ballet Institute, Inc., and Ballet International, Inc., NN, Yale.

31. See "Ballet Institute Will Open This Fall," *New York Times*, June 20, 1944, and John Martin, "The Dance: Another Ballet," *The New York Times*, July 23, 1944. *The Last Flower* is not among the ballets listed in Daguerre 1954, 87–128.

32. *Bagázh* typescript, Part 8, 55, DNA.

33. Ibid., 56; also "Tentative Outline of a Book entitled 'Ages of Lives'" (typescript), DNA.

34. A note in Nabokov's papers indicates that he had a brief love affair, about which nothing else is known, with a woman he identifies as "Greta B." See "Tentative Outline of a Book entitled 'Ages of Lives,'" DNA.

35. *Bagázh* typescript, Part 8 (2), 6–7, DNA.

36. Ibid., 2–4.

37. Nabokov to Calvin B. Hoover, August 11, 1942, DNA.

38. Nabokov 1975, 210.

39. Ignatieff 1998, 101.

40. Misidentified by the editor in Berlin 2004, 455n1. Berlin is not referring to Vladimir but to Vladimir's father V. D. Nabokov, who was indeed a "Cadet" (i.e., a Constitutional Democrat).

41. Isaiah Berlin to Marie and Mendel Berlin, August 16, 1943, cited from Berlin 2004, 455.

42. *The Times*, April 15, 1978, cited from Berlin 2009, 796.

43. Isaiah Berlin to Philip Graham, November 14, 1946, cited from Berlin 2009, 20.

44. See Isaiah Berlin to Marie Berlin, December 21, 1955, cited from Berlin 2009, 516.

45. See Nabokov 1975, 213, and *Bagázh* typescript, Part 8(2), 4, DNA.

46. *Bagázh* typescript, Part 8(2), 4, DNA.

47. See Charles Thayer's memoir of his mother (Thayer 1966).

48. See Kennan 1967, 62–3.

49. Isaacson and Thomas, 153.

50. *Bagázh* typescript, Part 8(2), 5, DNA.

51. George F. Kennan, *The Marquis de Custine and His Russia in 1839* (Princeton: Princeton University Press, 1971).

52. Nabokov 1975, 212.

53. See Bohlen 1973, 121–23.
54. *Bagázh* typescript, Part 8(2), 6, DNA.
55. Nabokov 1975, 213.
56. *Bagázh* typescript, Part 6, 123, DNA.
57. "Alexis de Saintléger Léger," manuscript of a talk, 19c–20, DNA.
58. Ibid.,12.
59. Ibid., 22.
60. Nabokov 1975, 216, 218.
61. *Bagázh* typescript, Part 8(2), 4–5, DNA.
62. Nabokov 1975, 217.
63. Nabokov 1975b, 134.
64. Ibid.
65. Nabokov 1941a, 436.
66. Ibid., 437.
67. Nabokov 1941b, 470.
68. Nabokov 1942.
69. Nabokov 1941b, 469.
70. Ibid., 469–70.
71. Nabokov 1942a, 92.
72. Ibid., 93.
73. Ibid., 94.
74. Ibid.
75. Ibid.
76. Ibid., 95.
77. Ibid.
78. Ibid., 97.
79. Ibid.
80. Ibid., 98.
81. Ibid.
82. Ibid., 99.
83. Nabokov 1942b, 70.
84. Ibid.
85. Nabokov 1943, 422.
86. Ibid., 423.
87. Ibid., 425.
88. Ibid., 426.
89. Ibid., 428.
90. Cited from Levitz 2013b, 274.
91. Nabokov 1943, 428–29.
92. Ibid., 429.
93. Ibid.
94. Ibid., 430.
95. Ibid.

96. See Nabokov 1942.

97. See David Fannin and Laurel Fay, "Shostakovich," *New Grove 2* via *Oxford Music Online* (accessed May 23, 2012).

98. *Bagázh* typescript, Part 6, 123.

99. See Nabokov 1951, 211, and Nabokov 1975, 171.

100. Igor Stravinsky to Nabokov, September 8, 1943, cited from Stravinsky 1984, 368–69.

101. Nabokov to Igor Stravinsky, September 2, 1943, cited from Stravinsky 1984, 368–69.

102. Nabokov 1944, 324–25.

103. Ibid., 325.

104. Ibid.

105. Nabokov 1944, 327.

106. Ibid., 328.

107. Ibid., 329.

108. Ibid., 332, 333.

109. Ibid., 333–34.

110. Stravinsky 1984, 365.

CHAPTER 10

1. Nabokov 1975, 218.

2. "Tentative Outline of of a Book entitled 'Ages of Lives,'" typescript, DNA.

3. Nabokov application is in the copy of his CIA files, DNA.

4. See Nabokov's testimony in *Nicolas Nabokov: L'invité du lundi*, INA.

5. Nabokov 1975, 218. Nabokov dates this visit "January 1945" but other sources suggest March or even April; see Carpenter 1981, 333.

6. Nabokov 1975, 218.

7. See Berlin 2004, 581.

8. Cited from Riding 2010, 161.

9. Cocteau's attitude during the Nazi Occupation is discussed at length in Arnaud 2003, 540–639.

10. Only the reunion with Remizov is mentioned in *Bagázh* typescript, Part 5, 43, DNA.

11. Nabokov's testimony in *Nicolas Nabokov: L'invité du lundi*, INA.

12. "Proposed outline of a 2nd book of reminiscences," typescript, DNA.

13. In "The Abomination of Desolation" typescript, 21, DNA, the name is given as Evgenii Pavlovich Mezentsev.

14. Nabokov 1975, 221, 223.

15. Ibid., 220. For a similarly bleak outlook on the morale division, see Galbraith 1981, 197.

16. The three camps are listed in "The Abomination of Desolation," typescript with annotations by Anna Kallin, 19, DNA.

17. Nabokov 1975, 221.

18. Early table of contents for autobiography, DNA.

19. See Spender 1986, 59.

20. Nabokov 1951, 243.

21. Nabokov 1975, 223–24.

22. Nabobov 2003, 11.

23. "Boris Blacher," manuscript of talk, NN, Yale.

24. Nabokov 2003, 14.

25. See Saunders 1999, 11–12. Contrary to what Saunders suggests, however, there is no evidence that Nabokov met Josselson in Berlin in the early 1920s.

26. *Bagázh* typescript, Part 7, 4, DNA.

27. "Boris Blacher," manuscript of talk, NN, Yale.

28. *Bagázh* typescript, Part 7, 4, DNA.

29. Ibid. According to Nabokov, "fellow travelers and what Germans call '*getarnte Kommunisten*' continued to occupy crucial jobs in the US military government's multiple enterprises well into 1946, if not 1947."

30. "Proposed outline of a 2nd book of reminiscences," typescript, DNA.

31. *Bagázh* typescript, Part 7, 4, DNA.

32. Nabokov 1951, 243.

33. Fischer 1956, 61–62.

34. Ibid., 63.

35. Ibid.

36. Ibid., 64.

37. *Bagázh* typescript, Part 7, 5, DNA.

38. Thomson 1966, 380.

39. See manuscript outline for *Bagázh*, DNA.

40. *Bagázh* typescript, Part 7, 5, DNA.

41. Nabokov 1951, 245.

42. "Proposed outline of a 2nd book of reminiscences," typescript, DNA.

43. See Thacker 2007, 40.

44. The name appears as Tulpanov in Nabokov 1951, 273ff. On Tiul'panov, see Naimark 1995, especially 318–52.

45. Michael Josselson to Nabokov, June 20, 1974, NN, Texas.

46. See Thacker 2007, 40.

47. Nabokov 1951, 281–82.

48. See Saunders 1999, 18, and Michael Josselson to Nabokov, June 20, 1974, NN, Texas.

49. Nabokov 1951, 263.

50. On Karajan's case, see Monod 2005, 86–92.

51. Ibid., 53ff.

52. See Nabokov 1951, 264, and Monod 2005, 75.

53. See Nabokov's testimony in *Nicolas Nabokov: L'invité du lundi*, INA.

54. Shirakawa 1992, 299. For an unsympathetic view, see Monod 2005, 128ff. An intermediate position is the one expressed by Leon Botstein when he sums up Furtwängler's behavior as "not as bad as some others'" (Botstein 1995, 227).

55. See Furtwängler's exchange of letters with Bruno Walter cited in Shirakawa 1992, 363–66.

56. Monod 2005, 135.

57. Shirakawa 1992, 257.

58. Cited in Monod 2005, 130.

59. The quotation is from Nabokov 1951, 264; Menuhin's letter is cited in Gillis 1970, 65–66.

60. See Thacker 2007, 53.

61. Wilhelm Furtwängler to Nabokov, September 7, 1946; Nabokov to Furtwängler, September 23, 1946, in German, NN, Yale.

62. Shirakawa 1992, 333.

63. Nabokov to Michael Josselson, October 20 [1974?], MJ, Texas.

64. Loose manuscript note in material for a second autobiographical volume, DNA.

65. On Josselson's intervention, see Monod 2005, 154.

66. See Thacker 2007, 103.

67. The word "machinations" used by Thacker 2003, 366, to describe Nabokov's activities in postwar Germany seems particularly out of place here, but is typical of the malevolence Nabokov clearly inspires in some modern scholars.

68. See Nabokov's portrait of Blacher in Nabokov 1951e, 39ff.

69. Nabokov 1951e, 39.

70. See Nabokov 2003, 18.

71. See Stuckenschmidt 1982, 178.

72. See ibid., 181.

73. Nabokov 1951, 264.

74. See the letter of Virgil Thomson to Major John Bittert, October 17, 1946, published Thomson 1988, 203.

75. See Thacker 2007, 94–95.

76. Nabokov 1951, 233.

77. See Walter Hinrichsen to Nabokov, June 27, 1946, DNA.

78. John Evarts to Nabokov, January 18, 1963, enclosing diary entries for August 23 and 26, 1946, NN, Texas.

79. Thomson 1966, 378.

80. Ibid., 248; see also 249.

81. Ibid., 379.

82. John Evarts to Nabokov, January 18, 1963, enclosing diary entries for August 23 and 26, 1946, NN, Texas.

83. Thomson 1966, 380. At the time, Thomson seemed doubtful about Blacher's claim: see Thomson 1947, 260–61.

84. Ibid., 381.

85. Collected in Thomson 1947.

86. Thomson 1947, 253.

87. Typescript translation of the review in *Das Volk*, January 17, 1946, DNA.

88. Typescript translation of Erwin Kroll's review in *Das Tagespiel*, December 29, 1945, DNA.

89. See Vladimir Nabokov to Elena Sikorski, February 24, 1946, in V. Nabokov 1989a, 66.

90. Nabokov to Igor Stravinsky, March 22, 1946, cited from Stravinsky 1984, 371–72.

91. See Saunders 1999, 196. Unfortunately, this undated, unreferenced allusion gives the impression that Nabokov indulged in witch-hunting at the height of McCarthyism, which is far from being the case.

92. Nabokov was thus not technically fired. The phrase in the FBI files is that his appointment was terminated "by reason of completion of employment agreement" (NN FBI files, file 123-359, June 25, 1946). According to Michael Hochgeschwender, one victim of Nabokov's campaign was the broadcaster Ruth Norden, who was accused of Communist sympathies, along with her colleague Gustave Mathieu, and eventually resigned from RIAS "for personal reasons" in early 1947; see Hochgeschwender 1998, 126; see also "Drahtlose Linkskurve: Ohne politische Hintergründe," *Der Spiegel* 2 (10 January 1948), accessed online at http://www.spiegel.de/spiegel/print/d-44415282.html on 6 September 2014.

93. The phrase was uttered by McClure in a May 1945 press conference; see Thacker 2007, 30.

94. Nabokov 1951, 262.

95. Ibid., 265.

96. Ibid., 266.

97. Ibid., 267–68.

98. Ibid., 270.

CHAPTER 11

1. Nabokov 1975, 232.

2. Edmund Wilson to Vladimir Nabokov, June 1, 1948, in Nabokov-Wilson 1979, 201.

3. See Todd 1997, especially 222–24, 371, 407.

4. Nabokov 1975, 232.

5. Ibid.

6. Vladimir Nabokov to Edmund Wilson, January 25, 1947, in Nabokov-Wilson 1979, 182.

7. See *Bagázh* typescript, Part 8, 18, DNA.

8. Thayer 1959, 188–89.

9. Alan L. Heil Jr., in Johson and Parta 2010, 29. On the VOA's Russian broadcasts, see also Hixson 1997, 32ff.

10. On this episode, see Pitzer 2013, 204–5.
11. Thayer 1959, 189. See also "Proposed outline of a 2d book of reminiscences," typescript, DNA.
12. Puddington 2000, 7; see also Thayer 1959, 187.
13. Thayer 1959, 189.
14. "On the Wings of the CIA, or the Congress for Cultural Freedom," provisional outline, DNA.
15. Argento 2004, 2–3.
16. A point evidently lost on Pitzer 2013, 394n26, who reports it as genuine witch-hunting. The same Prokofiev tune was subsequently used for the television show *This Is the FBI*.
17. *Bagázh* typescript, Part 6, 120, DNA.
18. Ansen 1989, 29.
19. Ibid., 30.
20. Thayer 1959, 189.
21. See Kennan 1967, 292–95 and 547–59.
22. See Jeffreys-Jones 1989, 24–41.
23. Saunders 1999, 43; see also *Bagázh* typescript, Part 7, 6, DNA.
24. *Bagázh* typescript, Part 8 (2), 5, DNA.
25. See autobiographical statement, Michael Josselson Papers, Texas, cited in Saunders 1999, 42.
26. Nabokov himself dates it from the fall of 1947 but the reference to his new marriage makes it clear that the security clearance interview could not have taken place before March 1948 at the earliest, while Kennan's letter of July 14, 1948, quoted below suggests that it happened in the early summer.
27. Saunders 1999, 43.
28. John Hunt, cited in Wise 2000, 163.
29. See *Bagázh* typescript, Part 7, 9, DNA.
30. Ibid., 12.
31. Ibid., 14.
32. Memorandum to FBI director and SAC, July 1, 1948, NN FBI files.
33. NN FBI files, file 77-15120 [June 1948].
34. According to a note in "Proposed outline of a new autobiography," DNA, Nabokov came to suspect that Brosse (who died in 2008) was "an FBI plant."
35. NN FBI file, file 77-15120 [June 1948].
36. On the obsession with homosexuality in that period, see, for instance, Whitfield 1991, 43–5.
37. George Kennan to Nabokov, July 14, 1948, NN, Texas.
38. *Bagázh* typescript, Part 7, 15, DNA.
39. See Nabokov to Harold Shapiro, July 5, 1951, NN, Texas.
40. Argento 2004, 2, 11. See also 12.
41. Ibid., 3–4.

42. Ibid., 144.

43. Igor Stravinsky to Nabokov, April 1, 1946, cited from Stravinsky 1984, 372.

44. Igor Stravinsky to Nabokov, November 24, 1947, NN, Texas.

45. Stravinsky's displeasure was first reported to Nabokov by Eugene Berman and confirmed by letter on December 15, 1949 (see Stravinsky 1984, 375–76). Robert Craft, though he had not entered the Stravinskys' lives then, describes Nabokov's account as "perfectly accurate" (Stravinsky 1984, 365), while noting that the description of the house (which was not, in any case, the main purpose of the piece) "left out a great deal" (Craft 1994, 9). While at Tanglewood in August 1948, Nabokov approached Edmund Wilson for advice on his article; see Wilson 2001, 155.

46. Nabokov 1951, 193, 201.

47. Ibid., 204.

48. Ibid., 206.

49. Ibid., 211.

50. Ibid., 214, 217.

51. Ibid., 217.

52. Igor Stravinsky to Nabokov, November 24, 1947, NN, Texas.

53. Nabokov to Igor Stravinsky, November 30, 1947, cited from Stravinsky 1984, 373.

54. Nabokov 1948b, 582.

55. Ibid.

56. Ibid., 583.

57. See Carroll 2003, 12.

58. Nabokov 1948b, 581.

59. Ibid., 584.

60. See Kiernan 2000, 288ff.

61. Schlesinger 2000, 377.

62. Ibid., 378.

63. "Outline of a New Book by Nicolas Nabokov," typescript, DNA.

64. See Wilford 1995, 188n36.

65. See Sumner 1996, 205.

66. Nabokov's use of "purge" has been criticized by a recent scholar, unduly in this author's view, since no one was physically eliminated; see Wellens 2002, 22. In fact the word is routinely used in political discourse without such terminal implications. See also Brody 1993, 174.

67. Nabokov 1948a, 102.

68. Ibid., 104.

69. See Schlesinger 1949, 79n.

70. Nabokov 1949c, 844.

71. Ibid., 847.

72. Ibid., 360.

73. Ibid.

74. See Nabokov 1951, 182.

75. Nabokov 1949c, 846.

76. Ibid., 847–48.

77. Ibid., 849.

78. Nabokov 1949b, 17.

79. Ibid., 18.

80. Ibid.

81. Ibid. In a May 1944 letter to Stravinsky, Nabokov referred, less diplomatically, to Prokofiev's recent output as "bourgeois infantilism" (see Stravinsky 1984, 376n31).

82. Nabokov 1949b, 19.

83. Ibid.

84. Dwight Macdonald writing in *Politics*, Winter 1949, cited in Kiernan 2000, 309.

85. Hook 1987, 384.

86. The phrase occurs in Epstein 1967.

87. See the full list of signatures in *The New York Times* for March 24, 1949.

88. As Sidney Hook mercilessly points out in his autobiography, the reference to "Joe McCarthy" in Nabokov 1975, 233, is implausible, since the Senator from Wisconsin came to prominence only in 1950. See Hook 1987, 396.

89. *Bagázh* typescript, Part 7, 86ff, DNA; also Nabokov 1975, 232–33.

90. Nabokov 1975, 233.

91. Ibid., 234.

92. Hook 1987, 396.

93. See Arthur M. Schlesinger Jr.'s perceptive assessment of Hook in Schlesinger 2000, 507–9.

94. See Levitz 2013b, 276.

95. *Bagázh* typescript, Part 7, 96–97, DNA.

96. See Wreszin 1994, 216. Hook disputes that there was "any policy, or differences about policy," but Nabokov's recollections are confirmed by other testimonies: see for instance Mary McCarthy, cited by Kiernan 2000, 308.

97. Nabokov 1951 [British edition], 204.

98. The date is given as "Thursday, 27 March" in Saunders 1999, 54, but March 27 was a Sunday; see William R. Conklin, "Soviet Is Attacked at Counter Rally," *The New York Times*, March 27, 1949. The text of Nabokov's speech was released with the date of March 27; there is a copy in NN, Texas.

99. The laundry metaphor is also found in Nabokov 1949c, 17.

100. *Bagázh* typescript, Part 7, 114, DNA.

101. Ibid., 115.

102. Saunders 1999, 40–41, 55.

103. Not the Parrot Room as Nabokov has it, confusing the arts panel and the press conference, in *Bagázh* typescript, Part 7, 107, DNA.

104. *Bagázh* typescript, Part 7, 108, DNA. On Downes as Shostakovich champion, see Downes 1944.

105. "Shostakovich Bids All Artists Lead War on New 'Fascists,'" *New York Times*, March 28, 1949.

106. "Peace Conference IV," *Time* (Research), March [28?] 1949, photocopy, DNA.

107. The quotations from Shostakovich's speech all come from the *New York Times* article cited in footnote 102 above.

108. Nabokov 1951 [British edition], 205.

109. *Bagázh* typescript, Part 7, 108, DNA. The enthusiastic reception given to Shostakovich's speech is confirmed by the *New York Times*.

110. The gist of Shostakovich's reply is also confirmed by the *New York Times* article, which refers to Nabokov's question.

111. See Levitz 2013b, 277.

112. "Peace Conference IV," *Time* (Research), March [28?] 1949, photocopy, DNA.

113. Miller 2005, 239.

114. Shostakovich 2004, 198. As for the suggestion, made since by Volkov and others, that Nabokov, "Stravinsky's man, completely under his control," spoke "at the great master's instigation," it is totally fanciful and no evidence is provided to support it; see Ho 1998, 339, 395–96. In Yevtushenko's mouth, it becomes "that question posed by Stravinsky" (ibid., 396).

115. Saunders 1999, 50.

116. For an eloquent rebuttal of the charge, see Longstaff 1989, 162.

117. Summarizing the conference in *Partisan Review*, Irving Howe (who briefly mentions Nabokov's participation) called it "a failure" (Howe 1949, 511).

118. Saunders 1999, 57.

119. Nabokov 1951, 236–37.

120. See Vladimir Nabokov 1975, 2:219.

121. See Nabokov's program note, Baltimore Symphony Orchestra concert program, October 31 and November 3, 1948, DNA.

122. *Bagázh* typescript, Part 2, 247, DNA.

123. Nabokov 1975, 105.

124. See Igor Stravinsky to Nabokov, January 2, 1948, in Stravinsky 1984, 374.

125. On Koshetz, see, for instance, Morrison 2013, 54ff.

126. There is no mention of *The Return of Pushkin* in Boyd 1992. See also Juliar 1986, 636, G04. Juliar, while admitting he has not seen the score, suggests that the work is "possibly an adaptation from the Pushkin poems translated in *Three Russian Poets*," which is not the case.

127. The earliest letter referring to the project is Nabokov to Vladimir Nabokov, September 23, 1947, Berg; by then the score was completed. Vladimir's translation has been reprinted in V. Nabokov 2008, 200–205.

128. Nabokov to Serge Koussevitzky, September 9, 1947, in Russian, Serge Koussevitzky Archive, LC. In his review, cited below (see n127), Thomson suggested Sauguet was a musical influence.

129. L. A. Sloper, "Nabokov Work Has Its First Performance," *The Christian Science Monitor*, January 5, 1948.
130. Alexander Williams, "Music: Symphony Concert," *The Boston Herald*, January 3, 1948.
131. Olin Downes, "Bostonians Play Nabokov Number," *The New York Times*, January 18, 1948.
132. Virgil Thomson, "Music: In Careless Vein," *New York Herald Tribune*, January 18, 1948.
133. *Bagázh* typescript, Part 2, 249, DNA.
134. See Nabokov to William Glock, March 15, 1966, NN, Texas.
135. Nabokov 1951, 238.
136. See *Bagázh* typescript, Part 8 (Auden), 11. It is not known whether Nabokov was familiar with Ermanno Wolf-Ferrari's 1901 cantata of the same title, for soprano, baritone, chorus, and orchestra, his opus 9, and the most successful of his non-operatic works.
137. Rudolph Elie, "Music. Symphony Hall. Symphony Concert," *The Boston Herald*, March 3, 1951.
138. Olin Downes, "Boston Symphony at Carnegie Hall: Miss Henderson, Soprano, and Herbert Handt, Tenor, in Debut of Nabokov Work," *New York Times*, January 15, 1953. Stravinsky's phrase is in his letter of December 15, 1949, to Nabokov, in Stravinsky 1984, 376.
139. Virgil Thomson, "Music: Boston Symphony," *New York Herald Tribune*, January 15, 1953.
140. See the review by H. T. in the *New York Times* for November 18, 1947.
141. Virgil Thomson, "Beauty, Distinction and Mastery," *New York Herald Tribune*, November 19, 1947.
142. Isaiah Berlin to Shirley Anglesey, January 21, 1949, cited from Berlin 2009, 75.
143. "The All of Me," typescript, 2/15, DNA.
144. See Barbara Horgan to Arlene Croce, November 30 and December 7, 1999, NN, Yale. A typescript copy of the scenario is also in the same archive.

CHAPTER 12

1. Nabokov 1975, 239.
2. *Bagázh* typescript, Part 7, 117, DNA.
3. Ibid., 118.
4. See Saunders 1999, 27–28. On the evolution of Lasky's politics, see Wald 1987, 278–79.
5. *Bagázh* typescript, Part 7, 119, DNA.
6. Cited from two passages canceled in *Bagázh* typescript, Part 7, 119, DNA.
7. *Bagázh* typescript, Part 7, 121, DNA. See also Nabokov 1975, 245–46.
8. See Grémion 1986, 270.
9. He was not involved in its planning, as claimed in Saunders 1999, 74.

10. See "Outline (continued). 1950. The Berlin Congress for Cultural Freedom, June 1950," NN, Texas. Unless otherwise noted, the quotations in the next page all come from this source.

11. Nabokov 1951f, 38.

12. Ibid.

13. *Fidelio*—but more likely *Leonore* II or III—according to Hook 1987, 433, *Egmont* according to Saunders 1999.

14. See Grémion 1995, 24. One could add that, Spender excepted, the English participants, like Ayer and Trevor-Roper, are difficult to fit into any of the four categories.

15. Nabokov was thus one of two composers who participated in the conference, and the only non-German (the other was Werner Egk). On the Berlin Congress, see also Pells 1997, 70–71.

16. On Silone and the CCF, see, in particular, Pugliese 2009, 201–05 and 222–50.

17. See Saunders 1999, 77, and Hook 1987, 439.

18. Sisman 2010, 200.

19. Hook 1987, 433. Hook's account of the Congress in his memoirs is substantially the same, except for the final paragraphs, as the one he wrote for the fall 1950 issue of *Partisan Review* (see Hook 1950).

20. "Outline (continued). 1950. The Berlin Congress for Cultural Freedom. June 1950." NN, Texas.

21. See Arthur M. Schlesinger Jr. to W. Averell Harriman, July 19, 1950, in Schlesinger 2013, 31–32.

22. IACF, Chicago. My translation is closer to the original than the version given in Saunders 1999, 93. Michael Hochgeschwender raises doubts on the spontaneity of Nabokov's call for a permanent organization, but the idea of "a permanent committee of anti-Communist intellectuals from Europe and America" was not his in any event: it preceded the Berlin Congress, as did the suggestion that it could be financed as a covert US operation; see Hochgeschwender 1998, 221, and Warner 1995, 92, 94.

23. See Nabokov 1975, 241.

24. Nabokov 1951f. This article was not reprinted in *Old Friends and New Music*.

25. Nabokov 1951f, 41.

26. Ibid.

27. Ibid., 42.

28. Ibid.

29. Ibid.

30. Ibid., 43.

31. Nabokov 1951b, 56.

32. Ibid.

33. Ibid., 58.

34. Ibid.

35. Ibid.
36. Nabokov 1951b, 84. Perhaps by osmosis with Dutilleux, Préger's first name is mistakenly given as Henri.
37. Ibid.
38. Ibid.
39. Ibid.
40. See Stravinsky 1984, 365.
41. "Les buts essentiels du Congrès," IACF, Chicago.
42. See Wilford 2003, 106.
43. See Scott-Smith 2002, 88 and 121. According to Scott-Smith, Fischer was backed by Brown and, to a lesser extent, by Silone and Altman.
44. Saunders 1999, 93.
45. On Lasky's unpopularity with OPC, see Warner 1995, 97.
46. Hook 1987, 444. See also Coleman 1987, 106–7.
47. "Outline of a new book by Nicolas Nabokov," typescript, DNA.
48. Phillips 1983, 189; Isaiah Berlin to Vera Weizmann, April 10, 1952, cited from Berlin 2009, 299. On Aron and the CCF, see also Aron 1990, 173–77.
49. Nabokov 1975, 242.
50. See Saunders 1999, 94 and 437n28.
51. See in particular Saunders 1999, 395–96.
52. Ibid., 128.
53. Nabokov 1975, 246.
54. See Nabokov's August 11, 1971, letter to J. E. Slater cited in Saunders 1999, 396.
55. Coleman 1989, 47.
56. Saunders 1999, 91.
57. George Kennan to Shepard Stone, November 9, 1967, cited from Wellens 2002, 69–70.
58. Wellens 2002, 69.
59. Epstein 1967.
60. *Bagázh* typescript, Part 7, 123, DNA.
61. "Outline of a new book by Nicolas Nabokov," typescript, DNA. Nabokov's actual phrasing is "'copies in reverse' of the enemy."
62. Phillips 1990, 8; see also 10.
63. Kramer 1999, 305.
64. *Bagázh* typescript, Part 7, 4, DNA.
65. Daniélou 1987, 241.
66. See Braden 1967.
67. See Coleman 1989, 46–48.
68. Contrary to what the slightly infelicitous title of Coleman 1989 suggests, the CCF was no "conspiracy" since there was nothing secret about any of its activities, only about its funding. The point is made by Hochgeschwender 2003, 323, among others.

69. *Bagázh* typescript, Part 7, 3, DNA.

70. Hook 1987, 451. See also Aron's own testimony in Aron 1990, 174–75.

71. See Wise 2000, 161.

72. See Nabokov to François Bondy, February 3, 1951, NN, Texas.

73. Stephen Walsh, "Stravinsky, Igor," *New Grove 2* via *Oxford Music Online*, accessed June 19, 2012.

74. See Craft 1994, 46, and Carpenter 1981, 366–67.

75. Stravinsky to Willi Strecker, March 28, 1951, cited in Stravinsky 1984, 379n41.

76. Stravinsky 1984, 378n41.

77. See Schiff 1999, 165.

78. Cecil Smith, *The New Republic*, April 2, 1951, 21.

79. Sebastian Haffner, "Symphonic Variations," *The Sunday Observer*, September 2, 1951.

80. Tamara Karsavina, *Tempo* 24 (Summer 1952): 39.

81. J. S. Harrison, *Notes* 8, no. 2 (March 1951): 347–8.

82. R. C., *Music & Letters* 32, no. 4 (October 1951): 379–81.

83. W. R. A., *The Musical Times* 92, no. 1305 (November 1951): 504–5.

84. Nabokov 2012, 62.

85. See Nabokov's correspondence with George Fisher, July 16 to August 22, 1951, NN, Texas.

86. Nabokov to Robert Joyce, October 10, 1951, NN, Texas.

87. Warburg 1973, 156.

88. Report to the American Committee, May 22, 1951, IACF, Chicago.

89. See Wilford 2003, 196.

90. Nabokov to James Burnham, June 27, 1951, cited from Saunders 1999, 101.

91. See Sutherland 2004, 320.

92. See Craft 2002, 94n99. According to Craft, Stravinsky, who expected the sole Auden to be present, was annoyed to discover that Rieti and Nabokov and his wife had been invited, presumably by Auden.

93. See Stravinsky 1984, 377.

94. "The Gracious Master," typescript, 181, NN, Yale.

95. Nabokov to Igor Stravinsky, April 27, 1951, cited from Stravinsky 1984, 379.

96. Nabokov 1951h, 22.

97. "The *Rake* Takes Off," typescript, NN, Texas.

98. Translated in 1953 as *Sociology and Psychology of Communism* and reprinted several times.

99. See Wreszin 1994, 219.

100. See Robert Joyce to Nabokov, November 23, 1951, NN, Texas, and Nabokov to Arthur Schlesinger Jr., April 21, 1952, ACCF, NYU. See also Margaret Storm Jameson to Arthur Koestler, January 19, 1951, ACCF, NYU.

101. Nabokov to Robert Joyce, January 13, 1952, NN, Texas.

102. Coleman 1989, 7. On the political climate in Cold War France, see, for instance, Wall 1991, 143–57, and Phillips 1983, 186–92.
103. "Outline of a new book by Nicolas Nabokov," typescript, DNA.
104. See my *French Opera: A Short History* (New Haven and London: Yale University Press, 2010), 297 and 302.
105. Jean Prodromidès, "Tribune libre," *Revue internationale de musique* 11 (Fall 1951): 513.
106. It may worth recalling that the condemnation of Shostakovich's *Lady Macbeth of the Mtsensk District* occurred out of the blue, in the middle of the opera's triumphal career, and at Stalin's personal initiative.
107. Jean Prodromidès, "Tribune libre," *Revue internationale de musique* 11 (Fall 1951): 517.
108. Ibid., 519.
109. Is one going too far by suggesting that an analogy would be an article on the situation of Jews in Nazi Germany in the late 1930s in an American journal accompanied, "for the sake of objective information," by an openly pro-Nazi rebuttal, with a concluding note suggesting that it was for readers alone to form their own opinion in this "debate"?
110. See Jacques Fontaine, "Le problème des ci-devant communistes," *Écrits de Paris* (February 1954): 44; see also Michael Josselson to Nabokov, sending him a copy of the "rather disagreeable article with a reference to you," March 13, 1954, IACF, Chicago.
111. Nabokov 1951f, 599.
112. See Wellens 2002,19. See Anna Kallin's obituary in *The Times*, October 16, 1984.

CHAPTER 13

1. See Hook 1950, 722.
2. See *Bagázh* typescript, Part 3, 34, DNA; see also Nabokov to International Rescue Committee, June 28, 1951, NN, Texas.
3. See Jerzy Giedroyc, "James Burnham, 1905-1987. II. Activist, Strategist," *The National Review* 39, no. 17 (September 11, 1987): 35.
4. See correspondence from the Association du Collège de l'Europe libre [ca. 1951–54], IACF, Chicago.
5. Coleman 1989, 51.
6. The essay by Milosz Nabokov mentions in his report, "Un païen devant la foi nouvelle," was published in *Preuves* in June 1951, under an essentially identical title (see Grémion 1989, 30–42).
7. On *Preuves*, see, especially, Grémion 1989.
8. Nabokov 1975, 243.
9. Undated memorandum from Nabokov to Irving Brown, IACF, Chicago, cited from Saunders 1999, 113. Nabokov particularly emphasized this point in the

presentation of the festival he wrote for the San Francisco-based musical journal *Counterpoint* (see Nabokov 1952c). No evidence has been presented to support the hypothesis, made by some (see for instance Coleman 1987, 109–10) that the idea of a festival originated from the CIA.

10. Cesarani 1998, 382. See also Hochgeschwender 1998, 273.
11. See Roger 2002.
12. The phrase is in Coleman 1989, 55.
13. See Saunders 1999, 126.
14. "Outline of a new book by Nicolas Nabokov," typescript, DNA.
15. Cited from Saunders 1999, 12–16.
16. Ross 2007, 385. See also Shreffler 2005, 227. Some recent music scholars have gone even further by suggesting—to quote one of them—that the festival was "a fairly simplistic propaganda exercise" comparable to what was done under the Nazi Occupation and that Nabokov exhibited "an aesthetic and ideological bias that differed from the Soviets only in its political complexion" (Carroll 2003, 24, 78, 91). It is best to let such disproportionate statements speak for themselves. As we have observed elsewhere, Nabokov, unlike the well-protected academics who breezily profess relativistic views of this kind, was well aware of what the suppression of freedom in totalitarian countries actually meant.
17. "Masterpieces of Our Century," typewritten proposal, marked "Not for Publication," n.d. [1951], NN, Texas.
18. Nabokov to Arthur Schlesinger Jr., July 19, 1951, NN, Texas.
19. Nabokov to Edward Weeks, November 23, 1951, NN, Texas.
20. "Masterpieces of the 20th Century: International Exposition of the Arts of the Western World: Progress Report of the Executive Secretary of the Congress for Cultural Freedom," December 17 [1951], IACF, Chicago; cited in Wellens 2002, 46.
21. See Julius Fleischmann to Albert Donnelly Jr., November 16, 1951, ACCF, NYU.
22. See Nabokov to Laurence Olivier, November 28, 1951, IACF, Chicago; Julius Fleishmann to Nabokov, December 13, 1951, NN, Texas.
23. Nabokov 1952c, 15.
24. See Whittfield 1991, 187–90.
25. Julius Fleishmann to Nabokov, n.d. [but probably January 1952], NN, Texas.
26. Nabokov to Julius Fleishmann, January 28, 1952, NN, Texas.
27. According to Scott-Smith 2002, 133, because Chaplin did not respond to the invitation.
28. *Bagázh* typescript, Part 6, 187, DNA.
29. See Igor Stravinsky to Ernst Roth of Boosey & Hawkes, February 15, 1952, in Stravinsky 1985, 356.
30. Nabokov to Henry Barraud, February 13, 1952, IACF, Chicago. See also Stravinsky 1984, 382.

31. Denise Tual to Jean Cocteau, January 21, 1952, in French, NN, Texas.
32. See Pearl Kluger to Nabokov, April 9, 1952, NYU, ACCF.
33. Igor Stravinsky to Ernst Roth, February 29, 1952, cited from Stravinsky 1985, 357.
34. Nabokov to Igor Stravinsky, February 13, 1951, cited from Stravinsky 1984, 383.
35. Nabokov to Igor Stravinsky, June 8, 1951, cited from Stravinsky 1984, 380.
36. "Report to the American Committee," May 22, 1951, NN, Texas.
37. Nabokov to Igor Stravinsky, June 27, 1951, cited from Stravinsky 1984, 381.
38. Igor Stravinsky to Nabokov, July 3, 1951, cited from Stravinsky 1984, 381.
39. Longer extracts were given in Nabokov's article for the special festival issue of *Preuves*: see Nabokov 1952b, 11–12.
40. Nabokov 1952b, 8.
41. Wellens 2002, 53–54.
42. See Nabokov's letter to Father Delos at the Vatican, August 8, 1952, and Nabokov to Igor Stravinsky, June 17, 1957, NN, Texas.
43. See Nabokov's notes in *L'oeuvre du XXe siècle: exposition internationale des arts sous les auspices du Congrès pour la liberté de la culture. 2. Concerts* (Paris: Mercure, 1952), 31–33.
44. See Saunders 1999, 113–28; Wellens 2002, a musically better informed but deeply unsympathetic account; even Coleman 1989, who generally gives a much more positive picture of the CCF, is needlessly dismissive (see 55–57)—though, as pointed out in Kramer 1999, 317 (and also in Lipman 1989), someone who evidently believed Pierre Monteux and Charles Münch were composers was poorly equipped to provide an objective assessment of an event of this nature.
45. Nabokov to Jacques Maritain, February 7, 1952, in French, IACF, Chicago.
46. This is missing in the supposedly complete list of works performed at the festival given in Wellens 2002, 135–39; other composers omitted include Badings, Dukas, d'Indy, Krenek, Pizzetti, Sibelius, and Zagwijn, while individual works by Copland, Fauré, Koechlin, and Strauss are also left out. More reliable is Carroll 2003, 177–85, though he too accidentally omits Sibelius (only mentioning his presence on p. 80) and a few others.
47. See René Dumesnil's complaints in "L'Œuvre du XXe siècle: concerts Fritz Münch et Bruno Walter," *Le Monde*, May 7, 1952; see also Luethy 1952, 72. Clarendon (a.k.a. Bernard Gavoty), the music critic of *Le Figaro*, was particularly vocal in deploring Schmitt's "exclusion" (see Carroll 2003, 84). It may be worth recalling here that in 2002—fifty years after the festival—the students and faculty of the Lycée Florent Schmitt in Saint-Cloud, outside Paris, demanded (and obtained) that the school be renamed Lycée Alexandre Dumas on account of Schmitt's collaborationist past.
48. On the omission of d'Indy from the initial program, see Jean-Claude Ledrut, "À propos de l'Œuvre du XXe siècle," *Combat*, May 6, 1952. Responding to Ledrut in the May 28 issue, Fred Goldbeck, who was in charge of the chamber

music programs, pointed out that out of the sixty-six composers represented, twenty-two were French.

49. Nabokov to Leopold Stokowski, January 25, 1952, IACF, Chicago.

50. Strauss was otherwise represented on the festival program by *Don Juan* and *Till Eulenspiegel*, both as ballets, and both nineteenth-, not twentieth-century pieces.

51. See René Dumesnil, "Les concerts: Clôture de L'Œuvre du vingtième siècle," *Le Monde*, June 3, 1952. The last-minute inclusion of Sibelius escaped the attention of Luethy 1952, 73.

52. It is superfluous to remind readers of this volume that the work is not an "adaptation of Gertrude Stein's *Four Saints in Three Acts*," as it is inaccurately labeled in Saunders 1999, 118.

53. "Confidentiel: Rapport sur le voyage de M. Nabokov aux États-Unis du 2 au 8 août 1951," IACF, Chicago.

54. Thomson 1966, 405.

55. See Virgil Thomson to John Houseman, October 30, 1951, in Thomson 1988, 253; and Nabokov to Virgil Thomson, October 18, 1951, IACF, Chicago.

56. The point is made in Saunders 1999, 118.

57. Nabokov to Virgil Thomson, October 18, 1951, IACF, Chicago.

58. Nabokov to Virgil Thomson, November 24, 1951, IACF, Chicago.

59. Nabokov to Virgil Thomson, February 26, 1952, IACF, Chicago. See also Nabokov to Mr. and Mrs. Chilsholm of Laurel, Mississippi, November 14, 1951, NN, Texas.

60. "Memorandum for Mr. Fleischmann, subject: Four Saints in Three Acts," n.d., NN, Texas. A similar argument is made in a November 15, 1951, letter to Fleischmann from Albert L. Donnelly Jr., "secretary to the Festival," IACF, Chicago; see Saunders 1999, 118–19.

61. Nabokov in *L'Œuvre du XXe siècle: exposition internationale des arts sous les auspices du Congrès poiur la liberté de la culture. 2. Concerts* (Paris: Mercure, 1952), 19.

62. See "En marge de l'Œuvre du XXe siècle: Lettre ouverte de Marc Chagall à Georges Balanchine," *Combat*, May 13, 1952.

63. Marcel Schneider, "Le Boston Symphony Orchestra avec Charles Münch et Pierre Monteux," *Combat*, May 13, 1952.

64. Nabokov, "Introduction à L'Œuvre du XXe siècle," 4.

65. Initial plans would have given it an even more prominent place, with Schoenberg's *The Survival from Warsaw* and Webern's *Das Augenlicht* listed as possibilities.

66. The work had only been heard in concert in 1950, admirably conducted by Jascha Horenstein, but in a French translation Pierre Jean Jouve described as "ghastly"; see his testimony in *Le Théâtre des Champs-Élysées*, 17: *les années cinquante*, INA.

67. See Pierre Jean Jouve, *Wozzeck ou le nouvel opéra* (Paris: Plon, 1953).

68. Marcel Schneider, "'Wozzeck' d'Alban Berg a fasciné Paris," *Combat*, May 6, 1952.

69. See Nabokov 1976b.

70. Luethy 1952, 71. On the lukewarm reception of *Billy Budd* by the French press, see Carroll 2003, 20.

71. See "The Paris Festival," *The Times*, June 10, 1952. That some booing was directed at the *tableaux vivants* is confirmed by Marcel Schneider's review of the first *Œdipus Rex* performance; see Marcel Schneider, "Strawinsky et Cocteau triomphent dans 'Œdipus Rex,'" *Combat*, May 21, 1952.

72. See René Dumesnil, "Les concerts: 'Erwartung' de Schoenberg aux Champs-Élysées," *Le Monde*, May 23, 1952. Janet Flanner considered *Oedipus Rex* one of the festival's musical and theatrical highlights; see Flanner 1952a, 76–77.

73. Henry Barraud's testimony in *Nicolas Nabokov ou le jardin des délices* 25, INA.

74. See Nabokov to Edward Weeks, November 23, 1951, and to James Johnson Sweeney, February 11, 1952, NN, Texas.

75. See James Johnson Sweeney, Avant-propos, in *L'Œuvre du XXe siècle: exposition internationale des arts sous les auspices du Congrès pour la liberté de la culture*, (Paris: Mercure, 1952).

76. See Craft 2002, 154.

77. See Pierre de Boisdeffre, "'L'Oeuvre du XXe siècle': Réflexions en marge d'un congrès," *Le Monde*, June 3, 1952.

78. Nabokov to André Malraux, in French, November 29, 1951, IACF, Chicago.

79. See Jean Carlier, "Triple arrivée à Orly: Charles Münch, Vittorio Rietiet Igor Strawinsky, qui a lu une déclaration préfabriquée et cherché Jean Cocteau du regard," *Combat*, April 30, 1952.

80. "Nicolas Nabokov présente son spectacle et indique le sens qu'il lui donne" [May 1952], INA.

81. Flanner 1952a, 72.

82. René Dumesnil, "L'Oeuvre du XXe siècle: concerts Fritz Münch et Bruno Walter," *Le Monde*, May 7, 1952.

83. See Olivier Merlin, "L'art chorégraphique américain se révèle à l'Opéra et s'implante aux Champs-Élysées," *Le Monde*, May 13, 1952. For an equally enthusiastic assessment of the New York City Ballet, see Dinah Maggie in *Combat*, May 12, 1952.

84. On the neutralism of *Le Monde*, see, for instance, Pells 1997, 67–68.

85. Cited in Saunders 1999, 119.

86. The point is made eloquently by the set designer Michel Brunet in his interview for *Nicolas Nabokov ou le jardin des délices* 25, INA.

87. Janet Flanner to Nabokov, August 7, 1952, NN, Texas.

88. Jean Kanapa, "Le festival du XXe siècle . . . américain," *L'Humanité*, April 26, 1952. English translation cited in part from Saunders 1999, 123. See similar quotations in Carroll 2003, 5, 8–9, 11–12, etc.

89. B. D. [Bernard Dort], "À propos de L'Oeuvre du vingtième siècle," *Les Temps Modernes* 8, no. 83 (September 1952): 574–76.

90. Serge Lifar, "En marge du 'Congrès pour la liberté de la culture': La France ne reçoit de conseils de personne: Elle en donne!", *Combat*, April 30, 1952. English translation partially cited from Saunders 1999, 123.

91. Balanchine himself, in a highly diplomatic interview he gave to Dinah Maggie, lavished praise both on Lifar and the Opéra ballet troupe: see "Une exclusivité *Combat*: À bâtons rompus avec . . . George Balanchine," *Combat*, May 16, 1952.

92. See Rieti 1987, 121; the opera has been premiered in Chicago, under Kubelík, in April of the same year.

93. Serge Lifar, "Post-scriptum à ma lettre à propos de 'l'Oeuvre du XXe siècle,'" *Combat*, May 5, 1952.

94. Cited from Coleman 1989, 56; see also Kuisel 1993, 28.

95. Guy Dumur, "L'Œuvre du XXe siècle et le dialogue France-U.S.A.," *Combat*, May 15, 1952. The phrase triggered a response by *Preuves*'s secretary general (see *Combat* for May 22), who pointed out, accurately from a strict accounting viewpoint, that the festival was financed independently from the Congress.

96. See Guy Dumur, "L'Œuvre du XXe siècle et le dialogue France-Amérique," *Combat*, May 16, 1952.

97. See Guy Dumur, "L'Œuvre du XXe siècle et le dialogue France-Amérique," *Combat*, May 18, 1952.

98. See "À propos de L'Œuvre du XXe siècle: Une lettre de MM. Denis de Rougemont et Nicolas Nabokov," *Combat*, June 2, 1952.

99. Kramer 1999, 316.

100. Hook 1987, 445.

101. See McAuliffe 1978, 121–23.

102. In a 1997 telephone interview, cited in Saunders 1999, 124–25.

103. Phillips 1990, 11.

104. Sidney Hook to Nabokov, June 12, 1952, ACCF, NYU.

105. See the testimonies of C. D. Jackson and Braden cited in Saunders 1999, 125. For an unsympathetic perspective, see also Cockfort 1992, 85.

106. Lipman 1989.

107. Luethy 1952, 71–72.

108. The term "manifesto" is actually used by Rougemont in his own presentation; see "Exposition internationale des arts sous les auspices du Congrès pour la liberté de la culture: L'Oeuvre du XXe siècle. 1. Opéras; Ballets" (Paris: Mercure, 1952).

109. Luethy 1952, 75.

110. Nadia Boulanger to Nabokov, September 23, 1952, in French, NN, Texas.

CHAPTER 14

1. Nabokov to Topazia Markevitch, June 23, 1952, in French, NN, Texas.

2. Nabokov to Arthur Schlesinger Jr., June 10, 1953, IACF, Chicago.

3. This is suggested by Nabokov's letter to Eugene Ormandy, October 28, 1952, NN, Texas.

4. Nabokov to Michael Josselson, November 13, 1953, IACF, Chicago.

5. Linton Martin, "Musical History Made at Academy Concert," *The Philadelphia Inquirer*, November 7, 1953.

6. Glenway Wescott to Nabokov, March 18, 1952, Glenway Wescott Papers, Yale.

7. See Nabokov to Leontyne Price, November 13, 1952, IACF, Chicago. Apparently Gold and Fitzdale were unhappy about their performance of the Waltz: see Fitzdale's letter of apology to Nabokov, November 24 [1952], NN, Texas.

8. See Nabokov to Hansi Lambert, October 8, 1952, in French, NN, Texas.

9. See Stravinsky 1984, 387.

10. See Nabokov to M. H. Fleming, October 28, 1952, NN, Texas.

11. Nabokov to Michael Josselson, September 20, 1952, AACF, NYU.

12. See Monod 2005, 222.

13. See "Arts Festival of Twentieth Century to be Held in Paris," *Tokyo Shimbun*, January 3, 1952, typed English translation, and Asahi Okura to Nabokov, January 10, 1952, ACCF, NYU.

14. Luethy 1952, 75.

15. Jay S. Harrison, "Forum of World's Music: Nabokov says '54 Symposium Will Give Young Composers Chance of Lifetime," *New York Herald Tribune*, February 8, 1953.

16. Nabokov to Michael Josselson, September 20, 1952, AACF, NYU.

17. See Stravinsky 1984, 384, 386.

18. Nabokov to Topazia Markevitch, June 23, 1952, in French, NN, Texas.

19. Nabokov to Sidney Hook, May 4, 1953, ACCF, NYU.

20. Nabokov to André Malraux, June 19, 1953, in French, IACF, Chicago.

21. Hamburg conference report, IACF, Chicago.

22. Coleman 1989, 98. See also Nabokov's letter to Cyril Darlington, September 29, 1953, IACF, Chicago.

23. See Coleman 1989, 93–95.

24. Ibid., 84–86.

25. Ibid., 60–61.

26. The date, wrongly given as May 1952 in Warburg 1973, 156, is rectified in Saunders 1999, 175.

27. Warburg 1973, 156.

28. See Spender's January 1953 conversation with Muggeridge as reported in Muggeridge 1981, 451.

29. Ibid., 157.

30. See Coleman 1989, 59.

31. "Draft statement for the Congress for Cultural Freedom," January 6, 1955, ACCF, NYU. According to Saunders 1999, 178, Nabokov intervened to dissuade

Kristol from including two contributions by Aron and Koestler in the first issue of *Encounter* because they were " too militantly anti-Communist."

32. Nabokov 1953, 49.
33. Ibid., 50.
34. Ibid., 51.
35. Ibid.
36. Ibid.
37. Ibid., 52.
38. See Carpenter 1981, 357ff.
39. *Bagázh* typescript, Part 8, 36, DNA.
40. Most of it is in NN, Texas.
41. Nabokov to Michael Josselson, December 24, 1953, IACF, Chicago.
42. See Berghahn 2001, 165 (but note that Berghahn confuses the Rome composers' conference Nabokov was preparing with the Milan conference on "The Future of Freedom").
43. Ibid., 171ff. See also McCarthy 1987.
44. See Nabokov to Michael Josselson, October 28, 1977, MJ, Texas.
45. See Nabokov to Maestro R. Leo, September 18, 1953, IACF, Chicago, and Nabokov to Eugene Ormandy, September 21, 1953.
46. Nabokov to Robert Whitney, September 17, 1953, IACF, Chicago.
47. See Nabokov 1975, 246–47.
48. Nabokov 1975, 247.
49. *Bagázh* typescript, Part 2, 303, DNA.
50. "The subject of the opera was suggested to me by Gian Carlo Menotti and Samuel Barber." Nabokov to Edward F. D'Arms, March 28, 1957, IACF, Chicago.
51. Nabokov to Arthur Schlesinger Jr., June 16, 1953, IACF, Chicago.
52. Nabokov to Gerald T. Robinson, July 16, 1953, IACF, Chicago.
53. Nabokov to George Weidenfeld, September 16, 1953, IACF, Chicago.
54. See Nabokov to Allan Moe, September 22, 1953, IACF, Chicago.
55. See Igor Stravinsky to Nabokov, November 7, 1953, cited from Stravinsky 1984, 388.
56. Nabokov to Igor Stravinsky, November 17, 1953, cited from Stravinsky 1984, 388. The word *foutriquet*, literally applied to a man of small size for his age, and figuratively to an insignificant person, seems to be used by Nabokov with an implied sexual connotation.
57. Rome conference documents, IACF, Chicago.
58. See Glock 1991, 59, and Paul Collaer to Nabokov, November 1, 1953, in French, AICF, Chicago.
59. Nabokov to Igor Markevitch, September 14, 1953, IACF, Chicago.
60. Allen Hughes, "Rome Conference Selects Prized Scores," *Musical America*, May 1954.

61. Prokofiev listed him among Koussevitzky's "illegitimate children" at the Russian Musical Editions; see Prokofiev 2012, 973.

62. Allen Hughes, "Rome Conference Selects Prized Scores," *Musical America*, May 1954.

63. It would be pointless to refute more recent negative appraisals such as Hochgeschwender 2003, 334, since the author apparently believes that the Rome Festival was "an exhibition of modern art," which is also how he characterizes the entire 1952 event.

64. Craft 1994, 108.

65. See "Composers Halted at Door: Dress Bars Stravinsky From Opera in Rome," *Los Angeles Times*, April 8, 1954.

66. See Michael Steiberg, "Rome Music Fête Upset by Turmoil: Tuxedo-Less Stravinsky Is Barred—Organized Jeers Greet Opera by Henze," *The New York Times*, April 9, 1954.

67. Translation cited from IACF, Chicago.

68. See Nabokov 1954.

69. Allen Hughes, "Rome Conference Selects Prized Scores," *Musical America*, May 1954.

70. Nabokov to Boulez, September 14, 1954, in French, IACF, Chicago.

71. See Pierre Boulez to John Cage, n.d. [but 1954], in Boulez-Cage 1993, 145.

72. Glock 1991, 58.

73. Nabokov to Ira Hirschmann, September 9, 1954, IACF, Chicago.

74. Nabokov to Michael Josselson, May 5 [1954], IACF, Chicago.

75. Nabokov to Michael Josselson, June 1, 1954, IACF, Chicago.

76. See Claudio Barigozzi to Nabokov, April 29, 1954, IACF, Chicago.

77. Nabokov to Edward Weeks, June 11, 1954, IACF, Chicago.

78. Nabokov to Grace W. Pierce, August 4, 1954, AICF, Chicago.

79. See Panufnik 1987, 200.

80. See Scarlet Panufnik to Nabokov, October 17, 1954, and Nabokov to Andzrej Panufnik, October 14, 1954, and January 19, 1955, IACF, Chicago.

81. Nabokov to Michael Josselson, March 22, 1954.

82. Nabokov to Alexander Schneider, August 6, 1954, IACF, Chicago.

83. Nabokov to Robert Craft, October 28, 1954, AICF, Chicago.

84. See Coleman 1989, 149.

85. "Buddha's Tooth" typescript, DNA.

86. Ibid.

87. "Outline of a new book by Nicolas Nabokov," typescript, DNA. See Coleman 1989, 150–51.

88. "Report on my trip to India, November 20th–December 1st, 1954," IACF, Chicago.

89. See Coleman 1989, 152.

90. Ibid., 92.

91. Herbert Passin to Michael Josselson, November 25, 1954, IACF, Chicago.

92. "People I met in India," IACF, Chicago.

93. See Nabokov 1965a, 23–24.

94. Nabokov does not specify whether it was the ten-year-old Rajiv or his younger brother Sanjay.

95. "Report on my trip to India, November 20th–December 1st, 1954," IACF, Chicago.

96. Ibid.

97. See Monroe Wheeler to Nabokov, March 20, 1956, Monroe Wheeler Papers, Yale.

98. "Persons I met in India," IACF, Chicago.

99. Nabokov to Edmund Wilson, January 7 [1955], NN, Texas.

100. Edmund Wilson to Nabokov, n.d. [but ca. January 1955], NN, Texas.

101. "Persons I met in India," IACF, Chicago.

102. "Report on my trip to India, November 20th–December 1st, 1954," IACF, Chicago.

CHAPTER 15

1. On this not universally accepted interpretation, see for instance Erik Zara, "Chrestians before Christians? An Old Inscription Revisited," http://www.text-excavation.com/documents/zarachrestianinscription.pdf (accessed on July 25, 2012).

2. "Symboli chrestiani: explanatory note," NN, Texas.

3. Ibid.

4. Daniélou 1987, 243.

5. Nabokov to Jacques Maritain, November 21, 1963, in French, NN, Texas.

6. Nabokov to "*tutti congressisti,*" IACF, Chicago.

7. Stravinsky 1984, 392.

8. See Eugene Ormandy to Nabokov, March 5, 1959, NN, Texas, and Edwin H. Schloss, "Gerard Souzay Sings In First Presentation Of Nabokov 'Symboli,'" *Philadelphia Inquirer*, March 7, 1959.

9. See Nabokov to E. Unger, April 15, 1958, NN, Texas; ibid., May 21, 1957, IACF, Chicago; and Eugene Ormandy to Nabokov, March 23, 1959, IACF, Chicago.

10. See Nabokov to Henry Moore, June 21, 1963, NN, Texas.

11. See the correspondence between Nabokov and Sidney Harth, July 2, October 12, and November 14, 1968, NN, Texas.

12. See Maria Cantacuzena-Enesco to Nabokov, December 4, 1954, thanking him for his visit and the roses he sent her afterward, IACF, Chicago.

13. See Julius Fleischmann to Nabokov, telegram, December 17, 1954, and Nabokov to Fleischmann, January 10, 1955, IACF, Chicago.

14. See Luigi Dallapiccola to Nabokov, August 9, 1956, NN, Texas, and Igor Stravinsky to Nabokov, August 4, 1956, IACF, Chicago.

15. On the Milan conference, see especially Grémion 1995, 153–226. A special issue of *Preuves,* coordinated by Tavernier, was devoted to the Milan conference in November 1955.

16. On the ties between the CCF and "Gaitskellite" Labour politicians, see, in particular, Wilford 2000; on Shils's involvement with the Congress, see Shils 1990.

17. Coleman 1989, 109; on Arendt's views on Hook, see Grémion 1995, 160. Gaitskell's opinion is reported in Spender 1985, 257.

18. "Assemblée générale, Milan, le 18 septembre 1955. Allocution de M. Nicolas Nabokov," IACF, Chicago.

19. Ibid.

20. See Coleman 1989, 127–30.

21. "Assemblée générale, Milan, le 18 septembre 1955. Allocution de M. Nicolas Nabokov," IACF, Chicago.

22. See his March 1956 correspondence with Monroe Wheeler at MoMA, Monroe Wheeler Papers, Yale.

23. "Buddha's Tooth," typescript, DNA.

24. Nabokov's report on his second visit to India, IACF, Chicago.

25. "Buddha's Tooth," typescript, DNA.

26. Ibid.

27. On these colorful figures, see Mait Talts, "'The First Buddhist Priest on the Baltic Coast': Karlis Tennison and the Introduction of Buddhism in Estonia," *Folklore* 38, 67–112, www.folklore.ee/folklore/vol38, accessed November 2, 2012.

28. "Days in Burma: The Bhan Party," MS, DNA.

29. See "Days in Burma, 9. Peter," MS, DNA.

30. "Days in Burma: Farewell to Burma," 3, DNA.

31. Ibid., 4.

32. See Coleman 1989, 146–49.

33. Daniélou 1987, 240.

34. Nabokov's report on his second visit to India, IACF, Chicago.

35. Nabokov to Igor Stravinsky, January 26, 1956, IACF, Chicago.

36. Nabokov to Michael Josselson, February 13, 1956, IACF, Chicago.

37. See John D. Rockefeller 2nd to Nabokov, March 8, 1956, IACF, Chicago.

38. Michael Josselson to Nabokov, February 17, 1956, IACF, Chicago.

39. John and Chantal Hunt, personal testimony, September 2010.

40. See George Tyler to Nabokov, October 7, 1956, IACF, Chicago.

41. Nabokov to Elliott Carter, June 28, 1956, cited from Meyer and Shreffler 2008, 127.

42. "Der Mord: Eine Oper in drei Akten. Musik: Nicolas Nabokov. Text: Heinz von Cramer," typescript with autograph corrections, DNA.

43. Nabokov 1975, 248.

44. Spender 1985, 171.

45. Ibid.

46. The parody comes from Stephen Spender to Nabokov, n.d. [1957?], NN, Texas.

47. See Nabokov to Giuseppe Paterno Landolina, November 9, 1962, NN, Texas.

48. Nabokov 1975, 248–49.
49. "The Holy Devil," typed presentation, NN, Yale.
50. Nabokov to Dr. Weitz, October 20 [1959], NN, Texas.
51. *Bagázh* typescript, Part 2, 309, DNA.
52. See the letter to Arthur Schlesinger cited above, 280.
53. *Bagázh* typescript, Part 2, 310, DNA.
54. See Coleman 1989, 131–32.
55. See "Memorandum de M. Nabokov à M. Jacques Enock," December 28, 1951, IACF, Chicago.
56. Coleman 1989, 133.
57. Curiously, there is no mention of Nabokov's involvement in the establishment of the Philharmonia Hungarica in Saunders 1999, where the orchestra is described, without any further reference, as an initiative of Josselson—who, though not at all ill-informed in musical matters, wisely left them in Nabokov's hands (see Saunders 1999, 305).
58. See Nabokov's report to Lawrence Dawson, September 5, IACF, Chicago.
59. Ernst Märzendorfer to Nabokov, July 12, 1957, IACF, Chicago.
60. Nabokov to Zoltán Rozsnyai, August 15, 1957, IACF, Chicago.
61. Nabokov to Gottfried von Einem, December 17, 1957, IACF, Chicago. See also the copy of the letter from Dorati to von Einem, December 3, 1957.
62. Nabokov to Antal Dorati, March 31, 1958, IACF, Chicago.
63. *Bagázh* typescript, Part 2, 318, DNA.
64. See Nabokov to Antal Dorati, November 21, 1958.
65. See Nabokov to Arthur Schlesinger, August 7 [1959], NN, Chicago, and to Elgie and Cummie Catherwood, September 18, 1959, IACF, Chicago. The shortfall was caused in part by the unions' refusal to waive their rule on radio and TV engagement of non-American orchestras.
66. "The Case of Mr. Rozsnyai," memorandum marked "Confidential," n.d. [late 1959 or early 1960], IACF, Chicago.
67. See Howard Taubman, "Gallant Players: 80-Piece Philharmonia Hungarica Bows," *The New York Times*, October 5, 1959.
68. Pawel Tchelitchew to Nabokov, March 3, 1957, in French, NN, Texas.
69. Nabokov to Igor Stravinsky, March 21 and February 28, 1958, cited from Stravinsky 1984, 397 and 395.
70. Nabokov to Rolf Liebermann, March 4, 1958, IACF, Chicago.
71. Nabokov to Moritz Bomhard, April 2, 1958, NN, Texas. The "Swiss boy" in question may have been Fernand Quattrocchi, later his assistant for the orchestration of *Don Quixote*.
72. Spender 1985, 185.
73. Nabokov 1975, 251.
74. Nabokov to Michael Josselson, April 18, 1958, IACF, Chicago.
75. Spender 1985, 185.

76. Nabokov 1975, 251.

77. Nabokov to Michael Josselson, April 18, 1958, IACF, Chicago.

78. Moritz Bomhard to Constance Loudon Mellen, May 1, 1957, NN, Texas.

79. Nabokov 1975, 250.

80. Spender 1985, 185.

81. Stephen Spender to Nabokov, April 17, 1958, NN, Texas.

82. Nabokov 1975, 251.

83. See Stephen Spender to Nabokov, April 2, 1959, NN, Yale.

84. Stephen Spender to Nabokov, n.d. [March or April 1959?], NN, Texas.

85. Igor Markevitch to Nabokov, March 15, 1958, NN, Texas.

86. Nabokov to Michael Mann, April 25, 1958, NN, Texas.

87. Nabokov to Moritz Bomhard, December 5, 1958, NN, Texas.

88. See Nabokov to Gisèle Dubuis, August 22, 1958, IACF, Chicago.

89. Moritz Bomhard to Nabokov, January 12 [1959], NN, Texas.

90. Nabokov to Vladimir Nabokov, December 19, 1958, NN, Texas.

91. Joseph Rosenstock to Nabokov, July 15, 1959, NN, Texas.

92. "Anders[s]son is very bad [underlined three times], Hanso [Lambert] Lucy [her daughter Lucie] and I all thought. He was the worst person in *Tristan*." Stephen Spender to Nabokov, n.d. [summer of fall 1959], NN, Texas.

93. Verrett 2003, 61.

94. Nabokov to Moritz Bomhard, November 3, 1959, NN, Texas.

95. Nabokov to Moritz Bomhard, December 12, 1959, NN, Texas.

96. Nabokov to Kay Halle, December 12, 1959, NN, Texas.

97. Nabokov to Moritz Bomhard, December 12, 1959, NN, Texas.

98. Nabokov to Igor Markevitch, November 30, 1959, NN, Texas.

99. Nabokov to Kay Halle, December 12, 1959, NN, Texas.

100. Nabokov to Kay Halle, December 12, 1959, NN, Texas.

101. Elliott Carter, personal testimony, August 19, 2011.

102. Nabokov to Dragutin Gostuski, January 28, 1963, NN, Texas; Daniélou 1987, 241.

103. See Nabokov to Massimo Bogianckino, March 12, 1963, NN, Texas; also Elliott Carter, personal testimony, August 19, 2011.

104. Nabokov to Jean Cocteau, March 14, 1963, NN, Texas.

105. See William Glock to Nabokov, October 21, 1963, NN, Texas.

106. See "The All of Me," typescript, 2/40, DNA.

107. Elliott Carter, personal testimony, New York, August 19, 2011.

108. Craft 2007, 43; see also Craft 2002, 269.

109. See Nabokov's letter of protest to Carl Ebert, the Stadische Oper Intendant, October 7, 1958, and Senator Tiburtius to Nabokov, October 24, 1958, NN, Texas.

110. See "W.B.," DNA.

111. Nabokov to Vladimir Nabokov, December 19, 1958, NN, Texas.

112. See Coleman 1989, 244.

113. See Arthur M. Schlesinger Jr. to Eleanor Roosevelt, November 1, 1958, in Schlesinger 2013, 165–66.
114. See Nabokov to Claude Gallimard, July 24 [1959] and Claude Gallimard to Nabokov, August 14 [1959], NN, Texas.
115. See Nabokov to Dragustin Gostucki, January 28, 1963, NN, Texas.
116. See Boris Carmeli to Nabokov, November 1, 1976, NN, Texas.
117. See Nabokov to Akeo Watanabe, April 9, 1965, NN, Texas.
118. See Nabokov to Carlo Maria Giulini, including a variant ending for one of the movements, February 22 [1969?], NN, Texas.

CHAPTER 16

1. See Coleman 1989, 171.
2. See "Outline of a new book by Nicolas Nabokov," typescript, DNA.
3. See for instance Shreffler 2005, 229. Characteristic of this kind of misperception is a sentence like: "It seems clear, moreover, that the CCF provided much, if not most, of the direct support for Stravinsky's late work."
4. Nabokov to Igor Stravinsky, June 17, 1957, cited from Stravinsky 1984, 393.
5. See Nabokov to Alessandro Piovesan, November 13, 1957, IACF, Chicago.
6. *Bagázh* typescript, Part 6, 197, DNA; see also Stravinsky 1964, 49–51 (there Nabokov claims he can't remember what the figure was). According to Liebermann's own account, Stravinsky had actually been offered $10,000 and demanded $1,000 more; see Liebermann 1976, 55–56.
7. See Nabokov 1976b.
8. See Liebermann 1976, 24–25.
9. "A Short Biographical Sketch of Igor Stravinsky," 41, NN, Yale.
10. See the conclusion of Nabokov 1964, 91.
11. *Bagázh* typescript, Part 6, 195, DNA; see also Stravinsky 1964, 52–54.
12. Liebermann 1976, 24.
13. *Bagázh* typescript, Part 6, 196, DNA.
14. Nabokov to Igor Stravinsky, March 11, 1958, cited from Stravinsky 1984, 397.
15. Nabokov to Igor Stravinsky, March 16, 1958, cited from Stravinsky 1984, 397.
16. Nabokov to Igor Stravinsky, March 21, 1958, cited from Stravinsky 1984, 397.
17. Igor Stravinsky to Nabokov, June 8, 1958, cited from Stravinsky 1984, 400.
18. See Nabokov to Igor Stravinsky, March 24, 1958, cited in Stravinsky 1984, 398.
19. Nabokov to Igor Stravinsky, November 22, 1955, cited from Stravinsky 1984, 391.
20. *Bagázh* typescript, Part 6, 167–68, DNA.
21. Stravinsky 1984, 349.
22. Nabokov 1975, 175–76.
23. See Nabokov 1975, 177.
24. *Bagázh* typescript, Part 6, 171, DNA.
25. Ernest Ansermet to Nabokov [early April 1958], and Nabokov to Ernest Ansermet, April 15, 1958, IACF, Chicago.

26. See Nabokov to Robert Craft, March 24, 1958, IACF, Chicago.

27. Nabokov 1975, 178–79.

28. Craft 2007, 40.

29. Nabokov 1975, 179.

30. *Bagázh* typescript, Part 6, 181, DNA.

31. See Mark Swed, "Marilyn Horne: Stravinsky and Me," *Los Angeles Times*, July 31, 2012.

32. Nabokov to Robert Craft, March 3, 1958.

33. Julius Fleischmann to Nabokov, September 18, 1958, IACF, Chicago.

34. See Meyer and Shreffler 2008, 176.

35. See Nabokov to Richard Wright, June 23 and July 10, 1959, and May 11, 1960, Richard Wright Papers, Yale.

36. Nabokov to Isaiah Berlin, July 31, 1959, IACF, Chicago.

37. Isaiah Berlin to Felix Frankfurter, July 15, 1960, cited from Berlin 2009, 739.

38. See Isaiah Berlin to Rowland Burdon-Muller, September 16, 1960, in Berlin 2013, 5.

39. Isaiah Berlin to Felix Frankfurter, July 15, 1960, cited from Berlin 2009, 740.

40. Kennan 1989, 201; and see 200–202.

41. "Alkestis in Monte-Carlo—Opera in three acts and an interlude. Music Nicolas Nabokov. Libretto George Steiner," typescript, n.d. [1960-1961], NN, Texas.

42. Christopher Sykes to Nabokov, March 30, 1962, NN, Texas.

43. Raimund von Hoffmannsthal to Nabokov, April 16, 1962, NN, Texas.

44. Christopher Sykes to Nabokov, March 19, 1963, NN, Texas.

45. See Grémion 1995, 381.

46. See the full text in Grémion 1995, 386–87.

47. Nabokov to Michael Josselson and John Hunt, February 15, 1961, IACF, Chicago.

48. See Saunders 1999, 342.

49. Craft 1994, 203, 215.

50. Ibid., 203.

51. See Nabokov 1964, 6–7; English original cited from "A Short Biographical Sketch of Igor Stravinsky," NN, Yale.

52. See Daniélou 1987, 303.

53. Elliott Carter, personal testimony, New York, August 19, 2011.

54. Stuckenschmidt 1982, 285.

55. See Roger Sessions to Luigi Dallapiccola, December 1, 1960, and to Felix Greissle, February 18, 1961, in Sessions 1992, 429, 434.

56. See Sidney Cowell to Ruby d'Archot, February 21, 1921, IACF, Chicago, and Sachs 2012, 463.

57. See Sachs 2012, 473.

58. "Outline of a new book by Nicolas Nabokov," typescript, DNA.

59. Stuckenschmidt 1982, 286.

60. Elliott Carter, personal testimony, New York, August 19, 2011.

61. Daniélou 1987, 303.
62. Glock 1991, 145.
63. Stuckenschmidt 1982, 286.
64. Translation cited from the Encounter report in IACF, Chicago.
65. See Sachs 2012, 473–74.
66. Nabokov to Herbert Passin, May 15, 1964, NN, Texas.
67. Nabokov to Prabhakar Padye, January 5, 1961, IACF, Chicago.
68. See Nabokov to Rockefeller Foundation, August 31, 1961, IACF, Chicago.
69. See Nabokov 1965a, 26.
70. Nabokov to Mantle Hood, July 25, 1962, NN, Texas.
71. Interview of Nabokov in *Delo* (Ljubljana), May 20, 1962, translation cited from NN, Texas.
72. See Coleman 1989, 154–55.
73. Isaiah Berlin to Robert Craft, June 5, 1961, cited from Craft 2002, 226.
74. Isaiah Berlin to Vera Weizmann, April 10, 1952, cited from Berlin 2009, 299. The word means, literally "a slave of the Jews."
75. Isaiah Berlin to Aline Berlin [September 7, 1962], cited from Berlin 2013, 59.
76. Isaiah Berlin to Stuart Hampshire, October 9, 1961, cited from Berlin 2013, 60.
77. Ibid., in Berlin 2013, 62.
78. Nabokov to Jean Zwerner, July 24, n.y., NN, Texas.
79. "Two Days," fragment of a diary, November 4–6, 1961, in French, holograph, DNA.
80. Ibid.
81. Nabokov to John Hunt, November 13, 1961, IACF, Chicago.
82. Nabokov to John Hunt, November 17, 1961, NN, Texas.
83. See Nabokov to John Hunt, November 28, 1961, NN, Texas.
84. See Liebermann 1976, 56; on the circumstances preceding Stravinsky's 1962 trip to Russia, see, especially, Levitz 2013b, 279–97. That Stravinsky was well aware of the political intentions of the invitation is borne out by his letter to Suvchinskii dated February 14, 1962, ibid., 289. According to Isaiah Berlin, Nabokov was "hysterically anxious" to stop Stravinsky from going; see Isaiah Berlin to Stuart Hampshire [September 7, 1962] in Berlin 2013, 63.
85. See Igor Stravinsky to Nabokov, January 3, 1962, NN, Texas.
86. Craft 1994, 284.
87. Nabokov to Michael Josselson, postcard, January 19, 1962, MJ, Texas.
88. Craft 1994, 284.
89. See Craft 1994, 286.
90. Nabokov 1964, 85; translation cited from "A Short Biographical Sketch of Igor Stravinsky," 77, DNA.
91. Schlesinger 2007, 146; see also Stravinsky to Petr Suvchinskii, February 14, 1962, in Levitz 2013b, 289.
92. "Outline of a new book by Nicolas Nabokov," typescript, DNA.
93. See Kennan's account of his embassy in Kennan 1972, 267–318.

94. Translation cited from NN, Texas.

95. Nabokov to Rolf Liebermann, June 5, 1962, NN, Texas.

96. Nabokov to Christopher Sykes, June 4, 1962, NN, Texas.

97. See Meyer and Shreffler 2008, 176.

98. Nabokov to Elgie and Cummins Catherwood, July 31, 1962, NN, Texas.

99. Nabokov to Milko Kelemen, August 23, 1962, in German, NN, Texas.

100. See Aleksandr Wat, "Pritcha o vorob'e, musyke i volke" [The Parable of the Sparrow, Music, and the Wolf], typescript, in Russian, dated September 7–8, 1962, NN, Texas.

101. See John Hunt to Nabokov, November 22, 1961, NN, Texas.

102. See Nabokov to Egon Seefehlner, February 23, 1962, NN, Texas.

103. Nabokov to John Hunt, November 13, 1961, IACF, Chicago.

104. Nabokov to Dragutin Gostuski, August 22, 1962, in French, NN, Texas.

105. Elizabeth Bishop to Robert Lowell, September 21, 1962, in Bishop and Lowell 2008, 419.

106. Elizabeth Hardwick to Nabokov, October 18, 1962, NN, Texas.

107. Report on 1962 trip to Brazil, September 18, 1962, MJ, Texas.

108. See Elizabeth Bishop to Elizabeth Hardwick Lowell, September 13, 1962, in Bishop 1994, 411. On this whole episode, see Hamilton 1982, 300–03, and Mariani 1994, 306–09.

109. Nabokov to Shepard Stone, April 8, 1963, NN, Texas.

110. Elizabeth Bishop to Robert Lowell, September 21, 1962, in Bishop and Lowell 2008, 419.

111. See Nabokov's correspondence with Simon Michael Bessie, 1958 and n.d., NN, Texas.

112. See Nabokov 1962b, 40–44. Rodin actually sculpted the head of Helene von Nostitz twice, in 1902 and 1907, and the site of the Rodin Museum mentions thirteen plasters of her head. The one Nabokov describes as damaged and unrecognizable may be, in fact, the version (much admired today) in which her features are largely covered with a thin plaster film like a *voilette* (see www.musee-rodin.fr/en/collections/sculptures/helene-von-nostitz, consulted 29 August 2014).

113. Nabokov to Oswald von Nostitz, January 29, 1963, NN, Texas. The passage in question is reprinted in Nabokov 1975a, 158–65, but is not present in either the English or the French editions of *Bagázh*.

114. Nabokov to Fred Warburg, December 12, 1964, NN, Texas.

115. Nabokov to Dragotin Gostuski, January 28, 1963, in French, NN, Texas.

116. Nabokov to John Hunt, November 13, 1961, NN, Texas.

117. Isaiah Berlin to Maurice Bowra, October 16, 1953, cited from Berlin 2009, 394. Berlin himself has been accused, contrary to all available evidence, of being aware of the CCF's CIA connection: see Berlin 2013, 432n1.

118. *Bagázh* typescript, Part 8, 123.

119. Nabokov to Igor Stravinsky, February 12, 1958, IACF, Chicago.
120. Daniélou 1987, 242.
121. See Saunders 1999, 357.
122. *Bagázh* typescript, Part 8, 123.
123. See Saunders 1999, 377–78.
124. John Hunt, personal testimony, Lyons, September 8, 2010.
125. Nabokov 1975, 255.
126. Ibid.
127. See "Arts Project for Berlin," memorandum [1962], MJ, Texas.
128. "Outline of a new book by Nicolas Nabokov," typescript, DNA.

CHAPTER 17

1. Craft 1994, 248. See also Stravinsky 1984, 406.
2. See memorandum from Scott Charles to John Hunt, November 14, 1962, IACF, Chicago.
3. See John Hunt to Nabokov, November 26, 1962, AICF, Chicago.
4. See John Hunt to Nabokov, n.d. [January 1964], NN, Texas.
5. Ruby d'Arschot to James Johnson Sweeney, March 15, 1963, NN, Texas.
6. See Nabokov to Michael Josselson, April 8, 1964, NN, Texas.
7. See Ford Foundation, *Berlin Confrontation: Künstler in Berlin; Artists in Berlin; Artistes à Berlin* (Berlin: Gebr. Mann Verlag, 1965).
8. Ibid.
9. Nabokov to Shepard Stone, April 8, 1963, NN, Texas.
10. Nabokov to Moritz Bomhard, January 25, 1963, NN, Texas.
11. See Jelenski's undated memorandum to Nabokov, NN, Texas. Jelenski also recommended Lawrence Durrell, Philippe Jacottet, André du Bouchet, Jacques Audiberti (who was approached and declined), Robert Pinget, and Mario Praz.
12. See Nabokov to Shepard Stone, November 21, 1963. See also R. Gombrowicz 1988, 155–252.
13. Gombrowicz's private assessment of the two works in his private diary was less than enthusiastic: see Gombrowicz 2013, 302.
14. Witold Gombrowicz to Nabokov, December 6, 1963, in French, NN, Texas.
15. Nabokov to Igor Stravinsky, September 2, 1963, cited from Stravinsky 1984, 407–8.
16. See Moritz Bomhard to Nabokov, April 3, 1963, NN, Texas.
17. Cited in Meyer and Shreffer 2008, 17–18.
18. Roger Sessions to Luigi Dallapiccola, April 23, 1964, cited from Sessions 1992, 451.
19. Daniélou 1987, 254.
20. Alain Daniélou to Nabokov, March 7, 1963, in French, NN, Texas.
21. Presentation of the Institute, typescript, 1965, NN, Texas.
22. Daniélou 1987, 303.

23. Craft 2007, 40. See under Audiovisual Documents in Bibliography.

24. This particular exchange was left untranslated by the Canadian producer. See Nabokov's testimony in *Nicolas Nabokov ou le jardin des délices*, 17, INA.

25. Igor Stravinsky to Nabokov, October 6, 1963, cited from Stravinsky 1984, 409.

26. See Wilford 2014.

27. Coleman 1989, 200, 203.

28. Robert Lowell to Nabokov, August 9,1963, cited from Lowell 2005, 432.

29. Nabokov to Igor Stravinsky, September 2, 1963, cited from Stravinsky 1984, 408. See also Nabokov to Leontyne Price, October 1963, NN, Texas.

30. Igor Stravinsky to Nabokov, October 6, 1963, cited from Stravinsky 1984, 409.

31. Robert Craft to Nabokov, October 18, 1963.

32. See Roger Sessions to Luigi Dallapiccola, April 23, 1964, cited from Sessions 1992, 448; also Elliott Carter, personal testimony, New York, August 19, 2011.

33. Nabokov 1975b, 148.Nabokov 1975b, 148.

34. *Bagázh* typescript, Part 8 (Auden), 37, DNA.

35. *Bagázh* typescript, Part 8, 11, DNA.

36. *Bagázh* typescript, Part 8, 12, DNA.

37. Nabokov to Michael Josselson, June 8, 1964, NN, Texas.

38. See Daniélou's version of their relations in Daniélou 1987, 255–56.

39. Wolverton 2008, 213.

40. Robert Lowell to Elizabeth Bishop, June 19, 1963, in Lowell 2005, 425; see also Bishop and Lowell 2008, 468–69.

41. See Monk 2012, 681–82.

42. "Tradition and Change in Music: East-West Conference in New Delhi," from a special correspondent, *The Times*, March 18, 1964.

43. Nabokov to Joseph Alsop, February 18, 1964, NN, Texas.

44. See Jacqueline Kennedy to Nabokov, February 13, 1964, NN, Texas.

45. See the account of this visit on the Berlin Festival website (www.archiv2.berlin-erfestspiele.de), accessed September 9, 2012.

46. Nabokov to Roger Klein, April 13, 1964, NN, Texas.

47. An incomplete typescript of the original English version, entitled "A Short Biographical Sketch of Igor Stravinsky," is in NN, Yale; there is a complete typescript in DNA.

48. Nabokov 1964, 38. Translation cited from "A Short Biographical Sketch of Igor Stravinsky," 33, NN, Yale.

49. At least in the German edition—the manuscript contains no such separate section.

50. Nabokov 1964, 90; translation cited from "A Short Autobiographical Sketch of Igor Stravinsky," 83, DNA.

51. Nabokov 1964, 91; translation cited from "A Short Autobiographical Sketch of Igor Stravinsky," 83, DNA.

52. Nabokov to Igor Stravinsky, November 1, 1964, in Stravinsky 1984, 416.

53. Igor Stravinsky to Nabokov, March 21, 1965, in Stravinsky 1984, 417.

54. Nabokov to Igor Stravinsky, April 5, 1965, in Stravinsky 1984, 418. The English version of Nabokov 1964, entitled "A Short Biographical Sketch of Igor Stravinsky," missing the last section, is in NN, Yale.

55. Nabokov to George Weidenfeld, September 16, 1965, NN, Texas.

56. A short extract of Nabokov's letter of apology to Stravinsky is printed in Stravinsky 1984, 415; see Craft's account of the episode in Craft 1994, 395, and Craft 2002, 274–76.

57. Nabokov to Igor Stravinsky, March 17, 1965, NN, Texas.

58. Igor Stravinsky to Nabokov, March 21, 1965, cited from Stravinsky 1984, 417.

59. Rampersad 2002, 380.

60. See Elliott Carter's testimony in *Nicolas Nabokov ou le jardin des délices*, 26, INA.

61. See Nabokov to Stella Holt, June 10, 1964, NN, Texas.

62. Already in the fall of 1961 Isaiah Berlin perceptively sensed that Nabokov's opposition to Stravinsky's visiting Soviet Russia was "connected with his own inability to go there" (Isaiah Berlin to Stuart Hampshire [September 7, 1961], in Berlin 2013, 63).

63. Igor Stravinsky to Nabokov, January 14, 1963, cited from Stravinsky 1984, 406.

64. Nabokov to Igor and Vera Stravinsky, February 3, 1963, cited from Stravinsky 1984, 407.

65. Nabokov to Dragotin Gostuski, January 28, 1963, NN, Texas.

66. See Nabokov's hilarious account of this visit in Nabokov 1975, 258–62.

67. See Nabokov's testimony in *Nicolas Nabokov: L'invité du lundi*, INA.

68. Nabokov 1975, 264.

69. *Bagázh* typescript, Part 9, 42, DNA.

70. Nabobov to Igor Stravinsky, June 9, 1964, NN, Texas.

71. Nabokov to Michael Josselson, June 8, 1964, NN, Texas.

72. Michael Josselson to Nabokov, June 29, 1964, NN, Texas.

73. Nabokov to Michael Josselson, July 3, 1964, NN, Texas.

74. See Nabokov to Alexandre Grunelius, September 3, 1963, NN, Texas. Nicolas Sombart (son of the eminent German sociologist Werner Sombart) is identified in the letter as a propagator of such rumors in Strasbourg.

75. Nabokov to Rufina Ampenoff, September 19 [1964], NN, Texas.

76. Michael Josselson to Nabokov, December 10, 1964, NN, Texas.

77. Ibid.

78. Nabokov to Michael Josselson, December 3, 1964, NN, Texas.

79. See the disgruntled letter from Paul, vicomte de Rozière (the financial backer of this original *Don Quixote*) to George Balanchine, November 26, 1964, NN, Yale. According to Rozière, Berman had received $2,500 for his set designs, while Nabokov had been paid an advance of $2,000, which he never repaid. The extant music had been recorded in Balanchine's Paris apartment; what happened to this recording, or to Nabokov's incomplete score, is not clear.

80. "Don Quixote: A Ballet in Two Acts," typescript, NN, Yale.

81. See Nabokov to José Brejc, January 28, 1963, in French, NN, Texas.

82. See his CV in NN, Texas. Though Balanchine did make a few suggestions on the orchestration (which Nabokov passed along), it is an exaggeration to claim that "to a sizable extent the choreographer dictated the score's actual orchestration" (Joseph 2002, 298).

83. George Balanchine to Nabokov, April 8, 1965, NN, Texas.

84. Nabokov to George Balanchine, April 6, 1965, NN, Texas.

85. George Balanchine to Nabokov, April 8, 1965, NN, Texas.

86. Farrell 2002, 107.

87. John Rockwell, "Balanchine's 'Don Quixote,' Revived by His Dulcinea," *The New York Times*, June 24, 2005.

88. George Balanchine to Nabokov, April 20, 1965, NN, Yale.

89. Joan Acocella, "Backstory," *The New Yorker*, July 25, 2005.

90. Farrell 2002, 115.

91. Ibid., 122.

92. Joan Acocella, "Backstory," *The New Yorker*, July 25, 2005.

93. Farrell 2002, 123.

94. Cited from *Dance News*, May 1965.

95. Betty Cage in Mason 1991, 295.

96. Martin Gottfried writing in *The Daily News Record* [1965], cited from *Congress News*, Autumn 1965, 14.

97. Suzanne Farrell to Nabokov, February 20, 1969, DNA.

98. Farrell 2002, 116.

99. John Rockwell, "Balanchine's 'Don Quixote,' Revived by His Dulcinea," *The New York Times*, June 24, 2005. Farrell's staging was also produced in 2007 by the National Ballet of Canada.

100. Nabokov to Fernand Quattrocchi, July 8, 1965, in French, NN, Texas.

101. The major changes are detailed in Balanchine 1983, 247–48.

102. Betty Cage in Mason 1991, 295.

103. Nabokov to Herbert Passin, May 15, 1964, NN, Texas.

104. Farrell 2002, 131.

105. See letter marked "Private and Confidential" to an unidentified correspondent in Rome [possibly Mario Labroca], n.d. [but 1966], NN, Texas.

106. Nabokov to Barbara Horgan, November 21 [1966], NN, Yale.

107. Arthur M. Schlesinger Jr., to Nabokov, December 27, 1965, NN, Texas.

108. Arthur M. Schlesinger Jr., to Nabokov, November 29, 1966, NN, Texas.

109. Nabokov to Simon Bessie, September 16, 1965, NN, Texas.

110. Isaiah Berlin to Nabokov, December 15, 1966, NN, Texas.

111. Nabokov to Isaiah Berlin, December 28, 1966, NN, Texas.

112. See especially Coleman 1989, 219–21 and Saunders 1999, 353–55.

113. See "Electronic Prying Grows," *The New York Times*, April 27, 1966, and Coleman 1989, 222.

114. Cited from NN, Texas.

115. See Coleman 1989, 223. Of the signers of the letter, at least one—Schlesinger—was well aware, because of his past White House appointment, of the CIA's involvement in the funding of the CCF; see Michael Josselson's interview with Thomas R. Bransten, *Ramparts*, May 1, 1967. As Michael Warner has noted, both President Kennedy and his brother Robert had been "enthusiastic about supporting the non-Communist left through the subtle pragmatism of covert action" (Warner 1996, 429).

116. Nabokov to Igor Stravinsky, May 12, 1966, NN, Texas.

117. See above, chapter 12.

118. Virgil Thomson to Nabokov, May 19, 1966, IACF, Chicago.

119. Robert Oppenheimer to Nabokov, October 28, 1966, NN, Texas.

120. See Nabokov to Aimée Kettaneh, June 24, 1966, NN, Texas.

121. See Berghahn 2001, 239–40.

122. Coleman 1989, 224. On the issue of Lasky's ties with the CIA, see Saunders's statements in Lucas 2003, 23.

123. Nabokov to Isaiah Berlin, November 5, 1966, NN, Texas.

124. Nabokov to Robert Oppenheimer, November 9, 1966, NN, Texas.

125. Stuart Hampshire to Nabokov, November 25, 1966, and Nabokov to Stuart Hampshire, December 5, 1966, NN, Texas.

126. See John Crewdson, "Worldwide Propaganda Network Built and Controlled by the CIA," *The New York Times*, December 25–26–27, 1977.

127. Warner 1996, 426.

128. John Hunt to Nabokov, February 22, 1967, NN, Texas.

129. Nabokov to John Hunt, March 16, 1967, NN, Texas.

130. See Coleman 1989, 233.

131. Press release of May 13, 1967, cited from the copy in NN, Texas.

132. See Coleman 1989, 229.

133. See Michael Josselson to Irving Kristol, May 7, 1967, and Diana Josselson to Tom Braden, May 5, 1967, MJ, Texas; see also Bloom 1986, 267, and Pells 1997, 72.

134. Cited from Coleman 1989, 233–34; see also Saunders 1999, 408.

CHAPTER 18

1. Stephen Spender to Nabokov, August 26, 1970, NN, Texas.

2. For a classic statement of such misrepresentations, see Lasch 1968 and 1969.

3. Isaiah Berlin to Aline Berlin [September 25, 1962], in Berlin 2013, 110.

4. Dr. Pierre Thirloix to Nabokov, n.d., 1966, in French, NN, Texas.

5. See Bird and Sherwin 2005, 564, 583–84, 586.

6. Nabokov to Anna Kallin, January 27, 1966, NN, Texas.

7. See Stravinsky 1984, 419n90.

8. Nabokov to Michael Raeburn, February 28, 1967, NN, Texas.

9. See Nabokov to Josselson, March 26 [1967] and April 16, 1967, NN, Texas.

10. "Vocabulary, semantics, facades" [1967 Russian visit diary], MS, DNA.
11. Nabokov 1975, 274–75.
12. Nabokov to George Kennan, September 13, 1967, NN, Texas.
13. Nabokov to Simon Michael Bessie, August 9, 1967, NN, Texas.
14. Nabokov to Igor Stravinsky, July 17, 1967, cited from Stravinsky 1984, 419.
15. Lafaye 1980, 115. Nabokov's replied that if he had remained in Russia he would be six feet under.
16. "Reise in die SU," typescript, DNA.
17. For a detailed, moving account of her ordeal, see Morrison 2013.
18. See Nabokov to André Malraux, December 8, 1968, NN, Texas, and Morrison 2013, 285–86.
19. See Morrison 2013, 287ff.
20. Nabokov to Elliott Carter, August 1, 1967, NN, Texas.
21. "Reise in die SU," typescript, DNA.
22. Nabokov 1975, 284.
23. Nabokov 1975, 285.
24. Nabokov to Igor Stravinsky, August 8, 1967, cited from Stravinsky 1984, 420.
25. Nabokov 1975, 285.
26. Nabokov's testimony in *Apostrophes* 73, INA.
27. "Reise in die SU," typsecript, DNA.
28. Nabokov to Simon Michael Bessie, August 9, 1967, NN, Texas.
29. Nabokov to Igor Stravinsky, August 8, 1967, cited from Stravinsky 1984, 420.
30. See Nabokov 1975, 284.
31. See Gaddis 2011, 599–602.
32. Nabokov to George Kennan, September 13, 1967, NN, Texas.
33. Nabokov to Isaiah Berlin, December 5, 1966, NN, Texas.
34. See Nabokov to Wolfgang Stresemann, February 6, 1968, NN, Yale.
35. Nabokov to Virgil Thomson, May 28 and June 16, 1967, NN, Texas.
36. See Nabokov to Mehdi Bousheri, n.d. [but 1968], NN, Texas.
37. Daniélou 1987, 305–6.
38. See Kustow 2005, 206–14; on Nabokov's fundraising efforts on behalf of Peter Brook, see Peter Brook files and correspondence with Micheline Rozan, Brook's agent, manager, and producer in Paris, NN, Texas.
39. See David Wesley to Nabokov, March 21, 1967, NN, Texas.
40. Harry Wofford to Nabokov, February 4, 1970, NN, Texas.
41. See "Trio: Nabokov and the Musical Psyche," *Intellectual Digest*, April 1973.
42. See Dominique Nabokov's testimony in *Nicolas Nabokov ou le jardin des délices*, 21, INA.
43. On the Aspen Institute, see, in particular, Berghahn 2001, 276ff.
44. See "Suggestions for Arts Council by N. Nabokov," January 1, 1970, NN, Texas.
45. Nabokov to Joseph Slater, November 8, 1970, NN, Texas.
46. Michael Josselson to Nabokov, June 20, 1974, NN, Texas.

47. Nabokov to Peter Diamand, June 12, 1970, NN, Texas.
48. Nabokov to Herbert and Joella Bayer, June 24, 1973, NN, Texas.
49. Nabokov to Michael Josselson, August 18, 1973, MJ, Texas.
50. Nabokov to Michael Josselson, June 6, 1974, MJ, Texas.
51. Nabokov to Armand Bartos, July 13, 1975, NN, Texas.
52. Or so Nabokov reported to Liebermann; see Nabokov to Rolf Liebermann, March 10, 1968, NN, Yale.
53. *Nicolas Nabokov: L'invité du lundi*, July 18, 1977, INA.
54. See Durand & Cie to Anatole Heller of Bureau artistique international, December 2, 1966, NN, Texas.
55. It is possible, of course, that Nabokov met her in Paris in the late 1920s or early 1930s, but no evidence of such contacts has been found.
56. Cited from the program of the world premiere in Monte-Carlo, August 5, 1970. There is no mention of the work—or of Nabokov—in Wilson 2007.
57. See Nabokov to Lucia [?] of the New York City Ballet, August 27, 1968, NN, Texas.
58. Nabokov to Eugene Ormandy, December 11, 1971, NN, Texas.
59. Nabokov to Philip Mayerson, January 16, 1977, NN, Texas.
60. See Nabokov to Katharine Graham, April 8, 1974, NN, Texas.
61. See "Une prière de Jean XXIII pour les Juifs," *Gazette de Lausanne*, September 9, 1966.
62. See Nabokov to Mgr John Quinn, November 2, 1966, and Mgr Quinn to Nabokov, December 14, 1966, NN, Texas.
63. Nabokov to Viola Hilpert, January 20, 1968, in German, NN, Yale.
64. Nabokov to A. Z. Propes, January 26, 1968, NN, Yale.
65. Nicole Klopfenstein to Nabokov, March 6, 1968, in French, NN, Yale.
66. See Craft 1992, 155.
67. Craft 2002, 41.
68. See Craft 1994, 506–7.
69. Craft 1994, 536.
70. Nabokov 1975, 180.
71. Craft 2002, 41.
72. Daniélou 1987, 300; as Daniélou also recalls, Stravinsky's children were nicknamed "les truffes du Père Igor," an atrocious pun on the French for Périgord truffles.
73. Robert Silvers, to whom Nabokov showed the manuscript in the hope it could be excerpted in *The New York Review of Books*, had a similar reaction. See his letter to Nabokov dated December 9, 1972, NN, Texas.
74. Saul Bellow to Nabokov, February 20, 1973, cited from Bellow 2010, 311–12.
75. See Nabokov 1978.
76. See Nabokov to Saul Bellow, March 7, 1973, NN, Texas.
77. Nabokov to Nadia Boulanger, July 8, 1971, in French, NN, Texas.
78. Nabokov to Michael Raeburn, August 9, 1966, NN, Texas.

79. Nabokov to Fred Goldbeck, August 25, 1970, NN, Texas.
80. See Yvonne Lefébure to Nabokov, October 22, 1970, NN, Texas.
81. See Fred Goldbeck to Nabokov, January 12, 1974, NN, Texas. Nabokov was not alone in having reservations on Goldbeck's volume: see Ned Rorem's "never-published" review sent to Nabokov at Christmas 1976, NN, Texas.
82. "The Slav Contribution," outline, NN, Texas.
83. See Nabokov to Shepard Stone, March 22, 1969, NN, Texas.
84. See Michael Josselson to Shepard Stone, May 18, 1972, MJ, Texas.
85. See Lasch 1968 and Lasch 1969.
86. Nabokov, Memorandum to Joseph Slater, August 11, 1971, NN, Texas.
87. Michael Josselson to John Hunt, January 21, 1972, MJ, Texas.
88. See Michael Josselson to Constantin Jelenski, January 20, 1972, MJ, Texas.
89. See Michael Josselson to Edward Shils, January 25, 1974, and to Sidney Hook, July 21, 1975, MJ, Texas.
90. See Nabokov to Saul Bellow, February 19, 1973, NN, Texas.
91. Undated memorandum to Jose de Azeredo Perdigao, NN, Texas.
92. See "New Dimensions for Autobiographical Research," NN, Texas.
93. Nabokov had helped him to get commissions in the 1950s.
94. See his *Two Leggings: The Making of a Crow Warrior* (1967, with several new editions) and *Tijerina and the Courthouse Raid* (1969).
95. *Bagázh* typescript, Part 8, 13–14, DNA.
96. See Kolding 1998, 7.
97. "Trio: Nabokov and the Musical Psyche," *Intellectual Digest*, April 1973.
98. See Edward Mendelson, Introduction, Auden and Kallman 1993, xxx.
99. Felix Apprahamian, "Brussels," *Sunday Times*, November 2, 1973.
100. See Kolding 1998, 20.
101. "Trio: Nabokov and the Musical Psyche," *Intellectual Digest*, April 1973.
102. On the genesis of the libretto *Love's Labour's Lost*, see, in particular, Mendelson's textual notes in Auden and Kallman 1993, 716–35.
103. Nabokov 1975, 228.
104. Nabokov 1975, 228.
105. See W. H. Auden to Nabokov, May 9, 1969, cited in Auden and Kallman 1993, 717.
106. Nabokov to Massimo Bogianckino, July 21 [1969], in French, NN, Texas.
107. W. H. Auden to Peter Heyworth, July 17, 1969, cited in Auden and Kallman 1993, 717.
108. See Edward Mendelson, textual notes, Auden and Kallman 1993, 717.
109. Alan Levy, "In the Autumn of the Age of Anxiety: On Audenstrasse," *The New York Times*, August 8, 1971.
110. See Edward Mendelson, Textual Notes, Auden and Kallman 1993, 719, and "Trio: Nabokov and the Musical Psyche," *Intellectual Digest*, April 1973.
111. See Edward Mendelson, Textual Notes, Auden and Kallman 1993, 727.

112. "Trio: Nabokov and the musical psyche," *Intellectual Digest*, April 1973. See also Nabokov 1975, 229.

113. See Nabokov's testimony in *Nabokov ou le jardin des délices*, 29, INA.

114. W. H. Auden and Chester Kallman, "Labour of Love," in Auden and Kallman 1993, 733.

115. "Trio: Nabokov and the Musical Psyche," *Intellectual Digest*, April 1973.

116. Felix Apprahamian, "Brussels," *Sunday Times*, November 2, 1973.

117. See full-score manuscript of this number, in pencil, DNA.

118. Nabokov 1975, 228.

119. On the opera's music, see, especially, Kolding 45–48.

120. Cited by Edward Mendelson, Introduction, Auden and Kallman 1993, xxx.

121. See Nabokov to Egon Seefehlner, n.d. [1971?], in German, NN, Texas.

122. W. H. Auden and Chester Kallman, "Labour of Love," in Auden and Kallman 1993, 735.

123. Daniélou 1987, 242.

124. Maurice Fleuret, "Deux sauts dans le futur," *Le Nouvel Observateur*, February 1973.

125. See Kenneth Loveland, "Genial Shakespeare Opera," *The Musical Times*, February 14, 1973.

126. Nabokov to Claus Henneberg, n.d. [summer 1970], NN, Texas.

127. See Nabokov to John Crosby, March 7, 1973, NN, Texas.

128. Nabokov 1975, 231.

129. John Evarts, "A Toast to Nicolas on His 70th Birthday," NN, Texas.

130. Spender 1985, 314–15.

131. Proffer 1984, 449.

132. Michael Josselson to Nabokov, May 5, 1973, NN, Texas.

133. Stephen Spender to Nabokov, November 16, 1972, NN, Texas.

134. Nabokov to Claus Henneberg, n.d. [summer 1973], NN, Texas.

135. There is a copy in NN, Texas.

136. See Nabokov to Michael Josselson, May 11, 1973, MJ, Texas.

137. According to Nabokov's own testimony, the project was still ongoing in July 1977; see *Nicolas Nabokov: L'invité du lundi*, July 18, 1977, INA.

138. See Nabokov to Janko von Musulin, August 1, 1965, NN, Texas.

139. Nabokov to John Hunt, March 17, 1973, NN, Texas.

140. See Nabokov 1975c.

141. The typescript of this section in DNA is incomplete and no other version has been traced.

142. Nabokov 1975, vii.

143. Nabokov 1976.

144. See Michael Josselson to Edward Shils, November 28, 1976, MJ, Texas.

145. Michael Josselson to Frank Platt, January 8, 1976, MJ, Texas.

146. Michael Josselson to Daniel Bell, October 22, 1976, MJ, Texas.

147. See Hook 1987, 396.
148. Raymond Mortimer, "Composer among the Castles," *The Sunday Times,* September 19, 1976.
149. Gabriele Annan, "Under the Apple Trees," *Times Literary Supplement,* October 22, 1976.
150. Clement Crisp, "A Pattern of Places," *The Financial Times,* November 13, 1976.
151. Clara Menck, "In allen Sätteln und zwischen allen Stühlen," *Frankfurter Allgemeines Zeitung,* November 22, 1975.
152. See H. Mayer 1975.
153. Ned Rorem, "The Promoter and the Composer," *The New York Book Review,* December 28, 1975. See also Rorem 1978.
154. Edward Crankshaw, "The Other Nabokov," *The Observer,* October 17, 1976.
155. Nabokov to McGeorge Bundy, March 14, 1976, NN, Texas.
156. Isaiah Berlin to Nabokov, December 21, 1976, NN, Texas.
157. "Outline of a second book of memoirs," DNA.
158. The same talk was subsequently given in Berlin, in German.
159. See Schiff 1999, 359.
160. Nabokov to Frederic St. Aubyn, July 18, 1977, NN, Texas.
161. Nabokov to Teddy Kollek, March 14, 1973, NN, Texas.
162. See Kollek 1978, 233–35.
163. Weil's name actually appears as "Wurst Keil" in the manuscript.
164. Craft 2002, 330.
165. The story about Nabokov's five wives attending his funeral, as reported in Saunders 1999, 418, is pure fiction.

EPILOGUE

1. Isaiah Berlin, interviewed by P. G., "Cosmopolitan Friend of Israel," *Jerusalem Post,* April 14, 1978.
2. See Aline, Lady Berlin, to Dominique Nabokov, April 8, 1978, DNA.
3. Isaiah Berlin, "Mr. Nicholas Nabokov," *The Times,* April 15, 1978. "Irrepressible" was printed as "irresistible" and is corrected by hand in the copy Berlin sent to Dominique Nabokov.
4. Arthur Schlesinger, cited from the typescript copy, DNA.
5. George Kennan, cited from a typescript copy, DNA.
6. The phrase *hortus deliciarum* (unfortunately misprinted) is in Nabokov 1975, viii.
7. Constantin Jelenski to Dominique Nabokov, April 7, 1978, in French, DNA.
8. Igor Markevitch, interview, in *Nabokov ou le jardin des délices,* 9, INA.
9. See Roger Sessions to David Diamond, December 9, 1972, in Sessions 1992, 479–80. Along with Nabokov, Sessions names Ross Lee Finney and Andrew Imbrie.
10. Fred Goldbeck, *La musique une et divisible,* INA.
11. See Nabokov's testimony in *Nicolas Nabokov: L'invité du lundi,* INA.

12. Nabokov's testimony in *Nicolas Nabokov ou le jardin des délices*, 19, INA.

13. Françoise Xenakis, "Au revoir Nicolas!", *Le Matin* [Paris], April 11, 1978.

14. Elliott Carter's testimony, *Nicolas Nabokov ou le jardin des délices*, 20, INA.

15. See for instance Rieti's testimony in Ricci 1987, 268.

16. Jean Daniel, testimony, *Nicolas Nabokov ou le jardin des délices*, 20, INA.

17. Elliott Carter, testimony, *Nicolas Nabokov ou le jardin des délices*, 30, INA.

Index

Chaney, Stewart, 163

Changalovich, Miro, 317

Chanler, Theodore, 110

Chapin, Katherine Garrison, 150

Chaplin, Charles, 176, 255–6, 506

Char, René, 267

Charbonnier, Pierre, 74, 77, 413

Charrat, Janine, 235

Chaudhuri, Joyanto Nath, 292, 299

Chaudhuri, Nirad C., 293

Chavchavadze, Helen, 335

Chávez, Carlos, 273

Chekhov, Anton Pavlovich, 27, 40,
    137, 148

Chekhova, Mariia Pavlovna, 40

Chiaromonte, Nicola, 239, 242,
    270, 328

Chopin, Frédéric, 14, 18, 37, 41, 94,
    95, 389

Christoff, Boris, 317

Churchill, Randolph, 165

Churchill, Winston, Sir, 199, 204

Citkowitz, Israel, 110

Claire, Jean, Dom, 66

Clarendon (pseudonym), see Gavoty

Clark, John Pepper, 349

Clay, Lucius D., 185, 187, 192, 195,
    199, 205

Cleveland, Grover, 152

Clift, Montgomery, 212

Cliquet-Pleyel, Henri, 59

Cloarec, Jacques, XI, 396

Cluytens, André, 257

Cocéa, Alice, 417

Cocteau, Jean, xiv, 57–8, 63, 70, 79–80,
    95, 97, 101, 108, 112, 120, 132, 142,
    181, 206, 207, 256–7, 263, 316,
    326, 348, 441, 474, 493, 507,
    509, 517,

Cœuroy, André, 96, 108, 480

Cohen, Elliott, 276

Colassi, Irma, 263

Collaer, Paul, 80, 236, 283–4, 347,
    476–9, 512

Colle, Pierre, 108–9, 119

Coolidge, Elizabeth Sprague, 162, 435, 491

Cooper, John Sherman, 299

Copland, Aaron, 110, 112–4, 140–2, 176,
    194, 211, 216, 260, 262, 284, 311,
    439, 483, 507

Copperie, [Germaine?], 421

Corle, Edwin, 209

Corneille, 297

Corre, Caroline (stepdaughter), 277, 385

Coton, A. V., 83

Counts, George S., 217, 219

Couturier, Marie-Alain, 63

Craft, Robert, 179, 210, 242, 284, 288,
    316, 323–4, 329, 333, 335, 343,
    348–9, 352, 354–5, 386, 387,
    405, 479, 498, 504, 513, 519–20,
    523–4

Croce, Arlene, 501

Croce, Benedetto, 217, 237, 286, 307

Crosby, Caresse, 118–9, 134, 485

Crosby, Harry, 118

Crosby, John, 530

Cowell, Henry, 208, 215, 283, 330–1

Cowell, Sidney, 519

Cramer, Johann Baptist, 121

Cramer, Heinz von, 195, 304, 515

Crankshaw, Edward, 402

Cravo, Mário, 338, 344

Crisp, Clement, 402

Crossman, Richard, 232, 297

Cuevas, George de, 163, 253, 266, 296

Custine, Astolphe, marquis de, 167, 391

Cui, César, 15

Cummings, E.E. (Edward Estlin), 133–4

Cushing, Mary, 119

Cuvelier, Marcel, 86, 478

Cvetko, Dragutin, 332, 336, 347

Czapski, Józef, 62, 65, 231, 250, 276, 336

Czerny, Carl, 121